Alpha Architecture Reference Manual
Third Edition

Alpha Architecture Reference Manual

Third Edition

The Alpha Architecture Committee

Contributing Authors for the Third Edition

Richard L. Sites, Co-Architect
Richard T. Witek, Co-Architect

Peter J. Bannon
Wayne M. Cardoza
John H. Edmondson
Kourosh Gharachorloo
Richard B. Grove
Michael S. Harvey
Steven O. Hobbs
James B. Keller
Daniel L. Leibholz
P. Geoffrey Lowney

Maurice P. Marks
Andrew H. Mason
William B. Noyce
Audrey R. Reith, chair
Eileen J. Samberg
Sridhar Samudrala
James B. Saxe
Robert M. Supnik
Dave Wagner
Yuan Yu

Digital Press

Boston • Oxford • Johannesburg • Melbourne • New Delhi • Singapore

Digital Press™ is an imprint of Butterworth-Heinemann, Publisher for Digital Equipment Corporation.

No part of this publication may be reproduced, stored in a retrieval system, or transmitted in any form or by any means, electronic, mechanical, photocopying, recording, or otherwise, without the prior written permission of the publisher.

Recognizing the importance of preserving what has been written, Butterworth–Heinemann prints its books on acid-free paper whenever possible.

Digital believes that the information in this publication is accurate as of its publication date; such information is subject to change without notice. DIGITAL is not responsible for any inadvertant errors.

The following are trademarks of Digital Equipment Corporation: DEC, DIGITAL, DIGITAL UNIX, OpenVMS, PDP-11, VAX, VMS, ULTRIX, and the DIGITAL logo. Cray is a registered trademark of Cray Research, Inc., a wholly-owned subsidiary of Silicon Graphics, Inc. IBM is a registered trademark of Open Software Foundation, Inc. UNIX is a registered trademark in the United States and other countries licensed exclusively through X/Open Company Ltd. Windows NT is a trademark of Microsoft Corporation. X Window System is a common law trademark of the Massachusetts Institute of Technology. All other trademarks and registered trademarks are the property of their respective owners.

This document was prepared using Adobe FrameMaker V5.1.2.

Technical Writer: Charles Greenman
Production Editor: Kathe Rhoades
Technical Illustrations: Lynne Kenison

Butterworth-Heinemann supports the efforts of American Forests and the Global ReLeaf program in its campaign for the betterment of trees, forests, and our environment.

Library of Congress Cataloging-in-Publication Data
ISBN 1-55558-202-8

British Library Cataloguing-in-Publication Data
A catalogue record for this book is available from the British Library.

The publisher offers special discounts on bulk orders of this book. For information, please contact:
Manager of Special Sales
Butterworth-Heinemann
225 Wildwood Avenue
Woburn, MA 01801-2041
Tel: 781-904-2500
Fax: 781-904-2620

For information on all Digital Press publications available, contact our World Wide Web home page at:
http://www.bh.com/digitalpress

Order number: EY-W938E-DP

10 9 8 7 6 5 4 3 2 1

Printed in the United States of America

Contents

Part III \Console Interface Architecture

Appendixes

Master Index

A Note on the Structure of This Book

The *Alpha Architecture Reference Manual* is divided into three Parts, four appendixes, and two indexes.

Each part or section of a part describes a major portion of the Alpha architecture. Each contains its own Table of Contents and Index. Additional sections will be incorporated as development proceeds on the architecture.

The following table outlines the contents of the manual:

Name	Symbol	Contents
Part One	(I)	Common Architecture This part describes the architecture that is common to and required by all implementations.
Part Two	(II)	Specific Operating System PALcode Architecture This part contains sections that describe how the following operating systems relate to the Alpha AXP architecture:

Section Name and Contents	Symbol
OpenVMS Alpha Software	(II–A)
DIGITAL UNIX Software	(II–B)
Windows NT Alpha Software	(II–C)

Name	Symbol	Contents
Part Three	(III)	Console Interface Architecture This part describes an architected console firmware implementation.
Appendixes		Because information in the appendixes can be shared by more than one section, appendixes are grouped together at the end of the manual.
Indexes		The index at the end of the manual is structured like a master index. Index entries are called out by the appropriate symbol: (I), (II), and so forth, associated with the corresponding part or section. Index entries for the appendixes are called out by appendix name and page number. Following the index for the entire manual is an index of the instructions. The instruction index is the easiest way to find primary documentation for the Alpha instruction set and the PALcode instructions for each operating system.

The Alpha architecture is a RISC architecture that was designed for longevity, high performance, scalability, and adaptability. Using the formulation of Amdahl, Blaauw, and Brooks,[1] architecture is distinguished from implementation as follows:

- *Computer architecture* is defined as the attributes of a computer seen by a machine-language programmer. This definition includes the instruction set, instruction formats, operation codes, addressing modes, and all registers and memory locations that may be directly manipulated by a machine-language programmer.

- *Implementation* is defined as the actual hardware structure, logic design, and data-path organization of the computer.

This book describes the Alpha architecture, the required behavior of all Alpha implementations as seen by a machine-language programmer. The architecture does not speak to implementation considerations such as how fast a program runs, what specific bit pattern is left in a hardware register after an unpredictable operation, how to schedule code for a specific chip, or how to wire up a specific chip. Those considerations are described in implementation-specific documents.

The Alpha architecture has now been implemented in three generations of CMOS VLSI microprocessors: the 21064 (and its variants, the 21064A and the 21066); the 21164 (and its variant, the 21164PC); and the 21264.

Defining the Alpha Architecture

When the Alpha project began in the fall of 1988, the architecture team (Dick Sites and Rich Witek) started with four goals:

1. Longevity, to maximize the investment for both customers and DIGITAL.
2. High performance, for both technical and commercial applications.
3. Scalability, across a wide range of system prices and form factors.
4. Adaptability, to a wide variety of operating systems and applications, with easy migration from prior architectures.

The architecture team's design decisions derived directly from these goals.

Longevity and Performance

Based on the life cycles of the 360 and VAX architectures, the architecture team assumed a 15–25 year design horizon and tried to avoid any architectural elements that would become limitations during this time. The design horizon led directly to the conclusion that Alpha could not be a 32-bit architecture: during the lifetime of the architecture, 32 bits would become too small to describe both virtual and physical address spaces in practical systems. Thus, Alpha was a full 64-bit architecture, with a minimal number of 32-bit operations for backward compatibility.

---

[1]G.M. Amdahl, G.A. Blaauw, and F.P. Brooks, Jr. "Architecture of the IBM System/360." *IBM Journal of Research and Development*, vol. 8, no. 2 (April 1964): 87-101.

The longevity goal also caused the team to examine how the performance of implementations would scale upward over 25 years. Over the previous decade, microprocessor-based systems had improved in performance at the rate of 60% per year. This suggested that Alpha implementations would have to do the same or better, resulting in a factor of 1000 performance improvements over the lifetime of the architecture. The architecture team was unwilling to bet that the future performance improvements would be less than the past and seriously examined the consequences of longevity on the architecture.

The team identified three dimensions to improving performance: clock speed, processor organization, and multiple instruction streams. For each dimension, an improvement by a factor of 10 over the lifetime of the architecture seemed reasonable, while an improvement by a factor of 100 did not; thus, improvements in all three dimensions were essential to meeting the longevity goal. Accordingly, the architecture had to gracefully support implementations with:

- Fast cycle times
- Multiple instruction issue and unconventional memory organizations
- Multiple instruction streams (multiple threads or multiple processors)

The cycle time goal led to an architectural design with few instruction formats, simple instruction definitions, and minimal interactions between instructions. The multiple instruction issue goal led to a design without specialized registers, architected delay slots, precise arithmetic traps, precise memory ordering, or byte writes (perceived to have an embedded read-modify-write bottleneck). The multiple instruction streams goal led to a design with a highly flexible atomic-update primitive and a relaxed memory ordering model.

Adaptability

To run multiple operating systems (OpenVMS, UNIX, Windows NT, and others) without burdening the hardware implementations with elaborate and sometimes conflicting operating system underpinnings, the architecture team incorporated an idea from a previous DIGITAL RISC design. The Alpha architecture places the underpinnings for interrupt delivery and return, exceptions, context switching, memory management, and error handling in a set of privileged software subroutines called PALcode. PALcode subroutines have controlled entries, with interrupts disabled, and have access to implementation-specific registers. By having different sets of PALcode for different operating systems, the architecture itself is not biased towards a specific operating system or computing style.

PALcode has several significant benefits:

- Separation of policy from mechanism. PALcode provides operating systems with an unchanging privileged interface to hardware, effectively disguising the unique properties of particular implementations.
- Fast adaptability to new environments. PALcode allows the Alpha architecture to implement mechanisms unique to particular operating systems without elaborate underlying hardware. For example, the OpenVMS PALcode provides interlocked queue and other VAX-derived primitives. The Windows NT PALcode implements a 32-bit view of Alpha's 64-bit page table descriptors.

- Isolation of impact. The complex primitives required for OpenVMS are unique to the OpenVMS PALcode and do not impact the UNIX or Windows NT implementations in any way.

To migrate user applications, the architecture team proposed the use of software translators that would convert VAX or MIPS code to Alpha code. The first software translators converted VAX OpenVMS images to functionally identical Alpha OpenVMS images; the second, MIPS ULTRIX images to functionally identical Alpha UNIX images. The architecture team adopted binary translation rather than hardware "compatibility modes" because the latter would have severely compromised the performance of initial implementations and would have provided no help with migration from other environments. The subsequent development of other translators (including SPARC SunOS to Alpha UNIX and x86 Win32 to Alpha Windows NT) has validated the choice of translation over hardware emulation.

Fundamentally, PALcode provided the Alpha architecture with a migration path for operating systems, and the translators (and native compilers) provided a migration path for appli cations. These two techniques facilitated a clean sheet of paper design for the bulk of the Alpha architecture. Other than an extra set of VAX floating-point formats (included for data compatibility reasons and subsettable later), the Alpha architecture does not include any VAX or MIPS features to support compatibility.

Evolving the Alpha Architecture

The Alpha architecture is not a static design; it has evolved, compatibly, based on accumulated experience and new requirements. Areas that have changed over the last five years include:

- IEEE floating point exception handling. The Alpha architecture optimized the normal cases and left the exception cases entirely to software. Efficient handling of exceptions requires additional architectural support for disabling individual exceptions.
- Software controlled memory accesses. Alpha was the first mainstream RISC architecture to implement a relaxed (weak consistency) memory model. As performance levels increase, software needs even more control over the memory hierarchy, requiring more forms of coherency management and explicit control of caching.
- Direct manipulation of byte-oriented I/O buses. The Alpha architecture envisioned that I/O buses would be accessed indirectly, via mailboxes. Instead, most systems implement direct access, requiring byte and word operations in I/O space.
- Windows NT support. The Alpha architecture specified longword granularity of sharing and 64-bit memory management. Windows applications assume byte granularity of sharing between threads, requiring byte and word operations in memory. In addition, Windows NT assumes a 32-bit memory management model, requiring new PALcode.
- Application specific requirements. The Alpha architecture focused on speed rather than specialization to obtain performance. With increasing silicon densities, application specific instruction extensions become feasible. Optional extensions to the architecture provide improved performance for multimedia and scientific applications.

To maintain compatibility, all new instructions are supported as traps (or, if appropriate, treated as no-operations) on earlier implementations. In addition, nonprivileged instructions allow software to test quickly and efficiently whether a particular architectural capability exists in an implementation.

Organization of this Book

Part One of this book describes the instruction set architecture and is largely self-contained. It provides basic information for readers who are involved with compilers or machine language programming. Part Two describes the supporting PALcode for three operating systems—OpenVMS, DIGITAL UNIX, and Windows NT (all other operating Systems ported to Alpha so far have used one of these three PALcode models). Part Three describes a particular console implementation that is specific to OpenVMS and DIGITAL UNIX. The console for Windows NT is discussed in the section on Windows NT PALcode.

Acknowledgments

The Alpha architecture is first and foremost the work of Dick Sites and Rich Witek, who shaped the philosophy, goals, outline, and details of the architecture through its first five years. Both drew on their extensive experiences in the field: Dick on his study of the landmark systems of (and in some cases, personal interaction with) Fred Brooks, John Cocke, and Seymour Cray; Rich from his work on the MicroVAX chip and on a prior DIGITAL RISC architecture. The architecture was reviewed and refined by dozens of DIGITAL engineers, whose vigorous and outspoken views sharpened the focus and smoothed the rough edges.

Since 1992, the Alpha architecture has been under the control of the Alpha Architecture Committee, which represents all the disciplines of computer engineering in DIGITAL. This committee is chaired by Audrey Reith, who has worked tirelessly to keep the architecture current, coherent, and correct. The organization, editing, and production of this text in final form remain largely the work of Charlie Greenman, whose clear writing is much appreciated.

Bob Supnik, October 3, 1997

Preface to the Second Edition

The Second Edition of the architecture manual continues to describe the required behavior for all Alpha implementations, as seen by the machine-level programmer.

A number of Alpha CPU implementations have been produced to date, designed according to the dictates of this architecture. The first generation implementation, the DECchip 21064, set new standards for high performance and was the basis for several chips that followed. The DECchip 21066 increased the level of integration on the chip by including the PCI interface and memory interface control logic on the chip itself. The DECchip 21064A further enhanced the performance by shrinking to the next generation CMOS process, providing an increase in operating frequency and doubling the internal cache size.

The second generation implementation, the DECchip 21164, has expanded beyond the DEC chip 21064A in width of issue and operating frequency, and provides a much higher-performance memory interface. In fact, since its introduction, an Alpha has been the highest performance microprocessor on the market. The third generation chip, currently under development, will continue that trend.

The first Alpha systems were workstations and midrange systems that were directed to the traditional VAX and MIPS customer base. Since then, the range of Alpha systems has been greatly expanded. Alpha systems have been designed in the PC price range to support Windows NT and X Window terminals. Alpha single-board computers have been introduced to cover the high-end embedded controller market. And Cray Research has introduced the Cray T3D, an Alpha-based MPP that can support up to 1024 Alpha CPU's in an MPP system.

PALcode has made much of this variety possible. By having different sets of PALcode for different operating systems, the architecture itself is not biased toward a specific operating system or computing style. PALcode has provided a flexible means, for example, of supporting Windows NT and the Cray T3D without hardware changes.

Organization

The organization of the Second Edition is similar to that of the first. Part One of this book describes the instruction-set architecture, and is largely self-contained for readers who work with compilers or assembly-language programs. Part Two describes the supporting PALcode routines for three operating systems—the specific operating system PALcode architecture. PALcode for Windows NT on Alpha is covered in this edition. Part Three describes a particular console implementation that is specific to platforms that support the OpenVMS AXP or DEC OSF/1 operating systems. A discussion of console issues for Windows NT is included with its PALcode description.

Acknowledgments

The list of people who have contributed to Alpha's current success has grown too large to itemize. Rather, we want to acknowledge the software and hardware engineers who have worked since long before Alpha's introduction to provide the whole system. On the software side, engineers have put in countless hours writing, porting, and optimizing code for the operating systems, compilers, run time libraries, CASE tools and applications.

Hardware engineers have spent long hours designing the broad range of products that today span a 2000X price range. We sincerely acknowledge their efforts.

The organization, editing, and production of this text in final form remain largely the work of Charlie Greenman, whose clear writing is much appreciated.

Richard L. Sites and Richard T. Witek, February 1995

Preface to the First Edition

The Alpha architecture is a RISC architecture that was designed for high performance and longevity. Following Amdahl, Blaauw, and Brooks[2], we distinguish between *architecture* and *implementation*:

- *Computer architecture* is defined as the attributes of a computer seen by a machine-language programmer. This definition includes the instruction set, instruction formats, operation codes, addressing modes, and all registers and memory locations that may be directly manipulated by a machine-language programmer.

- *Implementation* is defined as the actual hardware structure, logic design, and data-path organization.

This architecture book describes the required behavior of all Alpha implementations, as seen by the machine-language programmer. The architecture does not speak to implementation considerations such as how fast a program runs, what specific bit pattern is left in a hardware register after an unpredictable operation, how to schedule code for a particular chip, or how to wire up a given chip; those considerations are described in implementation-specific documents.

Various Alpha implementations are expected over the coming years, starting with the Digital 21064 chip.

Goals

When we started the Alpha project in the fall of 1988, we had a small number of goals:

1. High performance
2. Longevity
3. Run VMS and UNIX
4. Easy migration from VAX (and soon-to-be MIPS) customer base

As principal architects, Rich Witek and I made design decisions that were driven directly by these goals.

We assumed that high performance was needed to make a new architecture attractive in the marketplace, and to keep Digital competitive.

We set a 15–25 year design horizon (longevity) and tried to avoid any design elements that we thought would become limitations during this time. The design horizon led directly to the conclusion that Alpha could not be a 32-bit architecture: 32-bit addresses will be too small within 10 years. We thus adopted a full 64-bit architecture, with a minimal number of 32-bit operations for backward compatibility. Wherever possible, 32-bit operands are put in registers in a 64-bit canonical form and operated upon with 64-bit operations.

The longevity goal also caused us to examine how the performance of implementations would scale up over 25 years. Over the past 25 years, computers have become about 1000 times faster. This suggested to us that Alpha implementations would need to do the same, or we would have to bet that the industry would fall off the historical performance curve. We

---

[2]Amdahl, G.M., G.A. Blaauw, and F.P. Brooks. Jr. "Architecture of the IBM System/360." *IBM Journal of Research and Development*, vol. 8, no. 2 (April 1964): 87-101.

were unwilling to bet against the industry, and were unwilling to ignore the issue, so we seriously examined the consequences of longevity.

We thought that it would be realistic for implementors to improve clock speeds by a factor of 10 over 25 years, but not by a factor of 100 or 1000. (Clock speeds have improved by about a factor of 100 over the past 25 years, but physical limits are now slowing down the rate of increase.)

We concluded that the remaining factor of 100 would have to come from other design dimensions. If you cannot make the clock faster, the next dimension is to do more work per clock cycle. So the Alpha architecture is focused on allowing implementations that issue many instructions every clock cycle. We thought that it would be realistic for implementors to achieve about a factor of 10 over 25 years by using multiple instruction issue, but not a factor of 100. Even a factor of 10 will require perhaps a decade of compiler research.

We concluded that the remaining factor of 10 would have to come from some other design dimensions. If you cannot make the clock faster, and cannot do more work per clock, the next dimension is to have multiple clocked instruction streams, that is, multiple processors. So the Alpha architecture is focused on allowing implementations that apply multiple processors to a single problem. We thought that it would be realistic for implementors to achieve the remaining factor of 10 over 25 years by using multiple processors.

Overall, the factor-of-1000 increase in performance looked reasonable, but required factor-of-10 increases in three different dimensions. These three dimensions therefore formed part of our design framework:

- Gracefully allow fast cycle time implementations
- Gracefully allow multiple-instruction-issue implementations
- Gracefully allow multiple-processor implementations

The cycle-time goal encouraged us to keep the instruction definitions very simple, and to keep the interactions between instructions very simple. The multiple-instruction-issue goal encouraged us to eliminate specialized registers, architected delay slots, precise arithmetic traps, and byte writes (with their embedded read-modify-write bottleneck). The multiple-processor goal encouraged us to consider the memory model and atomic-update primitives carefully. We adopted load-locked/store-conditional sequences as the atomic-update primitive, and eliminated strict read-write ordering between processors.

All of the above design decisions were driven directly by the performance and longevity goals. The lack of byte writes, precise arithmetic traps, and multiprocessor read/write ordering have been the most controversial decisions, so far.

Clean Sheet of Paper

To run both OpenVMS and UNIX without burdening the hardware implementations with elaborate (and sometimes conflicting) operating system underpinnings, we adopted an idea from a previous Digital RISC design. Alpha places the underpinnings for interrupt delivery and return, exceptions, context switching, memory management, and error handling in a set of privileged software subroutines called PALcode, PALcode subroutines have controlled entries, run with interrupts turned off, and have access to real hardware (implementation) registers. By having different sets of PALcode for different operating systems, the architecture itself is not biased toward a specific operating system or computing style.

PALcode allowed us to design an architecture that could run OpenVMS gracefully without elaborate hardware and without massively rewriting the VMS synchronization and protection mechanisms. PALcode lets the Alpha architecture support some complex VAX primitives (such as the interlocked queue instructions) that are heavily used by OpenVMS, without burdening a UNIX implementation in any way.

Finally, we also considered how to move VAX and MIPS code to Alpha. We rejected various forms of "compatibility mode" hardware, because they would have severely compromised the performance and time-to-market of the first implementation. Alter some experimentation, we adopted the strategy of running existing binary code by building software translators. One translator converts OpenVMS VAX images to functionally identical OpenVMS Alpha images. A second translator converts MIPS ULTRIX images to functionally identical DEC OSF/1 Alpha images.

Fundamentally, PALcode gave us a migration path for existing operating systems, and the translators (and native compilers) gave us a migration path for existing user-mode code. PALcode and the translators provided a clean sheet of design paper for the bulk of the Alpha architecture. Other than an extra set of VAX floating-point formats (included for good business reasons, but subsettable later), no specific VAX or MIPS features are carried directly into the Alpha architecture for compatibility reasons.

These considerations substantially shaped the architecture described in the rest of this book.

Organization

The first part of this book describes the instruction-set architecture, and is largely self-contained for readers who are involved with compilers or with assembly language programming. The second and third parts describe the supporting PALcode routines for each operating system—the specific operating system PALcode architecture.

Acknowledgments

My collaboration with Rich Witek over the past few years has been extremely rewarding, both personally and professionally. By combining our backgrounds and viewpoints, we have produced an architecture that is substantially better than either of us could have produced alone. Thank you, Rich.

A work of this magnitude cannot be done on a shoestring or in isolation. Rich and I were blessed with a rich environment of dozens and later hundreds of bright, thoughtful, and outspoken professional peers. I thank the management of Digital Equipment Corporation for providing that rich environment, and those peers for making the architecture so much more robust and well-considered.

Three people have especially influenced my views of computer architecture, through personal interaction and landmark machine design: Fred Brooks, John Cocke, and Seymour Cray. This work is built directly upon theirs, and could not exist without them.

The organization, editing, and production of this text in final form is largely the work of Charlie Greenman, whose clear writing is much appreciated.

Richard L. Sites, May 1992

Common Architecture (I)

This part describes the common Alpha architecture and contains the following:

Contents

1 Introduction (I)

2 Basic Architecture (I)

3 Instruction Formats (I)

4   Instruction Descriptions (I)

5   System Architecture and Programming Implications (I)

6 Common PALcode Architecture (I)

Figures

Tables

Chapter 1

Introduction (I)

Alpha is a 64-bit load/store RISC architecture that is designed with particular emphasis on the three elements that most affect performance: clock speed, multiple instruction issue, and multiple processors.

The Alpha architects examined and analyzed current and theoretical RISC architecture design elements and developed high-performance alternatives for the Alpha architecture. The architects adopted only those design elements that appeared valuable for a projected 25-year design horizon. Thus, Alpha becomes the first 21st century computer architecture.

The Alpha architecture is designed to avoid bias toward any particular operating system or programming language. Alpha supports the OpenVMS Alpha, DIGITAL UNIX, and Windows NT Alpha operating systems and supports simple software migration for applications that run on those operating systems.

This manual describes in detail how Alpha is designed to be the leadership 64-bit architecture of the computer industry.

1.1 The Alpha Approach to RISC Architecture

Alpha Is a True 64-Bit Architecture

Alpha was designed as a 64-bit architecture. All registers are 64 bits in length and all operations are performed between 64-bit registers. It is not a 32-bit architecture that was later expanded to 64 bits.

Alpha Is Designed for Very High-Speed Implementations

The instructions are very simple. All instructions are 32 bits in length. Memory operations are either loads or stores. All data manipulation is done between registers.

The Alpha architecture facilitates pipelining multiple instances of the same operations because there are no special registers and no condition codes.

The instructions interact with each other only by one instruction writing a register or memory and another instruction reading from the same place. That makes it particularly easy to build implementations that issue multiple instructions every CPU cycle.

Alpha makes it easy to maintain binary compatibility across multiple implementations and easy to maintain full speed on multiple-issue implementations. For example, there are no implementation-specific pipeline timing hazards, no load-delay slots, and no branch-delay slots.

The Alpha Approach to Byte Manipulation

The Alpha architecture reads and writes bytes between registers and memory with the LDBU and STB instructions. (Alpha also supports word read/writes with the LDWU and STW instructions.)

Byte shifting and masking is performed with normal 64-bit register-to-register instructions, crafted to keep instruction sequences short.

The Alpha Approach to Multiprocessor Shared Memory

As viewed from a second processor (including an I/O device), a sequence of reads and writes issued by one processor may be arbitrarily reordered by an implementation. This allows implementations to use multibank caches, bypassed write buffers, write merging, pipelined writes with retry on error, and so forth. If strict ordering between two accesses must be maintained, explicit memory barrier instructions can be inserted in the program.

The basic multiprocessor interlocking primitive is a RISC-style load_locked, modify, store_conditional sequence. If the sequence runs without interrupt, exception, or an interfering write from another processor, then the conditional store succeeds. Otherwise, the store fails and the program eventually must branch back and retry the sequence. This style of interlocking scales well with very fast caches and makes Alpha an especially attractive architecture for building multiple-processor systems.

Alpha Instructions Include Hints for Achieving Higher Speed

A number of Alpha instructions include hints for implementations, all aimed at achieving higher speed.

- Calculated jump instructions have a target hint that can allow much faster subroutine calls and returns.

- There are prefetching hints for the memory system that can allow much higher cache hit rates.

- There are granularity hints for the virtual-address mapping that can allow much more effective use of translation lookaside buffers for large contiguous structures.

PALcode – Alpha's Very Flexible Privileged Software Library

A Privileged Architecture Library (PALcode) is a set of subroutines that are specific to a particular Alpha operating system implementation. These subroutines provide operating-system primitives for context switching, interrupts, exceptions, and memory management. PALcode is similar to the BIOS libraries that are provided in personal computers.

PALcode subroutines are invoked by implementation hardware or by software CALL_PAL instructions.

PALcode is written in standard machine code with some implementation-specific extensions to provide access to low-level hardware.

PALcode lets Alpha implementations run the full OpenVMS Alpha, DIGITAL UNIX, and Windows NT Alpha operating systems. PALcode can provide this functionality with little overhead. For example, the OpenVMS Alpha PALcode instructions let Alpha run OpenVMS with little more hardware than that found on a conventional RISC machine: the PAL mode bit itself, plus four extra protection bits in each translation buffer entry.

Other versions of PALcode can be developed for real-time, teaching, and other applications.

PALcode makes Alpha an especially attractive architecture for multiple operating systems.

Alpha and Programming Languages

Alpha is an attractive architecture for compiling a large variety of programming languages. Alpha has been carefully designed to avoid bias toward one or two programming languages. For example:

- Alpha does not contain a subroutine call instruction that moves a register window by a fixed amount. Thus, Alpha is a good match for programming languages with many parameters and programming languages with no parameters.

- Alpha does not contain a global integer overflow enable bit. Such a bit would need to be changed at every subroutine boundary when a FORTRAN program calls a C program.

1.2 Data Format Overview

Alpha is a load/store RISC architecture with the following data characteristics:

- All operations are done between 64-bit registers.
- Memory is accessed via 64-bit virtual byte addresses, using the little-endian or, optionally, the big-endian byte numbering convention.
- There are 32 integer registers and 32 floating-point registers.
- Longword (32-bit) and quadword (64-bit) integers are supported.
- Five floating-point data types are supported:
  - VAX F_floating (32-bit)
  - VAX G_floating (64-bit)
  - IEEE single (32-bit)
  - IEEE double (64-bit)
  - IEEE extended (128-bit)

1.3 Instruction Format Overview

As shown in Figure 1–1, Alpha instructions are all 32 bits in length. There are four major instruction format classes that contain 0, 1, 2, or 3 register fields. All formats have a 6-bit opcode.

Figure 1–1: Instruction Format Overview

31 26	25 21	20 16	15 5	4 0	
Opcode	Number				PALcode Format
Opcode	RA	Disp			Branch Format
Opcode	RA	RB	Disp		Memory Format
Opcode	RA	RB	Function	RC	Operate Format

- **PALcode instructions** specify, in the function code field, one of a few dozen complex operations to be performed.

- **Conditional branch instructions** test register Ra and specify a signed 21-bit PC-relative longword target displacement. Subroutine calls put the return address in register Ra.

- **Load and store instructions** move bytes, words, longwords, or quadwords between register Ra and memory, using Rb plus a signed 16-bit displacement as the memory address.

- **Operate instructions** for floating-point and integer operations are both represented in Figure 1–1 by the operate format illustration and are as follows:

  - Word and byte sign-extension operators.

  - Floating-point operations use Ra and Rb as source registers and write the result in register Rc. There is an 11-bit extended opcode in the function field.

  - Integer operations use Ra and Rb or an 8-bit literal as the source operand, and write the result in register Rc.

  - Integer operate instructions can use the Rb field and part of the function field to specify an 8-bit literal. There is a 7-bit extended opcode in the function field.

1.4 Instruction Overview

PALcode Instructions

As described in Section 1.1, a Privileged Architecture Library (PALcode) is a set of subroutines that is specific to a particular Alpha operating-system implementation. These subroutines can be invoked by hardware or by software CALL_PAL instructions, which use the function field to vector to the specified subroutine.

Branch Instructions

Conditional branch instructions can test a register for positive/negative or for zero/nonzero, and they can test integer registers for even/odd. Unconditional branch instructions can write a return address into a register.

There is also a calculated jump instruction that branches to an arbitrary 64-bit address in a register.

Load/Store Instructions

Load and store instructions move 8-bit, 16-bit, 32-bit, or 64-bit aligned quantities from and to memory. Memory addresses are flat 64-bit virtual addresses with no segmentation.

The VAX floating-point load/store instructions swap words to give a consistent register format for floating-point operations.

A 32-bit integer datum is placed in a register in a canonical form that makes 33 copies of the high bit of the datum. A 32 bit floating-point datum is placed in a register in a canonical form that extends the exponent by 3 bits and extends the fraction with 29 low-order zeros. The 32-bit operates preserve these canonical forms.

Compilers, as directed by user declarations, can generate any mixture of 32-bit and 64-bit operations. The Alpha architecture has no 32/64 mode bit.

Integer Operate Instructions

The integer operate instructions manipulate full 64-bit values and include the usual assortment of arithmetic, compare, logical, and shift instructions.

There are just three 32-bit integer operates: add, subtract, and multiply. They differ from their 64-bit counterparts only in overflow detection and in producing 32-bit canonical results.

There is no integer divide instruction.

The Alpha architecture also supports the following additional operations:

- Scaled add/subtract instructions for quick subscript calculation
- 128-bit multiply for division by a constant, and multiprecision arithmetic
- Conditional move instructions for avoiding branch instructions
- An extensive set of in-register byte and word manipulation instructions
- A set of multimedia instructions that support graphics and video

Integer overflow trap enable is encoded in the function field of each instruction, rather than kept in a global state bit. Thus, for example, both ADDQ/V and ADDQ opcodes exist for specifying 64-bit ADD with and without overflow checking. That makes it easier to pipeline implementations.

Floating-Point Operate Instructions

The floating-point operate instructions include four complete sets of VAX and IEEE arithmetic instructions, plus instructions for performing conversions between floating-point and integer quantities.

In addition to the operations found in conventional RISC architectures, Alpha includes conditional move instructions for avoiding branches and merge sign/exponent instructions for simple field manipulation.

The arithmetic trap enables and rounding mode are encoded in the function field of each instruction, rather than kept in global state bits. That makes it easier to pipeline implementations.

1.5 Instruction Set Characteristics

Alpha instruction set characteristics are as follows:

- All instructions are 32 bits long and have a regular format.

- There are 32 integer registers (R0 through R31), each 64 bits wide. R31 reads as zero, and writes to R31 are ignored.

- All integer data manipulation is between integer registers, with up to two variable register source operands (one may be an 8-bit literal) and one register destination operand.

- There are 32 floating-point registers (F0 through F31), each 64 bits wide. F31 reads as zero, and writes to F31 are ignored.

- All floating-point data manipulation is between floating-point registers, with up to two register source operands and one register destination operand.

- Instructions can move data in an integer register file to a floating-point register file, and data in a floating-point register file to an integer register file. The instructions do not interpret bits in the register files and do not access memory.

- All memory reference instructions are of the load/store type that moves data between registers and memory.

- There are no branch condition codes. Branch instructions test an integer or floating-point register value, which may be the result of a previous compare.

- Integer and logical instructions operate on quadwords.

- Floating-point instructions operate on G_floating, F_floating, and IEEE extended, double, and single operands. D_floating "format compatibility," in which binary files of D_floating numbers may be processed, but without the last 3 bits of fraction precision, is also provided.

- A minimal number of VAX compatibility instructions are included.

1.6 Terminology and Conventions

The following sections describe the terminology and conventions used in this book.

1.6.1 Numbering

All numbers are decimal unless otherwise indicated. Where there is ambiguity, numbers other than decimal are indicated with the name of the base in subscript form, for example, 10_{16}.

1.6.2 Security Holes

A security hole is an error of commission, omission, or oversight in a system that allows protection mechanisms to be bypassed.

Security holes exist when unprivileged software (software running outside of kernel mode) can:

- Affect the operation of another process without authorization from the operating system;
- Amplify its privilege without authorization from the operating system; or
- Communicate with another process, either overtly or covertly, without authorization from the operating system.

The Alpha architecture has been designed to contain no architectural security holes. Hardware (processors, buses, controllers, and so on) and software should likewise be designed to avoid security holes.

1.6.3 UNPREDICTABLE and UNDEFINED

The terms UNPREDICTABLE and UNDEFINED are used throughout this book. Their meanings are quite different and must be carefully distinguished.

In particular, only privileged software (software running in kernel mode) can trigger UNDEFINED operations. Unprivileged software cannot trigger UNDEFINED operations. However, either privileged or unprivileged software can trigger UNPREDICTABLE results or occurrences.

UNPREDICTABLE results or occurrences do not disrupt the basic operation of the processor; it continues to execute instructions in its normal manner. In contrast, UNDEFINED operation can halt the processor or cause it to lose information.

The terms UNPREDICTABLE and UNDEFINED can be further described as follows:

UNPREDICTABLE

- Results or occurrences specified as UNPREDICTABLE may vary from moment to moment, implementation to implementation, and instruction to instruction within implementations. Software can never depend on results specified as UNPREDICTABLE.

- An UNPREDICTABLE result may acquire an arbitrary value subject to a few constraints. Such a result may be an arbitrary function of the input operands or of any state information that is accessible to the process in its current access mode. UNPREDICTABLE results may be unchanged from their previous values.

  Operations that produce UNPREDICTABLE results may also produce exceptions.

- An occurrence specified as UNPREDICTABLE may happen or not based on an arbitrary choice function. The choice function is subject to the same constraints as are UNPREDICTABLE results and, in particular, must not constitute a security hole.

  Specifically, UNPREDICTABLE results must not depend upon, or be a function of, the contents of memory locations or registers that are inaccessible to the current process in the current access mode.

  Also, operations that may produce UNPREDICTABLE results must not:

  - Write or modify the contents of memory locations or registers to which the current process in the current access mode does not have access, or

  - Halt or hang the system or any of its components.

  For example, a security hole would exist if some UNPREDICTABLE result depended on the value of a register in another process, on the contents of processor temporary registers left behind by some previously running process, or on a sequence of actions of different processes.

UNDEFINED

- Operations specified as UNDEFINED may vary from moment to moment, implementation to implementation, and instruction to instruction within implementations. The operation may vary in effect from nothing to stopping system operation.

- UNDEFINED operations may halt the processor or cause it to lose information. However, UNDEFINED operations must not cause the processor to hang, that is, reach an unhalted state from which there is no transition to a normal state in which the machine executes instructions.

1.6.4 Ranges and Extents

Ranges are specified by a pair of numbers separated by two periods and are inclusive. For example, a range of integers 0..4 includes the integers 0, 1, 2, 3, and 4.

Extents are specified by a pair of numbers in angle brackets separated by a colon and are inclusive. For example, bits <7:3> specify an extent of bits including bits 7, 6, 5, 4, and 3.

1.6.5 ALIGNED and UNALIGNED

In this document the terms ALIGNED and NATURALLY ALIGNED are used interchangeably to refer to data objects that are powers of two in size. An aligned datum of size $2^{**}N$ is stored in memory at a byte address that is a multiple of $2^{**}N$, that is, one that has N low-order zeros. Thus, an aligned 64-byte stack frame has a memory address that is a multiple of 64.

If a datum of size $2^{**}N$ is stored at a byte address that is not a multiple of $2^{**}N$, it is called UNALIGNED.

1.6.6 Must Be Zero (MBZ)

Fields specified as Must be Zero (MBZ) must never be filled by software with a non-zero value. These fields may be used at some future time. If the processor encounters a non-zero value in a field specified as MBZ, an Illegal Operand exception occurs.

1.6.7 Read As Zero (RAZ)

Fields specified as Read as Zero (RAZ) return a zero when read.

1.6.8 Should Be Zero (SBZ)

Fields specified as Should be Zero (SBZ) should be filled by software with a zero value. Non-zero values in SBZ fields produce UNPREDICTABLE results and may produce extraneous instruction-issue delays.

1.6.9 Ignore (IGN)

Fields specified as Ignore (IGN) are ignored when written.

1.6.10 Implementation Dependent (IMP)

Fields specified as Implementation Dependent (IMP) may be used for implementation-specific purposes. Each implementation must document fully the behavior of all fields marked as IMP by the Alpha specification.

1.6.11 Illustration Conventions

Illustrations that depict registers or memory follow the convention that increasing addresses run right to left and top to bottom.

1.6.12 Macro Code Example Conventions

All instructions in macro code examples are either listed in Common Architecture (I), Chapter 4 or OpenVMS Software II-A, Chapter 2, or are stylized code forms found in Appendix A.

Chapter 2

Basic Architecture (I)

2.1 Addressing

The basic addressable unit in the Alpha architecture is the 8-bit byte. Virtual addresses are 64 bits long. An implementation may support a smaller virtual address space. The minimum virtual address size is 43 bits.

Virtual addresses as seen by the program are translated into physical memory addresses by the memory management mechanism.

Although the data types in Section 2.2 are described in terms of little-endian byte addressing, implementations may also include big-endian addressing support, as described in Section 2.3. All current implementations have some big-endian support.

2.2 Data Types

Following are descriptions of the Alpha architecture data types.

2.2.1 Byte

A byte is 8 contiguous bits starting on an addressable byte boundary. The bits are numbered from right to left, 0 through 7, as shown in Figure 2–1.

Figure 2–1: Byte Format

A byte is specified by its address A. A byte is an 8-bit value. The byte is only supported in Alpha by the load, store, sign-extend, extract, mask, insert, and zap instructions.

2.2.2 Word

A word is 2 contiguous bytes starting on an arbitrary byte boundary. The bits are numbered from right to left, 0 through 15, as shown in Figure 2–2.

Figure 2–2: Word Format

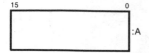

A word is specified by its address, the address of the byte containing bit 0.

A word is a 16-bit value. The word is only supported in Alpha by the load, store, sign-extend, extract, mask, and insert instructions.

2.2.3 Longword

A longword is 4 contiguous bytes starting on an arbitrary byte boundary. The bits are numbered from right to left, 0 through 31, as shown in Figure 2–3.

Figure 2–3: Longword Format

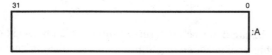

A longword is specified by its address A, the address of the byte containing bit 0. A longword is a 32-bit value.

When interpreted arithmetically, a longword is a two's-complement integer with bits of increasing significance from 0 through 30. Bit 31 is the sign bit. The longword is only supported in Alpha by sign-extended load and store instructions and by longword arithmetic instructions.

Note:

Alpha implementations will impose a significant performance penalty when accessing longword operands that are not naturally aligned. (A naturally aligned longword has zero as the low-order two bits of its address.)

2.2.4 Quadword

A quadword is 8 contiguous bytes starting on an arbitrary byte boundary. The bits are numbered from right to left, 0 through 63, as shown in Figure 2–4.

Figure 2–4: Quadword Format

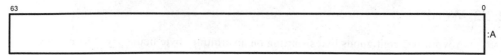

A quadword is specified by its address A, the address of the byte containing bit 0. A quadword is a 64-bit value. When interpreted arithmetically, a quadword is either a two's-complement integer with bits of increasing significance from 0 through 62 and bit 63 as the sign bit, or an unsigned integer with bits of increasing significance from 0 through 63.

Note:

> Alpha implementations will impose a significant performance penalty when accessing quadword operands that are not naturally aligned. (A naturally aligned quadword has zero as the low-order three bits of its address.)

2.2.5 VAX Floating-Point Formats

VAX floating-point numbers are stored in one set of formats in memory and in a second set of formats in registers. The floating-point load and store instructions convert between these formats purely by rearranging bits; no rounding or range-checking is done by the load and store instructions.

2.2.5.1 F_floating

An F_floating datum is 4 contiguous bytes in memory starting on an arbitrary byte boundary. The bits are labeled from right to left, 0 through 31, as shown in Figure 2–5 .

Figure 2–5: F_floating Datum

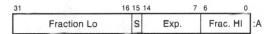

An F_floating operand occupies 64 bits in a floating register, left-justified in the 64-bit register, as shown in Figure 2–6.

Figure 2–6: F_floating Register Format

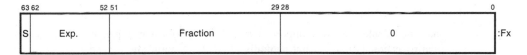

The F_floating load instruction reorders bits on the way in from memory, expands the exponent from 8 to 11 bits, and sets the low-order fraction bits to zero. This produces in the register an equivalent G_floating number suitable for either F_floating or G_floating operations. The mapping from 8-bit memory-format exponents to 11-bit register-format exponents is shown in Table 2–1. This mapping preserves both normal values and exceptional values.

Table 2–1: F_floating Load Exponent Mapping (MAP_F)

Memory <14:7>	Register <62:52>	
1 1111111	1 000 1111111	
1 xxxxxxx	1 000 xxxxxxx	(xxxxxxx not all 1's)
0 xxxxxxx	0 111 xxxxxxx	(xxxxxxx not all 0's)
0 0000000	0 000 0000000	

The F_floating store instruction reorders register bits on the way to memory and does no checking of the low-order fraction bits. Register bits <61:59> and <28:0> are ignored by the store instruction.

An F_floating datum is specified by its address A, the address of the byte containing bit 0. The memory form of an F_floating datum is sign magnitude with bit 15 the sign bit, bits <14:7> an excess-128 binary exponent, and bits <6:0> and <31:16> a normalized 24-bit fraction with the redundant most significant fraction bit not represented. Within the fraction, bits of increasing significance are from 16 through 31 and 0 through 6. The 8-bit exponent field encodes the values 0 through 255. An exponent value of 0, together with a sign bit of 0, is taken to indicate that the F_floating datum has a value of 0.

If the result of a VAX floating-point format instruction has a value of zero, the instruction always produces a datum with a sign bit of 0, an exponent of 0, and all fraction bits of 0. Exponent values of 1..255 indicate true binary exponents of −127..127. An exponent value of 0, together with a sign bit of 1, is taken as a reserved operand. Floating-point instructions processing a reserved operand take an arithmetic exception. The value of an F_floating datum is in the approximate range $0.29*10**-38$ through $1.7*10**38$. The precision of an F_floating datum is approximately one part in $2**23$, typically 7 decimal digits. See Section 4.7.

Note:

> Alpha implementations will impose a significant performance penalty when accessing F_floating operands that are not naturally aligned. (A naturally aligned F_floating datum has zero as the low-order two bits of its address.)

2.2.5.2 G_floating

A G_floating datum in memory is 8 contiguous bytes starting on an arbitrary byte boundary. The bits are labeled from right to left, 0 through 63, as shown in Figure 2–7.

Figure 2–7: G_floating Datum

A G_floating operand occupies 64 bits in a floating register, arranged as shown in Figure 2–8.

Figure 2–8: G_floating Register Format

A G_floating datum is specified by its address A, the address of the byte containing bit 0. The form of a G_floating datum is sign magnitude with bit 15 the sign bit, bits <14:4> an excess-1024 binary exponent, and bits <3:0> and <63:16> a normalized 53-bit fraction with the redundant most significant fraction bit not represented. Within the fraction, bits of increasing significance are from 48 through 63, 32 through 47, 16 through 31, and 0 through 3. The 11-bit exponent field encodes the values 0 through 2047. An exponent value of 0, together with a sign bit of 0, is taken to indicate that the G_floating datum has a value of 0.

If the result of a floating-point instruction has a value of zero, the instruction always produces a datum with a sign bit of 0, an exponent of 0, and all fraction bits of 0. Exponent values of 1..2047 indicate true binary exponents of –1023..1023. An exponent value of 0, together with a sign bit of 1, is taken as a reserved operand. Floating-point instructions processing a reserved operand take a user-visible arithmetic exception. The value of a G_floating datum is in the approximate range $0.56*10**–308$ through $0.9*10**308$. The precision of a G_floating datum is approximately one part in $2**52$, typically 15 decimal digits. See Section 4.7.

Note:

> Alpha implementations will impose a significant performance penalty when accessing G_floating operands that are not naturally aligned. (A naturally aligned G_floating datum has zero as the low-order three bits of its address.)

2.2.5.3 D_floating

A D_floating datum in memory is 8 contiguous bytes starting on an arbitrary byte boundary. The bits are labeled from right to left, 0 through 63, as shown in Figure 2–9.

Figure 2–9: D_floating Datum

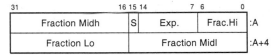

A D_floating operand occupies 64 bits in a floating register, arranged as shown in Figure 2–10.

Figure 2–10: D_floating Register Format

The reordering of bits required for a D_floating load or store is identical to that required for a G_floating load or store. The G_floating load and store instructions are therefore used for loading or storing D_floating data.

A D_floating datum is specified by its address A, the address of the byte containing bit 0. The memory form of a D_floating datum is identical to an F_floating datum except for 32 additional low significance fraction bits. Within the fraction, bits of increasing significance are from 48 through 63, 32 through 47, 16 through 31, and 0 through 6. The exponent conventions and approximate range of values is the same for D_floating as F_floating. The precision of a D_floating datum is approximately one part in $2**55$, typically 16 decimal digits.

Notes:

> D_floating is not a fully supported data type; no D_floating arithmetic operations are provided in the architecture. For backward compatibility, exact D_floating arithmetic may be provided via software emulation. D_floating "format compatibility" in which binary files of D_floating numbers may be processed, but without the last three bits of fraction precision, can be obtained via conversions to G_floating, G arithmetic operations, then conversion back to D_floating.
>
> Alpha implementations will impose a significant performance penalty on access to D_floating operands that are not naturally aligned. (A naturally aligned D_floating datum has zero as the low-order three bits of its address.)

2.2.6 IEEE Floating-Point Formats

The IEEE standard for binary floating-point arithmetic, ANSI/IEEE 754-1985, defines four floating-point formats in two groups, basic and extended, each having two widths, single and double. The Alpha architecture supports the basic single and double formats, with the basic double format serving as the extended single format. The values representable within a format are specified by using three integer parameters:

- P – the number of fraction bits
- Emax – the maximum exponent
- Emin – the minimum exponent

Within each format, only the following entities are permitted:

- Numbers of the form $(-1)**S \times 2**E \times b(0).b(1)b(2)..b(P-1)$ where:
  - S = 0 or 1
  - E = any integer between Emin and Emax, inclusive
  - b(n) = 0 or 1
- Two infinities – positive and negative
- At least one Signaling NaN
- At least one Quiet NaN

NaN is an acronym for Not-a-Number. A NaN is an IEEE floating-point bit pattern that represents something other than a number. NaNs come in two forms: Signaling NaNs and Quiet

NaNs. Signaling NaNs are used to provide values for uninitialized variables and for arithmetic enhancements. Quiet NaNs provide retrospective diagnostic information regarding previous invalid or unavailable data and results. Signaling NaNs signal an invalid operation when they are an operand to an arithmetic instruction, and may generate an arithmetic exception. Quiet NaNs propagate through almost every operation without generating an arithmetic exception.

Arithmetic with the infinities is handled as if the operands were of arbitrarily large magnitude. Negative infinity is less than every finite number; positive infinity is greater than every finite number.

2.2.6.1 S_Floating

An IEEE single-precision, or S_floating, datum occupies 4 contiguous bytes in memory starting on an arbitrary byte boundary. The bits are labeled from right to left, 0 through 31, as shown in Figure 2–11.

Figure 2–11: S_floating Datum

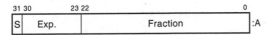

An S_floating operand occupies 64 bits in a floating register, left-justified in the 64-bit register, as shown in Figure 2–12.

Figure 2–12: S_floating Register Format

The S_floating load instruction reorders bits on the way in from memory, expanding the exponent from 8 to 11 bits, and sets the low-order fraction bits to zero. This produces in the register an equivalent T_floating number, suitable for either S_floating or T_floating operations. The mapping from 8-bit memory-format exponents to 11-bit register-format exponents is shown in Table 2–2.

Table 2–2: S_floating Load Exponent Mapping (MAP_S)

Memory <30:23>	Register <62:52>	
1 1111111	1 111 1111111	
1 xxxxxxx	1 000 xxxxxxx	(xxxxxx not all 1's)
0 xxxxxxx	0 111 xxxxxxx	(xxxxxx not all 0's)
0 0000000	0 000 0000000	

This mapping preserves both normal values and exceptional values. Note that the mapping for all 1's differs from that of F_floating load, since for S_floating all 1's is an exceptional value and for F_floating all 1's is a normal value.

The S_floating store instruction reorders register bits on the way to memory and does no checking of the low-order fraction bits. Register bits <61:59> and <28:0> are ignored by the store instruction. The S_floating load instruction does no checking of the input.

The S_floating store instruction does no checking of the data; the preceding operation should have specified an S_floating result.

An S_floating datum is specified by its address A, the address of the byte containing bit 0. The memory form of an S_floating datum is sign magnitude with bit 31 the sign bit, bits <30:23> an excess-127 binary exponent, and bits <22:0> a 23-bit fraction.

The value (V) of an S_floating number is inferred from its constituent sign (S), exponent (E), and fraction (F) fields as follows:

- If E=255 and F<>0, then V is NaN, regardless of S.
- If E=255 and F=0, then V = $(-1)^{**}S$ x Infinity.
- If 0 < E < 255, then V = $(-1)^{**}S$ x $2^{**}(E-127)$ x (1.F).
- If E=0 and F<>0, then V = $(-1)^{**}S$ x $2^{**}(-126)$ x (0.F).
- If E=0 and F=0, then V = $(-1)^{**}S$ x 0 (zero).

Floating-point operations on S_floating numbers may take an arithmetic exception for a variety of reasons, including invalid operations, overflow, underflow, division by zero, and inexact results.

Note:

Alpha implementations will impose a significant performance penalty when accessing S_floating operands that are not naturally aligned. (A naturally aligned S_floating datum has zero as the low-order two bits of its address.)

2.2.6.2 T_floating

An IEEE double-precision, or T_floating, datum occupies 8 contiguous bytes in memory starting on an arbitrary byte boundary. The bits are labeled from right to left, 0 through 63, as shown in Figure 2–13.

Figure 2–13: T_floating Datum

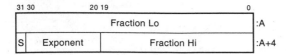

A T_floating operand occupies 64 bits in a floating register, arranged as shown in Figure 2–14.

Figure 2–14: T_floating Register Format

The T_floating load instruction performs no bit reordering on input, nor does it perform checking of the input data.

The T_floating store instruction performs no bit reordering on output. This instruction does no checking of the data; the preceding operation should have specified a T_floating result.

A T_floating datum is specified by its address A, the address of the byte containing bit 0. The form of a T_floating datum is sign magnitude with bit 63 the sign bit, bits <62:52> an excess-1023 binary exponent, and bits <51:0> a 52-bit fraction.

The value (V) of a T_floating number is inferred from its constituent sign (S), exponent (E), and fraction (F) fields as follows:

- If E=2047 and F<>0, then V is NaN, regardless of S.
- If E=2047 and F=0, then V = $(-1)^{**}S$ x Infinity.
- If $0 < E < 2047$, then V = $(-1)^{**}S$ x $2^{**}(E-1023)$ x (1.F).
- If E=0 and F<>0, then V = $(-1)^{**}S$ x $2^{**}(-1022)$ x (0.F).
- If E=0 and F=0, then V = $(-1)^{**}S$ x 0 (zero).

Floating-point operations on T_floating numbers may take an arithmetic exception for a variety of reasons, including invalid operations, overflow, underflow, division by zero, and inexact results.

Note:

Alpha implementations will impose a significant performance penalty when accessing T_floating operands that are not naturally aligned. (A naturally aligned T_floating datum has zero as the low-order three bits of its address.)

2.2.6.3 X_Floating

Support for 128-bit IEEE extended-precision (X_float) floating-point is initially provided entirely through software. This section is included to preserve the intended consistency of implementation with other IEEE floating-point data types, should the X_float data type be supported in future hardware.

An IEEE extended-precision, or X_floating, datum occupies 16 contiguous bytes in memory, starting on an arbitrary byte boundary. The bits are labeled from right to left, 0 through 127, as shown in Figure 2–15.

Figure 2–15: X_floating Datum

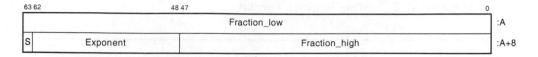

An X_floating datum occupies two consecutive even/odd floating-point registers (such as F4/F5), as shown in Figure 2–16.

Figure 2–16: X_floating Register Format

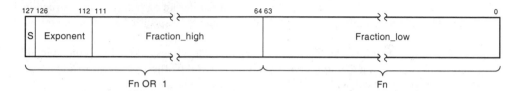

An X_floating datum is specified by its address A, the address of the byte containing bit 0. The form of an X_floating datum is sign magnitude with bit 127 the sign bit, bits <126:112> an excess–16383 binary exponent, and bits <111:0> a 112-bit fraction.

The value (V) of an X_floating number is inferred from its constituent sign (S), exponent (E), and fraction (F) fields as follows:

- If E=32767 and F<>0, then V is a NaN, regardless of S.

- If E=32767 and F=0, then V = $(-1)^{**}$S x Infinity.

- If $0 < E < 32767$, then V = $(-1)^{**}$S x 2^{**}(E–16383) x (1.F).

- If E=0 and F<> 0, then V = $(-1)^{**}$S x 2^{**}(–16382) x (0.F).

- If E = 0 and F = 0, then V = $(-1)^{**}$S x 0 (zero).

Note:

Alpha implementations will impose a significant performance penalty when accessing X_floating operands that are not naturally aligned. (A naturally aligned X_floating datum has zero as the low-order four bits of its address.)

X_Floating Big-Endian Formats

Section 2.3 describes Alpha support for big-endian data types. It is intended that software or hardware implementation for a big-endian X_float data type comply with that support and have the following formats.

Figure 2–17: X_floating Big-Endian Datum

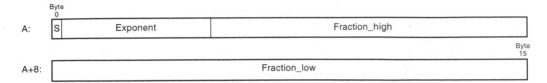

Figure 2–18: X_floating Big-Endian Register Format

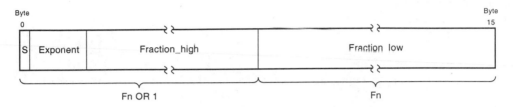

2.2.7 Longword Integer Format in Floating-Point Unit

A longword integer operand occupies 32 bits in memory, arranged as shown in Figure 2–19.

Figure 2–19: Longword Integer Datum

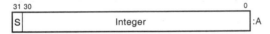

A longword integer operand occupies 64 bits in a floating register, arranged as shown in Figure 2–20.

Figure 2–20: Longword Integer Floating-Register Format

There is no explicit longword load or store instruction; the S_floating load/store instructions are used to move longword data into or out of the floating registers. The register bits <61:59> are set by the S_floating load exponent mapping. They are ignored by S_floating store. They are also ignored in operands of a longword integer operate instruction, and they are set to 000 in the result of a longword operate instruction.

The register format bit <62> "I" in Figure 2–20 is part of the Integer field in Figure 2–19 and represents the high-order bit of that field.

Note:

Alpha implementations will impose a significant performance penalty when accessing longwords that are not naturally aligned. (A naturally aligned longword datum has zero as the low-order two bits of its address.)

2.2.8 Quadword Integer Format in Floating-Point Unit

A quadword integer operand occupies 64 bits in memory, arranged as shown in Figure 2–21.

Figure 2–21: Quadword Integer Datum

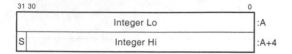

A quadword integer operand occupies 64 bits in a floating register, arranged as shown in Figure 2–22.

Figure 2–22: Quadword Integer Floating-Register Format

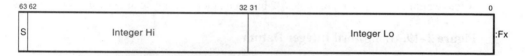

There is no explicit quadword load or store instruction; the T_floating load/store instructions are used to move quadword data between memory and the floating registers. (The ITOFT and FTOIT are used to move quadword data between integer and floating registers.)

The T_floating load instruction performs no bit reordering on input. The T_floating store instruction performs no bit reordering on output. This instruction does no checking of the data; when used to store quadwords, the preceding operation should have specified a quadword result.

Note:

Alpha implementations will impose a significant performance penalty when accessing quadwords that are not naturally aligned. (A naturally aligned quadword datum has zero as the low-order three bits of its address.)

2.2.9 Data Types with No Hardware Support

- The following VAX data types are not directly supported in Alpha hardware. Octaword
- H_floating
- D_floating (except load/store and convert to/from G_floating)
- Variable-Length Bit Field
- Character String

- Trailing Numeric String
- Leading Separate Numeric String
- Packed Decimal String

2.3 Big-Endian Addressing Support

Alpha implementations may include optional big-endian addressing support.

In a little-endian machine, the bytes within a quadword are numbered right to left:

Figure 2–23: Little-Endian Byte Addressing

In a big-endian machine, they are numbered left to right:

Figure 2–24: Big-Endian Byte Addressing

Bit numbering within bytes is not affected by the byte numbering convention (big-endian or little-endian).

The format for the X_floating big-endian data type is shown in Section 2.2.6.3.

The byte numbering convention does not matter when accessing complete aligned quadwords in memory. However, the numbering convention does matter when accessing smaller or unaligned quantities, or when manipulating data in registers, as follows:

- A quadword load or store of data at location 0 moves the same eight bytes under both numbering conventions. However, a longword load or store of data at location 4 must move the leftmost half of a quadword under the little-endian convention, and the rightmost half under the big-endian convention. Thus, to support both conventions, the convention being used must be known and it must affect longword load/store operations.

- A byte extract of byte 5 from a quadword of data into the low byte of a register requires a right shift of 5 bytes under the little-endian convention, but a right shift of 2 bytes under the big-endian convention.

- Manipulation of data in a register is almost the same for both conventions. In both, integer and floating-point data have their sign bits in the leftmost byte and their least significant bit in the rightmost byte, so the same integer and floating-point instructions are used unchanged for both conventions. Big-endian character strings have their most significant character on the left, while little-endian strings have their most significant character on the right.

- The compare byte (CMPBGE) instruction is neutral about direction, doing eight byte compares in parallel. However, following the CMPBGE instruction, the code is different that examines the byte mask to determine which string is larger, depending on whether the rightmost or leftmost unequal byte is used. Thus, compilers must be instructed to generate somewhat different code sequences for the two conventions.

Implementations that include big-endian support must supply all of the following features:

- A means at boot time to choose the byte numbering convention. The implementation is not required to support dynamically changing the convention during program execution. The chosen convention applies to all code executed, both operating-system and user.

- If the big-endian convention is chosen, the longword-length load/store instructions (LDF, LDL, LDL_L, LDS, STF, STL, STL_C, STS) invert bit va<2> (bit 2 of the virtual address). This has the effect of accessing the half of a quadword other than the half that would be accessed under the little-endian convention.

- If the big-endian convention is chosen, the word-length load instruction, LDWU, inverts bits va<1:2> (bits 1 and 2 of the virtual address). This has the effect of accessing the half of the longword that would be accessed under the little-endian convention.

- If the big-endian convention is chosen, the byte-length load instruction, LDBU, inverts bits va<0:2> (bits 0 through 2 of the virtual address). This has the effect of accessing the half of the word that would be accessed under the little-endian convention.

- If the big-endian convention is chosen, the byte manipulation instructions (EXTxx, INSxx, MSKxx) invert bits Rbv<2:0>. This has the effect of changing a shift of 5 bytes into a shift of 2 bytes, for example.

The instruction stream is always considered to be little-endian, and is independent of the chosen byte numbering convention. Compilers, linkers, and debuggers must be aware of this when accessing an instruction stream using data-stream load/store instructions. Thus, the rightmost instruction in a quadword is always executed first and always has the instruction-stream address 0 MOD 8. The same bytes accessed by a longword load/store instruction have data-stream address 0 MOD 8 under the little-endian convention, and 4 MOD 8 under the big-endian convention.

Using either byte numbering convention, it is sometimes necessary to access data that originated on a machine that used the other convention. When this occurs, it is often necessary to swap the bytes within a datum. See Appendix A, *Byte Swap*, for a suggested code sequence.

Chapter 3

Instruction Formats (I)

3.1 Alpha Registers

Each Alpha processor has a set of registers that hold the current processor state. If an Alpha system contains multiple Alpha processors, there are multiple per-processor sets of these registers.

3.1.1 Program Counter

The Program Counter (PC) is a special register that addresses the instruction stream. As each instruction is decoded, the PC is advanced to the next sequential instruction. This is referred to as the *updated PC*. Any instruction that uses the value of the PC will use the updated PC. The PC includes only bits <63:2> with bits <1:0> treated as RAZ/IGN. This quantity is a long-word-aligned byte address. The PC is an implied operand on conditional branch and subroutine jump instructions. The PC is not accessible as an integer register.

3.1.2 Integer Registers

There are 32 integer registers (R0 through R31), each 64 bits wide.

Register R31 is assigned special meaning by the Alpha architecture. When R31 is specified as a register source operand, a zero-valued operand is supplied.

For all cases except the Unconditional Branch and Jump instructions, results of an instruction that specifies R31 as a destination operand are discarded. Also, it is UNPREDICTABLE whether the other destination operands (implicit and explicit) are changed by the instruction. It is implementation dependent to what extent the instruction is actually executed once it has been fetched. An exception is never signaled for a load that specifies R31 as a destination operation. For all other operations, it is UNPREDICTABLE whether exceptions are signaled during the execution of such an instruction. Note, however, that exceptions associated with the instruction fetch of such an instruction are always signaled.

Implementation note:

As described in Appendix A, certain load instructions to an R31 destination are the preferred method for performing a cache block prefetch.

There are some interesting cases involving R31 as a destination:

- STx_C R31,disp(Rb)

   Although this might seem like a good way to zero out a shared location and reset the lock_flag, this instruction causes the lock_flag and virtual location {Rbv + SEXT(disp)} to become UNPREDICTABLE.

- LDx_L R31,disp(Rb)

   This instruction produces no useful result since it causes both lock_flag and locked_physical_address to become UNPREDICTABLE.

Unconditional Branch (BR and BSR) and Jump (JMP, JSR, RET, and JSR_COROUTINE) instructions, when R31 is specified as the Ra operand, execute normally and update the PC with the target virtual address. Of course, no PC value can be saved in R31.

3.1.3 Floating-Point Registers

There are 32 floating-point registers (F0 through F31), each 64 bits wide.

When F31 is specified as a register source operand, a true zero-valued operand is supplied. See Section 4.7.3 for a definition of true zero.

Results of an instruction that specifies F31 as a destination operand are discarded and it is UNPREDICTABLE whether the other destination operands (implicit and explicit) are changed by the instruction. In this case, it is implementation-dependent to what extent the instruction is actually executed once it has been fetched. An exception is never signaled for a load that specifies F31 as a destination operation. For all other operations, it is UNPREDICT-ABLE whether exceptions are signaled during the execution of such an instruction. Note, however, that exceptions associated with the instruction fetch of such an instruction are always signaled.

Implementation note:

   As described in Appendix A, certain load instructions to an F31 destination are the preferred method for signalling a cache block prefetch.

A floating-point instruction that operates on single-precision data reads all bits <63:0> of the source floating-point register. A floating-point instruction that produces a single-precision result writes all bits <63:0> of the destination floating-point register.

3.1.4 Lock Registers

There are two per-processor registers associated with the LDx_L and STx_C instructions, the lock_flag and the locked_physical_address register. The use of these registers is described in Section 4.2.

3.1.5 Processor Cycle Counter (PCC) Register

The PCC register consists of two 32-bit fields. The low-order 32 bits (PCC<31:0>) are an unsigned wrapping counter, PCC_CNT. The high-order 32 bits (PCC<63:32>), PCC_OFF, are operating system dependent in their implementation.

PCC_CNT is the base clock register for measuring time intervals and is suitable for timing intervals on the order of nanoseconds.

PCC_CNT increments once per N CPU cycles, where N is an implementation-specific integer in the range 1..16. The cycle counter frequency is the number of times the processor cycle counter gets incremented per second. The integer count wraps to 0 from a count of FFFF FFFF$_{16}$. The counter wraps no more frequently than 1.5 times the implementation's interval clock interrupt period (which is two thirds of the interval clock interrupt frequency), which guarantees that an interrupt occurs before PCC_CNT overflows twice

PCC_OFF need not contain a value related to time and could contain all zeros in a simple implementation. However, if PCC_OFF is used to calculate a per-process or per-thread cycle count, it must contain a value that, when added to PCC_CNT, returns the total PCC register count for that process or thread, modulo 2**32.

Implementation Note:

OpenVMS Alpha and DIGITAL UNIX supply a per-process value in PCC_OFF.

PCC is required on all implementations. It is required for every processor, and each processor on a multiprocessor system has its own private, independent PCC.

The PCC is read by the RPCC instruction. See Section 4.11.8.

3.1.6 Optional Registers

Some Alpha implementations may include optional memory prefetch or VAX compatibility processor registers.

3.1.6.1 Memory Prefetch Registers

If the prefetch instructions FETCH and FETCH_M are implemented, an implementation will include two sets of state prefetch registers used by those instructions. The use of these registers is described in Section 4.11. These registers are not directly accessible by software and are listed for completeness.

3.1.6.2 VAX Compatibility Register

The VAX compatibility instructions RC and RS include the intr_flag register, as described in Section 4.12.

3.2 Notation

The notation used to describe the operation of each instruction is given as a sequence of control and assignment statements in an ALGOL-like syntax.

3.2.1 Operand Notation

Tables 3–1, 3–2, and 3–3 list the notation for the operands, the operand values, and the other expression operands.

Table 3–1: Operand Notation

Notation	Meaning
Ra	An integer register operand in the Ra field of the instruction
Rb	An integer register operand in the Rb field of the instruction
#b	An integer literal operand in the Rb field of the instruction
Rc	An integer register operand in the Rc field of the instruction
Fa	A floating-point register operand in the Ra field of the instruction
Fb	A floating-point register operand in the Rb field of the instruction
Fc	A floating-point register operand in the Rc field of the instruction

Table 3–2: Operand Value Notation

Notation	Meaning
Rav	The value of the Ra operand. This is the contents of register Ra.
Rbv	The value of the Rb operand. This could be the contents of register Rb, or a zero-extended 8-bit literal in the case of an Operate format instruction.
Fav	The value of the floating point Fa operand. This is the contents of register Fa.
Fbv	The value of the floating point Fb operand. This is the contents of register Fb.

Table 3–3: Expression Operand Notation

Notation	Meaning
IPR_x	Contents of Internal Processor Register x)
IPR_SP[mode]	Contents of the per-mode stack pointer selected by mode
PC	Updated PC value
Rn	Contents of integer register n
Fn	Contents of floating-point register n
X[m]	Element m of array X

3.2.2 Instruction Operand Notation

The notation used to describe instruction operands follows from the operand specifier notation used in the *VAX Architecture Standard*. Instruction operands are described as follows:

```
<name>.<access type><data type>
```

3.2.2.1 Operand Name Notation

Specifies the instruction field (Ra, Rb, Rc, or disp) and register type of the operand (integer or floating). It can be one of the following:

Table 3–4: Operand Name Notation

Name	Meaning
disp	The displacement field of the instruction
fnc	The PALcode function field of the instruction
Ra	An integer register operand in the Ra field of the instruction
Rb	An integer register operand in the Rb field of the instruction
#b	An integer literal operand in the Rb field of the instruction
Rc	An integer register operand in the Rc field of the instruction
Fa	A floating-point register operand in the Ra field of the instruction
Fb	A floating-point register operand in the Rb field of the instruction
Fc	A floating-point register operand in the Rc field of the instruction

3.2.2.2 Operand Access Type Notation

A letter that denotes the operand access type:

Table 3–5: Operand Access Type Notation

Access Type	Meaning
a	The operand is used in an address calculation to form an effective address. The data type code that follows indicates the units of addressability (or scale factor) applied to this operand when the instruction is decoded. For example: ".al" means scale by 4 (longwords) to get byte units (used in branch displacements); ".ab" means the operand is already in byte units (used in load/store instructions).
i	The operand is an immediate literal in the instruction.

Table 3–5: Operand Access Type Notation (Continued)

Access Type	Meaning
r	The operand is read only.
m	The operand is both read and written.
w	The operand is write only.

3.2.2.3 Operand Data Type Notation

A letter that denotes the data type of the operand:

Table 3–6: Operand Data Type Notation

Data Type	Meaning
b	Byte
f	F_floating
g	G_floating
l	Longword
q	Quadword
s	IEEE single floating (S_floating)
t	IEEE double floating (T_floating)
w	Word
x	The data type is specified by the instruction

3.2.3 Operators

Table 3–7 describes the operators:

Table 3–7: Operators

Operator	Meaning
!	Comment delimiter
+	Addition
-	Subtraction
*	Signed multiplication
*U	Unsigned multiplication
**	Exponentiation (left argument raised to right argument)
/	Division
←	Replacement

Table 3–7: Operators (Continued)

Operator	Meaning
||	Bit concatenation
{ }	Indicates explicit operator precedence
(x)	Contents of memory location whose address is x
x <m:n>	Contents of bit field of x defined by bits n through m
x <m>	M'th bit of x
ACCESS(x,y)	Accessibility of the location whose address is x using the access mode y. Returns a Boolean value TRUE if the address is accessible, else FALSE.
AND	Logical product
ARITH_RIGHT_SHIFT(x,y)	Arithmetic right shift of first operand by the second operand. Y is an unsigned shift value. Bit 63, the sign bit, is copied into vacated bit positions and shifted out bits are discarded.
BYTE_ZAP(x,y)	X is a quadword, y is an 8-bit vector in which each bit corresponds to a byte of the result. The y bit to x byte correspondence is y <n> ↔ x <8n+7:8n>. This correspondence also exists between y and the result.
	For each bit of y from n = 0 to 7, if y <n> is 0 then byte <n> of x is copied to byte <n> of result, and if y <n> is 1 then byte <n> of result is forced to all zeros.

Table 3–7: Operators (Continued)

Operator	Meaning
CASE	The CASE construct selects one of several actions based on the value of its argument. The form of a case is:

```
CASE argument OF
     argvalue1: action_1
     argvalue2: action_2
       . . .
     argvaluen:action_n
     [otherwise: default_action]
ENDCASE
```

If the value of argument is argvalue1 then action_1 is executed; if argument = argvalue2, then action_2 is executed, and so forth.

Once a single action is executed, the code stream breaks to the ENDCASE (there is an implicit break as in Pascal). Each action may nonetheless be a sequence of pseudocode operations, one operation per line.

Optionally, the last argvalue may be the atom 'otherwise'. The associated default action will be taken if none of the other argvalues match the argument.

Operator	Meaning
DIV	Integer division (truncates)
LEFT_SHIFT(x,y)	Logical left shift of first operand by the second operand. Y is an unsigned shift value. Zeros are moved into the vacated bit positions, and shifted out bits are discarded.
LOAD_LOCKED	The processor records the target physical address in a per-processor locked_physical_address register and sets the per-processor lock_flag.
lg	Log to the base 2.
MAP_x	F_float or S_float memory-to-register exponent mapping function.
MAXS(x,y)	Returns the larger of x and y, with x and y interpreted as signed integers.
MAXU(x,y)	Returns the larger of x and y, with x and y interpreted as unsigned integers.
MINS(x,y)	Returns the smaller of x and y, with x and y interpreted as signed integers.
MINU(x,y)	Returns the smaller of x and y, with x and y interpreted as unsigned integers.
x MOD y	x modulo y

Table 3–7: Operators (Continued)

Operator	Meaning
NOT	Logical (ones) complement
OR	Logical sum
PHYSICAL_ADDRESS	Translation of a virtual address
PRIORITY_ENCODE	Returns the bit position of most significant set bit, interpreting its argument as a positive integer ($=int(lg(x))$). For example: `priority_encode( 255 ) = 7`

Relational Operators:

Operator	Meaning
LT	Less than signed
LTU	Less than unsigned
LE	Less or equal signed
LEU	Less or equal unsigned
EQ	Equal signed and unsigned
NE	Not equal signed and unsigned
GE	Greater or equal signed
GEU	Greater or equal unsigned
GT	Greater signed
GTU	Greater unsigned
LBC	Low bit clear
LBS	Low bit signed

RIGHT_SHIFT(x,y)	Logical right shift of first operand by the second operand. Y is an unsigned shift value. Zeros are moved into vacated bit positions, and shifted out bits are discarded.
SEXT(x)	X is sign-extended to the required size.
STORE_CONDITIONAL	If the lock_flag is set, then do the indicated store and clear the lock_flag.

Table 3–7: Operators (Continued)

Operator	Meaning
TEST(x,cond)	The contents of register x are tested for branch condition (cond) true. TEST returns a Boolean value TRUE if x bears the specified relation to 0, else FALSE is returned. Integer and floating test conditions are drawn from the preceding list of relational operators.
XOR	Logical difference
ZEXT(x)	X is zero-extended to the required size.

3.2.4 Notation Conventions

The following conventions are used:

- Only operands that appear on the left side of a replacement operator are modified.

- No operator precedence is assumed other than that replacement ($\leftarrow$) has the lowest precedence. Explicit precedence is indicated by the use of "{ }".

- All arithmetic, logical, and relational operators are defined in the context of their operands. For example, "+" applied to G_floating operands means a G_floating add, whereas "+" applied to quadword operands is an integer add. Similarly, "LT" is a G_floating comparison when applied to G_floating operands and an integer comparison when applied to quadword operands.

3.3 Instruction Formats

There are five basic Alpha instruction formats:

- Memory
- Branch
- Operate
- Floating-point Operate
- PALcode

All instruction formats are 32 bits long with a 6-bit major opcode field in bits <31:26> of the instruction.

Any unused register field (Ra, Rb, Fa, Fb) of an instruction must be set to a value of 31.

Software Note:

There are several instructions, each formatted as a memory instruction, that do not use the Ra and/or Rb fields. These instructions are: Memory Barrier, Fetch, Fetch_M, Read Process Cycle Counter, Read and Clear, Read and Set, and Trap Barrier.

3.3.1 Memory Instruction Format

The Memory format is used to transfer data between registers and memory, to load an effective address, and for subroutine jumps. It has the format shown in Figure 3–1.

Figure 3–1: Memory Instruction Format

A Memory format instruction contains a 6-bit opcode field, two 5-bit register address fields, Ra and Rb, and a 16-bit signed displacement field.

The displacement field is a byte offset. It is sign-extended and added to the contents of register Rb to form a virtual address. Overflow is ignored in this calculation.

The virtual address is used as a memory load/store address or a result value, depending on the specific instruction. The virtual address (va) is computed as follows for all memory format instructions except the load address high (LDAH):

    va ← {Rbv + SEXT(Memory_disp)}

For LDAH the virtual address (va) is computed as follows:

    va ← {Rbv + SEXT(Memory_disp*65536)}

3.3.1.1 Memory Format Instructions with a Function Code

Memory format instructions with a function code replace the memory displacement field in the memory instruction format with a function code that designates a set of miscellaneous instructions. The format is shown in Figure 3–2.

Figure 3–2: Memory Instruction with Function Code Format

The memory instruction with function code format contains a 6-bit opcode field and a 16-bit function field. Unused function codes produce UNPREDICTABLE but not UNDEFINED results; they are not security holes.

There are two fields, Ra and Rb. The usage of those fields depends on the instruction. See Section 4.11.

3.3.1.2 Memory Format Jump Instructions

For computed branch instructions (CALL, RET, JMP, JSR_COROUTINE) the displacement field is used to provide branch-prediction hints as described in Section 4.3.

3.3.2 Branch Instruction Format

The Branch format is used for conditional branch instructions and for PC-relative subroutine jumps. It has the format shown in Figure 3–3.

Figure 3–3: Branch Instruction Format

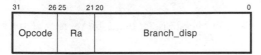

A Branch format instruction contains a 6-bit opcode field, one 5-bit register address field (Ra), and a 21-bit signed displacement field.

The displacement is treated as a longword offset. This means it is shifted left two bits (to address a longword boundary), sign-extended to 64 bits, and added to the updated PC to form the target virtual address. Overflow is ignored in this calculation. The target virtual address (va) is computed as follows:

$$va \leftarrow PC + \{4*SEXT(Branch\_disp)\}$$

3.3.3 Operate Instruction Format

The Operate format is used for instructions that perform integer register to integer register operations. The Operate format allows the specification of one destination operand and two source operands. One of the source operands can be a literal constant. The Operate format in Figure 3–4 shows the two cases when bit <12> of the instruction is 0 and 1.

Figure 3–4: Operate Instruction Format

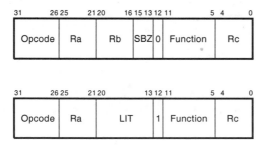

An Operate format instruction contains a 6-bit opcode field and a 7-bit function code field. Unused function codes for opcodes defined as reserved in the Version 5 Alpha architecture specification (May 1992) produce an illegal instruction trap. Those opcodes are 01, 02, 03, 04, 05, 06, 07, 0A, 0C, 0D, 0E, 14, 19, 1B, 1D, 1E, and 1F. For other opcodes, unused function codes produce UNPREDICTABLE but not UNDEFINED results; they are not security holes.

There are three operand fields, Ra, Rb, and Rc.

The Ra field specifies a source operand. Symbolically, the integer Rav operand is formed as follows:

```
IF inst<25:21> EQ 31 THEN
    Rav ← 0
ELSE
    Rav ← Ra
END
```

The Rb field specifies a source operand. Integer operands can specify a literal or an integer register using bit <12> of the instruction.

If bit <12> of the instruction is 0, the Rb field specifies a source register operand.

If bit <12> of the instruction is 1, an 8-bit zero-extended literal constant is formed by bits <20:13> of the instruction. The literal is interpreted as a positive integer between 0 and 255 and is zero-extended to 64 bits. Symbolically, the integer Rbv operand is formed as follows:

```
IF inst <12> EQ 1 THEN
    Rbv ← ZEXT(inst<20:13>)
ELSE
    IF inst <20:16> EQ 31 THEN
        Rbv ← 0
    ELSE
        Rbv ← Rb
    END
END
```

The Rc field specifies a destination operand.

3.3.4 Floating-Point Operate Instruction Format

The Floating-point Operate format is used for instructions that perform floating-point register to floating-point register operations. The Floating-point Operate format allows the specification of one destination operand and two source operands. The Floating-point Operate format is shown in Figure 3–5.

Figure 3–5: Floating-Point Operate Instruction Format

31	26 25	21 20	16 15	5 4	0
Opcode	Fa	Fb	Function	Fc	

A Floating-point Operate format instruction contains a 6-bit opcode field and an 11-bit function field. Unused function codes for those opcodes defined as reserved in the Version 5 Alpha architecture specification (May 1992) produce an illegal instruction trap. Those opcodes are 01, 02, 03, 04, 05, 06, 07, 14, 19, 1B, 1D, 1E, and 1F. For other opcodes, unused function codes produce UNPREDICTABLE but not UNDEFINED results; they are not security holes.

There are three operand fields, Fa, Fb, and Fc. Each operand field specifies either an integer or floating-point operand as defined by the instruction.

The Fa field specifies a source operand. Symbolically, the Fav operand is formed as follows:

```
IF inst<25:21> EQ 31 THEN
    Fav ← 0
ELSE
    Fav ← Fa
END
```

The Fb field specifies a source operand. Symbolically, the Fbv operand is formed as follows:

```
IF inst<20:16> EQ 31 THEN
    Fbv ← 0
ELSE
    Fbv ← Fb
END
```

Note:

Neither Fa nor Fb can be a literal in Floating-point Operate instructions.

The Fc field specifies a destination operand.

3.3.4.1 Floating-Point Convert Instructions

Floating-point Convert instructions use a subset of the Floating-point Operate format and perform register-to-register conversion operations. The Fb operand specifies the source; the Fa field must be F31.

3.3.4.2 Floating-Point/Integer Register Moves

Instructions that move data between a floating-point register file and an integer register file are a subset of of the Floating-point Operate format. The unused source field must be 31.

3.3.5 PALcode Instruction Format

The Privileged Architecture Library (PALcode) format is used to specify extended processor functions. It has the format shown in Figure 3–6.

Figure 3–6: PALcode Instruction Format

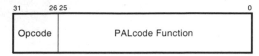

```
 31       26 25                                    0
┌─────────┬──────────────────────────────────────┐
│ Opcode  │          PALcode Function            │
└─────────┴──────────────────────────────────────┘
```

The 26-bit PALcode function field specifies the operation. The source and destination operands for PALcode instructions are supplied in fixed registers that are specified in the
individual instruction descriptions.

An opcode of zero and a PALcode function of zero specify the HALT instruction.

Chapter 4

Instruction Descriptions (I)

4.1 Instruction Set Overview

This chapter describes the instructions implemented by the Alpha architecture. The instruction set is divided into the following sections:

Instruction Type	Section
Integer load and store	4.2
Integer control	4.3
Integer arithmetic	4.4
Logical and shift	4.5
Byte manipulation	4.6
Floating-point load and store	4.7
Floating-point control	4.8
Floating-point branch	4.9
Floating-point operate	4.10
Miscellaneous	4.11
VAX compatibility	4.12
Multimedia (graphics and video)	4.13

Within each major section, closely related instructions are combined into groups and described together.

The instruction group description is composed of the following:

- The group name
- The format of each instruction in the group, which includes the name, access type, and data type of each instruction operand
- The operation of the instruction
- Exceptions specific to the instruction
- The instruction mnemonic and name of each instruction in the group

- Qualifiers specific to the instructions in the group

- A description of the instruction operation

- Optional programming examples and optional notes on the instruction

4.1.1 Subsetting Rules

An instruction that is omitted in a subset implementation of the Alpha architecture is not performed in either hardware or PALcode. System software may provide emulation routines for subsetted instructions.

4.1.2 Floating-Point Subsets

Floating-point support is optional on an Alpha processor. An implementation that supports floating-point must implement the following:

- The 32 floating-point registers

- The Floating-point Control Register (FPCR) and the instructions to access it

- The floating-point branch instructions

- The floating-point copy sign (CPYSx) instructions

- The floating-point convert instructions

- The floating-point conditional move instruction (FCMOV)

- The S_floating and T_floating memory operations

Software Note:

A system that will not support floating-point operations is still required to provide the 32 floating-point registers, the Floating-point Control Register (FPCR) and the instructions to access it, and the T_floating memory operations if the system intends to support the OpenVMS Alpha operating system. This requirement facilitates the implementation of a floating-point emulator and simplifies context-switching.

In addition, floating-point support requires at least one of the following subset groups:

1. VAX Floating-point Operate and Memory instructions (F_ and G_floating).

2. IEEE Floating-point Operate instructions (S_ and T_floating). Within this group, an implementation can choose to include or omit separately the ability to perform IEEE rounding to plus infinity and minus infinity.

Note:

If one instruction in a group is provided, all other instructions in that group must be provided. An implementation with full floating-point support includes both groups; a subset floating-point implementation supports only one of these groups. The individual instruction descriptions indicate whether an instruction can be subsetted.

4.1.3 Software Emulation Rules

General-purpose layered and application software that executes in User mode may assume that certain loads (LDL, LDQ, LDF, LDG, LDS, and LDT) and certain stores (STL, STQ, STF, STG, STL, and STT) of unaligned data are emulated by system software. General-purpose layered and application software that executes in User mode may assume that subsetted instructions are emulated by system software. Frequent use of emulation may be significantly slower than using alternative code sequences.

Emulation of loads and stores of unaligned data and subsetted instructions need not be provided in privileged access modes. System software that supports special-purpose dedicated applications need not provide emulation in User mode if emulation is not needed for correct execution of the special-purpose applications.

4.1.4 Opcode Qualifiers

Some Operate format and Floating-point Operate format instructions have several variants. For example, for the VAX formats, Add F_floating (ADDF) is supported with and without floating underflow enabled and with either chopped or VAX rounding. For IEEE formats, IEEE unbiased rounding, chopped, round toward plus infinity, and round toward minus infinity can be selected.

The different variants of such instructions are denoted by opcode qualifiers, which consist of a slash (/) followed by a string of selected qualifiers. Each qualifier is denoted by a single character as shown in Table 4–1. The opcodes for each qualifier are listed in Appendix C.

Table 4–1: Opcode Qualifiers

Qualifier	Meaning
C	Chopped rounding
D	Rounding mode dynamic
M	Round toward minus infinity
I	Inexact result enable
S	Exception completion enable
U	Floating underflow enable
V	Integer overflow enable

The default values are normal rounding, exception completion disabled, inexact result disabled, floating underflow disabled, and integer overflow disabled.

4.2 Memory Integer Load/Store Instructions

The instructions in this section move data between the integer registers and memory.

They use the Memory instruction format. The instructions are summarized in Table 4–2.

Table 4–2: Memory Integer Load/Store Instructions

Mnemonic	Operation
LDA	Load Address
LDAH	Load Address High
LDBU	Load Zero-Extended Byte from Memory to Register
LDL	Load Sign-Extended Longword
LDL_L	Load Sign-Extended Longword Locked
LDQ	Load Quadword
LDQ_L	Load Quadword Locked
LDQ_U	Load Quadword Unaligned
LDWU	Load Zero-Extended Word from Memory to Register
STB	Store Byte
STL	Store Longword
STL_C	Store Longword Conditional
STQ	Store Quadword
STQ_C	Store Quadword Conditional
STQ_U	Store Quadword Unaligned
STW	Store Word

4.2.1 Load Address

Format:

LDAx	Ra.wq,disp.ab(Rb.ab)	!Memory format

Operation:

```
Ra ← Rbv + SEXT(disp)              !LDA
Ra ← Rbv + SEXT(disp*65536)        !LDAH
```

Exceptions:

None

Instruction mnemonics:

LDA	Load Address
LDAH	Load Address High

Qualifiers:

None

Description:

The virtual address is computed by adding register Rb to the sign-extended 16-bit displacement for LDA, and 65536 times the sign-extended 16-bit displacement for LDAH. The 64-bit result is written to register Ra.

4.2.2 Load Memory Data into Integer Register

Format:

LDx   Ra.wq,disp.ab(Rb.ab)   !Memory format

Operation:

```
va ← {Rbv + SEXT(disp)}

CASE
  big_endian_data: va' ← va XOR 000₂      !LDQ
  big_endian_data: va' ← va XOR 100₂      !LDL
  big_endian_data: va' ← va XOR 110₂      !LDWU
  big_endian_data: va' ← va XOR 111₂      !LDBU
  little_endian_data: va' ← va
ENDCASE

Ra ← (va')<63:0>                           !LDQ
Ra ← SEXT((va')<31:0>)                     !LDL
Ra ← ZEXT((va')<15:0>)                     !LDWU
Ra ← ZEXT((va')<07:0>)                     !LDBU
```

Exceptions:

Access Violation

Alignment

Fault on Read

Translation Not Valid

Instruction mnemonics:

LDBU	Load Zero-Extended Byte from Memory to Register
LDL	Load Sign-Extended Longword from Memory to Register
LDQ	Load Quadword from Memory to Register
LDWU	Load Zero-Extended Word from Memory to Register

Qualifiers:

None

Description:

The virtual address is computed by adding register Rb to the sign-extended 16-bit displacement. For a big-endian access, the indicated bits are inverted, and any memory management fault is reported for va (not va').

In the case of LDQ and LDL, the source operand is fetched from memory, sign-extended, and written to register Ra.

In the case of LDWU and LDBU, the source operand is fetched from memory, zero-extended, and written to register Ra.

In all cases, if the data is not naturally aligned, an alignment exception is generated.

Notes:

- The word or byte that the LDWU or LDBU instruction fetches from memory is placed in the low (rightmost) word or byte of Ra, with the remaining 6 or 7 bytes set to zero.

- Accesses have byte granularity.

- For big-endian access with LDWU or LDBU, the word/byte remains in the rightmost part of Ra, but the va sent to memory has the indicated bits inverted. See Operation section, above.

- No sparse address space mechanisms are allowed with the LDWU and LDBU instructions.

Implementation Notes:

- The LDWU and LDBU instructions are supported in hardware on Alpha implementations for which the AMASK instruction returns bit 0 set. LDWU and LDBU are supported with software emulation in Alpha implementations for which AMASK does not return bit 0 set. Software emulation of LDWU and LDBU is significantly slower than hardware support.

- Depending on an address space region's caching policy, implementations may read a (partial) cache block in order to do word/byte stores. This may only be done in regions that have memory-like behavior.

- Implementations are expected to provide sufficient low-order address bits and length-of-access information to devices on I/O buses. But, strictly speaking, this is outside the scope of architecture.

4.2.3 Load Unaligned Memory Data into Integer Register

Format:

LDQ_U	Ra.wq,disp.ab(Rb.ab)	!Memory format

Operation:

```
va ← {{Rbv + SEXT(disp)} AND NOT 7}
Ra ← (va)<63:0>
```

Exceptions:

Access Violation

Fault on Read

Translation Not Valid

Instruction mnemonics:

LDQ_U   Load Unaligned Quadword from Memory to Register

Qualifiers:

None

Description:

The virtual address is computed by adding register Rb to the sign-extended 16-bit displacement, then the low-order three bits are cleared. The source operand is fetched from memory and written to register Ra.

4.2.4 Load Memory Data into Integer Register Locked

Format:

LDx_L   Ra.wq,disp.ab(Rb.ab)   !Memory format

Operation:

```
va ← {Rbv + SEXT(disp)}

CASE
  big_endian_data:  va' ← va XOR 000₂    ! LDQ_L
  big_endian_data:  va' ← va XOR 100₂    ! LDL_L
  little_endian_data: va' ← va           ! LDL_L
ENDCASE

lock_flag ← 1
locked_physical_address ← PHYSICAL_ADDRESS(va)

Ra ← SEXT((va')<31:0>)                    ! LDL_L
Ra ← (va)<63:0>                           ! LDQ_L
```

Exceptions:

Access Violation

Alignment

Fault on Read

Translation Not Valid

Instruction mnemonics:

LDL_L   Load Sign-Extended Longword from Memory to Register Locked

LDQ_L   Load Quadword from Memory to Register Locked

Qualifiers:

None

Description:

The virtual address is computed by adding register Rb to the sign-extended 16-bit displacement. For a big-endian longword access, va<2> (bit 2 of the virtual address) is inverted, and any memory management fault is reported for va (not va'). The source operand is fetched from memory, sign-extended for LDL_L, and written to register Ra.

When a LDx_L instruction is executed without faulting, the processor records the target physical address in a per-processor locked_physical_address register and sets the per-processor lock_flag.

If the per-processor lock_flag is (still) set when a STx_C instruction is executed (accessing within the same 16-byte naturally aligned block as the LDx_L), the store occurs; otherwise, it does not occur, as described for the STx_C instructions. The behavior of an STx_C instruction is UNPREDICTABLE, as described in Section 4.2.5, when it does not access the same 16-byte naturally aligned block as the LDx_L.

Processor A causes the clearing of a set lock_flag in processor B by doing any of the following in B's locked range of physical addresses: a successful store, a successful store_conditional, or executing a WH64 instruction that modifies data on processor B. A processor's locked range is the aligned block of $2^{**}N$ bytes that includes the locked_physical_address. The $2^{**}N$ value is implementation dependent. It is at least 16 (minimum lock range is an aligned 16-byte block) and is at most the page size for that implementation (maximum lock range is one physical page).

A processor's lock_flag is also cleared if that processor encounters a CALL_PAL REI, CALL_PAL rti, or CALL_PAL rfe instruction. It is UNPREDICTABLE whether or not a processor's lock_flag is cleared on any other CALL_PAL instruction. It is UNPREDICTABLE whether a processor's lock_flag is cleared by that processor executing a normal load or store instruction. It is UNPREDICTABLE whether a processor's lock_flag is cleared by that processor executing a taken branch (including BR, BSR, and Jumps); conditional branches that fall through do not clear the lock_flag. It is UNPREDICTABLE whether a processor's lock_flag is cleared by that processor executing a WH64 or ECB instruction.

The sequence:

    LDx_L
    Modify
    STx_C
    BEQ xxx

when executed on a given processor, does an atomic read-modify-write of a datum in shared memory if the branch falls through. If the branch is taken, the store did not modify memory and the sequence may be repeated until it succeeds.

Notes:

- LDx_L instructions do not check for write access; hence a matching STx_C may take an access-violation or fault-on-write exception.

  Executing a LDx_L instruction on one processor does not affect any architecturally visible state on another processor, and in particular cannot cause an STx_C on another processor to fail.

  LDx_L and STx_C instructions need not be paired. In particular, an LDx_L may be followed by a conditional branch: on the fall-through path an STx_C is executed, whereas on the taken path no matching STx_C is executed.

If two LDx_L instructions execute with no intervening STx_C, the second one overwrites the state of the first one. If two STx_C instructions execute with no intervening LDx_L, the second one always fails because the first clears lock_flag.

- Software will not emulate unaligned LDx_L instructions.

- If the virtual and physical addresses for a LDx_L and STx_C sequence are not within the same naturally aligned 16-byte sections of virtual and physical memory, that sequence may always fail, or may succeed despite another processor's store to the lock range; hence, no useful program should do this.

- If any other memory access (ECB, LDx, LDQ_U, STx, STQ_U, WH64) is executed on the given processor between the LDx_L and the STx_C, the sequence above may always fail on some implementations; hence, no useful program should do this.

- If a branch is taken between the LDx_L and the STx_C, the sequence above may always fail on some implementations; hence, no useful program should do this. (CMOVxx may be used to avoid branching.)

- If a subsetted instruction (for example, floating-point) is executed between the LDx_L and the STx_C, the sequence above may always fail on some implementations because of the Illegal Instruction Trap; hence, no useful program should do this.

- If an instruction with an unused function code is executed between the LDx_L and the STx_C, the sequence above may always fail on some implementations because an instruction with an unused function code is UNPREDICTABLE.

- If a large number of instructions are executed between the LDx_L and the STx_C, the sequence above may always fail on some implementations because of a timer interrupt always clearing the lock_flag before the sequence completes; hence, no useful program should do this.

- Hardware implementations are encouraged to lock no more than 128 bytes. Software implementations are encouraged to separate locked locations by at least 128 bytes from other locations that could potentially be written by another processor while the first location is locked.

- Execution of a WH64 instruction on processor A to a region within the lock range of processor B, where the execution of the WH64 changes the contents of memory, causes the lock_flag on processor B to be cleared. If the WH64 does not change the contents of memory on processor B, it need not clear the lock_flag.

Implementation Notes:

Implementations that impede the mobility of a cache block on LDx_L, such as that which may occur in a Read for Ownership cache coherency protocol, may release the cache block and make the subsequent STx_C fail if a branch-taken or memory instruction is executed on that processor.

All implementations should guarantee that at least 40 non-subsetted operate instructions can be executed between timer interrupts.

4.2.5 Store Integer Register Data into Memory Conditional

Format:

STx_C   Ra.mx,disp.ab(Rb.ab)   !Memory format

Operation:

```
va ← {Rbv + SEXT(disp)}

CASE
  big_endian_data:   va' ← va XOR 000₂    ! STQ_C
  big_endian_data:   va' ← va XOR 100₂    ! STL_C
  little_endian_data: va' ← va            ! STL_C
ENDCASE

IF lock_flag EQ 1 THEN
   (va')<31:0> ←  Rav<31:0>               ! STL_C
   (va)       ←  Rav                      ! STQ_C
Ra ← lock_flag
lock_flag ← 0
```

Exceptions:

Access Violation

Fault on Write

Alignment

Translation Not Valid

Instruction mnemonics:

STL_C   Store Longword from Register to Memory Conditional

STQ_C   Store Quadword from Register to Memory Conditional

Qualifiers:

None

Description:

The virtual address is computed by adding register Rb to the sign-extended 16-bit displacement. For a big-endian longword access, va<2> (bit 2 of the virtual address) is inverted, and any memory management fault is reported for va (not va').

If the lock_flag is set and the address meets the following constraints relative to the address specified by the preceding LDx_L instruction, the Ra operand is written to memory at this address. If the address meets the following constraints but the lock_flag is not set, a zero is returned in Ra and no write to memory occurs. The constraints are:

- The computed virtual address must specify a location within the naturally aligned 16-byte block in virtual memory accessed by the preceding LDx_L instruction.

- The resultant physical address must specify a location within the naturally aligned 16-byte block in physical memory accessed by the preceding LDx_L instruction.

If those addressing constraints are not met, it is UNPREDICTABLE whether the STx_C instruction succeeds or fails, regardless of the state of the lock_flag, unless the lock_flag is cleared as described in the next paragraph.

Whether or not the addressing constraints are met, a zero is returned and no write to memory occurs if the lock_flag was cleared by execution on a processor of a CALL_PAL REI, CALL_PAL rti, CALL_PAL rfe, or STx_C, after the most recent execution on that processor of a LDx_L instruction (in processor issue sequence).

In all cases, the lock_flag is set to zero at the end of the operation.

Notes:

- Software will not emulate unaligned STx_C instructions.

- Each implementation must do the test and store atomically, as illustrated in the following two examples. (See Section 5.6.1 for complete information.)

  - If two processors attempt STx_C instructions to the same lock range and that lock range was accessed by both processors' preceding LDx_L instructions, exactly one of the stores succeeds.

  - A processor executes a LDx_L/STx_C sequence and includes an MB between the LDx_L to a particular address and the *successful* STx_C to a different address (one that meets the constraints required for predictable behavior). That instruction sequence establishes an access order under which a store operation by another processor to that lock range occurs before the LDx_L or after the STx_C.

- If the virtual and physical addresses for a LDx_L and STx_C sequence are not within the same naturally aligned 16-byte sections of virtual and physical memory, that sequence may always fail, or may succeed despite another processor's store to the lock range; hence, no useful program should do this.

- The following sequence should not be used:

```
try_again: LDQ_L   R1, x
           <modify R1>
           STQ_C   R1, x
           BEQ     R1, try_again
```

That sequence penalizes performance when the STQ_C succeeds, because the sequence contains a backward branch, which is predicted to be taken in the Alpha architecture. In the case where the STQ_C succeeds and the branch will actually fall through, that sequence incurs unnecessary delay due to a mispredicted backward branch. Instead, a forward branch should be used to handle the failure case, as shown in Section 5.5.2.

Software Note:

If the address specified by a STx_C instruction does not match the one given in the preceding LDx_L instruction, an MB is required to guarantee ordering between the two instructions.

Hardware/Software Implementation Note:

STQ_C is used in the first Alpha implementations to access the MailBox Pointer Register (MBPR). In this special case, the effect of the STQ_C is well defined (that is, not UNPREDICTABLE) even though the preceding LDx_L did not specify the address of the MBPR. The effect of STx_C in this special case may vary from implementation to implementation.

Implementation Notes:

A STx_C must propagate to the point of coherency, where it is guaranteed to prevent any other store from changing the state of the lock bit, before its outcome can be determined.

If an implementation could encounter a TB or cache miss on the data reference of the STx_C in the sequence above (as might occur in some shared I- and D-stream direct-mapped TBs/caches), it must be able to resolve the miss and complete the store without always failing.

4.2.6 Store Integer Register Data into Memory

Format:

STx   Ra.rx,disp.ab(Rb.ab)   !Memory format

Operation:

va ← {Rbv + SEXT(disp)}

CASE
  big_endian_data: va' ← va XOR 000_2 !STQ
  big_endian_data: va' ← va XOR 100_2 !STL
  big_endian_data: va' ← va XOR 110_2 !STW
  big_endian_data: va' ← va XOR 111_2 !STD
  little_endian_data: va' ← va
ENDCASE

(va') ← Rav   !STQ
(va')<31:00> ← Rav<31:0>   !STL
(va')<15:00> ← Rav<15:0>   !STW
(va')<07:00> ← Rav<07:0>   !STB

Exceptions:

Access Violation

Alignment

Fault on Write

Translation Not Valid

Instruction mnemonics:

STB   Store Byte from Register to Memory

STL   Store Longword from Register to Memory

STQ   Store Quadword from Register to Memory

STW   Store Word from Register to Memory

Qualifiers:

None

Description:

The virtual address is computed by adding register Rb to the sign-extended 16-bit displacement. For a big-endian access, the indicated bits are inverted, and any memory management fault is reported for va (not va').

The Ra operand is written to memory at this address. If the data is not naturally aligned, an alignment exception is generated.

Notes:

- The word or byte that the STB or STW instruction stores to memory comes from the low (rightmost) byte or word of Ra.

- Accesses have byte granularity.

- For big-endian access with STB or STW, the byte/word remains in the rightmost part of Ra, but the va sent to memory has the indicated bits inverted. See Operation section, above.

- No sparse address space mechanisms are allowed with the STB and STW instructions.

Implementation Notes:

- The STB and STW instructions are supported in hardware on Alpha implementations for which the AMASK instruction returns bit 0 set. STB and STW are supported with software emulation in Alpha implementations for which AMASK does not return bit 0 set. Software emulation of STB and STW is significantly slower than hardware support.

- Depending on an address space region's caching policy, implementations may read a (partial) cache block in order to do byte/word stores. This may only be done in regions that have memory-like behavior.

- Implementations are expected to provide sufficient low-order address bits and length-of-access information to devices on I/O buses. But, strictly speaking, this is outside the scope of architecture.

4.2.7 Store Unaligned Integer Register Data into Memory

Format:

> STQ_U   Ra.rq,disp.ab(Rb.ab)   !Memory format

Operation:

```
va ← {{Rbv + SEXT(disp)} AND NOT 7}
(va)<63:0> ← Rav<63:0>
```

Exceptions:

> Access Violation
>
> Fault on Write
>
> Translation Not Valid

Instruction mnemonics:

> STQ_U   Store Unaligned Quadword from Register to Memory

Qualifiers:

> None

Description:

The virtual address is computed by adding register Rb to the sign-extended 16-bit displacement, then clearing the low order three bits. The Ra operand is written to memory at this address.

4.3 Control Instructions

Alpha provides integer conditional branch, unconditional branch, branch to subroutine, and jump instructions. The PC used in these instructions is the updated PC, as described in Section 3.1.1.

To allow implementations to achieve high performance, the Alpha architecture includes explicit hints based on a branch-prediction model:

- For many implementations of computed branches (JSR/RET/JMP), there is a substantial performance gain in forming a good guess of the expected target I-cache address before register Rb is accessed.

- For many implementations, the first-level (or only) I-cache is no bigger than a page (8 KB to 64 KB).

- Correctly predicting subroutine returns is important for good performance. Some implementations will therefore keep a small stack of predicted subroutine return I-cache addresses.

The Alpha architecture provides three kinds of branch-prediction hints: likely target address, return-address stack action, and conditional branch-taken.

For computed branches, the otherwise unused displacement field contains a function code (JMP/JSR/RET/JSR_COROUTINE), and, for JSR and JMP, a field that statically specifies the 16 low bits of the most likely target address. The PC-relative calculation using these bits can be exactly the PC-relative calculation used in unconditional branches. The low 16 bits are enough to specify an I-cache block within the largest possible Alpha page and hence are expected to be enough for branch-prediction logic to start an early I-cache access for the most likely target.

For all branches, hint or opcode bits are used to distinguish simple branches, subroutine calls, subroutine returns, and coroutine links. These distinctions allow branch-predict logic to maintain an accurate stack of predicted return addresses.

For conditional branches, the sign of the target displacement is used as a taken/fall-through hint. The instructions are summarized in Table 4–3.

Table 4–3: Control Instructions Summary

Mnemonic	Operation
BEQ	Branch if Register Equal to Zero
BGE	Branch if Register Greater Than or Equal to Zero
BGT	Branch if Register Greater Than Zero
BLBC	Branch if Register Low Bit Is Clear
BLBS	Branch if Register Low Bit Is Set
BLE	Branch if Register Less Than or Equal to Zero
BLT	Branch if Register Less Than Zero

Table 4–3: Control Instructions Summary (Continued)

Mnemonic	Operation
BNE	Branch if Register Not Equal to Zero
BR	Unconditional Branch
BSR	Branch to Subroutine
JMP	Jump
JSR	Jump to Subroutine
RET	Return from Subroutine
JSR_COROUTINE	Jump to Subroutine Return

4.3.1 Conditional Branch

Format:

Bxx   Ra.rq,disp.al   !Branch format

Operation:

```
{update PC}
va ← PC + {4*SEXT(disp)}
IF TEST(Rav, Condition_based_on_Opcode) THEN
    PC ← va
```

Exceptions:

None

Instruction mnemonics:

BEQ	Branch if Register Equal to Zero
BGE	Branch if Register Greater Than or Equal to Zero
BGT	Branch if Register Greater Than Zero
BLBC	Branch if Register Low Bit Is Clear
BLBS	Branch if Register Low Bit Is Set
BLE	Branch if Register Less Than or Equal to Zero
BLT	Branch if Register Less Than Zero
BNE	Branch if Register Not Equal to Zero

Qualifiers:

None

Description:

Register Ra is tested. If the specified relationship is true, the PC is loaded with the target virtual address; otherwise, execution continues with the next sequential instruction.

The displacement is treated as a signed longword offset. This means it is shifted left two bits (to address a longword boundary), sign-extended to 64 bits, and added to the updated PC to form the target virtual address.

The conditional branch instructions are PC-relative only. The 21-bit signed displacement gives a forward/backward branch distance of +/– 1M instructions.

The test is on the signed quadword integer interpretation of the register contents; all 64 bits are tested.

4.3.2 Unconditional Branch

Format:

BxR   Ra.wq,disp.al   !Branch format

Operation:

```
{update PC}
Ra ← PC
PC ← PC + {4*SEXT(disp)}
```

Exceptions:

None

Instruction mnemonics:

BR   Unconditional Branch

BSR   Branch to Subroutine

Qualifiers:

None

Description:

The PC of the following instruction (the updated PC) is written to register Ra and then the PC is loaded with the target address.

The displacement is treated as a signed longword offset. This means it is shifted left two bits (to address a longword boundary), sign-extended to 64 bits, and added to the updated PC to form the target virtual address.

The unconditional branch instructions are PC-relative. The 21-bit signed displacement gives a forward/backward branch distance of +/– 1M instructions.

PC-relative addressability can be established by:

```
        BR Rx,L1
L1:
```

Notes:

- BR and BSR do identical operations. They only differ in hints to possible branch-prediction logic. BSR is predicted as a subroutine call (pushes the return address on a branch-prediction stack), whereas BR is predicted as a branch (no push).

4.3.3 Jumps

Format:

mnemonic   Ra.wq,(Rb.ab),hint   !Memory format

Operation:

```
{update PC}
va ← Rbv AND {NOT 3}
Ra ← PC
PC ← va
```

Exceptions:

None

Instruction mnemonics:

JMP	Jump
JSR	Jump to Subroutine
RET	Return from Subroutine
JSR_COROUTINE	Jump to Subroutine Return

Qualifiers:

None

Description:

The PC of the instruction following the Jump instruction (the updated PC) is written to register Ra and then the PC is loaded with the target virtual address.

The new PC is supplied from register Rb. The low two bits of Rb are ignored. Ra and Rb may specify the same register; the target calculation using the old value is done before the new value is assigned.

All Jump instructions do identical operations. They only differ in hints to possible branch-prediction logic. The displacement field of the instruction is used to pass this information. The four different "opcodes" set different bit patterns in disp<15:14>, and the hint operand sets disp<13:0>

These bits are intended to be used as shown in Table 4–4.

Table 4–4: Jump Instructions Branch Prediction

disp<15:14>	Meaning	Predicted Target<15:0>	Prediction Stack Action
00	JMP	PC + {4*disp<13:0>}	–
01	JSR	PC + {4*disp<13:0>}	Push PC
10	RET	Prediction stack	Pop
11	JSR_COROUTINE	Prediction stack	Pop, push PC

The design in Table 4–4 allows specification of the low 16 bits of a likely longword target address (enough bits to start a useful I-cache access early), and also allows distinguishing call from return (and from the other two less frequent operations).

Note that the above information is used only as a hint; correct setting of these bits can improve performance but is not needed for correct operation. See Appendix A for more information on branch prediction.

An unconditional long jump can be performed by:
```
JMP R31,(Rb),hint
```

Coroutine linkage can be performed by specifying the same register in both the Ra and Rb operands. When disp<15:14> equals '10' (RET) or '11' (JSR_COROUTINE) (that is, the target address prediction, if any, would come from a predictor implementation stack), then bits <13:0> are reserved for software and must be ignored by all implementations. All encodings for bits <13:0> are used by DIGITAL software or Reserved to DIGITAL, as follows:

Encoding	Meaning
0000_{16}	Indicates non-procedure return
0001_{16}	Indicates procedure return
	All other encodings are reserved to DIGITAL.

4.4 Integer Arithmetic Instructions

The integer arithmetic instructions perform add, subtract, multiply, signed and unsigned compare, and bit count operations.

The integer instructions are summarized in Table 4–5

Table 4–5: Integer Arithmetic Instructions Summary

Mnemonic	Operation
ADD	Add Quadword/Longword
S4ADD	Scaled Add by 4
S8ADD	Scaled Add by 8
CMPEQ	Compare Signed Quadword Equal
CMPLT	Compare Signed Quadword Less Than
CMPLE	Compare Signed Quadword Less Than or Equal
CTLZ	Count leading zero
CTPOP	Count population
CTTZ	Count trailing zero
CMPULT	Compare Unsigned Quadword Less Than
CMPULE	Compare Unsigned Quadword Less Than or Equal
MUL	Multiply Quadword/Longword
UMULH	Multiply Quadword Unsigned High
SUB	Subtract Quadword/Longword
S4SUB	Scaled Subtract by 4
S8SUB	Scaled Subtract by 8

There is no integer divide instruction. Division by a constant can be done by using UMULH; division by a variable can be done by using a subroutine. See Appendix A.

4.4.1 Longword Add

Format:

ADDL	Ra.rl,Rb.rl,Rc.wq	!Operate format
ADDL	Ra.rl,#b.ib,Rc.wq	!Operate format

Operation:

Rc ← SEXT((Rav + Rbv)<31:0>)

Exceptions:

Integer Overflow

Instruction mnemonics:

ADDL   Add Longword

Qualifiers:

Integer Overflow Enable (/V)

Description:

Register Ra is added to register Rb or a literal and the sign-extended 32-bit sum is written to Rc.

The high order 32 bits of Ra and Rb are ignored. Rc is a proper sign extension of the truncated 32-bit sum. Overflow detection is based on the longword sum Rav<31:0> + Rbv<31:0>.

4.4.2 Scaled Longword Add

Format:

SxADDL	Ra.rl,Rb.rq,Rc.wq	!Operate format
SxADDL	Ra.rl,#b.ib,Rc.wq	!Operate format

Operation:

```
CASE
  S4ADDL: Rc ← SEXT (((LEFT_SHIFT(Rav,2)) + Rbv)<31:0>)
  S8ADDL: Rc ← SEXT (((LEFT_SHIFT(Rav,3)) + Rbv)<31:0>)
ENDCASE
```

Exceptions:

None

Instruction mnemonics:

S4ADDL	Scaled Add Longword by 4
S8ADDL	Scaled Add Longword by 8

Qualifiers:

None

Description:

Register Ra is scaled by 4 (for S4ADDL) or 8 (for S8ADDL) and is added to register Rb or a literal, and the sign-extended 32-bit sum is written to Rc.

The high 32 bits of Ra and Rb are ignored. Rc is a proper sign extension of the truncated 32-bit sum.

4.4.3 Quadword Add

Format:

ADDQ	Ra.rq,Rb.rq,Rc.wq	!Operate format
ADDQ	Ra.rq,#b.ib,Rc.wq	!Operate format

Operation:

$$Rc \leftarrow Rav + Rbv$$

Exceptions:

Integer Overflow

Instruction mnemonics:

ADDQ   Add Quadword

Qualifiers:

Integer Overflow Enable (/V)

Description:

Register Ra is added to register Rb or a literal and the 64-bit sum is written to Rc.

On overflow, the least significant 64 bits of the true result are written to the destination register.

The unsigned compare instructions can be used to generate carry. After adding two values, if the sum is less unsigned than either one of the inputs, there was a carry out of the most significant bit.

4.4.4 Scaled Quadword Add

Format:

SxADDQ	Ra.rq,Rb.rq,Rc.wq	!Operate format
SxADDQ	Ra.rq,#b.ib,Rc.wq	!Operate format

Operation:

```
CASE
  S4ADDQ: Rc ← LEFT_SHIFT(Rav,2) + Rbv
  S8ADDQ: Rc ← LEFT_SHIFT(Rav,3) + Rbv
ENDCASE
```

Exceptions:

None

Instruction mnemonics:

S4ADDQ	Scaled Add Quadword by 4
S8ADDQ	Scaled Add Quadword by 8

Qualifiers:

None

Description:

Register Ra is scaled by 4 (for S4ADDQ) or 8 (for S8ADDQ) and is added to register Rb or a literal, and the 64-bit sum is written to Rc.

On overflow, the least significant 64 bits of the true result are written to the destination register.

4.4.5 Integer Signed Compare

Format:

CMPxx	Ra.rq,Rb.rq,Rc.wq	!Operate format
CMPxx	Ra.rq,#b.ib,Rc.wq	!Operate format

Operation:

```
IF Rav SIGNED_RELATION Rbv THEN
  Rc ← 1
ELSE
  Rc ← 0
```

Exceptions:

None

Instruction mnemonics:

CMPEQ	Compare Signed Quadword Equal
CMPLE	Compare Signed Quadword Less Than or Equal
CMPLT	Compare Signed Quadword Less Than

Qualifiers:

None

Description:

Register Ra is compared to Register Rb or a literal. If the specified relationship is true, the value one is written to register Rc; otherwise, zero is written to Rc.

Notes:

- Compare Less Than A,B is the same as Compare Greater Than B,A; Compare Less Than or Equal A,B is the same as Compare Greater Than or Equal B,A. Therefore, only the less-than operations are included.

4.4.6 Integer Unsigned Compare

Format:

CMPUxx	Ra.rq,Rb.rq,Rc.wq	!Operate format
CMPUxx	Ra.rq,#b.ib,Rc.wq	!Operate format

Operation:

```
IF Rav UNSIGNED_RELATION Rbv THEN
   Rc ← 1
ELSE
   Rc ← 0
```

Exceptions:

None

Instruction mnemonics:

CMPULE	Compare Unsigned Quadword Less Than or Equal
CMPULT	Compare Unsigned Quadword Less Than

Qualifiers:

None

Description:

Register Ra is compared to Register Rb or a literal. If the specified relationship is true, the value one is written to register Rc; otherwise, zero is written to Rc.

4.4.7 Count Leading Zero

Format:

CTLZ   Rb.rq,Rc.wq   ! Operate format

Operation:

```
temp = 0
FOR i FROM 63 DOWN TO 0
 IF { Rbv<i> EQ 1 } THEN BREAK
 temp = temp + 1
END
 Rc<6:0> ← temp<6:0>
 Rc<63:7> ← 0
```

Exceptions:

None

Instruction mnemonics:

CTLZ   Count Leading Zero

Qualifiers:

None

Description:

The number of leading zeros in Rb, starting at the most significant bit position, is written to Rc. Ra must be R31.

4.4.8 Count Population

Format:

CTPOP   Rb.rq,Rc.wq   ! Operate format

Operation:

```
temp = 0
FOR i FROM 0 TO 63
 IF { Rbv<i> EQ 1 } THEN temp = temp + 1
END
Rc<6:0> ← temp<6:0>
Rc<63:7> ← 0
```

Exceptions:

None

Instruction mnemonics:

CTPOP   Count Population

Qualifiers:

None

Description:

The number of ones in Rb is written to Rc. Ra must be R31.

4.4.9 Count Trailing Zero

Format:

      CTTZ   Rb.rq,Rc.wq   ! Operate format

Operation:

```
temp = 0
FOR i FROM 0 TO 63
  IF { Rbv<i> EQ 1 } THEN BREAK
  temp = temp + 1
END
Rc<6:0> ← temp<6:0>
Rc<63:7> ← 0
```

Exceptions:

None

Instruction mnemonics:

      CTTZ   Count Trailing Zero

Qualifiers:

None

Description:

The number of trailing zeros in Rb, starting at the least significant bit position, is written to Rc. Ra must be R31.

4.4.10 Longword Multiply

Format:

MULL	Ra.rl,Rb.rl,Rc.wq	!Operate format
MULL	Ra.rl,#b.ib,Rc.wq	!Operate format

Operation:

```
Rc ← SEXT ((Rav * Rbv)<31:0>)
```

Exceptions:

Integer Overflow

Instruction mnemonics:

MULL   Multiply Longword

Qualifiers:

Integer Overflow Enable (/V)

Description:

Register Ra is multiplied by register Rb or a literal and the sign-extended 32-bit product is written to Rc.

The high 32 bits of Ra and Rb are ignored. Rc is a proper sign extension of the truncated 32-bit product. Overflow detection is based on the longword product Rav<31:0> * Rbv<31:0>. On overflow, the proper sign extension of the least significant 32 bits of the true result is written to the destination register.

The MULQ instruction can be used to return the full 64-bit product.

4.4.11 Quadword Multiply

Format:

MULQ	Ra.rq,Rb.rq,Rc.wq	!Operate format
MULQ	Ra.Rq,#b.ib,Rc.wq	!Operate format

Operation:

Rc ← Rav * Rbv

Exceptions:

Integer Overflow

Instruction mnemonics:

MULQ   Multiply Quadword

Qualifiers:

Integer Overflow Enable (/V)

Description:

Register Ra is multiplied by register Rb or a literal and the 64-bit product is written to register Rc. Overflow detection is based on considering the operands and the result as signed quantities. On overflow, the least significant 64 bits of the true result are written to the destination register.

The UMULH instruction can be used to generate the upper 64 bits of the 128-bit result when an overflow occurs.

4.4.12 Unsigned Quadword Multiply High

Format:

UMULH	Ra.rq,Rb.rq,Rc.wq	!Operate format
UMULH	Ra.rq,#b.ib,Rc.wq	!Operate format

Operation:

```
Rc ← {Rav * U Rbv}<127:64>
```

Exceptions:

None

Instruction mnemonics:

UMULH   Unsigned Multiply Quadword High

Qualifiers:

None

Description:

Register Ra and Rb or a literal are multiplied as unsigned numbers to produce a 128-bit result. The high-order 64-bits are written to register Rc.

The UMULH instruction can be used to generate the upper 64 bits of a 128-bit result as follows:

Ra and Rb are unsigned: result of UMULH
Ra and Rb are signed: (result of UMULH) – Ra<63>*Rb – Rb<63>*Ra

The MULQ instruction gives the low 64 bits of the result in either case.

4.4.13 Longword Subtract

Format:

SUBL	Ra.rl,Rb.rl,Rc.wq	!Operate format
SUBL	Ra.rl,#b.ib,Rc.wq	!Operate format

Operation:

Rc ← SEXT ((Rav - Rbv)<31:0>)

Exceptions:

Integer Overflow

Instruction mnemonics:

SUBL   Subtract Longword

Qualifiers:

Integer Overflow Enable (/V)

Description:

Register Rb or a literal is subtracted from register Ra and the sign-extended 32-bit difference is written to Rc.

The high 32 bits of Ra and Rb are ignored. Rc is a proper sign extension of the truncated 32-bit difference. Overflow detection is based on the longword difference $Rav<31:0> - Rbv<31:0>$.

4.4.14 Scaled Longword Subtract

Format:

SxSUBL	Ra.rl,Rb.rl,Rc.wq	!Operate format
SxSUBL	Ra.rl,#b.ib,Rc.wq	!Operate format

Operation:

```
CASE
  S4SUBL: Rc ← SEXT (((LEFT_SHIFT(Rav,2)) - Rbv)<31:0>)
  S8SUBL: Rc ← SEXT (((LEFT_SHIFT(Rav,3)) - Rbv)<31:0>)
ENDCASE
```

Exceptions:

None

Instruction mnemonics:

S4SUBL	Scaled Subtract Longword by 4
S8SUBL	Scaled Subtract Longword by 8

Qualifiers:

None

Description:

Register Rb or a literal is subtracted from the scaled value of register Ra, which is scaled by 4 (for S4SUBL) or 8 (for S8SUBL), and the sign-extended 32-bit difference is written to Rc.

The high 32 bits of Ra and Rb are ignored. Rc is a proper sign extension of the truncated 32-bit difference.

4.4.15 Quadword Subtract

Format:

SUBQ	Ra.rq,Rb.rq,Rc.wq	!Operate format
SUBQ	Ra.rq,#b.ib,Rc.wq	!Operate format

Operation:

Rc ← Rav - Rbv

Exceptions:

Integer Overflow

Instruction mnemonics:

SUBQ   Subtract Quadword

Qualifiers:

Integer Overflow Enable (/V)

Description:

Register Rb or a literal is subtracted from register Ra and the 64-bit difference is written to register Rc. On overflow, the least significant 64 bits of the true result are written to the destination register.

The unsigned compare instructions can be used to generate borrow. If the minuend (Rav) is less unsigned than the subtrahend (Rbv), a borrow will occur.

4.4.16 Scaled Quadword Subtract

Format:

SxSUBQ	Ra.rq,Rb.rq,Rc.wq	!Operate format
SxSUBQ	Ra.rq,#b.ib,Rc.wq	!Operate format

Operation:

```
CASE
  S4SUBQ: Rc ← LEFT_SHIFT(Rav,2) - Rbv
  S8SUBQ: Rc ← LEFT_SHIFT(Rav,3) - Rbv
ENDCASE
```

Exceptions:

None

Instruction mnemonics:

S4SUBQ	Scaled Subtract Quadword by 4
S8SUBQ	Scaled Subtract Quadword by 8

Qualifiers:

None

Description:

Register Rb or a literal is subtracted from the scaled value of register Ra, which is scaled by 4 (for S4SUBQ) or 8 (for S8SUBQ), and the 64-bit difference is written to Rc.

4.5 Logical and Shift Instructions

The logical instructions perform quadword Boolean operations. The conditional move integer instructions perform conditionals without a branch. The shift instructions perform left and right logical shift and right arithmetic shift. These are summarized in Table 4–6.

Table 4–6: Logical and Shift Instructions Summary

Mnemonic	Operation
AND	Logical Product
BIC	Logical Product with Complement
BIS	Logical Sum (OR)
EQV	Logical Equivalence (XORNOT)
ORNOT	Logical Sum with Complement
XOR	Logical Difference
CMOVxx	Conditional Move Integer
SLL	Shift Left Logical
SRA	Shift Right Arithmetic
SRL	Shift Right Logical

Software Note:

There is no arithmetic left shift instruction. Where an arithmetic left shift would be used, a logical shift will do. For multiplying by a small power of two in address computations, logical left shift is acceptable.

Integer multiply should be used to perform an arithmetic left shift with overflow checking.

Bit field extracts can be done with two logical shifts. Sign extension can be done with a left logical shift and a right arithmetic shift.

4.5.1 Logical Functions

Format:

mnemonic	Ra.rq,Rb.rq,Rc.wq	!Operate format
mnemonic	Ra.rq,#b.ib,Rc.wq	!Operate format

Operation:

```
Rc ← Rav AND Rbv                    !AND
Rc ← Rav OR Rbv                     !BIS
Rc ← Rav XOR Rbv                    !XOR
Rc ← Rav AND {NOT Rbv}              !BIC
Rc ← Rav OR {NOT Rbv}               !ORNOT
Rc ← Rav XOR {NOT Rbv}              !EQV
```

Exceptions:

None

Instruction mnemonics:

AND	Logical Product
BIC	Logical Product with Complement
BIS	Logical Sum (OR)
EQV	Logical Equivalence (XORNOT)
ORNOT	Logical Sum with Complement
XOR	Logical Difference

Qualifiers:

None

Description:

These instructions perform the designated Boolean function between register Ra and register Rb or a literal. The result is written to register Rc.

The NOT function can be performed by doing an ORNOT with zero (Ra = R31).

4.5.2 Conditional Move Integer

Format:

CMOVxx	Ra.rq,Rb.rq,Rc.wq	!Operate format
CMOVxx	Ra.rq,#b.ib,Rc.wq	!Operate format

Operation:

```
IF TEST(Rav, Condition_based_on_Opcode) THEN

    Rc ← Rbv
```

Exceptions:

None

Instruction mnemonics:

CMOVEQ	CMOVE if Register Equal to Zero
CMOVGE	CMOVE if Register Greater Than or Equal to Zero
CMOVGT	CMOVE if Register Greater Than Zero
CMOVLBC	CMOVE if Register Low Bit Clear
CMOVLBS	CMOVE if Register Low Bit Set
CMOVLE	CMOVE if Register Less Than or Equal to Zero
CMOVLT	CMOVE if Register Less Than Zero
CMOVNE	CMOVE if Register Not Equal to Zero

Qualifiers:

None

Description:

Register Ra is tested. If the specified relationship is true, the value Rbv is written to register Rc.

Notes:

Except that it is likely in many implementations to be substantially faster, the instruction:

```
CMOVEQ Ra,Rb,Rc
```

is exactly equivalent to:

```
       BNE Ra,label
       OR  Rb,Rb,Rc
 label: ...
```

For example, a branchless sequence for:

```
R1=MAX(R1,R2)
```

is:

```
CMPLT  R1,R2,R3        ! R3=1 if R1<R2
CMOVNE R3,R2,R1        ! Move R2 to R1 if R1<R2
```

4.5.3 Shift Logical

Format:

SxL	Ra.rq,Rb.rq,Rc.wq	!Operate format
SxL	Ra.rq,#b.ib,Rc.wq	!Operate format

Operation:

```
Rc ←  LEFT_SHIFT(Rav, Rbv<5:0>)      !SLL
Rc ←  RIGHT_SHIFT(Rav, Rbv<5:0>)     !SRL
```

Exceptions:

None

Instruction mnemonics:

SLL	Shift Left Logical
SRL	Shift Right Logical

Qualifiers:

None

Description:

Register Ra is shifted logically left or right 0 to 63 bits by the count in register Rb or a literal. The result is written to register Rc. Zero bits are propagated into the vacated bit positions.

4.5.4 Shift Arithmetic

Format:

SRA	Ra.rq,Rb.rq,Rc.wq	!Operate format
SRA	Ra.rq,#b.ib,Rc.wq	!Operate format

Operation:

```
Rc ← ARITH_RIGHT_SHIFT(Rav, Rbv<5:0>)
```

Exceptions:

None

Instruction mnemonics:

SRA   Shift Right Arithmetic

Qualifiers:

None

Description:

Register Ra is right shifted arithmetically 0 to 63 bits by the count in register Rb or a literal. The result is written to register Rc. The sign bit (Rav<63>) is propagated into the vacated bit positions.

4.6 Byte Manipulation Instructions

Alpha implementations that support the BWX extension provide the following instructions for loading, sign-extending, and storing bytes and words between a register and memory:

Instruction	Meaning	Described in Section
LDBU/LDWU	Load byte/word unaligned	4.2.2
SEXTB/SEXTW	Sign-extend byte/word	4.6.5
STB/STW	Store byte/word	4.2.6

The AMASK and IMPLVER instructions report whether a particular Alpha implementation supports the BWX extension. AMASK and IMPLVER are described in Sections 4.11.1 and 4.11.6, respectively, and in Appendix D.

LDBU and STB are the recommended way to perform byte load and store operations on Alpha implementations that support them; use them rather than the extract, insert, and mask byte instructions described in this section. In particular, the implementation examples in this section that illustrate byte operations are not appropriate for Alpha implementations that support the BWX extension – instead use the recommendations in Appendix A.

In addition to LDBU and STB, Alpha provides the instructions in Table 4–7 for operating on byte operands within registers.

Table 4–7: Byte-Within-Register Manipulation Instructions Summary

Mnemonic	Operation
CMPBGE	Compare Byte
EXTBL	Extract Byte Low
EXTWL	Extract Word Low
EXTLL	Extract Longword Low
EXTQL	Extract Quadword Low
EXTWH	Extract Word High
EXTLH	Extract Longword High
EXTQH	Extract Quadword High
INSBL	Insert Byte Low
INSWL	Insert Word Low
INSLL	Insert Longword Low

Table 4–7: Byte-Within-Register Manipulation Instructions Summary (Continued)

Mnemonic	Operation
INSQL	Insert Quadword Low
INSWH	Insert Word High
INSLH	Insert Longword High
INSQH	Insert Quadword High
MSKBL	Mask Byte Low
MSKWL	Mask Word Low
MSKLL	Mask Longword Low
MSKQL	Mask Quadword Low
MSKWH	Mask Word High
MSKLH	Mask Longword High
MSKQH	Mask Quadword High
SEXTB	Sign extend byte
SEXTW	Sign extend word
ZAP	Zero Bytes
ZAPNOT	Zero Bytes Not

4.6.1 Compare Byte

Format:

CMPBGE	Ra.rq,Rb.rq,Rc.wq	!Operate format
CMPBGE	Ra.rq,#b.ib,Rc.wq	!Operate format

Operation:

```
FOR i FROM 0 TO 7
  temp<8:0> ← 0 || Rav<i*8+7:i*8>} + {0 || NOT Rbv<i*8+7:i*8>} + 1
  Rc<i> ← temp<8>
END
Rc<63:8> ← 0
```

Exceptions:

None

Instruction mnemonics:

CMPBGE   Compare Byte

Qualifiers:

None

Description:

CMPBGE does eight parallel unsigned byte comparisons between corresponding bytes of Rav and Rbv, storing the eight results in the low eight bits of Rc. The high 56 bits of Rc are set to zero. Bit 0 of Rc corresponds to byte 0, bit 1 of Rc corresponds to byte 1, and so forth. A result bit is set in Rc if the corresponding byte of Rav is greater than or equal to Rbv (unsigned).

Notes:

The result of CMPBGE can be used as an input to ZAP and ZAPNOT.

To scan for a byte of zeros in a character string:

```
<initialize R1 to aligned QW address of string>
LOOP:
        LDQ    R2,  0(R1)      ; Pick up 8 bytes
        LDA    R1,  8(R1)      ; Increment string pointer
        CMPBGE R31, R2,R3      ; If NO bytes of zero, R3<7:0>=0
        BEQ    R3,  LOOP       ; Loop if no terminator byte found
        ...                    ; At this point, R3 can be used to
                               ; determine which byte terminated
```

To compare two character strings for greater/equal/less:

```
<initialize R1 to aligned QW address of string1>
<initialize R2 to aligned QW address of string2>
LOOP:
        LDQ     R3,   0(R1)        ; Pick up 8 bytes of string1
        LDA     R1,   8(R1)        ; Increment string1 pointer
        LDQ     R4,   0(R2)        ; Pick up 8 bytes of string2
        LDA     R2,   8(R2)        ; Increment string2 pointer
        CMPBGE  R31,  R3, R6       ; Test for zeros in string1
        XOR     R3,   R4, R5       ; Test for all equal bytes
        BNE     R6,   DONE         ; Exit if a zero found
        BEQ     R5,   LOOP         ; Loop if all equal
DONE:   CMPBGE  R31,  R5, R5               ;
        ...
; At this point, R5 can be used to determine the first not-equal
; byte position (if any), and R6 can be used to determine the
; position of the terminating zero in string1 (if any).
```

To range-check a string of characters in R1 for '0'...'9':

```
        LDQ     R2,   lit0s        ; Pick up 8 bytes of the character
                                   ; BELOW '0' '////////'
        LDQ     R3,   lit9s        ; Pick up 8 bytes of the character
                                   ; ABOVE '9' '::::::::'
        CMPBGE  R2,   R1, R4       ; Some R4<i>=1 if character is LT '0'
        CMPBGE  R1,   R3, R5       ; Some R5<i>=1 if character is GT '9'
        BNE     R4,   ERROR        ; Branch if some char too low
        BNE     R5,   ERROR        ; Branch if some char too high
```

4.6.2 Extract Byte

Format:

EXTxx	Ra.rq,Rb.rq,Rc.wq	!Operate format
EXTxx	Ra.rq,#b.ib,Rc.wq	!Operate format

Operation:

```
CASE
 big_endian_data:  Rbv' ← Rbv XOR 111₂
 little_endian_data: Rbv' ← Rbv
ENDCASE

CASE
  EXTBL: byte_mask ← 0000 0001₂
  EXTWx: byte_mask ← 0000 0011₂
  EXTLx: byte_mask ← 0000 1111₂
  EXTQx: byte_mask ← 1111 1111₂
ENDCASE

CASE
  EXTxL:
    byte_loc ← Rbv'<2:0>*8
    temp ← RIGHT_SHIFT(Rav, byte_loc<5:0>)
    Rc ← BYTE_ZAP(temp, NOT(byte_mask) )
  EXTxH:
    byte_loc ← 64 - Rbv'<2:0>*8
    temp ← LEFT_SHIFT(Rav, byte_loc<5:0>)
    Rc ← BYTE_ZAP(temp, NOT(byte_mask) )
ENDCASE
```

Exceptions:

None

Instruction mnemonics:

EXTBL	Extract Byte Low
EXTWL	Extract Word Low
EXTLL	Extract Longword Low
EXTQL	Extract Quadword Low
EXTWH	Extract Word High
EXTLH	Extract Longword High
EXTQH	Extract Quadword High

Qualifiers:

None

Description:

EXTxL shifts register Ra right by 0 to 7 bytes, inserts zeros into vacated bit positions, and then extracts 1, 2, 4, or 8 bytes into register Rc. EXTxH shifts register Ra left by 0 to 7 bytes, inserts zeros into vacated bit positions, and then extracts 2, 4, or 8 bytes into register Rc. The number of bytes to shift is specified by Rbv' <2:0>. The number of bytes to extract is specified in the function code. Remaining bytes are filled with zeros.

Notes:

The comments in the examples below assume that the effective address (ea) of X(R11) is such that (ea mod 8) = 5), the value of the aligned quadword containing X(R11) is CBAx xxxx, and the value of the aligned quadword containing X+7(R11) is yyyH GFED, and the datum is little-endian.

The examples below are the most general case unless otherwise noted; if more information is known about the value or intended alignment of X, shorter sequences can be used.

The intended sequence for loading a quadword from unaligned address X(R11) is:

```
LDQ_U   R1, X(R11)        ; Ignores va<2:0>, R1 = CBAx xxxx
LDQ_U   R2, X+7(R11)      ; Ignores va<2:0>, R2 = yyyH GFED
LDA     R3, X(R11)        ; R3<2:0> = (X mod 8) = 5
EXTQL   R1, R3, R1        ; R1 = 0000 0CBA
EXTQH   R2, R3, R2        ; R2 = HGFE D000
OR      R2, R1, R1        ; R1 = HGFE DCBA
```

The intended sequence for loading and zero-extending a longword from unaligned address X is:

```
LDQ_U   R1, X(R11)        ; Ignores va<2:0>, R1 = CBAx xxxx
LDQ_U   R2, X+3(R11)      ; Ignores va<2:0>, R2 = yyyy yyyD
LDA     R3, X(R11)        ; R3<2:0> = (X mod 8) = 5
EXTLL   R1, R3, R1        ; R1 = 0000 0CBA
EXTLH   R2, R3, R2        ; R2 = 0000 D000
OR      R2, R1, R1        ; R1 = 0000 DCBA
```

The intended sequence for loading and sign-extending a longword from unaligned address X is:

```
LDQ_U   R1,  X(R11)       ; Ignores va<2:0>, R1 = CBAx xxxx
LDQ_U   R2,  X+3(R11)     ; Ignores va<2:0>, R2 = yyyy yyyD
LDA     R3,  X(R11)       ; R3<2:0> = (X mod 8) = 5
EXTLL   R1,  R3, R1       ; R1 = 0000 0CBA
EXTLH   R2,  R3, R2       ; R2 = 0000 D000
OR      R2,  R1, R1       ; R1 = 0000 DCBA
ADDL    R31, R1, R1       ; R1 = ssss DCBA
```

For software that is not designed to use the BWX extension, the intended sequence for loading and zero-extending a word from unaligned address X is:

```
LDQ_U   R1, X(R11)       ; Ignores va<2:0>, R1 = yBAx xxxx
LDQ_U   R2, X+1(R11)     ; Ignores va<2:0>, R2 = yBAx xxxx
LDA     R3, X(R11)       ; R3<2:0> = (X mod 8) = 5
EXTWL   R1, R3, R1       ; R1 = 0000 00BA
EXTWH   R2, R3, R2       ; R2 = 0000 0000
OR      R2, R1, R1       ; R1 = 0000 00BA
```

For software that is not designed to use the BWX extension, the intended sequence for loading and sign-extending a word from unaligned address X is:

```
LDQ_U   R1, X(R11)       ; Ignores va<2:0>, R1 = yBAx xxxx
LDQ_U   R2, X+1(R11)     ; Ignores va<2:0>, R2 = yBAx xxxx
LDA     R3, X+1+1(R11)   ; R3<2:0> = 5+1+1 - 7
EXTQL   R1, R3, R1       ; R1 = 0000 000y
EXTQH   R2, R3, R2       ; R2 = BAxx xxx0
OR      R2, R1, R1       ; R1 = BAxx xxxy
SRA     R1, #48, R1      ; R1 = ssss ssBA
```

For software that is not designed to use the BWX extension, the intended sequence for loading and zero-extending a byte from address X is:

```
LDQ_U   R1, X(R11)       ; Ignores va<2:0>, R1 = yyAx xxxx
LDA     R3, X(R11)       ; R3<2:0> = (X mod 8) = 5
EXTBL   R1, R3, R1       ; R1 = 0000 000A
```

For software that is not designed to use the BWX extension, the intended sequence for loading and sign-extending a byte from address X is:

```
LDQ_U   R1, X(R11)       ; Ignores va<2:0>, R1 = yyAx xxxx
LDA     R3, X+1(R11)     ; R3<2:0> = (X + 1) mod 8, i.e.,
                         ; convert byte position within
                         ; quadword to one-origin based
EXTQH   R1, R3, R1       ; Places the desired byte into byte 7
                         ; of R1.final by left shifting
                         ; R1.initial by ( 8 - R3<2:0> ) byte
                         ; positions
SRA     R1, #56, R1      ; Arithmetic Shift of byte 7 down
                         ; into byte 0,
```

Optimized examples:

Assume that a word fetch is needed from 10(R3), where R3 is intended to contain a long-word-aligned address. The optimized sequences below take advantage of the known constant offset, and the longword alignment (hence a single aligned longword contains the entire word). The sequences generate a Data Alignment Fault if R3 does not contain a long-word-aligned address.

For software that is not designed to use the BWX extension, the intended sequence for loading and zero-extending an aligned word from 10(R3) is:

```
LDL    R1, 8(R3)          ; R1 = ssss BAxx
                          ; Faults if R3 is not longword aligned
EXTWL  R1, #2, R1         ; R1 = 0000 00BA
```

For software that is not designed to use the BWX extension, the intended sequence for loading and sign-extending an aligned word from 10(R3) is:

```
LDL    R1, 8(R3)          ; R1 = ssss BAxx
                          ; Faults if R3 is not longword aligned
SRA    R1, #16, R1        ; R1 = ssss ssBA
```

Big-endian examples:

For software that is not designed to use the BWX extension, the intended sequence for loading and zero-extending a byte from address X is:

```
LDQ_U  R1, X(R11)         ; Ignores va<2:0>, R1 = xxxx xAyy
LDA    R3, X(R11)         ; R3<2:0> = 5, shift will be 2 bytes
EXTBL  R1, R3, R1         ; R1 = 0000 000A
```

The intended sequence for loading a quadword from unaligned address X(R11) is:

```
LDQ_U  R1, X(R11)         ; Ignores va<2:0>, R1 = xxxxxABC
LDQ_U  R2, X+7(R11)       ; Ignores va<2:0>, R2 = DEFGHyyy
LDA    R3, X+7(R11)       ; R3<2:0> = 4, shift will be 3 bytes
EXTQH  R1, R3, R1         ; R1 = ABC0 0000
EXTQL  R2, R3, R2         ; R2 = 000D EFGH
OR     R1, R2, R1         ; R1 = ABCD EFGH
```

Note that the address in the LDA instruction for big-endian quadwords is X+7, for longwords is X+3, and for words is X+1; for little-endian, these are all just X. Also note that the EXTQH and EXTQL instructions are reversed with respect to the little-endian sequence.

4.6.3 Byte Insert

Format:

INSxx	Ra.rq,Rb.rq,Rc.wq	!Operate format
INSxx	Ra.rq,#b.ib,Rc.wq	!Operate format

Operation:

```
CASE
 big_endian_data:  Rbv' ← Rbv XOR 111_2
 little_endian_data: Rbv' ← Rbv
ENDCASE

CASE
  INSBL: byte_mask ← 0000 0000 0000 0001_2
  INSWx: byte_mask ← 0000 0000 0000 0011_2
  INSLx: byte_mask ← 0000 0000 0000 1111_2
  INSQx: byte_mask ← 0000 0000 1111 1111_2
ENDCASE
byte_mask ← LEFT_SHIFT(byte_mask, Rbv'<2:0>)

CASE
  INSxL:
    byte_loc ← Rbv'<2:0>*8
    temp ← LEFT_SHIFT(Rav, byte_loc<5:0>)
    Rc ← BYTE_ZAP(temp, NOT(byte_mask<7:0>))
  INSxH:
    byte_loc ← 64 - Rbv'<2:0>*8
    temp ← RIGHT_SHIFT(Rav, byte_loc<5:0>)
    Rc ← BYTE_ZAP(temp, NOT(byte_mask<15:8>))
ENDCASE
```

Exceptions:

None

Instruction mnemonics:

INSBL	Insert Byte Low
INSWL	Insert Word Low
INSLL	Insert Longword Low
INSQL	Insert Quadword Low
INSWH	Insert Word High
INSLH	Insert Longword High
INSQH	Insert Quadword High

Qualifiers:

None

Description:

INSxL and INSxH shift bytes from register Ra and insert them into a field of zeros, storing the result in register Rc. Register Rbv ′ <2:0> selects the shift amount, and the function code selects the maximum field width: 1, 2, 4, or 8 bytes. The instructions can generate a byte, word, longword, or quadword datum that is spread across two registers at an arbitrary byte alignment.

4.6.4 Byte Mask

Format:

MSKxx	Ra.rq,Rb.rq,Rc.wq	!Operate format
MSKxx	Ra.rq,#b.ib,Rc.wq	!Operate format

Operation:

```
CASE
  big_endian_data:  Rbv' ← Rbv XOR 111₂
  little_endian_data: Rbv' ← Rbv
ENDCASE

CASE
  MSKBL: byte_mask ← 0000 0000 0000 0001₂
  MSKWx: byte_mask ← 0000 0000 0000 0011₂
  MSKLx: byte_mask ← 0000 0000 0000 1111₂
  MSKQx: byte_mask ← 0000 0000 1111 1111₂
ENDCASE
byte_mask ← LEFT_SHIFT(byte_mask, Rbv'<2:0>)

CASE
  MSKxL:
    Rc ← BYTE_ZAP(Rav, byte_mask<7:0>)
  MSKxH:
    Rc ← BYTE_ZAP(Rav, byte_mask<15:8>)
ENDCASE
```

Exceptions:

None

Instruction mnemonics:

MSKBL	Mask Byte Low
MSKWL	Mask Word Low
MSKLL	Mask Longword Low
MSKQL	Mask Quadword Low
MSKWH	Mask Word High
MSKLH	Mask Longword High
MSKQH	Mask Quadword High

Qualifiers:

None

Description:

MSKxL and MSKxH set selected bytes of register Ra to zero, storing the result in register Rc. Register Rbv'<2:0> selects the starting position of the field of zero bytes, and the function code selects the maximum width: 1, 2, 4, or 8 bytes. The instructions generate a byte, word, longword, or quadword field of zeros that can spread across two registers at an arbitrary byte alignment.

Notes:

The comments in the examples below assume that the effective address (ea) of X(R11) is such that (ea mod 8) = 5, the value of the aligned quadword containing X(R11) is CBAx xxxx, the value of the aligned quadword containing X+7(R11) is yyyH GFED, the value to be stored from R5 is HGFE DCBA, and the datum is little-endian. Slight modifications similar to those in Section 4.6.2 apply to big-endian data.

The examples below are the most general case; if more information is known about the value or intended alignment of X, shorter sequences can be used.

The intended sequence for storing an unaligned quadword R5 at address X(R11) is:

```
LDA     R6, X(R11)          ; R6<2:0> = (X mod 8) = 5
LDQ_U   R2, X+7(R11)        ; Ignores va<2:0>, R2 = yyyH GFED
LDQ_U   R1, X(R11)          ; Ignores va<2:0>, R1 = CBAx xxxx
INSQH   R5, R6, R4          ; R4 = 000H GFED
INSQL   R5, R6, R3          ; R3 = CBA0 0000
MSKQH   R2, R6, R2          ; R2 = yyy0 0000
MSKQL   R1, R6, R1          ; R1 = 000x xxxx
OR      R2, R4, R2          ; R2 = yyyH GFED
OR      R1, R3, R1          ; R1 = CBAx xxxx
STQ_U   R2, X+7(R11)        ; Must store high then low for
STQ_U   R1, X(R11)          ; degenerate case of aligned QW
```

The intended sequence for storing an unaligned longword R5 at X is:

```
LDA     R6, X(R11)          ; R6<2:0> = (X mod 8) = 5
LDQ_U   R2, X+3(R11)        ; Ignores va<2:0>, R2 = yyyy yyyD
LDQ_U   R1, X(R11)          ; Ignores va<2:0>, R1 = CBAx xxxx
INSLH   R5, R6, R4          ; R4 = 0000 000D
INSLL   R5, R6, R3          ; R3 = CBA0 0000
MSKLH   R2, R6, R2          ; R2 = yyyy yyy0
MSKLL   R1, R6, R1          ; R1 = 000x xxxx
OR      R2, R4, R2          ; R2 = yyyy yyyD
OR      R1, R3, R1          ; R1 = CBAx xxxx
STQ_U   R2, X+3(R11)        ; Must store high then low for
STQ_U   R1, X(R11)          ; degenerate case of aligned
```

For software that is not designed to use the BWX extension, the intended sequence for storing an unaligned word R5 at X is:

```
LDA     R6, X(R11)          ; R6<2:0> = (X mod 8) = 5
LDQ_U   R2, X+1(R11)        ; Ignores va<2:0>, R2 = yBAx xxxx
LDQ_U   R1, X(R11)          ; Ignores va<2:0>, R1 = yBAx xxxx
INSWH   R5, R6, R4          ; R4 = 0000 0000
INSWL   R5, R6, R3          ; R3 = 0BA0 0000
MSKWH   R2, R6, R2          ; R2 = yBAx xxxx
MSKWL   R1, R6, R1          ; R1 = y00x xxxx
OR      R2, R4, R2          ; R2 = yBAx xxxx
OR      R1, R3, R1          ; R1 = yBAx xxxx
STQ_U   R2, X+1(R11)        ; Must store high then low for
STQ_U   R1, X(R11)          ; degenerate case of aligned
```

For software that is not designed to use the BWX extension, the intended sequence for storing a byte R5 at X is:

```
LDA     R6, X(R11)          ; R6<2:0> = (X mod 8) = 5
LDQ_U   R1, X(R11)          ; Ignores va<2:0>, R1 = yyAx xxxx
INSBL   R5, R6, R3          ; R3 = 00A0 0000
MSKBL   R1, R6, R1          ; R1 = yy0x xxxx
OR      R1, R3, R1          ; R1 = yyAx xxxx
STQ_U   R1, X(R11)          ;
```

4.6.5 Sign Extend

Format:

SEXTx	Rb.rq,Rc.wq	!Operate format
SEXTx	#b.ib,Rc.wq	!Operate format

Operation:

```
CASE
  SEXTB:  Rc ← SEXT(Rbv<07:0>)
  SEXTW:  Rc ← SEXT(Rbv<15:0>)
ENDCASE
```

Exceptions:

None

Instruction mnemonics:

SEXTB	Sign Extend Byte
SEXTW	Sign Extend Word

Qualifiers:

None

Description:

The byte or word in register Rb is sign-extended to 64 bits and written to register Rc. Ra must be R31.

Implementation Note:

The SEXTB and SEXTW instructions are supported in hardware on Alpha implementations for which the AMASK instruction returns bit 0 set. SEXTB and SEXTW are supported with software emulation in Alpha implementations for which AMASK does not return bit 0 set. Software emulation of SEXTB and SEXTW is significantly slower than hardware support.

4.6.6 Zero Bytes

Format:

ZAPx	Ra.rq,Rb.rq,Rc.wq	!Operate format
ZAPx	Ra.rq,#b.ib,Rc.wq	!Operate format

Operation:

```
CASE
  ZAP:
    Rc ← BYTE_ZAP(Rav, Rbv<7:0>)

  ZAPNOT:
    Rc ← BYTE_ZAP(Rav, NOT Rbv<7:0>)
ENDCASE
```

Exceptions:

None

Instruction mnemonics:

ZAP	Zero Bytes
ZAPNOT	Zero Bytes Not

Qualifiers:

None

Description:

ZAP and ZAPNOT set selected bytes of register Ra to zero and store the result in register Rc. Register Rb<7:0> selects the bytes to be zeroed. Bit 0 of Rbv corresponds to byte 0, bit 1 of Rbv corresponds to byte 1, and so on. A result byte is set to zero if the corresponding bit of Rbv is a one for ZAP and a zero for ZAPNOT.

4.7 Floating-Point Instructions

Alpha provides instructions for operating on floating-point operands in each of four data formats:

- F_floating (VAX single)
- G_floating (VAX double, 11-bit exponent)
- S_floating (IEEE single)
- T_floating (IEEE double, 11-bit exponent)

Data conversion instructions are also provided to convert operands between floating-point and quadword integer formats, between double and single floating, and between quadword and longword integers.

Note:

> D_floating is a partially supported datatype; no D_floating arithmetic operations are provided in the architecture. For backward compatibility, exact D_floating arithmetic may be provided via software emulation. D_floating "format compatibility," in which binary files of D_floating numbers may be processed but without the last 3 bits of fraction precision, can be obtained via conversions to G_floating, G arithmetic operations, then conversion back to D_floating.

The choice of data formats is encoded in each instruction. Each instruction also encodes the choice of rounding mode and the choice of trapping mode.

All floating-point operate instructions (*not* including loads or stores) that yield an F_floating or G_floating zero result must materialize a true zero.

4.7.1 Single-Precision Operation

Single-precision values (F_floating or S_floating) are stored in the floating-point registers in canonical form, as subsets of double-precision values, with 11-bit exponents restricted to the corresponding single-precision range, and with the 29 low-order fraction bits restricted to be all zero.

Single-precision operations applied to canonical single-precision values give single-precision results. Single-precision operations applied to non-canonical operands give UNPREDICTABLE results.

Longword integer values in floating-point registers are stored in bits <63:62,58:29>, with bits <61:59> ignored and zeros in bits <28:0>.

4.7.2 Subsets and Faults

All floating-point operations may take floating disabled faults. Any subsetted floating-point instruction may take an Illegal Instruction Trap. These faults are not explicitly listed in the description of each instruction.

All floating-point loads and stores may take memory management faults (access control violation, translation not valid, fault on read/write, data alignment).

The floating-point enable (FEN) internal processor register (IPR) allows system software to restrict access to the floating-point registers.

If a floating-point instruction is implemented and FEN = 0, attempts to execute the instruction cause a floating disabled fault.

If a floating-point instruction is not implemented, attempts to execute the instruction cause an Illegal Instruction Trap. This rule holds regardless of the value of FEN.

An Alpha implementation may provide both VAX and IEEE floating-point operations, either, or none.

Some floating-point instructions are common to the VAX and IEEE subsets, some are VAX only, and some are IEEE only. These are designated in the descriptions that follow. If either subset is implemented, all the common instructions must be implemented.

An implementation that includes IEEE floating-point may subset the ability to perform rounding to plus infinity and minus infinity. If not implemented, instructions requesting these rounding modes take Illegal Instruction Trap.

An implementation that includes IEEE floating-point may implement any subset of the Trap Disable flags (DNOD, DZED, INED, INVD, OVFD, and UNFD) and Denormal Control flags (DNZ and UNDZ) in the FPCR:

- If a Trap Disable flag is not implemented, then the corresponding trap occurs as usual.

- If DNZ is not implemented, then any IEEE operation with a denormal input must take an Invalid Operation Trap.

- If UNDZ is not implemented, then any IEEE operation that includes a /S qualifier that underflows must take an Underflow Trap.

- If DZED is implemented, then IEEE division of 0/0 must be treated as an invalid operation instead of a division by zero.

Any unimplemented bits in the FPCR arc read as zero and ignored when set.

4.7.3 Definitions

The following definitions apply to Alpha floating-point support.

Alpha finite number

A floating-point number with a definite, in-range value. Specifically, all numbers in the inclusive ranges –MAX through –MIN, zero, and +MIN through +MAX, where MAX is the largest non-infinite representable floating-point number and MIN is the smallest non-zero representable normalized floating-point number.

For VAX floating-point, finites do not include reserved operands or dirty zeros (this differs from the usual VAX interpretation of dirty zeros as finite). For IEEE floating-point, finites do not include infinites, NaNs, or denormals, but do include minus zero.

denormal

An IEEE floating-point bit pattern that represents a number whose magnitude lies between zero and the smallest finite number.

dirty zero

A VAX floating-point bit pattern that represents a zero value, but not in true-zero form.

infinity

An IEEE floating-point bit pattern that represents plus or minus infinity.

LSB

The least significant bit. For a positive finite representable number A, A + 1 LSB is the next larger representative number, and A + ½ LSB is exactly halfway between A and the next larger representable number. For a positive representable number A whose fraction field is not all zeros, A − 1 LSB is the next smaller representable number, and A − ½ LSB is exactly halfway between A and the next smaller representable number.

non-finite number

An IEEE infinity, NaN, denormal number, or a VAX dirty zero or reserved operand.

Not-a-Number

An IEEE floating-point bit pattern that represents something other than a number. This comes in two forms: signaling NaNs (for Alpha, those with an initial fraction bit of 0) and quiet NaNs (for Alpha , those with initial fraction bit of 1).

representable result

A real number that can be represented exactly as a VAX or IEEE floating-point number, with finite precision and bounded exponent range.

reserved operand

A VAX floating-point bit pattern that represents an illegal value.

trap shadow

The set of instructions potentially executed after an instruction that signals an arithmetic trap but before the trap is actually taken.

true result

The mathematically correct result of an operation, assuming that the input operand values are exact. The true result is typically rounded to the nearest representable result.

true zero

The value +0, represented as exactly 64 zeros in a floating-point register.

4.7.4 Encodings

Floating-point numbers are represented with three fields: sign, exponent, and fraction. The sign is 1 bit; the exponent is 8, 11, or 15 bits; and the fraction is 23, 52, 55, or 112 bits. Some encodings represent special values:

Sign	Exponent	Fraction	Vax Meaning	VAX Finite	IEEE Meaning	IEEE Finite
x	All-1's	Non-zero	Finite	Yes	+/–NaN	No
x	All-1's	0	Finite	Yes	+/–Infinity	No
0	0	Non-zero	Dirty zero	No	+Denormal	No
1	0	Non-zero	Resv. operand	No	–Denormal	No
0	0	0	True zero	Yes	+0	Yes
1	0	0	Resv. operand	No	–0	Yes
x	Other	x	Finite	Yes	finite	Yes

The values of MIN and MAX for each of the five floating-point data formats are:

Data Format	MIN	MAX
F_floating	$2^{**}-127 * 0.5$ (0.293873588e–38)	$2^{**}127 *(1.0 - 2^{**}-24)$ (1.7014117e38)
G_floating	$2^{**}-1023 * 0.5$ (0.5562684646268004e–308)	$2^{**}1023 * (1.0 - 2^{**}-53)$ (0.89884656743115785407e308)
S_floating	$2^{**}-126 * 1.0$ (1.17549435e–38)	$2^{**}127 * (2.0 - 2^{**}-23)$ (3.40282347e38)
T_floating	$2^{**}-1022 * 1.0$ (2.2250738585072013e–308)	$2^{**}1023 * (2.0 - 2^{**}-52)$ (1.7976931348623158e308)
X_floating	$2^{**}-16382*1.0$ (See below[†])	$2^{**}16383*(2.0-2^{**}-112)$ (See below[‡])

[†]   (1.18973149535723176508575932662800702e4932)

[‡]   (3.36210314311209350626267781732175260e–4932)

4.7.5 Rounding Modes

All rounding modes map a true result that is exactly representable to that representable value.

VAX Rounding Modes

For VAX floating-point operations, two rounding modes are provided and are specified in each instruction: normal (biased) rounding and chopped rounding.

Normal VAX rounding maps the true result to the nearest of two representable results, with true results exactly halfway between mapped to the larger in absolute value (sometimes called biased rounding away from zero); maps true results ≥ MAX + 1/2 LSB in magnitude to an overflow; maps true results < MIN − 1/4 LSB in magnitude to an underflow.

Chopped VAX rounding maps the true result to the smaller in magnitude of two surrounding representable results; maps true results ≥ MAX + 1 LSB in magnitude to an overflow; maps true results < MIN in magnitude to an underflow.

IEEE Rounding Modes

For IEEE floating-point operations, four rounding modes are provided: normal rounding (unbiased round to nearest), rounding toward minus infinity, round toward zero, and rounding toward plus infinity. The first three can be specified in the instruction. Rounding toward plus infinity can be obtained by setting the Floating-point Control Register (FPCR) to select it and then specifying dynamic rounding mode in the instruction (See Section 4.7.8). Alpha IEEE arithmetic does rounding before detecting overflow/underflow.

Normal IEEE rounding maps the true result to the nearest of two representable results, with true results exactly halfway between mapped to the one whose fraction ends in 0 (sometimes called unbiased rounding to even); maps true results ≥ MAX + 1/2 LSB in magnitude to an overflow; maps true results < MIN − 1/2 LSB in magnitude to an underflow.

Plus infinity IEEE rounding maps the true result to the larger of two surrounding representable results; maps true results > MAX in magnitude to an overflow; maps positive true results ≤ +MIN − 1 LSB to an underflow; and maps negative true results > −MIN to an underflow.

Minus infinity IEEE rounding maps the true result to the smaller of two surrounding representable results; maps true results > MAX in magnitude to an overflow; maps positive true results < +MIN to an underflow; and maps negative true results ≥ −MIN + 1 LSB to an underflow.

Chopped IEEE rounding maps the true result to the smaller in magnitude of two surrounding representable results; maps true results ≥ MAX + 1 LSB in magnitude to an overflow; and maps non-zero true results < MIN in magnitude to an underflow.

Dynamic rounding mode uses the IEEE rounding mode selected by the FPCR register and is described in more detail in Section 4.7.8.

The following tables summarize the floating-point rounding modes:

VAX Rounding Mode	Instruction Notation
Normal rounding	(No qualifier)
Chopped	/C

IEEE Rounding Mode	Instruction Notation
Normal rounding	(No qualifier)
Dynamic rounding	/D
Plus infinity	/D and ensure that FPCR<DYN> = '11'
Minus infinity	/M
Chopped	/C

4.7.6 Computational Models

The Alpha architecture provides a choice of floating-point computational models.

There are two computational models available on systems that implement the VAX floating-point subset:

- VAX-format arithmetic with precise exceptions
- High-performance VAX-format arithmetic

There are three computational models available on systems that implement the IEEE floating-point subset:

- IEEE compliant arithmetic
- IEEE compliant arithmetic without inexact exception
- High-performance IEEE-format arithmetic

4.7.6.1 VAX-Format Arithmetic with Precise Exceptions

This model provides floating-point arithmetic that is fully compatible with the floating-point arithmetic provided by the VAX architecture. It provides support for VAX non-finites and gives precise exceptions.

This model is implemented by using VAX floating-point instructions with the /S, /SU, and /SV trap qualifiers. Each instruction can determine whether it also takes an exception on underflow or integer overflow. The performance of this model depends on how often computations involve non-finite operands. Performance also depends on how an Alpha system chooses to trade off implementation complexity between hardware and operating system completion handlers (see Section 4.7.7.3).

4.7.6.2 High-Performance VAX-Format Arithmetic

This model provides arithmetic operations on VAX finite numbers. An imprecise arithmetic trap is generated by any operation that involves non-finite numbers, floating overflow, and divide-by-zero exceptions.

This model is implemented by using VAX floating-point instructions with a trap qualifier other than /S, /SU, or /SV. Each instruction can determine whether it also traps on underflow or integer overflow. This model does not require the overhead of an operating system completion handler and can be the faster of the two VAX models.

4.7.6.3 IEEE-Compliant Arithmetic

This model provides floating-point arithmetic that fully complies with the IEEE Standard for Binary Floating-Point Arithmetic. It provides all of the exception status flags that are in the standard. It provides a default where all traps and faults are disabled and where IEEE non-finite values are used in lieu of exceptions.

Alpha operating systems provide additional mechanisms that allow the user to specify dynamically which exception conditions should trap and which should proceed without trapping. The operating systems also include mechanisms that allow alternative handling of denormal values. See Appendix B and the appropriate operating system documentation for a description of these mechanisms.

This model is implemented by using IEEE floating-point instructions with the /SUI or /SVI trap qualifiers. The performance of this model depends on how often computations involve inexact results and non-finite operands and results. Performance also depends on how the Alpha system chooses to trade off implementation complexity between hardware and operating system completion handlers (see Section 4.7.7.3). This model provides acceptable performance on Alpha systems that implement the inexact disable (INED) bit in the FPCR. Performance may be slow if the INED bit is not implemented.

4.7.6.4 IEEE-Compliant Arithmetic Without Inexact Exception

This model is similar to the model in Section 4.7.6.3, except this model does not signal inexact results either by the inexact status flag or by trapping. Combining routines that are compiled with this model and routines that are compiled with the model in Section 4.7.6.3 can give an application better control over testing when an inexact operation will affect computational accuracy.

This model is implemented by using IEEE floating-point instructions with the /SU or /SV trap qualifiers. The performance of this model depends on how often computations involve non-finite operands and results. Performance also depends on how an Alpha system chooses to trade off implementation complexity between hardware and operating system completion handlers (see Section 4.7.7.3).

4.7.6.5 High-Performance IEEE-Format Arithmetic

This model provides arithmetic operations on IEEE finite numbers and notifies applications of all exceptional floating-point operations. An imprecise arithmetic trap is generated by any operation that involves non-finite numbers, floating overflow, divide-by-zero, and invalid operations. Underflow results are set to zero. Conversion to integer results that overflow are set to the low-order bits of the integer value.

This model is implemented by using IEEE floating-point instructions with a trap qualifier other than /SU, /SV, /SUI, or /SVI. Each instruction can determine whether it also traps on underflow or integer overflow. This model does not require the overhead of an operating system completion handler and can be the fastest of the three IEEE models.

4.7.7 Trapping Modes

There are six exceptions that can be generated by floating point operate instructions, all signaled by an arithmetic exception trap. These exceptions are:

- Invalid operation
- Division by zero
- Overflow
- Underflow
- Inexact result
- Integer overflow (conversion to integer only)

4.7.7.1 VAX Trapping Modes

This section describes the characteristics of the four VAX trapping modes, which are summarized in Table 4–8.

When no trap mode is specified (the default):
- Arithmetic is performed on VAX finite numbers.
- Operations give imprecise traps whenever the following occur:
    - an operand is a non-finite number
    - a floating overflow
    - a divide-by-zero
- Traps are imprecise and it is not always possible to determine which instruction triggered a trap or the operands of that instruction.
- An underflow produces a zero result without trapping.
- A conversion to integer that overflows uses the low-order bits of the integer as the result without trapping.
- The result of any operation that traps is UNPREDICTABLE.

When /U or /V mode is specified:

- Arithmetic is performed on VAX finite numbers.
- Operations give imprecise traps whenever the following occur:
  - an operand is a non-finite number
  - an underflow
  - an integer overflow
  - a floating overflow
  - a divide-by-zero
- Traps are imprecise and it is not always possible to determine which instruction triggered a trap or the operands of that instruction.
- An underflow trap produces a zero result.
- A conversion to integer trapping with an integer overflow produces the low-order bits of the integer value.
- The result of any other operation that traps is UNPREDICTABLE.

When /S mode is specified:

- Arithmetic is performed on all VAX values, both finite and non-finite.
- A VAX dirty zero is treated as zero.
- Exceptions are signaled for:
  - a VAX reserved operand, which generates an invalid operation exception
  - a floating overflow
  - a divide-by-zero
- Exceptions are precise and an application can locate the instruction that caused the exception, along with its operand values. See Section 4.7.7.3.
- An operation that underflows produces a zero result without taking an exception.
- A conversion to integer that overflows uses the low-order bits of the integer as the result, without taking an exception.
- When an operation takes an exception, the result of the operation is UNPREDICTABLE.

When /SU or /SV mode is specified:

- Arithmetic is performed on all VAX values, both finite and non-finite.
- A VAX dirty zero is treated as zero.
- Exceptions are signaled for:
  - a VAX reserved operand, which generates an invalid operation exception
  - an underflow
  - an integer overflow
  - a floating overflow
  - a divide-by-zero
- Exceptions are precise and an application can locate the instruction that caused the exception, along with its operand values. See Section 4.7.7.3.
- An underflow exception produces a zero.
- A conversion to integer exception with integer overflow produces the low-order bits of the integer value.
- The result of any other operation that takes an exception is UNPREDICTABLE.

A summary of the VAX trapping modes, instruction notation, and their meaning follows in Table 4–8:

Table 4–8: VAX Trapping Modes Summary

Trap Mode	Notation	Meaning
Underflow disabled	No qualifier	Imprecise
	/S	Precise exception completion
Underflow enabled	/U	Imprecise
	/SU	Precise exception completion
Integer overflow disabled	No qualifier	Imprecise
	/S	Precise exception completion
Integer overflow enabled	/V	Imprecise
	/SV	Precise exception completion

4.7.7.2 IEEE Trapping Modes

This section describes the characteristics of the four IEEE trapping modes, which are summarized in Table 4–9.

When no trap mode is specified (the default):
- Arithmetic is performed on IEEE finite numbers.
- Operations give imprecise traps whenever the following occur:
    - an operand is a non-finite number
    - a floating overflow
    - a divide-by-zero
    - an invalid operation
- Traps are imprecise, and it is not always possible to determine which instruction triggered a trap or the operands of that instruction.
- An underflow produces a zero result without trapping.
- A conversion to integer that overflows uses the low-order bits of the integer as the result without trapping.
- When an operation traps, the result of the operation is UNPREDICTABLE.

When /U or /V mode is specified :
- Arithmetic is performed on IEEE finite numbers.
- Operations give imprecise traps whenever the following occur:
    - an operand is a non-finite number
    - an underflow
    - an integer overflow
    - a floating overflow
    - a divide-by-zero
    - an invalid operation

- Traps are imprecise, and it is not always possible to determine which instruction triggered a trap or the operands of that instruction.
- An underflow trap produces a zero.
- A conversion to integer trap with an integer overflow produces the low-order bits of the integer.
- The result of any other operation that traps is UNPREDICTABLE.

When /SU or /SV mode is specified:
- Arithmetic is performed on all IEEE values, both finite and non-finite.
- Alpha systems support all IEEE features except inexact exception (which requires /SUI or /SVI):
  - The IEEE standard specifies a default where exceptions do not fault or trap.In combination with the FPCR, this mode allows disabling exceptions and producing IEEE compliant nontrapping results. See Sections 4.7.7.10 and 4.7.7.11.
  - Each Alpha operating system provides a way to optionally signal IEEE floating-point exceptions. This mode enables the IEEE status flags that keep a record of each exception that is encountered. An Alpha operating system uses the IEEE floating-point control (FP_C) quadword, described in Appendix B, to maintain the IEEE status flags and to enable calls to IEEE user signal handlers.
- Exceptions signaled in this mode are precise and an application can locate the instruction that caused the exception, along with its operand values. See Section 4.7.7.3.

When /SUI or /SVI mode is specified:
- Arithmetic is performed on all IEEE values, both finite and non-finite.
- Inexact exceptions are supported, along with all the other IEEE features supported by the /SU or /SV mode.

A summary of the IEEE trapping modes, instruction notation, and their meaning follows in Table 4–9:

Table 4–9: Summary of IEEE Trapping Modes

Trap Mode	Notation	Meaning
Underflow disabled and inexact disabled	No qualifier	Imprecise
Underflow enabled and inexact disabled	/U /SU	Imprecise Precise exception completion
Underflow enabled and inexact enabled	/SUI	Precise exception completion
Integer overflow disabled and inexact disabled	No qualifier	Imprecise

Table 4–9: Summary of IEEE Trapping Modes (Continued)

Trap Mode	Notation	Meaning
Integer overflow enabled and inexact disabled	/V /SV	Imprecise Precise exception completion
Integer overflow enabled and inexact enabled	/SVI	Precise exception completion

4.7.7.3 Arithmetic Trap Completion

Because floating-point instructions may be pipelined, the trap PC can be an arbitrary number of instructions past the one triggering the trap. Those instructions that are executed after the trigger instruction of an arithmetic trap are collectively referred to as the *trap shadow* of the trigger instruction.

Marking floating-point instructions for exception completion with any valid qualifier combination that includes the /S qualifier enables the completion of the triggering instruction. For any instruction so marked, the output register for the triggering instruction cannot also be one of the input registers, so that an input register cannot be overwritten and the input value is available after a trap occurs.

See Appendix B, Alpha Support for Operating System Completion Handlers, for more information.

The AMASK instruction reports how the arithmetic trap should be completed:

- If AMASK returns with bit 9 clear, floating-point traps are imprecise. Exception completion requires that generated code must obey the trap shadow rules in Section 4.7.7.3.1, with a trap shadow length as described in Section 4.7.7.3.2.

- If AMASK returns with bit 9 set, the hardware implements precise floating-point traps. If the instruction has any valid qualifier combination that includes /S, the trap PC points to the instruction that immediately follows the instruction that triggered the trap. The trap shadow contains zero instructions; exception completion does not require that the generated code follow the conditions in Section 4.7.7.3.1 and the length rules in Section 4.7.7.3.2.

4.7.7.3.1 Trap Shadow Rules

For an operating system (OS) completion handler to complete non-finite operands and exceptions, the following conditions must hold.

Conditions 1 and 2 allow an OS completion handler to locate the trigger instruction by doing a linear scan backwards from the trap PC while comparing destination registers in the trap shadow with the registers that are specified in the register write mask parameter to the arithmetic trap.

Condition 3 allows an OS completion handler to emulate the trigger instruction with its original input operand values.

Condition 4 allows the handler to re-execute instructions in the trap shadow with their original operand values.

Condition 5 prevents any unusual side effects that would cause problems on repeated execution of the instructions in the trap shadow.

Conditions:

1. The destination register of the trigger instruction may not be used as the destination register of any instruction in the trap shadow.

2. The trap shadow may not include any branch or jump instructions.

3. An instruction in the trap shadow may not modify an input to the trigger instruction.

4. The value in a register or memory location that is used as input to some instruction in the trap shadow may not be modified by a subsequent instruction in the trap shadow unless that value is produced by an earlier instruction in the trap shadow.

5. The trap shadow may not contain any instructions with side effects that interact with earlier instructions in the trap shadow or with other parts of the system. Examples of operations with prohibited side effects are:

    –   Modifications of the stack pointer or frame pointer that can change the accessibility of stack variables and the exception context that is used by earlier instructions in the trap shadow.

    –   Modifications of volatile values and access to I/O device registers.

    –   If order of exception reporting is important, taking an arithmetic trap by an integer instruction or by a floating-point instruction that does not include a /S qualifier, either of which can report exceptions out of order.

An instruction may be in the trap shadows of multiple instructions that include a /S qualifier. That instruction must obey all conditions for all those trap shadows. For example, the destination register of an instruction in multiple trap shadows must be different than the destination registers of each possible trigger instruction.

4.7.7.3.2 Trap Shadow Length Rules

The trap shadow length rules in Table 4–10 apply only to those floating-point instructions with any valid qualifier combination that includes a /S trap qualifier. Further, the instruction to which the trap shadow extends is not part of the trap shadow and that instruction is not executed prior to the arithmetic trap that is signaled by the trigger instruction.

Implementation notes:

•   On Alpha implementations for which the IMPLVER instruction returns the value 0, the trap shadow of an instruction may extend after the result is consumed by a floating-point STx instruction. On all other implementations, the trap shadow ends when a result is consumed.

•   Because Alpha implementations need not execute instructions that have R31 or F31 as the destination operand, instructions with such an destination should not be thought to end a trap shadow.

Table 4–10: Trap Shadow Length Rules

Floating-Point Instruction Group	Trap Shadow Extends Until Any of the Following Occurs:
Floating-point operate (except DIVx and SQRTx)	• Encountering a CALL_PAL, EXCB, or TRAPB instruction.
	• The result is consumed by any instruction except floating-point STx.
	• The fourth instruction[†] after the result is consumed by a floating-point STx instruction.
	Or, following the floating-point STx of the result, the result of a LDx that loads the stored value is consumed by any instruction.
	• The result of a subsequent floating-point operate instruction is consumed by any instruction except floating-point STx.
	• The second instruction[†] after the result of a subsequent floating-point operate instruction is consumed by a floating-point STx instruction.
	• The result of a subsequent floating-point DIVx or SQRTx instruction is consumed by any instruction.
Floating-point DIVx	• Encountering a CALL_PAL, EXCB, or TRAPB instruction.
	• The result is consumed by any instruction except floating-point STx.
	• The fourth instruction[†] after the result is consumed by a floating-point STx instruction.
	Or, following the floating-point STx of the result, the result of a LDx that loads the stored value is consumed by any instruction.
	• The result of a subsequent floating-point DIVx is consumed by any instruction.

Table 4-10: Trap Shadow Length Rules (Continued)

Floating-Point Instruction Group	Trap Shadow Extends Until Any of the Following Occurs:
Floating-point SQRTx	
	• Encountering a CALL_PAL, EXCB, or TRAPB instruction.
	• The result is consumed by any instruction.
	• The result of a subsequent SQRTx instruction is consumed by any instruction.

† The length of four instructions is a conservative estimate of how far the trap shadow may extend past a consuming floating-point STx instruction. The length of two instructions is a conservative estimate of how far the trap shadow may extend after a subsequent floating-point operate instruction is consumed by a floating-point STx instruction. Compilers can make a more precise estimate by consulting the *DECchip 21064 and DECchip 21064A Alpha AXP Microprocessors Hardware Reference Manual, EC-QD2RA-TE.*

4.7.7.4 Invalid Operation (INV) Arithmetic Trap

An invalid operation arithmetic trap is signaled if an operand is a non-finite number or if an operand is invalid for the operation to be performed. (Note that CMPTxy does not trap on plus or minus infinity.) Invalid operations are:

- Any operation on a signaling NaN.
- Addition of unlike-signed infinities or subtraction of like-signed infinities, such as (+infinity + –infinity) or (+infinity – +infinity).
- Multiplication of 0*infinity.
- IEEE division of 0/0 or infinity/infinity.
- Conversion of an infinity or NaN to an integer.
- CMPTLE or CMPTLT when either operand is a NaN.
- SQRTx of a negative non-zero number.

The instruction cannot disable the trap and, if the trap occurs, an UNPREDICTABLE value is stored in the result register. However, under some conditions, the FPCR can dynamically disable the trap, as described in Section 4.7.7.10, producing a correct IEEE result, as described in Section 4.7.10.

IEEE-compliant system software must also supply an invalid operation indication to the user for x REM 0 and for conversions to integer that take an integer overflow trap.

If an implementation does not support the DZED (division by zero disable) bit, it may respond to the IEEE division of 0/0 by delivering a division by zero trap to the operating system, which IEEE compliant software must change to an invalid operation trap for the user.

An implementation may choose not to take an INV trap for a valid IEEE operation that involves denormal operands if:

- The instruction is modified by any valid qualifier combination that includes the /S (exception completion) qualifier.

- The implementation supports the DNZ (denormal operands to zero) bit and DNZ is set.

- The instruction produces the result and exceptions required by Section 4.7.10, as modified by the DNZ bit described in Section 4.7.7.11.

An implementation may choose not to take an INV trap for a valid IEEE operation that involves denormal operands, and direct hardware implementation of denormal arithmetic is permitted if:

- The instruction is modified by any valid qualifier combination that includes the /S (exception completion) qualifier.

- The implementation supports both the DNOD (denormal operand exception disable) bit and the DNZ (denormal operands to zero) bit and DNOD is set while DNZ is clear.

- The instruction produces the result and exceptions required by Section 4.7.10, possibly modified by the UDNZ bit described in Section 4.7.7.11.

Regardless of the setting of the INVD (invalid operation disable) bit, the implementation may choose not to trap on valid operations that involve quiet NaNs and infinities as operands for IEEE instructions that are modified by any valid qualifier combination that includes the /S (exception completion) qualifier.

4.7.7.5 Division by Zero (DZE) Arithmetic Trap

A division by zero arithmetic trap is taken if the numerator does not cause an invalid operation trap and the denominator is zero.

The instruction cannot disable the trap and, if the trap occurs, an UNPREDICTABLE value is stored in the result register. However, under some conditions, the FPCR can dynamically disable the trap, as described in Section 4.7.7.10, producing a correct IEEE result, as described in Section 4.7.10.

If an implementation does not support the DZED (division by zero disable) bit, it may respond to the IEEE division of 0/0 by delivering a division by zero trap to the operating system, which IEEE compliant software must change to an invalid operation trap for the user.

4.7.7.6 Overflow (OVF) Arithmetic Trap

An overflow arithmetic trap is signaled if the rounded result exceeds in magnitude the largest finite number of the destination format.

The instruction cannot disable the trap and, if the trap occurs, an UNPREDICTABLE value is stored in the result register. However, under some conditions, the FPCR can dynamically disable the trap, as described in Section 4.7.7.10, producing a correct IEEE result, as described in Section 4.7.10.

4.7.7.7 Underflow (UNF) Arithmetic Trap

An underflow occurs if the rounded result is smaller in magnitude than the smallest finite number of the destination format.

If an underflow occurs, a true zero (64 bits of zero) is always stored in the result register. In the case of an IEEE operation that takes an underflow arithmetic trap, a true zero is stored even if the result after rounding would have been −0 (underflow below the negative denormal range).

If an underflow occurs and underflow traps are enabled by the instruction, an underflow arithmetic trap is signaled. However, under some conditions, the FPCR can dynamically disable the trap, as described in Section 4.7.7.10, producing the result described in Section 4.7.10, as modified by the UNDZ bit described in Section 4.7.7.11.

4.7.7.8 Inexact Result (INE) Arithmetic Trap

An inexact result occurs if the infinitely precise result differs from the rounded result.

If an inexact result occurs, the normal rounded result is still stored in the result register. If an inexact result occurs and inexact result traps are enabled by the instruction, an inexact result arithmetic trap is signaled. However, under some conditions, the FPCR can dynamically disable the trap; see Section 4.7.7.10 for information.

4.7.7.9 Integer Overflow (IOV) Arithmetic Trap

In conversions from floating to quadword integer, an integer overflow occurs if the rounded result is outside the range $-2**63..2**63-1$. In conversions from quadword integer to longword integer, an integer overflow occurs if the result is outside the range $-2**31..2**31-1$.

If an integer overflow occurs in CVTxQ or CVTQL, the true result truncated to the low-order 64 or 32 bits respectively is stored in the result register.

If an integer overflow occurs and integer overflow traps are enabled by the instruction, an integer overflow arithmetic trap is signaled.

4.7.7.10 IEEE Floating-Point Trap Disable Bits

In the case of IEEE exception completion modes, any of the traps described in Sections 4.7.7.4 through 4.7.7.9 may be disabled by setting the appropriate trap disable bit in the FPCR. The trap disable bits only affect the IEEE trap modes when the instruction is modified by any valid qualifier combination that includes the /S (exception completion) qualifier. The trap disable bits (DNOD, DZED, INED, INVD, OVFD, and UNFD) do not affect any of the VAX trap modes.

If a trap disable bit is set and the corresponding trap condition occurs, the hardware implementation sets the result of the operation to the nontrapping result value as specified in the IEEE standard and Section 4.7.10 and modified by the denormal control bits. If the implementation is unable to calculate the required result, it ignores the trap disable bit and signals a trap as usual.

Note that a hardware implementation may choose to support any subset of the trap disable bits, including the empty subset.

4.7.7.11 IEEE Denormal Control Bits

In the case of IEEE exception completion modes, the handling of denormal operands and results is controlled by the DNZ and UNDZ bits in the FPCR. These denormal control bits only affect denormal handling by IEEE instructions that are modified by any valid qualifier combination that includes the /S (exception completion) qualifier.

The denormal control bits apply only to the IEEE operate instructions – ADD, SUB, MUL, DIV, SQRT, CMPxx, and CVT with floating-point source operand.

If both the UNFD (underflow disable) bit and the UNDZ (underflow to zero) bit are set in the FPCR, the implementation sets the result of an underflow operation to a true zero result. The zeroing of a denormal result by UNDZ must also be treated as an inexact result.

If the DNZ (denormal operands to zero) bit is set in the FPCR, the implementation treats each denormal operand as if it were a signed zero value. The source operands in the register are not changed. If DNZ is set, IEEE operations with any valid qualifier combination that includes a /S qualifier signal arithmetic traps as if any denormal operand were zero; that is, with DNZ set:

- An IEEE operation with a denormal operand never generates an overflow, underflow, or inexact result arithmetic trap.

- Dividing by a denormal operand is a division by zero or invalid operation as appropriate.

- Multiplying a denormal by infinity is an invalid operation.

- A SQRT of a negative denormal produces a –0 instead of an invalid operation.

- A denormal operand, treated as zero, does not take the denormal operand exception trap controlled by the DNOD bit in the FPCR.

Note that a hardware implementation may choose to support any subset of the denormal control bits, including the empty subset.

4.7.8 Floating-Point Control Register (FPCR)

When an IEEE floating-point operate instruction specifies dynamic mode (/D) in its function field (function field bits <12:11> = 11), the rounding mode to be used for the instruction is derived from the FPCR register. The layout of the rounding mode bits and their assignments matches exactly the format used in the 11-bit function field of the floating-point operate instructions. The function field is described in Section 4.7.9.

In addition, the FPCR gives a summary of each exception type for the exception conditions detected by all IEEE floating-point operates thus far, as well as an overall summary bit that indicates whether any of these exception conditions has been detected. The individual exception bits match exactly in purpose and order the exception bits found in the exception summary quadword that is pushed for arithmetic traps. However, for each instruction, these exception bits are set independent of the trapping mode specified for the instruction. Therefore, even though trapping may be disabled for a certain exceptional condition, the fact that the exceptional condition was encountered by an instruction is still recorded in the FPCR.

Floating-point operates that belong to the IEEE subset and CVTQL, which belongs to both VAX and IEEE subsets, appropriately set the FPCR exception bits. It is UNPREDICTABLE whether floating-point operates that belong only to the VAX floating-point subset set the FPCR exception bits.

Alpha floating-point hardware only transitions these exception bits from zero to one. Once set to one, these exception bits are only cleared when software writes zero into these bits by writing a new value into the FPCR.

Section 4.7.2 allows certain of the FPCR bits to be subsetted.

The format of the FPCR is shown in Figure 4–1 and described in Table 4–11.

Figure 4–1: Floating-Point Control Register (FPCR) Format

```
63 62 61 60 59  58 57 56 55 54 53 52 51 50 49 48 47 46                      0
┌──┬──┬──┬──┬────┬──┬──┬──┬──┬──┬──┬──┬──┬──┬──┬──┬───────────────────────────┐
│S │I │U │U │DYN │I │I │U │O │D │I │O │D │I │D │D │                           │
│U │N │N │N │_RM │O │N │N │V │Z │N │V │Z │N │N │N │         RAZ/IGN           │
│M │E │F │D │    │V │E │F │F │E │V │F │E │V │Z │O │                           │
│  │D │D │Z │    │  │  │  │  │  │  │D │D │D │  │D │                           │
└──┴──┴──┴──┴────┴──┴──┴──┴──┴──┴──┴──┴──┴──┴──┴──┴───────────────────────────┘
```

Table 4–11: Floating-Point Control Register (FPCR) Bit Descriptions

Bit	Description (Meaning When Set)
63	Summary Bit (SUM). Records bitwise OR of FPCR exception bits. Equal to FPCR<57 |56 | 55 | 54 | 53 | 52>.
62	Inexact Disable (INED)[†]. Suppress INE trap and place correct IEEE nontrapping result in the destination register
61	Underflow Disable (UNFD)[†]. Suppress UNF trap and place correct IEEE nontrapping result in the destination register if the implementation is capable of producing correct IEEE nontrapping result. The correct result value is determined according to the value of the UNDZ bit.
60	Underflow to Zero (UNDZ)[†]. When set together with UNFD, on underflow, the hardware places a true zero (64 bits of zero) in the destination register rather than the result specified by the IEEE standard.
59–58	Dynamic Rounding Mode (DYN). Indicates the rounding mode to be used by an IEEE floating-point operate instruction when the instruction's function field specifies dynamic mode (/D). Assignments are:

DYN	IEEE Rounding Mode Selected
00	Chopped rounding mode
01	Minus infinity
10	Normal rounding
11	Plus infinity

Bit	Description (Meaning When Set)
57	Integer Overflow (IOV). An integer arithmetic operation or a conversion from floating to integer overflowed the destination precision.
56	Inexact Result (INE). A floating arithmetic or conversion operation gave a result that differed from the mathematically exact result.
55	Underflow (UNF). A floating arithmetic or conversion operation underflowed the destination exponent.
54	Overflow (OVF). A floating arithmetic or conversion operation overflowed the destination exponent.
53	Division by Zero (DZE). An attempt was made to perform a floating divide operation with a divisor of zero.
52	Invalid Operation (INV). An attempt was made to perform a floating arithmetic, conversion, or comparison operation, and one or more of the operand values were illegal.
51	Overflow Disable (OVFD)[†]. Suppress OVF trap and place correct IEEE nontrapping result in the destination register if the implementation is capable of producing correct IEEE nontrapping results.
50	Division by Zero Disable (DZED)[†]. Suppress DZE trap and place correct IEEE nontrapping result in the destination register if the implementation is capable of producing correct IEEE nontrapping results.
49	Invalid Operation Disable (INVD)[†]. Suppress INV trap and place correct IEEE nontrapping result in the destination register if the implementation is capable of producing correct IEEE nontrapping results.
48	Denormal Operands to Zero (DNZ)[†]. Treat all denormal operands as a signed zero value with the same sign as the denormal.
47	Denormal Operand Exception Disable (DNOD)[†]. Suppress INV trap for valid operations that involve denormal operand values and place the correct IEEE nontrapping result in the destination register if the implementation is capable of processing the denormal operand. If the result of the operation underflows, the correct result is determined according to the value of the UNDZ bit. If DNZ is set, DNOD has no effect because a denormal operand is treated as having a zero value instead of a denormal value.
46–0	Reserved. Read as Zero. Ignored when written.

[†] Bit only has meaning for IEEE instructions when any valid qualifier combination that includes exception completion (/S) is specified.

FPCR is read from and written to the floating-point registers by the MT_FPCR and MF_FPCR instructions respectively, which are described in Section 4.7.8.1.

FPCR and the instructions to access it are required for an implementation that supports floating-point (see Section 4.7.8). On implementations that do not support floating-point, the instructions that access FPCR (MF_FPCR and MT_FPCR) take an Illegal Instruction Trap.

Software Note:

Support for FPCR is required on a system that supports the OpenVMS Alpha operating system even if that system does not support floating-point.

4.7.8.1 Accessing the FPCR

Because Alpha floating-point hardware can overlap the execution of a number of floating-point instructions, accessing the FPCR must be synchronized with other floating-point instructions. An EXCB instruction must be issued both prior to and after accessing the FPCR to ensure that the FPCR access is synchronized with the execution of previous and subsequent floating-point instructions; otherwise synchronization is not ensured.

Issuing an EXCB followed by an MT_FPCR followed by another EXCB ensures that only floating-point instructions issued after the second EXCB are affected by and affect the new value of the FPCR. Issuing an EXCB followed by an MF_FPCR followed by another EXCB ensures that the value read from the FPCR only records the exception information for floating-point instructions issued prior to the first EXCB.

Consider the following example:

```
ADDT/D
EXCB                        ;1
MT_FPCR F1,F1,F1
EXCB                        ;2
SUBT/D
```

Without the first EXCB, it is possible in an implementation for the ADDT/D to execute in parallel with the MT_FPCR. Thus, it would be UNPREDICTABLE whether the ADDT/D was affected by the new rounding mode set by the MT_FPCR and whether fields cleared by the MT_FPCR in the exception summary were subsequently set by the ADDT/D.

Without the second EXCB, it is possible in an implementation for the MT_FPCR to execute in parallel with the SUBT/D. Thus, it would be UNPREDICTABLE whether the SUBT/D was affected by the new rounding mode set by the MT_FPCR and whether fields cleared by the MT_FPCR in the exception summary field of FPCR were previously set by the SUBT/D.

Specifically, code should issue an EXCB before and after it accesses the FPCR if that code needs to see valid values in FPCR bits <63> and <57:52>. An EXCB should be issued before attempting to write the FPCR if the code expects changes to bits <59:52> not to have dependencies with prior instructions. An EXCB should be issued after attempting to write the FPCR if the code expects subsequent instructions to have dependencies with changes to bits <59:52>.

4.7.8.2 Default Values of the FPCR

Processor initialization leaves the value of FPCR UNPREDICTABLE.

Software Note:

DIGITAL software should initialize FPCR<DYN> = 10 during program activation. Using this default, a program can be coded to use only dynamic rounding without the need to explicitly set the rounding mode to normal rounding in its start-up code.

Program activation normally clears all other fields in the FPCR. However, this behavior may depend on the operating system.

4.7.8.3 Saving and Restoring the FPCR

The FPCR must be saved and restored across context switches so that the FPCR value of one process does not affect the rounding behavior and exception summary of another process.

The dynamic rounding mode put into effect by the programmer (or initialized by image activation) is valid for the entirety of the program and remains in effect until subsequently changed by the programmer or until image run-down occurs.

Software Notes:

The following software notes apply to saving and restoring the FPCR:

1. The IEEE standard precludes saving and restoring the FPCR across subroutine calls.

2. The IEEE standard requires that an implementation provide status flags that are set whenever the corresponding conditions occur and are reset only at the user's request. The exception bits in the FPCR do not satisfy that requirement, because they can be spuriously set by instructions in a trap shadow that should not have been executed had the trap been taken synchronously.

   The IEEE status flags can be provided by software (as software status bits) as follows:

   > Trap interface software (usually the operating system) keeps a set of software status bits and a mask of the traps that the user wants to receive. Code is generated with the /SUI qualifiers. For a particular exception, the software clears the corresponding trap disable bit if either the corresponding software status bit is 0 or if the user wants to receive such traps. If a trap occurs, the software locates the offending instruction in the trap shadow, simulates it and sets any of the software status bits that are appropriate. Then, the software either delivers the trap to the user program or disables further delivery of such traps. The user program must interface to this trap interface software to set or clear any of the software status bits or to enable or disable floating-point traps. See Appendix B.

   When such a scheme is being used, the trap disable bits and denormal control bits should be modified only by the trap interface software. If the disable bits are spuriously cleared, unnecessary traps may occur. If they are spuriously set, the software may fail to set the correct values in the software status bits. Programs should call routines in the trap interface software to set or clear bits in the FPCR.

DIGITAL software may choose to initialize the software status bits and the trap disable bits to all 1's to avoid any initial trapping when an exception condition first occurs. Or, software may choose to initialize those bits to all 0's in order to provide a summary of the exception behavior when the program terminates.

In any event, the exception bits in the FPCR are still useful to programs. A program can clear all of the exception bits in the FPCR, execute a single floating-point instruction, and then examine the status bits to determine which hardware-defined exceptions the instruction encountered. For this operation to work in the presence of various implementation options, the single instruction should be followed by a TRAPB or EXCB instruction, and exception completion by the system software should save and restore the FPCR registers without other modifications.

3. Because of the way the LDS and STS instructions manipulate bits <61:59> of floating-point registers, they should not be used to manipulate FPCR values.

4.7.9 Floating-Point Instruction Function Field Format

The function code for IEEE and VAX floating-point instructions, bits <15..5>, contain the function field. That field is shown in Figure 4–2 and described for IEEE floating-point in Table 4–12 and for VAX floating-point in Table 4–13. Function codes for the independent floating-point instructions, those with opcode 17_{16}, do not correspond to the function fields below.

The function field contains subfields that specify the trapping and rounding modes that are enabled for the instruction, the source datatype, and the instruction class.

Figure 4–2: Floating-Point Instruction Function Field

31	26 25	21 20	16 15	13 12 11	10 9 8	5 4	0
Opcode	Fa	Fb	T R P	R N D	S R C	F N C	Fc

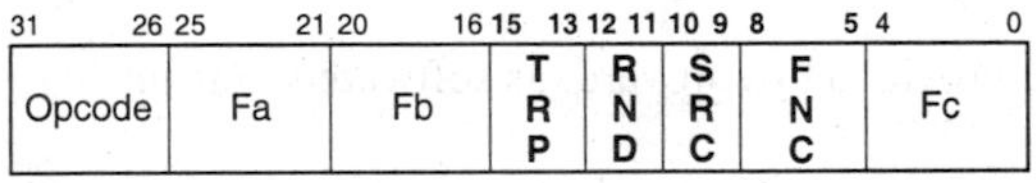

Table 4–12: IEEE Floating-Point Function Field Bit Summary

Bits	Field	Meaning[†]
15–13	TRP	Trapping modes:

Contents	Meaning for Opcodes 14_{16} and 16_{16}
000	Imprecise (default)
001	Underflow enable (/U) — floating-point output Integer overflow enable (/V) — integer output
010	UNPREDICTABLE for opcode 16_{16} instructions Reserved for opcode 14_{16} instructions
011	UNPREDICTABLE for opcode 16_{16} instructions Reserved for opcode 14_{16} instructions
100	UNPREDICTABLE for opcode 16_{16} instructions Reserved for opcode 14_{16} instructions
101	/SU — floating-point output /SV — integer output
110	UNPREDICTABLE for opcode 16_{16} instructions Reserved for opcode 14_{16} instructions
111	/SUI — floating-point output /SVI — integer output

Bits	Field	Meaning
12–11	RND	Rounding modes:

Contents	Meaning for Opcodes 16_{16} and 14_{16}
00	Chopped (/C)
01	Minus infinity (/M)
10	Normal (default)
11	Dynamic (/D)

Bits	Field	Meaning
10–9	SRC	Source datatype:

Contents	Meaning for Opcode 16_{16}	Meaning for Opcode 14_{16}
00	S_floating	S_floating
01	Reserved	Reserved
10	T_floating	T_floating
11	Q_fixed	Reserved

Table 4–12: IEEE Floating-Point Function Field Bit Summary (Continued)

Bits	Field	Meaning[†]
8–5	FNC	Instruction class:

Contents	Meaning for Opcode 16_{16}	Meaning for Opcode 14_{16}
0000	ADDx	Reserved
0001	SUBx	Reserved
0010	MULx	Reserved
0011	DIVx	Reserved
0100	CMPxUN	ITOFS/ITOFT
0101	CMPxEQ	Reserved
0110	CMPxLT	Reserved
0111	CMPxLE	Reserved
1000	Reserved	Reserved
1001	Reserved	Reserved
1010	Reserved	Reserved
1011	Reserved	SQRTS/SQRTT
1100	CVTxS	Reserved
1101	Reserved	Reserved
1110	CVTxT	Reserved
1111	CVTxQ	Reserved

[†] Encodings for the instructions CVTST and CVTST/S are exceptions to this table; use the encodings in Appendix C.

Table 4–13: VAX Floating-Point Function Field Bit Summary

Bits	Field	Meaning
15–13	TRP	Trapping modes:

		Contents	Meaning for Opcodes 14_{16} and 15_{16}
		000	Imprecise (default)
		001	Underflow enable (/U) – floating-point output
			Integer overflow enable (/V) – integer output
		010	UNPREDICTABLE for opcode 15_{16} instructions
			Reserved for opcode 14_{16} instructions
		011	UNPREDICTABLE for opcode 15_{16} instructions
			Reserved for opcode 14_{16} instructions
		100	/S – Exception completion enable
		101	/SU – floating-point output
			/SV – integer output
		110	UNPREDICTABLE for opcode 15_{16} instructions
			Reserved for opcode 14_{16} instructions
		111	UNPREDICTABLE for opcode 15_{16} instructions
			Reserved for opcode 14_{16} instructions

12–11	RND	Rounding modes:

		Contents	Meaning for Opcodes 15_{16} and 14_{16}
		00	Chopped (/C)
		01	UNPREDICTABLE
		10	Normal (default)
		11	UNPREDICTABLE

10–9	SRC	Source datatype:[†]

		Contents	Meaning for Opcode 15_{16}	Meaning for Opcode 14_{16}
		00	F_floating	F_floating
		01	D_floating	F_floating
		10	G_floating	G_floating
		11	Q_fixed	Reserved

Table 4–13: VAX Floating-Point Function Field Bit Summary (Continued)

Bits	Field	Meaning		
8–5	FNC	Instruction class:		
		Contents	**Meaning for Opcode 15_{16}**	**Meaning for Opcode 14_{16}**
		0000	ADDx	Reserved
		0001	SUBx	Reserved
		0010	MULx	Reserved
		0011	DIVx	Reserved
		0100	CMPxUN	ITOFF
		0101	CMPxEQ	Reserved
		0110	CMPxLT	Reserved
		0111	CMPxLE	Reserved
		1000	Reserved	Reserved
		1001	Reserved	Reserved
		1010	Reserved	SQRTF/SQRTG
		1011	Reserved	Reserved
		1100	CVTxF	Reserved
		1101	CVTxD	Reserved
		1110	CVTxG	Reserved
		1111	CVTxQ	Reserved

† In the SRC field, both 00 and 01 specify the F_floating source datatype for opcode 14_{16}.

4.7.10 IEEE Standard

The IEEE Standard for Binary Floating-Point Arithmetic (ANSI/IEEE Standard 754-1985) is included by reference.

This standard leaves certain operations as implementation dependent. The remainder of this section specifies the behavior of the Alpha architecture in these situations. Note that this behavior may be supplied by either hardware (if the invalid operation disable, or INVD, bit is implemented) or by software. See Sections 4.7.7.10, 4.7.7.11, 4.7.8, 4.7.8.3, and Appendix B.

4.7.10.1 Conversion of NaN and Infinity Values

Conversion of a NaN or an Infinity value to an integer gives a result of zero.

Conversion of a NaN value from S_floating to T_floating gives a result identical to the input, except that the most significant fraction bit (bit 51) is set to indicate a quiet NaN.

Conversion of a NaN value from T_floating to S_floating gives a result identical to the input, except that the most significant fraction bit (bit 51) is set to indicate a quiet NaN, and bits <28:0> are cleared to zero.

4.7.10.2 Copying NaN Values

Copying a NaN value without changing its precision does not cause an invalid operation exception.

4.7.10.3 Generating NaN Values

When an operation is required to produce a NaN and none of its inputs are NaN values, the result of the operation is the quiet NaN value that has the sign bit set to one, all exponent bits set to one (to indicate a NaN), the most significant fraction bit set to one (to indicate that the NaN is quiet), and all other fraction bits cleared to zero. This value is referred to as "the canonical quiet NaN."

4.7.10.4 Propagating NaN Values

When an operation is required to produce a NaN and one or both of its inputs are NaN values, the IEEE standard requires that quiet NaN values be propagated when possible. With the Alpha architecture, the result of such an operation is a NaN generated according to the first of the following rules that is applicable:

1. If the operand in the Fb register of the operation is a quiet NaN, that value is used as the result.

2. If the operand in the Fb register of the operation is a signaling NaN, the result is the quiet NaN formed from the Fb value by setting the most significant fraction bit (bit 51) to a one bit.

3. If the operation uses its Fa operand and the value in the Fa register is a quiet NaN, that value is used as the result.

4. If the operation uses its Fa operand and the value in the Fa register is a signaling NaN, the result is the quiet NaN formed from the Fa value by setting the most significant fraction bit (bit 51) to a one bit.

5. The result is the canonical quiet NaN.

4.8 Memory Format Floating-Point Instructions

The instructions in this section move data between the floating-point registers and memory. They use the Memory instruction format. They do not interpret the bits moved in any way; specifically, they do not trap on non-finite values.

The instructions are summarized in Table 4–14.

Table 4–14: Memory Format Floating-Point Instructions Summary

Mnemonic	Operation	Subset
LDF	Load F_floating	VAX
LDG	Load G_floating (Load D_floating)	VAX
LDS	Load S_floating (Load Longword Integer)	Both
LDT	Load T_floating (Load Quadword Integer)	Both
STF	Store F_floating	VAX
STG	Store G_floating (Store D_floating)	VAX
STS	Store S_floating (Store Longword Integer)	Both
STT	Store T_floating (Store Quadword Integer)	Both

4.8.1 Load F_floating

Format:

> LDF   Fa.wf,disp.ab(Rb.ab)   !Memory format

Operation:

```
va ←   {Rbv + SEXT(disp)}

CASE
 big_endian_data:  va' ← va XOR 100₂
 little_endian_data: va' ← va
ENDCASE

Fa ← (va')<15> || MAP_F((va')<14:7>) || (va')<6:0> ||
     (va')<31:16> || 0<28:0>
```

Exceptions:

Access Violation

Fault on Read

Alignment

Translation Not Valid

Instruction mnemonics:

> LDF   Load F_floating

Qualifiers:

None

Description:

LDF fetches an F_floating datum from memory and writes it to register Fa. If the data is not naturally aligned, an alignment exception is generated.

The MAP_F function causes the 8-bit memory-format exponent to be expanded to an 11-bit register-format exponent according to Table 2–1.

The virtual address is computed by adding register Rb to the sign-extended 16-bit displacement. For a big-endian longword access, va<2> (bit 2 of the virtual address) is inverted, and any memory management fault is reported for va (not va'). The source operand is fetched from memory and the bytes are reordered to conform to the F_floating register format. The result is then zero-extended in the low-order longword and written to register Fa.

4.8.2 Load G_floating

Format:

LDG   Fa.wg,disp.ab(Rb.ab)   !Memory format

Operation:

```
va ← {Rbv + SEXT(disp)}
Fa ← (va)<15:0> || (va)<31:16> || (va)<47:32> || (va)<63:48>
```

Exceptions:

Access Violation
Fault on Read
Alignment
Translation Not Valid

Instruction mnemonics:

LDG   Load G_floating (Load D_floating)

Qualifiers:

None

Description:

LDG fetches a G_floating (or D_floating) datum from memory and writes it to register Fa. If the data is not naturally aligned, an alignment exception is generated.

The virtual address is computed by adding register Rb to the sign-extended 16-bit displacement. The source operand is fetched from memory, the bytes are reordered to conform to the G_floating register format (also conforming to the D_floating register format), and the result is then written to register Fa.

4.8.3 Load S_floating

Format:

LDS	Fa.ws,disp.ab(Rb.ab)	!Memory format

Operation:

```
va ← {Rbv + SEXT(disp)}

CASE
 big_endian_data:  va' ← va XOR 100₂
 little_endian_data: va' ← va
ENDCASE

Fa ← (va')<31> || MAP_S((va')<30:23>) || (va')<22:0> || 0<28:0>
```

Exceptions:

Access Violation
Fault on Read
Alignment
Translation Not Valid

Instruction mnemonics:

LDS   Load S_floating (Load Longword Integer)

Qualifiers:

None

Description:

LDS fetches a longword (integer or S_floating) from memory and writes it to register Fa. If the data is not naturally aligned, an alignment exception is generated. The MAP_S function causes the 8-bit memory-format exponent to be expanded to an 11-bit register-format exponent according to Table 2–2.

The virtual address is computed by adding register Rb to the sign-extended 16-bit displacement. For a big-endian longword access, va<2> (bit 2 of the virtual address) is inverted, and any memory management fault is reported for va (not va'). The source operand is fetched from memory, is zero-extended in the low-order longword, and then written to register Fa. Longword integers in floating registers are stored in bits <63:62,58:29>, with bits <61:59> ignored and zeros in bits <28:0>.

4.8.4 Load T_floating

Format:

> LDT   Fa.wt,disp.ab(Rb.ab)   !Memory format

Operation:

```
va ← {Rbv + SEXT(disp)}

Fa ← (va)<63:0>
```

Exceptions:

> Access Violation
> Fault on Read
> Alignment
> Translation Not Valid

Instruction mnemonics:

> LDT   Load T_floating (Load Quadword Integer)

Qualifiers:

> None

Description:

LDT fetches a quadword (integer or T_floating) from memory and writes it to register Fa. If the data is not naturally aligned, an alignment exception is generated.

The virtual address is computed by adding register Rb to the sign-extended 16-bit displacement. The source operand is fetched from memory and written to register Fa.

4.8.5 Store F_floating

Format:

STF   Fa.rf,disp.ab(Rb.ab)   !Memory format

Operation:

```
va ← {Rbv + SEXT(disp)}

CASE
 big_endian_data:   va' ← va XOR 100₂
 little_endian_data: va' ← va
ENDCASE

(va')<31:0> ← Fav<44:29> || Fav<63:62> || Fav<58:45>
```

Exceptions:

Access Violation

Fault on Write

Alignment

Translation Not Valid

Instruction mnemonics:

STF   Store F_floating

Qualifiers:

None

Description:

STF stores an F_floating datum from Fa to memory. If the data is not naturally aligned, an alignment exception is generated.

The virtual address is computed by adding register Rb to the sign-extended 16-bit displacement. For a big-endian longword access, va<2> (bit 2 of the virtual address) is inverted, and any memory management fault is reported for va (not va'). The bits of the source operand are fetched from register Fa, the bits are reordered to conform to F_floating memory format, and the result is then written to memory. Bits <61:59> and <28:0> of Fa are ignored. No checking is done.

4.8.6 Store G_floating

Format:

STG   Fa.rg,disp.ab(Rb.ab)   !Memory format

Operation:

```
va ← {Rbv + SEXT(disp)}
(va)<63:0> ← Fav<15:0> || Fav<31:16> || Fav<47:32> || Fav<63:48>
```

Exceptions:

> Access Violation
> Fault on Write
> Alignment
> Translation Not Valid

Instruction mnemonics:

STG   Store G_floating (Store D_floating)

Qualifiers:

> None

Description:

STG stores a G_floating (or D_floating) datum from Fa to memory. If the data is not naturally aligned, an alignment exception is generated.

The virtual address is computed by adding register Rb to the sign-extended 16-bit displacement. The source operand is fetched from register Fa, the bytes are reordered to conform to the G_floating memory format (also conforming to the D_floating memory format), and the result is then written to memory.

4.8.7 Store S_floating

Format:

STS	Fa.rs,disp.ab(Rb.ab)	!Memory format

Operation:

```
va ← {Rbv + SEXT(disp)}

CASE
 big_endian_data:  va' ← va XOR 100₂
 little_endian_data: va' ← va
ENDCASE

(va')<31:0> ← Fav<63:62> || Fav<58:29>
```

Exceptions:

Access Violation
Fault on Write
Alignment
Translation Not Valid

Instruction mnemonics:

STS	Store S_floating (Store Longword Integer)

Qualifiers:

None

Description:

STS stores a longword (integer or S_floating) datum from Fa to memory. If the data is not naturally aligned, an alignment exception is generated.

The virtual address is computed by adding register Rb to the sign-extended 16-bit displacement. For a big-endian longword access, va<2> (bit 2 of the virtual address) is inverted, and any memory management fault is reported for va (not va'). The bits of the source operand are fetched from register Fa, the bits are reordered to conform to S_floating memory format, and the result is then written to memory. Bits <61:59> and <28:0> of Fa are ignored. No checking is done.

4.8.8 Store T_floating

Format:

STT	Fa.rt,disp.ab(Rb.ab)	!Memory format

Operation:

```
va ← {Rbv + SEXT(disp)}
(va)<63:0> ← Fav<63:0>
```

Exceptions:

Access Violation
Fault on Write
Alignment
Translation Not Valid

Instruction mnemonics:

STT   Store T_floating (Store Quadword Integer)

Qualifiers:

None

Description:

STT stores a quadword (integer or T_floating) datum from Fa to memory. If the data is not naturally aligned, an alignment exception is generated.

The virtual address is computed by adding register Rb to the sign-extended 16-bit displacement. The source operand is fetched from register Fa and written to memory.

4.9 Branch Format Floating-Point Instructions

Alpha provides six floating conditional branch instructions. These branch-format instructions test the value of a floating-point register and conditionally change the PC.

They do not interpret the bits tested in any way; specifically, they do not trap on non-finite values.

The test is based on the sign bit and whether the rest of the register is all zero bits. All 64 bits of the register are tested. The test is independent of the format of the operand in the register. Both plus and minus zero are equal to zero. A non-zero value with a sign of zero is greater than zero. A non-zero value with a sign of one is less than zero. No reserved operand or non-finite checking is done.

The floating-point branch operations are summarized in Table 4–15:

Table 4–15: Floating-Point Branch Instructions Summary

Mnemonic	Operation	Subset
FBEQ	Floating Branch Equal	Both
FBGE	Floating Branch Greater Than or Equal	Both
FBGT	Floating Branch Greater Than	Both
FBLE	Floating Branch Less Than or Equal	Both
FBLT	Floating Branch Less Than	Both
FBNE	Floating Branch Not Equal	Both

4.9.1 Conditional Branch

Format:

FBxx   Fa.rq,disp.al   !Branch format

Operation:

```
{update PC}
va ← PC + {4*SEXT(disp)}
IF TEST(Fav, Condition_based_on_Opcode) THEN
    PC ← va
```

Exceptions:

None

Instruction mnemonics:

FBEQ	Floating Branch Equal
FBGE	Floating Branch Greater Than or Equal
FBGT	Floating Branch Greater Than
FBLE	Floating Branch Less Than or Equal
FBLT	Floating Branch Less Than
FBNE	Floating Branch Not Equal

Qualifiers:

None

Description:

Register Fa is tested. If the specified relationship is true, the PC is loaded with the target virtual address; otherwise, execution continues with the next sequential instruction.

The displacement is treated as a signed longword offset. This means it is shifted left two bits (to address a longword boundary), sign-extended to 64 bits, and added to the updated PC to form the target virtual address.

The conditional branch instructions are PC-relative only. The 21-bit signed displacement gives a forward/backward branch distance of +/–1M instructions.

Notes:

- To branch properly on non-finite operands, compare to F31, then branch on the result of the compare.

- The largest negative integer ($8000\ 0000\ 0000\ 0000_{16}$) is the same bit pattern as floating minus zero, so it is treated as equal to zero by the branch instructions. To branch properly on the largest negative integer, convert it to floating or move it to an integer register and do an integer branch.

4.10 Floating-Point Operate Format Instructions

The floating-point bit-operate instructions perform copy and integer convert operations on 64-bit register values. The bit-operate instructions do not interpret the bits moved in any way; specifically, they do not trap on non-finite values.

The floating-point arithmetic-operate instructions perform add, subtract, multiply, divide, compare, register move, squre root, and floating convert operations on 64-bit register values in one of the four specified floating formats.

Each instruction specifies the source and destination formats of the values, as well as the rounding mode and trapping mode to be used. These instructions use the Floating-point Operate format.

The floating-point operate instructions are summarized in Table 4–16.

Table 4–16: Floating-Point Operate Instructions Summary

Mnemonic	Operation	Subset
Bit and FPCR Operations:		
CPYS	Copy Sign	Both
CPYSE	Copy Sign and Exponent	Both
CPYSN	Copy Sign Negate	Both
CVTLQ	Convert Longword to Quadword	Both
CVTQL	Convert Quadword to Longword	Both
FCMOVxx	Floating Conditional Move	Both
MF_FPCR	Move from Floating-point Control Register	Both
MT_FPCR	Move to Floating-point Control Register	Both

Table 4–16: Floating-Point Operate Instructions Summary (Continued)

Mnemonic	Operation	Subset
Arithmetic Operations:		
ADDF	Add F_floating	VAX
ADDG	Add G_floating	VAX
ADDS	Add S_floating	IEEE
ADDT	Add T_floating	IEEE
CMPGxx	Compare G_floating	VAX
CMPTxx	Compare T_floating	IEEE
CVTDG	Convert D_floating to G_floating	VAX
CVTGD	Convert G_floating to D_floating	VAX
CVTGF	Convert G_floating to F_floating	VAX
CVTGQ	Convert G_floating to Quadword	VAX
CVTQF	Convert Quadword to F_floating	VAX
CVTQG	Convert Quadword to G_floating	VAX
CVTQS	Convert Quadword to S_floating	IEEE
CVTQT	Convert Quadword to T_floating	IEEE
CVTST	Convert S_floating to T_floating	IEEE
CVTTQ	Convert T_floating to Quadword	IEEE
CVTTS	Convert T_floating to S_floating	IEEE
DIVF	Divide F_floating	VAX
DIVG	Divide G_floating	VAX
DIVS	Divide S_floating	IEEE
DIVT	Divide T_floating	IEEE
FTOIS	Floating-point to integer register move, S_floating	IEEE
FTOIT	Floating-point to integer register move, T_floating	IEEE
ITOFF	Integer to floating-point register move, F_floating	VAX
ITOFS	Integer to floating-point register move, S_floating	IEEE

Table 4–16: Floating-Point Operate Instructions Summary (Continued)

Mnemonic	Operation	Subset
ITOFT	Integer to floating-point register move, T_floating	IEEE
MULF	Multiply F_floating	VAX
MULG	Multiply G_floating	VAX
MULS	Multiply S_floating	IEEE
MULT	Multiply T_floating	IEEE
SQRTF	Square root F_floating	VAX
SQRTG	Square root G_floating	VAX
SQRTS	Square root S_floating	IEEE
SQRTT	Square root T_floating	IEEE
SUBF	Subtract F_floating	VAX
SUBG	Subtract G_floating	VAX
SUBS	Subtract S_floating	IEEE
SUBT	Subtract T_floating	IEEE

4.10.1 Copy Sign

Format:

CPYSy   Fa.rq,Fb.rq,Fc.wq   !Floating-point Operate format

Operation:

```
CASE
   CPYS:   Fc ← Fav<63> || Fbv<62:0>
   CPYSN:  Fc ← NOT(Fav<63>) || Fbv<62:0>
   CPYSE:  Fc ← Fav<63:52> || Fbv<51:0>
ENDCASE
```

Exceptions:

None

Instruction mnemonics:

CPYS	Copy Sign
CPYSE	Copy Sign and Exponent
CPYSN	Copy Sign Negate

Qualifiers:

None

Description:

For CPYS and CPYSN, the sign bit of Fa is fetched (and complemented in the case of CPYSN) and concatenated with the exponent and fraction bits from Fb; the result is stored in Fc.

For CPYSE, the sign and exponent bits from Fa are fetched and concatenated with the fraction bits from Fb; the result is stored in Fc.

No checking of the operands is performed.

Notes:

- Register moves can be performed using CPYS Fx,Fx,Fy. Floating-point absolute value can be done using CPYS F31,Fx,Fy. Floating-point negation can be done using CPYSN Fx,Fx,Fy. Floating values can be scaled to a known range by using CPYSE.

4.10.2 Convert Integer to Integer

Format:

CVTxy   Fb.rq,Fc.wx   !Floating-point Operate format

Operation:

```
CASE
    CVTQL: Fc ← Fbv<31:30> || 0<2:0> || Fbv<29:0> ||0<28:0>
    CVTLQ: Fc ← SEXT(Fbv<63:62> || Fbv<58:29>)
ENDCASE
```

Exceptions:

Integer Overflow, CVTQL only

Instruction mnemonics:

CVTLQ   Convert Longword to Quadword
CVTQL   Convert Quadword to Longword

Qualifiers:

Trapping: Exception Completion (/S) (CVTQL only)
        Integer Overflow Enable (/V) (CVTQL only)

Description:

The two's-complement operand in register Fb is converted to a two's-complement result and written to register Fc. Register Fa must be F31.

The conversion from quadword to longword is a repositioning of the low 32 bits of the operand, with zero fill and optional integer overflow checking. Integer overflow occurs if Fb is outside the range $-2^{**}31..2^{**}31-1$. If integer overflow occurs, the truncated result is stored in Fc, and an arithmetic trap is taken if enabled.

The conversion from longword to quadword is a repositioning of 32 bits of the operand, with sign extension.

4.10.3 Floating-Point Conditional Move

Format:

FCMOVxx   Fa.rq,Fb.rq,Fc.wq   !Floating-point Operate format

Operation:

```
IF TEST(Fav, Condition_based_on_Opcode) THEN

    Fc ← Fbv
```

Exceptions:

None

Instruction mnemonics:

FCMOVEQ	FCMOVE if Register Equal to Zero
FCMOVGE	FCMOVE if Register Greater Than or Equal to Zero
FCMOVGT	FCMOVE if Register Greater Than Zero
FCMOVLE	FCMOVE if Register Less Than or Equal to Zero
FCMOVLT	FCMOVE if Register Less Than Zero
FCMOVNE	FCMOVE if Register Not Equal to Zero

Qualifiers:

None

Description:

Register Fa is tested. If the specified relationship is true, register Fb is written to register Fc; otherwise, the move is suppressed and register Fc is unchanged. The test is based on the sign bit and whether the rest of the register is all zero bits, as described for floating branches in Section 4.9.

Notes:

Except that it is likely in many implementations to be substantially faster, the instruction:

        FCMOVxx Fa,Fb,Fc

is exactly equivalent to:

        FByy Fa,label   ! yy = NOT xx
        CPYS Fb,Fb,Fc
    label: ...

For example, a branchless sequence for:

        F1=MAX(F1,F2)

is:

        CMPxLT   F1,F2,F3   ! F3=one if F1<F2; x=F/G/S/T
        FCMOVNE F3,F2,F1   ! Move F2 to F1 if F1<F2

4.10.4 Move from/to Floating-Point Control Register

Format:

      Mx_FPCR   Fa.rq,Fa.rq,Fa.wq   !Floating-point Operate format

Operation:
```
CASE
    MF_FPCR: Fa   ← FPCR
    MT_FPCR: FPCR ← Fav
ENDCASE
```

Exceptions:

    None

Instruction mnemonics:

    MF_FPCR   Move from Floating-point Control Register
    MT_FPCR   Move to Floating-point Control Register

Qualifiers:

    None

Description:

The Floating-point Control Register (FPCR) is read from (MF_FPCR) or written to (MT_FPCR), a floating-point register. The floating-point register to be used is specified by the Fa, Fb, and Fc fields all pointing to the same floating-point register. If the Fa, Fb, and Fc fields do not all point to the same floating-point register, then it is UNPREDICTABLE which register is used. If the Fa, Fb, and Fc fields do not all point to the same floating-point register, the resulting values in the Fc register and in FPCR are UNPREDICTABLE.

If the Fc field is F31 in the case of MT_FPCR, the resulting value in FPCR is UNPREDICTABLE.

The use of these instructions and the FPCR are described in Section 4.7.8.

4.10.5 VAX Floating Add

Format:

ADDx   Fa.rx,Fb.rx,Fc.wx   !Floating-point Operate format

Operation:

Fc ← Fav + Fbv

Exceptions:

Invalid Operation
Overflow
Underflow

Instruction mnemonics:

ADDF   Add F_floating
ADDG   Add G_floating

Qualifiers:

Rounding: Chopped (/C)
Trapping: Exception Completion (/S)
Underflow Enable (/U)

Description:

Register Fa is added to register Fb, and the sum is written to register Fc.

The sum is rounded or chopped to the specified precision, and then the corresponding range is checked for overflow/underflow. The single-precision operation on canonical single-precision values produces a canonical single-precision result.

An invalid operation trap is signaled if either operand has exp=0 and is not a true zero (that is, VAX reserved operands and dirty zeros trap). The contents of Fc are UNPREDICTABLE if this occurs. See Section 4.7.7 for details of the stored result on overflow or underflow.

4.10.6 IEEE Floating Add

Format:

ADDx   Fa.rx,Fb.rx,Fc.wx   !Floating-point Operate format

Operation:

Fc ← Fav + Fbv

Exceptions:

Invalid Operation
Overflow
Underflow
Inexact Result

Instruction mnemonics:

ADDS   Add S_floating
ADDT   Add T_floating

Qualifiers:

Rounding: Dynamic (/D)
                Minus infinity (/M)
                Chopped (/C)
Trapping: Exception Completion (/S)
                Underflow Enable (/U)
                Inexact Enable (/I)

Description:

Register Fa is added to register Fb, and the sum is written to register Fc.

The sum is rounded to the specified precision and then the corresponding range is checked for overflow/underflow. The single-precision operation on canonical single-precision values produces a canonical single-precision result.

See Section 4.7.7 for details of the stored result on overflow, underflow, or inexact result.

4.10.7 VAX Floating Compare

Format:

CMPGyy   Fa.rg,Fb.rg,Fc.wq   !Floating-point Operate format

Operation:

```
IF Fav SIGNED_RELATION Fbv THEN
    Fc ← 4000 0000 0000 0000₁₆
ELSE
    Fc ← 0000 0000 0000 0000₁₆
```

Exceptions:

Invalid Operation

Instruction mnemonics:

CMPGEQ	Compare G_floating Equal
CMPGLE	Compare G_floating Less Than or Equal
CMPGLT	Compare G_floating Less Than

Qualifiers:

Trapping: Exception Completion (/S)

Description:

The two operands in Fa and Fb are compared. If the relationship specified by the qualifier is true, a non-zero floating value (0.5) is written to register Fc; otherwise, a true zero is written to Fc.

Comparisons are exact and never overflow or underflow. Three mutually exclusive relations are possible: less than, equal, and greater than.

An invalid operation trap is signaled if either operand has exp=0 and is not a true zero (that is, VAX reserved operands and dirty zeros trap). The contents of Fc are UNPREDICTABLE if this occurs.

Notes:

- Compare Less Than A,B is the same as Compare Greater Than B,A; Compare Less Than or Equal A,B is the same as Compare Greater Than or Equal B,A. Therefore, only the less-than operations are included.

4.10.8 IEEE Floating Compare

Format:

CMPTyy   Fa.rx,Fb.rx,Fc.wq   !Floating-point Operate format

Operation:

```
IF Fav SIGNED_RELATION Fbv THEN
    Fc ← 4000 0000 0000 0000₁₆
ELSE
    Fc ← 0000 0000 0000 0000₁₆
```

Exceptions:

Invalid Operation

Instruction mnemonics:

CMPTEQ   Compare T_floating Equal
CMPTLE   Compare T_floating Less Than or Equal
CMPTLT   Compare T_floating Less Than
CMPTUN   Compare T_floating Unordered

Qualifiers:

Trapping: Exception Completion (/SU)

Description:

The two operands in Fa and Fb are compared. If the relationship specified by the qualifier is true, a non-zero floating value (2.0) is written to register Fc; otherwise, a true zero is written to Fc.

Comparisons are exact and never overflow or underflow. Four mutually exclusive relations are possible: less than, equal, greater than, and unordered. The unordered relation is true if one or both operands are NaN. (This behavior must be provided by an operating system (OS) completion handler, since NaNs trap.) Comparisons ignore the sign of zero, so +0 = –0.

Comparisons with plus and minus infinity execute normally and do not take an invalid operation trap.

Notes:

- In order to use CMPTxx with exception completion handling, it is necessary to specify the /SU IEEE trap mode, even though an underflow trap is not possible.

- Compare Less Than A,B is the same as Compare Greater Than B,A; Compare Less Than or Equal A,B is the same as Compare Greater Than or Equal B,A. Therefore, only the less-than operations are included.

4.10.9 Convert VAX Floating to Integer

Format:

> CVTGQ   Fb.rx,Fc.wq   !Floating-point Operate format

Operation:

> Fc ← {conversion of Fbv}

Exceptions:

> Invalid Operation
> Integer Overflow

Instruction mnemonics:

> CVTGQ   Convert G_floating to Quadword

Qualifiers:

> Rounding: Chopped (/C)
> Trapping: Exception Completion (/S)
>   Integer Overflow Enable (/V)

Description:

The floating operand in register Fb is converted to a two's-complement quadword number and written to register Fc. The conversion aligns the operand fraction with the binary point just to the right of bit zero, rounds as specified, and complements the result if negative. Register Fa must be F31.

An invalid operation trap is signaled if the operand has exp=0 and is not a true zero (that is, VAX reserved operands and dirty zeros trap). The contents of Fc are UNPREDICTABLE if this occurs.

See Section 4.7.7 for details of the stored result on integer overflow.

4.10.10 Convert Integer to VAX Floating

Format:

CVTQy   Fb.rq,Fc.wx   !Floating-point Operate format

Operation:

Fc ← {conversion of Fbv<63:0>}

Exceptions:

None

Instruction mnemonics:

CVTQF   Convert Quadword to F_floating
CVTQG   Convert Quadword to G_floating

Qualifiers:

Rounding: Chopped (/C)

Description:

The two's-complement quadword operand in register Fb is converted to a single- or double-precision floating result and written to register Fc. The conversion complements a number if negative, normalizes it, rounds to the target precision, and packs the result with an appropriate sign and exponent field. Register Fa must be F31.

4.10.11 Convert VAX Floating to VAX Floating

Format:

> CVTxy   Fb.rx,Fc.wx   !Floating-point Operate format

Operation:

> Fc ← {conversion of Fbv}

Exceptions:

> Invalid Operation
> Overflow
> Underflow

Instruction mnemonics:

CVTDG	Convert D_floating to G_floating
CVTGD	Convert G_floating to D_floating
CVTGF	Convert G_floating to F_floating

Qualifiers:

Rounding:	Chopped (/C)
Trapping:	Exception Completion (/S)
	Underflow Enable (/U)

Description:

The floating operand in register Fb is converted to the specified alternate floating format and written to register Fc. Register Fa must be F31.

An invalid operation trap is signaled if the operand has exp=0 and is not a true zero (that is, VAX reserved operands and dirty zeros trap). The contents of Fc are UNPREDICTABLE if this occurs.

See Section 4.7.7 for details of the stored result on overflow or underflow.

Notes:

- The only arithmetic operations on D_floating values are conversions to and from G_floating. The conversion to G_floating rounds or chops as specified, removing three fraction bits. The conversion from G_floating to D_floating adds three low-order zeros as fraction bits, then the 8-bit exponent range is checked for overflow/underflow.

- The conversion from G_floating to F_floating rounds or chops to single precision, then the 8-bit exponent range is checked for overflow/underflow.

- No conversion from F_floating to G_floating is required, since F_floating values are always stored in registers as equivalent G_floating values.

4.10.12 Convert IEEE Floating to Integer

Format:

CVTTQ   Fb.rx,Fc.wq   !Floating-point Operate format

Operation:

Fc ← {conversion of Fbv}

Exceptions:

Invalid Operation
Inexact Result
Integer Overflow

Instruction mnemonics:

CVTTQ   Convert T_floating to Quadword

Qualifiers:

Rounding:	Dynamic (/D)
	Minus infinity (/M)
	Chopped (/C)
Trapping:	Exception Completion (/S)
	Integer Overflow Enable (/V)
	Inexact Enable (/I)

Description:

The floating operand in register Fb is converted to a two's-complement number and written to register Fc. The conversion aligns the operand fraction with the binary point just to the right of bit zero, rounds as specified, and complements the result if negative. Register Fa must be F31.

See Section 4.7.7 for details of the stored result on integer overflow and inexact result.

4.10.13 Convert Integer to IEEE Floating

Format:

CVTQy   Fb.rq,Fc.wx   !Floating-point Operate format

Operation:

Fc ← {conversion of Fbv<63:0>}

Exceptions:

Inexact Result

Instruction mnemonics:

CVTQS   Convert Quadword to S_floating
CVTQT   Convert Quadword to T_floating

Qualifiers:

Rounding: Dynamic (/D)
                  Minus infinity (/M)
                  Chopped (/C)
Trapping: Exception Completion (/S)
                  Inexact Enable (/I)

Description:

The two's-complement operand in register Fb is converted to a single- or double-precision floating result and written to register Fc. The conversion complements a number if negative, normalizes it, rounds to the target precision, and packs the result with an appropriate sign and exponent field. Register Fa must be F31.

See Section 4.7.7 for details of the stored result on inexact result.

Notes:

- In order to use CVTQS or CVTQT with exception completion handling, it is necessary to specify the /SUI IEEE trap mode, even though an underflow trap is not possible.

4.10.14 Convert IEEE S_Floating to IEEE T_Floating

Format:

       CVTST   Fb.rx,Fc.wx   ! Floating-point Operate format

Operation:

```
Fc ← {conversion of Fbv}
```

Exceptions:

Invalid Operation

Instruction mnemonics:

       CVTST   Convert S_floating to T_floating

Qualifiers:

       Trapping: Exception Completion (/S)

Description:

The S_floating operand in register Fb is converted to T_floating format and written to register Fc. Register Fa must be F31.

Notes:

- The conversion from S_floating to T_floating is exact. No rounding occurs. No underflow, overflow, or inexact result can occur. In fact, the conversion for finite values is the identity transformation.

- A trap handler can convert an S_floating denormal value into the corresponding T_floating finite value by adding 896 to the exponent and normalizing.

4.10.15 Convert IEEE T_Floating to IEEE S_Floating

Format:

> CVTTS   Fb.rx,Fc.wx   !Floating-point Operate format

Operation:

> Fc ← {conversion of Fbv}

Exceptions:

> Invalid Operation
> Overflow
> Underflow
> Inexact Result

Instruction mnemonics:

> CVTTS   Convert T_floating to S_floating

Qualifiers:

> Rounding: Dynamic (/D)
>   Minus infinity (/M)
>   Chopped (/C)
> Trapping: Exception Completion (/S)
>   Underflow Enable (/U)
>   Inexact Enable (/I)

Description:

The T_floating operand in register Fb is converted to S_floating format and written to register Fc. Register Fa must be F31.

See Section 4.7.7 for details of the stored result on overflow, underflow, or inexact result.

4.10.16 VAX Floating Divide

Format:

DIVx   Fa.rx,Fb.rx,Fc.wx   !Floating-point Operate format

Operation:

Fc ← Fav / Fbv

Exceptions:

Invalid Operation
Division by Zero
Overflow
Underflow

Instruction mnemonics:

DIVF   Divide F_floating
DIVG   Divide G_floating

Qualifiers:

Rounding: Chopped (/C)
Trapping: Exception Completion (/S)
                Underflow Enable (/U)

Description:

The dividend operand in register Fa is divided by the divisor operand in register Fb and the quotient is written to register Fc.

The quotient is rounded or chopped to the specified precision and then the corresponding range is checked for overflow/underflow. The single-precision operation on canonical single-precision values produces a canonical single-precision result.

An invalid operation trap is signaled if either operand has exp=0 and is not a true zero (that is, VAX reserved operands and dirty zeros trap). The contents of Fc are UNPREDICTABLE if this occurs.

A division by zero trap is signaled if Fbv is zero. The contents of Fc are UNPREDICTABLE if this occurs.

See Section 4.7.7 for details of the stored result on overflow or underflow.

4.10.17 IEEE Floating Divide

Format:

DIVx   Fa.rx,Fb.rx,Fc.wx   !Floating-point Operate format

Operation:

Fc ← Fav / Fbv

Exceptions:

Invalid Operation
Division by Zero
Overflow
Underflow
Inexact Result

Instruction mnemonics:

DIVS   Divide S_floating
DIVT   Divide T_floating

Qualifiers:

Rounding: Dynamic (/D)
                    Minus infinity (/M)
                    Chopped (/C)
Trapping: Exception Completion (/S)
                    Underflow Enable (/U)
                    Inexact Enable (/I)

Description:

The dividend operand in register Fa is divided by the divisor operand in register Fb and the quotient is written to register Fc.

The quotient is rounded to the specified precision and then the corresponding range is checked for overflow/underflow. The single-precision operation on canonical single-precision values produces a canonical single-precision result.

See Section 4.7.7 for details of the stored result on overflow, underflow, or inexact result.

4.10.18 Floating-Point Register to Integer Register Move

Format:

FTOIx   Fa.rq,Rc.wq   !Floating-point Operate format

Operation:

```
CASE:
   FTOIS:
      Rc<63:32> ← SEXT(Fav<63>)
      Rc<31:0> ← Fav<63:62> || Fav <58:29>
   FTOIT:
      Rc <- Fav
ENDCASE
```

Exceptions:

None

Instruction mnemonics:

FTOIS   Floating-point to Integer Register Move, S_floating
FTOIT   Floating-point to Integer Register Move, T_floating

Qualifiers:

None

Description:

Data in a floating-point register file is moved to an integer register file.

The Fb field must be F31.

The instructions do not interpret bits in the register files; specifically, the instructions do not trap on non-finite values. Also, the instructions do not access memory.

FTOIS is exactly equivalent to the sequence:

```
STS
LDL
```

FTOIT is exactly equivalent to the sequence:

```
STT
LDQ
```

Software Note:

FTOIS and FTOIT are no slower than the corresponding store/load sequence and can be significantly faster.

4.10.19 Integer Register to Floating-Point Register Move

Format:

> ITOFx   Ra.rq,Fc.wq   !Floating-point Operate format

Operation:

```
CASE:
  ITOFF:
     Fc ← Rav<31> || MAP_F(Rav<30:23>) || Rav<22:0> || 0<28:0>
  ITOFS:
     Fc ← Rav<31> || MAP_S(Rav<30:23>) || Rav<22:0> || 0<28:0>
  ITOFT:
     Fc <- Rav
ENDCASE
```

Exceptions:

> None

Instruction mnemonics:

> ITOFF   Integer to Floating-point Register Move, F_floating
> ITOFS   Integer to Floating-point Register Move, S_floating
> ITOFT   Integer to Floating-point Register Move, T_floating

Qualifiers:

> None

Description:

Data in an integer register file is moved to a floating-point register file.

The Rb field must be R31.

The instructions do not interpret bits in the register files; specifically, the instructions do not trap on non-finite values. Also, the instructions do not access memory.

ITOFF is equivalent to the following sequence, except that the word swapping that LDF normally performs is not performed by ITOFF:

```
STL
LDF
```

ITOFS is exactly equivalent to the sequence:

    STL
    LDS

ITOFT is exactly equivalent to the sequence:

    STQ
    LDT

Software Note:

ITOFF, ITOFS, and ITOFT are no slower than the corresponding store/load sequence and can be significantly faster.

4.10.20 VAX Floating Multiply

Format:

> MULx   Fa.rx,Fb.rx,Fc.wx   !Floating-point Operate format

Operation:

> Fc ← Fav * Fbv

Exceptions:

> Invalid Operation
> Overflow
> Underflow

Instruction mnemonics:

> MULF   Multiply F_floating
> MULG   Multiply G_floating

Qualifiers:

> Rounding: Chopped (/C)
> Trapping: Exception Completion (/S)
>   Underflow Enable (/U)

Description:

The multiplicand operand in register Fb is multiplied by the multiplier operand in register Fa and the product is written to register Fc.

The product is rounded or chopped to the specified precision and then the corresponding range is checked for overflow/underflow. The single-precision operation on canonical single-precision values produces a canonical single-precision result.

An invalid operation trap is signaled if either operand has exp=0 and is not a true zero (that is, VAX reserved operands and dirty zeros trap). The contents of Fc are UNPREDICTABLE if this occurs.

See Section 4.7.7 for details of the stored result on overflow or underflow.

4.10.21 IEEE Floating Multiply

Format:

MULx   Fa.rx,Fb.rx,Fc.wx   !Floating-point Operate format

Operation:

Fc ← Fav * Fbv

Exceptions:

Invalid Operation
Overflow
Underflow
Inexact Result

Instruction mnemonics:

MULS   Multiply S_floating
MULT   Multiply T_floating

Qualifiers:

Rounding: Dynamic (/D)
                  Minus infinity (/M)
                  Chopped (/C)
Trapping: Exception Completion (/S)
                  Underflow Enable (/U)
                  Inexact Enable (/I)

Description:

The multiplicand operand in register Fb is multiplied by the multiplier operand in register Fa and the product is written to register Fc.

The product is rounded to the specified precision and then the corresponding range is checked for overflow/underflow. The single-precision operation on canonical single-precision values produces a canonical single-precision result.

See Section 4.7.7 for details of the stored result on overflow, underflow, or inexact result.

4.10.22 VAX Floating Square Root

Format:

SQRTx   Fb.rx,Fc.wx   !Floating-point Operate format

Operation:

Fc ← Fb ** (1/2)

Exceptions:

Invalid operation

Instruction mnemonics:

SQRTF   Square root F_floating
SQRTG   Square root G_floating

Qualifiers:

Rounding: Chopped (/C)
Trapping: Exception Completion (/S)
               Underflow Enable (/U) — See Notes below

Description:

The square root of the floating-point operand in register Fb is written to register Fc. (The Fa field of this instruction must be set to a value of F31.)

The result is rounded or chopped to the specified precision. The single-precision operation on a canonical single-precision value produces a canonical single-precision result.

An invalid operation is signaled if the operand has exp=0 and is not a true zero (that is, VAX reserved operands and dirty zeros trap). An invalid operation is signaled if the sign of the operand is negative.

The contents of the Fc are UNPREDICTABLE if an invalid operation is signaled.

Notes:

- Floating-point overflow and underflow are not possible for square root operation. The underflow enable qualifier is ignored.

4.10.23 IEEE Floating Square Root

Format:

> SQRTx   Fb.rx,Fc.wx   !Floating-point Operate format

Operation:

> Fc ← Fb ** (1/2)

Exceptions:

> Inexact result
> Invalid operation

Instruction mnemonics:

> SQRTS   Square root S_floating
> SQRTT   Square root T_floating

Qualifiers:

> Rounding: Chopped (/C)
>   Dynamic (/D)
>   Minus infinity (/M)
> Trapping: Inexact Enable (/I)
>   Exception Completion (/S)
>   Underflow Enable (/U) — See Notes below

Description:

The square root of the floating-point operand in register Fb is written to register Fc. (The Fa field of this instruction must be set to a value of F31.)

The result is rounded to the specified precision. The single-precision operation on a canonical single-precision value produces a canonical single-precision result.

An invalid operation is signaled if the sign of the operand is less than zero. However, SQRT (–0) produces a result of –0.

Notes:

- Floating-point overflow and underflow are not possible for square root operation. The underflow enable qualifier is ignored.

4.10.24 VAX Floating Subtract

Format:

SUBx   Fa.rx,Fb.rx,Fc.wx   !Floating-point Operate format

Operation:

$Fc \leftarrow Fav - Fbv$

Exceptions:

Invalid Operation
Overflow
Underflow

Instruction mnemonics:

SUBF   Subtract F_floating
SUBG   Subtract G_floating

Qualifiers:

Rounding: Chopped (/C)
Trapping: Exception Completion (/S)
                 Underflow Enable (/U)

Description:

The subtrahend operand in register Fb is subtracted from the minuend operand in register Fa and the difference is written to register Fc.

The difference is rounded or chopped to the specified precision and then the corresponding range is checked for overflow/underflow. The single-precision operation on canonical single-precision values produces a canonical single-precision result.

An invalid operation trap is signaled if either operand has exp=0 and is not a true zero (that is, VAX reserved operands and dirty zeros trap). The contents of Fc are UNPREDICTABLE if this occurs.

See Section 4.7.7 for details of the stored result on overflow or underflow.

4.10.25 IEEE Floating Subtract

Format:

SUBx   Fa.rx,Fb.rx,Fc.wx   !Floating-point Operate format

Operation:

$Fc \leftarrow Fav - Fbv$

Exceptions:

Invalid Operation
Overflow
Underflow
Inexact Result

Instruction mnemonics:

SUBS	Subtract S_floating
SUBT	Subtract T_floating

Qualifiers:

Rounding:	Dynamic (/D)
	Minus infinity (/M)
	Chopped (/C)
Trapping:	Exception Completion (/S)
	Underflow Enable (/U)
	Inexact Enable (/I)

Description:

The subtrahend operand in register Fb is subtracted from the minuend operand in register Fa and the difference is written to register Fc.

The difference is rounded to the specified precision and then the corresponding range is checked for overflow/underflow. The single-precision operation on canonical single-precision values produces a canonical single-precision result.

See Section 4.7.7 for details of the stored result on overflow, underflow, or inexact result.

4.11 Miscellaneous Instructions

Alpha provides the miscellaneous instructions shown in Table 4–17.

Table 4–17: Miscellaneous Instructions Summary

Mnemonic	Operation
AMASK	Architecture Mask
CALL_PAL	Call Privileged Architecture Library Routine
ECB	Evict Cache Block
EXCB	Exception Barrier
FETCH	Prefetch Data
FETCH_M	Prefetch Data, Modify Intent
IMPLVER	Implementation Version
MB	Memory Barrier
RPCC	Read Processor Cycle Counter
TRAPB	Trap Barrier
WH64	Write Hint — 64 Bytes
WMB	Write Memory Barrier

4.11.1 Architecture Mask

Format:

AMASK	Rb.rq,Rc.wq	!Operate format
AMASK	#b.ib,Rc.wq	!Operate format

Operation:

```
Rc ← Rbv AND {NOT CPU_feature_mask}
```

Exceptions:

None

Instruction mnemonics:

AMASK   Architecture Mask

Qualifiers:

None

Description:

Rbv represents a mask of the requested architectural extensions. Bits are cleared that correspond to architectural extensions that are present. Reserved bits and bits that correspond to absent extensions are copied unchanged. In either case, the result is placed in Rc. If the result is zero, all requested features are present.

Software may specify an Rbv of all 1's to determine the complete set of architectural extensions implemented by a processor. Assigned bit definitions are located in Appendix D.

Ra must be R31 or the result in Rc is UNPREDICTABLE and it is UNPREDICTABLE whether an exception is signaled.

Software Note:

Use this instruction to make instruction-set decisions; use IMPLVER to make code-tuning decisions.

Implementation Note:

Instruction encoding is implemented as follows:

- On 21064/21064A/21066/21068/21066A (EV4/EV45/LCA/LCA45 chips), AMASK copies Rbv to Rc.

- On 21164 (EV5), AMASK copies Rbv to Rc.

- On 21164A (EV56), 21164PC (PCA56), and 21264 (EV6), AMASK correctly indicates support for architecture extensions by copying Rbv to Rc and clearing appropriate bits.

Bits are assigned and placed in Appendix D for architecture extensions as ECOs for those extensions are passed. The low 8 bits are reserved for standard architecture extensions so they can be tested with a literal; application-specific extensions are assigned from bit 8 upward.

4.11.2 Call Privileged Architecture Library

Format:

    CALL_PAL   fnc.ir   !PAL format

Operation:

```
{Stall instruction issuing until all
prior instructions are guaranteed to
complete without incurring exceptions.}
{Trap to PALcode.}
```

Exceptions:

None

Instruction mnemonics:

CALL_PAL   Call Privileged Architecture Library

Qualifiers:

None

Description:

The CALL_PAL instruction is not issued until all previous instructions are guaranteed to complete without exceptions. If an exception occurs, the continuation PC in the exception stack frame points to the CALL_PAL instruction. The CALL_PAL instruction causes a trap to PALcode.

4.11.3 Evict Data Cache Block

Format:

ECB   (Rb.ab)   ! Misc format

Operation:

```
va ← Rbv

IF { va maps to memory space } THEN
  Prepare to reuse cache resources that are occupied by the
  the addressed byte.
END
```

Exceptions:

None

Instruction mnemonics:

ECB   Evict Cache Block

Qualifiers:

None

Description:

The ECB instruction provides a hint that the addressed location will not be referenced again in the near future, so any cache space it occupies should be made available to cache other memory locations. If the cache copy of the location is dirty, the processor may start writing it back; if the cache has multiple sets, the processor may arrange for the set containing the addressed byte to be the next set allocated.

The ECB instruction does not generate exceptions; if it encounters data address translation errors (access violation, translation not valid, and so forth) during execution, it is treated as a NOP.

If the address maps to non-memory-like (I/O) space, ECB is treated as a NOP.

Software Note:

- ECB makes a particular cache location available for reuse by evicting and invalidating its contents. The intent is to give software more control over cache allocation policy in set-associative caches so that "useful" blocks can be retained in the cache.

- ECB is a performance hint — it does not serialize the eviction of the addressed cache block with any preceding or following memory operation.

- ECB is not intended for flushing caches prior to power failure or low power operation — CFLUSH is intended for that purpose.

Implementation Note:

Implementations with set-associative caches are encouraged to update their allocation pointer so that the next D-stream reference that misses the cache and maps to this line is allocated into the vacated set.

4.11.4 Exception Barrier

Format:

> EXCB   ! Memory format

Operation:

```
{EXCB does not appear to issue until completion of all
 exceptions and dependencies on the Floating-point Control
 Register (FPCR) from prior instructions.}
```

Exceptions:

> None

Instruction mnemonics:

> EXCB   Exception Barrier

Qualifiers:

> None

Description:

The EXCB instruction allows software to guarantee that in a pipelined implementation, all previous instructions have completed any behavior related to exceptions or rounding modes before any instructions after the EXCB are issued.

In particular, all changes to the Floating-point Control Register (FPCR) are guaranteed to have been made, whether or not there is an associated exception. Also, all potential floating-point exceptions and integer overflow exceptions are guaranteed to have been taken. EXCB is thus a superset of TRAPB.

If a floating-point exception occurs for which trapping is enabled, the EXCB instruction acts like a fault. In this case, the value of the Program Counter reported to the program may be the address of the EXCB instruction (or earlier) but is never the address of an instruction following the EXCB.

The relationship between EXCB and the FPCR is described in Section 4.7.8.1.

4.11.5 Prefetch Data

Format:

FETCHx   0(Rb.ab)   !Memory format

Operation:

```
va ← {Rbv}
{Optionally prefetch aligned 512-byte block surrounding va.}
```

Exceptions:

None

Instruction mnemonics:

FETCH   Prefetch Data
FETCH_M   Prefetch Data, Modify Intent

Qualifiers:

None

Description:

The virtual address is given by Rbv. This address is used to designate an aligned 512-byte block of data. An implementation may optionally attempt to move all or part of this block (or a larger surrounding block) of data to a part of the memory hierarchy that has faster-access, in anticipation of subsequent Load or Store instructions that access that data.

Implementation Note:

FETCHx is intended to help software overlap memory latencies when such latencies are on the order of at least 100 cycles. FETCHx is unlikely to help (or be implemented) for significantly shorter memory latencies. Code scheduling and cache-line prefetching (See Appendix A.3.5) should be used to overlap such shorter latencies.

Existing Alpha implementations (through the 21264) have memory latencies that are too short to profitably implement FETCHx. Therefore, FETCHx does not improve memory performance in existing Alpha implementations.

The FETCH instruction is a hint to the implementation that may allow faster execution. An implementation is free to ignore the hint. If prefetching is done in an implementation, the order of fetch within the designated block is UNPREDICTABLE.

The FETCH_M instruction gives the additional hint that modifications (stores) to some or all of the data block are anticipated.

No exceptions are generated by FETCHx. If a Load (or Store in the case of FETCH_M) that uses the same address would fault, the prefetch request is ignored. It is UNPREDICTABLE whether a TB-miss fault is ever taken by FETCHx.

Implementation Note:

Implementations are encouraged to take the TB-miss fault, then continue the prefetch.

4.11.6 Implementation Version

Format:

IMPLVER   Rc   !Operate format

Operation:

Rc ← value, which is defined in Appendix D

Exceptions:

None

Instruction mnemonics:

IMPLVER   Implementation Version

Description:

A small integer is placed in Rc that specifies the major implementation version of the processor on which it is executed. This information can be used to make code-scheduling or tuning decisions, or the information can be used to branch to different pieces of code optimized for different implementations.

Notes:

- The value returned by IMPLVER does not identify the particular processor type. Rather, it identifies a group of processors that can be treated similarly for performance characteristics such as scheduling. Ra must be R31 and Rb must be the literal #1 or the result in Rc is UNPREDICTABLE and it is UNPREDICTABLE whether an exception is signaled.

Software Note:

Use this instruction to make code-tuning decisions; use AMASK to make instruction-set decisions.

4.11.7 Memory Barrier

Format:

MB   !Memory format

Operation:

```
{Guarantee that all subsequent loads or stores
will not access memory until after all previous
loads and stores have accessed memory, as
observed by other processors.}
```

Exceptions:

None

Instruction mnemonics:

MB   Memory Barrier

Qualifiers:

None

Description:

The use of the Memory Barrier (MB) instruction is required only in multiprocessor systems.

In the absence of an MB instruction, loads and stores to different physical locations are allowed to complete out of order on the issuing processor as observed by other processors. The MB instruction allows memory accesses to be serialized on the issuing processor as observed by other processors. See Chapter 5 for details on using the MB instruction to serialize these accesses. Chapter 5 also details coordinating memory accesses across processors.

Note that MB ensures serialization only; it does not necessarily accelerate the progress of memory operations.

4.11.8 Read Processor Cycle Counter

Format:

RPCC   Ra.wq   !Memory format

Operation:

```
Ra ← {cycle counter}
```

Exceptions:

None

Instruction mnemonics:

RPCC   Read Processor Cycle Counter

Qualifiers:

None

Description:

Register Ra is written with the processor cycle counter (PCC). The PCC register consists of two 32-bit fields. The low-order 32 bits (PCC<31:0>) are an unsigned, wrapping counter, PCC_CNT. The high-order 32 bits (PCC<63:32>), PCC_OFF, are operating-system dependent in their implementation.

See Section 3.1.5 for a description of the PCC.

If an operating system uses PCC_OFF to calculate the per-process or per-thread cycle count, that count must be derived from the 32-bit sum of PCC_OFF and PCC_CNT. The following example computes that cycle count, modulo 2**32, and returns the count value in R0. Notice the care taken not to cause an unwanted sign extension.

```
RPCC   R0              ; Read the process cycle counter
SLL    R0, #32, R1     ; Line up the offset and count fields
ADDQ   R0, R1, R0      ; Do add
SRL    R0, #32, R0     ; Zero extend the count to 64  bits
```

The following example code returns the value of PCC_CNT in R0<31:0> and all zeros in R0<63:32>.

```
RPCC   R0
ZAPNOT R0,#15,R0
```

4.11.9 Trap Barrier

Format:

TRAPB   !Memory format

Operation:

{TRAPB does not appear to issue until all prior instructions
 are guaranteed to complete without causing any arithmetic traps}.

Exceptions:

None

Instruction mnemonics:

TRAPB   Trap Barrier

Qualifiers:

None

Description:

The TRAPB instruction allows software to guarantee that in a pipelined implementation, all previous arithmetic instructions will complete without incurring any arithmetic traps before the TRAPB or any instructions after it are issued.

If an arithmetic exception occurs for which trapping is enabled, the TRAPB instruction acts like a fault. In this case, the value of the Program Counter reported to the program may be the address of the TRAPB instruction (or earlier) but is never the address of the instruction following the TRAPB.

This fault behavior by TRAPB allows software, using one TRAPB instruction for each exception domain, to isolate the address range in which an exception occurs. If the address of the instruction following the TRAPB were allowed, there would be no way to distinguish an exception in the address range preceding a label from an exception in the range that includes the label along with the faulting instruction and a branch back to the label. This case arises when the code is not following exception completion rules but is inserting TRAPB instructions to isolate exceptions to the proper scope.

Use of TRAPB should be compared with use of the EXCB instruction; see Section 4.11.4.

4.11.10 Write Hint

Format:

WH64   (Rb.ab)   ! Misc format

Operation:

```
va ← Rbv
IF { va maps to memory space } THEN
 Write UNPREDICTABLE data to the aligned 64-byte region
 containing the addressed byte.
END
```

Exceptions:

None

Instruction mnemonics:

WH64   Write Hint - 64 Bytes

Qualifiers:

None

Description:

The WH64 instruction provides a hint that the current contents of the aligned 64-byte block containing the addressed byte will never be read again but will be overwritten in the near future.

The processor may allocate cache resources to hold the block without reading its previous contents from memory; the contents of the block may be set to any value that does not introduce a security hole, as described in Section 1.6.3.

The WH64 instruction does not generate exceptions; if it encounters data address translation errors (access violation, translation not valid, and so forth), it is treated as a NOP.

If the address maps to non-memory-like (I/O) space, WH64 is treated as a NOP.

Software Note:

This instruction is a performance hint that should be used when writing a large continuous region of memory. The intended code sequence consists of one WH64 instruction followed by eight quadword stores for each aligned 64-byte region to be written.

Sometimes, the UNPREDICTABLE data will exactly match some or all of the previous contents of the addressed block of memory.

Implementation Note:

If the 64-byte region containing the addressed byte is not in the data cache, implementations are encouraged to allocate the region in the data cache without first reading it from memory. However, if any of the addressed bytes exist in the caches of other processors, they must be kept coherent with respect to those processors.

Processors with cache blocks smaller than 64 bytes are encouraged to implement WH64 as defined. However, they may instead implement the instruction by allocating a smaller aligned cache block for write access or by treating WH64 as a NOP.

Processors with cache blocks larger than 64 bytes are also encouraged to implement WH64 as defined. However, they may instead treat WH64 as a NOP.

4.11.11 Write Memory Barrier

Format:

WMB   !Memory format

Operation:

```
{ Guarantee that
{   All preceding stores that access memory-like
{      regions are ordered before any subsequent stores
{      that access memory-like regions and
{   All preceding stores that access non-memory-like
{      regions are ordered before any subsequent stores
{      that access non-memory-like regions.
```

Exceptions:

None

Instruction mnemonics:

WMB   Write Memory Barrier

Qualifiers:

None

Description:

The WMB instruction provides a way for software to control write buffers. It guarantees that writes preceding the WMB are not aggregated with writes that follow the WMB.

WMB guarantees that writes to memory-like regions that precede the WMB are ordered before writes to memory-like regions that follow the WMB. Similarly, WMB guarantees that writes to non-memory-like regions that precede the WMB are ordered before writes to non-memory-like regions that follow the WMB. It does not order writes to memory-like regions relative to writes to non-memory-like regions.

WMB causes writes that are contained in buffers to be completed without unnecessary delay. It is particularly suited for batching writes to high-performance I/O devices.

WMB prevents writes that precede the WMB from being merged with writes that follow the WMB. In particular, two writes that access the same location and are separated by a WMB cause two distinct and ordered write events.

In the absence of a WMB (or IMB or MB) instruction, stores to memory-like or non-memory-like regions can be aggregated and/or buffered and completed in any order.

The WMB instruction is the preferred method for providing high-bandwidth write streams where order must be preserved between writes in that stream.

Notes:

WMB is useful for ordering streams of writes to a non-memory-like region, such as to memory-mapped control registers or to a graphics frame buffer. While both MB and WMB can ensure that writes to a non-memory-like region occur in order, without being aggregated or reordered, the WMB is usually faster and is never slower than MB.

WMB can correctly order streams of writes in programs that operate on shared sections of data if the data in those sections are protected by a classic semaphore protocol. The following example illustrates such a protocol:

Processor i	Processor j
<Acquire lock>	
MB	
<Read and write data in shared section>	
WMB	
<Release lock> ⇒	<Acquire lock>
	MB
	<Read and write data in shared section>
	WMB

The example above is similar to that in Section 5.5.4, except a WMB is substituted for the second MB in the lock-update-release sequence. It is correct to substitute WMB for the second MB only if:

1. All data locations that are read or written in the critical section are accessed only after acquiring a software lock by using lock_variable (and before releasing the software lock).

2. For each read u of shared data in the critical section, there is a write v such that:

   a. v is BEFORE the WMB

   b. v follows u in processor issue sequence (see Section 5.6.1.1)

   c. v either depends on u (see Section 5.6.1.7) or overlaps u (see Section 5.6.1), or both.

3. Both lock_variable and all the shared data are in memory-like regions (or lock_variable and all the shared data are in non-memory-like regions). If the lock_variable is in a non-memory-like region, the atomic lock protocol must use some implementation-specific hardware support.

The substitution of a WMB for the second MB is usually faster and never slower.

4.12 VAX Compatibility Instructions

Alpha provides the instructions shown in Table 4–18 for use in translated VAX code. These instructions are not a permanent part of the architecture and will not be available in some future implementations. They are intended to preserve customer assumptions about VAX instruction atomicity in porting code from VAX to Alpha.

These instructions should be generated only by the VAX-to-Alpha software translator; they should never be used in native Alpha code. Any native code that uses them may cease to work.

Table 4–18: VAX Compatibility Instructions Summary

Mnemonic	Operation
RC	Read and Clear
RS	Read and Set

4.12.1 VAX Compatibility Instructions

Format:

Rx   Ra.wq   !Memory format

Operation:

```
Ra ← intr_flag
intr_flag ← 0                          !RC
intr_flag ← 1                          !RS
```

Exceptions:

None

Instruction mnemonics:

RC   Read and Clear

RS   Read and Set

Qualifiers:

None

Description:

The intr_flag is returned in Ra and then cleared to zero (RC) or set to one (RS).

These instructions may be used to determine whether the sequence of Alpha instructions between RS and RC (corresponding to a single VAX instruction) was executed without interruption or exception.

Intr_flag is a per-processor state bit. The intr_flag is cleared if that processor encounters a CALL_PAL REI instruction.

It is UNPREDICTABLE whether a processor's intr_flag is affected when that processor executes an LDx_L or STx_C instruction. A processor's intr_flag is not affected when that processor executes a normal load or store instruction.

A processor's intr_flag is not affected when that processor executes a taken branch.

Notes:

- These instructions are intended *only* for use by the VAX-to-Alpha software translator; they should never be used by native code.

4.13 Multimedia (Graphics and Video) Support

Alpha provides the following instructions that enhance support for graphics and video algorithms:

Mnemonic	Operation
MINUB8	Vector Unsigned Byte Minimum
MINSB8	Vector Signed Byte Minimum
MINUW4	Vector Unsigned Word Minimum
MINSW4	Vector Signed Word Minimum
MAXUB8	Vector Unsigned Byte Maximum
MAXSB8	Vector Signed Byte Maximum
MAXUW4	Vector Unsigned Word Maximum
MAXSW4	Vector Signed Word Maximum
PERR	Pixel Error
PKLB	Pack Longwords to Bytes
PKWB	Pack Words to Bytes
UNPKBL	Unpack Bytes to Longwords
UNPKBW	Unpack Bytes to Words

The MIN and MAX instructions allow the clamping of pixel values to maximium values that are allowed in different standards and stages of the CODECs.

The PERR instruction accelerates the macroblock search in motion estimation.

The pack and unpack (PKxB and UNPKBx) instructions accelerate the blocking of interleaved YUV coordinates for processing by the CODEC.

Implementation Note:

Alpha processors for which the AMASK instruction returns bit 8 set implement these instructions. Those processors for which AMASK does not return bit 8 set can take an Illegal Instruction trap, and software can emulate their function, if required.

4.13.1 Byte and Word Minimum and Maximum

Format:

MINxxx	Ra.rq,Rb.rq,Rc.wq	! Operate Format
MAXxxx	Ra.rq,#b.ib,Rc.wq	! Operate Format

Operation:

```
CASE
  MINUB8:
    FOR i FROM 0 TO 7
    Rcv<i*8+7:i*8> = MINU(Rav<i*8+7:i*8>,Rbv<i*8+7:i*8>)
    END
  MINSB8:
    FOR i FROM 0 TO 7
    Rcv<i*8+7:i*8> = MINS(Rav<i*8+7:i*8>,Rbv<i*8+7:i*8>)
    END
  MINUW4:
    FOR i FROM 0 TO 3
    Rcv<i*16+15:i*16> = MINU(Rav<i*16+15:i*16>,Rbv<i*16+15:i*16>)
    END
  MINSW4:
    FOR i FROM 0 TO 3
    Rcv<i*16+15:i*16> = MINS(Rav<i*16+15:i*16>,Rbv<i*16+15:i*16>)
    END
  MAXUB8:
    FOR i FROM 0 TO 7
    Rcv<i*8+7:i*8> = MAXU(Rav<i*8+7:i*8>,Rbv<i*8+7:i*8>)
    END
  MAXSB8:
    FOR i FROM 0 TO 7
    Rcv<i*8+7:i*8> = MAXS(Rav<i*8+7:i*8>,Rbv<i*8+7:i*8>)
    END
  MAXUW4:
    FOR i FROM 0 TO 3
    Rcv<i*16+15:i*16> = MAXU(Rav<i*16+15:i*16>,Rbv<i*16+15:i*16>)
    END
  MAXSW4:
    FOR i FROM 0 TO 3
    Rcv<i*16+15:i*16> = MAXS(Rav<i*16+15:i*16>,Rbv<i*16+15:i*16>)
    END
ENDCASE:
```

Exceptions:

None

Instruction mnemonics:

MINUB8	Vector Unsigned Byte Minimum
MINSB8	Vector Signed Byte Minimum
MINUW4	Vector Unsigned Word Minimum
MINSW4	Vector Signed Word Minimum
MAXUB8	Vector Unsigned Byte Maximum
MAXSB8	Vector Signed Byte Maximum
MAXUW4	Vector Unsigned Word Maximum
MAXSW4	Vector Signed Word Maximum

Qualifiers:

None

Description:

For MINxB8, each byte of Rc is written with the smaller of the corresponding bytes of Ra or Rb. The bytes may be interpreted as signed or unsigned values.

For MINxW4, each word of Rc is written with the smaller of the corresponding words of Ra or Rb. The words may be interpreted as signed or unsigned values.

For MAXxB8, each byte of Rc is written with the larger of the corresponding bytes of Ra or Rb. The bytes may be interpreted as signed or unsigned values.

For MAXxW4, each word of Rc is written with the larger of the corresponding words of Ra or Rb. The words may be interpreted as signed or unsigned values.

4.13.2 Pixel Error

Format:

> PERR   Ra.rq,Rb.rq,Rc.wq   ! Operate Format

Operation:

```
temp = 0
FOR i FROM 0 TO 7
 IF { Rav<i*8+7:i*8> GEU Rbv<i*8+7:i*8>} THEN
  temp ← temp + (Rav<i*8+7:i*8> - Rbv<i*8+7:i*8>)
 ELSE
  temp ← temp + (Rbv<i*8+7:i*8> - Rav<i*8+7:i*8>)
END
Rc ← temp
```

Exceptions:

None

Instruction mnemonics:

PERR   Pixel Error

Qualifiers:

None

Description:

The absolute value of the difference between each of the bytes in Ra and Rb is calculated. The sum of the resulting bytes is written to Rc.

4.13.3 Pack Bytes

Format:

PKxB   Rb.rq,Rc.wq   ! Operate Format

Operation:

```
CASE
 PKLB:
  BEGIN
  Rc<07:00> ← Rbv<07:00>
  Rc<15:08> ← Rbv<39:32>
  Rc<63:16> ← 0
  END
 PKWB:
  BEGIN
  Rc<07:00> ← Rbv<07:00>
  Rc<15:08> ← Rbv<23:16>
  Rc<23:16> ← Rbv<39:32>
  Rc<31:24> ← Rbv<55:48>
  Rc<63:32> ← 0
  END
 ENDCASE
```

Exceptions:

None

Instruction mnemonics:

PKLB   Pack Longwords to Bytes
PKWB   Pack Words to Bytes

Qualifiers:

None

Description:

For PKLB, the component longwords of Rb are truncated to bytes and written to the lower two byte positions of Rc. The upper six bytes of Rc are written with zero.

For PKWB, the component words of Rb are truncated to bytes and written to the lower four byte positions of Rc. The upper four bytes of Rc are written with zero.

4.13.4 Unpack Bytes

Format:

UNPKBx   Rb.rq,Rc.wq   ! Operate Format

Operation:

```
temp = 0
CASE
 UNPKBL:
  BEGIN
  temp<07:00> = Rbv<07:00>
  temp<39:32> = Rbv<15:08>
  END
 UNPKBW:
  BEGIN
  temp<07:00> = Rbv<07:00>
  temp<23:16> = Rbv<15:08>
  temp<39:32> = Rbv<23:16>
  temp<55:48> = Rbv<31:24>
  END
ENDCASE
Rc ← temp
```

Exceptions:

None

Instruction mnemonics:

UNPKBL   Unpack Bytes to Longwords

UNPKBW   Unpack Bytes to Words

Qualifiers:

None

Description:

For UNPKBL, the lower two component bytes of Rb are zero-extended to longwords. The resulting longwords are written to Rc.

For UNPKBW, the lower four component bytes of Rb are zero-extended to words. The resulting words are written to Rc.

Chapter 5

System Architecture and Programming Implications (I)

5.1 Introduction

Portions of the Alpha architecture have implications for programming, and the system structure, of both uniprocessor and multiprocessor implementations. Architectural implications considered in the following sections are:

- Physical address space behavior
- Caches and write buffers
- Translation buffers and virtual caches
- Data sharing
- Read/write ordering
- Arithmetic traps

To meet the requirements of the Alpha architecture, software and hardware implementors need to take these issues into consideration.

5.2 Physical Address Space Characteristics

Alpha physical address space is divided into four equal-size regions. The regions are delineated by the two most significant, implemented, physical address bits. Each region's characteristics are distinguished by the coherency, granularity, and width of memory accesses, and whether the region exhibits memory-like behavior or non-memory-like behavior.

5.2.1 Coherency of Memory Access

Alpha implementations must provide a coherent view of memory, in which each write by a processor or I/O device (hereafter, called "processor") becomes visible to all other processors. No distinction is made between coherency of "memory space" and "I/O space."

Memory coherency may be provided in different ways for each of the four physical address regions.

Possible per-region policies include, but are not restricted to:

- No caching

  No copies are kept of data in a region; all reads and writes access the actual data location (memory or I/O register), but a processor may elide multiple accesses to the same data (see Section 5.2.3).

- Write-through caching

  Copies are kept of any data in the region; reads may use the copies, but writes update the actual data location and either update or invalidate all copies.

- Write-back caching

  Copies are kept of any data in the region; reads and writes may use the copies, and writes use additional state to determine whether there are other copies to invalidate or update.

Software/Hardware Note:

To produce separate and distinct accesses to a specific location, the location must be a region with no caching and a memory barrier instruction must be inserted between accesses. See Section 5.2.3.

Part of the coherency policy implemented for a given physical address region may include restrictions on excess data transfers (performing more accesses to a location than is necessary to acquire or change the location's value) or may specify data transfer widths (the granularity used to access a location).

Independent of coherency policy, a processor may use different hardware or different hardware resource policies for caching or buffering different physical address regions.

5.2.2 Granularity of Memory Access

For each region, an implementation must support aligned quadword access and may optionally support aligned longword access or byte access. If byte access is supported in a region, aligned word access and aligned longword access are also supported.

For a quadword access region, accesses to physical memory must be implemented such that independent accesses to adjacent aligned quadwords produce the same results regardless of the order of execution. Further, an access to an aligned quadword must be done in a single atomic operation.

For a longword access region, accesses to physical memory must be implemented such that independent accesses to adjacent aligned longwords produce the same results regardless of the order of execution. Further, an access to an aligned longword must be done in a single atomic operation, and an access to an aligned quadword must also be done in a single atomic operation.

For a byte access region, accesses to physical memory must be implemented such that independent accesses to adjacent bytes or adjacent aligned words produce the same results, regardless of the order of execution. Further, an access to a byte, an aligned word, an aligned longword, or an aligned quadword must be done in a single atomic operation.

In this context, "atomic" means that the following is true if different processors do simultaneous reads and writes of the same data:

- The result of any set of writes must be the same as if the writes had occurred sequentially in some order, and

- Any read that observes the effect of a write on some part of memory must observe the effect of that write (or of a later write or writes) on the entire part of memory that is accessed by both the read and the write.

When a write accesses only part of a given word, longword, or quadword, a read of the entire structure may observe the effect of that partial write without observing the effect of an earlier write of another byte or bytes to the same structure. See Sections 5.6.1.5 and 5.6.1.6.

5.2.3 Width of Memory Access

Subject to the granularity, ordering, and coherency constraints given in Sections 5.2.1, 5.2.2, and 5.6, accesses to physical memory may be freely cached, buffered, and prefetched.

A processor may read more physical memory data (such as a full cache block) than is actually accessed, writes may trigger reads, and writes may write back more data than is actually updated. A processor may elide multiple reads and/or writes to the same data.

5.2.4 Memory-Like and Non-Memory-Like Behavior

Memory-like regions obey the following rules:

- Each page frame in the region either exists in its entirety or does not exist in its entirety; there are no holes within a page frame.

- All locations that exist are read/write.

- A write to a location followed by a read from that location returns precisely the bits written; all bits act as memory.

- A write to one location does not change any other location.

- Reads have no side effects.

- Longword access granularity is provided, and if the byte/word extension is implemented, byte access granularity is provided.

- Instruction-fetch is supported.

- Load-locked and store-conditional are supported.

Non-memory-like regions may have much more arbitrary behavior:

- Unimplemented locations or bits may exist anywhere.

- Some locations or bits may be read-only and others write-only.

- Address ranges may overlap, such that a write to one location changes the bits read from a different location.

- Reads may have side effects, although this is strongly discouraged.

- Longword granularity need not be supported and, even if the byte/word extension is implemented, byte access granularity need not be implemented.

- Instruction-fetch need not be supported.

- Load-locked and store-conditional need not be supported.

Hardware/Software Coordination Note:

The details of such behavior are outside the scope of the Alpha architecture. Specific processor and I/O device implementations may choose and document whatever behavior they need. It is the responsibility of system designers to impose enough consistency to allow processors successfully to access matching non-memory devices in a coherent way.

5.3 Translation Buffers and Virtual Caches

A system may choose to include a virtual instruction cache (virtual I-cache) or a virtual data cache (virtual D-cache). A system may also choose to include either a combined data and instruction translation buffer (TB) or separate data and instruction TBs (DTB and ITB). The contents of these caches and/or translation buffers may become invalid, depending on what operating system activity is being performed.

Whenever a non-software field of a valid page table entry (PTE) is modified, copies of that PTE must be made coherent. PALcode mechanisms are available to clear all TBs, both DTB and ITB entries for a given VA, either DTB or ITB entries for a given VA, or all entries with the address space match (ASM) bit clear. Virtual D-cache entries are made coherent whenever the corresponding DTB entry is requested to be cleared by any of the appropriate PALcode mechanisms. Virtual I-cache entries can be made coherent via the IMB instruction.

If a processor implements address space numbers (ASNs), and the old PTE has the Address Space Match (ASM) bit clear (ASNs in use) and the Valid bit set, then entries can also effectively be made coherent by assigning a new, unused ASN to the currently running process and not reusing the previous ASN before calling the appropriate PALcode routine to invalidate the translation buffer (TB).

In a multiprocessor environment, making the TBs and/or caches coherent on only one processor is not always sufficient. An operating system must arrange to perform the above actions on each processor that could possibly have copies of the PTE or data for any affected page.

5.4 Caches and Write Buffers

A hardware implementation may include mechanisms to reduce memory access time by making local copies of recently used memory contents (or those expected to be used) or by buffering writes to complete at a later time. Caches and write buffers are examples of these mechanisms. They must be implemented so that their existence is transparent to software (except for timing, error reporting/control/recovery, and modification to the I-stream).

The following requirements must be met by all cache/write-buffer implementations. All processors must provide a coherent view of memory.

- Write buffers may be used to delay and aggregate writes. From the viewpoint of another processor, buffered writes appear not to have happened yet. (Write buffers must not delay writes indefinitely. See Section 5.6.1.9.)

- Write-back caches must be able to detect a later write from another processor and invalidate or update the cache contents.

- A processor must guarantee that a data store to a location followed by a data load from the same location reads the updated value.

- Cache prefetching is allowed, but virtual caches must not prefetch from invalid pages. See Sections 5.6.1.3, 5.6.4.3, and 5.6.4.4.

- A processor must guarantee that all of its previous writes are visible to all other processors before a HALT instruction completes. A processor must guarantee that its caches are coherent with the rest of the system before continuing from a HALT.

- If battery backup is supplied, a processor must guarantee that the memory system remains coherent across a powerfail/recovery sequence. Data that was written by the processor before the powerfail may not be lost, and any caches must be in a valid state before (and if) normal instruction processing is continued after power is restored.

- Virtual instruction caches are not required to notice modifications of the virtual I-stream (they need not be coherent with the rest of memory). Software that creates or modifies the instruction stream must execute a CALL_PAL IMB before trying to execute the new instructions.

  In this context, to "modify the virtual I-stream" means either:

  - any Store to the same physical address that is subsequently fetched as an instruction by some corresponding (virtual address, ASN) pair, or

  - any change to the virtual-to-physical address mapping so that different values are fetched.

  For example, if two different virtual addresses, VA1 and VA2, map to the same page frame, a store to VA1 modifies the virtual I-stream fetched by VA2.

  However, the following sequence does not modify the virtual I-stream (this might happen in soft page faults).

  1. Change the mapping of an I-stream page from valid to invalid.

  2. Copy the corresponding page frame to a new page frame.

  3. Change the original mapping to be valid and point to the new page frame.

- Physical instruction caches are not required to notice modifications of the physical I-stream (they need not be coherent with the rest of memory), except for certain paging activity. (See Section 5.6.4.4.) Software that creates or modifies the instruction stream must execute a CALL_PAL IMB before trying to execute the new instructions.

  In this context, to "modify the physical I-stream" means any Store to the same physical address that is subsequently fetched as an instruction.

5.5 Data Sharing

In a multiprocessor environment, writes to shared data must be synchronized by the programmer.

5.5.1 Atomic Change of a Single Datum

The ordinary STL and STQ instructions can be used to perform an atomic change of a shared aligned longword or quadword. ("Change" means that the new value is not a function of the old value.) In particular, an ordinary STL or STQ instruction can be used to change a variable that could be simultaneously accessed via an LDx_L/STx_C sequence.

5.5.2 Atomic Update of a Single Datum

The load-locked/store-conditional instructions may be used to perform an atomic update of a shared aligned longword or quadword. ("Update" means that the new value is a function of the old value.)

The following sequence performs a read-modify-write operation on location x. Only register-to-register operate instructions and branch fall-throughs may occur in the sequence:

```
try_again:
        LDQ_L   R1,x
        <modify R1>
        STQ_C   R1,x
        BEQ     R1,no_store
        :
no_store:
        <code to check for excessive iterations>
        BR      try_again
```

If this sequence runs with no exceptions or interrupts, and no other processor writes to location x (more precisely, the locked range including x) between the LDQ_L and STQ_C instructions, then the STQ_C shown in the example stores the modified value in x and sets R1 to 1. If, however, the sequence encounters exceptions or interrupts that eventually continue the sequence, or another processor writes to x, then the STQ_C does not store and sets R1 to 0. In this case, the sequence is repeated by the branches to no_store and try_again. This repetition continues until the reasons for exceptions or interrupts are removed and no interfering store is encountered.

To be useful, the sequence must be constructed so that it can be replayed an arbitrary number of times, giving the same result values each time. A sufficient (but not necessary) condition is that, within the sequence, the set of operand destinations and the set of operand sources are disjoint.

Note:

A sufficiently long instruction sequence between LDx_L and STx_C will never complete, because periodic timer interrupts will always occur before the sequence completes. The rules in Appendix A describe sequences that will eventually complete in *all* Alpha implementations.

This load-locked/store-conditional paradigm may be used whenever an atomic update of a shared aligned quadword is desired, including getting the effect of atomic byte writes.

5.5.3 Atomic Update of Data Structures

Before accessing shared writable data structures (those that are not a single aligned longword or quadword), the programmer can acquire control of the data structure by using an atomic update to set a software lock variable. Such a software lock can be cleared with an ordinary store instruction.

A software-critical section, therefore, may look like the sequence:

```
stq_c_loop:
spin_loop:
        LDQ   R1,lock_variable      ; This optional spin-loop code
        BLBS  R1,already_set        ;   should be used unless the
                                    ;   lock is known to be low-contention.
        LDQ_L R1,lock_variable      ; \
        BLBS  R1,already_set        ;  \
        OR    R1,#1,R2              ;   > Set lock bit
        STQ_C R2,lock_variable      ;  /
        BEQ   R2,stq_c_fail         ; /

        MB
        <critical section: updates various data structures>
        MB                          ; Second MB
        STQ   R31,lock_variable     ; Clear lock bit
         :
         :
already_set:
        <code to block or reschedule or test for too many iterations>
        BR  spin_loop
stq_c_fail:
        <code to test for too many iterations>
        BR  stq_c_loop
```

This code has a number of subtleties:

- If the lock_variable is already set, the spin loop is done without doing any stores. This avoidance of stores improves memory subsystem performance and avoids the deadlock described below. The loop uses an ordinary load. This code sequence is preferred unless the lock is known to be low-contention, because the sequence increases the probability that the LDQ_L hits in the cache and the LDQ_L/STQ_C sequence complete quickly and successfully.

- If the lock_variable is actually being changed from 0 to 1, and the STQ_C fails (due to an interrupt, or because another processor simultaneously changed lock_variable), the entire process starts over by reading the lock_variable again.

- Only the fall-through path of the BLBS instructions does a STx_C; some implementations may not allow a successful STx_C after a branch-taken.

- Only register-to-register operate instructions are used to do the modify.

- Both conditional branches are forward branches, so they are properly predicted not to be taken (to match the common case of no contention for the lock).

- The OR writes its result to a second register; this allows the OR and the BLBS to be interchanged if that would give a faster instruction schedule.

- Other operate instructions (from the critical section) may be scheduled into the LDQ_L..STQ_C sequence, so long as they do not fault or trap and they give correct results if repeated; other memory or operate instructions may be scheduled between the STQ_C and BEQ.

- The memory barrier instructions are discussed in Section 5.5.4. It is correct to substitute WMB for the second MB only if:

  – All data locations that are read or written in the critical section are accessed only after acquiring a software lock by using lock_variable (and before releasing the software lock).

  – For each read u of shared data in the critical section, there is a write v such that:

    1. v is BEFORE the WMB

    2. v follows u in processor issue sequence (see Section 5.6.1.1)

    3. v either depends on u (see Section 5.6.1.7) or overlaps u (see Section 5.6.1), or both.

  – Both lock_variable and all the shared data are in memory-like regions (or lock_variable and all the shared data are in non-memory-like regions). If the lock_variable is in a non-memory-like region, the atomic lock protocol must use some implementation-specific hardware support.

  Generally, the substitution of a WMB for the second MB increases performance.

- An ordinary STQ instruction is used to clear the lock_variable.

It would be a performance mistake to spin-wait by repeating the full LDQ_L..STQ_C sequence (to move the BLBS after the BEQ) because that sequence may repeatedly change the software lock_variable from "locked" to "locked," with each write causing extra access delays in all other caches that contain the lock_variable. In the extreme, spin-waits that contain writes may deadlock as follows:

If, when one processor spins with writes, another processor is modifying (not changing) the lock_variable, then the writes on the first processor may cause the STx_C of the modify on the second processor always to fail.

This deadlock situation is avoided by:

- Having only one processor execute a store (no STx_C), or

- Having no write in the spin loop, or

- Doing a write *only* if the shared variable actually changes state (1 → 1 does not change state).

5.5.4 Ordering Considerations for Shared Data Structures

A critical section sequence, such as shown in Section 5.5.3, is conceptually only three steps:

1. Acquire software lock

2. Critical section — read/write shared data

3. Clear software lock

In the absence of explicit instructions to the contrary, the Alpha architecture allows reads and writes to be reordered. While this may allow more implementation speed and overlap, it can also create undesired side effects on shared data structures. Normally, the critical section just described would have two instructions added to it:

```
<acquire software lock>
MB (memory barrier #1)
<critical section - read/write shared data>
MB (memory barrier #2)
<clear software lock>
<endcode_example>
```

The first memory barrier prevents any reads (from within the critical section) from being prefetched before the software lock is acquired; such prefetched reads would potentially contain stale data.

The second memory barrier prevents any writes and reads in the critical section being delayed past the clearing of the software lock. Such delayed accesses could interact with the next user of the shared data, defeating the purpose of the software lock entirely. It is correct to substitute WMB for the second MB only if:

1. All data locations that are read or written in the critical section are accessed only after acquiring a software lock by using lock_variable (and before releasing the software lock).

2. For each read u of shared data in the critical section, there is a write v such that:

   a. v is BEFORE the WMB

   b. v follows u in processor issue sequence (see Section 5.6.1.1)

   c. v either depends on u (see Section 5.6.1.7) or overlaps u (see Section 5.6.1), or both.

3. Both lock_variable and all the shared data are in memory-like regions (or lock_variable and all the shared data are in non-memory-like regions). If the lock_variable is in a non-memory-like region, the atomic lock protocol must use some implementation-specific hardware support.

Generally, the substitution of a WMB for the second MB increases performance.

Software Note:

In the VAX architecture, many instructions provide noninterruptable read-modify-write sequences to memory variables. Most programmers never regard data sharing as an issue.

In the Alpha architecture, programmers must pay more attention to synchronizing access to shared data; for example, to AST routines. In the VAX architecture, a programmer can use an ADDL2 to update a variable that is shared between a "MAIN" routine and an AST routine, if running on a single processor. In the Alpha architecture, a programmer must deal with AST shared data by using multiprocessor shared data sequences.

5.6 Read/Write Ordering

This section applies to programs that run on multiple processors or on one or more processors that are interacting with DMA I/O devices. To a program running on a single processor and not interacting with DMA I/O devices, all memory accesses appear to happen in the order specified by the programmer. This section deals with predictable read/write ordering across multiple processors and/or DMA I/O devices.

The order of reads and writes done in an Alpha implementation may differ from that specified by the programmer.

For any two memory accesses A and B, either A must occur before B in all Alpha implementations, B must occur before A, or they are UNORDERED. In the last case, software cannot depend upon one occurring first: the order may vary from implementation to implementation, and even from run to run or moment to moment on a single implementation.

If two accesses cannot be shown to be ordered by the rules given, they are UNORDERED and implementations are free to do them in any order that is convenient. Implementations may take advantage of this freedom to deliver substantially higher performance.

The discussion that follows first defines the architectural issue sequence of memory accesses on a single processor, then defines the (partial) ordering on this issue sequence that *all* Alpha implementations are required to maintain.

The individual issue sequences on multiple processors are merged into access sequences at each shared memory location. The discussion defines the (partial) ordering on the individual access sequences that *all* Alpha implementations are required to maintain.

The net result is that for any code that executes on multiple processors, one can determine which memory accesses are required to occur before others on *all* Alpha implementations and hence can write useful shared-variable software.

Software writers can force one access to occur before another by inserting a memory barrier instruction (MB, WMB, or CALL_PAL IMB) between the accesses.

5.6.1 Alpha Shared Memory Model

An Alpha system consists of a collection of processors, I/O devices (and possibly a bridge to connect remote I/O devices), and shared memories that are accessible by all processors.

Note:

> An example of an unshared location is a physical address in I/O space that refers to a CSR that is local to a processor and not accessible by other processors.

A processor is an Alpha CPU.

In most systems, DMA I/O devices or other agents can read or write shared memory locations. The order of accesses by those agents is not completely specified in this document. It is possible in some systems for read accesses by I/O devices or other agents to give results indicating some reordering of accesses. However, there are guarantees that apply in all systems. See Section 5.6.4.7.

A shared memory is the primary storage place for one or more locations.

A location is a byte, specified by its physical address. Multiple virtual addresses may map to the same physical address. Ordering considerations are based only on the physical address. This definition of location specifically includes locations and registers in memory mapped I/O devices and bridges to remote I/O (for example, Mailbox Pointer Registers, or MBPRs).

Implementation Note:

An implementation may allow a location to have multiple physical addresses, but the rules for accesses via mixtures of the addresses are implementation-specific and outside the scope of this section. Accesses via exactly one of the physical addresses follow the rules described next.

Each processor may generate accesses to shared memory locations. There are six types of accesses:

1. Instruction fetch by processor i to location x, returning value a, denoted Pi:I<4>(x,a).

2. Data read (including load-locked) by processor i to location x, returning value a, denoted Pi:R<size>(x,a).

3. Data write (including successful store-conditional) by processor i to location x, storing value a, denoted Pi:W<size>(x,a).

4. Memory barrier issued by processor i, denoted Pi:MB.

5. Write memory barrier issued by processor i, denoted Pi:WMB.

6. I-stream memory barrier issued by processor i, denoted Pi:IMB.

The first access type is also called an I-stream access or I-fetch. The next two are also called D-stream accesses. The first three types are collectively called read/write accesses, denoted Pi:Op<m>(x,a), where m is the size of the access in bytes, x is the (physical) address of the access, and a is a value representable in m bytes; for any k in the range 0..m−1, byte k of value a (where byte 0 is the low-order byte) is the value written to or read from location x+k by the access. This relationship reflects little-endian addressing; big-endian addressing representation is as described in Chapter 2.

The last three types collectively are called barriers or memory barriers.

The size of a read/write access is 8 for a quadword access, 4 for a longword access (including all instruction fetches), 2 for a word access, or 1 for a byte access. All read/write accesses in this chapter are naturally aligned. That is, they have the form Pi:Op<m>(x,a), where the address x is divisible by size m.

The word "access" is also used as a verb; a read/write access Pi:Op<m>(x,a) accesses byte z if $x \leq z < x+m$. Two read/write accesses Op1<m>(x,a) and Op2<n>(y,b) are defined to overlap if there is at least one byte that is accessed by both, that is, if max(x,y) < min(x+m,y+n).

5.6.1.1 Architectural Definition of Processor Issue Sequence

The issue sequence for a processor is architecturally defined with respect to a hypothetical simple implementation that contains one processor and a single shared memory, with no caches or buffers. This is the instruction execution model:

1. I-fetch: An Alpha instruction is fetched from memory.

2. Read/Write: That instruction is executed and runs to completion, including a single data read from memory for a Load instruction or a single data write to memory for a Store instruction.

3. Update: The PC for the processor is updated.

4. Loop: Repeat the above sequence indefinitely.

If the instruction fetch step gets a memory management fault, the I-fetch is not done and the PC is updated to point to a PALcode fault handler. If the read/write step gets a memory management fault, the read/write is not done and the PC is updated to point to a PALcode fault handler.

5.6.1.2 Definition of Before and After

The ordering relation BEFORE ($\Leftarrow$) is a partial order on memory accesses. It is further defined in Sections 5.6.1.3 through 5.6.1.9.

The ordering relation BEFORE ($\Leftarrow$), being a partial order, is acyclic.

The BEFORE order cannot be observed directly, nor fully predicted before an actual execution, nor reproduced exactly from one execution to another. Nonetheless, some useful ordering properties must hold in all Alpha implementations.

If u $\Leftarrow$ v, then v is said to be AFTER u.

5.6.1.3 Definition of Processor Issue Constraints

Processor issue constraints are imposed on the processor issue sequence defined in Section 5.6.1.1, as shown in Table 5–1:

Table 5–1: Processor Issue Constraints

1st↓ 2nd →	Pi:I<n=4>(y,b)	Pi:R<n>(y,b)	Pi:W<n>(y,b)	Pi:MB	Pi:IMB
Pi:I<m=4>(x,a)	$\Leftarrow$ if overlap		$\Leftarrow$ if overlap	$\Leftarrow$	$\Leftarrow$
Pi:R<m>(x,a)		$\Leftarrow$ if overlap	$\Leftarrow$ if overlap	$\Leftarrow$	$\Leftarrow$
Pi:W<m>(x,a)			$\Leftarrow$ if overlap	$\Leftarrow$	$\Leftarrow$
Pi:MB		$\Leftarrow$	$\Leftarrow$	$\Leftarrow$	$\Leftarrow$
Pi:IMB	$\Leftarrow$	$\Leftarrow$	$\Leftarrow$	$\Leftarrow$	$\Leftarrow$

Where "overlap" denotes the condition max(x,y) < min(x+m,y+n).

For two accesses u and v issued by processor Pi, if u precedes v by processor issue constraint, then u precedes v in BEFORE order. u and v on Pi are ordered by processor issue constraint if any of the following applies:

1. The entry in Table 5–1 indicated by the access type of u (1st) and v (2nd) indicates the accesses are ordered.

2. u and v are both writes to memory-like regions and there is a WMB between u and v in processor issue sequence.

3. u and v are both writes to non-memory-like regions and there is a WMB between u and v in processor issue sequence.

4. u is a TB fill that updates a PTE, for example, a PTE read in order to satisfy a TB miss, and v is an I- or D-stream access using that PTE (see Sections 5.6.4.3 and 5.6.4.4).

In Table 5–1, *1st* and *2nd* refer to the ordering of accesses in the processor issue sequence. Note that Table 5–1 imposes no direct constraint on the ordering relationship between non-overlapping read/write accesses, though there may be indirect constraints due to the transitivity of BEFORE ($\Leftarrow$). Conditions 2 through 4, above, impose ordering constraints on some pairs of nonoverlapping read/write accesses.

Table 5–1 permits a read access Pi:R<n>(y,b) to be ordered BEFORE an overlapping write access Pi:W<m>(x,a) that precedes the read access in processor issue order. This asymmetry for reads allows reads to be satisfied by using data from an earlier write in processor issue sequence by the same processor (for example, by hitting in a write buffer) before the write completes. The write access remains "visible" to the read access; "visibility" is described in Sections 5.6.1.5 and 5.6.1.6 and illustrated in Litmus Test 11 in Section 5.6.2.11.

An I-fetch Pi:I<4>(y,b) may also be ordered BEFORE an overlapping write Pi:W<m>(x,a) that precedes it in processor issue sequence. In that case, the write may, but need not, be visible to the I-fetch. This asymmetry in Table 5–1 allows writes to the I-stream to be incoherent until a CALL_PAL IMB is executed.

Implementations are free to perform memory accesses from a single processor in any sequence that is consistent with processor issue constraints.

5.6.1.4 Definition of Location Access Constraints

Location access constraints are imposed on overlapping read/write accesses. If u and v are overlapping read/write accesses, at least one of which is a write, then u and v must be comparable in the BEFORE ($\Leftarrow$) ordering, that is, either u $\Leftarrow$ v or v $\Leftarrow$ u.

There is no direct requirement that nonoverlapping accesses be comparable in the BEFORE ($\Leftarrow$) ordering.

All writes accessing any given byte are totally ordered, and any read or I-fetch accessing a given byte is ordered with respect to all writes accessing that byte.

5.6.1.5 Definition of Visibility

If u is a write access Pi:W<m>(x,a) and v is an overlapping read access Pj:R<n>(y,b), u is visible to v only if:

$u \Leftarrow v$, or

u precedes v in processor issue sequence (possible only if Pi=Pj).

If u is a write access Pi:W<m>(x,a) and v is an overlapping instruction fetch Pj:I<4>(y,b), there are the following rules for visibility:

1. If $u \Leftarrow v$, then u is visible to v.

2. If u precedes v in processor issue sequence, then:

   a. If there is a write w such that:

   u overlaps w and precedes w in processor issue sequence, and
   w is visible to v,

       then u is visible to v.

   b. If there is an instruction fetch w such that:

   u is visible to w, and
   w overlaps v and precedes v in processor issue sequence,

       then u is visible to v.

3. If u does not precede v in either processor issue sequence or BEFORE order, then u is not visible to v.

Note that the rules of visibility for reads and instruction fetches are slightly different. If a write u precedes an overlapping instruction fetch v in processor issue sequence, but u is not BEFORE v, then u may or may not be visible to v.

5.6.1.6 Definition of Storage

The property of storage applies only to memory-like regions.

The value read from any byte by a read access or instruction fetch v, is the value written by the latest (in BEFORE order) write u to that byte that is visible to v. More formally:

If u is Pi:W<m>(x,a), and v is either Pj:I<4>(y,b) or Pj:R<n>(y,b), and z is a byte accessed by both u and v, and u is visible to v; and there is no write that is AFTER u, is visible to v, and accesses byte z; then the value of byte z read by v is exactly the value written by u. In this situation, u is a source of v.

The only way to communicate information between different processors is for one to write a shared location and the other to read the shared location and receive the newly written value. (In this context, the sending of an interrupt from processor Pi to Pj is modeled as Pi writing to a location INTij, and Pj reading from INTij.)

5.6.1.7 Definition of Dependence Constraint

The depends relation (DP) is defined as follows. Given u and v issued by processor Pi, where u is a read or an instruction fetch and v is a write, u precedes v in DP order (written u DP v, that is, v depends on u) in either of the following situations:

- u determines the execution of v, the location accessed by v, or the value written by v.

- u determines the execution or address or value of another memory access z that precedes v or might precede v (that is, would precede v in some execution path depending on the value read by u) by processor issue constraint (see Section 5.6.1.3).

Note that the DP relation does not directly impose a BEFORE ($\Leftarrow$) ordering between accesses u and v.

The dependence constraint requires that the union of the DP relation and the "is a source of" relation (see Section 5.6.1.6) be acyclic. That is, there must not exist reads and/or I-fetches R1, ..., Rn, and writes W1, ..., Wn, such that:

1. $n \geq 1$,

2. For each i, $1 \leq i \leq n$, Ri DP Wi,

3. For each i, $1 \leq i < n$, Wi is a source of Ri + 1, and

4. Wn is a source of R1.

That constraint eliminates the possibility of "causal loops." A simple example of a "causal loop" is when the execution of a write on Pi depends on the execution of a write on Pj and vice versa, creating a circular dependence chain. The following simple example of a "causal loop" is written in the style of the litmus tests in Section 5.6.2, where initially x and y are 1:

Processor Pi executes:

```
LDQ    R1,x
STQ    R1,y
```

Processor Pj executes:

```
LDQ    R1,y
STQ    R1,x
```

Representing those code sequences in the style of the litmus tests in Section 5.6.2, it is impossible for the following sequence to result:

Pi	Pj
[U1] Pi:R<8>(x,0)	[V1] Pj:R<8>(y,0)
[U2] Pi:W<8>(y,0)	[V2] Pj:W<8>(x,0)

Analysis:

<1> By the definitions of storage and visibility, U2 is the source of V1, and V2 is the source of U1.

<2> By the definition of DP and examination of the code, U1 DP U2, and V1 DP V2.

<3> Thus, U1 DP U2, U2 is the source of V1, V1 DP V2, and V2 is the source of U1. This circular chain is forbidden by the dependence constraint.

Given the initial condition x, y = 1, the access sequence above would also be impossible if the code were:

Processor Pi's program:

```
      LDQ    R1,x
      BNE    R1,done
      STQ    R31,y
done:
```

Processor Pj's program:

```
      LDQ    R1,y
      BNE    R1,done
      STQ    R31,x
done:
```

5.6.1.8 Definition of Load-Locked and Store-Conditional

The property of load-locked and store-conditional applies only to memory-like regions.

For each successful store-conditional v, there exists a load-locked u such that the following are true:

1. u precedes v in the processor issue sequence.

2. There is no load-locked or store-conditional between u and v in the processor issue sequence.

3. If u and v access within the same naturally aligned 16-byte physical and virtual block in memory, then for every write w by a different processor that accesses within u's lock range (where w is either a store or a successful store conditional), it must be true that $w \Leftarrow u$ or $v \Leftarrow w$.

u's lock range contains the region of physical memory that u accesses. See Sections 4.2.4 and 4.2.5, which define the lock range and conditions for success or failure of a store conditional.

5.6.1.9 Timeliness

Even in the absence of a barrier after the write, no write by a processor may be delayed indefinitely in the BEFORE ordering.

5.6.2 Litmus Tests

Many issues about writing and reading shared data can be cast into questions about whether a write is before or after a read. These questions can be answered by rigorously checking whether any ordering satisfies the rules in Sections 5.6.1.3 through 5.6.1.8.

In litmus tests 1–9 below, all initial quadword memory locations contain 1. In all these litmus tests, it is assumed that initializations are performed by a write or writes that are BEFORE all the explicitly listed accesses, that all relevant writes other than the initializations are explicitly shown, and that all accesses shown are to memory-like regions (so the definition of storage applies).

5.6.2.1 Litmus Test 1 (Impossible Sequence)

Initially, location x contains 1:

Pi	Pj
[U1]Pi:W<8>(x,2)	[V1]Pj:R<8>(x,2)
	[V2]Pj:R<8>(x,1)

Analysis:

<1> By the definition of storage (Section 5.6.1.6), V1 reading 2 implies that U1 is visible to V1.

<2> By the rules for visibility (Section 5.6.1.5), U1 being visible to V1, but being issued by a different processor, implies that U1 $\Leftarrow$ V1.

<3> By the processor issue constraints (Section 5.6.1.3), V1 $\Leftarrow$ V2.

<4> By the transitivity of the partial order $\Leftarrow$, it follows from <2> and <3> that U1 $\Leftarrow$ V2.

<5> By the rules for visibility, it follows from U1 $\Leftarrow$ V2 that U1 is visible to V2.

<6> Since U1 is AFTER the initialization of x, U1 is the latest (in the $\Leftarrow$ ordering) write to x that is visible to V1.

<7> By the definition of storage, it follows that V2 should read the value written by U1, in contradiction to the stated result.

Thus, once a processor reads a new value from a location, it must never see an old value – time must not go backward. V2 must read 2.

5.6.2.2 Litmus Test 2 (Impossible Sequence)

Initially, location x contains 1:

Pi	Pj
[U1]Pi:W<8>(x,2)	[V1]Pj:W<8>(x,3)
	[V2]Pj:R<8>(x,2)
	[V3]Pj:R<8>(x,3)

Analysis:

<1> Since V1 precedes V2 in processor issue sequence, V1 is visible to V2.

<2> V2 reading 2 implies U1 is the latest (in $\Leftarrow$ order) write to x visible to V2.

<3> From <1> and <2>, V1 $\Leftarrow$ U1.

<4> Since U1 is visible to V2, and they are issued by different processors, U1 $\Leftarrow$ V2.

<5> By the processor issue constraints, V2 $\Leftarrow$ V3.

<6> From <4> and <5>, U1 $\Leftarrow$ V3.

<7> From <6> and the visibility rules, U1 is visible to V3.

<8> Since both V1 and the initialization of x are BEFORE U1, U1 is the latest write to x that is visible to V3.

<9> By the definition of storage, it follows that V3 should read the value written by U1, in contradiction to the stated result.

Thus, once processor Pj reads a new value written by U1, any other writes that must precede the read must also precede U1. V3 must read 2.

5.6.2.3 Litmus Test 3 (Impossible Sequence)

Initially, location x contains 1:

Pi	Pj	Pk
[U1]Pi:W<8>(x,2)	[V1]Pj:W<8>(x,3)	[W1]Pk:R<8>(x,3)
[U2]Pi:R<8>(x,3)		[W2]Pk:R<8>(x,2)

Analysis:

<1> U2 reading 3 implies V1 is the latest write to x visible to U2, therefore U1 $\Leftarrow$ V1.

<2> W1 reading 3 implies V1 is visible to W1, so V1 $\Leftarrow$ W1 $\Leftarrow$ W, therefore V1 is also visible to W2.

<3> W2 reading 2 implies U1 is the latest write to x visible to W2, therefore V1 $\Leftarrow$ U1.

<4> From <1> and <3>, U1 $\Leftarrow$ V1 $\Leftarrow$ U1.

Again, time cannot go backwards. If V1 is ordered before U1, then processor Pk cannot read first the later value 3 and then the earlier value 2. Alternatively, if V1 is ordered before U1, U2 must read 2.

5.6.2.4 Litmus Test 4 (Sequence Okay)

Initially, locations x and y contain 1:

Pi	Pj
[U1]Pi:W<8>(x,2)	[V1]Pj:R<8>(y,2)
[U2]Pi:W<8>(y,2)	[V2]Pj:R<8>(x,1)

Analysis:

<1> V1 reading 2 implies U2 $\Leftarrow$ V1, by storage and visibility.

<2> Since V2 does not read 2, there cannot be U1 $\Leftarrow$ V2.

<3> By the access order constraints, it follows from <2> that V2 $\Leftarrow$ U1.

There are no conflicts in the sequence. There are no violations of the definition of BEFORE.

5.6.2.5 Litmus Test 5 (Sequence Okay)

Initially, locations x and y contain 1:

Pi	Pj
[U1]Pi:W<8>(x,2)	[V1]Pj:R<8>(y,2)
	[V2]Pj:MB
[U2]Pi:W<8>(y,2)	[V3]Pj:R<8>(x,1)

Analysis:

<1> V1 reading 2 implies U2 $\Leftarrow$ V1, by storage and visibility.

<2> V1 $\Leftarrow$ V2 $\Leftarrow$ V3, by processor issue constraints.

<3> V3 reading 1 implies V3 $\Leftarrow$ U1, by storage and visibility.

There is U2 $\Leftarrow$ V1 $\Leftarrow$ V2 $\Leftarrow$ V3 $\Leftarrow$ U1. There are no conflicts in this sequence. There are no violations of the definition of BEFORE.

5.6.2.6 Litmus Test 6 (Sequence Okay)

Initially, locations x and y contain 1:

Pi	Pj
[U1]Pi:W<8>(x,2)	[V1]Pj:R<8>(y,2)
[U2]Pi:MB	
[U3]Pi:W<8>(y,2)	[V2]Pj:R<8>(x,1)

Analysis:

<1> U1 $\Leftarrow$ U2 $\Leftarrow$ U3, by processor issue constraints.

<2> V1 reading 2 implies U3 $\Leftarrow$ V1, by storage and visibility.

<3> V2 reading 1 implies V2 $\Leftarrow$ U1, by storage and visibility.

There is V2 $\Leftarrow$ U1 $\Leftarrow$ U2 $\Leftarrow$ U3 $\Leftarrow$ V1. There are no conflicts in this sequence. There are no violations of the definition of BEFORE.

In litmus tests 4, 5, and 6, writes to two different locations x and y are observed (by another processor) to occur in the opposite order than that in which they were performed. An update to y propagates quickly to Pj, but the update to x is delayed, and Pi and Pj do not both have MBs.

5.6.2.7 Litmus Test 7 (Impossible Sequence)

Initially, locations x and y contain 1:

Pi	Pj
[U1]Pi:W<8>(x,2)	[V1]Pj:R<8>(y,2)
[U2]Pi:MB	[V2]Pj:MB
[U3]Pi:W<8>(y,2)	[V3]Pj:R<8>(x,1)

Analysis:

<1> V3 reading 1 implies V3 $\Leftarrow$ U1, by storage and visibility.

<2> V1 reading 2 implies U3 $\Leftarrow$ V1, by storage and visibility.

<3> U1 $\Leftarrow$ U2 $\Leftarrow$ U3, by processor issue constraints.

<4> V1 $\Leftarrow$ V2 $\Leftarrow$ V3, by processor issue constraints.

<5> By <2>, <3>, and <4>, U1 $\Leftarrow$ U2 $\Leftarrow$ U3 $\Leftarrow$ V1 $\Leftarrow$ V2 $\Leftarrow$ V3.

Both <1> and <5> cannot be true, so if V1 reads 2, then V3 must also read 2.

If both x and y are in memory-like regions, the sequence remains impossible if U2 is changed to a WMB. Similarly, if both x and y are in non-memory-like regions, the sequence remains impossible if U2 is changed to a WMB.

5.6.2.8 Litmus Test 8 (Impossible Sequence)

Initially, locations x and y contain 1:

Pi	Pj
[U1]Pi:W<8>(x,2)	[V1]Pj:W<8>(y,2)
[U2]Pi:MB	[V2]Pj:MB
[U3]Pi:R<8>(y,1)	[V3]Pj:R<8>(x,1)

Analysis:

<1>   V3 reading 1 implies V3 $\Leftarrow$ U1, by storage and visibility.

<2>   U3 reading 1 implies U3 $\Leftarrow$ V1, by storage and visibility.

<3>   U1 $\Leftarrow$ U2 $\Leftarrow$ U3, by processor issue constraints.

<4>   V1 $\Leftarrow$ V2 $\Leftarrow$ V3, by processor issue constraints.

<5>   By <2>, <3>, and <4>, U1 $\Leftarrow$ U2 $\Leftarrow$ U3 $\Leftarrow$ V1 $\Leftarrow$ V2 $\Leftarrow$ V3.

Both <1> and <5> cannot be true, so if U3 reads 1, then V3 must read 2, and vice versa.

5.6.2.9 Litmus Test 9 (Impossible Sequence)

Initially, location x contains 1:

Pi	Pj
[U1]Pi:W<8>(x,2)	[V1]Pj:W<8>(x,3)
[U2]Pi:R<8>(x,2)	[V2]Pj:R<8>(x,3)
[U3]Pi:R<8>(x,3)	[V3]Pj:R<8>(x,2)

Analysis:

<1>   V3 reading 2 implies U1 is the latest write to x visible to V3, therefore V1 $\Leftarrow$ U1.

<2>   U3 reading 3 implies V1 is the latest write to x visible to U3, therefore U1 $\Leftarrow$ V1.

Both <1> and <2> cannot be true. Time cannot go backwards. If V3 reads 2, then U3 must read 2. Alternatively, if U3 reads 3, then V3 must read 3.

5.6.2.10 Litmus Test 10 (Sequence Okay)

For an aligned quadword location, x, initially 100000001_{16}:

Pi	Pj
[U1]Pi:W<4>(x,2)	[V1]Pj:W<4>(x+4,2)
[U2]Pi:R<8>(x,100000002_{16})	[V2]Pj:R<8>(x,200000001_{16})

Analysis:

<1> Since U2 reads 1 from x+4, V1 is not visible to U2. Thus U2 $\Leftarrow$ V1.

<2> Similarly, V2 $\Leftarrow$ U1.

<3> U1 is visible to U2, but since they are issued by the same processor, it is not necessarily the case that U1 $\Leftarrow$ U2.

<4> Similarly, it is not necessarily the case that V1 $\Leftarrow$ V2.

There is no ordering cycle, so the sequence is permitted.

5.6.2.11 Litmus Test 11 (Impossible Sequence)

For an aligned quadword location, x, initially 100000001_{16}:

Pi	Pj
[U1]Pi:W<4>(x,2)	[V1]Pj:R<8>(x,200000001_{16})
[U2]Pi:MB or WMB	
[U3]Pi:W<4>(x+4,2)	

Analysis:

<1> V1 reading 200000001_{16} implies U3 $\Leftarrow$ V1 $\Leftarrow$ U1 by storage and visibility.

<2> U1 $\Leftarrow$ U2 $\Leftarrow$ U3, by processor issue constraints.

Both <1> and <2> cannot be true.

5.6.3 Implied Barriers

There are no implied barriers in Alpha. If an implied barrier is needed for functionally correct access to shared data, it must be written as an explicit instruction. (Software must explicitly include any needed MB, WMB, or CALL_PAL IMB instructions.)

Alpha transitions such as the following have no built-in implied memory barriers:

- Entry to PALcode

- Sending and receiving interrupts

- Returning from exceptions, interrupts, or machine checks

- Swapping context

- Invalidating the Translation Buffer (TB)

Depending on implementation choices for maintaining cache coherency, some PALcode/cache implementations may have an implied CALL_PAL IMB in the I-stream TB fill routine, but this is transparent to the non-PALcode programmer.

5.6.4 Implications for Software

Software must explicitly include MB, WMB, or CALL_PAL IMB instructions according to the following circumstances.

5.6.4.1 Single Processor Data Stream

No barriers are ever needed. A read to physical address x will always return the value written by the immediately preceding write to x in the processor issue sequence.

5.6.4.2 Single Processor Instruction Stream

An I-fetch from virtual or physical address x does not necessarily return the value written by the immediately preceding write to x in the issue sequence. To make the I-fetch reliably get the newly written instruction, a CALL_PAL IMB is needed between the write and the I-fetch.

5.6.4.3 Multiprocessor Data Stream (Including Single Processor with DMA I/O)

Generally, the only way to reliably communicate shared data is to write the shared data on one processor or DMA I/O device, execute an MB (or the logical equivalent[1] if it is a DMA I/O device), then write a flag (equivalently, send an interrupt) signaling the other processor that the shared data is ready. Each receiving processor must read the new flag (equivalently, receive the interrupt), execute an MB, then read or update the shared data. In the special case in which data is communicated through just one location in memory, memory barriers are not necessary.

Software Note:

> Note that this section does not describe how to reliably communicate data from a processor to a DMA device. See Section 5.6.4.7.

Leaving out the first MB removes the assurance that the shared data is written before the flag is written.

Leaving out the second MB removes the assurance that the shared data is read or updated only after the flag is seen to change; in this case, an early read could see an old value, and an early update could be overwritten.

---

1   In this context, the logical equivalent of an MB for a DMA device is whatever is necessary under the applicable I/O subsystem architecture to ensure that preceding writes will be BEFORE (see Section 5.6.1.2) the subsequent write of a flag or transmission of an interrupt. Not all I/O devices behave exactly as required by the Alpha architecture. To interoperate properly with those devices, some special action might be required by the program executing on the CPU. For example, PCI bus devices require that after the CPU has received an interrupt, the CPU must read a CSR location on the PCI device, execute an MB, then read or update the shared data. From the perspective of the Alpha architecture, this CSR read can be regarded as a necessary assist to help the DMA I/O device complete its logical equivalent of an MB.

This implies that after a DMA I/O device has written some data to memory (such as paging in a page from disk), the DMA device must logically execute an MB[1] before posting a completion interrupt, and the interrupt handler software must execute an MB before the data is guaranteed to be visible to the interrupted processor. Other processors must also execute MBs before they are guaranteed to see the new data.

An important special case occurs when a write is done (perhaps by an I/O device) to some physical page frame, then an MB is executed, and then a previously invalid PTE is changed to be a valid mapping of the physical page frame that was just written. In this case, all processors that access virtual memory by using the newly valid PTE must guarantee to deliver the newly written data after the TB miss, for both I-stream and D-stream accesses.

5.6.4.4 Multiprocessor Instruction Stream (Including Single Processor with DMA I/O)

The only way to update the I-stream reliably is to write the shared I-stream on one processor or DMA I/O device, then execute a CALL_PAL IMB (or an MB if the processor is not going to execute the new I-stream, or the logical equivalent of an MB if it is a DMA I/O device), then write a flag (equivalently, send an interrupt) signaling the other processor that the shared I-stream is ready. Each receiving processor must read the new flag (equivalently, receive the interrupt), execute a CALL_PAL IMB, then fetch the shared I-stream.

Software Note:

> Note that this section does not describe how to reliably communicate I-stream from a processor to a DMA device. See Section 5.6.4.7.

Leaving out the first CALL_PAL IMB (or MB) removes the assurance that the shared I-stream is written before the flag.

Leaving out the second CALL_PAL IMB removes the assurance that the shared I-stream is read only *after* the flag is seen to change; in this case, an early read could see an old value.

This implies that after a DMA I/O device has written some I-stream to memory (such as paging in a page from disk), the DMA device must logically execute an MB[1] before posting a completion interrupt, and the interrupt handler software must execute a CALL_PAL IMB before the I-stream is guaranteed to be visible to the interrupted processor. Other processors must also execute CALL_PAL IMB instructions before they are guaranteed to see the new I-stream.

An important special case occurs under the following circumstances:

1. A write (perhaps by an I/O device) is done to some physical page frame.

2. A CALL_PAL IMB (or MB) is executed.

3. A previously invalid PTE is changed to be a valid mapping of the physical page frame that was written in step 1.

In this case, all processors that access virtual memory by using the newly valid PTE must guarantee to deliver the newly written I-stream after the TB miss.

---

1 See Footnote 1 on page 5-23.

5.6.4.5 Multiprocessor Context Switch

If a process migrates from executing on one processor to executing on another, the context switch operating system code must include a number of barriers.

A process migrates by having its context stored into memory, then eventually having that context reloaded on another processor. In between, some shared mechanism must be used to communicate that the context saved in memory by the first processor is available to the second processor. This could be done by using an interrupt, by using a flag bit associated with the saved context, or by using a shared-memory multiprocessor data structure, as follows:

First Processor	Second Processor
:	
Save state of current process.	
MB [1]	
Pass ownership of process context data structure memory. ⇒	Pick up ownership of process context data structure memory.
	MB [2]
	Restore state of new process context data structure memory.
	Make I-stream coherent [3].
	Make TB coherent [4].
	:
	Execute code for new process that accesses memory that is not common to all processes.

MB [1] ensures that the writes done to save the state of the current process happen before the ownership is passed.

MB [2] ensures that the reads done to load the state of the new process happen after the ownership is picked up and hence are reliably the values written by the processor saving the old state. Leaving this MB out makes the code fail if an old value of the context remains in the second processor's cache and invalidates from the writes done on the first processor are not delivered soon enough.

The TB on the second processor must be made coherent with any write to the page tables that may have occurred on the first processor just before the save of the process state. This must be done with a series of TB invalidate instructions to remove any nonglobal page mapping for this process, or by assigning an ASN that is unused on the second processor to the process. One of these actions must occur sometime before starting execution of the code for the new process that accesses memory (instruction or data) that is not common to all processes. A common method is to assign a new ASN after gaining ownership of the new process and before loading its context, which includes its ASN.

The D-cache on the second processor must be made coherent with any write to the D-stream that may have occurred on the first processor just before the save of process state. This is ensured by MB [2] and does not require any additional instructions.

The I-cache on the second processor must be made coherent with any write to the I-stream that may have occurred on the first processor just before the save of process state. This can be done with a CALL_PAL IMB sometime before the execution of any code that is not common to all processes, More commonly, this can be done by forcing a TB miss (via the new ASN or via TB invalidate instructions) and using the TB-fill rule (see Section 5.6.4.3). This latter approach does not require any additional instruction.

Combining all these considerations gives the following, where, on a single processor, there is no need for the barriers:

First Processor	Second Processor
:	
Pick up ownership of process context data structure memory.	
MB	
Assign new ASN or invalidate TBs.	
Save state of current process.	
Restore state of new process.	
MB	
Pass ownership of process context data structure memory. $\Rightarrow$:	: Pickup ownership of new process context data structure memory.
:	MB
	Assign new ASN or invalidate TBs.
	Save state of current process.
	Restore state of new process.
	MB
	Pass ownership of old process context data structure memory.
	:
	Execute code for new process that accesses memory that is not common to all processes.

5.6.4.6 Multiprocessor Send/Receive Interrupt

If one processor writes some shared data, then sends an interrupt to a second processor, and that processor receives the interrupt, then accesses the shared data, the sequence from Section 5.6.4.3 must be used:

First Processor		Second Processor
:		
Write data		
MB		
Send interrupt	$\Rightarrow$	Receive interrupt
		MB
		Access data
		:

Leaving out the MB at the beginning of the interrupt-receipt routine causes the code to fail if an old value of the context remains in the second processor's cache, and invalidates from the writes done on the first processor are not delivered soon enough.

5.6.4.7 Implications for Memory Mapped I/O

Sections 5.6.4.3 and 5.6.4.4 describe methods for communicating data from a processor or DMA I/O device to another processor that work reliably in all Alpha systems. Special considerations apply to the communication of data or I-stream from a processor to a DMA I/O device. These considerations arise from the use of bridges to connect to I/O buses with devices that are accessible by memory accesses to non-memory-like regions of physical memory.

The following communication method works in all Alpha systems.

To reliably communicate shared data from a processor to an I/O device:

1. Write the shared data to a memory-like physical memory region on the processor.

2. Execute an MB instruction.

3. Write a flag (equivalently, send an interrupt or write a register location implemented in the I/O device).

The receiving I/O device must:

1. Read the flag (equivalently, detect the interrupt or detect the write to the register location implemented in the I/O device).

2. Execute the equivalent of an MB[1]

---

1 In this context, the logical equivalent of an MB for a DMA device is whatever is necessary under the applicable I/O subsystem architecture to ensure that preceding writes will be BEFORE (see Section 5.6.1.2) the subsequent reads of shared data. Typically, this action is defined to be present between every read and write access done by the I/O device, according to the applicable I/O subsystem architecture.

3. Read the shared data.

As shown in Section 5.6.4.3, leaving out the memory barrier removes the assurance that the shared data is written before the flag is. Unlike the case in Section 5.6.4.3, writing the shared data to a non-memory-like physical memory region removes the assurance that the I/O device will detect the writes of the shared data before detecting the flag write, interrupt, or device register write.

This implies that after a processor has prepared a data buffer to be read from memory by a DMA I/O device (such as writing a buffer to disk), the processor must execute an MB before starting the I/O. The I/O device, after receiving the start signal, must logically execute an MB before reading the data buffer, and the buffer must be located in a memory-like physical memory region.

There are methods of communicating data that may work in some systems but are not guaranteed in all systems. Two notable examples are:

1. If an Alpha processor writes a location implemented in a component located on an I/O bus in the system, then executes a memory barrier, then writes a flag in some memory location (in a memory-like or non-memory-like region), a device on the I/O bus may be able to detect (via read access) the result of the flag in memory write and the write of the location on the I/O bus out of order (that is, in a different order than the order in which the Alpha processor wrote those locations).

2. If an Alpha processor writes a location that is a control register within an I/O device, then executes a memory barrier, then writes a location in memory (in a memory-like or non-memory-like region), the I/O device may be able to detect (via read access) the result of the memory write before receiving and responding to the write of its own control register.

In almost every case, a mechanism that ensures the completion of writes to control register locations within I/O devices is provided. The normal and strongly recommended mechanism is to read a location after writing it, which guarantees that the write is complete. In any case, all systems that use a particular I/O device should provide the same mechanism for that device.

5.6.4.8 Multiple Processors Writing to a Single I/O Device

Generally, for multiple processors to cooperate in writing to a single I/O device, the first processor must write to the device, execute an MB, then notify other processors. Another processor that intends to write the same I/O device after the first processor must receive the notification, execute an MB, and then write to the I/O device. For example:

First Processor		Second Processor
:		
Write CSR_A		
MB		
Write flag (in memory)	$\Rightarrow$	Read flag (in memory)
		MB
		Write CSR_B
		:

The MB on the first processor guarantees that the write to CSR_A precedes the write to flag in memory, as perceived on other processors. (The MB does not guarantee that the write to CSR_A has completed. See Section 5.6.4.7 for a discussion of how a processor can guarantee that a write to an I/O device has completed at that device.) The MB on the second processor guarantees that the write to CSR_B will reach the I/O device after the write to CSR_A.

5.6.5 Implications for Hardware

The coherency point for physical address x is the place in the memory subsystem at which accesses to x are ordered. It may be at a main memory board, or at a cache containing x exclusively, or at the point of winning a common bus arbitration.

The coherency point for x may move with time, as exclusive access to x migrates between main memory and various caches.

MB and CALL_PAL IMB force all preceding writes to at least reach their respective coherency points. This does not mean that main-memory writes have been done, just that the *order* of the eventual writes is committed. For example, on the XMI with retry, this means getting the writes acknowledged as received with good parity at the inputs to memory board queues; the actual RAM write happens later.

MB and CALL_PAL IMB also force all queued cache invalidates to be delivered to the local caches before starting any subsequent reads (that may otherwise cache hit on stale data) or writes (that may otherwise write the cache, only to have the write effectively overwritten by a late-delivered invalidate).

WMB ensures that the final order of writes to memory-like regions is committed and that the final order of writes to non-memory-like regions is committed. This does not imply that the final order of writes to memory-like regions relative to writes to non-memory-like regions is committed. It also prevents writes that precede the WMB from merging with writes that follow the WMB. For example, an implementation with a write buffer might implement WMB by closing all valid write buffer entries from further merging and then drain the write buffer entries in order.

Implementations may allow reads of x to hit (by physical address) on pending writes in a write buffer, even before the writes to x reach the coherency point for x. If this is done, it is still true that no earlier value of x may subsequently be delivered to the processor that took the hit on the write buffer value.

Virtual data caches are allowed to deliver data before doing address translation, but only if there cannot be a pending write under a synonym virtual address. Lack of a write-buffer match on untranslated address bits is sufficient to guarantee this.

Virtual data caches must invalidate or otherwise become coherent with the new value whenever a PALcode routine is executed that affects the validity, fault behavior, protection behavior, or virtual-to-physical mapping specified for one or more pages. Becoming coherent can be delayed until the next subsequent MB instruction or TB fill (using the new mapping) if the implementation of the PALcode routine always forces a subsequent TB fill.

5.7 Arithmetic Traps

Alpha implementations are allowed to execute multiple instructions concurrently and to forward results from one instruction to another. Thus, when an arithmetic trap is detected, the PC may have advanced an arbitrarily large number of instructions past the instruction T (calculating result R) whose execution triggered the trap.

When the trap is detected, any or all of these subsequent instructions may run to completion before the trap is actually taken. The set of instructions subsequent to T that complete before the trap is taken are collectively called the trap shadow of T. The PC pushed on the stack when the trap is taken is the PC of the first instruction past the trap shadow.

The instructions in the trap shadow of T may use the UNPREDICTABLE result R of T, they may generate additional traps, and they may completely change the PC (branches, JSR).

Thus, by the time a trap is taken, the PC pushed on the stack may bear no useful relationship to the PC of the trigger instruction T, and the state visible to the programmer may have been updated using the UNPREDICTABLE result R. If an instruction in the trap shadow of T uses R to calculate a subsequent register value, that register value is UNPREDICTABLE, even though there may be no trap associated with the subsequent calculation. Similarly:

- If an instruction in the trap shadow of T stores R or any subsequent UNPREDICTABLE result, the stored value is UNPREDICTABLE.

- If an instruction in the trap shadow of T uses R or any subsequent UNPREDICTABLE result as the basis of a conditional or calculated branch, the branch target is UNPREDICTABLE.

- If an instruction in the trap shadow of T uses R or any subsequent UNPREDICTABLE result as the basis of an address calculation, the memory address actually accessed is UNPREDICTABLE.

Software can follow the rules in Section 4.7.7.3 to reliably bound how far the PC may advance before taking a trap, how far an UNPREDICTABLE result may propagate or continue from a trap by supplying a well-defined result R within an arithmetic trap handler. Arithmetic instructions that do not use the /S exception completion qualifier can reliably produce that behavior by inserting TRAPB instructions at appropriate points.

Chapter 6

Common PALcode Architecture (I)

6.1 PALcode

In a family of machines, both users and operating system developers require functions to be implemented consistently. When functions conform to a common interface, the code that uses those functions can be used on several different implementations without modification.

These functions range from the binary encoding of the instruction and data to the exception mechanisms and synchronization primitives. Some of these functions can be implemented cost effectively in hardware, but others are impractical to implement directly in hardware. These functions include low-level hardware support functions such as Translation Buffer miss fill routines, interrupt acknowledge, and vector dispatch. They also include support for privileged and atomic operations that require long instruction sequences.

In the VAX, these functions are generally provided by microcode. This is not seen as a problem because the VAX architecture lends itself to a microcoded implementation.

One of the goals of Alpha architecture is to implement functions consistently without microcode. However, it is still desirable to provide an architected interface to these functions that will be consistent across the entire family of machines. The Privileged Architecture Library (PALcode) provides a mechanism to implement these functions without microcode.

6.2 PALcode Instructions and Functions

PALcode is used to implement the following functions:

- Instructions that require complex sequencing as an atomic operation
- Instructions that require VAX style interlocked memory access
- Privileged instructions
- Memory management control, including translation buffer (TB) management
- Context swapping
- Interrupt and exception dispatching
- Power-up initialization and booting
- Console functions
- Emulation of instructions with no hardware support

The Alpha architecture lets these functions be implemented in standard machine code that is resident in main memory. PALcode is written in standard machine code with some implementation-specific extensions to provide access to low-level hardware. This lets an Alpha implementation make various design trade-offs based on the hardware technology being used to implement the machine. The PALcode can abstract these differences and make them invisible to system software.

For example, in a MOS VLSI implementation, a small (32-entry) fully associative TB can be the right match to the media, given that chip area is a costly resource. In an ECL version, a large (1024 entry) direct-mapped TB can be used because it will use RAM chips and does not have fast associative memories available. This difference would be handled by implementation-specific versions of the PALcode on the two systems, both versions providing transparent TB miss service routines. The operating system code would not need to know there were any differences.

An Alpha Privileged Architecture Library (PALcode) of routines and environments is supplied by DIGITAL. Other systems may use a library supplied by DIGITAL or architect and implement a different library of routines. Alpha systems are required to support the replacement of PALcode defined by DIGITAL with an operating system-specific version.

6.3 PALcode Environment

The PALcode environment differs from the normal environment in the following ways:

- Complete control of the machine state.
- Interrupts are disabled.
- Implementation-specific hardware functions are enabled, as described below.
- I-stream memory management traps are prevented (by disabling I-stream mapping, mapping PALcode with a permanent TB entry, or by other mechanisms).

Complete control of the machine state allows all functions of the machine to be controlled. Disabling interrupts allows the system to provide multi-instruction sequences as atomic operations. Enabling implementation-specific hardware functions allows access to low-level system hardware. Preventing I-stream memory management traps allows PALcode to implement memory management functions such as translation buffer fill.

6.4 Special Functions Required for PALcode

PALcode uses the Alpha instruction set for most of its operations. A small number of additional functions are needed to implement the PALcode. Five opcodes are reserved to implement PALcode functions: PAL19, PAL1B, PAL1D, PAL1E, and PAL1F. These instructions produce an trap if executed outside the PALcode environment.

- PALcode needs a mechanism to save the current state of the machine and dispatch into PALcode.
- PALcode needs a set of instructions to access hardware control registers.

- PALcode needs a hardware mechanism to transition the machine from the PALcode environment to the non-PALcode environment. This mechanism loads the PC, enables interrupts, enables mapping, and disables PALcode privileges.

An Alpha implementation may also choose to provide additional functions to simplify or improve performance of some PALcode functions. The following are some examples:

- An Alpha implementation may include a read/write virtual function that allows PALcode to perform mapped memory accesses using the mapping hardware rather than providing the virtual-to-physical translation in PALcode routines. PALcode may provide a special function to do physical reads and writes and have the Alpha loads and stores continue to operate on virtual address in the PALcode environment.

- An Alpha implementation may include hardware assists for various functions, such as saving the virtual address of a reference on a memory management error rather than having to generate it by simulating the effective address calculation in PALcode.

- An Alpha implementation may include private registers so it can function without having to save and restore the native general registers.

6.5 PALcode Effects on System Code

PALcode will have one effect on system code. Because PALcode may reside in main memory and maintain privileged data structures in main memory, the operating system code that allocates physical memory cannot use all of physical memory.

The amount of memory PALcode requires is small, so the loss to the system is negligible.

6.6 PALcode Replacement

Alpha systems are required to support the replacement of PALcode supplied by DIGITAL with an operating system-specific version. The following functions must be implemented in PALcode, *not* directly in hardware, to facilitate replacement with different versions.

- Translation Buffer fill. Different operating systems will want to replace the Translation Buffer (TB) fill routines. The replacement routines will use different data structures. Page tables will not be present in these systems. Therefore, no portion of the TB fill flow that would change with a change in page tables may be placed in hardware, unless it is placed in a manner that can be overridden by PALcode.

- Process structure. Different operating systems might want to replace the process context switch routines. The replacement routines will use different data structures. The HWPCB or PCB will not be present in these systems. Therefore, no portion of the context switching flows that would change with a change in process structure may be placed in hardware.

PALcode can be viewed as consisting of the following somewhat intertwined components:

- Chip/architecture component
- Hardware platform component
- Operating system component

PALcode should be written modularly to facilitate the easy replacement or conditional building of each component. Such a practice simplifies the integration of CPU hardware, system platform hardware, console firmware, operating system software, and compilers.

PALcode subsections that are commonly subject to modification include:

- Translation Buffer fill
- Process structure and context switch
- Interrupt and exception frame format and routine dispatch
- Privileged PALcode instructions
- Transitions to and from console I/O mode
- Power-up reset

6.7 Required PALcode Instructions

The PALcode instructions listed in Table 6–1 and Appendix C must be recognized by mnemonic and opcode in all operating system implementations, but the effect of each instruction is dependent on the implementation. DIGITAL defines the operation of these PALcode instructions for operating system implementations supplied by DIGITAL.

Table 6–1: PALcode Instructions that Require Recognition

Mnemonic	Name
BPT	Breakpoint trap
BUGCHK	Bugcheck trap
CSERVE	Console service
GENTRAP	Generate trap
RDUNIQUE	Read unique value
SWPPAL	Swap PALcode
WRUNIQUE	Write unique value

The PALcode instructions listed in Table 6–2 and described in the following sections must be supported by all Alpha implementations:

Table 6–2: Required PALcode Instructions

Mnemonic	Type	Operation
DRAINA	Privileged	Drain aborts
HALT	Privileged	Halt processor
IMB	Unprivileged	I-stream memory barrier

6.7.1 Drain Aborts

Format:

> CALL_PAL   DRAINA   !PALcode format

Operation:

```
IF PS<literal>(<)CM> NE 0 THEN
    {privileged instruction exception}

{Stall instruction issuing until all prior
 instructions are guaranteed to complete
 without incurring aborts.}
```

Exceptions:

> Privileged Instruction

Instruction mnemonics:

> CALL_PAL DRAINA   Drain Aborts

Description:

If aborts are deliberately generated and handled (such as nonexistent memory aborts while sizing memory or searching for I/O devices), the DRAINA instruction forces any outstanding aborts to be taken before continuing.

Aborts are necessarily implementation dependent. DRAINA stalls instruction issue at least until all previously issued instructions have completed and any associated aborts have been signaled, as follows:

- For operate instructions, this usually means stalling until the result register has been written.

- For branch instructions, this usually means stalling until the result register and PC have been written.

- For load instructions, this usually means stalling until the result register has been written.

- For store instructions, this usually means stalling until at least the first level in a potentially multilevel memory hierarchy has been written.

For load instructions, DRAINA does not necessarily guarantee that the unaccessed portions of a cache block have been transferred error free before continuing.

For store instructions, DRAINA does not necessarily guarantee that the ultimate target location of the store has received error-free data before continuing. An implementation-specific technique must be used to guarantee the ultimate completion of a write in implementations that have multilevel memory hierarchies or store-and-forward bus adapters.

6.7.2 Halt

Format:

CALL_PAL   HALT   !PALcode format

Operation:

```
IF PS<literal>(<)CM> NE 0 THEN
    {privileged instruction exception}

CASE {halt_action} OF
   ! Operating System or Platform dependent choice
     halt:                    {halt}
     restart/boot/halt:       {restart/boot/halt}
     boot/halt:               {boot/halt}
     debugger/halt:           {debugger/halt}
     restart/halt:            {restart/halt}
ENDCASE
```

Exceptions:

Privileged Instruction

Instruction mnemonics:

CALL_PAL HALT   Halt Processor

Description:

The HALT instruction stops normal instruction processing and initiates some other operating system or platform-specific behavior, depending on the HALT action setting. The choice of behavior typically includes the initiation of a restart sequence, a system bootstrap, or entry into console mode. See Console Interface (III), Chapter 3.

6.7.3 Instruction Memory Barrier

Format:

CALL_PAL   IMB   !PALcode format

Operation:

```
{Make instruction stream coherent with data stream}
```

Exceptions:

None

Instruction mnemonics:

CALL_PAL IMB   I-stream Memory Barrier

Description:

An IMB instruction must be executed after software or I/O devices write into the instruction stream or modify the instruction stream virtual address mapping, and before the new value is fetched as an instruction. An implementation may contain an instruction cache that does not track either processor or I/O writes into the instruction stream. The instruction cache and memory are made coherent by an IMB instruction.

If the instruction stream is modified and an IMB is not executed before fetching an instruction from the modified location, it is UNPREDICTABLE whether the old or new value is fetched.

Software Note:

In a multiprocessor environment, executing an IMB on one processor does not affect instruction caches on other processors. Thus, a single IMB on one processor is insufficient to guarantee that all processors see a modification of the instruction stream.

The cache coherency and sharing rules are described in Console Interface (III), Chapter 2.

Chapter 7

Console Subsystem Overview (I)

On an Alpha system, underlying control of the system platform hardware is provided by a *console subsystem*. The console subsystem:

- Initializes, tests, and prepares the system platform hardware for Alpha system software.

- Bootstraps (loads into memory and starts the execution of) system software.

- Controls and monitors the state and state transitions of each processor in a multiprocessor system.

- Provides services to system software that simplify system software control of and access to platform hardware.

- Provides a means for a *console operator* to monitor and control the system.

The console subsystem interacts with system platform hardware to accomplish the first three tasks. The actual mechanisms of these interactions are specific to the platform hardware; however, the net effects are common to all systems.

The console subsystem interacts with system software once control of the system platform hardware has been transferred to that software.

The console subsystem interacts with the console operator through a virtual display device or *console terminal*. The console operator may be a person or a management application.

Chapter 8

Input/Output Overview (I)

Conceptually, Alpha systems can consist of processors, memory, a processor-memory interconnect (PMI), I/O buses, bridges, and I/O devices.

Figure 8–1 shows the Alpha system overview.

Figure 8–1: Alpha System Overview

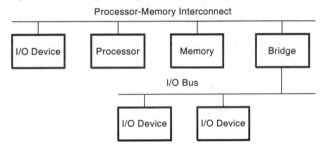

As shown in Figure 8–1, processors, memory, and possibly I/O devices, are connected by a PMI.

A bridge connects an I/O bus to the system, either directly to the PMI or through another I/O bus. The I/O bus address space is available to the processor either directly or indirectly. Indirect access is provided through either an I/O mailbox or an I/O mapping mechanism. The I/O mapping mechanism includes provisions for mapping between PMI and I/O bus addresses and access to I/O bus operations.

Alpha I/O operations can include:

- Accesses between the processor and an I/O device across the PMI
- Accesses between the processor and an I/O device across an I/O bus
- DMA accesses — I/O devices initiating reads and writes to memory
- Processor interrupts requested by devices
- Bus-specific I/O accesses

Common Architecture Index

MAXU(x,y) operator, 3–8

MAXUB8 instruction, 4–152

MAXUW4 instruction, 4–152

MB (Memory barrier) instruction, 4–142
    compared with WMB, 4–148
    multiprocessors only, 4–142
    with DMA I/O, 5–23
    with LDx_L/STx_C, 4–14
    with multiprocessor D-stream, 5–22
    with shared data structures, 5–9
    See also IMB, WMB

MBZ (must be zero), 1–9

Memory access
    coherency of, 5–1
    granularity of, 5–2
    width of, 5–3
    with WMB instruction, 4–147

Memory alignment, requirement for, 5–2

Memory barrier instructions. See MB, IMB
    (PALcode), and WMB instructions

Memory barriers, 5–22

Memory instruction format, 3–11

Memory jump instruction format, 3–12

Memory management
    support in PALcode, 6–2

Memory prefetch registers
    defined, 3–3

Memory-like behavior, 5–3

MF_FPCR instruction, 4–109

MIN, defined for floating-point, 4–65

MINS(x,y) operator, 3–8

MINSB8 instruction, 4–152

MINSW4 instruction, 4–152

MINU(x,y) operator, 3–8

MINUB8 instruction, 4–152

MINUW4 instruction, 4–152

Miscellaneous instructions, 4–132

Move instructions (conditional). See Conditional
    move instructions

MSKBL instruction, 4–57

MSKLH instruction, 4–57

MSKLL instruction, 4–57

MSKQL instruction, 4–57

MSKWH instruction, 4–57

MSKWL instruction, 4–57

MT_FPCR instruction, 4–109
    synchronization requirement, 4–82

MULF instruction, 4–126

MULG instruction, 4–126

MULL instruction, 4–34
    with MULQ, 4–34

MULQ instruction, 4–35
    with MULL, 4–34
    with UMULH, 4–35

MULS instruction, 4–127

MULT instruction, 4–127

Multimedia instructions, 4–151

Multiply instructions
    multiply longword, 4–34
    multiply quadword, 4–35
    multiply unsigned quadward high, 4–36
    See also Floating-point operate

Multiprocessor environment
    cache coherency in, 5–6
    context switching, 5–25
    I-stream reliability, 5–24
    MB and WMB with, 5–23
    no implied barriers, 5–22
    read/write ordering, 5–10
    serialization requirements in, 4–142
    shared data, 5–6

N

NaN (Not-a-Number)
    conversion to integer, 4–88
    copying, generating, propogating, 4–89
    defined, 2–6
    quiet, 4–64
    signaling, 4–64

NATURALLY ALIGNED data objects, 1–9

Non-finite number, 4–64

Nonmemory-like behavior, 5–3

NOT instruction, ORNOT with zero, 4–42

NOT operator, 3–9

O

Opcode qualifiers
    default values, 4–3
    notation, 4–3
    See also specific qualifiers

Operand expressions, 3–4

Operand notation
    defined, 3–4

Operand values, 3–4

Operate instruction format
    unused function codes with, 3–13

Operate instructions, convert with integer overflow,
    4–78

Operators, instruction format, 3–6

OR operator, 3–9

ORNOT instruction, 4–42

Overlap
    with location access constraints, 5–13
    with processor issue constraints, 5–13
    with visibility, 5–14

OVF bit. See Arithmetic traps, overflow

OVFD bit. See Trap disable bits, overflow disable

P

Pack to bytes instructions, 4–155

PALcode
    barriers with, 5–22
    CALL_PAL instruction, 4–135
    compared to hardware instructions, 6–1
    implementation-specific, 6–2
    instead of microcode, 6–1
    instruction format, 3–14
    overview, 6–1
    recognized instructions, 6–4
    replacing, 6–3
    required, 6–2
    required instructions, 6–4
    running environment, 6–2
    special functions function support, 6–2

PALcode instructions, required privileged, 6–4

PALcode instructions, required unprivileged, 6–4

PCC_CNT, 3–3, 4–143

PCC_OFF, 3–3, 4–143

Performance tuning
    IMPLVER instruction with, 4–141

PERR (Pixel error) instruction, 4–154

Physical address space
    described, 5–1

PHYSICAL_ADDRESS operator, 3–9

Pipelined implementations, using EXCB instruction
    with, 4–138

Pixel error instruction, 4–154

PKLB (Pack longwords to bytes) instruction, 4–155

PKWB (Pack words to bytes) instruction, 4–155

Prefetch data (FETCH instruction), 4–139

PRIORITY_ENCODE operator, 3–9

Privileged Architecture Library. See PALcode

Processor communication, 5–14

Processor cycle counter (PCC) register, 3–3
    RPCC instruction with, 4–143

Processor issue constraints, 5–12

Processor issue sequence, 5–12

Program counter (PC) register, 3–1

with EXCB instruction, 4–138

Q

Quadword data type, 2–2
    alignment of, 2–3, 2–12
    atomic access of, 5–2
    integer floating-point format, 2–12
    T_floating with, 2–12

R

R31
    restrictions, 3–1

RAZ (read as zero), 1–9

RC (read and clear) instruction, 4–150

RDUNIQUE (PALcode) instruction
    required recognition of, 6–4

Read/write ordering (multiprocessor), 5–10
    determining requirements, 5–10
    hardware implications for, 5–29
    memory location defined, 5–11

Regions in physical address space, 5–1

Registers, 3–1
    floating-point, 3–2
    integer, 3–1
    lock, 3–2
    memory prefetch, 3–3
    optional, 3–3
    processor cycle counter, 3–3
    program counter (PC), 3–1
    value when unused, 3–10
    VAX compatibility, 3–3
    See also specific registers

Relational Operators, 3–9

Representative result, 4–64

RET instruction, 4–22

RIGHT_SHIFT(x,y) operator, 3–9

Rounding modes. See Floating-point rounding modes

RPCC (read processor cycle counter) instruction,
    4–143

RS (read and set) instruction, 4–150

S

S_floating data type
    alignment of, 2–8
    compared to F_floating, 2–8
    exceptions, 2–8
    format, 2–7
    mapping, 2–7
    MAX/MIN, 4–65
    NaN with T_floating convert, 4–88
    operations, 4–62

S4ADDQ instruction, 4–28

Specific Operating System PALcode Architecture (II)

This part describes how operating systems supplied by DIGITAL relate to the Alpha architecture. It is made up of the following sections:

- OpenVMS Alpha Software (II–A)
- DIGITAL UNIX Software (II–B)
- Windows NT Alpha Software (II–C)

OpenVMS Alpha Software (II-A)

This section describes how the OpenVMS Alpha operating system relates to the Alpha architecture and contains the following chapters:

- Chapter 1, Introduction to OpenVMS Alpha (II–A)
- Chapter 2, PALcode Instruction Descriptions (II–A)
- Chapter 3, Memory Management (II–A)
- Chapter 4, Process Structure (II-A)
- Chapter 5, Internal Processor Registers (II–A)
- Chapter 6, Exceptions, Interrupts, and Machine Checks (II–A)

Contents

1 Introduction to OpenVMS Alpha (II–A)

2 PALcode Instruction Descriptions (II–A)

3 Memory Management (II-A)

4 Process Structure (II-A)

5 Internal Processor Registers (II–A)

6 Exceptions, Interrupts, and Machine Checks (II–A)

Figures

Tables

Chapter 1

Introduction to OpenVMS Alpha (II–A)

The goals of this design are to provide a hardware-implementation independent interface between the OpenVMS Alpha operating system and the hardware. Further, the design provides the needed abstractions to minimize the impact between OpenVMS Alpha and different hardware implementations. Finally, the design must contain only that overhead necessary to satisfy those requirements, while still supporting high-performance systems.

1.1 Register Usage

In addition to those registers described in Part I, Common Architecture, OpenVMS Alpha defines the registers described in the following sections.

1.1.1 Processor Status

The Processor Status (PS) is a special register that contains the current status of the processor. It can be read by the CALL_PAL RD_PS instruction. The software field PS<SW> can be written by the CALL_PAL WR_PS_SW routine. See Chapter 6 for a description of the PS register.

1.1.2 Stack Pointer (SP)

Integer register R30 is the Stack Pointer (SP).

The SP contains the address of the top of the stack in the current mode.

Certain PALcode instructions, such as CALL_PAL REI, use R30 as an implicit operand. During such operations, the address value in R30, interpreted as an unsigned 64-bit integer, decreases (predecrements) when items are pushed onto the stack and increases (postincrements) when they are popped from the stack. After pushing (writing) an item to the stack, SP points to that item.

1.1.3 Internal Processor Registers (IPRs)

The IPRs provide an architected mapping to internal hardware or provide other specialized uses. They are available only to privileged software through PALcode routines and allow OpenVMS Alpha to interrogate or modify system state. The IPRs are described in Chapter 5.

1.1.4 Processor Cycle Counter (PCC)

The PCC register consists of two 32-bit fields. The low-order 32 bits (PCC<31:0>) are an unsigned, wrapping counter, PCC_CNT. The high-order 32 bits (PCC<63:32>) are an offset, PCC_OFF. PCC_OFF is a value that, when added to PCC_CNT, gives the total PCC register count for this process, modulo 2**32.

Chapter 2

PALcode Instruction Descriptions (II–A)

This chapter describes the PALcode instructions that are implemented for the OpenVMS Alpha environment. The PALcode instructions are a set of unprivileged and privileged CALL_PAL instructions that are used to match specific operating system requirements to the underlying hardware implementation.

For example, privileged PALcode instructions switch the hardware context of a process structure. Unprivileged PALcode instructions implement the uninterruptible queue operations. Also, PALcode instructions provide mechanisms for standard interrupt and exception reporting that are independent of the underlying hardware implementation.

Table 2–1 lists all the unprivileged and privileged OpenVMS Alpha PALcode instructions and the section in this chapter in which they are described.

Table 2–1: OpenVMS Alpha PALcode Instructions

Mnemonic	Operation	Section
AMOVRM	Atomic move register/memory	2.4.1
AMOVRR	Atomic move register/register	2.4.1
BPT	Breakpoint	2.1.1
BUGCHK	Bugcheck	2.1.2
CFLUSH	Cache flush	2.6.1
CHME	Change mode to executive	2.1.3
CHMK	Change mode to kernel	2.1.4
CHMS	Change mode to supervisor	2.1.5
CHMU	Change mode to user	2.1.6
CLRFEN	Clear floating-point enable	2.1.7
CSERVE	Console service	2.6.2
DRAINA	Drain aborts	Common Architecture, Chap. 6
GENTRAP	Generate software trap	2.1.8
HALT	Halt processor	Common Architecture, Chap. 6
IMB	I-stream memory barrier	Common Architecture, Chap. 6

Table 2–1: OpenVMS Alpha PALcode Instructions (Continued)

Mnemonic	Operation	Section
INSQxxx	Insert in specified queue	2.3
LDQP	Load quadword physical	2.6.3
MFPR	Move from processor register	2.6.4
MTPR	Move to processor register	2.6.5
PROBER	Probe read access	2.1.9
PROBEW	Probe write access	2.1.9
RD_PS	Read processor status	2.1.10
READ_UNQ	Read unique context	2.5.1
REI	Return from exception or interrupt	2.1.11
REMQxxx	Remove from specified queue	2.3
RSCC	Read system cycle counter	2.1.12
STQP	Store quadword physical	2.6.6
SWASTEN	Swap AST enable	2.1.13
SWPCTX	Swap privileged context	2.6.7
SWPPAL	Swap PALcode image	2.6.8
WRITE_UNQ	Write unique context	2.5.2
WR_PS_SW	Write processor status software field	2.1.14
WTINT	Wait for interrupt	2.6.9

2.1 Unprivileged General PALcode Instructions

The general unprivileged instructions in this section, together with those in Sections 2.3, 2.4, and 2.5, provide support for the underlying OpenVMS Alpha model.

Table 2–2: Unprivileged General PALcode Instruction Summary

Mnemonic	Operation
BPT	Breakpoint
BUGCHK	Bugcheck
CHME	Change mode to executive
CHMK	Change mode to kernel
CHMS	Change mode to supervisor
CHMU	Change mode to user
CLRFEN	Clear floating-point enable
GENTRAP	Generate software trap
IMB	I-stream memory barrier. See Common Architecture, Chapter 6.
PROBER	Probe read access
PROBEW	Probe write access
RD_PS	Read processor status
REI	Return from exception or interrupt
RSCC	Read system cycle counter
SWASTEN	Swap AST enable
WR_PS_SW	Write processor status software field

2.1.1 Breakpoint

Format:

CALL_PAL   BPT   ! PALcode format

Operation:

{initiate BPT exception with new_mode=kernel}

Exceptions:

Kernel Stack Not Valid Halt

Instruction mnemonics:

CALL_PAL BPT   Breakpoint

Description:

The BPT instruction is provided for program debugging. It switches to kernel mode and pushes R2..R7, the updated PC, and PS on the kernel stack. It then dispatches to the address in the Breakpoint SCB vector. See Section 6.3.3.2.1.

2.1.2 Bugcheck

Format:

> CALL_PAL   BUGCHK   ! PALcode format

Operation:

```
{initiate BUGCHK exception with new_mode=kernel}
! R16 contains a value encoding for the bugchk trap
```

Exceptions:

> Kernel Stack Not Valid Halt

Instruction mnemonics:

> CALL_PAL   BUGCHK   Bugcheck

Description:

The BUGCHK instruction is provided for error reporting. It switches to kernel mode and pushes R2..R7, the updated PC, and PS on the kernel stack. It then dispatches to the address in the Bugcheck SCB vector. See Section 6.3.3.2.2.

The value in R16 identifies the particular bugcheck type. Interpretation of the encoded value determines the course of action by the operating system.

2.1.3 Change Mode Executive

Format:

CALL_PAL   CHME   ! PALcode format

Operation:

```
tmp1 ← MINU( 1, PS<CM>)
{initiate CHME exception with new_mode=tmp1}
```

Exceptions:

Kernel Stack Not Valid Halt

Instruction mnemonics:

CALL_PAL   CHME   Change Mode to Executive

Description:

The CHME instruction lets a process change its mode in a controlled manner.

A change in mode also results in a change of stack pointers: the old pointer is saved, the new pointer is loaded. R2..R7, PC, and PS are pushed onto the selected stack. The saved PC addresses the instruction following the CHME instruction. Registers R22, R23, R24, and R27 are available for use by PALcode as scratch registers. The contents of these registers are not preserved across a CHME.

2.1.4 Change Mode to Kernel

Format:

CALL_PAL   CHMK   ! PALcode format

Operation:

{initiate CHMK exception with new_mode=kernel}

Exceptions:

Kernel Stack Not Valid Halt

Instruction mnemonics:

CALL_PAL CHMK   Change Mode to Kernel

Description:

The CHMK instruction lets a process change its mode to kernel in a controlled manner.

A change in mode also results in a change of stack pointers: the old pointer is saved, the new pointer is loaded. R2..R7, PC, and PS are pushed onto the kernel stack. The saved PC addresses the instruction following the CHMK instruction. Registers R22, R23, R24, and R27 are available for use by PALcode as scratch registers. The contents of these registers are not preserved across a CHMK.

2.1.5 Change Mode Supervisor

Format:

> CALL_PAL   CHMS   ! PALcode format

Operation:

> tmp1 ← MINU(2, PS<CM>)
> {initiate CHMS exception with new_mode=tmp1}

Exceptions:

> Kernel Stack Not Valid Halt

Instruction mnemonics:

> CALL_PAL   CHMS   Change Mode to Supervisor

Description:

The CHMS instruction lets a process change its mode in a controlled manner.

A change in mode also results in a change of stack pointers: the old pointer is saved, the new pointer is loaded. R2..R7, PC, and PS are pushed onto the selected stack. The saved PC addresses the instruction following the CHMS instruction.

2.1.6 Change Mode User

Format:

CALL_PAL   CHMU   ! PALcode format

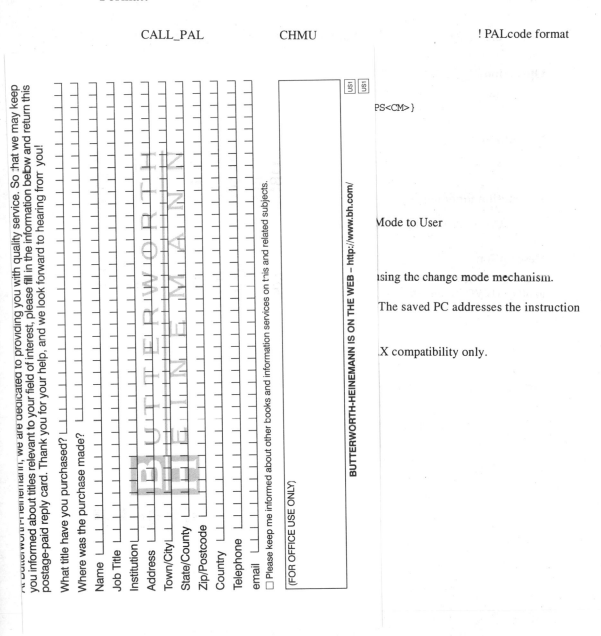

PS<CM> }

Mode to User

ısing the change mode mechanism.

The saved PC addresses the instruction

.X compatibility only.

2.1.7 Clear Floating-Point Enable

Format:

CALL_PAL   CLRFEN   ! PALcode format

Operation:

```
FEN ← 0
(HWPCB+56)<0> ← 0                    ! Update HWPCB on Write
```

Exceptions:

None

Instruction mnemonics:

CALL_PAL   CLRFEN   Clear floating-point enable

Description:

The CLRFEN instruction writes a zero to the floating-point enable register and to the HWPCB at offset (HWPCB+56)<0>.

2.1.8 Generate Software Trap

Format:

> CALL_PAL   GENTRAP   ! PALcode format

Operation:

```
{initiate GENTRAP exception with new_mode=kernel}
! R16 contains the value encoding of the software trap
```

Exceptions:

> Kernel Stack Not Valid Halt

Instruction mnemonics:

> CALL_PAL   GENTRAP   Generate Software Trap

Description:

The GENTRAP instruction is provided for reporting run-time software conditions. It switches to kernel mode and pushes R2...R7, the updated PC, and PS on the kernel stack. It then dispatches to the address in the GENTRAP SCB Vector. See Section 6.6.

The value in R16 identifies the particular software condition that has occurred. The encoding for the software trap values is given in the software calling standard for the system.

2.1.9 Probe Memory Access

Format:

```
CALL_PAL          PROBE                              ! PALcode format
```

Operation:

```
! R16 contains the base address
! R17 contains the signed offset
! R18 contains the access mode
! R0 receives the completion status
!    ← 1 if success
!    ← 0 if failure

first ← R16
last  ← {R16+R17}

IF R18<1:0> GTU PS<CM> THEN
    probe_mode ← R18<1:0>
ELSE
    probe_mode ← PS<CM>

IF ACCESS(first, probe_mode) AND ACCESS(last, probe_mode) THEN
    R0 ← 1
ELSE
    R0 ← 0
```

Exceptions:

Translation Not Valid

Instruction mnemonics:

```
CALL_PAL   PROBER          Probe for Read Access
CALL_PAL   PROBEW          Probe for Write Access
```

Description:

The PROBE instruction checks the read or write accessibility of the first and last byte specified by the base address and the signed offset; the bytes in between are not checked.

System software must check all pages between the two bytes if they are to be accessed. If both bytes are accessible, PROBE returns the value 1 in R0; otherwise, PROBE returns 0. The Fault on Read and Fault on Write PTE bits are not checked. A Translation Not Valid exception is signaled only if the mapping structures cannot be accessed. A Translation Not Valid exception is signaled only if a higher-level PTE (above Level 3) is invalid.

The protection is checked against the less privileged of the modes specified by R18<1:0> and the Current Mode (PS<CM>). See Section 6.2 for access mode encodings.

PROBE is only intended to check a single datum for accessibility. It does not check all intervening pages because this could result in excessive interrupt latency.

2.1.10 Read Processor Status

Format:

     CALL_PAL   RD_PS   ! PALcode format

Operation:

    R0 ← PS

Exceptions:

    None

Instruction mnemonics:

    CALL_PAL   RD_PS   Read Processor Status

Description:

The RD_PS instruction returns the Processor Status (PS) in register R0. The Processor Status is described in Section 6.2. The PS<SP_ALIGN> field is always a zero on a RD_PS.

2.1.11 Return from Exception or Interrupt

Format:

```
CALL_PAL              REI                              ! PALcode format
```

Operation:

```
! See Chapter 6
!  for information on interrupted registers

IF SP<5:0> NE 0 THEN
    {illegal operand }
tmp1 ← (SP)                            ! Get saved R2
tmp2 ← (3P+8)                          ! Get saved R3
tmp3 ← (SP+16)                         ! Get saved R4
tmp4 ← (SP+24)                         ! Get saved R5
tmp5 ← (SP+32)                         ! Get saved R6
tmp6 ← (SP+40)                         ! Get saved R7
tmp7 ← (SP+48)                         ! Get new PC
tmp8 ← (SP+56)                         ! Get new PS

ps_chk ← tmp8                          ! Copy new ps
ps_chk<cm> ← 0                         ! Clear cm field
ps_chk<sp_align> ← 0                   ! Clear sp_align field
ps_chk<sw> ← 0                         ! Clear Software Field
intr_flag ← 0                         ! Clear except/inter/mcheck flag
{ clear lock_flag}

! If current mode is not kernel check the new ps is valid.
IF {ps<cm> NE 0} AND
   {{tmp8<cm> LT ps<cm>} OR {ps_chk NE 0}} THEN
  BEGIN
   {illegal operand}
  END

sp ← {sp + 8*8} OR tmp8<sp_align>
IF {internal registers for stack pointers}  THEN
   CASE ps<cm>  BEGIN
    [0]: ipr_ksp ← sp
    [1]: ipr_esp ← sp
    [2]: ipr_ssp ← sp
    [3]: ipr_usp ← sp
   ENDCASE
   CASE tmp8<cm>  BEGIN
    [0]: sp ← ipr_ksp
    [1]: sp ← ipr_esp
    [2]: sp ← ipr_ssp
    [3]: sp ← ipr_usp
   ENDCASE
```

```
ELSE
   (pcbb + 8*ps<cm>) ← sp
   sp ← (pcbb + 8*tmp8<cm>)
ENDIF

R2 ← tmp1
R3 ← tmp2
R4 ← tmp3
R5 ← tmp4
R6 ← tmp5
R7 ← tmp6
PC ← tmp7
PS ← tmp8 <12:00>
```

{Initiate interrupts or AST interrupts that are now pending}

Exceptions:

Access Violation

Fault on Read

Illegal Operand

Kernel Stack Not Valid Halt

Translation Not Valid

Instruction mnemonics:

CALL_PAL   REI   Return from Exception or Interrupt

Description:

The REI instruction pops the PS, PC, and saved R2...R7 from the current stack and holds them in temporary registers. The new PS is checked for validity and consistency. If it is invalid or inconsistent, an illegal operand exception occurs; otherwise the operation continues. A kernel to nonkernel REI with a new PS<IPL> not equal to zero may yield UNDEFINED results.

The current stack pointer is then saved and a new stack pointer is selected according to the new PS<CM> field. R2 through R7 are restored using the saved values held in the temporary registers. A check is made to determine if an AST or other interrupt is pending (see Section 6.7.6).

If the enabling conditions are present for an interrupt or AST interrupt at the completion of this instruction, the interrupt or AST interrupt occurs before the next instruction.

When an REI is issued, the current stack must be writeable from the current mode or an Access Violation may occur.

Implementation Note:

This is necessary so that an implementation can choose to clear the lock_flag by doing a STx_C to above the top-of-stack after popping PS, PC, and saved R2..R7 off the current stack.

2.1.12 Read System Cycle Counter

Format:

CALL_PAL   RSCC   ! PALcode format

Operation:

```
R0 ← {System Cycle Counter}
```

Exceptions:

None

Instruction mnemonics:

CALL_PAL   RSCC   Read System Cycle Counter

Description:

The RSCC instruction writes register R0 with the value of the system cycle counter. This counter is an unsigned 64-bit integer that increments at the same rate as the process cycle counter. The cycle counter frequency, which is the number of times the system cycle counter gets incremented per second rounded to a 64-bit integer, is given in the HWRPB. (See Console Interface (III), Chapter 2).

The system cycle counter is suitable for timing a general range of intervals to within 10% error and may be used for detailed performance characterization. It is required on all implementations. SCC is required for every processor, and each processor in a multiprocessor system has its own private, independent SCC.

Notes:

- Processor initialization starts the SCC at 0.

- SCC is monotonically increasing. On the same processor, the values returned by two successive reads of SCC must either be equal or the value of the second must be greater (unsigned) than the first.

- SCC ticks are never lost so long as the SCC is accessed at least once per each PCC overflow period (2**32 PCC increments) during periods when the hardware clock interrupt remains blocked. The hardware clock interrupt is blocked whenever the IPL is at or above CLOCK_IPL or whenever the processor enters console I/O mode from program I/O mode.

- The 64-bit SCC may be constructed from the 32-bit PCC hardware counter and a 32-bit PALcode software counter. As part of the hardware clock interrupt processing, PALcode increments the software counter whenever a PCC wrap is detected. Thus, SCC ticks may be lost only when PALcode fails to detect PCC wraps. In a machine where the PCC is incremented at a 1 ns rate, this may occur when hardware clock interrupts are blocked for greater than 4 seconds.

- An implementation-dependent mechanism must exist so that, when enabled, it causes the RSCC instruction, as implemented by standard PALcode, always to return a zero in R0. This mechanism must be usable by privileged system software. A similar mechanism must exist for RPCC. Implementations are allowed to have only a single mechanism, which when enabled causes both RSCC and RPCC to return zero.

2.1.13 Swap AST Enable

Format:

CALL_PAL   SWASTEN   ! PALcode format

Operation:

```
R0 ← ZEXT(ASTEN<PS<CM>>)
ASTEN<PS<CM>> ← R16<0>

{check for pending ASTs}
```

Exceptions:

None

Instruction mnemonics:

CALL_PAL   SWASTEN   Swap AST Enable for Current Mode

Description:

The SWASTEN instruction swaps the AST enable bit for the current mode. The new state for the enable bit is supplied in register R16<0> and previous state of the enable bit is returned, zero extended, in R0.

A check is made to determine if an AST interrupt is pending (see Section 6.7.6.5).

If the enabling conditions are present for an AST interrupt at the completion of this instruction, the AST occurs before the next instruction.

2.1.14 Write Processor Status Software Field

Format:

> CALL_PAL   WR_PS_SW   ! PALcode format

Operation:

> PS<SW> ← R16<1:0>

Exceptions:

> None

Instruction mnemonics:

> CALL_PAL   WR_PS_SW   Write Processor Status Software Field

Description:

The WR_PS_SW instruction writes the Processor Status software field (PS<SW>) with the low-order two bits of R16. The Processor Status is described in Section 6.2.

2.2 Queue Data Types

The following sections describe the queue data types that are manipulated by the OpenVMS Alpha queue PALcode. Section 2.3 describes the PALcode instructions that perform the manipulation.

2.2.1 Absolute Longword Queues

A longword queue is a circular, doubly linked list. A longword queue entry is specified by its address. Each longword queue entry is linked to the next with a pair of longwords. A queue is classified by the type of link it uses. Absolute longword queues use absolute addresses as links.

The first (lowest addressed) longword is the forward link; it specifies the address of the succeeding longword queue entry. The second (highest addressed) longword is the backward link; it specifies the address of the preceding longword queue entry.

A longword queue is specified by a longword queue header, which is identical to a pair of longword queue linkage longwords. The forward link of the header is the address of the entry termed the head of the longword queue. The backward link of the header is the address of the entry termed the tail of the longword queue. The forward link of the tail points to the header.

An empty longword queue is specified by its header at address H, as shown in Figure 2–1. If an entry at address B is inserted into an empty longword queue (at either the head or tail), the longword queue shown in Figure 2–2 results. Figures 2–3, 2–4, and 2–5, respectively, illustrate the results of subsequent insertion of an entry at address A at the head, insertion of an entry at address C at the tail, and removal of the entry at address B.

The queue header and all entries in absolute longword queues need only be byte aligned. For better performance, quadword alignment (or higher) is recommended.

2.2.2 Self-Relative Longword Queues

Self-relative longword queues use displacements from longword queue entries as links. Longword queue entries are linked by a pair of longwords. The first longword (lowest addressed) is the forward link; it is a displacement of the succeeding longword queue entry from the present entry. The second longword (highest addressed) is the backward link; it is the displacement of the preceding longword queue entry from the present entry. A longword queue is specified by a longword queue header, which also consists of two longword links.

An empty longword queue is specified by its header at address H. Since the longword queue is empty, the self-relative links are zero, as shown in Figure 2–6.

Four types of operations can be performed on self-relative queues: insert at head, insert at tail, remove from head, and remove from tail. Furthermore, these operations are interlocked to allow cooperating processes in a multiprocessor system to access a shared list without additional synchronization. A hardware-supported, interlocked memory-access mechanism is used to modify the queue header. Bit <0> of the queue header is used as a secondary interlock and is set when the queue is being accessed.

If an interlocked queue CALL_PAL instruction encounters the secondary interlock set, then, in the absence of exceptions, it terminates after setting R0 to −1 to indicate failure to gain access to the queue. If the secondary interlock bit is not set, then it is set during the interlocked queue operation and is cleared upon completion of the operation. This prevents other interlocked queue CALL_PAL instructions from operating on the same queue.

If both the secondary interlock is set and an exception condition occurs, it is UNPREDICTABLE whether the exception will be reported.

The queue header and all entries in self-relative longword queues must be at least quadword aligned.

Figures 2–7, 2–8, and 2–9, respectively, illustrate the results of subsequent insertion of an entry at address B at the head, insertion of an entry at address A at the tail, and insertion of an entry at address C at the tail.

Figures 2–9, 2–8, and 2–7 (in that order) illustrate the effect of removal at the tail and removal at the head.

Figure 2–1: Empty Absolute Longword Queue

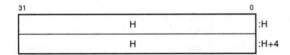

Figure 2–2: Absolute Longword Queue with One Entry

Figure 2–3: Absolute Longword Queue with Two Entries

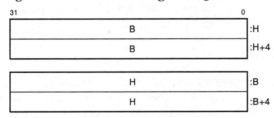

Figure 2–4: Absolute Longword Queue with Three Entries

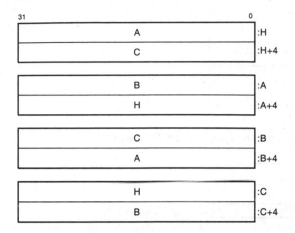

Figure 2–5: Absolute Longword Queue with Three Entries After Removing the Second Entry

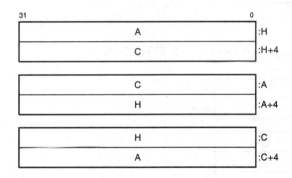

Figure 2–6: Empty Self-Relative Longword Queue

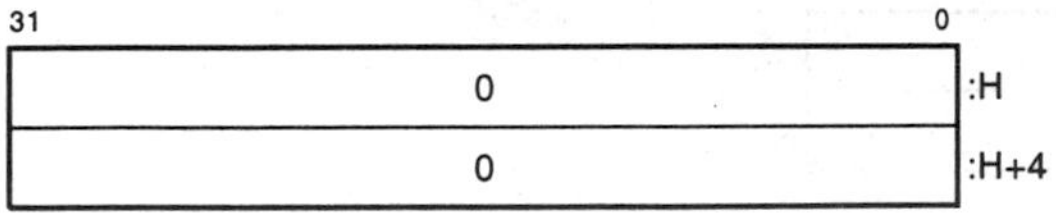

```
31                              0
┌──────────────────────┬────
│          0           │ :H
├──────────────────────┼────
│          0           │ :H+4
└──────────────────────┴────
```

Figure 2–7: Self-Relative Longword Queue with One Entry

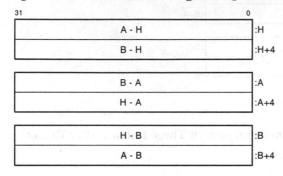

```
31                                              0
┌──────────────────────────────┐
│            B - H             │ :H
├──────────────────────────────┤
│            B - H             │ :H+4
└──────────────────────────────┘

┌──────────────────────────────┐
│            H - B             │ :B
├──────────────────────────────┤
│            H - B             │ :B+4
└──────────────────────────────┘
```

Figure 2–8: Self-Relative Longword Queue with Two Entries

```
31                                              0
┌──────────────────────────────┐
│            A - H             │ :H
├──────────────────────────────┤
│            B - H             │ :H+4
└──────────────────────────────┘

┌──────────────────────────────┐
│            B - A             │ :A
├──────────────────────────────┤
│            H - A             │ :A+4
└──────────────────────────────┘

┌──────────────────────────────┐
│            H - B             │ :B
├──────────────────────────────┤
│            A - B             │ :B+4
└──────────────────────────────┘
```

Figure 2–9: Self-Relative Longword Queue with Three Entries

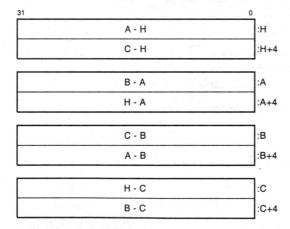

```
31                                              0
┌──────────────────────────────┐
│            A - H             │ :H
├──────────────────────────────┤
│            C - H             │ :H+4
└──────────────────────────────┘

┌──────────────────────────────┐
│            B - A             │ :A
├──────────────────────────────┤
│            H - A             │ :A+4
└──────────────────────────────┘

┌──────────────────────────────┐
│            C - B             │ :B
├──────────────────────────────┤
│            A - B             │ :B+4
└──────────────────────────────┘

┌──────────────────────────────┐
│            H - C             │ :C
├──────────────────────────────┤
│            B - C             │ :C+4
└──────────────────────────────┘
```

2.2.3 Absolute Quadword Queues

A quadword queue is a circular, doubly linked list. A quadword queue entry is specified by its address. Each quadword queue entry is linked to the next with a pair of quadwords. A queue is classified by the type of link it uses. Absolute quadword queues use absolute addresses as links.

The first (lowest addressed) quadword is the forward link; it specifies the address of the succeeding quadword queue entry. The second (highest addressed) quadword is the backward link; it specifies the address of the preceding quadword queue entry.

A quadword queue is specified by a quadword queue header, which is identical to a pair of quadword queue linkage quadwords. The forward link of the header is the address of the entry termed the head of the quadword queue. The backward link of the header is the address of the entry termed the tail of the quadword queue. The forward link of the tail points to the header.

An empty quadword queue is specified by its header at address H, as shown in Figure 2–10. If an entry at address B is inserted into an empty quadword queue (at either the head or tail), the quadword queue shown in Figure 2–11 results. Figures 2–12, 2–13, and 2–14, respectively, illustrate the results of subsequent insertion of an entry at address A at the head, insertion of an entry at address C at the tail, and removal of the entry at address B.

The queue header and all entries in absolute quadword queues must be at least octaword aligned.

2.2.4 Self-Relative Quadword Queues

Self-relative quadword queues use displacements from quadword queue entries as links. Quadword queue entries are linked by a pair of quadwords. The first quadword (lowest addressed) is the forward link; it is a displacement of the succeeding quadword queue entry from the present entry. The second quadword (highest addressed) is the backward link; it is the displacement of the preceding quadword queue entry from the present entry. A quadword queue is specified by a quadword queue header, which also consists of two quadword links.

An empty quadword queue is specified by its header at address H. Since the quadword queue is empty, the self-relative links are zero, as shown in Figure 2–15.

Four types of operations can be performed on self-relative queues: insert at head, insert at tail, remove from head, and remove from tail. Furthermore, these operations are interlocked to allow cooperating processes in a multiprocessor system to access a shared list without additional synchronization. A hardware-supported, interlocked memory-access mechanism is used to modify the queue header. Bit <0> of the queue header is used as a secondary interlock and is set when the queue is being accessed.

If an interlocked queue CALL_PAL instruction encounters the secondary interlock set, then, in the absence of exceptions, it terminates after setting R0 to –1 to indicate failure to gain access to the queue. If the secondary interlock bit is not set, it is set during the interlocked queue operation and is cleared upon completion of the operation. This prevents other interlocked queue CALL_PAL instructions from operating on the same queue.

If both the secondary interlock is set and an exception condition occurs, it is UNPREDICTABLE whether the exception will be reported.

The queue header and all entries in self-relative quadword queues must be at least octaword aligned.

Figures 2–16, 2–17, and 2–18, respectively, illustrate the results of subsequent insertion of an entry at address B at the head, insertion of an entry at address A at the tail, and insertion of an entry at address C at the tail.

Figures 2–18, 2–17, and 2–16, (in that order) illustrate the effect of removal at the tail and removal at the head.

Figure 2–10: Empty Absolute Quadword Queue

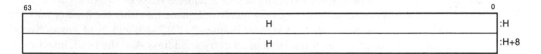

Figure 2–11: Absolute Quadword Queue with One Entry

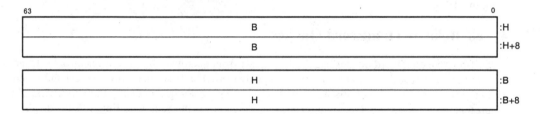

Figure 2–12: Absolute Quadword Queue with Two Entries

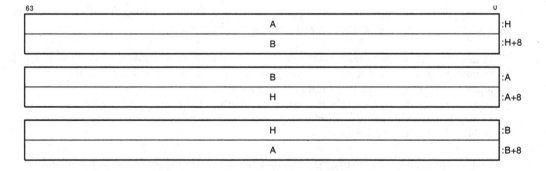

Figure 2–13: Absolute Quadword Queue with Three Entries

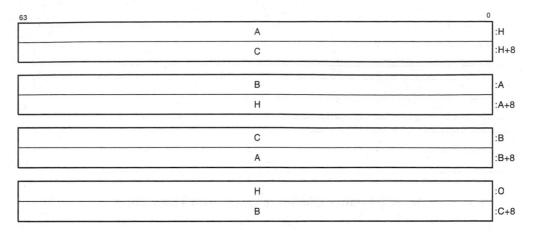

Figure 2–14: Absolute Quadword Queue with Three Entries After Removing the Second Entry

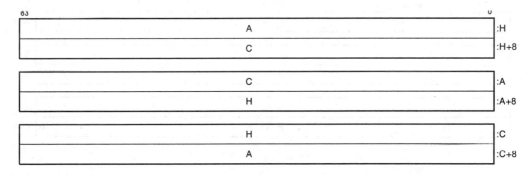

Figure 2–15: Empty Self-Relative Quadword Queue

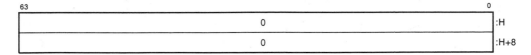

Figure 2–16: Absolute Quadword Queue with One Entry

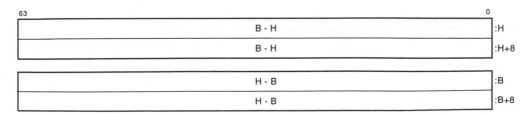

Figure 2–17: Self-Relative Quadword Queue with Two Entries

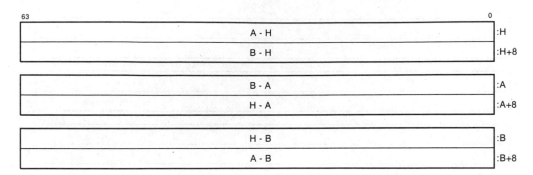

Figure 2–18: Self-Relative Quadword Queue with Three Entries

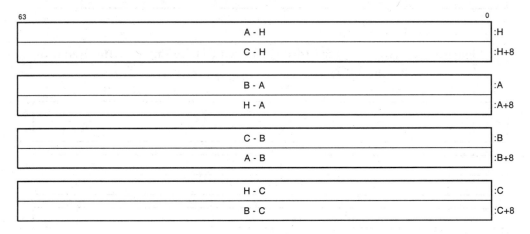

2.3 Unprivileged Queue PALcode Instructions

The following unprivileged PALcode instructions perform atomic modification of the queue data types that are described in Section 2.2.

Table 2–3: Queue PALcode Instruction Summary

Mnemonic	Operation
INSQHIL	Insert into longword queue at head, interlocked
INSQHILR	Insert into longword queue at head, interlocked, resident
INSQHIQ	Insert into quadword queue at head, interlocked
INSQHIQR	Insert into quadword queue at head, interlocked, resident
INSQTIL	Insert into longword queue at tail, interlocked
INSQTILR	Insert into longword queue at tail, interlocked, resident
INSQTIQ	Insert into quadword queue at tail, interlocked
INSQTIQR	Insert into quadword queue at tail, interlocked, resident
INSQUEL	Insert into longword queue
INSQUEQ	Insert into quadword queue
REMQHIL	Remove from longword queue at head, interlocked
REMQHILR	Remove from longword queue at head, interlocked, resident
REMQHIQ	Remove from quadword queue at head, interlocked
REMQHIQR	Remove from quadword queue at head, interlocked, resident
REMQTIL	Remove from longword queue at tail, interlocked
REMQTILR	Remove from longword queue at tail, interlocked, resident
REMQTIQ	Remove from quadword queue at tail, interlocked
REMQTIQR	Remove from quadword queue at tail, interlocked, resident
REMQUEL	Remove from longword queue
REMQUEQ	Remove from quadword queue

2.3.1 Insert Entry into Longword Queue at Head Interlocked

Format:

```
CALL_PAL              INSQHIL                        ! PALcode format
```

Operation:

```
! R16 contains the address of the queue header
! R17 contains the address of the new entry
! R0 receives status:
!    -1 if the secondary interlock was set
!     0 if the queue was not empty before adding this entry
!     1 if the queue was empty before adding this entry
!
! Must have write access to header and queue entries
! Header and entries must be quadword aligned.
! Header cannot be equal to entry.
!
! check entry and header alignment and
! that the header and entry not same location and
! that the header and entry are valid 32 bit addresses

IF {R16<2:0> NE 0} OR {R17<2:0> NE 0} OR {R16 EQ R17} OR
   {SEXT(R16<31:0>) NE R16} OR {SEXT(R17<31:0>) NE R17} THEN
   BEGIN
      {illegal operand exception}
   END


N <- {retry_amount}                    ! Implementation-specific
REPEAT
      LOAD_LOCKED (tmp0 ← (R16))        ! Acquire hardware interlock.
      IF tmp0<0> EQ 1 THEN             ! Try to set secondary interlock
         R0 ← -1, {return}            ! Already set
      done ←STORE_CONDITIONAL ((R16) ←{tmp0 OR 1} )
      N ← N - 1
UNTIL {done EQ 1} OR {N EQ 0}
IF done NEQ 1, R0 ← -1, {return}       ! Retry exceeded

MB
tmp1 ← SEXT(tmp0<31:0>)
IF {tmp1<2:1> NE 0} THEN BEGIN         ! Check alignment
   BEGIN                               ! Release secondary interlock.
      (R16) ← tmp0
      {illegal operand exception}
   END

! Check if following addresses can be written
! without causing a memory management exception:
!              entry
!              header + tmp1
```

```
IF {all memory accesses can NOT be completed} THEN
    BEGIN                                    ! Release secondary interlock.
      (R16) ← tmp0
      {initiate memory management fault}
    END


! All accesses can be done so enqueue the entry

tmp2 ← SEXT({R16 - R17}<31:0>)
(R17)<31:0> ← tmp1 + tmp2                 ! Forward link
(R17 + 4)<31:0> ← tmp2                     ! Backward link
(R16 + tmp1 + 4)<31:0> ← -tmp1 - tmp2! Successor back link


MB

(R16)<31:0> ← -tmp2                        ! Forward link of header
                                          ! Release lock
IF tmp1 EQ 0 THEN
    R0 ← 1                                 ! Queue was empty
ELSE
    R0 ← 0                                 ! Queue was not empty
END
```

Exceptions:

Access Violation

Fault on Read

Fault on Write

Illegal Operand

Translation Not Valid

Instruction mnemonics:

CALL_PAL   INSQHIL   Insert into Longword Queue at Head Interlocked

Description:

If the secondary interlock is clear, INSQHIL inserts the entry specified in R17 into the self-relative queue following the header specified in R16.

If the entry inserted was the first one in the queue, R0 is set to 1; otherwise it is set to 0. The insertion is a non-interruptible operation. The insertion is interlocked to prevent concurrent interlocked insertions or removals at the head or tail of the same queue by another process, in a multiprocessor environment. Before the insertion, the processor validates that the entire operation can be completed. This ensures that if a memory management exception occurs, the queue is left in a consistent state (see Chapters 3 and 6). If the instruction fails to acquire the secondary interlock after "N" retry attempts, then (in the absence of exceptions) R0 is set to −1. The value "N" is implementation dependent.

2.3.2 Insert Entry into Longword Queue at Head Interlocked Resident

Format:

CALL_PAL   INSQHILR   ! PALcode format

Operation:

```
! R16 contains the address of the queue header
! R17 contains the address of the new entry
! R0 receives status:
!     -1 if the secondary interlock was set
!      0 if the queue was not empty before adding this entry
!      1 if the queue was empty before adding this entry
!
! Must have write access to header and queue entries
! Header and entries must be quadword aligned.
! Header cannot be equal to entry.
! All parts of the Queue must be memory resident

N <- {retry_amount}                  ! Implementation-specific
REPEAT
    LOAD_LOCKED (tmp0 ← (R16))       ! Acquire hardware interlock.
    IF tmp0<0> EQ 1 THEN             ! Try to set secondary interlock.
        R0 ← -1, {return}           ! Already set
    done ←STORE_CONDITIONAL ((R16) ←{tmp0 OR 1} )
    N ← N - 1
UNTIL {done EQ 1} OR {N EQ 0}
IF done NEQ 1, R0 ← -1, {return}     ! Retry exceeded

MB

tmp1 ← SEXT(tmp0<31:0>)
tmp2 ← SEXT({R16 - R17}<31:0>)       ! Enqueue the entry
(R17)<31:0> ←tmp1 + tmp2             ! Forward link of entry.
(R17 + 4)<31:0> ←tmp2                ! Backward link of entry.
(R16 + tmp1 + 4)<31:0> ← -tmp1 - tmp2  ! Successor back link

MB
(R16)<31:0> ← -tmp2                  ! Forward link of header
                                     ! Release the lock
IF tmp1 EQ 0 THEN
    R0 ←1                            ! Queue was empty
ELSE
    R0 ← 0                           ! Queue was not empty
END
```

Exceptions:

Illegal Operand

Instruction mnemonics:

CALL_PAL   INSQHILR   Insert Entry into Longword Queue at Head
                           Interlocked Resident

Description:

If the secondary interlock is clear, INSQHILR inserts the entry specified in R17 into the self-relative queue following the header specified in R16.

If the entry inserted was the first one in the queue, R0 is set to 1; otherwise, it is set to 0. The insertion is a non-interruptible operation. The insertion is interlocked to prevent concurrent interlocked insertions or removals at the head or tail of the same queue by another process, in a multiprocessor environment. If the instruction fails to acquire the secondary interlock after "N" retry attempts, then (in the absence of exceptions) R0 is set to −1. The value "N" is implementation dependent.

This instruction requires that the queue be memory resident and that the queue header and elements are quadword aligned. No alignment or memory management checks are made before starting queue modifications to verify these requirements. Therefore, if any of these requirements are not met, the queue may be left in an UNPREDICTABLE state and an illegal operand fault may be reported.

2.3.3 Insert Entry into Quadword Queue at Head Interlocked

Format:

```
CALL_PAL            INSQHIQ                    ! PALcode format
```

Operation:

```
! R16 contains the address of the queue header
! R17 contains the address of the new entry
! R0 receives status:
!       -1 if the secondary interlock was set
!        0 if the entry was not empty before adding this entry
!        1 if the entry was empty before adding this entry
!
! Must have write access to header and queue entries
! Header and entries must be octaword aligned.
! Header cannot be equal to entry.
!
! check entry and header alignment and
! that the header and entry not same location
IF {R16<3:0> NE 0} OR {R17<3:0> NE 0} OR {R16 EQ R17} THEN
   BEGIN
     {illegal operand exception}
   END


N <- {retry_amount}                    ! Implementation-specific
REPEAT
    LOAD_LOCKED (tmp1 ← (R16))         ! Acquire hardware interlock.
    IF tmp1<0> EQ 1 THEN               ! Try to set secondary interlock.
       R0 ← -1, {return}               ! Already set
    done ←STORE_CONDITIONAL ((R16) ←{tmp1 OR 1} )
    N ← N - 1
UNTIL {done EQ 1} OR {N EQ 0}
IF done NEQ 1, R0 ← -1, {return}       ! Retry exceeded

MB

IF {tmp1<3:1> NE 0} THEN BEGIN          ! Check Alignment
   BEGIN                                ! Release secondary interlock
     (R16) ← tmp1
     {illegal operand exception}
   END

! Check if following addresses can be written
!  without causing a memory management exception:
!             entry
!             header + tmp1
```

```
        IF {all memory accesses can NOT be completed} THEN
           BEGIN                                    ! Release secondary interlock
            (R16) ← tmp1
            {initiate memory management fault}
           END

        ! All accesses can be done so enqueue the entry
        tmp2 ← R16 - R17
        (R17) ← tmp1 + tmp2                         ! Forward link
        (R17 + 8) ← tmp1                            ! Backward link
        (R16 + tmp1 + 8) ← -tmp1 - tmp2             ! Successor back link

        MB

        (R16) ← -tmp2                               ! Forward link of header
                                                    ! Release the lock.
        IF tmp1 EQ 0 THEN
           R0 ← 1                                   ! Queue was empty
        ELSE
           R0 ← 0                                   ! Queue was not empty
        END
```

Exceptions:

> Access Violation
> Fault on Read
> Fault on Write
> Illegal Operand
> Translation Not Valid

Instruction mnemonics:

CALL_PAL	INSQHIQ	Insert into Quadword Queue at Head Interlocked

Description:

If the secondary interlock is clear, INSQHIQ inserts the entry specified in R17 into the self-relative queue following the header specified in R16.

If the entry inserted was the first one in the queue, R0 is set to 1; otherwise, it is set to 0. The insertion is a non-interruptible operation. The insertion is interlocked to prevent concurrent interlocked insertions or removals at the head or tail of the same queue by another process, in a multiprocessor environment. Before the insertion, the processor validates that the entire operation can be completed. This ensures that if a memory management exception occurs, the queue is left in a consistent state (see Chapters 3 and 6). If the instruction fails to acquire the secondary interlock after "N" retry attempts, then (in the absence of exceptions) R0 is set to −1. The value "N" is implementation dependent.

2.3.4 Insert Entry into Quadword Queue at Head Interlocked Resident

Format:

      CALL_PAL   INSQHIQR   ! PALcode format

Operation:

```
! R16 contains the address of the queue header
! R17 contains the address of the new entry
! R0 receives status:
!       -1 if the secondary interlock was set
!        0 if the entry was not empty before adding this entry
!        1 if the entry was empty before adding this entry
!
! Must have write access to header and queue entries
! Header and entries must be octaword aligned.
! Header cannot be equal to entry.
! All parts of the Queue must be memory resident

N <- {retry_amount}                   ! Implementation-specific
REPEAT
   LOAD_LOCKED (tmp1 ← (R16))          ! Acquire hardware interlock.
   IF tmp1<0> EQ 1 THEN                ! Try to set secondary interlock.
       R0 ← -1, {return}              ! Already set
   done ←STORE_CONDITIONAL ((R16) ←{tmp1 OR 1} )
   N ← N - 1
UNTIL {done EQ 1} OR {N EQ 0}
IF done NEQ 1, R0 ← -1, {return}       ! Retry exceeded

MB

tmp2 ← R16 - R17                       ! Enqueue the entry
(R17) ← tmp1 + tmp2                    ! Forward link of entry.
(R17 + 8) ← tmp2                       ! Backward link of entry.
(R16 + tmp1 + 8) ← -tmp1 - tmp2        ! Successor back link

MB
(R16) ← -tmp2                          ! Forward link of header,
                                       ! Release the lock
IF tmp1 EQ 0 THEN
    R0 ← 1                             ! Queue was empty
ELSE
    R0 ← 0                             ! Queue was not empty
END
```

Exceptions:

Illegal Operand

Instruction mnemonics:

CALL_PAL   INSQHIQR   Insert Entry into Quadword Queue at Head
                             Interlocked Resident

Description:

If the secondary interlock is clear, INSQHIQR inserts the entry specified in R17 into the self-relative queue following the header specified in R16.

If the entry inserted was the first one in the queue, R0 is set to 1; otherwise, it is set to 0. The insertion is a non interruptible operation. The insertion is interlocked to prevent concurrent interlocked insertions or removals at the head or tail of the same queue by another process, in a multiprocessor environment. If the instruction fails to acquire the secondary interlock after "N" retry attempts, then (in the absence of exceptions) R0 is set to −1. The value "N" is implementation dependent.

This instruction requires that the queue be memory resident and that the queue header and elements are octaword aligned. No alignment or memory management checks are made before starting queue modifications to verify these requirements. Therefore, if any of these requirements are not met, the queue may be left in an UNPREDICTABLE state and an illegal operand fault may be reported.

2.3.5 Insert Entry into Longword Queue at Tail Interlocked

Format:

CALL_PAL INSQTIL ! PALcode format

Operation:

```
! R16 contains the address of the queue header
! R17 contains the address of the new entry
! R0 receives status:
!    -1 if the secondary interlock was set
!     0 if the entry was not empty before adding this entry
!     1 if the entry was empty before adding this entry
!
! Must have write access to header and queue entries
! Header and entries must be quadword aligned.
! Header cannot be equal to entry.
!
! check entry and header alignment and
! that the header and entry not same location and
! that the header and entry are valid 32 bit addresses
IF {R16<2:0> NE 0} OR {R17<2:0> NE 0} OR {R16 EQ R17} OR
    {SEXT(R16<31:0>) NE R16} OR {SEXT(R17<31:0>) NE R16} THEN
    BEGIN
      {illegal operand exception}
    END
N <- {retry_amount}                    ! Implementation-specific
REPEAT
    LOAD_LOCKED (tmp0 ← (R16))         ! Acquire hardware interlock.
    IF tmp0<0> EQ 1 THEN               ! Try to set secondary interlock.
        R0 ← -1, {return}             ! Already set
    done ←STORE_CONDITIONAL ((R16) ←{tmp0 OR 1} )
    N ← N - 1
UNTIL {done EQ 1} OR {N EQ 0}
IF done NEQ 1, R0 ← -1, {return}      ! Retry exceeded

MB

tmp1 ← SEXT(tmp0<31:0>)
tmp2 ← SEXT(tmp0<63:32>)

IF {tmp1<2:1> NE 0} OR {tmp2<2:0> NE 0} THEN   ! Check Alignment
    BEGIN                              ! Release secondary interlock
      (R16) ← tmp0
      {illegal operand exception}
    END

! Check if following addresses can be written
!  without causing a memory management exception:
!          entry
!          header + (header + 4)
```

```
IF {all memory accesses can NOT be completed} THEN
    BEGIN                               ! Release secondary interlock
     (R16) ← tmp0
     {initiate memory management fault}
    END


! All Accesses can be done so enqueue entry
tmp3 ← SEXT( {R16 - R17}<31:0>)
(R17)<31:0> ← tmp3                      ! Forward link
(R17 + 4)<31:0> ← tmp2 + tmp3           ! Backward link
IF {tmp2 NE 0} THEN                     ! Forward link of predecessor
    (R16+tmp2)<31:0> ← -tmp3 - tmp2
ELSE
    tmp1 ← SEXT({-tmp3 - tmp2}<31:0>)
    (R16+4)<31:0> ← -tmp3               ! Backward link of header
MB
(R16)<31:0> ← tmp1                      ! Forward link, release lock
IF tmp1 EQ -tmp3 THEN
    R0 ← 1                              ! Queue was empty
ELSE
    R0 ← 0                              ! Queue was not empty
END
```

Exceptions:

Access Violation

Fault on Read

Fault on Write

Illegal Operand

Translation Not Valid

Instruction mnemonics:

CALL_PAL   INSQTIL   Insert into Longword Queue at Tail Interlocked

Description:

If the secondary interlock is clear, INSQTIL inserts the entry specified in R17 into the self-relative queue preceding the header specified in R16.

If the entry inserted was the first one in the queue, R0 is set to 1; otherwise, it is set to 0. The insertion is a non-interruptible operation. The insertion is interlocked to prevent concurrent interlocked insertions or removals at the head or tail of the same queue by another process, in a multiprocessor environment. Before performing any part of the operation, the processor validates that the insertion can be completed. This ensures that if a memory management exception occurs, the queue is left in a consistent state (see Chapters 3 and 6). If the instruction fails to acquire the secondary interlock after "N" retry attempts, then (in the absence of exceptions) R0 is set to -1. The value "N" is implementation dependent.

2.3.6 Insert Entry into Longword Queue at Tail Interlocked Resident

Format:

```
CALL_PAL              INSQTILR                    ! PALcode format
```

Operation:

```
! R16 contains the address of the queue header
! R17 contains the address of the new entry
! R0 receives status:
!    -1 if the secondary interlock was set
!     0 if the entry was not empty before adding this entry
!     1 if the entry was empty before adding this entry
!
! Must have write access to header and queue entries
! Header and entries must be quadword aligned.
! Header cannot be equal to entry.
! All parts of the Queue must be memory resident

N <- {retry_amount}                   ! Implementation-specific
REPEAT
    LOAD_LOCKED (tmp0 ← (R16))         ! Acquire hardware interlock.
    IF tmp0<0> EQ 1 THEN               ! Try to set secondary interlock.
        R0 ← -1, {return}             ! Already set
    done ←STORE_CONDITIONAL ((R16) ←{tmp0 OR 1} )
    N ← N - 1
UNTIL {done EQ 1} OR {N EQ 0}
IF done NEQ 1, R0 ← -1, {return}      ! Retry exceeded


MB

tmp1 ← SEXT(tmp0<31:0>)
tmp2 ← SEXT(tmp0<63:32>)
tmp3 ← SEXT( {R16 - R17}<31:0>)
(R17)<31:0> ← tmp3                     ! Forward link
(R17 + 4)<31:0> ← tmp2 + tmp3          ! Backward link
IF {tmp2 NE 0} THEN                    ! Forward link of predecessor
    (R16+tmp2)<31:0> ← -tmp3 - tmp2
ELSE
    tmp1 ← <- SEXT({-tmp3 - tmp2}<31:0>)

(R16+4)<31:0> ← -tmp3                  ! Backward link of header

MB

(R16)<31:0> ← tmp1                     ! Forward link
                                       ! Release the lock
```

```
IF tmp1 EQ -tmp3 THEN
   R0 ← 1                                     ! Queue was empty
ELSE
   R0 ← 0                                     ! Queue was not empty
END
```

Exceptions:

Illegal Operand

Instruction mnemonics:

CALL_PAL   INSQTILR   Insert Entry into Longword Queue at Tail
                             Interlocked Resident

Description:

If the secondary interlock is clear, INSQTILR inserts the entry specified in R17 into the
self-relative queue preceding the header specified in R16.

If the entry inserted was the first one in the queue, R0 is set to 1; otherwise, it is set to 0. The
insertion is a non-interruptible operation. The insertion is interlocked to prevent concurrent
interlocked insertions or removals at the head or tail of the same queue by another process, in
a multiprocessor environment. If the instruction fails to acquire the secondary interlock after
"N" retry attempts, then (in the absence of exceptions) R0 is set to –1. The value "N" is implementation dependent.

This instruction requires that the queue be memory resident and that the queue header and elements are quadword aligned. No alignment or memory management checks are made before
starting queue modifications to verify these requirements. Therefore, if any of these requirements are not met, the queue may be left in an UNPREDICTABLE state and an illegal
operand fault may be reported.

2.3.7 Insert Entry into Quadword Queue at Tail Interlocked

Format:

    CALL_PAL   INSQTIQ   ! PALcode format

Operation:

```
! R16 contains the address of the queue header
! R17 contains the address of the new entry
! R0 receives status:
!     -1 if the secondary interlock was set
!      0 if the entry was not empty before adding this entry
!      1 if the entry was empty before adding this entry
!
! Must have write access to header and queue entries
! Header and entries must be octaword aligned.
! Header cannot be equal to entry.
!
! check entry and header alignment and
! that the header and entry not same location
IF {R16<3:0> NE 0} OR {R17<3:0> NE 0} OR {R16 EQ R17} THEN
   BEGIN
     {illegal operand exception}
   END

N <- {retry_amount}                    ! Implementation-specific
REPEAT
     LOAD_LOCKED (tmp1 <- (R16))        ! Acquire hardware interlock.
     IF tmp1<0> EQ 1 THEN              ! Try to set secondary interlock.
        R0 <- -1, {return}             ! Already set
     done <-STORE_CONDITIONAL ((R16) <-{tmp1 OR 1} )
     N <- N - 1
UNTIL {done EQ 1} OR {N EQ 0}
IF done NEQ 1, R0 <- -1, {return}      ! Retry exceeded

MB

tmp2 <- (R16+8)
IF {tmp1<3:1> NE 0} OR {tmp2<3:0> NE 0} THEN  ! Check Alignment.
   BEGIN                                ! Release secondary interlock.
     (R16) <- tmp1
     {illegal operand exception}
   END

! Check if following addresses can be written
!  without causing a memory management exception:
. !          entry
  !          header + (header + 8)
```

```
IF {all memory accesses can NOT be completed} THEN
    BEGIN                                      ! Release secondary interlock.
     (R16) ← tmp1
     {initiate memory management fault}
    END

! All accesses can be done so enqueue the entry
tmp3 ← R16 - R17
(R17) ← tmp3                              ! Forward link
(R17 + 8) ← tmp2 + tmp3                   ! Backward link
IF {tmp2 NE 0} THEN                       ! Forward link of predecessor
    (R16+tmp2) ← -tmp3 - tmp2
ELSE
    tmp1 ← {-tmp3 - tmp2}
(R16+8) ← -tmp3                           ! Backward link of header

MB

(R16) ← tmp1                              ! Forward link
                                          ! Release the lock
IF tmp1 EQ -tmp3  THEN
  R0 ← 1                                  ! Queue was empty
ELSE
  R0 ← 0                                  ! Queue was not empty
END
```

Exceptions:

Access Violation
Fault on Read
Fault on Write
Illegal Operand
Translation Not Valid

Instruction mnemonics:

CALL_PAL INSQTIQ   Insert into Quadword Queue at Tail Interlocked

Description:

If the secondary interlock is clear, INSQTIQ inserts the entry specified in R17 into the self-relative queue preceding the header specified in R16.

If the entry inserted was the first one in the queue, R0 is set to 1; otherwise, it is set to 0. The insertion is a non-interruptible operation. The insertion is interlocked to prevent concurrent interlocked insertions or removals at the head or tail of the same queue by another process, in a multiprocessor environment. Before performing any part of the operation, the processor validates that the insertion can be completed. This ensures that if a memory management exception occurs, the queue is left in a consistent state (see Chapters 3 and 6). If the instruction fails to acquire the secondary interlock after "N" retry attempts, then (in the absence of exceptions) R0 is set to –1. The value "N" is implementation dependent.

2.3.8 Insert Entry into Quadword Queue at Tail Interlocked Resident

Format:

```
CALL_PAL              INSQTIQR                          ! PALcode format
```

Operation:

```
! R16 contains the address of the queue header
! R17 contains the address of the new entry
! R0 receives status:
!     -1 if the secondary interlock was set
!      0 if the entry was not empty before adding this entry
!      1 if the entry was empty before adding this entry
!
! Must have write access to header and queue entries
! Header and entries must be octaword aligned.
! Header cannot be equal to entry.
! All parts of the Queue must be memory resident


N <- {retry_amount}                     ! Implementation-specific
REPEAT
   LOAD_LOCKED (tmp1 ← (R16))            ! Acquire hardware interlock.
   IF tmp1<0> EQ 1 THEN                  ! Try to set secondary interlock.
      R0 ← -1, {return}                  ! Already set
   done ←STORE_CONDITIONAL ((R16) ←{tmp1 OR 1} )
   N ← N - 1
UNTIL {done EQ 1} OR {N EQ 0}
IF done NEQ 1, R0 ← -1, {return}        ! Retry exceeded

MB

tmp2 ← (R16+8)
tmp3 ← R16 - R17
(R17) ← tmp3                            ! Forward link
(R17 + 8) ← tmp2 + tmp3                 ! Backward link
IF {tmp2 NE 0} THEN                     ! Forward link of predecessor
     (R16+tmp2) ← -tmp3 - tmp2
ELSE
     tmp1 ← {-tmp3 - tmp2}
(R16+8) ← -tmp3                         ! Backward link of header

MB

(R16) ← tmp1                            ! Forward link and release the lock
IF tmp1 EQ -tmp3 THEN
   R0 ← 1                               ! Queue was empty
ELSE
   R0 ← 0                               ! Queue was not empty
END
```

Exceptions:

Illegal Operand

Instruction mnemonics:

CALL_PAL   INSQTIQR   Insert Entry into Quadword Queue at Tail
                          Interlocked Resident

Description:

If the secondary interlock is clear, INSQTIQR inserts the entry specified in R17 into the self-relative queue preceding the header specified in R16.

If the entry inserted was the first one in the queue, R0 is set to 1; otherwise, it is set to 0. The insertion is a non-interruptible operation. The insertion is interlocked to prevent concurrent interlocked insertions or removals at the head or tail of the same queue by another process, in a multiprocessor environment. If the instruction fails to acquire the secondary interlock after "N" retry attempts, then (in the absence of exceptions) R0 is set to −1. The value "N" is implementation dependent.

This instruction requires that the queue be memory resident and that the queue header and elements are octaword aligned. No alignment or memory management checks are made before starting queue modifications to verify these requirements. Therefore, if any of these requirements are not met, the queue may be left in an UNPREDICTABLE state and an illegal operand fault may be reported.

2.3.9 Insert Entry into Longword Queue

Format:

```
CALL_PAL            INSQUEL                      ! PALcode format
```

Operation:

```
! R16 contains the address of the predecessor entry
!     or the 32 bit address of the 32 bit address of the
!     predecessor entry for INSQUEL/D
! R17 contains the address of the new entry
! R0 receives status:
!        0 if the queue was not empty before adding this entry
!        1 if the queue was empty before adding this entry
!
! Header and entries need only be byte aligned
! Must have write access to header and queue entries
IF opcode EQ INSQUEL/D THEN
      tmp2 ← SEXT((R16)<31:0>)        ! Address of predecessor
ELSE
      tmp2 ← R16

IF {all memory accesses can be completed} THEN
   BEGIN
     tmp1<31:0> ← SEXT((tmp2)<31:0>) ! Get Forward Link
     (R17)<31:0> ← tmp1              ! Set forward link
     (R17 + 4)<31:0> ← tmp2          ! Backward link
     (SEXT((tmp2)<31:0>) + 4)<31:0> ← R17
                                     ! Backward link of Successor
     (tmp2)<31:0> ← R17              ! Forward link of Predecessor
     IF tmp1 EQ tmp2 THEN
        R0 ← 1
     ELSE
        R0 ← 0
     END
ELSE
   BEGIN
    {initiate fault}
   END
END
```

Exceptions:

Access Violation

Fault on Read

Fault on Write

Translation Not Valid

Instruction mnemonics:

CALL_PAL	INSQUEL	Insert Entry into Longword Queue
CALL_PAL	INSQUEL/D	Insert Entry into Longword Queue Deferred

Description:

INSQUEL inserts the entry specified in R17 into the absolute queue following the entry specified by the predecessor addressed by R16. INSQUEL/D performs the same operation on the entry specified by the contents of the longword addressed by R16. The queue header and entry need only be byte aligned.

In either case, if the entry inserted was the first one in the queue, a 1 is returned in R0; otherwise, a 0 is returned in R0. The insertion is a non-interruptible operation. Before performing any part of the insertion, the processor validates that the entire operation can be completed. This ensures that if a memory management exception occurs, the queue is left in a consistent state (see Chapters 3 and 6).

2.3.10 Insert Entry into Quadword Queue

Format:

CALL_PAL   INSQUEQ   ! PALcode format

Operation:

```
! R16 contains the address of the predecessor entry
!     or the address of the address of the
!     predecessor entry for INSQUEQ/D
! R17 contains the address of the new entry
! R0 receives status:
!        0 if the queue was not empty before adding this entry
!        1 if the queue was empty before adding this entry
!
! Must have write access to header and queue entries
! Header and entries must be octaword aligned

IF opcode EQ INSQUEQ/D THEN
   IF {R16<3:0> NE 0} THEN
     BEGIN
       {illegal operand exception}
     END
   tmp2 ← (R16)                       ! Address of predecessor
ELSE
   tmp2 ← R16
END
IF {tmp2<3:0> NE 0} OR {R17<3:0> NE 0} THEN
   BEGIN
     {illegal operand exception}
   END
IF {all memory accesses can be completed} THEN
   BEGIN
     tmp1 ← (tmp2)                     ! Get forward link of entry
     IF {tmp1<3:0> NE 0} THEN
       BEGIN                           ! Check alignment
         {illegal operand exception}
       END
     (R17) ← tmp1                      ! Set forward link of entry
     (R17 + 8) ← tmp2                  ! Backward link of entry
     (tmp1 + 8) ← R17                  ! Backward link of successor
     (tmp2) ← R17                      ! Forward link of predecessor
     IF tmp1 EQ tmp2 THEN
       R0 ← 1
     ELSE
       R0 ← 0
   END
```

```
ELSE
  BEGIN
   {initiate fault}
  END
END
```

Exceptions:

Access Violation

Fault on Read

Fault on Write

Translation Not Valid

Illegal Operand

Instruction mnemonics:

CALL_PAL	INSQUEQ	Insert Entry into Quadword Queue
CALL_PAL	INSQUEQ/D	Insert Entry into Quadword Queue Deferred

Description:

INSQUEQ inserts the entry specified in R17 into the absolute queue following the entry speci-fied by the predecessor addressed by R16. INSQUEQ/D performs the same operation on the entry specified by the contents of the quadword addressed by R16.

In either case, if the entry inserted was the first one in the queue, a 1 is returned in R0; other-wise, a 0 is returned in R0. The insertion is a non-interruptible operation. Before performing any part of the insertion, the processor validates that the entire operation can be completed. This ensures that if a memory management exception occurs, the queue is left in a consistent state (see Chapters 3 and 6). R0 is UNPREDICTABLE if an exception occurs. The relative order of reporting memory management and illegal operand exceptions is UNPREDICTABLE.

2.3.11 Remove Entry from Longword Queue at Head Interlocked

Format:

CALL_PAL   REMQHIL   ! PALcode format

Operation:

```
! R16 contains the address of the queue header
! R0 receives status:
!        -1 if the secondary interlock was set
!         0 if the queue was empty
!         1 if entry removed and queue still not empty
!         2 if entry removed and queue empty
! R1 receives the address of the removed entry
!
! Must have write access to header and queue entries
! Header and entries must be quadword aligned.
!
! Check header alignment and
! that the header is a valid 32 bit address
IF {R16<2:0> NE 0} OR {SEXT(R16<31:0>) NE R16} THEN
   BEGIN
     {illegal operand exception}
   END

N <- {retry_amount}                   ! Implementation-specific
REPEAT
   LOAD_LOCKED (tmp0 ← (R16))          ! Acquire hardware interlock.
   IF tmp0<0> EQ 1 THEN               ! Try to set secondary interlock.
      R0 ← -1, {return}               ! Already set
   done ←STORE_CONDITIONAL ((R16) ←{tmp0 OR 1} )
   N ← N - 1
UNTIL {done EQ 1} OR {N EQ 0}
IF done NEQ 1, R0 ← -1, {return}       ! Retry exceeded

MB

tmp1 ← SEXT(tmp0<31:0>)
IF tmp1<2:0> NE 0 THEN                 ! Check Alignment
   BEGIN                               ! Release secondary interlock
     (R16) ← tmp0
     {illegal operand exception}
   END
```

```
! Check if the following can be done without
! causing a memory management exception:
!  read contents of header + tmp1 {if tmp1 NE 0}
!  write into header + tmp1 + (header + tmp1) {if tmp1 NE 0}
IF {all memory accesses can NOT be completed} THEN
  BEGIN                                    ! Release secondary interlock
    (R16) ← tmp0
    {initiate memory management fault}
  END


tmp2 ← SEXT({R16 + tmp1}<31:0>)
IF {tmp1 EQL 0} THEN
  tmp3 ← R16
ELSE
  tmp3 ← SEXT({tmp2 + SEXT((tmp2)<31:0>)})


IF tmp3<2:0> NE 0 THEN                     ! Check Alignment
  BEGIN                                    ! Release secondary interlock
    (R16) ← tmp0
    {illegal operand exception}
  END


(tmp3 + 4)<31:0> ← R16 - tmp3             ! Backward link of successor

MB

(R16)<31:0> ← tmp3 - R16                  ! Forward link of header
                                          ! Release lock
IF tmp1 EQ 0 THEN
  R0 ← 0                                  ! Queue was empty
ELSE
  BEGIN
    IF {tmp3 - R16} EQ 0 THEN
      R0 ← 2                              ! Queue now empty
    ELSE
      R0 ← 1                              ! Queue not empty
  END
END
R1 ← tmp2                                 ! Address of removed entry
```

Exceptions:

Access Violation
Fault on Read
Fault on Write
Illegal Operand
Translation Not Valid

Instruction mnemonics:

CALL_PAL   REMQHIL   Remove from Longword Queue at Head
                                 Interlocked

Description:

If the secondary interlock is clear, REMQHIL removes from the self-relative queue the entry following the header, pointed to by R16, and the address of the removed entry is returned in R1.

If the queue was empty prior to this instruction and secondary interlock succeeded, a 0 is returned in R0. If the interlock succeeded and the queue was not empty at the start of the removal and the queue is empty after the removal, a 2 is returned in R0. If the instruction fails to acquire the secondary interlock after "N" retry attempts, then (in the absence of exceptions) R0 is set to −1. The value "N" is implementation dependent.

The removal is interlocked to prevent concurrent interlocked insertions or removals at the head or tail of the same queue by another process, in a multiprocessor environment. The removal is a non-interruptible operation. Before performing any part of the removal, the processor validates that the entire operation can be completed. This ensures that if a memory management exception occurs, the queue is left in a consistent state (see Chapters 3 and 6).

2.3.12 Remove Entry from Longword Queue at Head Interlocked Resident

Format:

        CALL_PAL   REMQHILR   ! PALcode format

Operation:

```
! R16 contains the address of the queue header
! R0 receives status:
!         -1 if the secondary interlock was set
!          0 if the queue was empty
!          1 if entry removed and queue still not empty
!          2 if entry removed and queue empty
! R1 receives the address of the removed entry
!
! Must have write access to header and queue entries
! Header and entries must be quadword aligned.
! All parts of the Queue must be memory resident

N <- {retry_amount}                   ! Implementation-specific
REPEAT
   LOAD_LOCKED (tmp0 ← (R16))          ! Acquire hardware interlock.
   IF tmp0<0> EQ 1 THEN                ! Try to set secondary interlock.
      R0 ← -1, {return}                ! Already set
   done ←STORE_CONDITIONAL ((R16) ←{tmp0 OR 1} )
   N ← N - 1
UNTIL {done EQ 1} OR {N EQ 0}
IF done NEQ 1, R0 ← -1, {return}       ! Retry exceeded

MB

tmp1 ← SEXT(tmp0<31:0>)
tmp2 ← SEXT({R16 + tmp1}<31:0>)
IF {tmp1 EQL 0} THEN
   tmp3 ← R16
ELSE
   tmp3 ← SEXT({tmp2 + SEXT((tmp2)<31:0>)})
END

(tmp3 + 4)<31:0> ← R16 - tmp3         ! Backward link of successor

MB
(R16)<31:0> ← tmp3 - R16              ! Forward link of header
                                      ! Release lock
IF tmp1 EQ 0 THEN
  R0 ← 0                              ! Queue was empty
```

```
    ELSE
       BEGIN
       IF {tmp3 - R16} EQ 0 THEN
          R0 ← 2                           ! Queue now empty
       ELSE
          R0 ← 1                           ! Queue not empty
       END
    END
    R1 ← tmp2                              ! Address of removed entry
```

Exceptions:

Illegal Operand

Instruction mnemonics:

CALL_PAL   REMQHILR   Remove Entry from Longword Queue at Head
                           Interlocked Resident

Description:

If the secondary interlock is clear, REMQHILR removes from the self-relative queue the entry following the header, pointed to by R16, and the address of the removed entry is returned in R1.

If the queue was empty prior to this instruction and secondary interlock succeeded, a 0 is returned in R0. If the interlock succeeded and the queue was not empty at the start of the removal and the queue is empty after the removal, a 2 is returned in R0. If the instruction fails to acquire the secondary interlock after "N" retry attempts, then (in the absence of exceptions) R0 is set to −1. The value "N" is implementation dependent.

The removal is interlocked to prevent concurrent interlocked insertions or removals at the head or tail of the same queue by another process, in a multiprocessor environment. The removal is a non-interruptible operation.

This instruction requires that the queue be memory resident and that the queue header and elements are quadword aligned. No alignment or memory management checks are made before starting queue modifications to verify these requirements. Therefore, if any of these requirements are not met, the queue may be left in an UNPREDICTABLE state and an illegal operand fault may be reported.

2.3.13 Remove Entry from Quadword Queue at Head Interlocked

Format:

CALL_PAL   REMQHIQ   ! PALcode format

Operation:

```
! R16 contains the address of the queue header
! R0 receives status:
!        -1 if the secondary interlock was set
!         0 if the queue was empty
!         1 if entry removed and queue still not empty
!         2 if entry removed and queue empty
! R1 receives the address of the removed entry
!
! Must have write access to header and queue entries
! Header and entries must be octaword aligned.
!
! Check header alignment
IF {R16<3:0> NE 0} THEN
    BEGIN
      {illegal operand exception}
    END


N <- {retry_amount}                   ! Implementation-specific
REPEAT
    LOAD_LOCKED (tmp1 ← (R16))        ! Acquire hardware interlock.
    IF tmp1<0> EQ 1 THEN             ! Try to set secondary interlock.
        R0 ← -1, {return}            ! Already set
    done ←STORE_CONDITIONAL ((R16) ←{tmp1 OR 1} )
    N ← N - 1
UNTIL {done EQ 1} OR {N EQ 0}
IF done NEQ 1, R0 ← -1, {return}      ! Retry exceeded


MB


IF tmp1<3:0> NE 0 THEN                 ! Check Alignment
    BEGIN                             ! Release secondary interlock
      (R16) ← tmp1
      {illegal operand exception}
    END


! Check if the following can be done without
!   causing a memory management exception:
!   read contents of header + tmp1 {if tmp1 NE 0}
!   write into header + tmp1 + (header + tmp1) {if tmp1 NE 0}
```

```
IF {all memory accesses can NOT be completed} THEN
    BEGIN                               ! Release secondary interlock
      (R16) ← tmp0
      {initiate memory management fault}
    END


tmp2 ← R16 + tmp1
IF {tmp1 EQL 0} THEN
    tmp3 ← R16
ELSE
    tmp3 ← tmp2 + (tmp2)


IF tmp3<3:0> NE 0 THEN               ! Check Alignment
    BEGIN                               ! Release secondary interlock
      (R16) ← tmp1
      {illegal operand exception}
    END


(tmp3 + 8) ← R16 - tmp3              ! Backward link of successor

MB

(R16) ← tmp3 - R16                   ! Forward link of header
                                     ! Release lock
IF tmp1 EQ 0 THEN
    R0 ← 0                           ! Queue was empty
ELSE
  BEGIN
    IF {tmp3 - R16} EQ 0 THEN
      R0 ← 2                         ! Queue now empty
    ELSE
      R0 ← 1                         ! Queue not empty
  END
END
R1 ← tmp2                            ! Address of removed entry
```

Exceptions:

Access Violation

Fault on Read

Fault on Write

Illegal Operand

Translation Not Valid

Instruction mnemonics:

CALL_PAL   REMQHIQ   Remove from Quadword Queue at Head
                            Interlocked

Description:

If the secondary interlock is clear, REMQHIQ removes from the self-relative queue the entry following the header, pointed to by R16, and the address of the removed entry is returned in R1.

If the queue was empty prior to this instruction and secondary interlock succeeded, a 0 is returned in R0. If there was an entry to remove and the queue is not empty at the end of this instruction, R0 is set to 1. If the interlock succeeded and the queue was not empty at the start of the removal, and the queue is empty after the removal, a 2 is returned in R0. If the instruction fails to acquire the secondary interlock after "N" retry attempts, then (in the absence of exceptions) R0 is set to –1. The value "N" is implementation dependent.

The removal is interlocked to prevent concurrent interlocked insertions or removals at the head or tail of the same queue by another process, in a multiprocessor environment. The removal is a non-interruptible operation. Before performing any part of the removal, the processor validates that the entire operation can be completed. This ensures that if a memory management exception occurs, the queue is left in a consistent state (see Chapters 3 and 6).

2.3.14 Remove Entry from Quadword Queue at Head Interlocked Resident

Format:

CALL_PAL   REMQHIQR   ! PALcode format

Operation:

```
! R16 contains the address of the queue header
! R0 receives status:
!           -1 if the secondary interlock was set
!            0 if the queue was empty
!            1 if entry removed and queue still not empty
!            2 if entry removed and queue empty
! R1 receives the address of the removed entry
!
! Must have write access to header and queue entries
! Header and entries must be octaword aligned.
! All parts of the Queue must be memory resident

N ← {retry_amount}                      ! Implementation-specific
REPEAT
    LOAD_LOCKED (tmp1 ← (R16))          ! Acquire hardware interlock.
    IF tmp1<0> EQ 1 THEN                ! Try to set secondary interlock.
        R0 ← -1, {return}              ! Already set
    done ←STORE_CONDITIONAL ((R16) ←{tmp1 OR 1} )
    N ← N - 1
UNTIL {done EQ 1} OR {N EQ 0}
IF done NEQ 1, R0 ← -1, {return}        ! Retry exceeded

MB

tmp2 ← R16 + tmp1
IF {tmp1 EQL 0} THEN
    tmp3 ← R16
ELSE
    tmp3 ← tmp2 + (tmp2)
END
(tmp3 + 8) ← R16 - tmp3                  ! Backward link of successor

MB

(R16) ← tmp3 - R16                       ! Forward link of header
                                         ! Release lock
```

```
IF tmp1 EQ 0 THEN
    R0 ← 0                              ! Queue was empty
ELSE
  IF {tmp3 - R16} EQ 0 THEN
      R0 ← 2                            ! Queue now empty
  ELSE
      R0 ← 1                            ! Queue not empty
END
R1 ← tmp2                               ! Address of removed entry
```

Exceptions:

Illegal Operand

Instruction mnemonics:

CALL_PAL   REMQHIQR   Remove Entry from Quadword Queue at Head
                             Interlocked Resident

Description:

If the secondary interlock is clear, REMQHIQR removes from the self-relative queue the entry
following the header, pointed to by R16, and the address of the removed entry is returned in
R1.

If the queue was empty prior to this instruction and secondary interlock succeeded, a 0 is
returned in R0. If there was an entry to remove and the queue is not empty at the end of this
instruction, R0 is set to 1. If the interlock succeeded and the queue was not empty at the start
of the removal, and the queue is empty after the removal, a 2 is returned in R0. If the instruction fails to acquire the secondary interlock after "N" retry attempts, then (in the absence of
exceptions) R0 is set to –1. The value "N" is implementation dependent.

The removal is interlocked to prevent concurrent interlocked insertions or removals at the
head or tail of the same queue by another process, in a multiprocessor environment. The
removal is a non-interruptible operation.

This instruction requires that the queue be memory resident and that the queue header and elements are octaword aligned. No alignment or memory management checks are made before
starting queue modifications to verify these requirements. Therefore, if any of these requirements are not met, the queue may be left in an UNPREDICTABLE state and an illegal
operand fault may be reported.

2.3.15 Remove Entry from Longword Queue at Tail Interlocked

Format:

CALL_PAL   REMQTIL   ! PALcode format

Operation:

```
! R16 contains the address of the queue header
! R0 receives status:
!          -1 if the secondary interlock was set
!           0 if the queue was empty
!           1 if entry removed and queue still not empty
!           2 if entry removed and queue empty
! R1 receives the address of the removed entry
!
! Must have write access to header and queue entries
! Header and entries must be quadword aligned.
!
! Check header alignment and
! that the header is a valid 32 bit address
IF {R16<2:0> NE 0} OR {SEXT(R16<31:0>) NE R16} THEN
   BEGIN
    {illegal operand exception}
   END

N <- {retry_amount}                   ! Implementation-specific
REPEAT
   LOAD_LOCKED (tmp0 ← (R16))          ! Acquire hardware interlock.
   IF tmp0<0> EQ 1 THEN                ! Try to set secondary interlock.
      R0 ← -1, {return}                ! Already set
   done ←STORE_CONDITIONAL ((R16) ←{tmp0 OR 1} )
   N ← N - 1
UNTIL {done EQ 1} OR {N EQ 0}
IF done NEQ 1, R0 ← -1, {return}       ! Retry exceeded

MB

tmp1 ← SEXT(tmp0<31:0>)
tmp5 ← SEXT(tmp0<63:32>)
IF tmp5<2:0> NE 0 THEN                 ! Check alignment
   BEGIN                               ! Release secondary interlock
    (R16) ← tmp0
    {illegal operand exception}
   END

!Check if the following can be done without
! causing a memory management exception:
!  read contents of header + (header + 4) {if tmp1 NE 0}
!  write into header + (header + 4)
!    + (header + 4 + (header + 4)){if tmp1 NE 0}
```

```
IF {all memory accesses can NOT be completed} THEN
  BEGIN                                      ! Release secondary interlock
    (R16) ← tmp0
    {initiate memory management fault}
  END


addr ← SEXT( {R16 + tmp5}<31:0> )
tmp2 ← SEXT( {addr + SEXT( (addr+4)<31:0>)}<31:0> )
IF tmp2<2:0> NE 0 THEN                       ! Check alignment
  BEGIN                                      ! Release secondary interlock
    (R16) ← tmp0
    {illegal operand exception}
  END


(R16 + 4)<31:0> ← tmp2 - R16                 ! Backward link of header
IF {tmp2 EQL R16} THEN
    (R16)<31:0> ← 0                          ! Forward link, release lock
ELSE
  BEGIN
    (tmp2)<31:0> ← R16 - tmp2                ! Forward link of predecessor
  MB
    (R16)<31:0> ← tmp1                       ! Release lock
  END
IF tmp1 EQ 0 THEN
    R0 ← 0                                   ! Queue was empty
ELSE
  BEGIN
    IF {tmp2 - R16} EQ 0 THEN
      R0 ← 2                                 ! Queue now empty
    ELSE
      R0 ← 1                                 ! Queue not empty
  END
R1 ← addr                                    ! Address of removed entry
```

Exceptions:

Access Violation
Fault on Read
Fault on Write
Illegal Operand
Translation Not Valid

Instruction mnemonics:

CALL_PAL   REMQTIL   Remove from Longword Queue at Tail Inter-
                            locked

Description:

If the secondary interlock is clear, REMQTIL removes from the self-relative queue the entry preceding the header, pointed to by R16, and the address of the removed entry is returned in R1.

If the queue was empty prior to this instruction and secondary interlock succeeded, a 0 is returned in R0. If there was an entry to remove and the queue is not empty at the end of this instruction, R0 is set to 1. If the interlock succeeded and the queue was not empty at the start of the removal, and the queue is empty after the removal, a 2 is returned in R0. If the instruction fails to acquire the secondary interlock after "N" retry attempts, then (in the absence of exceptions) R0 is set to −1. The value "N" is implementation dependent.

The removal is interlocked to prevent concurrent interlocked insertions or removals at the head or tail of the same queue by another process, in a multiprocessor environment. The removal is a non-interruptible operation. Before performing any part of the removal, the processor validates that the entire operation can be completed. This ensures that if a memory management exception occurs, the queue is left in a consistent state (see Chapters 3 and 6).

2.3.16 Remove Entry from Longword Queue at Tail Interlocked Resident

Format:

```
CALL_PAL              REMQTILR                    ! PALcode format
```

Operation:

```
! R16 contains the address of the queue header
! R0 receives status:
!         -1 if the secondary interlock was set
!          0 if the queue was empty
!          1 if entry removed and queue still not empty
!          2 if entry removed and queue empty
! R1 receives the address of the removed entry
!
! Must have write access to header and queue entries
! Header and entries must be quadword aligned.
! All parts of the Queue must be memory resident


N ← {retry_amount}                  ! Implementation-specific
REPEAT
    LOAD_LOCKED (tmp0 ← (R16))       ! Acquire hardware interlock.
    IF tmp0<0> EQ 1 THEN             ! Try to set secondary interlock.
        R0 ← -1, {return}            ! Already set
    done ←STORE_CONDITIONAL ((R16) ←{tmp0 OR 1} )
    N ← N - 1
UNTIL {done EQ 1} OR {N EQ 0}
IF done NEQ 1, R0 ← -1, {return}     ! Retry exceeded

MB

tmp1 ← SEXT(tmp0<31:0>)
tmp5 ← SEXT(tmp0<63:32>)
addr ← SEXT( {R16 + tmp5}<31:0> )
tmp2 ← SEXT( {addr + SEXT( (addr+4)<31:0>)}<31:0> )
(R16 + 4)<31:0> ← tmp2 - R16         ! Backward link of header
IF {tmp2 EQL R16} THEN
    (R16)<31:0> ← 0                  ! Forward link, release lock
ELSE
  BEGIN
    (tmp2)<31:0> ← R16 - tmp2        ! Forward link of predecessor
    MB
    (R16)<31:0> ← tmp1               ! Release lock
  END
```

```
          IF tmp1 EQ 0 THEN
              R0 ← 0                              ! Queue was empty
          ELSE
            IF {tmp2 - R16} EQ 0 THEN
                  R0 ← 2                          ! Queue now empty
            ELSE
                  R0 ← 1                          ! Queue not empty
          END
       END
       R1 ← addr                                  ! Address of removed entry
```

Exceptions:

Illegal Operand

Instruction mnemonics:

CALL_PAL   REMQTILR   Remove Entry from Longword Queue at Tail
                             Interlocked Resident

Description:

If the secondary interlock is clear, REMQTILR removes from the self-relative queue the entry preceding the header, pointed to by R16, and the address of the removed entry is returned in R1.

If the queue was empty prior to this instruction and secondary interlock succeeded, a 0 is returned in R0. If there was an entry to remove and the queue is not empty at the end of this instruction, R0 is set to 1. If the interlock succeeded and the queue was not empty at the start of the removal, and the queue is empty after the removal, a 2 is returned in R0. If the instruction fails to acquire the secondary interlock after "N" retry attempts, then (in the absence of exceptions) R0 is set to –1. The value "N" is implementation dependent.

The removal is interlocked to prevent concurrent interlocked insertions or removals at the head or tail of the same queue by another process, in a multiprocessor environment. The removal is a non-interruptible operation.

This instruction requires that the queue be memory resident and that the queue header and elements are quadword aligned. No alignment or memory management checks are made before starting queue modifications to verify these requirements. Therefore, if any of these requirements are not met, the queue may be left in an UNPREDICTABLE state and an illegal operand fault may be reported.

2.3.17 Remove Entry from Quadword Queue at Tail Interlocked

Format:

CALL_PAL   REMQTIQ   ! PALcode format

Operation:

```
! R16 contains the address of the queue header
! R0 receives status:
!          -1 if the secondary interlock was set
!           0 if the queue was empty
!           1 if entry removed and queue still not empty
!           2 if entry removed and queue empty
! R1 receives the address of the removed entry
!
! Must have write access to header and queue entries
! Header and entries must be octaword aligned.
!
! Check header alignment
IF {R16<3:0> NE 0} THEN
  BEGIN
    {illegal operand exception}
  END


N ←{retry_amount}                    ! Implementation-specific
REPEAT
    LOAD_LOCKED (tmp1 ← (R16))        ! Acquire hardware interlock.
    IF tmp1<0> EQ 1 THEN             ! Try to set secondary interlock.
        R0 ← -1, {return}            ! Already set
    done ←STORE_CONDITIONAL ((R16) ←{tmp1 OR 1} )
    N ← N - 1
UNTIL {done EQ 1} OR {N EQ 0}
IF done NEQ 1, R0 ← -1, {return}      ! Retry exceeded


MB


tmp5 ← (R16+8)
IF tmp5<3:0> NE 0 THEN                ! Check Alignment
    BEGIN                            ! Release secondary interlock
      (R16) ← tmp1
      {illegal operand exception}
    END
! Check if the following can be done without
!  causing a memory management exception:
!   read contents of header + (header + 8) {if tmp1 NE 0}
!   write into header + (header + 8)
!    + (header + 8 + (header + 8)){if tmp1 NE 0}
```

```
IF {all memory accesses can NOT be completed} THEN
   BEGIN                                  ! Release secondary interlock
      (R16) ← tmp1
      {initiate memory management fault}
   END

addr ← R16 + tmp5
tmp2 ← addr + (addr + 8)
IF tmp2<3:0> NE 0 THEN                    ! Check alignment
   BEGIN                                  ! Release secondary interlock
      (R16) ← tmp1
      {illegal operand exception}
   END

(R16 + 8) ← tmp2 - R16                    ! Backward link of header
IF {tmp2 EQL R16} THEN
      (R16) ← 0                           ! Forward link, release lock
ELSE
   BEGIN
      (tmp2) ← R16 - tmp2                 ! Forward link of predecessor
      MB
      (R16) ← tmp1                        ! Release lock
   END
END
IF tmp1 EQ 0 THEN
   R0 ← 0                                 ! Queue was empty
ELSE
   BEGIN
      IF {tmp2 - R16} EQ 0 THEN
         R0 ← 2                           ! Queue now empty
      ELSE
         R0 ← 1                           ! Queue not empty
   END
END
R1 ← addr                                 ! Address of removed entry
```

Exceptions:

Access Violation
Fault on Read
Fault on Write
Illegal Operand
Translation Not Valid

Instruction mnemonics:

CALL_PAL   REMQTIQ   Remove from Quadword Queue at Tail
                               Interlocked

Description:

If the secondary interlock is clear, REMQTIQ removes from the self-relative queue the entry preceding the header, pointed to by R16, and the address of the removed entry is returned in R1.

If the queue was empty prior to this instruction and secondary interlock succeeded, a 0 is returned in R0. If there was an entry to remove and the queue is not empty at the end of this instruction, R0 is set to 1. If the interlock succeeded and the queue was not empty at the start of the removal, and the queue is empty after the removal, a 2 is returned in R0. If the instruction fails to acquire the secondary interlock after "N" retry attempts, then (in the absence of exceptions) R0 is set to –1. The value "N" is implementation dependent.

The removal is interlocked to prevent concurrent interlocked insertions or removals at the head or tail of the same queue by another process, in a multiprocessor environment. The removal is a non-interruptible operation. Before performing any part of the removal, the processor validates that the entire operation can be completed. This ensures that if a memory management exception occurs, the queue is left in a consistent state (see Chapters 3 and 6).

2.3.18 Remove Entry from Quadword Queue at Tail Interlocked Resident

Format:

CALL_PAL   REMQTIQR   ! PALcode format

Operation:

```
! R16 contains the address of the queue header
! R0 receives status:
!           -1 if the secondary interlock was set
!            0 if the queue was empty
!            1 if entry removed and queue still not empty
!            2 if entry removed and queue empty
! R1 receives the address of the removed entry
!
! Must have write access to header and queue entries
! Header and entries must be octaword aligned.
! All parts of the Queue must be memory resident

N ←{retry_amount}                     ! Implementation-specific
REPEAT
   LOAD_LOCKED (tmp1 ← (R16))         ! Acquire hardware interlock.
   IF tmp1<0> EQ 1 THEN               ! Try to set secondary interlock.
      R0 ← -1, {return}               ! Already set
   done ←STORE_CONDITIONAL ((R16) ←{tmp1 OR 1} )
      N ← N - 1
UNTIL {done EQ 1} OR {N EQ 0}
IF done NEQ 1, R0 ← -1, {return}      ! Retry exceeded

MB

tmp5 ← (R16+8)
addr ← R16 + tmp5
tmp2 ← addr + (addr + 8)
(R16 + 8) ← tmp2 - R16                ! Backward link of header
IF {tmp2 EQL R16} THEN
   (R16) ← 0                          ! Forward link, release lock
ELSE
  BEGIN
   (tmp2) ← R16 - tmp2                ! Forward link of predecessor
   MB
   (R16) ← tmp1                       ! Release lock
  END
END
```

```
IF tmp1 EQ 0 THEN
    R0 ← 0                              ! Queue was empty
ELSE
    IF {tmp2 - R16} EQ 0 THEN
        R0 ← 2                          ! Queue now empty
    ELSE
        R0 ← 1                          ! Queue not empty
END
R1 ← addr                              ! Address of removed entry
```

Exceptions:

Illegal Operand

Instruction mnemonics:

CALL_PAL   REMQTIQR   Remove Entry from Quadword Queue at Tail Interlocked Resident

Description:

If the secondary interlock is clear, REMQTIQR removes from the self-relative queue the entry preceding the header, pointed to by R16, and the address of the removed entry is returned in R1.

If the queue was empty prior to this instruction and secondary interlock succeeded, a 0 is returned in R0. If there was an entry to remove and the queue is not empty at the end of this instruction, R0 is set to 1. If the interlock succeeded and the queue was not empty at the start of the removal, and the queue is empty after the removal, a 2 is returned in R0. If the instruction fails to acquire the secondary interlock after "N" retry attempts, then (in the absence of exceptions) R0 is set to –1. The value "N" is implementation dependent.

The removal is interlocked to prevent concurrent interlocked insertions or removals at the head or tail of the same queue by another process, in a multiprocessor environment. The removal is a non-interruptible operation.

This instruction requires that the queue be memory resident and that the queue header and elements are octaword aligned. No alignment or memory management checks are made before starting queue modifications to verify these requirements. Therefore, if any of these requirements are not met, the queue may be left in an UNPREDICTABLE state and an illegal operand fault may be reported.

2.3.19 Remove Entry from Longword Queue

Format:

CALL_PAL   REMQUEL   ! PALcode format

Operation:

```
! R16 contains the address of the entry to remove
!     or the address of the 32 bit address of the
!     entry for REMQUEL/D
! R0 receives status:
!       -1 if the queue was empty
!        0 if the queue is empty after removing an entry
!        1 if the queue is not empty after removing an entry
! R1 receives the address of the removed entry
!
! Header and entries need only be byte aligned
! Must have write access to header and queue entries
IF opcode EQ REMQUEL/D THEN
    R1 ← SEXT((R16)<31:0>)
ELSE
    R1 ← SEXT(R16<31:0>)

IF {all memory accesses can be completed} THEN
    BEGIN
        tmp1 ← (R1)<31:0>                 ! Forward Link of Predecessor
        ((R1+4)<31:0>)<31:0> ← tmp1
        tmp2 ← (R1+4)<31:0>               ! Backward Link of Successor
        ((R1)<31:0>+4)<31:0> ← tmp2
        R0 ← 1                           ! Queue not empty
        IF {tmp1 EQ tmp2} THEN
          R0 ← 0                         ! Queue now empty
        IF {R1 EQ tmp2} THEN
          R0 ← -1                        ! Queue was empty
    END
ELSE
  BEGIN
   {initiate fault}
  END
END
```

Exceptions:

Access Violation

Fault on Read

Fault on Write

Translation Not Valid

Instruction mnemonics:

CALL_PAL	REMQUEL	Remove Entry from Longword Queue
CALL_PAL	REMQUEL/D	Remove Entry from Longword Queue Deferred

Description:

REMQUEL removes the entry addressed by R16 from the longword absolute queue. The address of the removed entry is returned in R1. REMQUEL/D performs the same operation on the queue entry addressed by the longword addressed by R16. The queue header and entry need only be byte aligned.

In either case, if there was no entry in the queue to be removed, R0 is set to −1. If there was an entry to remove and the queue is empty at the end of this instruction, R0 is set to 0. If there was an entry to remove and the queue is not empty at the end of this instruction, R0 is set to 1. The removal is a non-interruptible operation. Before performing any part of the removal, the processor validates that the entire operation can be completed. This ensures that if a memory management exception occurs, the queue is left in a consistent state (see Chapters 3 and 6).

2.3.20 Remove Entry from Quadword Queue

Format:

CALL_PAL   REMQUEQ   ! PALcode format

Operation:

```
! R16 contains the address of the entry to remove
!     or address of address of entry for REMQUEQ/D
! R0 receives status:
!       -1 if the queue was empty
!        0 if the queue is empty after removing an entry
!        1 if the queue is not empty after removing an entry
! R1 receives the address of the removed entry
! Must have write access to header and queue entries
! Header and entries must be octaword aligned
IF opcode EQ REMQUEQ/D THEN
   IF {R16<3:0> NE 0} THEN
     BEGIN
       {illegal operand exception}
     END
   R1 ← (R16)
ELSE
   R1 ← R16
IF {R1<3:0> NE 0} THEN                   ! Check alignment
   BEGIN
     {illegal operand exception}
   END
 IF {all memory accesses can be completed} THEN
   BEGIN
   tmp1 ← (R1)                           ! Forward link of Predecessor
   IF {tmp1<3:0> NE 0} THEN
    BEGIN                                ! Check alignment
      {illegal operand exception}
    END
   tmp2 ← (R1+8)                         ! Find predecessor
   IF {tmp2<3:0> NE 0} THEN
    BEGIN                                ! Check alignment
      {illegal operand exception}
    END
   (tmp2) ← tmp1                         ! Update Forward link of predecessor
   ((R1)+8) ← tmp2
```

```
                    R0 ← 1                        ! Queue not empty
              IF {tmp1 EQ tmp2} THEN
                    R0 ← 0                        ! Queue now empty
              IF {R1 EQ tmp2} THEN
                    R0 ← -1                       ! Queue was empty
          END
     ELSE
          BEGIN
          {initiate fault}
          END
     END
```

Exceptions:

Access Violation
Fault on Read
Fault on Write
Translation Not Valid
Illegal Operand

Instruction mnemonics:

CALL_PAL	REMQUEQ	Remove Entry from Quadword Queue
CALL_PAL	REMQUEQ/D	Remove Entry from Quadword Queue Deferred

Description:

REMQUEQ removes the queue entry addressed by R16 from the quadword absolute queue. The address of the removed entry is returned in R1. REMQUEL/D performs the same operation on the queue entry addressed by the quadword addressed by R16.

In either case, if there was no entry in the queue to be removed, R0 is set to –1. If there was an entry to remove and the queue is empty at the end of this instruction, R0 is set to 0. If there was an entry to remove and the queue is not empty at the end of this instruction, R0 is set to 1. The removal is a non-interruptible operation. Before performing any part of the removal, the processor validates that the entire operation can be completed. This ensures that if a memory management exception occurs, the queue is left in a consistent state (see Chapters 3 and 6). R0 and R1 are UNPREDICTABLE if an exception occurs. The relative order of reporting memory management and illegal operand exceptions is UNPREDICTABLE.

2.4 Unprivileged VAX Compatibility PALcode Instructions

The Alpha architecture provides the following PALcode instructions for use in translated VAX code. These instructions are not a permanent part of the architecture and will not be available in some future implementations. They are provided to help customers preserve VAX instruction atomicity assumptions in porting code from VAX to Alpha. These calls should be user mode. They must not be used by any code other than that generated by the VEST software translator and its supporting run-time code (TIE).

2.4.1 Atomic Move Operation

Format:

AMOVRR   ! PALcode format

AMOVRM   ! PALcode format

Operation:

```
! R16 contains the first source
! R17 contains the first destination address
! R18 contains the first length
! R19 contains the second source
! R20 contains the second destination address
! R21 contains the second length
CASE
  AMOVRR:
        IF intr_flag EQ 0 THEN
            R18 ← 0
            {return}
        END

        intr_flag ← 0
        (R17) ← R16                 ! length specified by R18<1:0>
        (R20) ← R19                 ! length specified by R21<1:0>
        IF {both moves successful} THEN
            R18 ← 1
        ELSE
            R18 ← 0
        END
  AMOVRM:
        IF intr_flag EQ 0 THEN
            R18 ← 0
            {return}
        END

        intr_flag ← 0
        (R17) ← R16                 ! length specified by R18<1:0>
        IF R21<5:0> NE 0 THEN
            BEGIN
                IF R19<1:0> NE 0 OR R20<1:0> NE 0
                    {Illegal operand exception}
                ELSE
                    (R20) ← (R19)    ! length specified by R21<5:0>
            END
        IF {both moves successful} THEN
            R18 ← 1
        ELSE
            R18 ← 0
        END
ENDCASE
```

Exceptions:

AMOVRR: Access Violation

Fault On Write

Translation Not Valid

AMOVRM: Access Violation

Fault On Read

Fault On Write

Illegal Operand

Translation Not Valid

Instruction mnemonics:

CALL_PAL	AMOVRR	Atomic Move Register/Register
CALL_PAL	AMOVRM	Atomic Move Register/Memory

Description:

Note:

The CALL_PAL AMOVxx instructions exist *only* for the support of translated VAX code. They will be removed from the architecture at some time in the future. They must be used *only* in translated VAX code and its support routines (TIE).

CALL_PAL AMOVRR

The CALL_PAL AMOVRR instruction specifies two multiprocessor-safe register stores to arbitrary byte addresses. Either both stores are done or neither store is done. R18 is set to 1 if both stores are done, and 0 otherwise. The two source registers are R16 and R19. The two destination byte addresses are in R17 and R20. The two lengths are specified in R18<1:0> and R21<1:0>. The length encoding is as follows: 00 is store byte, 01 is store word, 10 is store longword, 11 is store quadword. The low 1, 2, 4, or 8 bytes of the source register are used, respectively. The unused bytes of the source registers are ignored. The unused bits of the length registers (R18<63:2> and R21<63:2>) should be zero (SBZ).

If, upon entry to the PALcode routine, the intr_flag is clear then the instruction sets R18 to zero and exits, doing no stores. Otherwise, intr_flag is cleared and the PALcode routine proceeds. This is the same per-processor intr_flag used by the RS and RC instructions.

The AMOVRR memory addresses may be unaligned. If either store would result in a Translation Not Valid fault, Fault on Write, or Access Violation fault, neither store is done and the corresponding fault is taken. If both stores would result in faults, it is UNPREDICTABLE which one is taken.

Note:

A fault does not set R18, since the instruction has not been completed.

If both stores can be completed without faulting, they are both attempted using multiprocessor-safe LDQ_L..STQ_C sequences. If all the sequences store successfully with no interruption, the PALcode routine completes with R18 set to one. Otherwise, the PALcode routine completes with R18 set to zero. In addition, R16, R17, R19, R20, and R21 are UNPREDICTABLE upon return from the PALcode routine, even if an exception has occurred.

If the destinations overlap, the stores must appear to be done in the order specified.

CALL_PAL AMOVRM

The CALL_PAL AMOVRM instruction specifies one multiprocessor safe register store to an arbitrary byte address, plus an atomic memory-to-memory move of 0 to 63 aligned longwords. Either the store and the move are both done in their entirety or neither is done. R18 is set to one if both are done, and zero otherwise.

The first source register is in R16, the first destination address is in R17, and the first length is in R18. These three are specified exactly as in AMOVRR.

The second source address is in R19, the second destination address is in R20, and the second length is in R21<5:0>. The length is a longword length, in the range 0 to 63 longwords (0 to 252 bytes). The unused bytes of the source register R16 are ignored. The unused bits of the length registers (R18<63:2> and R21<63:6>) should be zero (SBZ).

If, upon entry to the PALcode routine, the intr_flag is clear, the instruction sets R18 to zero and exits, doing no stores. Otherwise, intr_flag is cleared and the PALcode routine proceeds. This is the same per-processor intr_flag used by the RS and RC instructions.

The memory address in R17 may be unaligned.

If the length for the move is zero, no move is done, no memory accesses are made via R19 and R20, and no fault checking of these addresses is done. In this case, the move is always considered to have succeeded in determining the setting of R18.

If the length in R21 is non-zero, the two addresses in R19 and R20 must be aligned longword addresses; otherwise, an Illegal Operand exception is taken.

If either the store or the move would result in a Translation Not Valid, Fault on Read, Fault on Write, or Access Violation fault, neither is done and the corresponding fault is taken. If both would result in faults, it is UNPREDICTABLE which one is taken.

Note:
  A fault does not set R18, since the instruction has not been completed.

If both the store and the move can be completed without faulting, they are both attempted, using multiprocessor-safe LDQ_L..STQ_C sequences for the store. If all the operations store successfully with no interruption, the PALcode routine completes with R18 set to one. Otherwise, the PALcode routine completes with R18 set to zero. In addition, R16, R17, R19, R20, and R21 are UNPREDICTABLE upon return from the PALcode routine, even if an exception has occurred.

If the memory fields overlap, the store must appear to be done first, followed by the move. The ordering of the reads and writes of the move is unspecified. Thus, if the move destination overlaps the move source, the move results are UNPREDICTABLE.

These instructions contain no implicit MB.

Notes:

- Typically, these instructions would be used in a sequence starting with CALL_PAL RS and ending with CALL_PAL AMOVxx, Bxx R18,label. The failure path from the conditional branch would eventually go back to the RS instruction. When such a sequence succeeds, it has done everything from the RS up to and including the CALL_PAL AMOVxx completely with no interrupts or exceptions.

- The CALL_PAL AMOVxx instruction is typically followed by a conditional branch on R18. If the CALL_PAL AMOVxx is likely to succeed, the conditional branch should be a forward branch on failure (BEQ R18,forward_label) or backward branch on success (BNE R18, backward_label), to match the architected branch-prediction rule.

- The CALL_PAL AMOVxx instruction must either do both stores or neither. If R18=0 upon return, then memory state must be unchanged. If the first STQ_C inside AMOVRR succeeds (and thus has changed programmer-visible state in memory), the PALcode routine must complete the second STQ_C also, and exit with R18=1. In particular, if the failure loop around the second STQ_C is executed an excessive number of times (due to perverse interference from another processor), the PALcode may not "give up" and return with R18=0.

2.5 Unprivileged PALcode Thread Instructions

The PALcode thread instructions provide support for multithread implementations, which require that a given thread be able to generate a reproduciable unique value in a "timely" fashion. This value can then be used to index into a structure or otherwise generate additional thread unique data.

The two instructions in Table 2–4 are provided to read and write a process unique value from the process's hardware context.

Table 2–4: Unprivileged PALcode Thread Instructions

Mnemonic	Operation
READ_UNQ	Read unique context
WRITE_UNQ	Write unique context

The process-unique value is stored in the HWPCB at [HWPCB+72] when the process is not active. When the process is active, the process unique value can be cached in hardware internal storage or reside in the HWPCB only.

2.5.1 Read Unique Context

Format:

CALL_PAL	READ_UNQ	! PALcode format

Operation:

```
IF {internal storage for process unique context} THEN
    R0 ← {process unique context}
ELSE
    R0 ← (HWPCB+72)
```

Exceptions:

None

Instruction mnemonics:

CALL_PAL   READ_UNQ   Read Unique Context

Description:

The READ_UNQ instruction causes the hardware process (thread) unique context value to be placed in R0. If this value has not previously been written using a CALL_PAL WRITE_UNQ or stored into the quadword in the HWPCB at [HWPCB+72] while the thread was inactive, the result returned in R0 is UNPREDICTABLE. Implementations can cache this unique context value while the hardware process is active. The unique context may be thought of as a "slow register." Typically, this value will be used by software to establish a unique context for a given thread of execution.

2.5.2 Write Unique Context

Format:

CALL_PAL   WRITE_UNQ   ! PALcode format

Operation:

```
!R16 contains value to be written to the hardware process
!   unique context

IF {internal storage for process unique context} THEN
    {process unique context} ← R16
ELSE
    (HWPCB+72) ← R16
```

Exceptions:

None

Instruction mnemonics:

CALL_PAL   WRITE_UNQ   Write Unique Context

Description:

The WRITE_UNQ instruction causes the value of R16 to be stored in internal storage for hardware process (thread) unique context, if implemented, or in the HWPCB at [HWPCB+72], if the internal storage is not implemented. When the process is context switched, SWPCTX ensures that this value is stored in the HWPCB at [HWPCB+72]. Implementations can cache this unique context value in internal storage while the hardware process is active. The unique context may be thought of as a "slow register." Typically, this value will be used by software to establish a unique context for a given thread of execution.

2.6 Privileged PALcode Instructions

Privileged instructions can be called in kernel mode only; otherwise, a privileged instruction exception occurs. The following privileged instructions are provided:

Table 2–5: PALcode Privileged Instructions Summary

Mnemonic	Operation
CFLUSH	Cache flush
CSERVE	Console service
DRAINA	Drain abort. See Common Architecture, Chapter 6.
HALT	Halt processor. See Common Architecture, Chapter 6.
LDQP	Load quadword physical
MFPR	Move from processor register
MTPR	Move to processor register
STQP	Store quadword physical
SWPCTX	Swap privileged context
SWPPAL	Swap PALcode image

2.6.1 Cache Flush

Format:

```
CALL_PAL              CFLUSH                    ! PALcode format
```

Operation:

```
! R16 contains the Page Frame Number (PFN)
!   of the page to be flushed

IF  PS<CM> NE 0  THEN
    {privileged instruction exception}

{Flush page out of cache(s)}
```

Exceptions:

Privileged Instruction

Instruction mnemonics:

CALL_PAL   CFLUSH   Cache Flush

Description:

The CFLUSH instruction may be used to flush an entire physical page specified by the PFN in R16 from any data caches associated with the current processor. All processors must implement this instruction.

On processors that implement a backup power option that maintains only the contents of memory during a powerfail, this instruction is used by the powerfail interrupt handler to force data written by the handler to the battery backed-up main memory. After a CFLUSH, the first subsequent load (on the same processor) to an arbitrary address in the target page is either fetched from physical memory or from the data cache of another processor.

In some multiprocessor systems, CFLUSH is not sufficient to ensure that the data are actually written to memory and not exchanged between processor caches. Additional platform-specific cooperation between the powerfail interrupt handlers executing on each processor may be required.

On systems that implement other backup power options (including none), CFLUSH may return without affecting the data cache contents. To order CFLUSH properly with respect to preceding writes, an MB instruction is needed before the CFLUSH; to order CFLUSH properly with respect to subsequent reads, an MB instruction is needed after the CFLUSH.

2.6.2 Console Service

Format:

    CALL_PAL   CSERVE   ! PALcode format

Operation:

```
! Implementation specific

IF  PS<CM> NE 0  THEN
{Privileged instruction exception}

ELSE
{Implementation-dependent action}
```

Exceptions:

Privileged Instruction

Instruction Mnemonics:

CALL_PAL   CSERVE   Console Service

Description:

This instruction is specific to each PALcode and console implementation and is not intended for operating system use

2.6.3 Load Quadword Physical

Format:

      CALL_PAL   LDQP   ! PALcode format

Operation:

```
! R16 contains the quadword-aligned physical address
! R0 receives the data from memory

IF PS<CM> NE 0 THEN
  {Privileged Instruction exception}

R0 ← (R16) {physical access}
```

Exceptions:

Privileged Instruction

Instruction mnemonics:

CALL_PAL   LDQP   Load Quadword Physical

Description:

The LDQP instruction fetches and writes to R0 the quadword-aligned memory operand, whose physical address is in R16.

If the operand address in R16 is not quadword aligned, the result is UNPREDICTABLE.

2.6.4 Move from Processor Register

Format:

CALL_PAL   MFPR_IPR_Name   ! PALcode format

Operation:

```
IF  PS<CM> NE 0  THEN
   {privileged instruction exception}

! R16 may contain an IPR specific source operand
R0 ← result of IPR specific function
```

Exceptions:

Privileged Instruction

Instruction mnemonics:

CALL_PAL   MFPR_*xxx*   Move from Processor Register *xxx*

Description:

The MFPR_xxx instruction reads the internal processor register specified by the PALcode function field and writes it to R0.

Registers R1, R16, and R17 contain UNPREDICTABLE results after an MFPR.

See Chapter 5 for a description of each IPR.

2.6.5 Move to Processor Register

Format:

CALL_PAL   MTPR_IPR_Name   ! PALcode format

Operation:

```
IF  PS<CM> NE 0  THEN
   {privileged instruction exception}
! R16 may contain an IPR specific source operand

R0 ← result of IPR specific function
IPR ← result of IPR specific function
```

Exceptions:

Privileged Instruction

Instruction mnemonics:

CALL_PAL MTPR_xxx   Move to Processor Register xxx

Description:

The MTPR_xxx instruction writes the IPR-specific source operands in integer registers R16 and R17 (R17 reserved for future use) to the internal processor register specified by the PAL-code function field. The effect produced by loading a processor register is guaranteed to be active on the next instruction.

Registers R1, R16, and R17 contain UNPREDICTABLE results after an MTPR. The MTPR may return results in R0. If the specific IPR being accessed does not return results in R0, then R0 contains an UNPREDICTABLE result after an MTPR.

See Chapter 5 for a description of each IPR.

2.6.6 Store Quadword Physical

Format:

> CALL_PAL STQP   ! PALcode format

Operation:

```
! R16 contains the quadword aligned physical address
! R17 contains the data to be written

IF PS<CM> NE 0 then
  {Privileged Instruction exception}

(R16) ← R17 {physical access}
```

Exceptions:

Privileged Instruction

Instruction mnemonics:

CALL_PAL STQP   Store Quadword Physical

Description:

The STQP instruction writes the quadword contents of R17 to the memory location whose physical address is in R16.

If the operand address in R16 is not quadword aligned, the result is UNPREDICTABLE.

2.6.7 Swap Privileged Context

Format:

    CALL_PAL   SWPCTX   ! PALcode format

Operation:

```
! R16 contains the physical address of the new HWPCB.

! check HWPCB alignment

IF R16<6:0> NE 0 THEN
  {reserved operand exception}
IF {PS<CM> NE 0} THEN
  {privileged instruction exception}

! Store old HWPCB contents

(IPR_PCBB + HWPCB_KSP) ← SP
IF {internal registers for stack pointers}  THEN
  BEGIN
    (IPR_PCBB + HWPCB_ESP) ← IPR_ESP
    (IPR_PCBB + HWPCB_SSP) ← IPR_SSP
    (IPR_PCBB + HWPCB_USP) ← IPR_USP
  END

IF {internal registers for ASTxx}  THEN
  BEGIN
    (IPR_PCBB + HWPCB_ASTSR) ← IPR_ASTSR
    (IPR_PCBB + HWPCB_ASTEN) ← IPR_ASTEN
  END
tmp1 ← PCC
tmp2 ← ZEXT(tmp1<31:0>)
tmp3 ← ZEXT(tmp1<63:32>)
(IPR_PCBB + HWPCB_PCC) ← {tmp2 + tmp3}<31:0>
IF {internal storage for process unique value} THEN
  BEGIN
    (IPR_PCBB + HWPCB_UNQ) ← process unique value
  END

! Load new HWPCB contents

IPR_PCBB ← R16

IF {ASNs not implemented in virtual instruction cache} THEN
  {flush instruction cache}
```

```
IF {ASNs not implemented in TB} THEN
    IF {IPR_PTBR NE (IPR_PCBB + HWPCB_PTBR)} THEN
        {invalidate trans. buffer entries with PTE<ASM> EQ 0}
ELSE
    IPR_ASN ← (IPR_PCBB + HWPCB_ASN)


SP ← (IPR_PCBB + HWPCB_KSP)
IF {internal registers for stack pointers} THEN
  BEGIN
   IPR_ESP ← (IPR_PCBB + HWPCB_ESP)
   IPR_SSP ← (IPR_PCBB + HWPCB_SSP)
   IPR_USP ← (IPR_PCBB + HWPCB_USP)
  END


IPR_PTBR  ← (IPR_PCBB + HWPCB_PTBR)

IF {internal registers for ASTxx}  THEN
 BEGIN
  IPR_ASTSR ← (IPR_PCBB + HWPCB_ASTSR)
  IPR_ASTEN ← (IPR_PCBB + HWPCB_ASTEN)
 END

IPR_FEN ← (IPR_PCBB + HWPCB_FEN)
  tmp4 ← ZEXT((IPR_PCBB + HWPCB_PCC)<31:0>)
  tmp4 ← tmp4 - tmp2
  PCC<63:32> ← tmp4<31:0>
IF {internal storage for process unique value} THEN
  BEGIN
    process unique value ← (IPR_PCBB + HWPCB_UNQ)
  END
IF {internal storage for Data Alignment trap setting} THEN
  BEGIN
    DAT ← (IPR_PCBB + HWPCB_DAT)
  END
```

Exceptions:

Reserved Operand

Privileged Instruction

Instruction mnemonics:

CALL_PAL   SWPCTX   Swap Privileged Context

Description:

The SWPCTX instruction returns ownership of the current Hardware Privileged Context Block (HWPCB) to the operating system and passes ownership of the new HWPCB to the processor. The HWPCB is described in Chapter 4.

SWPCTX saves the privileged context from the internal processor registers into the HWPCB specified by the physical address in the PCBB internal processor register. It then loads the privileged context from the new HWPCB specified by the physical address in R16. The actual sequence of the save and restore operation is not specified, so any overlap of the current and new HWPCB storage areas produces UNDEFINED results.

The privileged context includes the four stack pointers, the Page Table Base Register (PTBR), the Address Space Number (ASN), the AST enable and summary registers, the Floating-point Enable Register (FEN), the Performance Monitor (PME) register, the Data Alignment Trap (DAT) register, and the Charged Process Cycles — the number of PCC register counts that are charged to a process (modulo $2^{**}32$).

PTBR is never saved in the HWPCB and it is UNPREDICTABLE whether or not ASN is saved. These values cannot be changed for a running process. The process integer and floating registers are saved and restored by the operating system. See Figure 4–1 for the HWPCB format.

Notes:

- Any change to the current HWPCB while the processor has ownership results in UNDEFINED operation.

- All the values in the current HWPCB can be read through IPRs, except the Charged Process Cycles.

- If the HWPCB is read while ownership resides with the processor, it is UNPREDICTABLE whether the original or an updated value of a field is read. The processor can update an HWPCB field at any time. The decision as to whether or not a field is updated is made individually for each field.

- If the enabling conditions are present for an interrupt at the completion of this instruction, the interrupt occurs before the next instruction.

- PALcode sets up the PCBB at boot time to point to the HWPCB storage area in the Hardware Restart Parameter Block (HWRPB). See Console Interface (III), Chapter 2.

- The operation is UNDEFINED if SWPCTX accesses a non-memory-like region.

- A reference to nonexistent memory causes a machine check. Unimplemented physical address bits are SBZ. The operation is UNDEFINED if any of these bits are set.

  Note:

  Processors may keep a copy of each of the per-process stack pointers in internal registers. In those processors, SWPCTX stores the internal registers into the HWPCB. Processors that do not keep a copy of the stack pointers in internal registers keep only the stack pointer for the current access mode in SP and switch this with the HWPCB contents whenever the current access mode changes.

2.6.8 Swap PALcode Image

Format:

CALL_PAL   SWPPAL   ! PALcode format

Operation:

```
! R16 contains the new PALcode identifier
! R17-R21 contain implementation-specific entry parameters
! R0  receives status:
!          0 Success (PALcode was switched)
!          1 Unknown PALcode variant
!          2 Known PALcode variant, but PALcode not loaded

IF  (PS<CM> NE 0)  then
      {Privileged instruction exception}

ELSE
      IF {R16 < 256} THEN
          BEGIN
             IF {R16 invalid} THEN
                R0 ← 1
                {Return}
             ELSE IF {PALcode not loaded} THEN
                R0 ← 2
                {Return}
             ELSE
                tmp1 ← {PALcode base}
          END
      ELSE
          tmp1 = R16
      {Flush instruction cache}
      {Invalidate all translation buffers}
      {Perform additional PALcode variant-specific initialization}
      {Transfer control to PALcode entry at physical address in tmp1}
```

Exceptions:

Privileged Instruction

Instruction mnemonics:

CALL_PAL   SWPPAL   Swap PALcode Image

Description:

The SWPPAL instruction causes the current (active) PALcode to be replaced by the specified new PALcode image. This instruction is intended for use by operating systems only during bootstraps and by consoles during transitions to console I/O mode.

The PALcode descriptor contained in R16 is interpreted as either a PALcode variant or the base physical address of the new PALcode image. If a variant, the PALcode image must have been previously loaded. No PALcode loading occurs as a result of this instruction.

After successful PALcode switching, the register contents are determined by the parameters passed in R17 through R21 or are UNPREDICTABLE. A common parameter is the address of a new HWPCB. In this case, the stack pointer register and PTBR are determined by the contents of that HWPCB; the contents of other registers such as R16 through R21 may be UNPREDICTABLE.

See Console Interface Architecture (III), for information on using this instruction.

2.6.9 Wait for Interrupt

Format:

```
CALL_PAL              WTINT                              ! PALcode format
```

Operation:

```
! R16 contains the maximum number of interval clock ticks to skip
! R0  receives the number of interval clock ticks actually skipped

IF (implemented)
BEGIN
  IF {Implementation supports skipping multiple
      clock interrupts} THEN
    {Ticks_to_skip ←R16}

  {Wait no longer than any non-clock interrupt or the first clock
    interrupt after ticks_to_skip ticks have been skipped}

  IF {Implementation supports skipping multiple}
      {clock interrupts} THEN
    R0 ←number of interval clock ticks actually skipped
  ELSE
    R0 ←0
END
ELSE
  R0 ←0
{return}
```

Exceptions:

Privileged Instruction

Instruction mnemonics:

```
CALL_PAL  WTINT          Wait for Interrupt
```

Description:

The WTINT instruction requests that, if possible, the PALcode wait for the first of either of the following conditions before returning:

- Any interrupt other than a clock tick
- The first clock tick after a specified number of clock ticks has been skipped

The WTINT instruction returns in R0 the number of clock ticks that are skipped. The number returned in R0 is zero on hardware platforms that implement this instruction, but where it is not possible to skip clock ticks.

The operating system can specify a full 64-bit integer value in R16 as the maximum number of interval clock ticks to skip. A value of zero in R16 causes no clock ticks to be skipped.

Note the following if specifying in R16 the maximum number of interval clock ticks to skip:

- Adherence to a specified value in R16 is at the discretion of the PALcode; the PALcode may complete execution of WTINT and proceed to the next instruction at any time up to the specified maximum, even if no interrupt or interval-clock tick has occurred. That is, WTINT may return before all requested clock ticks are skipped.

- The PALcode must complete execution of WTINT if an interrupt occurs or if an interval-clock tick occurs after the requested number of interval-clock ticks has been skipped.

In a multiprocessor environment, only the issuing processor is affected by an issued WTINT instruction. The counters, SCC and PCC, may increment at a lower rate or may stop entirely during WTINT execution. This side effect is implementation dependent.

Chapter 3

Memory Management (II-A)

3.1 Introduction

Memory management consists of the hardware and software that control the allocation and use of physical memory. Typically, in a multiprogramming system, several processes may reside in physical memory at the same time (see Chapter 4). OpenVMS Alpha uses memory protection and multiple address spaces to ensure that one process will not affect other processes or the operating system.

To further improve software reliability, four hierarchical access modes provide memory access control. They are, from most to least privileged: kernel, executive, supervisor, and user. Protection is specified at the individual page level, where a page may be inaccessible, read-only, or read/write for each of the four access modes. Accessible pages can be restricted to have only data or instruction access.

A program uses virtual addresses to access its data and instructions. However, before these virtual addresses can be used to access memory, they must be translated into physical addresses. Memory management software maintains hierarchical tables of mapping information (page tables) that keep track of where each virtual page is located in physical memory. The processor utilizes this mapping information when it translates virtual addresses to physical addresses.

Therefore, memory management provides mechanisms for both memory protection and memory mapping. The OpenVMS Alpha memory management architecture is designed to meet several goals:

- Provide a large address space for instructions and data
- Allow programs to run on hardware with physical memory smaller than the virtual memory used
- Provide convenient and efficient sharing of instructions and data
- Allow sparse use of a large address space without excessive page table overhead
- Contribute to software reliability
- Provide independent read and write access protection

3.2 Virtual Address Space

A virtual address is a 64-bit unsigned integer that specifies a byte location within the virtual address space. Implementations subset the address space supported to one of several sizes, as a function of page size and page table depth. The minimal virtual address size supported is 43 bits. If an implementation supports less than 64-bit virtual addresses, it must check that all the VA<63:VA_SIZE> bits are equal to VA<VA_SIZE-1>. That gives two disjoint ranges for valid virtual addresses. For example, for a 43-bit virtual address space, valid virtual address ranges are $0 \ldots 3FF\ FFFF\ FFFF_{16}$ and $FFFF\ FC00\ 0000\ 0000_{16} \ldots FFFF\ FFFF\ FFFF\ FFFF_{16}$. Accesses to virtual addresses outside of the valid virtual address ranges for an implementation cause an access violation exception.

The virtual address space is broken into pages, which are the units of relocation, sharing, and protection. The page size ranges from 8K bytes to 64K bytes. System software should, therefore, allocate regions with differing protection on 64K-byte virtual address boundaries to ensure image compatibility across all Alpha implementations.

Memory management provides the mechanism to map the active part of the virtual address space to the available physical address space. The operating system controls the virtual-to-physical address mapping tables and saves the inactive parts of the virtual address space on external storage media.

3.3 Virtual Address Format

The processor generates a 64-bit virtual address for each instruction and operand in memory. The virtual address consists of three or four level-number fields and a byte_within_page field, as shown in Figures 3–1 and 3–2 .

Figure 3–1: Virtual Address Format, Three-Level Mode

Figure 3–2: Virtual Address Format, Four-Level Mode

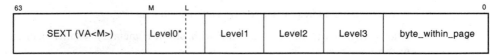

* Level0 <M:L+1> contains SEXT(VA<L>), where L is the highest numbered implemented VA bit.

The byte_within_page field can be either 13, 14, 15, or 16 bits depending on a particular implementation. Thus, the allowable page sizes are 8K bytes, 16K bytes, 32K bytes, and 64K bytes. Each level-number field contains n bits, where n is, for example, 10 with an 8K-byte page size. The level-number fields are the same size for a given implementation.

Implementations must support a mode of operation such that the virtual address format consists of at least three level-number fields (Level1, Level2, Level3) and a byte_within_page field. Optionally, implementations may support an extended mode of operation, such that the virtual address format includes a fourth level-number field, Level0. Determination of a three-versus four-level mode of operation occurs during system bootstrap. The selected mode affects all processes identically and remains in effect until the next bootstrap.

An implementation that supports the fourth level-number field may further subset the supported address space to include only a subset of low-order bits within that field. That subset must be at least two bits[1], and may be as large as *n* bits, where *n* is the full bit count of any given level-number field. The most significant bit in the chosen subset is sign-extended to VA<63> for any valid virtual address.

The level-number fields are a function of the page size; all page table entries at any given level do not exceed one page. The PFN field in the PTE is always 32 bits wide. Thus, as the page size grows, the virtual and physical address size also grows (Table 3–1).

Table 3–1: Virtual Address Options

Page Size (bytes)	Byte Offset (bits)	Level Size (bits)	Virtual Address (bits[1])	Physical Address (bits)
8 K	13	10	43, 45–53	45
16 K	14	11	47, 49–58	46
32 K	15	12	51, 53–63	47
64 K	16	13	55, 57–64[2]	48

[1] Bit counts for three, or four levels, respectively (VA_SIZE)

[2] Level 0 page table not fully utilized for this page size.

3.4 Physical Address Space

Physical addresses are at most 48 bits. A processor may choose to implement a smaller physical address space by not implementing some number of high-order bits.

The two most significant implemented physical address bits delineate the four regions in the physical address space. Implementations use these bits as appropriate for their systems. For example, in a workstation with a 30-bit physical address space, bit <29> might select between memory and non-memory-like regions, and bit <28> could enable or disable cacheing. See Common Architecture (I), Chapter 5.

3.5 Memory Management Control

Memory management is always enabled. Implementations must provide an environment for PALcode to service exceptions and to initialize and boot the processor. For example, PALcode might run with I-stream mapping disabled and use the privileged CALL_PAL LDQP and STQP instructions to access data stored in physical addresses.

---

1 OpenVMS requires at least three PTEs in the highest-level page table. The lowest-order PTE must map process space, the highest-order PTE must map system space, and the penultimate PTE maps the page table structure. See Section 3.8.2.

3.6 Page Table Entries

The processor uses a quadword Page Table Entry (PTE), as shown in Figure 3–3, to translate virtual addresses to physical addresses. A PTE contains hardware and software control information and the physical Page Frame Number.

Figure 3–3: Page Table Entry

63 PFN 32	31 Reserved for Software 16	15 U W E	S W E	E W E	K W E	U R E	S R E	E R E	K R E	R S V	8 7 6 G H	5 4 A S M	3 F O E	2 F O W	1 F O R	0 V

Fields in the page table entry are interpreted as shown in Table 3–2.

Table 3–2: Page Table Entry

Bits	Description
63–32	Page Frame Number (PFN) The PFN field always points to a page boundary. If V is set, the PFN is concatenated with the byte_within_page bits of the virtual address to obtain the physical address (see Section 3.8). If V is clear, this field may be used by software.
31–16	Reserved for software.
15	User Write Enable (UWE) This bit enables writes from user mode. If this bit is a 0 and a STORE is attempted while in user mode, an Access Violation occurs. This bit is valid even when V=0. **Note:** If a write-enable bit is set and the corresponding read-enable bit is not, the operation of the processor is UNDEFINED.
14	Supervisor Write Enable (SWE) This bit enables writes from supervisor mode. If this bit is a 0 and a STORE is attempted while in supervisor mode, an Access Violation occurs. This bit is valid even when V=0.
13	Executive Write Enable (EWE) This bit enables writes from executive mode. If this bit is a 0 and a STORE is attempted while in executive mode, an Access Violation occurs. This bit is valid even when V=0.
12	Kernel Write Enable (KWE) This bit enables writes from kernel mode. If this bit is a 0 and a STORE is attempted while in kernel mode, an Access Violation occurs. This bit is valid even when V=0.
11	User Read Enable (URE) This bit enables reads from user mode. If this bit is a 0 and a LOAD or instruction fetch is attempted while in user mode, an Access Violation occurs. This bit is valid even when V=0.

Table 3–2: Page Table Entry (Continued)

Bits	Description
10	**Supervisor Read Enable (SRE)** This bit enables reads from supervisor mode. If this bit is a 0 and a LOAD or instruction fetch is attempted while in supervisor mode, an Access Violation occurs. This bit is valid even when V=0.
9	**Executive Read Enable (ERE)** This bit enables reads from executive mode. If this bit is a 0 and a LOAD or instruction fetch is attempted while in executive mode, an Access Violation occurs. This bit is valid even when V=0.
8	**Kernel Read Enable (KRE)** This bit enables reads from kernel mode. If this bit is a 0 and a LOAD or instruction fetch is attempted while in kernel mode, an Access Violation occurs. This bit is valid even when V=0.
7	Reserved for future use by DIGITAL. **Programming Note:** The reserved bit will be used by future hardware systems and should not be used by software even if PTE<V> is clear.
6–5	**Granularity hint (GH)** Software may set these bits to a non-zero value to supply a hint to translation buffer implementations that a block of pages can be treated as a single larger page: 1. The block is an aligned group of 8**N pages, where N is the value of PTE<6:5>, that is, a group of 1, 8, 64, or 512 pages starting at a virtual address with page_size + 3*N low-order zeros. 2. The block is a group of physically contiguous pages that are aligned both virtually and physically. Within the block, the low 3*N bits of the PFNs describe the identity mapping and the high 32-3*N PFN bits are all equal. 3. Within the block, all PTEs have the same values for bits <15:0>, that is, protection, fault, granularity, and valid bits. Hardware may use this hint to map the entire block with a single TB entry, instead of 8, 64, or 512 separate TB entries. It is UNPREDICTABLE which PTE values within the block are used if the granularity bits are set inconsistently. **Programming Note:** A granularity hint might be appropriate for a large memory structure such as a frame buffer or nonpaged pool that, in fact, is mapped into contiguous virtual pages with identical protection, fault, and valid bits.
4	**Address Space Match (ASM)** When set, this PTE matches all Address Space Numbers. For a given VA, ASM must be set consistently in all processes; otherwise, the address mapping is UNPREDICTABLE.

Table 3–2: Page Table Entry (Continued)

Bits	Description
3	Fault on Execute (FOE) When set, a Fault on Execute exception occurs on an attempt to execute an instruction in the page.
2	Fault on Write (FOW) When set, a Fault on Write exception occurs on an attempt to write any location in the page.
1	Fault on Read (FOR) When set, a Fault on Read exception occurs on an attempt to read any location in the page.
0	Valid (V) Indicates the validity of the the PFN field. When V is set, the PFN field is valid for use by hardware. When V is clear, the PFN field is reserved for use by software. The V bit does not affect the validity of PTE<15:1> bits.

3.6.1 Changes to Page Table Entries

The operating system changes PTEs as part of its memory management functions. For example, the operating system may set or clear the valid bit, change the PFN field as pages are moved to and from external storage media, or modify the software bits. The processor hardware never changes PTEs.

Software must guarantee that each PTE is always internally consistent. Changing a PTE one field at a time may give incorrect system operation, for example, setting PTE<V> with one instruction before establishing PTE<PFN> with another. Execution of an interrupt service routine between the two instructions could use an address that would map using the inconsistent PTE. Software can solve this problem by building a complete new PTE in a register and then moving the new PTE to the page table using a Store Quadword instruction (STQ).

Multiprocessing complicates the problem. Another processor could be reading (or even changing) the same PTE that the first processor is changing. Such concurrent access must produce consistent results. Software must use some form of software synchronization to modify PTEs that are already valid. Once a processor has modified a valid PTE, it is possible that other processors in a multiprocessor system may have old copies of that PTE in their Translation Buffer. Software must notify other processors of changes to PTEs.

Software may write new values into invalid PTEs using quadword store instructions (STQ). Hardware must ensure that aligned quadword reads and writes are atomic operations. The following procedure must be used to change any of the PTE bits <15:0> of a shared valid PTE (PTE<0>=1) such that an access that was allowed before the change is not allowed after the change.

1. The PTE<0> is cleared without changing any of the PTE bits <63:32> and <15:1>.

2. All processors do a TBIS for the VA mapped by the PTE that changed. The VA used in the TBIS must assume that the PTE granularity hint bits are zero.

3. After all processors have done the TBIS, the new PTE may be written changing any or all fields.

Programming Note:

The procedure above allows queue instructions that have probed in order to check that all can complete, to service a TB miss. The queue instructions use the PTE even though the V bit is clear, if the V bit was set during the instruction's initial probe flow.

3.7 Memory Protection

Memory protection is the function of validating whether a particular type of access is allowed to a specific page from a particular access mode. Access to each page is controlled by a protection code that specifies, for each access mode, whether read or write references are allowed.

The processor uses the following to determine whether an intended access is allowed:

- The virtual address, which is used to index page tables

- The intended access type (read data, write data, or instruction fetch)

- The current access mode from the Processor Status

If the access is allowed and the address can be mapped (the Page Table Entry is valid), the result is the physical address that corresponds to the specified virtual address.

For protection checks, the intended access is read for data loads and instruction fetch, and write for data stores.

If an operand is an address operand, then no reference is made to memory. Hence, the page need not be accessible nor map to a physical page.

3.7.1 Processor Access Modes

There are four processor modes:

- Kernel

- Executive

- Supervisor

- User

The access mode of a running process is stored in the Current Mode bits of the Processor Status (PS) (see Section 6–2).

3.7.2 Protection Code

Every page in the virtual address space is protected according to its use. A program may be prevented from reading or writing portions of its address space. Each page has an associated protection code that describes the accessibility of the page for each processor mode. The code allows a choice of read or write protection for each processor mode.

- Each mode's access can be read/write, read-only, or no-access.

- Read and write accessibility are specified independently.
- The protection of each mode can be specified independently.

The protection code is specified by 8 bits in the PTE (see Table 3–2).

The OpenVMS Alpha architecture allows a page to be designated as execute only by setting the read enable bit for the access mode and by setting the fault on read and write bits in the PTE.

3.7.3 Access Violation Fault

An Access Violation fault occurs if an illegal access is attempted, as determined by the current processor mode and the page's protection field.

3.8 Address Translation

The page tables can be accessed from physical memory, or (to reduce overhead) through a mapping to a linear region of the virtual address space. All implementations must support the virtual access method and are expected to use it as the primary access method to enhance performance.

The following sections describe both access methods.

3.8.1 Physical Access for Page Table Entries

Physical address translation is performed by accessing entries in a multilevel page table structure. The Page Table Base Register (PTBR) contains the physical Page Frame Number (PFN) of the highest-level page table. If the system was booted with three levels of page table, this is the Level 1 page table. If the system was booted with four levels of page table, this is the Level 0 page table. In that case, bits <Level0> of the virtual address are used to index into the Level 0 page table to obtain the physical PFN of the base of the Level 1 page table.

With either a three-level or four-level page table, bits <Level1> of the virtual address are used to index into the Level 1 page table to obtain the physical PFN of the base of the next level (Level 2) page table. Bits <Level2> of the virtual address are used to index into the Level 2 page table to obtain the physical PFN of the base of the next level (Level 3) page table. Bits <Level3> of the virtual address are used to index into the Level 3 page table to obtain the physical PFN of the page being referenced. The PFN is concatenated with virtual address bits <byte_within_page> to obtain the physical address of the location being accessed.

If part of any page table resides in I/O space, or in nonexistent memory, the operation of the processor is UNDEFINED.

If all the higher-level PTEs (those PTEs that map higher-significance portions of the virtual address space than is mapped by Level 3) are valid, the protection bits are ignored; the protection code in the Level 3 PTE is used to determine accessibility. If a higher-level PTE is invalid, an access-violation fault occurs if the PTE<KRE> equals zero. An Access-Violation fault on any higher-level PTE implies that all lower-level page tables mapped by that PTE do not exist.

Programming Note:

This mapping scheme does not require multiple contiguous physical pages. There are no length registers. With a page size of 8K bytes and three levels of page table, 3 pages (24K bytes) map 8M bytes of virtual address space; 1026 pages (approximately 8M bytes) map an 8G-byte address space; and 1,049,601 pages (approximately 8G bytes) map the entire 8T byte 2**43 byte address space.

The algorithm to generate a physical address from a virtual address follows:

```
IF {SEXT(VA<63:VA_SIZE>) NEQ SEXT(VA<VA_SIZE-1>} THEN
    {initiate Access Violation fault}

IF {booted with 4 levels of page table} THEN

    ! Read Physical
    level0_pte ← ({PTBR * page_size} + {8 * VA<level0>})

    IF level0_pte<V> EQ 0 THEN
        IF level0_pte<KRE> EQ 0 THEN
            {initiate Access Violation fault}
        ELSE
            {initiate Translation Not Valid fault}

    ! Read Physical
    level1_pte ← ({level0_pte<PFN> * page_size} + {8 * VA<level1>})

ELSE

    ! Read Physical
    level1_pte ← ({PTBR * page_size} + {8 * VA<level1>})

IF level1_pte<V> EQ 0 THEN
    IF level1_pte<KRE> EQ 0 THEN
        {initiate Access Violation fault}
    ELSE
        {initiate Translation Not Valid fault}

! Read Physical
level2_pte ← ({level1_pte<PFN> * page_size} + {8 * VA<level2>})

IF level2_pte<V> EQ 0 THEN
    IF level2_pte<KRE> EQ 0 THEN
        {initiate Access Violation fault}
    ELSE
        {initiate Translation Not Valid fault}

! Read Physical
level3_pte ← ({level2_pte<PFN> * page_size} + {8 * VA<level3>})
```

```
IF {{{level3_pte<UWE> EQ 0} AND {write access} AND {PS<CM> EQ 3}} OR
    {{level3_pte<URE> EQ 0} AND {read  access} AND {PS<CM> EQ 3}} OR
    {{level3_pte<SWE> EQ 0} AND {write access} AND {PS<CM> EQ 2}} OR
    {{level3_pte<SRE> EQ 0} AND {read  access} AND {PS<CM> EQ 2}} OR
    {{level3_pte<EWE> EQ 0} AND {write access} AND {PS<CM> EQ 1}} OR
    {{level3_pte<ERE> EQ 0} AND {read  access} AND {PS<CM> EQ 1}} OR
    {{level3_pte<KWE> EQ 0} AND {write access} AND {PS<CM> EQ 0}} OR
    {{level3_pte<KRE> EQ 0} AND {read  access} AND {PS<CM> EQ 0}}}}
THEN
    {initiate Access Violation fault}
ELSE
    IF level3_pte<V> EQ 0 THEN
        {initiate Translation Not Valid fault}

IF {level3_pte<FOW> EQ 1} AND { write   access} THEN
    {initiate Fault On Write fault}
IF {level3_pte<FOR> EQ 1} AND { read    access} THEN
    {initiate Fault On Read fault}
IF {level3_pte<FOE> EQ 1} AND { execute access} THEN
    {initiate Fault On Execute fault}

Physical_Address ← {level3_pte<PFN> * page_size} OR VA<byte_within_page>
```

3.8.2 Virtual Access for Page Table Entries

To reduce the overhead associated with the address translation in a multilevel page table structure, the page tables are mapped into a linear region of the virtual address space. The virtual address of the base of the page table structure is set on a system-wide basis and is contained in the VPTB IPR.

When a native mode DTB or ITB miss occurs, the TBMISS flows attempt to load the Level 3 page table entry using a single virtual mode load instruction.

The algorithm involving the manipulation of the missing VA follows, where L_c represents Level_count and pS represents pageSize:

```
! If booted with 3 level fields in the VA format, L_c=3
! If booted with 4 level fields in the VA format, L_c=4

tmp ← LEFT_SHIFT (va, {64 - {{lg(pS)*{L_c+1}} - {L_c*3}}})
tmp ← RIGHT_SHIFT (tmp, {64 - {{lg(pS)*{L_c+1}} - {L_c*3}} + lg(pS)-3})
tmp ← VPTB OR tmp
tmp<2:0> ← 0
```

At this point, *tmp* contains the VA of the Level 3 page table entry. A LDQ from that VA will result in the acquistion of the PTE needed to satisfy the initial TBMISS condition.

However, in the PALcode environment, if a TBMISS occurs during an attempt to fetch the Level 3 PTE, it is necessary to use the longer sequence of multiple dependent loads described in Section 3.8.1.

Chapter 5 contains the description of the VPTB IPR used to contain the virtual address of the base of the page table structure.

The necessary mapping of the page tables for the correct function of the algorithm is done as follows. In the algorithm, if the system is booted with three level fields in the virtual address format, Level_count=3. If the system is booted with four level fields in the virtual address format, Level_count=4.

1. Select a $2^{(Level\_count*lg(pageSize/8))+3)}$ byte-aligned region (an address with Level_count*lg(pageSize/8)+3) low-order zeros) in the virtual address space. This value will be written into the VPTB register.

2. Create a PTE to map the page tables as follows:

```
PTE = 0                         ! Initialize all fields to zero
PTE<63:32> = pfn_of_most_significant_pagetable
                                ! Set the PFN to the PFN of
                                !  the most significant pagetable
PTE<8>  = 1                     ! Set the kernel read enable bit
PTE<0>  = 1                     ! Set the valid bit
```

3. Write the created PTE into the page table entry that corresponds to the VPTB value. If operating in the mode of three levels of page table, this is the Level 1 page table. If operating in the mode of four levels of page table, this is the Level 0 page table.

4. Set all higher-level, Valid PTEs that map the Level 3 page tables to allow kernel read access.

5. Write the VPTB register with the selected base value.

Note:

No validity checks need be made on the value stored in the VPTB in a running system. Therefore, if the VPTB contains an invalid address, the operation is UNDEFINED.

3.9 Translation Buffer

In order to save actual memory references when repeatedly referencing the same pages, hardware implementations include a translation buffer to remember successful virtual address translations and page states.

When the process context is changed, a new value is loaded into the Address Space Number (ASN) internal processor register with a Swap Privileged Context instruction (CALL_PAL SWPCTX). (see Section 2.6 and Chapter 4.) This causes address translations for pages with PTE<ASM> clear to be invalidated on a processor that does not implement address space numbers. Additionally, when the software changes any part (except for the Software field) of a valid Page Table Entry, it must also move a virtual address within the corresponding page to the Translation Buffer Invalidate Single (TBIS) internal processor register with the MTPR instruction (see Chapter 5).

Implementation Note:

> Some implementations may invalidate the entire Translation Buffer on an MTPR to TBIS. In general, implementations may invalidate more than the required translations in the TB.

The entire Translation Buffer can be invalidated by doing a write to Translation Buffer Invalidate All register (CALL_PAL MTPR_TBIA), and all ASM=0 entries can be invalidated by doing a write to Translation Buffer Invalidate All Process register (CALL_PAL MTPR_TBIAP). (See Chapter 5.)

The Translation Buffer must not store invalid PTEs. Therefore, the software is not required to invalidate Translation Buffer entries when making changes for PTEs that are already invalid.

After software changes a valid zero-, first- or second-level PTE, software must flush the translation for the corresponding page in the virtual page table. Then software must flush the translations of all valid pages mapped by that page. In the case of a change to a first-level PTE, this action must be taken through a second iteration. In the case of a change to a zero-level PTE, this action must be taken through a second and third iteration.

The TBCHK internal processor register is available for interrogating the presence of a valid translation in the Translation Buffer (see Chapter 5).

Implementation Note:

> Hardware implementors should be aware that a single, direct-mapped TB has a potential problem when a load/store instruction and its data map to the same TB location. If TB misses are handled in PALcode, there could be an endless loop unless the instruction is held in an instruction buffer or a translated physical PC is maintained by the hardware.

3.10 Address Space Numbers

The Alpha architecture allows a processor to optionally implement address space numbers (process tags) to reduce the need for invalidation of cached address translations for process specific addresses when a context switch occurs. The supported ASN range is 0...MAX_ASN. MAX_ASN is provided in the HWRPB MAX_ASN field. See Console Interface (III), Chapter 2, for a detailed description of the HWRPB.

Note:

> If an ASN outside of the range 0...MAX_ASN is assigned to a process, the operation of the processor is UNDEFINED.

The address space number for the current process is loaded by software in the Address Space Number (ASN) internal processor register with a Swap Privileged Context instruction. ASNs are processor specific and the hardware makes no attempt to maintain coherency across multiple processors. In a multiprocessor system, software is responsible for ensuring the consistency of TB entries for processes that might be rescheduled on different processors.

Systems that support ASNs should have MAX_ASN in the range 13...65535. The number of ASNs should be determined by the market a system is targeting.

Programming Note:

System software should not assume that the number of ASNs is a power of two. This allows, for example, hardware to use N TB tag bits to encode (2**N)−3 ASN values, one value for ASM=1 PTEs, and one for invalid.

There are several possible ways of using ASNs that result from several complications in a multiprocessor system. Consider the case in which a process that executed on processor 1 is rescheduled on processor 2. If a page is deleted or its protection is changed, the TB in processor 1 has stale data. One solution is to send an interprocessor interrupt to all the processors on which this process could have run and cause them to invalidate the changed PTE. That results in significant overhead in a system with several processors. Another solution is to have software invalidate all TB entries for a process on a new processor before it can begin execution, if the process executed on another processor during its previous execution. That ensures the deletion of possibly stale TB entries on the new processor. A third solution is to assign a new ASN whenever a process is run on a processor that is not the same as the last processor on which it ran.

3.11 Memory Management Faults

Five types of faults are associated with memory access and protection:

- Access Control Violation (ACV)

  Taken when the protection field of the third-level PTE that maps the data indicates that the intended page reference would be illegal in the specified access mode. An Access Control Violation fault is also taken if the KRE bit is zero in an invalid Level 0 (if one exists), Level 1, or Level 2 PTE.

- Fault on Read (FOR)

  Occurs when a read is attempted with PTE<FOR> set.

- Fault on Write (FOW)

  Occurs when a write is attempted with PTE<FOW> set.

- Fault on Execute (FOE)

  Occurs when instruction execution is attempted with PTE<FOE> set.

- Translation Not Valid (TNV)

  Taken when a read or write reference is attempted through an invalid PTE in a Level 0 (if one exists), Level 1, Level 2, or Level 3 page table.

See Chapter 6 for a detailed description of these faults.

Those five faults have distinct vectors in the System Control Block. The Access Violation (ACV) fault takes precedence over the faults TNV, FOR, FOW, and FOE. The Translation Not Valid (TNV) fault takes precedence over the faults FOR, FOW, and FOE.

The faults FOR and FOW can occur simultaneously in the CALL_PAL queue instructions, in which case the order that the exceptions are taken is UNPREDICTABLE (see Section 2.1).

Chapter 4

Process Structure (II-A)

4.1 Process Definition

A process is the basic entity that is scheduled for execution by the processor. A process represents a single thread of execution and consists of an address space and both hardware and software context.

The hardware context of a process is defined by:

- Thirty-one integer registers and 31 floating-point registers
- Processor Status (PS)
- Program Counter (PC)
- Four stack pointers
- Asynchronous System Trap Enable and summary registers (ASTEN, ASTSR)
- Process Page Table Base Register (PTBR)
- Address Space Number (ASN)
- Floating Enable Register (FEN)
- Charged Process Cycles
- Process Unique value
- Data Alignment Trap (DAT)
- Performance Monitoring Enable Register (PME)

The software context of a process is defined by operating system software and is system dependent.

A process may share the same address space with other processes or have an address space of its own. There is, however, no separate address space for system software, and therefore, the operating system must be mapped into the address space of each process (see Chapter 3).
In order for a process to execute, its hardware context must be loaded into the integer registers, floating-point registers, and internal processor registers. When a process is being executed, its hardware context is continuously updated. When a process is not being executed, its hardware context is stored in memory.

Saving the hardware context of the current process in memory, followed by loading the hardware context for a new process, is termed context switching. Context switching occurs as one process after another is scheduled by the operating system for execution.

4.2 Hardware Privileged Process Context

The hardware context of a process is defined by a privileged part that is context switched with the Swap Privileged Context instruction (SWPCTX) (see Section 2.6), and a nonprivileged part that is context switched by operating system software.

When a process is not executing, its privileged context is stored in a 128-byte naturally aligned memory structure called the Hardware Privileged Context Block (HWPCB). (See Figure 4–1.)

Figure 4–1: Hardware Privileged Context Block

63 62 61	32 31	16 15	8 7	4 3 1 0	
Kernel Stack Pointer (KSP)					:HWPCB
Executive Stack Pointer (ESP)					:+8
Supervisor Stack Pointer (SSP)					:+16
User Stack Pointer (USP)					:+24
Page Table Base Register (PTBR)					:+32
		ASN			:+40
			AST SR	AST EN	:+48
D P A M T E				F E N	:+56
	Charged Process Cycles				:+64
Process Unique Value					:+72
PALcode Scratch Area of 6 Quadwords					:+80

The Hardware Privileged Context Block (HWPCB) for the current process is specified by the Privileged Context Block Base register (PCBB). (See Chapter 5.)

The Swap Privileged Context instruction (SWPCTX) saves the privileged context of the current process into the HWPCB specified by PCBB, loads a new value into PCBB, and then loads the privileged context of the new process into the appropriate hardware registers.

The new value loaded into PCBB, as well as the contents of the Privileged Context Block, must satisfy certain constraints or an UNDEFINED operation results:

- The physical address loaded into PCBB must be 128-byte aligned and describes 16 contiguous quadwords that are in a memory-like region. (See Common Architecture (I), Chapter 5.)

- The value of PTBR must be the Page Frame Number of an existent page that is in a memory-like region.

It is the responsibility of the operating system to save and load the nonprivileged part of the hardware context.

The SWPCTX instruction returns ownership of the current HWPCB to operating system software and passes ownership of the new HWPCB from the operating system to the processor. Any attempt to write a HWPCB while ownership resides with the processor has UNDEFINED results. If the HWPCB is read while ownership resides with the processor, it is UNPREDICTABLE whether the original or an updated value of a field is read. The processor can update an HWPCB field at any time. The decision as to whether or not a field is updated is made individually for each field.

If ASNs are not implemented, the ASN field is not read or written by PALcode.

The FEN bit reflects the setting of the FEN IPR.

Setting the PME bit alerts any performance hardware or software in the system to monitor the performance of this process.

The DAT bit controls whether data alignment traps that are fixed up in PALcode are reported to the operating system. If the bit is clear, the trap is reported. If the bit is set, after the fixup, return is to the user. See Section 6.6.

The Charged Process Cycles is the total number of PCC register counts that are charged to the process (modulo $2**32$). When a process context is loaded by the SWPCTX instructions, the contents of the PCC count field (PCC_CNT) are subtracted from the contents of HWPCB[64]<31:0> and the result is written to the PCC offset field (PCC_OFF):

$$PCC<63:32> \leftarrow (HWPCB[64]<31:0> - PCC<31:0>)$$

When a process context is saved by the SWPCTX instruction, the charged process cycles is computed by performing an unsigned add of PCC<63:32> and PCC<31:0>. That value is written to HWPCB[64]<31:0>.

Software Programming Note:

The following example returns in R0 the current PCC register count (modulo $2**32$) for a process. Care is taken not to cause an unwanted sign extension.

```
RPCC    R0              ; Read the processor cycle counter
SLL     R0, #32, R1     ; Line up the offset and count fields
ADDQ    R0, R1, R0      ; Do add
SRL     R0, #32, R0     ; Zero extend the cycle count to 64 bits
```

The Process Unique value is that value used in support of multithread implementations. The value is stored in the HWPCB when the process is not active. When the process is active, the value may be cached in hardware internal storage or kept only in the HWPCB.

4.3 Asynchronous System Traps (AST)

Asynchronous System Traps (ASTs) are a means of notifying a process of events that are not synchronized with its execution but that must be dealt with in the context of the process with minimum delay.

Asynchronous System Traps (ASTs) interrupt process execution and are controlled by the AST Enable (ASTEN) and AST Summary (ASTSR) internal processor registers. (See Chapter 5.)

The AST Enable register (ASTEN) contains an enable bit for each of the four processor access modes. When the bit corresponding to an access mode is set, ASTs for that mode are enabled. The AST enable bit for an access mode may be changed by executing a Swap AST Enable instruction (SWASTEN; see Section 2.6), or by executing a Move to Processor Register instruction specifying ASTEN (MTPR ASTEN; see Chapter 5).

The AST Summary Register (ASTSR) contains a pending bit for each of the four processor access modes. When the bit corresponding to an access mode is set, an AST is pending for that mode.

Kernel mode software may request an AST for a particular access mode by executing a Move to Processor Register instruction specifying ASTSR (MTPR ASTSR; see Chapter 5).

Hardware or PALcode monitors the state of ASTEN, ASTSR, PS<CM>, and PS<IPL>. If PS<IPL> is less than 2, and there is an AST pending and enabled for an access mode that is less than or equal to PS<CM> (that is, an equal or more privileged access mode), an AST is initiated at IPL 2.

ASTs that are pending and enabled for a less privileged access mode are not allowed to interrupt execution in a more privileged access mode.

4.4 Process Context Switching

Process context switching occurs as one process after another is scheduled for execution by operating system software. Context switching requires the hardware context of one process to be saved in memory followed by the loading of the hardware context for another process into the hardware registers.

The privileged hardware context is swapped with the CALL_PAL Swap Privileged Context instruction (SWPCTX). Other hardware context must be saved and restored by operating system software.

The sequence in which process context is changed is important because the SWPCTX instruction changes the environment in which the context switching software itself is executing. Also, although hardware does not enforce this, it is advisable to execute the actual context switching software in an environment that cannot be context switched (that is, at an IPL high enough that rescheduling cannot occur).

The SWPCTX instruction is the only method provided for loading certain internal processor registers. The SWPCTX instruction always saves the privileged context of the old process and loads the privileged context of a new process. Therefore, a valid HWPCB must be available to save the privileged context of the old process as well as load the privileged context of the new process.

At system initialization, a valid HWPCB is constructed in the Hardware Restart Parameter Block (HWRPB) for the primary processor. (See Console Interface (III), Chapter 2.) Thereafter, it is the responsibility of operating system software to ensure a valid HWPCB when executing a SWPCTX instruction.

Chapter 5

Internal Processor Registers (II–A)

5.1 Internal Processor Registers

This chapter describes the OpenVMS Alpha Internal Processor Registers (IPRs). These registers are read and written with Move from Processor Register (MFPR) and Move to Processor Register (MTPR) instructions. See Section 2.6.

Those instructions accept an input operand in R16 and return a result, if any, in R0. Registers R1, R16, and R17 are UNPREDICTABLE after a CALL_PAL MxPR routine. If a CALL_PAL MxPR routine does not return a result in R0, then R0 is also UNPREDICTABLE on return.

Some IPRs (for example, ASTSR, ASTEN, IPL) may be both read and written in a combined operation by performing an MTPR instruction.

Internal Processor Registers may or may not be implemented as actual hardware registers. An implementation may choose any combination of PALcode and hardware to produce the architecturally specified function.

Internal Processor Registers are only accessible from kernel mode.

5.2 Stack Pointer Internal Processor Registers

The stack pointers for user, supervisor, and executive stacks are accessible as IPRs through the CALL_PAL MTPR and MFPR instructions. An implementation may retain some or all of these stack pointers only in the HWPCB. In this case, MTPR and MFPR for these registers must access the corresponding PCB locations. However, implementations that have these stack pointers in internal hardware registers are not required to access the corresponding HWPCB locations for MTPR and MFPR. The HWPCB locations get updated when a SWPCTX instruction is executed.

An implementation may also choose to keep the kernel stack pointer (KSP) in an internal hardware register (labeled IPR_KSP); however, this register is not directly accessible through MTPR and MFPR instructions. Because access to the KSP requires kernel mode, the actual KSP is the current mode stack pointer (R30); thus access to KSP is provided through R30, and no MTPR or MFPR access is required. PALcode routines can directly access IPR_KSP as needed.

At system initialization, the value of the KSP is taken from the initial HWPCB (see Chapter 4). Table 5–1 summarizes the IPRs.

5.3 IPR Summary

Table 5-1: Internal Processor Register (IPR) Summary

Register Name	Mnemonic	Access[1]	Input R16	Output R0	Context Switched
Address Space Number	ASN	R	—	Number	Yes
AST Enable	ASTEN	R/W*	Mask	Mask	Yes
AST Summary Register	ASTSR	R/W*	Mask	Mask	Yes
Data Align Trap Fixup	DATFX	W	Value	—	Yes
Exec Stack Pointer	ESP	R/W	Address	Address	Yes
Floating-point Enable	FEN	R/W	Value	Value	Yes
Interprocessor Int. Request	IPIR	W	Number	—	No
Interrupt Priority Level	IPL	R/W*	Value	Value	No
Kernel Stack Pointer	KSP	None	—	—	Yes
Machine Check Error Summary	MCES	R/W	Value	Value	No
Performance Monitor	PERFMON	W*	IMP	IMP	No
Privileged Context Block Base	PCBB	R	—	Address	No
Processor Base Register	PRBR	R/W	Value	Value	No
Page Table Base Register	PTBR	R	—	Frame	Yes
System Control Block Base	SCBB	R/W	Frame	Frame	No
Software Int. Request Register	SIRR	W	Level	—	No
Software Int. Summary Register	SISR	R	—	Mask	No
Supervisor Stack Pointer	SSP	R/W	Address	Address	Yes
TB Check	TBCHK	R	Number	Status	No
TB Invalid. All	TBIA	W	—	—	No
TB Invalid. All Process	TBIAP	W	—	—	No
TB Invalid. Single	TBIS	W	Address	—	No
TB Invalid. Single Data	TBISD	W	Address	—	No
TB Invalid. Single Instruct.	TBISI	W	Address	—	No
User Stack Pointer	USP	R/W	Address	Address	Yes
Virtual Page Table Base	VPTB	R/W	Address	Address	No
Who-Am-I	WHAMI	R	—	Number	No

[1] Access symbols are defined in Table 5-2.

Table 5–2: Internal Processor Register (IPR) Access Summary

Access Type	Meaning
R	Access by MFPR only.
W	Access by MTPR only.
R/W	Access by MFPR or MTPR.
W*	Read and Write access accomplished by MTPR. See Section 5.1 for details.
R/W*	Access by MFPR or MTPR. Read and Write access accomplished by MTPR. See Section 5.1 for details.
None	Not accessible by MTPR or MFPR; accessed by PALcode routines as needed.

5.3.1 Address Space Number (ASN)

Access:

> Read

Operation:

```
IF {ASN are implemented} THEN
    R0 ← ZEXT(ASN)
ELSE
    R0 ← 0
```

Value at System Initialization:

> Zero

Format:

Figure 5–1: Address Space Number (ASN) Register

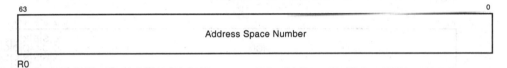

Description:

Address Space Numbers (ASNs) are used to further qualify Translation Buffer references. See Chapter 3. If ASNs are implemented, the current ASN may be read by executing an MFPR instruction specifying ASN.

As processes are scheduled for execution, the ASN for the next process to execute is loaded using the Swap Privileged Context (SWPCTX) instruction. See Section 2.6.7 and Chapter 4.

The ASN register is an implicit operand to the CALL_PAL MFPR_IPR, TBCHK, and TBISx PALcode instructions, in which it is used to qualify the virtual address supplied in R16.

5.3.2 AST Enable (ASTEN)

Access:

Read

Write*

Operation:

```
R0 ← ZEXT (ASTEN<3:0>)                    ! Read (MFPR)
R0 ← ZEXT (ASTEN<3:0>)                    ! Write* (MTPR)
ASTEN<3:0> ← {{ASTEN<3:0> AND R16<3:0>} OR R16<7:4>}
{check for pending ASTs}
```

Value at System Initialization:

Zero

Format:

Figure 5–2: AST Enable (ASTEN) Register

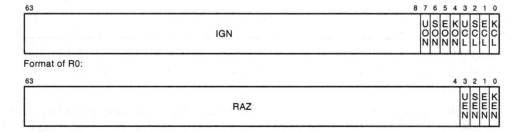

Description:

The AST Enable Register records the AST enable state for each of the modes: kernel (KEN), executive (EEN), supervisor (SEN), and user (UEN). By writing R16 appropriately and then executing an MTPR instruction specifying ASTEN, the value of ASTEN may be simultaneously read and modified. R16 contains bit masks that are used to determine the new value of ASTEN:

- Bits R16<0> and R16<4> control the new state of kernel enable.

- Bits R16<1> and R16<5> control the new state of executive enable.

- Bits R16<2> and R16<6> control the new state of supervisor enable.

- Bits R16<3> and R16<7> control the new state of user enable.

An MFPR to ASTEN reads the current value of the ASTEN and returns this value in R0.

An MTPR to ASTEN begins by reading the current value of ASTEN and returning this value in R0. The current value of ASTEN is then ANDed with bits R16<3:0>; these bits preserve (if set to 1) or clear (if equal to 0) the current state of their corresponding enable modes. The value produced by this operation is then ORed with bits R16<7:4>; these bits turn on (if set to 1) or do not affect (if equal to 0) their corresponding enable modes. The resulting value is then written to the ASTEN.

Note:

All AST enables can be cleared by loading a zero into R16 and executing an MTPR instruction specifying ASTEN. To enable an AST for a given mode, load R16 with a mask that has bits <3:0> set and one of the bits <7:4> corresponding to the AST mode to be set. Then execute an MTPR instruction specifying ASTEN.

As processes are scheduled for execution, the state of the AST enables for the next process to execute is loaded using the Swap Privileged Context (SWPCTX) instruction. The Swap AST Enable (SWASTEN) instruction can be used to change the enable state for the current access mode. See Section 2.1.13 and Chapter 4.

5.3.3 AST Summary Register (ASTSR)

Access:

> Read
> Write*

Operation:

```
R0 ← ZEXT(ASTSR<3:0>)                    ! Read (MFPR)
R0 ← ZEXT(ASTSR<3:0>)                    ! Write* (MTPR)
ASTSR<3:0> ← {{ASTSR<3:0> AND R16<3:0>} OR R16<7:4>}
{check for pending ASTs}
```

Value at System Initialization:

> Zero

Format:

Figure 5–3: AST Summary Register (ASTSR)

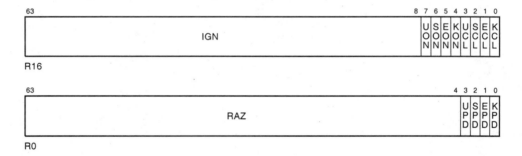

Description:

The AST Summary Register records the AST pending state for each of the modes: kernel (KPD), executive (EPD), supervisor (SPD), and user (UPD).

By writing R16 appropriately and then executing an MTPR instruction specifying ASTSR, the value of ASTSR may be simultaneously read and modified. R16 contains bit masks used to determine the new value of ASTSR:

- Bits R16<0> and R16<4> control the new state of kernel pending.

- Bits R16<1> and R16<5> control the new state of executive pending.

- Bits R16<2> and R16<6> control the new state of supervisor pending.

- Bits R16<3> and R16<7> control the new state of user pending.

An MFPR reads the current value of ASTSR and returns this value in R0.

An MTPR to ASTSR begins by reading the current value of ASTSR and returning this value in R0. The current value of ASTSR is then ANDed with bits R16<3:0>; these bits preserve (if set to 1) or clear (if equal to 0) the current state of their corresponding pending modes. The value produced by this operation is then ORed with bits R16<7:4>; these bits turn on (if set to 1) or do not affect (if equal to 0) their corresponding pending modes. The resulting value is then written to the ASTSR.

Note:

> All AST requests can be cleared by loading a zero in R16 and executing an MTPR instruction specifying ASTSR. To request an AST for a given mode, load R16 with a mask that has bits <3:0> set and one of the bits <7:4> corresponding to the AST mode to be set. Then execute an MTPR instruction specifying ASTSR.

As processes are scheduled for execution, the pending AST state for the next process to execute is loaded using the Swap Privileged Context (SWPCTX) instruction. See Section 2.6.7 and Chapter 4.

When the processor IPL is less than 2, and proper enabling conditions are present, an AST interrupt is initiated at IPL 2 and the corresponding access mode bit in ASTSR is cleared. See Section 6.7.6.

5.3.4 Data Alignment Trap Fixup (DATFX)

Access:

Write

Operation:

```
DATFX ← R16<0>
(HWPCB+56)<63> ← DATFX
```

Value at System Initialization:

Zero

Format:

Figure 5–4: Data Alignment Trap Fixup (DATFX)

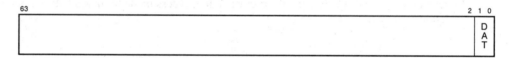

Description:

Data Alignment traps are fixed up in PALcode and are reported to the operating system under the control of the DAT bit. If the bit is zero, the trap is reported. For the LDx_L and STx_C instructions, no fixup is possible and an illegal operand exception is generated.

For the description of the data alignment traps, see Section 6.6.

5.3.5 Executive Stack Pointer (ESP)

Access:

Read/Write

Operation:

```
IF {internal registers for stack pointers}  THEN      ! Read
    R0 ← ESP
ELSE
    R0 ← (IPR_PCBB + HWPCB_ESP)

IF {internal registers for stack pointers}  THEN      ! Write
    ESP ← R16
ELSE
    (IPR_PCBB + HWPCB_ESP) ← R16
```

Value at System Initialization:

Value in the initial HWPCB

Format:

Figure 5–5: Executive Stack Pointer (ESP)

Description:

This register allows the stack pointer for executive mode (ESP) to be read and written via MFPR and MTPR instructions that specify ESP.

The current stack pointer may be read and written directly by specifying scalar register SP (R30).

As processes are scheduled for execution, the stack pointers for the next process to execute are loaded using the Swap Privileged Context (SWPCTX) instruction. See Section 2.6.7 and Chapter 4.

5.3.6 Floating Enable (FEN)

Access:

Read/Write

Operation:

```
R0 ← ZEXT(FEN)                    ! Read

FEN ← R16<0>                      ! Write
(HWPCB+56)<0> ← FEN               ! Update PCB on Write
```

Value at System Initialization:

Zero

Format:

Figure 5–6: Floating Enable (FEN) Register

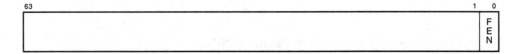

Description:

The floating-point unit can be disabled with the CALL_PAL CLRFEN instruction. If the Floating Enable Register (FEN) is zero, all instructions that have floating registers as operands cause a floating-point disabled fault. See Section 6.3.1.1.

5.3.7 Interprocessor Interrupt Request (IPIR)

Access:

Write

Operation:

IPIR ← R16

Value at System Initialization:

Not applicable

Format:

Figure 5–7: Interprocessor Interrupt Request (IPIR) Register

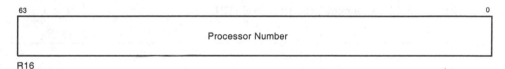

63   0

Processor Number

R16

Description:

An interprocessor interrupt can be requested on a specified processor by writing that processor's number into the IPIR register through an MTPR instruction. The interrupt request is recorded on the target processor and is initiated when proper enabling conditions are present.

Programming Note:

The interrupt need not be initiated before the next instruction is executed on the requesting processor, even if the requesting processor is also the target processor for the request.

For additional information on interprocessor interrupts, see Section 6.4.6.

5.3.8 Interrupt Priority Level (IPL)

Access:

Read/Write*

Operation:

```
R0 ← ZEXT(PS<IPL>)              ! Read
R0 ← ZEXT(PS<IPL>)              ! Write*
PS<IPL> ← R16<4:0>             ! Write
{check for pending ASTs or interrupts}
```

Value at System Initialization:

31

Format:

Figure 5–8: Interrupt Priority Level (IPL)

Description:

An MFPR IPL returns the current interrupt priority level in R0. An MTPR IPL returns the current interrupt priority level in R0 and sets the interrupt priority level to the value in R16. If proper enabling conditions are present, an interrupt or AST is initiated prior to issuing the next instruction. See Sections 6.4.2 and 6.7.6. R16<63:5> are defined as RAZ/SBZ. Therefore, the presence of nonzero bits upon write in R16<63:5> may cause UNDEFINED results.

5.3.9 Machine Check Error Summary Register (MCES)

Access:

Read/Write

Operation:

```
RO ← ZEXT(MCES)                        ! Read

IF {R16<0> EQ 1} THEN MCES<0> ← 0      ! Write
IF {R16<1> EQ 1} THEN MCES<1> ← 0
IF {R16<2> EQ 1} THEN MCES<2> ← 0
MCES<3> ← R16<3>
MCES<4> ← R16<4>
```

Value at System Initialization:

Zero

Format:

Figure 5–9: Machine Check Error Summary (MCES) Register

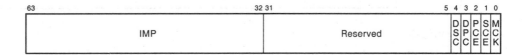

Description:

The use of the MCES IPR is described in Section 6.5.

MCK (MCES<0>) is set by the hardware or PALcode when a processor or system machine check occurs. SCE (MCES<1>) is set by the hardware or PALcode when a system correctable error occurs. PCE (MCES<2>) is set by the hardware or PALcode when a processor correctable error occurs.

Setting the corresponding bit(s) in R16 clears MCK, SCE, and PCE. MCK is cleared by the operating system machine check error handler and used by the hardware or PALcode to detect double machine checks. SCE and PCE are cleared by the operating system or processor system correctable error handlers; these bits are used to indicate that the associated correctable error logout area may be reused by hardware or PALcode. In the event of double correctable errors, PALcode does not overwrite the logout area and does not force the processor to enter console I/O mode. See Section 6.5.1.

DPC (MCES<3>) and DSC (MCES<4>) are used to disable reporting of correctable errors to system software. The generation and correction of the machine check are not affected; only the report to system software is disabled. Setting DPC disables reporting of processor-correctable machine checks. Setting DSC disables reporting of system-correctable machine checks. Implementation-dependent (IMP) bits may be used to report implementation-specific errors.

5.3.10 Performance Monitoring Register (PERFMON)

Access:

Write*

Operation:

```
! R16 contains implementation specific input values
! R17 contains implementation specific input values
! R0 may return implementation specific values
! Operations and actions taken are implementation specific
```

Value at System Initialization:

Implementation Dependent

Format:

Figure 5–10: Performance Monitoring (PERFMON) Register

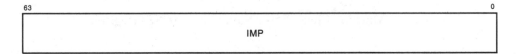

Description:

The arguments and actions of this performance monitoring function are platform and chip dependent. The functions, when defined for an implementation, are described in Appendix E.

R16 and R17 contain implementation-dependent input values. Implementation-specific values may be returned in R0.

5.3.11 Privileged Context Block Base (PCBB)

Access:

Read

Operation:

R0 ← ZEXT(PCBB)

Value at System Initialization:

Address of processor's bootstrap HWPCB

Format:

Figure 5–11: Privileged Context Block Base (PCBB) Register

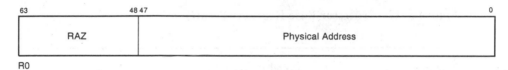

63	48 47	0
RAZ	Physical Address	

R0

Description:

The Privileged Context Block Base Register contains the physical address of the privileged context block for the current process. It may be read by executing an MFPR instruction specifying PCBB.

PCBB is written by the Swap Privileged Context (SWPCTX) instruction. See Section 2.6.7 and Chapter 4.

5.3.12 Processor Base Register (PRBR)

Access:

Read/Write

Operation:

```
R0 ← PRBR                        ! Read

PRBR ← R16                       ! Write
```

Value at System Initialization:

UNPREDICTABLE

Format:

Figure 5–12: Processor Base Register (PRBR)

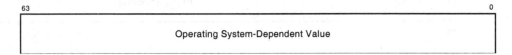

Description:

In a multiprocessor system, it is desirable for the operating system to be able to locate a processor-specific data structure in a simple and straightforward manner. The Processor Base Register provides a quadword of operating system-dependent state that can be read and written via MFPR and MTPR instructions that specify PRBR.

5.3.13 Page Table Base Register (PTBR)

Access:

Read

Operation:

R0 ← PTBR

Value at System Initialization:

Value in the bootstrap HWPCB

Format:

Figure 5–13: Page Table Base Register (PTBR)

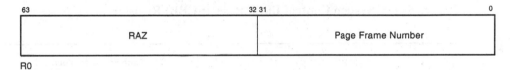

R0

Description:

The Page Table Base Register contains the page frame number of the highest-level page table for the current process. It may be read by executing an MFPR instruction specifying PTBR. See Chapter 3.

As processes are scheduled for execution, the PTBR for the next process to execute is loaded using the Swap Privileged Context (SWPCTX) instruction. See Section 2.6.7 and Chapter 4.

5.3.14 System Control Block Base (SCBB)

Access:

Read/Write

Operation:

```
R0 ← ZEXT(SCBB)              ! Read

SCBB ← R16                   ! Write
```

Value at System Initialization:

UNPREDICTABLE

Format:

Figure 5–14: System Control Block Base (SCBB) Register

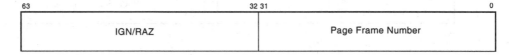

63 32 31	0
IGN/RAZ	Page Frame Number

Description:

The System Control Block Base Register holds the Page Frame Number (PFN) of the System Control Block, which is used to dispatch exceptions and interrupts, and may be read and written by executing MFPR and MTPR instructions that specify SCBB. See Section 6.6.

When SCBB is written, the specified physical address must be the PFN of a page that is neither in I/O space nor nonexistent memory, or UNDEFINED operation will result.

5.3.15 Software Interrupt Request Register (SIRR)

Access:

Write

Operation:

```
IF R16<3:0> NE 0 THEN
    SISR<R16<3:0>> ← 1
```

Value at System Initialization:

Not applicable

Format:

Figure 5–15: Software Interrupt Request Register (SIRR)

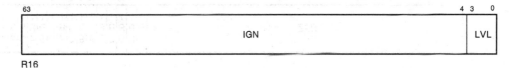

R16

Description:

A software interrupt may be requested for a particular Interrupt Priority Level (IPL) by executing an MTPR instruction specifying SIRR. Software interrupts may be requested at levels 0 through 15 (requests at level 0 are ignored).

An MTPR SIRR sets the bit corresponding to the specified interrupt level in the Software Interrupt Summary Register (SISR).

If proper enabling conditions are present, a software interrupt is initiated prior to issuing the next instruction. See Sections 6.4.1 and 6.7.6.

5.3.16 Software Interrupt Summary Register (SISR)

Access:

Read

Operation:

R0 ← ZEXT(SISR<15:0>)

Value at System Initialization:

Zero

Format:

Figure 5–16: Software Interrupt Summary Register (SISR)

63																			
	16	15	14	13	12	11	10	9	8	7	6	5	4	3	2	1	0		

```
63                                  16 15 14 13 12 11 10 9 8 7 6 5 4 3 2 1 0
┌──────────────────────────────────┬──┬──┬──┬──┬──┬──┬──┬─┬─┬─┬─┬─┬─┬─┬─┬─┬──┐
│                                  │I │I │I │I │I │I │I │I│I│I│I│I│I│I│I│I│R │
│                RAZ               │R │R │R │R │R │R │R │R│R│R│R│R│R│R│R│R│A │
│                                  │F │E │D │C │B │A │9 │8│7│6│5│4│3│2│1│ │Z │
└──────────────────────────────────┴──┴──┴──┴──┴──┴──┴──┴─┴─┴─┴─┴─┴─┴─┴─┴─┴──┘
```

Description:

The Software Interrupt Summary Register records the interrupt pending state for each of the interrupt levels 1 through 15. The current interrupt pending state may be read by executing an MFPR instruction specifying SISR.

MTPR SIRR (see SIRR) requests an interrupt at a particular interrupt level and sets the corresponding pending bit in SISR.

When the processor IPL falls below the level of a pending request, an interrupt is initiated and the corresponding bit in SISR is cleared. See Sections 6.4.1 and 6.7.6.

5.3.17 Supervisor Stack Pointer (SSP)

Access:

Read/Write

Operation:

```
IF {internal registers for stack pointers}  THEN      ! Read
    R0 ← SSP
ELSE
    R0 ← (IPR_PCBB + HWPCB_SSP)

IF {internal registers for stack pointers}  THEN      ! Write
    SSP ← R16
ELSE
    (IPR_PCBB + HWPCB_SSP) ← R16
```

Value at System Initialization:

Value in the initial HWPCB

Format:

Figure 5–17: Supervisor Stack Pointer (SSP)

Description:

The Supervisor Stack Pointer register allows the stack pointer for supervisor mode (SSP) to be read and written by using MFPR and MTPR instructions that specify SSP.

The current stack pointer may be read and written directly by specifying scalar register SP (R30).

As processes are scheduled for execution, the stack pointers for the next process to execute are loaded using the Swap Privileged Context (SWPCTX) instruction. See Section 2.6.7 and Chapter 4.

5.3.18 Translation Buffer Check (TBCHK)

Access:

> Read

Operation:

```
R0 ← 0
IF {implemented} THEN
    R0<0> ← {indicator that VA in R16 is in TB}
ELSE
    R0<63> ← 1
```

Value at System Initialization:

> Correct results are always returned

Format:

Figure 5–18: Translation Buffer Check Register (TBCHK)

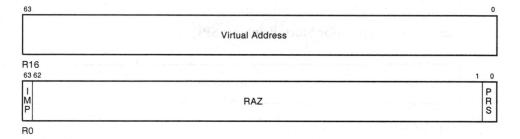

Description:

The Translation Buffer Check Register provides the capability to determine if a virtual address is present in the Translation Buffer by executing an MFPR instruction specifying TBCHK. See Chapter 3.

The virtual address to be checked is specified in R16 and may be any address within the desired page. If ASNs are implemented, only those Translation Buffer entries that are associated with the current value of the ASN IPR will be checked for the virtual address. The value read contains an indication of whether the function is implemented and whether the virtual address is present in the Translation Buffer.

If the function is not implemented, a one is returned in bit <63> and bit <0> is clear. Otherwise, bit <63> is clear and bit <0> indicates the presence or absence of the virtual address in the Translation Buffer. Bit <0> set indicates the virtual address is present; bit <0> clear indicates it is absent.

The TBCHK register can be used by system software for working set management.

5.3.19 Translation Buffer Invalidate All (TBIA)

Access:

Write

Operation:

{Invalidate all TB entries}

Value at System Initialization:

Not applicable

Format:

Figure 5–19: Translation Buffer Invalidate All (TBIA) Register

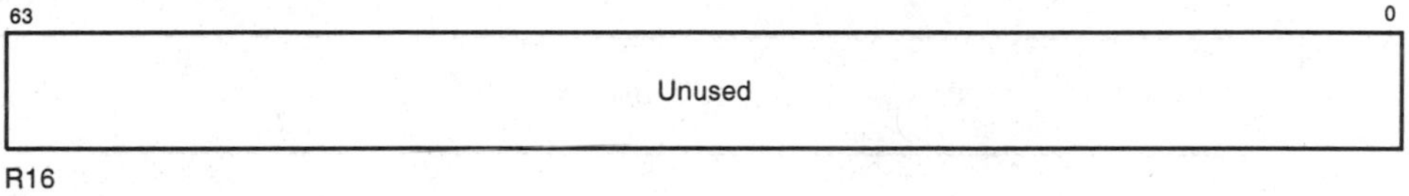

```
63                                                                              0
┌───────────────────────────────────────────────────────────────────────────────┐
│                                                                               │
│                                    Unused                                      │
│                                                                               │
└───────────────────────────────────────────────────────────────────────────────┘
R16
```

Description:

The Translation Buffer Invalidate All Register provides the capability to invalidate all entries in the Translation Buffer by executing an MTPR instruction specifying TBIA. See Chapter 3.

5.3.20 Translation Buffer Invalidate All Process (TBIAP)

Access:

> Write

Operation:

> {Invalidate all TB entries with PTE<ASM> clear}

Value at System Initialization:

> Not applicable

Format:

Figure 5–20: Translation Buffer Invalidate All Process (TBIAP) Register

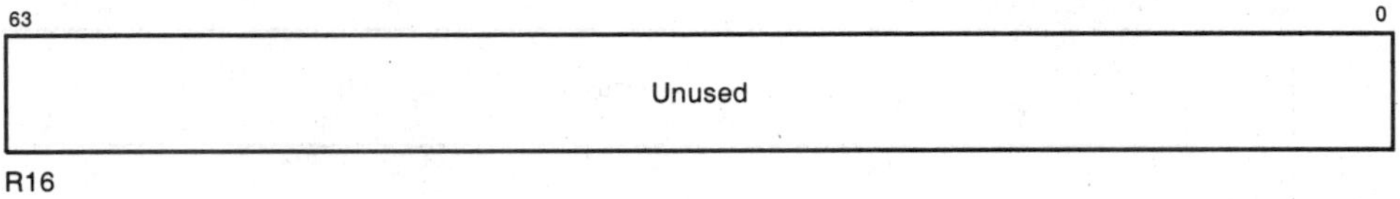

63	0
Unused	

R16

Description:

The Translation Buffer Invalidate All Process Register provides the capability to invalidate all entries in the Translation Buffer that do not have the ASM bit set by executing an MTPR instruction specifying TBIAP. See Chapter 3.

Notes:

> More entries may be invalidated by this operation. For example, some implementations may flush the entire TB on a TBIAP.

5.3.21 Translation Buffer Invalidate Single (TBISx)

Access:

Write

Operation:

```
TBIS:
     {Invalidate single Data TB entry using R16}
     {Invalidate single Instruction TB entry using R16}
TBISD:
     {Invalidate single Data TB entry using R16}
TBISI:
     {Invalidate single Instruction TB entry using R16}
```

Value at System Initialization:

Not applicable

Format:

Figure 5–21: Translation Buffer Invalidate Single (TBIS)

R16

Description:

The Translation Buffer Invalidate Single Registers provide the capability to invalidate a single entry in the Instruction Translation Buffer (TBISI), the Data Translation Buffer (TBISD), or both translation buffers (TBIS). The virtual address to be invalidated is passed in R16 and may be any address within the desired page.

Notes:

More than the single entry may be invalidated by this operation. For example some implementations may flush the entire TB on a TBIS. As a result, if the specified address does not match any entry in the Translation Buffer, then it is implementation dependent whether the state of the Translation Buffer is affected by the operation.

5.3.22 User Stack Pointer (USP)

Access:

Read/Write

Operation:

```
IF {internal registers for stack pointers}  THEN      ! Read
    R0 ← USP
ELSE
    R0 ← (IPR_PCBB + HWPCB_USP)

IF {internal registers for stack pointers}  THEN      ! Write
    USP ← R16
ELSE
    (IPR_PCBB + HWPCB_USP) ← R16
```

Value at System Initialization:

Value in the initial HWPCB

Format:

Figure 5–22: User Stack Pointer (USP)

63   0

Stack Address

Description:

This register allows the stack pointer for user mode (USP) to be read and written via MFPR and MTPR instructions that specify USP.

The current stack pointer may be read and written directly by specifying scalar register SP (R30).

As processes are scheduled for execution, the stack pointers for the next process to execute are loaded using the Swap Privileged Context (SWPCTX) instruction. See Section 2.6.7 and Chapter 4.

5.3.23 Virtual Page Table Base (VPTB)

Access:

Read/Write

Operation:

```
R0 ← VPTB                           ! Read

VPTB ← R16                          ! Write
```

Value at System Initialization:

Initialized by the console in the bootstrap address space.

Format:

Figure 5–23: Virtual Page Table Base (VPTB) Register

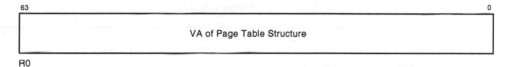

Description:

The Virtual Page Table Base Register contains the virtual address of the base of the entire multi-level page table structure. It may be read by executing an MFPR instruction specifying VPTB. It is written at system initialization using an MTPR instruction specifying VPTB. See Section 3.8.2 and Console Interface (III), Chapter 3, for initialization considerations.

5.3.24 Who-Am-I (WHAMI)

Access:

Read

Operation:

R0 ← WHAMI

Value at System Initialization:

Processor number

Format:

Figure 5–24: Who-Am-I (WHAMI) Register

```
63                                                                    0
┌──────────────────────────────────────────────────────────────────┐
│                        Processor Number                            │
└──────────────────────────────────────────────────────────────────┘
R0
```

Description:

The Who-Am-I Register provides the capability to read the current processor number by executing an MFPR instruction specifying WHAMI. The processor number returned is in the range 0 to the number of processors minus one that can be configured in the system. Processor number FFFF FFFF FFFF FFFF$_{16}$ is reserved.

The current processor number is useful in a multiprocessing system to index arrays that store per processor information. Such information is operating system dependent.

Chapter 6

Exceptions, Interrupts, and Machine Checks (II–A)

6.1 Introduction

At certain times during the operation of a system, events within the system require the execution of software outside the explicit flow of control. When such an exceptional event occurs, an Alpha processor forces a change in control flow from that indicated by the current instruction stream. The notification process for such events is of one of three types:

- Exceptions

  These events are relevant primarily to the currently executing process and normally invoke software in the context of the current process. The three types of exceptions are faults, arithmetic traps, and synchronous traps. Exceptions are described in Section 6.3.

- Interrupts

  These events are primarily relevant to other processes or to the system as a whole and are typically serviced in a system-wide context.

  Some interrupts are of such urgency that they require high-priority service, while others must be synchronized with independent events. To meet these needs, each processor has priority logic that grants interrupt service to the highest priority event at any point in time. Interrupts are described in Section 6.4.

- Machine Checks

  These events are generally the result of serious hardware failure. The registers and memory are potentially in an indeterminate state such that the instruction execution cannot necessarily be correctly restarted, completed, simulated, or undone. Machine checks are described in Section 6.5.

For all such events, the change in flow of control involves changing the Program Counter (PC), possibly changing the execution mode (current mode) and/or interrupt priority level (IPL) in the Processor Status (PS), and saving the old values of the PC and PS. The old values are saved on the target stack as part of an Exception, Interrupt, or Machine Check Stack Frame. Collectively, those elements are described in Section 6.2.

The service routines that handle exceptions, interrupts, and machine checks are specified by entry points in the System Control Block (SCB), described in Section 6.6.

Return from an exception, interrupt, or machine check is done via the CALL_PAL REI instruction. As part of its work, CALL_PAL REI restores the saved values of PC and PS and pops them off the stack.

6.1.1 Differences Between Exceptions, Interrupts, and Machine Checks

Generally, exceptions, interrupts, and machine checks are similar. However, there are four important differences:

1. An exception is caused by the execution of an instruction. An interrupt is caused by some activity in the system that may be independent of any instruction. A machine check is associated with a hardware error condition.

2. The IPL of the processor is not changed when the processor initiates an exception. The IPL is always raised when an interrupt is initiated. The IPL is always raised when a machine check is initiated, and for all machine checks other than system correctable, is raised to 31 (highest priority level). (For system correctable machine checks, the IPL is raised to 20.)

3. Exceptions are always initiated immediately, no matter what the processor IPL is. Interrupts are deferred until the processor IPL drops below the IPL of the requesting source. Machine checks can be initiated immediately or deferred, depending on error conditions.

4. Some exceptions can be selectively disabled by selecting instructions that do not check for exception conditions. If an exception condition occurs in such an instruction, the condition is totally ignored and no state is saved to signal that condition at a later time.

    If an interrupt request occurs while the processor IPL is equal to or greater than that of the interrupting source, the condition will eventually initiate an interrupt if the interrupt request is still present and the processor IPL is lowered below that of the interrupting source.

    Machine checks cannot be disabled. Machine checks can be initiated immediately or deferred, depending on the error condition. Also, they can be deliberately generated by software.

6.1.2 Exceptions, Interrupts, and Machine Checks Summary

Table 6–1 summarizes the actions taken on an exception, interrupt, or machine check. The remaining sections in this chapter describe those actions in greater detail.

*   The "SavedPC" column describes what is saved in the "PC" field of the exception or interrupt or machine check stack frame.

    1. "Current" indicates the PC of the instruction at which the exception or interrupt or machine check was taken,

    2. "Next" indicates the PC of the successor instruction.

*   The "NewMode" column specifies the mode and stack that the exception or interrupt or machine check routine will start with. For change mode traps, "MostPrv" indicates the more privileged of the current and new modes.

- The "R2" column specifies the value with which R2 is loaded, after its original value has been saved in the exception or interrupt or machine check stack frame. The SCB vector quadword, "SCBv", is loaded into R2 for all interrupts and exceptions and machine checks.

- The "R3" column specifies the value with which R3 is loaded, after its original value has been saved in the exception or interrupt or machine check stack frame. The SCB parameter quadword, "SCBp", is loaded into R3 for all interrupts and exceptions and machine checks.

- The "R4" column specifies the value with which R4 is loaded, after its original value has been saved in the exception or interrupt or machine check stack frame. If the "R4" column is blank, the value in R4 is UNPREDICTABLE on entry to an interrupt or exception.

  1. "VA" indicates the exact virtual address that triggered a memory management fault or data alignment trap.

  2. "Mask" indicates the Register Write Mask.

  3. "LAOff" indicates the offset from the base of the logout area in the HWRPB (see Section 6.5.2).

- The "R5" column specifies the value with which R5 is loaded, after its original value has been saved in the exception or interrupt or machine check stack frame. If the "R5" column is blank, the value in R5 is UNPREDICTABLE on entry to an interrupt or exception or machine check.

  1. "MMF" indicates the Memory Management Flags.

  2. "Exc" indicates the Exception Summary parameter.

  3. "RW" indicates Read/Load =0 Write/Store =1 for data alignment traps

Table 6–1: Exceptions, Interrupts, and Machine Checks Summary

	SavedPC	NewMode	R2	R3	R4	R5
Exceptions – Faults :						
Floating Disabled Fault	Current	Kernel	SCBv	SCBp		
Memory Management Faults :						
Access Control Violation	Current	Kernel	SCBv	SCBp	VA	MMF
Translation Not Valid	Current	Kernel	SCBv	SCBp	VA	MMF
Fault on Read	Current	Kernel	SCBv	SCBp	VA	MMF
Fault on Write	Current	Kernel	SCBv	SCBp	VA	MMF
Fault on Execute	Current	Kernel	SCBv	SCBp	VA	MMF
Exceptions – Arithmetic Traps:						
Arithmetic Traps	Next	Kernel	SCBv	SCBp	Mask	Exc
Exceptions - Synchronous Traps :						
Breakpoint Trap	Next	Kernel	SCBv	SCBp		
Bugcheck Trap	Next	Kernel	SCBv	SCBp		
Change Mode to K/E/S/U	Next	MostPrv	SCBv	SCBp		
Illegal Instruction	Next	Kernel	SCBv	SCBp		
Illegal Operand	Next	Kernel	SCBv	SCBp		
Data Alignment Trap	Next	Kernel	SCBv	SCBp	VA	RW
Interrupts :						
Asynch System Trap (4)	Current	Kernel	SCBv	SCBp		
Interval Clock	Current	Kernel	SCBv	SCBp		
Interprocessor Interrupt	Current	Kernel	SCBv	SCBp		
Software Interrupts	Current	Kernel	SCBv	SCBp		
Performance monitor	Current	Kernel	SCBv	SCBp	IMP	IMP
Passive Release	Current	Kernel	SCBv	SCBp		
Powerfail	Current	Kernel	SCBv	SCBp		
I/O Device	Current	Kernel	SCBv	SCBp		
Machine Checks :						
Processor Correctable	Current	Kernel	SCBv	SCBp	LAOff	
System Correctable	Current	Kernel	SCBv	SCBp	LAOff	
System	Current	Kernel	SCBv	SCBp	LAOff	
Processor	Current	Kernel	SCBv	SCBp	LAOff	

6.2 Processor State and Exception/Interrupt/Machine Check Stack Frame

Processor state consists of a quadword of privileged information called the Processor Status (PS) and a quadword containing the Program Counter (PC), which is the virtual address of the next instruction.

When an exception, interrupt, or machine check is initiated, the current processor state during the exception, interrupt, or machine check must be preserved. This is accomplished by automatically pushing the PS and the PC on the target stack.

Subsequently, instruction execution can be continued at the point of the exception, interrupt, or machine check by executing a CALL PAL REI instruction (see Section 2.1.11).

Process context such as memory mapping information is not saved or restored on each exception, interrupt, or machine check. Instead, it is saved and restored when process context switching is performed. Other processor status is changed even less frequently (see Chapter 4).

6.2.1 Processor Status

The PS can be explicitly read with the CALL_PAL RD_PS instruction. The PS<SW> field can be explicitly written with the CALL_PAL WR_PS_SW instruction. See Section 2.1.

The terms current PS and saved PS are used to distinguish between this status information when it is stored internal to the processor and when copies of it are materialized in memory. The current PS is shown in Figure 6–1, the saved PS in Figure 6–2, and the bits for both are described in Table 6–2.

Figure 6–1: Current Processor Status (PS Register)

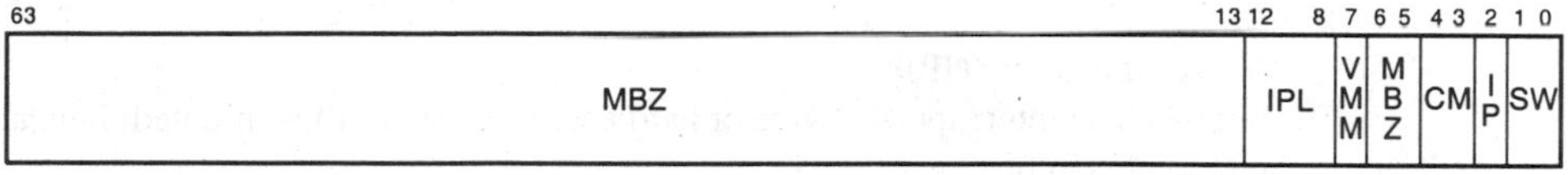

Figure 6–2: Saved Processor Status (PS on Stack)

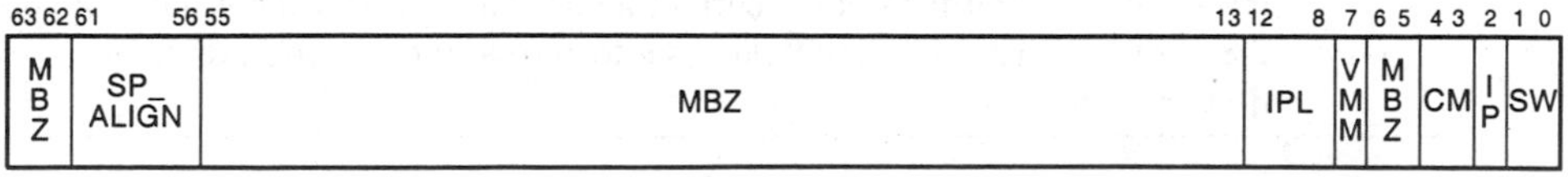

Table 6–2: Processor Status Register Summary

Bits	Description
63–62	Reserved to DIGITAL, MBZ.
61–56	Stack alignment (SP_ALIGN) The previous stack byte alignment within a 64-byte aligned area, in the range 0 to 63. This field is set in the saved PS during the act of taking an exception or interrupt; it is used by the CALL_PAL REI instruction to restore the previous stack byte alignment.
55–13	Reserved to DIGITAL, MBZ.
12–8	Interrupt priority level (IPL) The current processor priority, in the range 0 to 31.
7	Virtual machine monitor (VMM). When set, the processor is executing in a virtual machine monitor. When clear, the processor is running in either real or virtual machine mode. **Programming Note:** This bit is only meaningful when running with PALcode that implements virtual machine capabilities.
6–5	Reserved to DIGITAL, MBZ.
4–3	Current mode (CM) The access mode of the currently executing process as follows: 0 Kernel 1 Executive 2 Supervisor 3 User
2	Interrupt pending (IP) Set when an interrupt (software or hardware but not AST) is initiated; indicates an interrupt is in progress.
1–0	Reserved for Software (SW) These bits are reserved for software use and can be read and written at any time by the software, regardless of the current mode. The value of these bits is ignored by the hardware. The software field is set to zero at the initiation of either an exception or an interrupt.

At bootstrap, the initial value of PS is set to $1F00_{16}$. Previous stack alignment is zero, IPL is 31, VMM is clear, CM is kernel, and the SW and IP fields are zero.

6.2.2 Program Counter

The PC (Figure 6–3) is a 64-bit virtual address. All instructions are aligned on longword boundaries and, therefore, hardware can assume zero for the two low-order PC bits. The PC is discussed in Section 6.2.6.

The PC can be explicitly read with the Unconditional Branch (BR) instruction. All branching instructions also load a new value into the PC.

Figure 6–3: Program Counter (PC)

6.2.3 Processor Interrupt Priority Level (IPL)

Each processor has 32 interrupt priority levels (IPLs) divided into 16 software levels (numbered 0 to 15), and 16 hardware levels (numbered 16 to 31). User applications and most operating system software run at IPL 0, which may be thought of as process level. Higher numbered interrupt levels have higher priority; that is, any request at an interrupt level higher than the processor's current IPL will interrupt immediately, but requests at lower or equal levels are deferred.

Interrupt levels 0 to 15 exist solely for use by software. No hardware event can request an interrupt on these levels. Conversely, interrupt levels 16 to 31 exist solely for use by hardware. Serious system failures, such as a machine check abort, however, raise the IPL to the highest level (31) to minimize processor interruption until the problem is corrected, and execute in kernel mode on the kernel stack.

6.2.4 Protection Modes

Each processor has four protection modes: kernel, executive, supervisor, and user. Per-page memory protection varies as a function of mode (for example, a page can be made read-only in user mode, but read-write in supervisor, executive, or kernel mode).

For each process, a separate stack is associated with each mode. Corruption of one stack does not affect use of the other stacks.

Some instructions, termed privileged instructions, may be executed only in kernel mode.

6.2.5 Processor Stacks

Each processor has four stacks. There are four process-specific stacks associated with the four modes of the current process. At any given time, only one of these stacks is actively used as the current stack.

6.2.6 Stack Frames

When an exception, interrupt, or machine check occurs, a stack frame (Figure 6–4) is pushed on the target stack. Regardless of the type of event notification, this stack frame consists of a 64-byte-aligned structure that contains the saved contents of registers R2..R7, the Program Counter (PC), and the Processor Status (PS). Registers R2 and R3 are then loaded with vector and parameter from the SCB for the exception, interrupt, or machine check. Registers R4 and

R5 may be loaded with data pertaining to the exception, interrupt, or machine check. The specific data loaded is described below in conjunction with each exception, interrupt, or machine check; if no specific data is specified, the contents of R4 and R5 are UNPREDICTABLE. After the stack is built, the contents of registers R6 and R7 are UNPREDICTABLE.

The Program Counter value that is saved in the stack frame is:

- For faults, the instruction that encountered the exception.

- For traps, the next instruction.

- For interrupts and (on a best-effort basis) machine checks, the instruction that would have been issued if the interrupt or machine-check condition had not occurred.

Return from an exception, interrupt, or machine check is done via the CALL_PAL REI instruction, which restores the saved values of PC, PS, and R2..R7. Thus, the CALL_PAL REI instruction:

- For faults, re-executes the faulting instruction.

- For traps, executes the next instruction.

- For interrupts, executes the instruction that would have been executed if the interrupt had not occurred.

- For machine checks, continues execution from the point at which the machine check was taken.

Figure 6–4: Stack Frame

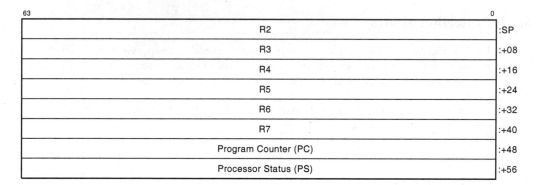

6.3 Exceptions

Exception service routines execute in response to exception conditions caused by software. Most exception service routines execute in kernel mode, on the kernel stack; all exception service routines execute at the current processor IPL. Change mode exception routines for CHMU/CHMS/CHME execute in the more privileged of the current mode or the target mode (U/S/E) on the matching stack. Exception service routines are usually coded to avoid exceptions; however, nested exceptions can occur.

Types of Exceptions

There are three types of exceptions:

- A fault is an exception condition that occurs during an instruction and leaves the registers and memory in a consistent state such that elimination of the fault condition and subsequent re-execution of the instruction will give correct results. Faults are not guaranteed to leave the machine in exactly the same state it was in immediately prior to the fault, but rather in a state such that the instruction can be correctly executed if the fault condition is removed. The PC saved in the exception stack frame is the address of the faulting instruction. A CALL_PAL REI instruction to this PC will reexecute the faulting instruction.

- An arithmetic trap is an exception condition that occurs at the completion of the operation that caused the exception. Because several instructions may be in various stages of execution at any time, it is possible for multiple arithmetic traps to occur simultaneously. The PC that is saved in the exception frame on traps is that of the next instruction that would have been issued if the trapping condition(s) had not occurred. This is not necessarily the address of the instruction immediately following the one(s) that encountered the trap condition, and the intervening instructions are collectively called the *trap shadow*. See Common Architecture, Chapter 4, Arithmetic Trap Completion, for information.

  The intervening instructions may have changed operands or other state used by the instruction(s) encountering the trap condition(s). If such is the case, a CALL_PAL REI instruction to this PC does not reexecute the trapping instruction(s), nor does it reexecute any intervening instructions; it simply continues execution from the point at which the trap was taken.

  In general, it is difficult to fix up results and continue program execution at the point of an arithmetic trap. Software can force a trap to be continued more easily without the need for complicated fixup code. This is accomplished by specifying any valid qualifier combination that includes the /S qualifier with each such instruction and following a set of code-generation restrictions in the code that could cause arithmetic traps, allowing those traps to be completed by an OS completion handler.

  The AND of all the exception completion qualifiers for trapping instructions is provided to the OS completion handler in the exception summary SWC bit. If SWC is set, the OS completion handler may find the trigger instruction by scanning backward from the trap PC until each register in the register write mask has been an instruction destination. The trigger instruction is the last instruction in I-stream order to get a trap before the trap shadow. If the SWC bit is clear, no fixup is possible. (The trigger instruction may have been followed by a taken branch, so the trap PC cannot be used to find it.)

- A synchronous trap is an exception condition that occurs at the completion of the operation that caused the exception (or, if the operation can only be partially carried out, at the completion of that part of the operation), and no subsequent instruction is issued before the trap occurs.

  Synchronous traps are divided into data alignment traps and all other synchronous traps.

6.3.1 Faults

The six types of faults signal that an instruction or its operands are in some way illegal. These faults are all initiated in kernel mode and push an exception stack frame onto the stack. Upon entry to the exception routine, the saved PC (in the exception stack frame) is the virtual address of the faulting instruction.
The six faults include the Floating Disable Fault described in the next section and five memory management faults.

Memory management faults occur when a virtual address translation encounters an exception condition. This can occur as the result of instruction fetch or during a load or store operation.

Immediately following a memory management fault, register R4 contains the exact virtual address encountering the fault condition.

The register R5 contains the "MM Flag" quadword.

"MM Flag" is set as follows:

$0000\ 0000\ 0000\ 0000_{16}$ for a faulting data read

$0000\ 0000\ 0000\ 0001_{16}$ for a faulting I-fetch operation

$8000\ 0000\ 0000\ 0000_{16}$ for a faulting write operation

The faulting instruction is the instruction whose fetch faulted, or the load, store, or PALcode instruction that encountered the fault condition.

Chapter 3 describes the Alpha memory management architecture in more detail.

6.3.1.1 Floating Disabled Fault

A Floating Disabled Fault is an exception that occurs when an attempt is made to execute a floating-point instruction and the floating-point enable (FEN) bit in the HWPCB is not set.

6.3.1.2 Access Control Violation (ACV) Fault

An ACV fault is a memory management fault that indicates that an attempted access to a virtual address was not allowed in the current mode.

ACV faults usually indicate program errors, but in some cases, such as automatic stack expansion, can indicate implicit operating system functions.

ACV faults take precedence over Translation Not Valid, Fault on Read, Fault on Write, and Fault on Execute faults.

ACV faults take precedence over Translation Not Valid faults so that a malicious user could not degrade system performance by causing spurious page faults to pages for which no access is allowed.

6.3.1.3 Translation Not Valid (TNV)

A TNV fault is a memory management fault that indicates that an attempted access was made to a virtual address whose Page Table Entry (PTE) was not valid.

Software may use TNV faults to implement virtual memory capabilities.

6.3.1.4 Fault on Read (FOR)

An FOR fault is a memory management fault that indicates that an attempted data read access was made to a virtual address whose Page Table Entry (PTE) had the Fault on Read bit set.

As a part of initiating the FOR fault, the processor invalidates the Translation Buffer entry that caused the fault to be generated.

Implementation Note:

> This allows an implementation to invalidate entries only from the Data-stream Translation Buffer on Fault on Read faults.

The Translation Buffer may reload and cache the old PTE value between the time the FOR fault invalidates the old value from the Translation Buffer and the time software updates the PTE in memory. Software that depends on the processor-provided invalidate must thus be prepared to take another FOR fault on a page after clearing the page's PTE<FOR> bit. The second fault will invalidate the stale PTE from the Translation Buffer, and the processor cannot load another stale copy. Thus, in the worst case, a multiprocessor system will take an initial FOR fault and then an additional FOR fault on each processor. In practice, even a single repetition is unlikely.

Software may use FOR faults to implement watchpoints, to collect page usage statistics, and to implement execute-only pages.

6.3.1.5 Fault on Write (FOW)

A FOW fault is a memory management fault that indicates that an attempted data write access was made to a virtual address whose Page Table Entry (PTE) had the Fault On Write bit set.

As a part of initiating the FOW fault, the processor invalidates the Translation Buffer entry that caused the fault to be generated.

Implementation Note:

> This allows an implementation to invalidate entries only from the Data-stream Translation Buffer on Fault on Write faults.

Note that the Translation Buffer may reload and cache the old PTE value between the time the FOW fault invalidates the old value from the Translation Buffer and the time software updates the PTE in memory. Software that depends on the processor-provided invalidate must thus be prepared to take another FOW fault on a page after clearing the page's PTE<FOW> bit. The second fault will invalidate the stale PTE from the Translation Buffer, and the processor cannot load another stale copy. Thus, in the worst case, a multiprocessor system will take an initial FOW fault and then an additional FOW fault on each processor. In practice, even a single repetition is unlikely.

Software may use FOW faults to maintain modified page information, to implement copy on write and watchpoint capabilities, and to collect page usage statistics.

6.3.1.6 Fault on Execute (FOE)

An FOE fault is a memory management fault that indicates that an attempted instruction stream access was made to a virtual address whose Page Table Entry (PTE) had the Fault On Execute bit set.

As a part of initiating the FOE fault, the processor invalidates the Translation Buffer entry that caused the fault to be generated.

Implementation Note:

This allows an implementation to invalidate entries only from the Instruction-stream Translation Buffer on Fault on Execute faults.

Note that the Translation Buffer may reload and cache the old PTE value between the time the FOE fault invalidates the old value from the Translation Buffer and the time software updates the PTE in memory. Software that depends on the processor-provided invalidate must thus be prepared to take another FOE fault on a page after clearing the page's PTE<FOE> bit. The second fault will invalidate the stale PTE from the Translation Buffer, and the processor cannot load another stale copy. Thus, in the worst case, a multiprocessor system will take an initial FOE fault and then an additional FOE fault on each processor. In practice, even a single repetition is unlikely.

Software may use FOE faults to implement access mode changes and protected entry to kernel mode, to collect page usage statistics, and to detect programming errors that try to execute data.

6.3.2 Arithmetic Traps

An arithmetic trap is an exception that occurs as the result of performing an arithmetic or conversion operation.

If integer register R31 or floating-point register F31 is specified as the destination of an operation that can cause an arithmetic trap, it is UNPREDICTABLE whether the trap will actually occur, even if the operation would definitely produce an exceptional result. If the operation causes an arithmetic trap, the bit that corresponds to R31 or F31 in the Register Write Mask is UNPREDICTABLE.

Arithmetic traps are initiated in kernel mode and push the exception stack frame on the kernel stack. The Register Write Mask is saved in R4, and the Exception Summary parameter is saved in R5. These are described in Section 6.3.2.1.

6.3.2.1 Exception Summary Parameter

The Exception Summary parameter shown in Figure 6–5 and described in Table 6–3 records the various types of arithmetic traps that can occur together. These types of traps are described in subsections below.

Figure 6–5: Exception Summary

63									7	6	5	4	3	2	1	0
Zero										IOV	INE	UNF	OVF	DZE	INV	SWC

Table 6–3: Exception Summary

Bit	Description
63–7	Zero.
6	Integer Overflow (IOV) An integer arithmetic operation or a conversion from floating to integer overflowed the destination precision.
5	Inexact Result (INE) A floating arithmetic or conversion operation gave a result that differed from the mathematically exact result.
4	Underflow (UNF) A floating arithmetic or conversion operation underflowed the destination exponent.
3	Overflow (OVF) A floating arithmetic or conversion operation overflowed the destination exponent.
2	Division by Zero (DZE) An attempt was made to perform a floating divide operation with a divisor of zero.
1	Invalid Operation (INV) An attempt was made to perform a floating arithmetic, conversion, or comparison operation, and one or more of the operand values were illegal.
0	Software Completion (SWC) Set when all of the other arithmetic exception bits were set by floating-operate instructions with the /S exception completion qualifier set. See Common Architecture, Chapter 4, Arithmetic Trap Completion, for rules about setting the /S qualifier in code that may cause an arithmetic trap, and Section 6.3 for rules about using the SWC bit in a trap handler.

6.3.2.2 Register Write Mask

The Register Write Mask parameter records all registers that were targets of instructions that set the bits in the exception summary register. There is a one-to-one correspondence between bits in the Register Write Mask quadword and the register numbers. The quadword records, starting at bit 0 and proceeding right to left, which of the registers R0 through R31, then F0 through F31, received an exceptional result.

Note:

For a sequence such as:

```
ADDF F1,F2,F3
MULF F4,F5,F3
```

If the add overflows and the multiply does not, the OVF bit is set in the exception summary, and the F3 bit is set in the register mask, even though the overflowed sum in F3 can be overwritten with an in-range product by the time the trap is taken. (This code violates the destination reuse rule for software completion. See Common Architecture, Chapter 4, Arithmetic Trap Completion, for the destination reuse rules.)

The PC value saved in the exception stack frame is the virtual address of the next instruction. This is defined as the virtual address of the first instruction not executed after the trap condition was recognized.

6.3.2.3 Invalid Operation (INV) Trap

An INV trap is reported for most floating-point operate instructions with an input operand that is a VAX reserved operand, VAX dirty zero, IEEE NaN, IEEE infinity, or IEEE denormal.

Floating INV traps are always enabled. If this trap occurs, the result register is written with an UNPREDICTABLE value.

6.3.2.4 Division by Zero (DZE) Trap

A DZE trap is reported when a finite number is divided by zero. Floating DZE traps are always enabled. If this trap occurs, the result register is written with an UNPREDICTABLE value.

6.3.2.5 Overflow (OVF) Trap

An OVF trap is reported when the destination's largest finite number is exceeded in magnitude by the rounded true result. Floating OVF traps are always enabled. If this trap occurs, the result register is written with an UNPREDICTABLE value.

6.3.2.6 Underflow (UNF) Trap

A UNF trap is reported when the destination's smallest finite number exceeds in magnitude the non-zero rounded true result. Floating UNF trap enable can be specified in each floating-point operate instruction. If underflow occurs, the result register is written with a true zero.

6.3.2.7 Inexact Result (INE) Trap

An INE trap is reported if the rounded result of an IEEE operation is not exact. INE trap enable can be specified in each IEEE floating-point operate instruction. The unchanged result value is stored in all cases.

6.3.2.8 Integer Overflow (IOV) Trap

An IOV trap is reported for any integer operation whose true result exceeds the destination register size. IOV trap enable can be specified in each arithmetic integer operate instruction and each floating-point convert-to-integer instruction. If integer overflow occurs, the result register is written with the truncated true result.

6.3.3 Synchronous Traps

A synchronous trap is an exception condition that occurs at the completion of the operation that caused the exception (or, if the operation can only be partially carried out, at the completion of that part of the operation), but no successor instruction is allowed to start. All traps that are not arithmetic traps are synchronous traps.

Some synchronous traps are caused by PALcode instructions: BPT, BUGCHK, CHMU, CIIMS, CIIME, and CIIMK. For synchronous traps, the PC saved in the exception stack frame is the address of the instruction immediately following the one causing the trap condition. A CALL_PAL REI instruction to this PC will continue without reexecuting the trapping instruction. The following subsections describe the synchronous traps in detail.

6.3.3.1 Data Alignment Trap

All data must be naturally aligned or an alignment trap may be generated. Natural alignment means that data bytes are on byte boundaries, data words are on word boundaries, data longwords are on longword boundaries, and data quadwords are on quadword boundaries.

A Data Alignment trap is generated by the hardware when an attempt is made to load or store a word, a longword, or a quadword to/from a register using an address that does not have the natural alignment of the particular data reference.

Data Alignment traps are fixed up by the PALcode and are optionally reported to the operating system under the control of the DAT bit. If the bit is zero, the trap will be reported. If the bit is set, after the alignment is corrected, control is returned to the user. In either case, if the PALcode detects a LDx_L or STx_C instruction, no correction is possible and an illegal operand exception is generated.

Note:

In the case of concurrently pending data alignment and arithmetic traps, it is assumed that the arithmetic trap is reported before PALcode data alignment fixup is performed. Otherwise, it would not be possible to back up the PC for the synchronous data alignment trap as required by Section 6.7.4.

The system software is notified via the generation of a kernel mode exception through the Unaligned_Access SCB vector (280_{16}) The virtual address of the unaligned data being accessed is stored in R4. R5 indicates whether the operation was a read or a write (0 = read/load 1 = write/store).

PALcode may write partial results to memory without probing to make sure all writes will succeed when dealing with unaligned store operations.

If a memory management exception condition occurs while reading or writing part of the unaligned data, the appropriate memory management fault is generated.

Software should avoid data misalignment whenever possible since the emulation performance penalty may be as large as 100-to-1.

The Data Alignment trap control bit is included in the HWPCB at offset HWPCB[56], bit 63. In order to change this bit for the currently executing process, the DATFX IPR may be written by using a CALL_PAL MTPR_DATFX instruction. This operation will also update the value in the HWPCB.

6.3.3.2 Other Synchronous Traps

With the traps described in this subsection, the SCB vector quadword is saved in R2 and the SCB parameter quadword is saved in R3. The change mode traps are initiated in the more privileged of the current mode and the target mode, while the other traps are initiated in kernel mode.

6.3.3.2.1 Breakpoint Trap

A Breakpoint trap is an exception that occurs when a CALL_PAL BPT instruction is executed (see Section 2.1.1). Breakpoint traps are intended for use by debuggers and can be used to place breakpoints in a program.

Breakpoint traps are initiated in kernel mode so that system debuggers can capture breakpoint traps that occur while the user is executing system code.

6.3.3.2.2 Bugcheck Trap

A Bugcheck trap is an exception that occurs when a CALL_PAL BUGCHK instruction is executed (see Section 2.1.2). Bugchecks are used to log errors detected by software.

6.3.3.2.3 Illegal Instruction Trap

An Illegal Instruction trap is an exception that occurs when an attempt is made to execute an instruction when:

- It has an opcode that is reserved to DIGITAL or reserved to PALcode.
- It is a subsetted opcode that requires emulation on the host implementation.
- It is a privileged instruction and the current mode is not kernel.
- It has an unused function code for those opcodes defined as reserved in the Version 5 Alpha architecture specification (May 1992).

6.3.3.2.4 Illegal Operand Trap

An Illegal Operand trap occurs when an attempt is made to execute PALcode with operand values that are illegal or reserved for future use by DIGITAL. Illegal operands include:

- An invalid combination of bits in the PS restored by the CALL_PAL REI instruction.
- An unaligned operand passed to PALcode.

6.3.3.2.5 Generate Software Trap

A Generate Software trap is an exception that occurs when a CALL_PAL GENTRAP instruction is executed (see Section 2.1.8). The intended use is for low-level compiler-generated code that detects conditions such as divide-by-zero, range errors, subscript bounds, and negative string lengths.

6.3.3.2.6 Change Mode to Kernel Trap

A Change Mode to Kernel trap is an exception that occurs when a CALL_PAL CHMK instruction is executed (see Section 2.1.4). Change Mode to Kernel traps are initiated in kernel mode and push the exception frame on the kernel stack.

6.3.3.2.7 Change Mode to Executive Trap

A Change Mode to Executive trap is an exception that occurs when a CALL_PAL CHME instruction is executed (see Section 2.1.3). Change Mode to Executive traps are initiated in the more privileged of the current mode and Executive mode, and push the exception frame on the target stack.

6.3.3.2.8 Change Mode to Supervisor Trap

A Change Mode to Supervisor trap is an exception that occurs when a CALL_PAL CHMS instruction is executed (see Section 2.1.5). Change Mode to Supervisor traps are initiated in the more privileged of the current mode and supervisor mode, and push the exception frame on the target stack.

6.3.3.2.9 Change Mode to User Trap

A Change Mode to User trap is an exception that occurs when a CALL_PAL CHMU instruction is executed (see Section 2.1.6). Change Mode to User traps are initiated in the more privileged of the current mode and user mode, and push the exception frame on the target stack.

6.4 Interrupts

The processor arbitrates interrupt requests according to priority. When the priority of an interrupt request is higher than the current processor IPL, the processor will raise the IPL and service the interrupt request. The interrupt service routine is entered at the IPL of the interrupting source, in kernel mode, and on the kernel stack. Interrupt requests can come from I/O devices, memory controllers, other processors, or the processor itself.

The priority level of one processor does not affect the priority level of other processors. Thus, in a multiprocessor system, interrupt levels alone cannot be used to synchronize access to shared resources.

Synchronization with other processors in a multiprocessor system involves a combination of raising the IPL and executing an interlocking instruction sequence. Raising the IPL prevents the synchronization sequence itself from being interrupted on a single processor while the interlock sequence guarantees mutual exclusion with other processors. Alternately, one processor can issue explicit interprocessor interrupts (and wait for acknowledgment) to put other processors in a known software state, thus achieving mutual exclusion.

In some implementations, several instructions may be in various stages of execution simultaneously. Before the processor can service an interrupt request, all active instructions must be allowed to complete without exception. Thus, when an exception occurs in a currently active instruction, the exception is initiated and the exception stack frame built immediately before the interrupt is initiated and its stack frame built.

The following events will cause an interrupt:

- Software interrupts — IPL 1 to 15
- Asynchronous System Traps — IPL 2
- Passive Release interrupts — IPL 20 to 23
- I/O Device interrupts — IPL 20 to 23
- Interval Clock interrupt — IPL 22
- Interprocessor interrupt — IPL 22
- Performance Monitor interrupt — IPL 29
- Powerfail interrupt — IPL 30

Interrupts are initiated in kernel mode and push the interrupt stack frame of eight quadwords onto the kernel stack. The PC saved in the interrupt stack frame is the virtual address of the first instruction not executed after the interrupt condition was recognized. A CALL_PAL REI instruction to the saved PC/PS will continue execution at the point of interrupt.

Each interrupt source has a separate vector location (offset) within the System Control Block (SCB). (See Section 6.6.) With the exception of I/O device interrupts, each of the above events has a unique fixed vector. I/O device interrupts occupy a range of vectors that can be both statically and dynamically assigned. Upon entry to the interrupt service routine, R2 contains the SCB vector quadword and R3 contains the SCB parameter quadword. For Corrected Error interrupts, R4 optionally locates additional information (see Section 6.5.2).

In order to reduce interrupt overhead, no memory mapping information is changed when an interrupt occurs. Therefore, the instructions, data, and the contents of the interrupt vector for the interrupt service routine must be present in every process at the same virtual address.

Interrupt service routines should follow the discipline of not lowering IPL below their initial level. Lowering IPL in this way could result in an interrupt at an intermediate level, which would cause the stack nesting to be incorrect.

Kernel mode software may need to raise and lower IPL during certain instruction sequences that must synchronize with possible interrupt conditions (such as powerfail). This can be accomplished by specifying the desired IPL and executing a CALL_PAL MTPR_IPL instruction or by executing a CALL_PAL REI instruction that restores a PS that contains the desired IPL (see Section 2.6.5).

6.4.1 Software Interrupts — IPLs 1 to 15

6.4.1.1 Software Interrupt Summary Register

The architecture provides fifteen priority interrupt levels for use by software (level 0 is also available for use by software but interrupts can never occur at this level). The Software Interrupt Summary Register (SISR) stores a mask of pending software interrupts. Bit positions in this mask that contain a 1 correspond to the levels on which software interrupts are pending.

When the processor IPL drops below that of the highest requested software interrupt, a software interrupt is initiated and the corresponding bit in the SISR is cleared.

The SISR is a read-only internal processor register that may be read by kernel mode software by executing a CALL_PAL MFPR_SISR instruction (see Section 5.3).

6.4.1.2 Software Interrupt Request Register

The Software Interrupt Request Register (SIRR) is a write-only internal processor register used for making software interrupt requests.

Kernel mode software may request a software interrupt at a particular level by executing a CALL_PAL MTPR_SIRR instruction (see Section 5.3).

If the requested interrupt level is greater than the current IPL, the interrupt will occur before the execution of the next instruction. If, however, the requested level is equal to or less than the current processor IPL, the interrupt request will be recorded in the Software Interrupt Summary Register (SISR) and deferred until the processor IPL drops to the appropriate level.
Note that no indication is given if there is already a request at the specified level. Therefore, the respective interrupt service routine must not assume that there is a one-to-one correspondence between interrupts requested and interrupts generated. A valid protocol for generating this correspondence is:

1. The requester places information in a control block and then inserts the control block in a queue associated with the respective software interrupt level.

2. The requester uses CALL_PAL MTPR_SIRR to request an interrupt at the appropriate level.

3. When enabling conditions arise, processor HW clears the appropriate SISR bit as part of initiating the software interrupt.

4. The interrupt service routine attempts to remove a control block from the request queue. If there are no control blocks in the queue, the interrupt is dismissed with a CALL_PAL REI instruction.

5. If a valid control block is removed from the queue, the requested service is performed and step 3 is repeated.

6.4.2 Asynchronous System Trap — IPL 2

Asynchronous System Traps (ASTs) are a means of notifying a process of events that are not synchronized with its execution, but that must be dealt with in the context of the process. An AST is initiated in kernel mode at IPL 2 when the current mode is less privileged than or equal to a mode for which an AST is pending and not disabled, with PS<IPL> less than 2 (see Sections 6.7.6 and 4.3).

There are four separate per-mode SCB vectors, one for each of kernel, executive, supervisor, and user modes.

On encountering an AST, the interrupt stack frame is pushed on the kernel stack. The value of the PC saved in this stack frame is the address of the next instruction to have been executed if the interrupt had not occurred. The SCB vector quadword is saved in R2 and the SCB parameter quadword in R3.

6.4.3 Passive Release Interrupts — IPLs 20 to 23

Passive releases occur when the source of an interrupt granted by a processor cannot be determined. This can happen when the requesting I/O device determines that it no longer requires an interrupt after requesting one or when a previously requested interrupt has already been serviced by another processor in some multiprocessor configurations. The interrupt handler for passive releases executes at the priority level of the interrupt request.

6.4.4 I/O Device Interrupts — IPLs 20 to 23

The architecture provides four priority levels for use by I/O devices. I/O device interrupts are requested when the device encounters a completion, attention, or error condition and the respective interrupt is enabled. See Console Interface (III), Chapter 2, for more information.

6.4.5 Interval Clock Interrupt — IPL 22

The interval clock requests an interrupt periodically.

At least 1000 interval clock interrupts occur per second. An entry in the HWRPB contains the number of interval clock interrupts per second that occur in an actual Alpha implementation, scaled up by 4096, and rounded to a 64-bit integer. (See Console Interface (III), Chapter 2.)

The accuracy of the interval clock must be at least 50 parts per million (ppm).

Hardware/Software Note:

> For example, an interval of 819.2 usec derived from a 10 MHz Ethernet clock and a 13-bit counter is acceptable.
>
> To guarantee software progress, the interval clock interrupt should be no more frequent than the time it takes to do 500 main memory accesses. Over the life of the architecture, this interval may well decrease much more slowly than CPU cycle time decreases.
>
> Other constraints may apply to secure kernel systems.

6.4.6 Interprocessor Interrupt — IPL 22

Interprocessor interrupts are provided to enable operating system software running on one processor to interrupt activity on another processor and cause operating system-dependent actions to be performed.

6.4.6.1 Interprocessor Interrupt Request Register

The Interprocessor Interrupt Request Register (IPIR) is a write-only internal processor register used for making a request to interrupt a specific processor.

Kernel mode software may request to interrupt a particular processor by executing a CALL_PAL MTPR_IPIR instruction (see Section 5.3.)

If the specified processor is the same as the current processor and the current IPL is less than 22, then the interrupt may be delayed and not initiated before the execution of the next instruction.

Note that, as with software interrupts, no indication is given as to whether there is already an interprocessor interrupt pending when one is requested. Therefore, the interprocessor interrupt service routine must not assume there is a one-to-one correspondence between interrupts requested and interrupts generated. A valid protocol similar to the one for software interrupts for generating this correspondence is:

1. The requester places information in a control block and then inserts the control block in a queue associated with the target processor.

2. The requester uses CALL_PAL MTPR_IPIR to request an interprocessor interrupt on the target processor.

3. The interprocessor interrupt service routine on the target processor attempts to remove a control block from its request queue. If there are no control blocks remaining, the interrupt is dismissed with a CALL_PAL REI instruction.

4. If a valid control block is removed from the queue, the specified action is performed and step 3 is repeated.

6.4.7 Performance Monitor Interrupts — IPL 29

These interrupts provide some of the support for processor or system performance measurements. The implementation is processor or system specific.

6.4.8 Powerfail Interrupt — IPL 30

If the system power supply backup option permits powerfail recovery, a powerfail interrupt is generated to each processor when power is about to fail. See Console Interface (III), Chapter 3 for a description of powerfail recovery requirements and for a description of the interactions between system software and the console during system restarts.

In systems in which the backup option maintains only the contents of memory and keeps system time with the BB_WATCH, the power supply requests a powerfail interrupt to permit volatile system state to be saved. Prior to dispatching to the powerfail interrupt service routine, PALcode is responsible for saving all system state that is not visible to system software. Such state includes, but is not limited to, processor internal registers and PALcode temporary variables.

PALcode is also responsible for saving the contents of any write-back caches or buffers, including the powerfail interrupt stack frame. System software is responsible for saving all other system state. Such state includes, but is not limited to, processor registers and write-back cache contents. State can be saved by forcing all written data to a backed-up part of the memory subsystem; software may use the CALL_PAL CFLUSH instruction.

The powerfail interrupt will not be initiated until the processor IPL drops below 30. Thus, critical code sequences can block the power-down sequence by raising the IPL to 31. Software, however, must take extra care not to lock out the power-down sequence for an extended period of time. The time interval is platform specific.

Explicit state is not provided by the architecture for software to directly determine whether there were outstanding interrupts when powerfail occurred. It is the responsibility of software to leave sufficient information in memory so that it may determine the proper action on power-up.

6.5 Machine Checks

A machine check, or mcheck, indicates that a hardware error condition was detected and may or may not be successfully corrected by hardware or PALcode. Such error conditions can occur either synchronously or asynchronously with respect to instruction execution. There are four types:

1. System Machine Check (IPL 31)

   These machine checks are generated by error conditions that are detected asynchronously to processor execution but are not successfully corrected by hardware or PALcode. Examples of system machine check conditions include protocol errors on the processor-memory-interconnect (PMI) and unrecoverable memory errors.

   System machine checks are always maskable and deferred until processor IPL drops below IPL 31.

2. Processor Machine Check (IPL 31)

   These machine checks indicate that a processor internal error was detected and not successfully corrected by hardware or PALcode. Examples of processor machine check conditions include processor internal cache errors, translation buffer parity errors, or read access to a nonexistent local I/O space location (NXM).

   Processor machine checks may be nonmaskable or maskable. If nonmaskable, they are initiated immediately, even if the processor IPL is 31. If maskable, they are deferred until processor IPL drops below IPL 31.

3. System Correctable Machine Check (IPL 20)

These machine checks are generated by error conditions that are detected asynchronously to processor execution and are successfully corrected by hardware or PALcode. Examples of system correctable machine check conditions include single-bit errors within the memory subsystem.

System correctable machine checks are always maskable and deferred until processor IPL drops below IPL 20.

4. Processor Correctable Machine Check (IPL 31)

These machine checks indicate that a processor internal error was detected and successfully corrected by hardware or PALcode. Examples of processor correctable machine check conditions include corrected processor internal cache errors and corrected translation buffer table errors.

Processor correctable machine checks may be nonmaskable or maskable. If nonmaskable, they are initiated immediately, even if the processor IPL is 31. If maskable, they are deferred until processor IPL drops below IPL 31.

Machine checks are initiated in kernel mode, on the kernel stack, and cannot be disabled.

Correctable machine checks permit the pattern and frequency of certain errors to be captured. The delivery of these machine checks to system software can be disabled by setting IPR MCES<4:3>, as described in Section 5.3.9. Note that setting IPR MCES<4:3> does not disable the generation of the machine check or the correction of the error, but rather suppresses the reporting of that correction to system software.

The PC in the machine check stack frame is that of the next instruction that would have issued if the machine check condition had not occurred. This is not necessarily the address of the instruction immediately following the one encountering the error, and intervening instructions may have changed operands or other state used by the instruction encountering the error condition. A CALL_PAL REI instruction to this PC will simply continue execution from the point at which the machine check was taken.

Note:

On machine checks, a meaningful PC is delivered on a best-effort basis. The machine state, processor registers, memory, and I/O devices may be indeterminate.

Machine checks may be deliberately generated by software, such as by probing nonexistent memory during memory sizing or searching for local I/O devices. In such a case, the DRAINA PALcode instruction can be called to force any outstanding machine checks to be taken before continuing.

6.5.1 Software Response

The reaction of system software to machine checks is specific to the characteristics of the processor, platform, and system software. System software must determine if operation should be discontinued on an implementation-specific basis.

To assist system software, PALcode provides a retry flag in the machine check logout frame (see Figure 6–6). If the retry flag is set, the state of the processor and platform hardware has not been compromised; system software operation should be able to continue.

If the retry flag is clear, the state of the processor is either unknown or is known to have been updated during partial execution of one or more instructions. System software operation can continue only after system software determines that the hardware state change permits and/or takes corrective action.

PALcode should take appropriate implementation-specific actions prior to setting the retry flag. PALcode should also attempt to ensure that each encountered error condition generates only one machine check.

Implementation Note:

> An important example of using the retry flag is read NXM. Also, a read NXM should not generate both a Processor Machine Check and a System Machine Check.

PALcode sets an internal Machine-Check-In-Progress flag in the Machine Check Error Summary (MCES) register prior to initiating a system or processor machine check. System software must clear that flag to dismiss the machine check. If a second uncorrectable machine check hardware error condition is detected while the flag is set, or if PALcode cannot deliver the machine check, PALcode forces the processor to enter console I/O mode, and subsequent actions, such as processor restart, are taken by the console. The REASON FOR HALT code is "double error abort encountered."See Console Interface (III), Chapter 3.

Similarly, PALcode sets an internal correctable Machine-Check-In-Progress flag in the Machine Check Error Summary (MCES) register prior to initiating a system-correctable error interrupt or processor-correctable machine check. System software must clear that flag to dismiss the condition and permit the reuse of the logout area. If a second correctable hardware error condition is detected while the flag is set, the error is corrected, but not reported. PALcode does not overwrite the logout area and the processor remains in program I/O mode.

6.5.2 Logout Areas

When a hardware error condition is encountered, PALcode optionally builds a logout frame prior to passing control to the machine check service routine. The logout frame is shown in Figure 6–6 and described in Table 6–4. The logout frame is built in the logout area located by the processor's per-CPU slot in the HWRPB (see Console Interface (III), Chapter 2).

Figure 6–6: Corrected Error and Machine Check Logout Frame

63 62 61	32 31	0	
R S	SBZ	Frame Size	:FRAME
System Offset		CPU Offset	:+8
PALcode-Specific Information			:+16
CPU-Specific Information			:+CPU Offset
System-Specific Information			:+SYS Offset
			:+FRAME SIZE

Table 6–4: Corrected Error and Machine Check Logout Frame Fields

Offset	Description
FRAME	FRAME SIZE — Size in bytes of the logout frame, including the FRAME SIZE longword.
+04	FRAME FLAGS — Informational flags.

Bit	Description
31	RETRY FLAG — Indicates whether execution can be resumed after dismissing this machine check. Set on Corrected Error interrupts; may be set on machine checks.
30	SECOND ERROR FLAG — Indicates that a second correctable error was encountered. Set on Corrected Error interrupts when a correctable error was encountered while the relevant correctable error bit (PCE or SCE) is set in the MCES register. Clear on machine checks.
29–0	SBZ.

Offset	Description
+08	CPU OFFSET — Offset in bytes from the base of the logout frame to the CPU-specific information. If CPU OFFSET is equal to 16, the frame contains no PALcode-specific information. If CPU OFFSET is equal to SYS OFFSET, the frame contains no CPU-specific information.
+12	SYS OFFSET — Offset in bytes from the base of the logout frame to the system-specific information. If SYS OFFSET is equal to FRAME SIZE, the frame contains no system-specific information.
+16	PALCODE INFORMATION — PALcode-specific logout information.
+CPU OFFSET	CPU INFORMATION — CPU-specific logout information.
+SYS OFFSET	SYS INFORMATION — System platform-specific logout information.

The logout frame is optional; the service routine uses R4 to locate the frame, if any. Upon entry to the service routine, R4 contains the byte offset of the logout frame from the base of the logout area. If no frame was built, R4 contains –1.

6.6 System Control Block

The System Control Block (SCB) specifies the entry points for exception, interrupt, and machine check service routines. The block is from 8K to 32K bytes long, must be page aligned, and must be physically contiguous. The PFN is specified by the value of the System Control Block Base (SCBB) internal register.

The SCB, shown in Figure 6–7, consists of from 512 to 2048 entries, each 16 bytes long. The first eight bytes of an entry, the vector, specify the virtual address of the service routine associated with that entry. The second eight bytes, the parameter, are an arbitrary quadword value to be passed to the service routine.

Figure 6–7: System Control Block Summary

Faults	000-0F0
Arithmetic Traps	200-230
Asynchronous System Traps	240-270
Data Alignment Traps	280-3F0
Other Synchronous Traps	400-4F0
Software Interrupts	500-5F0
Processor Hardware Interrupts and Machine Checks	600-6F0
Unused	700-7F0
I/O Hardware Interrupts	800-7FF0

The SCB entries are grouped as follows:

- Faults
- Arithmetic traps
- Asynchronous system traps
- Data alignment trap
- Other synchronous traps
- Processor software interrupts
- Processor hardware interrupts and machine checks
- I/O device interrupts

The first 512 entries (offsets 0000 through 800_{16}) contain all architecturally defined and any statically allocated entries. All remaining SCB entries, if any, are used only for those I/O device interrupt vectors that are assigned dynamically by system software. It is the responsibility of that software to ensure the consistency of the assigned vector and the SCB entry.

6.6.1 SCB Entries for Faults

The exception handler for a fault executes with the IPL unchanged, in kernel mode, on the kernel stack. Table 6–5 lists the SCB entries for faults.

Table 6–5: SCB Entries for Faults

Byte offset$_{16}$	Entry name
000	Unused
010	Floating Disabled fault
020–070	Unused
080	Access Control Violation fault
090	Translation Not Valid fault
0A0	Fault on Read fault
0B0	Fault on Write fault
0C0	Fault on Execute fault
0A0–0F0	Unused

6.6.2 SCB Entries for Arithmetic Traps

The exception handler for an arithmetic trap executes with the IPL unchanged, in kernel mode, on the kernel stack. Table 6–6 lists the SCB entries for arithmetic traps.

Table 6–6: SCB Entries for Arithmetic Traps

Byte offset$_{16}$	Entry name
200	Arithmetic Trap
210–230	Unused

6.6.3 SCB Entries for Asynchronous System Traps (ASTs)

The interrupt handler for an asynchronous system trap executes at IPL 2, in kernel mode, on the kernel stack. Table 6–7 lists the SCB entries for asynchronous system traps.

Table 6–7: SCB Entries for Asynchronous System Traps

Byte offset$_{16}$	Entry name
240	Kernel Mode AST
250	Executive Mode AST

Table 6–7: SCB Entries for Asynchronous System Traps (Continued)

Byte offset$_{16}$	Entry name
260	Supervisor Mode AST
270	User Mode AST

6.6.4 SCB Entries for Data Alignment Traps

The exception handler for a data alignment trap executes with the IPL unchanged in kernel mode, on the kernel stack. Table 6–8 lists the SCB entries for data alignment traps.

Table 6–8: SCB Entries for Data Alignment Trap

Byte offset$_{16}$	Entry name
280	Unaligned_Access
290-3F0	Unused

6.6.5 SCB Entries for Other Synchronous Traps

The exception handler for a synchronous trap, other than those described above, executes with the IPL unchanged, in the mode and on the stack indicated below. "MostPriv" indicates that the handler executes in either the original mode or the new mode, whichever is the most privileged. Table 6–9 lists the SCB entries for other synchronous traps.

Table 6–9: SCB Entries for Other Synchronous Traps

Byte Offset$_{16}$	Entry Name	Mode
400	Breakpoint Trap	Kernel
410	Bugcheck Trap	Kernel
420	Illegal Instruction Trap	Kernel
430	Illegal Operand Trap	Kernel
440	Generate Software Trap	Kernel
450	Unused	
460	Unused	
470	Unused	
480	Change Mode to Kernel	Kernel
490	Change Mode to Executive	MostPriv
4A0	Change Mode to Supervisor	MostPriv

Table 6–9: SCB Entries for Other Synchronous Traps (Continued)

Byte Offset$_{16}$	Entry Name	Mode
4B0	Change Mode to User	Current
4C0–4F0	Reserved for DIGITAL	

6.6.6 SCB Entries for Processor Software Interrupts

The exception handler for a processor software interrupt executes at the target IPL, in kernel mode, on the kernel stack. Table 6–10 lists the SCB entries for processor software interrupts.

Table 6–10: SCB Entries for Processor Software Interrupts

Byte Offset$_{16}$	Entry Name	Target IPL$_{10}$
500	Unused	
510	Software interrupt level 1	1
520	Software interrupt level 2	2
530	Software interrupt level 3	3
540	Software interrupt level 4	4
550	Software interrupt level 5	5
560	Software interrupt level 6	6
570	Software interrupt level 7	7
580	Software interrupt level 8	8
590	Software interrupt level 9	9
5A0	Software interrupt level 10	10
5B0	Software interrupt level 11	11
5C0	Software interrupt level 12	12
5D0	Software interrupt level 13	13
5E0	Software interrupt level 14	14
5F0	Software interrupt level 15	15

6.6.7 SCB Entries for Processor Hardware Interrupts and Machine Checks

The interrupt handler for a processor hardware interrupt executes at the target IPL, in kernel mode, on the kernel stack.

The handler for machine checks executes in kernel mode, on the kernel stack. The handler for system-correctable machine checks executes at IPL 20; the handler for all other machine

Exceptions, Interrupts, and Machine Checks (II–A) **6–29**

checks executes at IPL 31. Table 6–11 lists the SCB entries for processor hardware interrupts and machine checks.

Table 6–11: SCB Entries for Processor Hardware Interrupts and Machine Checks

Byte Offset$_{16}$	Entry name	Target IPL$_{10}$
600	Interval clock interrupt	22
610	Interprocessor interrupt	22
620	System correctable machine check	20
630	Processor correctable machine check	31
640	Powerfail interrupt	30
650	Performance monitor	29
660	System machine check	31
670	Processor machine check	31
680–6E0	Reserved — processor specific	
6F0	Passive release	20-23

Processor-specific SCB entries include those used by console devices (if any) or other peripherals dedicated to system support functions.

6.6.8 SCB Entries for I/O Device Interrupts

The interrupt handler for an I/O device interrupt executes at the target IPL, in kernel mode, on the kernel stack. SCB entries for offsets of 800_{16} through $7FF0_{16}$ are reserved for I/O device interrupts.

6.7 PALcode Support

6.7.1 Stack Writeability

In response to various exceptions, interrupts, and machine checks, PALcode pushes information on the kernel stack. PALcode may write this information without first probing to ensure that all such writes to the kernel stack will succeed. If a memory management exception occurs while pushing information, PALcode forces the processor to enter console I/O mode, and subsequent actions, such as processor restart, are taken by the console. The REASON FOR HALT code is "processor halted due to kernel-stack-not-valid." See Console Interface (III), Chapter 3.

6.7.2 Stack Residency

The user, supervisor, and executive stacks for the current process do not need to be resident. Software running in kernel mode can bring in or allocate stack pages as TNV faults occur.

However, since this activity is taking place in kernel mode, the kernel stack must be fully resident.

When the faults TNV, ACV, FOR, and FOW occur on kernel mode references to the kernel stack, they are considered serious system failures from which recovery is not possible. If any of those faults occur, PALcode forces the processor to enter console I/O mode, and subsequent actions, such as processor restart, are taken by the console. The REASON FOR HALT code is "processor halted due to kernel-stack-not-valid." See Console Interface (III), Chapter 3.

6.7.3 Stack Alignment

Stacks may have arbitrary byte alignment, but performance may suffer if at least octaword alignment is not maintained by software.

PALcode creates stack frames in response to exceptions and interrupts. Before doing so, the target stack is aligned to a 64-byte boundary by setting the six low bits of the target SP to 000000_2. The previous value of these bits is stored in the SP_ALIGN field of the saved PS in memory, for use by a CALL_PAL REI instruction.

Software-constructed stack frames must be 64-byte aligned and have SP_ALIGN properly set; otherwise, a CALL_PAL REI instruction will take an illegal operand trap.

6.7.4 Initiate Exception or Interrupt or Machine Check

Exceptions, interrupts, and machine checks are initiated by PALcode with interrupts disabled. When an exception, interrupt, or machine check is initiated, the associated SCB vector is read to determine the address of the service routine. PALcode then attempts to push the PC, PS, and R2..R7 onto the target stack. When an interrupt (software or hardware but not AST) is initiated, PS<IP> is set to 1 to indicate an interrupt is in progress. Additional parameters may be passed in R4 and R5 on exceptions and machine checks.

During the attempt to push this information, the exceptions (faults) TNV, ACV, and FOW can occur:

- If any of those faults occur when the target stack is user, supervisor, or executive, then the fault is taken on the kernel stack.

- If any of those faults occur when the target stack is the kernel stack, PALcode forces the processor to enter console I/O mode, and subsequent actions, such as processor restart, are taken by the console. The REASON FOR HALT code is "processor halted due to kernel-stack-not-valid." See Console Interface (III), Chapter 3.

6.7.5 Initiate Exception or Interrupt or Machine Check Model

```
check_for_exception_or_interrupt_or_mcheck:
    IF NOT {ready_to_initiate_exception OR
            ready_to_initiate_interrupt OR
            ready_to_initiate_mcheck} THEN
        BEGIN
          {fetch next instruction}
          {decode and execute instruction}
        END
    ELSE
        BEGIN
          {wait for instructions in progress to complete}
                             ! clear interrupt pending
          tmp ← 0
          IF {exception pending} THEN
             BEGIN
               {back up implementation specific state if necessary,
                this includes the PC if synchronous trap pending}
               new_ipl ← PS<IPL>
               new_mode ← Kernel
             END

          ELSE IF {unmaskable mcheck pending} THEN
             BEGIN
               {back up implementation specific state if necessary}
               {attempt correction if appropriate}
               IF {uncorrectable AND MCES<0> = 1} THEN
                   {enter console}
               ELSE IF {uncorrectable} THEN
                   new_mode ← Kernel
                   new_ipl ← 31
                                      ! set mcheck error flag
                   MCES<0> ← 1
               ELSE IF {reporting enabled} THEN
                   new_mode ← Kernel
                   new_ipl ← 31
                   MCES<2> ← 1
             END
          END

          ELSE IF {data alignment trap} THEN
             new_mode ← Kernel

          ELSE IF {synchronous trap} THEN
             CASE {opcode} OF
               {back up implementation specific state if necessary}
               CHME: new_mode ← min(PS<CM>,Executive)
               CHMS: new_mode ← min(PS<CM>,Supervisor)
               CHMU: new_mode ← min(PS<CM>,User)
               otherwise: new_mode ← Kernel
             ENDCASE
```

```
ELSE IF {maskable uncorrectable mcheck pending and IPL < 31} THEN
   BEGIN
      {back up implementation specific state if necessary}
      IF {MCES<0> = 1} THEN
          {enter console}
      ELSE
          new_mode ← Kernel
          new_ipl  ← 31
          MCES<0> ← 1 ! set mcheck error flag
      END
   END

ELSE IF {interrupt pending} THEN
      new_ipl ← {interrupt source IPL}
      tmp ← 1 ! set interrupt pending
      new_mode ← Kernel

ELSE IF {maskable correctable  mcheck pending AND
         reporting enabled} THEN
      new_ipl ← 20
      MCES<1> ← 1
      new_mode ← Kernel
END

IPR_SP[PS<CM>] ← SP
new_sp ← IPR_SP[new_mode]
save_align ← new_sp<5:0>
new_sp<5:0> ← 0

PUSH(PS OR LEFT_SHIFT(save_align,56), old_pc, new_mode)
PUSH(R7, R6, new_mode)
PUSH(R5, R4, new_mode)
PUSH(R3, R2, new_mode)

PS<SW> ← 0
PS<CM> ← new_mode
PS<IP> ← tmp
PS<IPL> ← new_ipl
SP ← new_sp

IF {memory management fault} THEN
    R4 ← VA
    R5 ← MMF
END

IF {data alignment trap} THEN
    R4 ← VA
    R5 ← { 0 if read/load  1 if write/store }
END
```

```
          IF {mcheck or correctable error interrupt} THEN
               IF {logout frame built}
                    R4 ← logout_area_offset
               ELSE
                    R4 ← -1
               END
          END

          IF {arithmetic Trap} THEN
               R4 ← register write mask
               R5 ← exception summary
          END

          IF {software interrupt} THEN
               SISR ← SISR AND NOT{ 2**{ PRIORITY_ENCODE(SISR) } }
          END

          vector ← {exception or interrupt or mcheck SCB offset}

          R2 ← (SCBB + vector)
          R3 ← (SCBB + vector + 8)
          PC ← R2

     END

     GOTO check_for_exception_or_interrupt_or_mcheck

PROCEDURE PUSH(first, last, mode)
     BEGIN
       IF ACCESS(new_sp - 16, mode) THEN
          BEGIN
             (new_sp - 8) ← first
             (new_sp - 16) ← last
             new_sp ← new_sp - 16
             RETURN
          END
       ELSE
             {initiate ACV, TNV, or FOW fault, or
             Kernel Stack Not Valid restart sequence}
          END
     END
```

6.7.6 PALcode Interrupt Arbitration

The following sections describe the logic for the interrupt conditions produced by the specified operation.

6.7.6.1 Writing the AST Summary Register

Writing the ASTSR internal processor register (Section 5.3) requests an AST for any of the four processor modes. This operation may request an AST on a formerly inactive level and thus cause an AST interrupt. The logic required to check for this condition is:

```
ASTSR<3:0> ← {ASTSR<3:0> AND R16<3:0>} OR R16<7:4>
IF ASTEN<0> AND ASTSR<0> AND {PS<IPL> LT 2} THEN
   {initiate AST interrupt at IPL 2}
```

6.7.6.2 Writing the AST Enable Register

Writing the ASTEN internal processor register (Section 5.3) enables ASTs for any of the four processor modes. This operation may enable an AST on a formerly inactive level and thus cause an AST interrupt. The logic required to check for this condition is:

```
ASTEN<3:0> ← {ASTEN<3:0> AND R16<3:0>} OR R16<7:4>
IF ASTEN<0> AND ASTSR<0> AND {PS<IPL> LT 2} THEN
   {initiate AST interrupt at IPL 2}
```

6.7.6.3 Writing the IPL Register

Writing the IPL internal processor register (Section 5.3) changes the current IPL. This operation may enable an AST or software interrupt on a formerly inactive level and thus cause an AST or software interrupt. The logic required to check for this condition is:

```
PS<IPL> ← R16<4:0>

! check for software interrupt at level 2..15

IF {RIGHT_SHIFT({SISR AND FFFC₁₆ }, PS<IPL> + 1) NE 0} THEN
   {initiate software interrupt at IPL of high bit set in SISR}

! check for AST

IF ASTEN<0> AND ASTSR<0> AND {PS<IPL> LT 2} THEN
   {initiate AST interrupt at IPL 2}

! check for software interrupt at level 1

IF SISR<1> AND {PS<IPL> EQ 0} THEN
   {initiate software interrupt at IPL 1}
```

6.7.6.4 Writing the Software Interrupt Request Register

Writing the SIRR internal processor register (Section 5.3) requests a software interrupt at one of the fifteen software interrupt levels. This operation may cause a formerly inactive level to cause a software interrupt. The logic required to check for this condition is:

```
SISR<level> ← 1
IF level GT PS<IPL> THEN
 {initiate software interrupt at IPL level}
```

6.7.6.4.1 Return from Exception or Interrupt

The CALL_PAL REI instruction (Section 2.1.11) writes both the Current Mode and IPL fields of the PS (see Section 6.2). This may enable a formerly disabled AST or software interrupt to occur. The logic required to check for this condition is:

```
PS ← New PS

! check for software interrupt at level 2..15

IF {RIGHT_SHIFT({SISR AND FFFC₁₆ }, PS<IPL> + 1) NE 0} THEN
{initiate software interrupt at IPL of high bit set in SISR}

! check for AST

tmp ← NOT LEFT_SHIFT(1110(bin), PS<CM>)
IF {{tmp AND ASTEN AND ASTSR}<3:0> NE 0} AND {PS<IPL> LT 2} THEN
 {initiate AST interrupt at IPL 2}

! check for software interrupt at level 1

IF SISR<1> AND {PS<IPL> EQ 0} THEN
 {initiate software interrupt at IPL 1}
```

6.7.6.5 Swap AST Enable

Swapping the AST enable state for the Current Mode results in writing the ASTEN internal processor register (see Section 5.3). This operation may enable a formerly disabled AST to cause an AST interrupt. The logic required to check for this condition is:

```
R0 ← ZEXT(ASTEN<PS<CM>>)
ASTEN<PS<CM>> ← R16<0>

IF ASTEN<PS<CM>> AND ASTSR<PS<CM>> AND {PS<IPL> LT 2} THEN
 {initiate AST interrupt at IPL 2}
```

6.7.7 Processor State Transition Table

Table 6–12 shows the operations that can produce a state transition and the specific transition produced. For example, if a processor's initial state is supervisor mode, it is not possible for the processor to transition to a program halt condition. A processor can only transition to program halt from kernel mode.

In Table 6–12:

- "REI" increases mode or lowers IPL.
- "MTPR" changes IPL or is a CALL_PAL MTPR_ASTSR or CALL_PAL MTPR_ASTEN instruction that causes an interrupt request.
- "Exc" is a state change caused by an exception.
- "Int" is a state change caused by an interrupt.
- "Mcheck" is a state change caused by a machine check.

Table 6–12: Processor State Transitions

Initial State:	Final State:				
	User	**Super.**	**Exec.**	**Kernel**	**Program Halt**
User	CHMU REI	CHMS	CHME	CHMK Exc Int Mcheck SWASTEN	Not Possible
Supervisor	REI	CHMS REI	CHME	CHMK Exc Int Mcheck SWASTEN	Not Possible
Executive	REI	REI	CHME REI	CHMK Exc Int Mcheck SWASTEN	Not Possible
Kernel	REI	REI	REI	CHMK REI Exc Int Mcheck MTPR SWASTEN	HALT

OpenVMS Alpha Software Index

C

Caches
   flushing physical page from, 2–83
CFLUSH (PALcode) instruction, 2–83
   with powerfail, 6–22
Charged process cycles register, 2–91
   in HWPCB, 4–2
   PCC register and, 4–3
CHME (PALcode) instruction, 2–6
   service routine entry point, 6–28
   trap initiation, 6–17
CHMK (PALcode) instruction, 2–7
   service routine entry point, 6–28
   trap initiation, 6–17
CHMS (PALcode) instruction, 2–8
   service routine entry point, 6–28
   trap initiation, 6–17
CHMU (PALcode) instruction, 2–9
   service routine entry point, 6–28
   trap initiation, 6–17
CLRFEN (PALcode) instruction, 2–10
Context switching
   defined, 4–1
   hardware, 4–2
   initiating, 2–91
   raising IPL while, 4–4
   software, 4–2
   See also Hardware
Corrected error interrupts, logout area for, 6–24
CSERVE (PALcode) instruction, 2–84
Current mode field, in PS register, 6–6
Current PC, 6–2

D

Data alignment trap (DAT) register
   privileged context, 2–91
Data alignment traps, 6–15
   fixup (DAT) bit, in HWPCB, 4–2
   fixup (DATFX) register, 5–10
   registers used, 6–15
   service routine entry point, 6–28
   when concurrent with arithmetic, 6–15
Division by zero trap, 6–14
DPC bit, machine check error summary register, 5–15
DSC bit, machine check error summary register, 5–15
DZE bit
   exception summary parameter, 6–13

E

Exception service routines
   entry point, 6–26
   introduced, 6–8
Exception summary parameter, 6–12
Exceptional events
   actions, summarized, 6–2
   defined, 6–1
Exceptions
   actions, summarized, 6–2
   initiated before interrupts, 6–18
   initiated by PALcode, 6–31
   introduced, 6–8
   processor state transitions, 6–37
   stack frames for, 6–7
   See also Arithmetic traps
Executive read enable (ERE), bit in PTE, 3–5
Executive stack pointer (ESP) register, 5–11
   as internal processor register, 5–1
   in HWPCB, 4–2
Executive write enable (EWE), bit in PTE, 3–4

F

F_floating data type
   when data is unaligned, 6–28
Fault on execute (FOE), 6–12
   bit in PTE, 3–6
   service routine entry point, 6–27
   software usage of, 6–12
Fault on read (FOR), 6–11
   bit in PTE, 3–6
   service routine entry point, 6–27
   software usage of, 6–11
Fault on write (FOW), 6–11
   bit in PTE, 3–6
   service routine entry point, 6–27
   software usage of, 6–11
Faults, 6–9
   access control violation, 6–10
   defined, 6–9
   fault on execute, 6–12
   fault on read, 6–11
   fault on write, 6–11
   floating-point disabled, 6–10
   MM flag, 6–10
   program counter (PC) value, 6–9
   REI instruction with, 6–9
   translation not valid, 6–10
Floating-point disabled fault, 6–10
   service routine entry point, 6–27
Floating-point enable (FEN) register
   clearing, 2–10
   described, 5–12
   in HWPCB, 4–2
   privileged context, 2–91

T

T_floating data type
    when data is unaligned, 6–28

TB. See Translation buffer

Translation buffer (TB)
    address space number with, 3–11
    fault on execute, 6–12
    fault on read, 6–11
    fault on write, 6–11
    granularity hint in PTE, 3–5
    with invalid PTEs, 3–12

Translation buffer check (TBCHK) register
    described, 5–25
    with translation buffer, 3–12

Translation buffer invalidate all (TBIA) register
    described, 5–26
    with translation buffer, 3–12

Translation buffer invalidate all process (TBIAP)
      register
    described, 5–27
    with translation buffer, 3–12

Translation buffer invalidate single (TBIS) register,
    5–28

Translation not valid fault, 6–10
    service routine entry point, 6–27

Traps
    See also Arithmetic traps

U

Underflow trap, 6–14

UNF bit
    exception summary parameter, 6–13

User read enable (URE)
    bit in PTE, 3–4

User stack pointer (USP) register, 5–29
    in HWPCB, 4–2
    internal processor register, 5–1

User write enable (UWE)
    bit in PTE, 3–4

V

Valid (V)
    bit in PTE, 3–6

Virtual address format, 3–2

Virtual address space, 3–1, 3–2
    minimum and maximum, 3–2
    page size with, 3–2

Virtual address translation, 3–10

Virtual machine monitor (VMM), bit in PS register,
    6–6

Virtual page table base (VPTB) register, 5–30

W

Watchpoints
    with fault on read, 6–11
    with fault on write, 6–11

Who-Am-I (WHAMI) register Processor number,
    reading, 5–31

WR_PS_SW (PALcode) instruction, 2–20

WRITE_UNQ (PALcode) instruction, 2–81

DIGITAL UNIX Software (II–B)

This section describes how the DIGITAL UNIX operating system relates to the Alpha architecture, and includes the following chapters:

- Chapter 1, Introduction to DIGITAL UNIX (II–B)
- Chapter 2, PALcode Instruction Descriptions (II–B)
- Chapter 3, Memory Management (II–B)
- Chapter 4, Process Structure (II–B)
- Chapter 5, Exceptions and Interrupts (II–B)

Contents

1 Introduction to DIGITAL UNIX (II–B)

2 PALcode Instruction Descriptions (II–B)

3   Memory Management (II–B)

4   Process Structure (II–B)

5   Exceptions and Interrupts (II–B)

Figures

Tables

Chapter 1

Introduction to DIGITAL UNIX (II–B)

The goals of this design are to provide a hardware interface between the hardware and DIGITAL UNIX that is implementation independent. The interface needs to provide the required abstractions to minimize the impact of different hardware implementations on the operating system. The interface also needs to be low in overhead to support high-performance systems. Finally, the interface needs to support only the features used by DIGITAL UNIX.

The register usage in this interface is based on the current calling standard used by DIGITAL UNIX. If the calling standard changes, this interface will be changed accordingly. The current calling standard register usage is shown in Table 1–1.

Table 1–1: DIGITAL UNIX Register Usage

Register Name	Software Name	Use and Linkage
r0	v0	Used for expression evaluations and to hold integer function results.
r1...r8	t0...t7	Temporary registers; not preserved across procedure calls.
r9...r14	s0...s5	Saved registers; their values must be preserved across procedure calls.
r15	FP or s6	Frame pointer or a saved register.
r16...r21	a0...a5	Argument registers; used to pass the first six integer type arguments; their values are not preserved across procedure calls.
r22...r25	t8...t11	Temporary registers; not preserved across procedure calls.
r26	ra	Contains the return address; used for expression evaluation.
r27	pv or t12	Procedure value or a temporary register.
r28	at	Assembler temporary register; not preserved across procedure calls.
r29	GP	Global pointer.
r30	SP	Stack pointer.
r31	zero	Always has the value 0.

1.1 Programming Model

The programming model of the machine is the combination of the state visible either directly via instructions, or indirectly via actions of the machine. Tables 1–2 and 1–3 and define code flow constants, state variables, terms, subroutines, and code flow terms that are used in the rest of the document.

1.1.1 Code Flow Constants and Terms

DIGITAL UNIX uses the following constants and terms

Table 1–2: Code Flow Constants and Terms

Term	Meaning and value
IPL = 2:0	The range 2:0 used in the PS to access the IPL field of the PS (PS <IPL>).
maxCPU	The maximum number of processors in a given system.
mode = 3	Used as a subscript in PS to select current mode (PS <mode>).
opDec	An attempt was made to execute a reserved instruction or execute a privileged instruction in user mode.
pageSize	Size of a page in an implementation in bytes.
vaSize	Size of virtual address in bits in a given implementation.

1.1.2 Machine State Terms

Table 1–3: Machine State Terms

Term	Meaning
ASN	An implementation-dependent size register to hold the current address space number (ASN). The size and existence of ASN is an implementation choice.
entArith <63:0>	The arithmetic trap entry address register. The entArith is an internal processor register that holds the dispatch address on an arithmetic trap. There can be a hardware register for the entArith or the PALcode can use private scratch memory.
entIF <63:0>	The instruction fault or synchronous trap entry address register. The entIF is an internal processor register that holds the dispatch address on an instruction fault or synchronous trap. There can be a hardware register for the entIF or the PALcode can use private scratch memory.
entInt <63:0>	The interrupt entry address register. The entInt is an internal processor register that holds the dispatch address on an interrupt. There can be a hardware register for the entInt or the PALcode can use private scratch memory.
entMM <63:0>	The memory-management fault entry address register. The entMM is an internal processor register that holds the dispatch address on a memory-management fault. There can be a hardware register for the entMM or the PALcode can use private scratch memory.
entSys <63:0>	The system call entry address register. The entSys is an internal processor register that holds the dispatch address on an callsys instruction. There can be a hardware register for the entSys or the PALcode can use private scratch memory.
entUna <63:0>	The unaligned fault entry address register. The entUna is an internal processor register that holds the dispatch address on an unaligned fault. There can be a hardware register for the entUna or the PALcode can use private scratch memory.
FEN <0>	The floating-point enable register. The FEN is a one-bit register, located at bit 0 of PCB[40], that is used to enable or disable floating-point instructions. If a floating-point instruction is executed with FEN equal to zero, a FEN fault is initiated.
instruction <31:0>	The current instruction being executed. This is a fake register used in the flows to CASE on different instructions.
intr_flag	A per-processor state bit. The intr_flag bit is cleared if that processor executes an rti or retsys instruction.
KGP <63:0>	The kernel global pointer. The KGP is an internal processor register that holds the kernel global pointer that is loaded into R15, the GP, when an exception is initiated. There can be a hardware register for the KGP or the PALcode can use private scratch memory.

Table 1–3: Machine State Terms (Continued)

Term	Meaning
KSP <63:0>	The kernel stack pointer. The KSP is an internal processor register that holds the kernel stack pointer while in user mode. There can be a hardware register for the KSP or the storage space in the PCB can be used.
lock_flag <0>	A one-bit register that is used by the load locked and store conditional instructions.
MCES <2:0>	The machine check error summary register. The MCES is a 3-bit register that contains controls for machine check and system-correctable error handling.
PC <63:0>	The program counter. The PC is a pointer to the next instruction in the flows. The low-order two bits of the PC always read as zero and writes to them are ignored.
PCB	The process control block. The PCB holds the state of the process.
PCBB <63:0>	The process control block base address register. The PCBB holds the address of the PCB for the current process.
PCC	The PCC register consists of two 32-bit fields. The low-order 32 bits (PCC <31:0>) are an unsigned, wrapping counter, PCC_CNT. The high-order 32 bits (PCC <63:32>) are an offset, PCC_OFF. PCC_OFF is a value that, when added to PCC_CNT, gives the total PCC register count for this process, modulo 2**32.
PME <62>	The performance monitoring enable bit. The PME is a one-bit register, located at bit 62 of PCB[40], that alerts any performance monitoring software/hardware in the system that this process is to have its performance monitored. The implementation mechanism for this bit is not specified; it is implementation dependent (IMP).
PS <3:0>	The processor status. The PS is a four-bit register that stores the current mode in bit <3> and stores the three-bit IPL in bits <2:0>. The mode is 0 for kernel and 1 for user.
PTBR <63:0>	The page table base register. The PTBR contains the physical page frame number (PFN) of the highest level page table.
SP <63:0>	Another name for R30. The SP points to the top of the current stack.
	PALcode only accesses the kernel stack. The kernel stack must be quadword aligned whenever PALcode reads or writes it. If the PALcode accesses the kernel stack and the stack is not aligned, a kernel-stack-not-valid halt is initiated. Although PALcode does not access the user stack, that stack should also be at least quadword aligned for best performance.

Table 1–3: Machine State Terms (Continued)

Term	Meaning
sysvalue <63:0>	The system value register. The sysvalue holds the per-processor unique value. There can be a hardware register for the sysvalue register or the storage space in the PALcode scratch memory can be used. The sysvalue register can only be accessed by kernel mode code and there is one sysvalue register per CPU.
unique <63:0>	The process unique value register. The unique register holds the per-process unique value. There can be a hardware register for the unique register or the storage space in the PCB can be used. The unique register can be accessed by both user and kernel code and there is one unique register per process.
USP <63:0>	The user stack pointer. The USP is an internal processor register that holds the user stack pointer while in kernel mode. There can be a hardware register for the USP or the storage space in the PCB can be used.
VPTPTR <63:0>	The virtual page table pointer. The VPTPTR holds the virtual address of the first level page table.
whami <63:0>	The processor number of the current processor. This number is in the range 0…maxCPU–1.

Chapter 2

PALcode Instruction Descriptions (II–B)

2.1 Unprivileged PALcode Instructions

Table 2–1 lists the DIGITAL UNIX PALcode unprivileged instruction mnemonics, names, and the environment from which they can be called.

Table 2–1: Unprivileged PALcode Instructions

Mnemonic	Name	Calling environment
bpt	Breakpoint trap	Kernel and user modes
bugchk	Bugcheck trap	Kernel and user modes
callsys	System call	User mode
clrfen	Clear floating-point enable	User mode
gentrap	Generate trap	Kernel and user modes
imb	I-stream memory barrier	Kernel and user modes Described in Common Architecture, Chapter 6.
rdunique	Read unique	Kernel and user modes
urti	Return from user mode trap	User mode
wrunique	Write unique	Kernel and user modes

2.1.1 Breakpoint Trap

Format:

```
bpt                                                    ! PALcode format
```

Operation:

```
temp ← PS
if (ps<mode> NE 0)  then
        USP ← SP              !  Mode is user so switch to kernel
        SP  ← KSP
        PS  ← 0
endif
SP ← SP - {6 * 8}
(SP+00) ← temp
(SP+08) ← PC
(SP+16) ← GP
(SP+24) ← a0
(SP+32) ← a1
(SP+40) ← a2
a0 ← 0
GP ← KGP
PC ← entIF
```

Exceptions:

Kernel stack not valid

Instruction Mnemonics:

bpt   Breakpoint trap

Description:

The breakpoint trap (bpt) instruction switches mode to kernel, builds a stackframe on the kernel stack, loads the GP with the KGP, loads a value of 0 into a0, and dispatches to the breakpoint code pointed to by the entIF register. The registers a1...a2 are UNPREDICTABLE on entry to the trap handler. The saved PC at (SP+08) is the address of the instruction following the trap instruction that caused the trap.

2.1.2 Bugcheck Trap

Format:

      bugchk   ! PALcode format

Operation:

```
temp ← PS
if (PS<mode> NE 0)  then
        USP ← SP              !  Mode is user so switch to kernel
        SP  ← KSP
        PS  ← 0
endif
SP ← SP - (6 ^ 8)
(SP+00) ← temp
(SP+08) ← PC
(SP+16) ← GP
(SP+24) ← a0
(SP+32) ← a1
(SP+40) ← a2
a0 ← 1
GP ← KGP
PC ← entIF
```

Exceptions:

Kernel stack not valid

Instruction Mnemonics:

bugchk   Bugcheck trap

Description:

The bugcheck trap (bugchk) instruction switches mode to kernel, builds a stackframe on the kernel stack, loads the GP with the KGP, loads a value of 1 into a0, and dispatches to the breakpoint code pointed to by the entIF register. The registers a1...a2 are UNPREDICT-ABLE on entry to the trap handler. The saved PC at (SP+08) is the address of the instruction following the trap instruction that caused the trap.

2.1.3 System Call

Format:

callsys   ! PALcode format)

Operation:

```
if (PS<mode> EQ 0)  then
        machineCheck
endif
USP ← SP
SP  ← KSP
PS  ← 0                   ! Mode=kernel
SP  ← SP - {6*8}
(SP+00) ← 8              ! PS of mode=user, IPL=0
(SP+08) ← PC
(SP+08) ← GP
GP ← KGP
PC ← entSys
```

Exceptions:

Machine check – invalid kernel mode callsys

Kernel stack not valid

Instruction Mnemonics:

callsys   System call

Description:

The system call (callsys) instruction is supported only from user mode. (Issuing a callsys from kernel mode causes a machine check exception.)

The callsys instruction switches mode to kernel and builds a callsys stack frame. The GP is loaded with the KGP. The exception then dispatches to the system call code pointed to by the entSys register. On entry to the callsys code, the scratch registers t0 and t8...t11 are UNPREDICTABLE.

2.1.4 Clear Floating-Point Enable

Format:

clrfen   ! PALcode format

Operation:

$$FEN \leftarrow 0$$
$$(PCBB+40)<0> \leftarrow 0$$

Exceptions:

None

Instruction Mnemonics:

clrfen   Clear floating-point enable

Description:

The clear floating-point enable (clrfen) instruction writes a zero to the floating-point enable register and to the PCB at offset (PCBB+40)<0>. On return from the clrfen instruction, the scratch registers t0 and t8...t11 are UNPREDICTABLE.

2.1.5 Generate Trap

Format:

```
gentrap                                                    ! PALcode format
```

Operation:

```
temp ← PS
if (PS<mode> NE 0)  then
        USP ← SP             !  Mode is user so switch to kernel
        SP  ← KSP
        PS  ← 0
endif
SP ← SP - {6 * 8}
(SP+00) ← temp
(SP+08) ← PC
(SP+16) ← GP
(SP+24) ← a0
(SP+32) ← a1
(SP+40) ← a2
a0 ← 2
GP ← KGP
PC ← entIF
```

Exceptions:

Kernel stack not valid

Instruction Mnemonics:

gentrap   Generate trap

Description:

The generate trap (gentrap) instruction switches mode to kernel, builds a stackframe on the kernel stack, loads the GP with the KGP, loads a value of 2 into a0, and dispatches to the breakpoint code pointed to by the entIF register. The registers a1...a2 are UNPREDICT-ABLE on entry to the trap handler. The saved PC at (SP+08) is the address of the instruction following the trap instruction that caused the trap.

2.1.6 Read Unique Value

Format:

rdunique   ! PALcode format

Operation:

v0 ← unique

Exceptions:

None

Instruction Mnemonics:

rdunique   Read unique value

Description:

The read unique value (rdunique) instruction returns the process unique value in v0. The write unique value (wrunique) instruction, described in Section 2.1.8, scts the process unique value register.

2.1.7 Return from User Mode Trap

Format:

```
urti                                              ! PALcode format
```

Operation:

```
if (PS<mode> EQ 0) then
        {machineCheck}
endif
if (SP<5:0> NE 0)
        {Initiate illegal operand exception}
endif
tempps ← (SP+16)

if (( tempps<mode> EQ 0 ) OR ( tempps<IPL> NE 0 )) then
        {Initiate illegal operand exception}
endif

at      ← (SP+0)
tempsp ← (SP+8)
temppc ← (SP+24)
GP      ← (SP+32)
a0      ← (SP+40)
a1      ← (SP+48)
a2      ← (SP+56)

intr_flag = 0            ! Clear the interrupt flag
lock_flag = 0            ! Clear the load lock flag

SP      ← tempsp
PC      ← temppc
```

Exceptions:

Machine check - invalid kernel mode urti
Illegal operand
Translation not valid
Access violation
Fault on read

Instruction Mnemonics:

urti   Return from user mode trap

Description:

The return from user trap (urti) instruction pops registers (a0...a2, and GP), the new user at, SP, PC, and the PS, from the user stack.

2.1.8 Write Unique Value

Format:

wrunique   ! PALcode format

Operation:

unique ← a0

Exceptions:

None

Instruction Mnemonics:

wrunique   Write unique value

Description:

The write unique value (wrunique) instruction sets the process unique register to the value passed in a0. The read unique value (rdunique) instruction, described in Section 2.1.6, returns the process unique value.

2.2 Privileged PALcode Instructions

The Privileged DIGITAL UNIX PALcode instructions (Table 2–2) provide an abstracted interface to control the privileged state of the machine.

Table 2–2: Privileged PALcode Instructions

Mnemonic	Name
cflush	Cache flush
cserve	Console service
draina	Drain aborts. Described in Common Architecture, Chapter 6.
halt	Halt the processor. Described in Common Architecture, Chapter 6.
rdmces	Read machine check error summary register
rdps	Read processor status
rdusp	Read user stack pointer
rdval	Read system value
retsys	Return from system call
rti	Return from trap, fault, or interrupt
swpctx	Swap process context
swppal	Swap PALcode image
swpipl	Swap IPL
tbi	TB (translation buffer) invalidate
whami	Who am I
wrent	Write system entry address
wrfen	Write floating-point enable
wripir	Write interprocessor interrupt request
wrkgp	Write kernal global pointer
wrmces	Write machine check error summary register
wrperfmon	Performance monitoring function
wrusp	Write user stack pointer
wrval	Write system value
wrvptptr	Write virtual page table pointer
wtint	Wait for interrupt

2.2.1 Cache Flush

Format:

cflush   !PALcode format

Operation:

```
! a0 contains the page frame number (PFN)
!       of the page to be flushed

IF  PS<mode> EQ 1  THEN
   {Initiate opDec fault}

{Flush page out of cache(s)}
```

Exceptions:

Opcode reserved to DIGITAL

Instruction Mnemonics:

cflush   Cache flush

Description:

The cflush instruction may be used to flush an entire physical page specified by the PFN in a0 from any data caches associated with the current processor. All processors must implement this instruction.

On processors that implement a backup power option that maintains only the contents of memory if a powerfail occurs, this instruction is used by the powerfail interrupt handler to force data written by the handler to the battery backed-up main memory. After a cflush, the first subsequent load (on the same processor) to an arbitrary address in the target page is either fetched from physical memory or from the data cache of another processor.

In some multiprocessor systems, cflush is not sufficient to ensure that the data are actually written to memory and not exchanged between processor caches. Additional platform-specific cooperation between the powerfail interrupt handlers executing on each processor may be required.

On systems that implement other backup power options (including none), cflush may return without affecting the data cache contents.

To order cflush properly with respect to preceding writes, an MB instruction is needed before the cflush; to order cflush properly with respect to subsequent reads, an MB instruction is needed after the cflush.

2.2.2 Console Service

Format:

cserve   !PALcode format

Operation:

```
! implementation specific

if  PS<mode> EQ 1  then
{initiate opDec fault}

else
{implementation-dependent action}
```

Exceptions:

Opcode reserved to DIGITAL

Instruction Mnemonics:

cserve   Console service

Description:

This instruction is specific to each PALcode and console implementation and is not intended for operating system use.

2.2.3 Read Machine Check Error Summary

Format:

rdmces   ! PALcode format

Operation:

```
if (PS<mode> EQ 1) then
        {Initiate opDec fault}
endif
v0 ← MCES
```

Exceptions:

Opcode reserved to DIGITAL

Instruction Mnemonics:

rdmces   Read machine check error summary

Description:

The read machine check error summary (rdmces) instruction returns the MCES (machine check error summary) register in v0. On return from the rdmces instruction, registers t0 and t8...t11 are UNPREDICTABLE.

2.2.4 Read Processor Status

Format:

```
rdps                                                    ! PALcode format
```

Operation:

```
if (PS<mode> EQ 1) then
        {Initiate opDec fault}
endif
v0 ← PS
```

Exceptions:

Opcode reserved to DIGITAL

Instruction Mnemonics:

rdps   Read processor status

Description:

The read processor status (rdps) instruction returns the PS in v0. On return from the rdps instruction, registers t0 and t8...t11 are UNPREDICTABLE.

2.2.5 Read User Stack Pointer

Format:

rdusp   ! PALcode format

Operation:

```
if (PS<mode> EQ 1) then
        {Initiate opDec fault}
endif
v0 ← USP
```

Exceptions:

Opcode reserved to DIGITAL

Instruction Mnemonics:

rdusp   Read user stack pointer

Description:

The read user stack pointer (rdusp) instruction returns the user stack pointer in v0. The user stack pointer is written by the wrusp instruction, described in Section 2.2.20. On return from the rdusp instruction, registers t0 and t8...t11 are UNPREDICTABLE.

2.2.6 Read System Value

Format:

rdval   !PALcode format

Operation:

```
if (PS<mode> EQ 1) then
        {Initiate opDec fault}
endif
v0 ← sysvalue
```

Exceptions:

Opcode reserved to DIGITAL

Instruction Mnemonics:

rdval   Read system value

Description:

The read system value (rdval) instruction returns the sysvalue in v0, allowing access to a 64-bit per-processor value for use by the operating system. On return from the rdval instruction, registers t0 and t8...t11 are UNPREDICTABLE.

2.2.7 Return from System Call

Format:

retsys   ! PALcode format

Operation:

```
if {PS<mode> EQ 1} then
        {Initiate opDec fault}
endif
tmp ← (SP+08)
GP  ← (SP+16)
KSP ← SP + {6*8}
SP  ← UOP
intr_flag = 0              ! Clear the interrupt flag
lock_flag = 0              ! Clear the load lock flag
PS  ← 8                    ! Mode=user
PC  ← tmp
```

Exceptions:

Opcode reserved to DIGITAL
Kernel stack not valid (halt)

Instruction Mnemonics:

retsys   Return from system call

Description:

The return from system call (retsys) instruction pops the return address and the user mode global pointer from the kernel stack. It then saves the kernel stack pointer, sets the mode to user, sets the IPL to zero, and enters the user mode code at the address popped off the stack. On return from the retsys instruction, registers t0 and t8...t11 are UNPREDICTABLE.

2.2.8 Return from Trap, Fault or Interrupt

Format:

rti   ! PALcode format

Operation:

```
if (PS<mode> EQ 1) then
        {Initiate opDec fault}
endif
tempps ← (SP+0)
temppc ← (SP+8)
GP ← (SP+16)
a0 ← (SP+24)
a1 ← (SP+32)
a2 ← (SP+40)
SP ← SP + {6 * 8}
if { tempps<3> EQ 1} then
        KSP ← SP            !  New mode is user
        SP ← USP
        tempps ← 8
endif
intr_flag = 0              ! Clear the interrupt flag
lock_flag = 0             ! Clear the load lock flag
PS ← tempps<3:0>          ! Set new PS
PC ← temppc
```

Exceptions:

Opcode reserved to DIGITAL

Kernel stack not valid (halt)

Instruction Mnemonics:

rti   Return from trap, fault, or interrupt

Description:

The return from fault, trap, or interrupt (rti) instruction pops registers (a0...a2, and GP), the PC, and the PS, from the kernel stack. If the new mode is user, the kernel stack is saved and the user stack is restored.

2.2.9 Swap Process Context

Format:

swpctx   ! PALcode format

Operation:

```
if (PS<mode> EQ 1)
        {Initiate opDec fault}
endif
(PCBB) ← SP                              ! Save current state
(PCBB+8) ← USP
tmp ← PCC
tmp1 ← tmp<31:0> + tmp<63:32>
(PCBB+24)<31:0> ← tmp1<31:0>
v0 ← PCBB                                ! Return old PCBB
PCBB ← a0                                ! Switch PCBB
SP ← (PCBB)                              ! Restore new state
USP ← (PCBB+8)
oldPTBR ← PTBR
PTBR ← (PCBB+16)
tmp1 ← (PCBB+24)
PCC<63:32> ← {tmp1 - tmp}<31:0>
FEN ← (PCBB+40)
if {process unique register implemented} then
        (v0+32) ← unique
        unique ← (PCBB+32)
endif
if {ASN implemented}
        ASN ← tmp1<63:32>
else
        if (oldPTBR  NE PTBR)
                {Invalidate all TB entries with ASM=0}
        endif
endif
```

Exceptions:

Opcode reserved to DIGITAL

Instruction Mnemonics:

swpctx   Swap process context

Description:

The swap process context (swpctx) instruction saves the current process data in the current PCB. Then swpctx switches to the PCB passed in a0 and loads the new process context. The old PCBB is returned in v0.

The process context and the PCB are described in Chapter 4.

On return from the swpctx instruction, registers t0, t8...t11, and a0 are UNPREDICTABLE.

2.2.10 Swap IPL

Format:

swpipl   ! PALcode format

Operation:

```
if (PS<mode> EQ 1) then
        {Initiate opDec fault}
endif
v0 ← PS<IPL>
PS<IPL> ← a0<2:0>
```

Exceptions:

Opcode reserved to DIGITAL

Instruction Mnemonics:

swpipl   Swap IPL

Description:

The swap IPL (swpipl) instruction returns the current value of the PS<IPL> bits in v0 and sets the IPL to the value passed in a0. On return from the spwipl instruction, registers t0, t8...t11, and a0 are UNPREDICTABLE.

2.2.11 Swap PALcode Image

Format:

    swppal   !PALcode format

Operation:

```
! a0 contains the new PALcode identifier
! a1:a5 contain implementation-specific entry parameters
! v0 receives the following status:
!        0 success (PALcode was switched)
!        1 unknown PALcode variant
!        2 known PALcode variant, but PALcode not loaded

if  (PS<mode> EQ 1)  then
     (Initiate opDec fault)

else
    if {a0 < 256} then
        begin
            if {a0 invalid} then
                v0 ← 1
                {return}
            else if {PALcode not loaded} then
                v0 ← 2
                {return}
            else
                tmp1 ← {PALcode base}
        end
    else
        tmp1 = a0
    {flush instruction cache}
    {invalidate all translation buffers}
    {perform additional PALcode variant-specific initialization}
    {transfer control to PALcode entry at physical address in tmp1}
```

Exceptions:

    Opcode reserved to DIGITAL

Instruction Mnemonics:

    swppal   Swap PALcode image

Description:

The swap Palcode image (swppal) instruction causes the current (active) PALcode to be replaced by the specified new PALcode image. The swppal instruction is intended for use by operating systems only during bootstraps and by consoles during transitions to console I/O mode.

The PALcode descriptor contained in a0 is interpreted as either a PALcode variant or the base physical address of the new PALcode image. If a variant, the PALcode image must have been loaded previously. No PALcode loading occurs as a result of this instruction.

After successful PALcode switching, the register contents are determined by the parameters passed in a1...a5 or are UNPREDICTABLE. A common parameter is the address of a new PCB. In this case, the stack pointer register and PTBR are determined by the contents of that PCB; the contents of other registers such as a0...a5 may be UNPREDICTABLE.

See Console Interface Architecture, for information on using this instruction.

2.2.12 TB Invalidate

Format:

> tbi   ! PALcode format

Operation:

```
if (PS<mode> EQ 1) then
        {Initiate opDec fault}
endif
case a0 begin
        1: ! tbisi
                {Invalidate ITB entry for va=a1}
                break;
        2: ! tbisd
                {Invalidate DTB entry for va=a1}
                break;
        3: ! tbis
                {Invalidate both ITB and DTB entry for va=a1}
                break;
       -1: ! tbiap
                {Invalidate all TB entries with ASM=0}
                break;
       -2: ! tbia
                {Flush all TBs}
                break;
        otherwise:
                break;
endcase
```

Exceptions:

> Opcode reserved to DIGITAL

Instruction Mnemonics:

> tbi   TB (translation buffer) invalidate

Description:

The TB invalidate (tbi) instruction removes specified entries from the I and D translation buffers (TBs) when the mapping changes. The tbi instruction removes specific entry types based on a CASE selection of the value passed in register a0. On return from the tbi instruction, registers t0, t8…t11, a0, and a1 are UNPREDICTABLE.

2.2.13 Who Am I

Format:

whami   ! PALcode format

Operation:

```
if (PS<mode> EQ 1) then
          {Initiate opDec fault}
endif
v0 ← whami
```

Exceptions:

Opcode reserved to DIGITAL

Instruction Mnemonics:

whami   Who am I

Description:

The who am I (whami) instruction returns the processor number for the current processor in
v0. The processor number is in the range 0 to the number of processors minus one (0...max-
CPU–1) that can be configured in the system. On return from the whami instruction, registers
t0 and t8...t11 are UNPREDICTABLE.

2.2.14 Write System Entry Address

Format:

wrent   ! PALcode format

Operation:

```
if (PS<mode> EQ 1) then
        {Initiate opDec fault}
endif
case a1 begin
        0:  ! Write the EntInt:
                entInt ← a0
                break;
        1:  ! Write the EntArith:
                entArith ← a0
                break;
        2:  ! Write the EntMM:
                entMM ← a0
                break;
        3: ! Write the EntIF:
                entIF ← a0
                break;
        4: ! Write the EntUna:
                entUna ← a0
                break;
        5: ! Write the EntSys:
                entSys ← a0
                break;
        otherwise:
                break;
endcase;
```

Exceptions:

Opcode reserved to DIGITAL

Instruction Mnemonics:

wrent   Write system entry address

Description:

The write system entry address (wrent) instruction determines the specific system entry point based on a CASE selection of the value passed in register a1. The wrent instruction then sets the virtual address of the specified system entry point to the value passed in a0.

For best performance, all the addresses should be kseg addresses. (See Chapter 3 for a definition of kseg addresses.) On return from the wrent instruction, registers t0, t8…t11, a0, and a1 are UNPREDICTABLE.

2.2.15 Write Floating-Point Enable

Format:

      wrfen   ! PALcode format

Operation:

```
if (PS<mode> EQ 1) then
        {Initiate opDec fault}
endif
FEN ← a0<0>
(PCBB+40)<0> ← a0 AND 1
```

Exceptions:

Opcode reserved to DIGITAL

Instruction Mnemonics:

wrfen   Write floating-point enable

Description:

The write floating-point enable (wrfen) instruction writes bit zero of the value passed in a0 to the floating-point enable register. The wrfen instruction also writes the value for FEN to the PCB at offset (PCBB+40)<0>. On return from the wrfen instruction, registers t0, t8...t11, and a0 are UNPREDICTABLE.

2.2.16 Write Interprocessor Interrupt request

Format:

    wripir   ! PALcode format

Operation:

```
if (PS<mode> EQ 1) then
        {Initiate opDec fault}
endif
IPIR ← a0
```

Exceptions:

Opcode reserved to DIGITAL

Instruction Mnemonics:

    wripir   Write interprocessor interrupt request

Description:

The write interprocessor interrupt request (wripir) instruction generates an interprocessor interrupt on the processor number passed in register a0. The interrupt request is recorded on the target processor and is initiated when the proper enabling conditions are present. On return from wripir, registers t0, t8...t11, and a0 are UNPREDICTABLE.

Programming Note:

The interrupt need not be initiated before the next instruction is executed on the requesting processor, even if the requesting processor is also the target processor for the request.

2.2.17 Write Kernel Global Pointer

Format:

wrkgp   ! PALcode format

Operation:

```
if (PS<mode> EQ 1) then
        {Initiate opDec fault}
endif
KGP ← a0
```

Exceptions:

Opcode reserved to DIGITAL

Instruction Mnemonics:

wrkgp   Write kernal global pointer

Description:

The write kernel global pointer (wrkgp) instruction writes the value passed in a0 to the kernel global pointer (KGP) internal register. The KGP is used to load the GP on exceptions. On return from the wrkgp instruction, registers t0, t8...t11, and a0 are UNPREDICTABLE.

2.2.18 Write Machine Check Error Summary

Format:

    wrmces   ! PALcode format

Operation:

```
if (PS<mode> EQ 1) then
        {Initiate opDec fault}
endif
if (a0<0> EQ 1) then MCES<0> ← 0
if (a0<1> EQ 1) then MCES<1> ← 0
if (a0<2> EQ 1) then MCES<2> ← 0
MCES<3> ← a0<3>
MCES<4> ← a0<4>
```

Exceptions:

Opcode reserved to DIGITAL

Instruction Mnemonics:

    wrmces   Write machine check error summary

Description:

The write machine check error summary (wrmces) instruction clears the machine check in progress bit and clears the processor- or system-correctable error in progress bit in the MCES register. The instruction also sets or clears the processor- or system-correctable error reporting enabled bit in the MCES register. On return from the wrmces instruction, registers t0, t8...t11 are UNPREDICTABLE.

2.2.19 Performance Monitoring Function

Format:

wrperfmon   ! PALcode format

Operation:

```
if (PS<mode> EQ 1) then
        {Initiate opDec fault}
! a0 contains implementation specific input values
! a1 contains implementation specific output values
! v0 may return implementation specific values
! Operations and actions taken are implementation specific
```

Exceptions:

Opcode reserved to DIGITAL

Instruction Mnemonics:

wrperfmon   Performance monitoring

Description:

The performance monitoring instruction (wrperfmon) alerts any performance monitoring software/hardware in the system to monitor the performance of this process. The wrperfmon function arguments and actions are platform and chip dependent, and when defined for an implementation, are described in Appendix E.

Registers a0 and a1 contain implementation-specific input values. Implementation-specific values may be returned in register v0. On return from the wrperfmon instruction, registers a0, a1, t0, and t8...t11 are UNPREDICTABLE.

2.2.20 Write User Stack Pointer

Format:

    wrusp   ! PALcode format

Operation:

```
if (PS<mode> EQ 1) then
        {Initiate opDec fault}
endif
USP ← a0
```

Exceptions:

Opcode reserved to DIGITAL

Instruction Mnemonics:

    wrusp   Write user stack pointer

Description:

The write user stack pointer (wrusp) instruction writes the value passed in a0 to the user stack pointer. On return from the wrusp instruction, registers t0, t8...t11, and a0 are UNPREDICTABLE.

2.2.21 Write System Value

Format:

wrval   !PALcode format

Operation:

```
if (PS<mode> EQ 1) then
        {Initiate opDec fault}
endif
sysvalue ← a0
```

Exceptions:

Opcode reserved to DIGITAL

Instruction Mnemonics:

wrval   Write system value

Description:

The write system value (wrval) instruction writes the value passed in a0 to a 64-bit system value register. The combination of wrval with the rdval instruction, described in Section 2.2.6, allows access by the operating system to a 64-bit per-processor value. On return from the wrval instruction, registers t0, t8...t11, and a0 are UNPREDICTABLE.

2.2.22 Write Virtual Page Table Pointer

Format:

wrvptptr   ! PALcode format

Operation:

```
if (PS<mode> EQ 1) then
        {Initiate opDec fault}
endif
VPTPTR ← a0
```

Exceptions:

Opcode reserved to DIGITAL

Instruction Mnemonics:

wrvptptr   Write virtual page table pointer

Description:

The write virtual page table pointer (wrvptptr) instruction writes the pointer passed in a0 to the virtual page table pointer register (VPTPTR). The VPTPTR is described in Section 3.6.2. On return from the wrvptptr instruction, registers t0, t8...t11, and a0 are UNPREDICTABLE.

2.2.23 Wait For Interrupt

Format:

wtint   ! PALcode format

Operation:

```
! a0 contains the maximum number of interval clock ticks to skip
! v0  receives the number of interval clock ticks actually skipped

IF (implemented)
BEGIN
  IF {Implementation supports skipping multiple
      clock interrupts} THEN
    {Ticks_to_skip ← a0}

  {Wait no longer than any non-clock interrupt or the first clock
    interrupt after ticks_to_skip ticks have been skipped}

  IF {Implementation supports skipping multiple
      clock interrupts} THEN
    v0 ←number of interval clock ticks actually skipped
  ELSE
    v0 ← 0
END
ELSE
  v0 ← 0
{return}
```

Exceptions:

Opcode reserved to DIGITAL

Instruction Mnemonics:

wtint   Wait for interrupt

Description:

The wait for interrupt instruction (wtint) requests that, if possible, the PALcode wait for the first of either of the following conditions before returning:

- Any interrupt other than a clock tick

- The first clock tick after a specified number of clock ticks has been skipped

The wtint instruction returns in v0 the number of clock ticks that are skipped. The number returned in v0 is zero on hardware platforms that implement this instruction, but where it is not possible to skip clock ticks.

The operating system can specify a full 64-bit integer value in a0 as the maximum number of interval clock ticks to skip. A value of zero in a0 causes no clock ticks to be skipped

Note the following if specifying in a0 the maximum number of interval clock ticks to skip:

- Adherence to a specified value in a0 is at the discretion of the PALcode; the PALcode may complete execution of wtint and proceed to the next instruction at any time up to the specified maximum, even if no interrupt or interval-clock tick has occurred. That is, wtint may return before all requested clock ticks are skipped.

- The PALcode must complete execution of wtint if an interrupt occurs or if an interval-clock tick occurs after the requested number of interval-clock ticks has been skipped.

In a multiprocessor environment, only the issuing processor is affected by an issued wtint instruction.

The counter, PCC, may increment at a lower rate or may stop entirely during wtint execution. This side effect is implementation dependent.

Chapter 3

Memory Management (II–B)

3.1 Virtual Address Spaces

A virtual address is a 64-bit unsigned integer that specifies a byte location within the virtual address space. Implementations subset the supported address space to one of several sizes, as a function of page size and page table depth. The minimal supported virtual address size is 43 bits. If an implementation supports less than 64-bit virtual addresses, it must check that all the VA<63:vaSize> bits are equal to VA<vaSize–1>. This gives two disjoint ranges for valid virtual addresses. For example, for a 43-bit virtual address space, valid virtual address ranges are $0 \cdots 3FFFFFFFFFF_{16}$ and $FFFFFC0000000000_{16} \cdots FFFFFFFFFFFFFFFF_{16}$. Access to virtual addresses outside an implementation's valid virtual address range cause an access-violation fault.

.The virtual address space is divided into three segments.

The two bits, va<vaSize–1:vaSize–2>, select a segment as shown in Table 3–1.

Table 3–1: Virtual Address Space Segments

VA<vaSize–1:vaSize–2>	Name	Mapping	Access Control
0x	seg0	3- or 4-level page tables	Programmed in PTE
10	kseg	PA ← SEXT(VA<(vaSize–3):0>)	Kernel Read/Write
11	seg1	3- or 4-level page tables	Programmed in PTE

For kseg, the relocation, sharing, and protection are fixed. The base of kseg is located at LEFT_SHIFT(FFFFFC0000000000$_{16}$, (vaSize–43)).

For seg0 and seg1, the virtual address space is broken into pages, which are the units of relocation, sharing, and protection. The page size ranges from 8K bytes to 64K bytes. Therefore, system software should allocate regions with differing protection on 64K-byte virtual address boundaries to ensure image compatibility across all Alpha implementations.

Memory management provides the mechanism to map the active part of the virtual address space to the available physical address space. The operating system controls the virtual-to-physical address mapping tables and saves the inactive (but used) parts of the virtual address space on external storage media.

3.1.1 Segment Seg0 and Seg1 Virtual Address Format

The processor generates a 64-bit virtual address for each instruction and operand in memory. A seg0 or seg1 virtual address consists of three or four level-number fields and a byte_within_page field, as shown in Figures 3-1 and 3-2 .

Figure 3-1: Virtual Address Format, Three-Level Mode

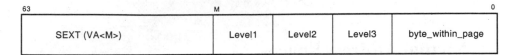

| SEXT (VA<M>) | Level1 | Level2 | Level3 | byte_within_page |

Figure 3-2: Virtual Address Format, Four-Level Mode

| SEXT (VA<M>) | Level0* | Level1 | Level2 | Level3 | byte_within_page |

* Level0 <M:L+1> contains SEXT(VA<L>), where L is the highest numbered implemented VA bit.

The byte_within_page field can be either 13, 14, 15, or 16 bits depending on a particular implementation. Thus, the allowable page sizes are 8K bytes, 16K bytes, 32K bytes, and 64K bytes. The low-order bit in each level-number field is 0 and each field is 0···n bits, where for example, n is 9 for an 8K page size. Level-number fields are the same size for a given implementation.

The level-number fields are a function of the page size; all page table entries at any given level do not exceed one page. The PFN field in the PTE is always 32 bits wide. Thus, as the page size grows, the virtual and physical address size also grows.

Table 3-2 shows the virtual address options and physical address size (in bits) calculations. The physical address (bits) column is the maximum physical address allowed by the smaller of the kseg size or available physical address bits for a given page size. The available physical address bits is calculated by combining the number of bits in the PFN (always 32) with the number of bits in the byte_within_page field. The kseg segment size is calculated from the virtual address size minus 2.

Table 3–2: Virtual Address Options

Page Size (bytes)	Byte_within_page (bits)	Level Size (bits)	Virtual Address (bits)[1]	Physical Address (bits)
8K	13	10	43, 45–53	41, 43–45
16K	14	11	47, 49–58	45,46
32K	15	12	51, 53–63	47
64K	16	13	55, 57-64[2]	48

[1] Bit counts for three levels or four levels, respectively (vaSize)

[2] Level 0 page table not fully utilized for this page size

3.1.2 Kseg Virtual Address Format

The processor generates a 64-bit virtual address for each instruction and operand in memory. A kseg virtual address consists of segment select field with a value of 10_2 and a physical address field. The segment select field is the two bits va<vaSize–1:vaSize–2>. The physical address field is va<vaSize–3:0>.

Figure 3–3: Kseg Virtual Address Format

63		0
SEXT (segment_select<1>)	Segment Select=10_2	Physical Address

3.2 Physical Address Space

Physical addresses are at most vaSize–2 bits. This allows all of physical memory to be accessed via kseg. A processor may choose to implement a smaller physical address space by not implementing some number of high-order bits.

The two most significant implemented physical address bits delineate the four regions in the physical address space. Implementations use these bits as appropriate for their systems. For example, in a workstation with a 30-bit physical address space, bit<29> might select between memory and non-memory-like regions, and bit <28> could enable or disable cacheing (see Common Architecture, Chapter 5).

3.3 Memory Management Control

Memory management is always enabled. Implementations must provide an environment for PALcode to service exceptions and to initialize and boot the processor. For example PALcode might run with I-stream mapping disabled.

3.4 Page Table Entries

The processor uses a quadword page table entry (PTE) to translate seg0 and seg1 virtual addresses to physical addresses. A PTE contains hardware and software control information and the physical page frame number (PFN). A PTE is a quadword with fields as shown in Figure 3–4 and described in Table 3–3.

Figure 3–4: Page Table Entry (PTE)

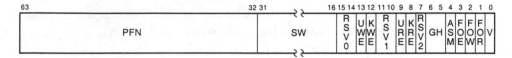

Table 3–3: Page Table Entry (PTE) Bit Summary

Bits	Name	Meaning
63–32	PFN	Page frame number The PFN field always points to a page boundary. If V is set, the PFN is concatenated with the byte_within_page bits of the virtual address to obtain the physical address.
31–16	SW	Reserved for software.
15–14	RSV0	Reserved for hardware; SBZ.
13	UWE	User write enable. Enables writes from user mode. If this bit is 0 and a store is attempted while in user mode, an access-violation fault occurs. This bit is valid even when V=0. **Note:** If a write enable bit is set and the corresponding read enable bit is not, the operation of the processor is UNDEFINED.
12	KWE	Kernel write enable. Enables writes from kernel mode. If this bit is 0 and a store is attempted while in kernel mode, an access-violation fault occurs. This bit is valid even when V=0.
11–10	RSV1	Reserved for hardware; SBZ.
9	URE	User read enable. Enables reads from user mode. If this bit is 0 and a load or instruction fetch is attempted while in user mode, an Access Violation occurs. This bit is valid even when V=0.
8	KRE	Kernel read enable. Enables reads from kernel mode. If this bit is 0 and a load or instruction fetch is attempted while in kernel mode, an access-violation fault occurs. This bit is valid even when V=0.

Table 3–3: Page Table Entry (PTE) Bit Summary (Continued)

Bits	Name	Meaning
7	RSV2	Reserved for hardware; SBZ.
6–5	GH	Granularity hint. Software may set these bits to a non-zero value to supply a hint to translation buffer implementations that a block of pages can be treated as a single larger page:

1. A block is an aligned group of 8**N pages, where N is the value of PTE<6:5>, for example, a group of 1, 8, 64, or 512 pages starting at a virtual address with page_size + 3*N low-order zeros.

2. The block is a group of physically contiguous pages that are aligned both virtually and physically. Within the block, the low 3*N bits of the PFNs describe the identity mapping and the high 32–3*N PFN bits are all equal.

3. Within the block, all PTEs have the same values for bits <15:0>. Hardware may use this hint to map the entire block with a single TB entry, instead of 8, 64, or 512 separate TB entries.

Bits	Name	Meaning
4	ASM	Address space match. When set, this PTE matches all address space numbers. For a given VA, ASM must he set consistently in all processes; otherwise, the address mapping is UNPREDICTABLE.
3	FOE	Fault on execute. When set, a Fault on Execute exception occurs on an attempt to execute any location in the page.
2	FOW	Fault on write. When set, a Fault on Write exception occurs on an attempt to write any location in the page.
1	FOR	Fault on read. When set, a Fault on Read exception occurs on an attempt to read any location in the page.
0	V	Valid. Indicates the validity of the PFN field. When V is set, the PFN field is valid for use by hardware. When V is clear, the PFN field is reserved for use by software. The V bit does not affect the validity of PTE<15:1> bits.

3.4.1 Changes to Page Table Entries

The operating system changes PTEs as part of its memory management functions. For example, the operating system may set or clear the V bit, change the PFN field as pages are moved to and from external storage media, or modify the software bits. The processor hardware never changes PTEs.

Software must guarantee that each PTE is always internally consistent. Changing a PTE one field at a time can cause incorrect system operation, such as setting PTE<V> with one instruction before establishing PTE<PFN> with another. Execution of an interrupt service routine between the two instructions could use an address that would map using the inconsistent PTE. Software can solve this problem by building a complete new PTE in a register and then moving the new PTE to the page table by using an STQ instruction.

Multiprocessing complicates the problem. Another processor could be reading (or even changing) the same PTE that the first processor is changing. Such concurrent access must produce consistent results. Software must use some form of software synchronization to modify PTEs that are already valid. Whenever a processor modifies a valid PTE, it is possible that other processors in a multiprocessor system may have old copies of that PTE in their translation buffer. Software must inform other processors of changes to PTEs. Hardware must ensure that aligned quadword reads and writes are atomic operations. Hardware must not cache invalid PTEs (PTEs with the V bit equal to 0) in translation buffers. See Section 3.7 for more information.

3.5 Memory Protection

Memory protection is the function of validating whether a particular type of access is allowed to a specific page from a particular access mode. Access to each page is controlled by a protection code that specifies, for each access mode, whether read or write references are allowed. The processor uses the following to determine whether an intended access is allowed:

- The virtual address, which is used to either select kseg mapping or provide the index into the page tables.

- The intended access type (read or write).

- The current access mode base on processor mode.

For protection checks, the intended access is read for data loads and instruction fetches, and write for data stores.

3.5.1 Processor Access Modes

There are two processor modes, user and kernel. The access mode of a running process is stored in the processor status mode bit (PS<mode>).

3.5.2 Protection Code

Every page in the virtual address space is protected according to its use. A program may be prevented from reading or writing portions of its address space. A protection code associated with each page describes the accessibility of the page for each processor mode.

For seg0 and seg1, the code allows a choice of read or write protection for each processor mode. For each mode, access can be read/write, read-only, or no-access. Read and write accessibility and the protection for each mode are specified independently.

For kseg, the protection code is kernel read/write, user no-access.

3.5.3 Access-Violation Faults

An access-violation memory-management fault occurs if an illegal access is attempted, as determined by the current processor mode and the page's protection.

3.6 Address Translation for Seg0 and Seg1

The page tables can be accessed from physical memory, or (to reduce overhead) can be mapped to a linear region of the virtual address space. The following sections describe both access methods.

3.6.1 Physical Access for Seg0 and Seg1 PTEs

Seg0 and seg1 address translation can be performed by accessing entries in a multilevel page table structure. The page table base register (PTBR) contains the physical page frame number (PFN) of the highest-level page table. If the system was booted with three levels of page table, this is the Level 1 page table. If the system was booted with four levels of page table, this is the Level 0 page table. In that case, bits <Level0> of the virtual address are used to index into the Level 0 page table to obtain the physical page frame number of the base of the Level 1 page table.

With either a three-level or four-level page table, bits <Level1> of the virtual address are used to index into the Level 1 page table to obtain the physical PFN of the base of the next level (Level 2) page table. Bits <Level2> of the virtual address are used to index into the Level 2 page table to obtain the physical PFN of the base of the next level (Level 3) page table. Bits <Level3> of the virtual address are used to index the Level 3 page table to obtain the physical PFN of the page being referenced. The PFN is concatenated with virtual address bits <byte_within_page> to obtain the physical address of the location being accessed.

If part of any page table does not reside in a memory-like region, or does reside in nonexistent memory, the operation of the processor is UNDEFINED.

If all the higher-level PTEs (those PTEs that map higher-significance portions of the virtual address space than is mapped by Level 3) are valid, the protection bits are ignored; the protection code in the Level 3 PTE is used to determine accessibility. If a higher-level PTE (numerically, any below Level 3) is invalid, an access-violation fault occurs if the PTE<KRE> equals zero. An access-violation fault on any higher-level PTE implies that all lower-level page tables mapped by that PTE do not exist.

The algorithm to generate a physical address from a seg0 or seg1 virtual address follows:

```
IF {SEXT(VA<(vaSize-1):0>) neq VA} THEN
        { initiate access-violation fault}
IF {booted with 4 levels of page table} THEN

    ! Read physical:
    level0_pte ← ({PTBR * page_size} + {8 * VA<level0>})

    IF level0_pte<V> eq 0 THEN
    IF level0_pte<KRE> eq 0 THEN
            {initiate access-violation fault}
        ELSE
            {initiate translation-not-valid fault}
    ! Read physical:
    level1_pte ← ({level0_pte<PFN> * page_size} + {8 * VA<level1>})

ELSE
    ! Read physical:
    level1_pte ← (PTBR * page_size) + {8 * VA<level1>})

! Read physical:
level1_PTE ← ({PTBR * page_size} + {8 * VA<level1>} )
IF level1_PTE<v> EQ 0 THEN
        IF level1_PTE<KRE> eq 0 THEN
                { initiate access-violation fault}
        ELSE
                { initiate translation-not-valid fault}
! Read physical:
level2_PTE ← ({level1_PTE<PFN> * page_size} + {8 * VA<level2>} )
IF level2_PTE<v> EQ 0 THEN
        IF level2_PTE<KRE> eq 0 THEN
                { initiate access-violation fault}
        ELSE
                { initiate translation-not-valid fault}
! Read physical:
level3_PTE ← ({level2_PTE<PFN> * page_size} + {8 * VA<level3>} )

IF {{{level3_PTE<UWE> eq 0}AND {write access} AND {ps<mode> EQ 1}} OR
   {{level3_PTE<URE> eq 0} AND {read access} AND {ps<mode> EQ 1}} OR
   {{level3_PTE<KWE> eq 0}AND {write access} AND {ps<mode> EQ 0}} OR
   {{level3_PTE<KRE> eq 0}AND {read access} AND {ps<mode> EQ 0}}}
        THEN
                {initiate memory-management fault}
        ELSE
                IF level3_PTE<v> EQ 0 THEN
                        {initiate memory-management fault}
```

```
IF { level3_PTE<FOW> eq 1} AND {write access} THEN
        {initiate memory-management fault}
IF { level3_PTE<FOR> eq 1} AND {read access} THEN
        {initiate memory-management fault}
IF { level3_PTE<FOE> eq 1} AND {execute access} THEN
        {initiate memory-management fault}


Physical_address ← {level3_PTE<PFN> * page_size} OR VA<byte_within_page>
```

3.6.2 Virtual Access for Seg0 or Seg1 PTEs

The page tables can be mapped into a linear region of the virtual address space, reducing the overhead for seg0 and seg1 PTE accesses. The mapping is done as follows, where, if the system is booted with three level fields in the virtual address format, Level_count=3. If the system is booted with four level fields in the virtual address format, Level_count=4.

1. Select a $2^{(Level\_count*lg(pageSize/8))+3}$ byte-aligned region (an address with Level_count*lg(pageSize/8)+3 low-order zeros) in the seg0 or seg1 address space.

2. Create a PTE to map the page tables as follows.

    ```
    PTE = 0                          ! Initialize all fields to zero
    ! Set the PFN to the PFN of the most-significant pagetable:
    PTE<63:32> = pfn_of_most-significant_pagetable
    PTE<8>  = 1                      ! Set the kernel read enable bit
    PTE<0>  = 1                      ! Set the valid bit
    ```

3. Set the page table entry that corresponds to the VPTPTR to the created PTE. If operating in the mode of three levels of page table, this is a Level 1 page table. If operating in the mode of four levels of page table, this is a Level 0 page table.

4. Set all higher level, valid PTEs that map the Level 3 page tables to allow kernel read access. With this setup in place, the algorithm to fetch a seg0 or seg1 PTE is as follows, where L_c represents Level_count and pS represents pageSize:

    ```
    ! If booted with 3 level fields in the VA format, L_c=3
    ! If booted with 4 level fields in the VA format, L_c=4

    tmp ← LEFT_SHIFT (va, {64 - {{lg(pS)*{L_c+1}} - {L_c*3}}})
    tmp ← RIGHT_SHIFT (tmp, {64 - {{lg(pS)*{L_c+1}} - {L_c*3}} + lg(pS)-3})
    tmp ← VPTB OR tmp
    tmp<2:0> ← 0
    level3_PTE ← (tmp)              ! Load PTE using its virtual address
    ```

5. Set the virtual page table pointer (VPTPTR) with a write virtual page table pointer instruction (wrvptptr) to the selected value.

The virtual access method is used by PALcode for most TB fills.

Implementation Note:

Assume the following:

- A system with a 52-bit virtual address size
- VPTB is the index of the top-level page table entry, which is self-referencing.
- The virtual address is in seg0 or seg1.

For a virtual address B, mapped with a three-level page table, the address to virtually access the Level 3 PTE is as follows. The double-miss TB fill flow is a three-level flow.

Figure 3–5: Three-Level Page Table Mapping

63	43 42	33 32	23 22	13 12	03 02 0
SEXT (VPTB)	VPTB	B<42:33>	B<32:23>	B<22:13>	0

For a virtual address A, mapped with a four-level page table, the address to virtually access the Level 3 PTE is shown in Figure 3–6. The double-miss TB fill flow is a four-level flow.

Figure 3–6: Four-Level Page Table Mapping

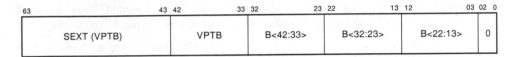

63	53 52	43 42	33 32	23 22	13 12	03 02 0
SEXT (VPTB)	VPTB	A<52:43>	A<42:33>	A<32:23>	A<22:13>	0

3.7 Translation Buffer

In order to save actual memory references when repeatedly referencing the same pages, hardware implementations include a translation buffer to remember successful virtual address translations and page states.

When the process context is changed, a new value is loaded into the address space number (ASN) internal processor register with a swap process context (swpctx) instruction. This causes address translations for pages with PTE<ASM> clear to be invalidated on a processor that does not implement address space numbers.

Additionally, when the software changes any part (except the software field) of a valid PTE, it must also execute a tbi instruction. The entire translation buffer can be invalidated by tbia, and all ASM=0 entries can be invalidated by tbiap. The translation buffer must not store invalid PTEs. Therefore, the software is not required to invalidate translation buffer entries when making changes for PTEs that are already invalid.

After software changes a valid zero-, first-, or second-level PTE, software must flush the translation for the corresponding page in the virtual page table. Then software must flush the translations of all valid pages mapped by that page. In the case of a change to a first-level PTE, this action must be taken through a second iteration. In the case of a change to a zero-level PTE, this action must be taken through a second and third iteration.

3.8 Address Space Numbers

The Alpha architecture allows a processor to optionally implement address space numbers (process tags) to reduce the need for invalidation of cached address translations for process-specific addresses when a context switch occurs. The supported address space number (ASN) range is 0···MAX_ASN; MAX_ASN is provided in the HWRPB MAX_ASN field.

The address space number for the current process is loaded by software in the address space number (ASN) with a swpctx instruction. ASNs are processor specific and the hardware makes no attempt to maintain coherency across multiple processors. In a multiprocessor system, software is responsible for ensuring the consistency of TB entries for processes that might be rescheduled on different processors. Systems that support ASNs should have MAX_ASN in the range 13···65535. The number of ASNs should be determined by the market a system is targeting.

Programming Note:

System software should not assume that the number of ASNs is a power of two. This allows hardware, for example, to use N TB tag bits to encode (2**N)–3 ASN values, one value for ASM=1 PTEs, and one for invalid.

There are several possible ways of using ASNs that result from several complications in a multiprocessor system. Consider the case where a process that executed on processor–1 is rescheduled on processor–2. If a page is deleted or its protection is changed, the TB in processor–1 has stale data.

- One solution is to send an interprocessor interrupt to all the processors on which this process could have run and cause them to invalidate the changed PTE. That results in significant overhead in a system with several processors.

- Another solution is to have software invalidate all TB entries for a process on a new processor before it can begin execution, if the process executed on another processor during its previous execution. This ensures the deletion of possibly stale TB entries on the new processor.

- A third solution is to assign a new ASN whenever a process is run on a processor that is not the same as the last processor on which it ran.

3.9 Memory-Management Faults

On a memory-management fault, the fault code (MMCSR) is passed in a1 to specify the type of fault encountered, as shown in Table 3–4.

Table 3–4: Memory-Management Fault Type Codes

Fault	MMCSR value
Translation not valid	0
Access-violation	1
Fault on read	2
Fault on execute	3
Fault on write	4

- A translation-not-valid fault is taken when a read or write reference is attempted through an invalid PTE in a zero (if one exists), first, second, or third-level page table.

- An access-violation fault is taken on a reference to a seg0 or seg1 address when the protection field of the third-level PTE that maps the data indicates that the intended page reference would be illegal in the specified access mode. An access-violation fault is also taken if the KRE bit is a zero in an invalid zero (if one exists), first, or second-level PTE. An access-violation fault is generated for any access to a kseg address when the mode is user (PS<mode> EQ 1).

- A fault-on-read (FOR) fault occurs when a read is attempted with PTE<FOR> set.

- A fault-on-execute (FOE) fault occurs when an instruction fetch is attempted with PTE<FOE> set.

- A fault-on-write (FOW) fault occurs when a write is attempted with PTE<FOW> set.

Chapter 4

Process Structure (II–B)

4.1 Process Definition

A process is a single thread of execution. It is the basic entity that can be scheduled and is executed by the processor. A process consists of an address space and both software and hardware context. The hardware context of a process is defined by the the following:

- Thirty integer registers (excludes R31 and SP)

- Thirty-one floating-point registers (excludes F31)

- The program counter (PC)

- The two per-process stack pointers (USP/KSP)

- The processor status (PS)

- The address space number (ASN)

- The charged process cycles

- The page table base register (PTBR)

- The process unique value (unique)

- The floating-point enable register (FEN)

- The performance monitoring enable bit (PME)

This information must be loaded if a process is to execute.

While a process is executing, some of its hardware context is being updated in the internal registers. When a process is not being executed, its hardware context is stored in memory in a software structure called the process control block (PCB). Saving the process context in the PCB and loading new values from another PCB for a new context is called context switching. Context switching occurs as one process after another is scheduled for execution.

4.2 Process Control Block (PCB)

As shown in Figure 4–1, the PCB holds the state of a process.

Figure 4–1: Process Control Block (PCB)

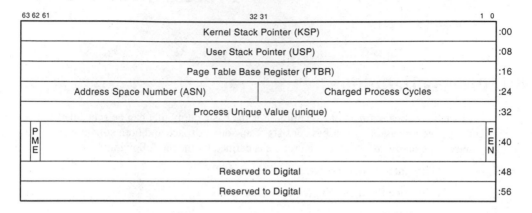

The contents of the PCB are loaded and saved by the swap process context (swpctx) instruction. The PCB must be quadword aligned and lie within a single page of physical memory. It should be 64-byte aligned for best performance.

The PCB for the current process is specified by the process control block base address register (PCBB); see Table 1–3.

The swap privileged context instruction (swpctx) saves the privileged context of the current process into the PCB specified by PCBB, loads a new value into PCBB, and then loads the privileged context of the new process into the appropriate hardware registers.

The new value loaded into PCBB, as well as the contents of the PCB, must satisfy certain constraints or an UNDEFINED operation results:

1. The physical address loaded into PCBB must be quadword aligned and describes eight contiguous quadwords that are in a memory-like region (see Common Architecture, Chapter 5).

2. The value of PTBR must be the page frame number (PFN) of an existent page that is in a memory-like region.

It is the responsibility of the operating system to save and load the non-privileged part of the hardware context.

The swpctx instruction returns ownership of the current PCB to operating system software and passes ownership of the new PCB from the operating system to the processor. Any attempt to write a PCB while ownership resides with the processor has UNDEFINED results. If the PCB is read while ownership resides with the processor, it is UNPREDICTABLE whether the original or an updated value of a field is read. The processor is free to update a PCB field at any time. The decision as to whether or not a field is updated is made individually for each field.

The charged process cycles is the total number of PCC register counts that are charged to the process (modulo 2**32). When a process context is loaded by the swpctx instructions, the contents of the PCC count field (PCC_CNT) is subtracted from the contents of PCB[24]<31:0> and the result is written to the PCC offset field (PCC_OFF):

$$\text{PCC<63:32>} \leftarrow (\text{PCB[24]<31:0>} - \text{PCC<31:0>})$$

When a process context is saved by the swpctx instruction, the charged process cycles is computed by performing an unsigned add of PCC<63:32> and PCC<31:0>. That value is written to PCB[24]<31:0>.

Software Programming Note:

The following example returns in R0 the current PCC register count (modulo 2**32) for a process. Notice the care taken not to cause an unwanted sign extension.

```
RPCC    R0              ; Read the processor cycle counter
SLL     R0, #32, R1     ; Line up the offset and count fields
ADDQ    R0, R1, R0      ; Do add
SRL     R0, #32, R0     ; Zero extend the cycle count to 64 bits
```

If ASNs are not implemented, the ASN field is not read or written by PALcode.

The process unique value is that value used in support of multithread implementations. The value is stored in the PCB when the process is not active. When the process is active, the value may be cached in hardware internal storage or kept in the PCB only.

The FEN bit reflects the setting of the FEN IPR.

Setting the PME bit alerts any performance hardware or software in the system to monitor the performance of this process.

Kernel mode code must use the rdusp/wrusp instructions to access the USP. Kernel mode code can read the PTBR, the ASN, the FEN, and the PME for the current process from the PCB. The unique value can be accessed with the rdunique and wrunique instructions.

Chapter 5

Exceptions and Interrupts (II–B)

5.1 Introduction

At certain times during the operation of a system, events within the system require the execution of software outside the explicit flow of control. When such an event occurs, an Alpha processor forces a change in control flow from that indicated by the current instruction stream. The notification process for such an event is either an exception or an interrupt.

5.1.1 Exceptions

Exceptions occur primarily in relation to the currently executing process. Exception service routines execute in response to exception conditions caused by software. All exception service routines execute in kernel mode on the kernel stack. Exception conditions consist of faults, arithmetic traps, and synchronous traps:

- A fault occurs during an instruction and leaves the registers and memory in a consistent state such that elimination of the fault condition and subsequent reexecution of the instruction gives correct results. Faults are not guaranteed to leave the machine in exactly the same state it was in immediately prior to the fault, but rather in a state such that the instruction can be correctly executed if the fault condition is removed. The PC saved in the exception stack frame is the address of the faulting instruction. An rti instruction to that PC reexecutes the faulting instruction.

- An arithmetic trap occurs at the completion of the operation that caused the exception. Since several instructions may be in various stages of execution at any point in time, it is possible for multiple arithmetic traps to occur simultaneously.

  The PC that is saved in the exception frame on traps is that of the next instruction that would have been issued if the trapping conditions had not occurred. However, that PC is not necessarily the address of the instruction immediately following the instruction that encountered the trap condition, and the intervening instructions are collectively called the *trap shadow*. See Common Architecture, Chapter 4, Arithmetic Trap Completion, for information.

  The intervening instructions may have changed operands or other state used by the instructions encountering the trap conditions. If such is the case, an rti instruction to that PC does not reexecute the trapping instructions, nor does it reexecute any intervening instructions; it simply continues execution from the point at which the trap was taken.

  In general, it is difficult to fix up results and continue program execution at the point of an arithmetic trap. Software can force a trap to be continued more easily without the need for complicated fixup code. This is accomplished by specifying any valid qualifier combination that includes the /S qualifier with each such instruction and following a set of code-generation restrictions in the code that could cause arithmetic traps, allowing those traps to be completed by an OS completion handler.

The AND of all the exception completion qualifiers for trapping instructions is provided to the OS completion handler in the exception summary SWC bit. If SWC is set, a completion handler may find the trigger instruction by scanning backward from the trap PC until each register in the register write mask has been an instruction destination. The trigger instruction is the last instruction in I-stream order to get a trap before the trap shadow. If the SWC bit is clear, no fixup is possible.

- A synchronous trap occurs at the completion of the operation that caused the exception. No instructions can be issued between the completion of the operation that caused the exception and the trap.

5.1.2 Interrupts

The processor arbitrates interrupt requests. When the interrupt priority level (IPL) of an outstanding interrupt is greater than the current IPL, the processor raises IPL to the level of the interrupt and dispatches to entInt, the interrupt entry to the OS. Interrupts are serviced in kernel mode on the kernel stack. Interrupts can come from one of five sources: interprocessor interrupts, I/O devices, the clock, performance counters, or machine checks.

5.2 Processor Status

The processor status (PS) is a four-bit register that contains the current mode (PS<mode>) in bit <3> and a three-bit interrupt priority level (PS<IPL>) in bits <2...0>. The PS<mode> bit is zero for kernel mode and one for user mode. The PS<IPL> bits are always zero if the mode is user and can be zero to 7 if the mode is kernel. The PS is changed when an interrupt or exception is initiated and by the rti, retsys, and swpipl instructions.

The uses of the PS values are shown in Table 5–1.

Table 5–1: Processor Status Summary

PS<mode>	PS<IPL>	Mode	Use
1	0	User	User software
0	0	Kernel	System software
0	1	Kernel	System software
0	2	Kernel	System software
0	3	Kernel	Low priority device interrupts
0	4	Kernel	High priority device interrupts
0	5	Kernel	Clock, and interprocessor interrupts
0	6	Kernel	Real-time devices

Table 5–1: Processor Status Summary (Continued)

PS<mode>	PS<IPL>	Mode	Use
0	6	Kernel	Correctable error reporting
0	7	Kernel	Machine checks

5.3 Stack Frames

There are three types of system entries: entries for the callsys instruction from user mode, entries for exceptions and interrupts from kernel mode, and entries for interrupts from user mode.

Those three types of system entries use one of two stack frame layouts, as follows

Entries for the .callsys instruction from user mode, and entries for exceptions and interrupts from kernel mode use the same stack frame layout, as shown in Figure 5–1. The stack frame contains space for the PC, the PS, the saved GP, and the saved registers a0, a1, a2. On entry, the SP points to the saved PS.

The callsys entry saves the PC, the PS, and the GP. The exception and interrupt entries save the PC, the PS, the GP, and also save the registers a0...a2.

Figure 5–1: Stack Frame Layout for callsys and rti

63	0	
PS		:00
PC		:08
GP		:16
a0		:24
a1		:32
a2		:40

Entries for interrupts from user mode use the stack frame layout as shown in Figure 5–2. The stack frame must be aligned on a 64-byte boundary and contains the registers, at, SP, PS, PC, GP, and saved registers a0, a1, and a2.

Figure 5–2: Stack Frame Layout for urti

63		0
at		:00
SP		:08
PS		:16
PC		:24
GP		:32
a0		:40
a1		:48
a2		:56

5.4 System Entry Addresses

All system entries are in kernel mode. The interrupt priority PS bits (PS<IPL>) are set as shown in the following table. The system entry point address is set by the wrent instruction, as described in Section 2.2.14.

Table 5–2: Entry Point Address Registers

Entry Point	Value in a0	Value in a1	Value in a2	PS<IPL>
entArith	Exception summary	Register mask	UNPREDICTABLE	Unchanged
entIF	Fault or trap type code	UNPREDICTABLE	UNPREDICTABLE	Unchanged
entInt	Interrupt type	Vector	Interrupt parameter	Priority of interrupt
entMM	VA	MMCSR	Cause	Unchanged
entSys	p0	p1	p2	Unchanged
entUna	VA	Opcode	Src/Dst	Unchanged

5.4.1 System Entry Arithmetic Trap (entArith)

The arithmetic trap entry, entArith, is called when an arithmetic trap occurs. On entry, a0 contains the exception summary register and a1 contains the exception register write mask. Section 5.4.1.1 describes the exception summary register and Section 5.4.1.2 describes the register write mask.

5.4.1.1 Exception Summary Register

The exception summary register, shown in Figure 5–3 and described in Table 5–3, records the various types of arithmetic exceptions that can occur together.

Figure 5–3: Exception Summary Register

63		7	6	5	4	3	2	1	0
Zero			IOV	INE	UNF	OVF	DZE	INV	SWC

Table 5–3: Exception Summary Register Bit Definitions

Bit	Description
63–7	Zero.
6	**Integer overflow (IOV)** An integer arithmetic operation or a conversion from floating to integer overflowed the destination precision. An IOV trap is reported for any integer operation whose true result exceeds the destination register size. Integer overflow trap enable can be specified in each arithmetic integer operate instruction and each floating-point convert-to-integer instruction. If integer overflow occurs, the result register is written with the truncated true result.
5	**Inexact result (INE)** A floating arithmetic or conversion operation gave a result that differed from the mathematically exact result. An INE trap is reported if the rounded result of an IEEE operation is not exact. Inexact result trap enable can be specified in each IEEE floating-point operate instruction. The rounded result value is stored in all cases.
4	**Underflow (UNF)** A floating arithmetic or conversion operation underflowed the destination exponent. An UNF trap is reported when the destination's smallest finite number exceeds in magnitude the non-zero rounded true result. Floating underflow trap enable can be specified in each floating-point operate instruction. If underflow occurs, the result register is written with a true zero.
3	**Overflow (OVF)** A floating arithmetic or conversion operation overflowed the destination exponent. An OVF trap is reported when the destination's largest finite number is exceeded in magnitude by the rounded true result. Floating overflow traps are always enabled. If this trap occurs, the result register is written with an UNPREDICTABLE value.

Table 5–3: Exception Summary Register Bit Definitions (Continued)

Bit	Description
2	Division by zero (DZE) An attempt was made to perform a floating divide operation with a divisor of zero. A DZE trap is reported when a finite number is divided by zero. Floating divide by zero traps are always enabled. If this trap occurs, the result register is written with an UNPREDICTABLE value.
1	Invalid operation (INV) An attempt was made to perform a floating arithmetic, conversion, or comparison operation, and one or more of the operand values were illegal. An INV trap is reported for most floating-point operate instructions with an input operand that is an IEEE NaN, IEEE infinity, or IEEE denormal. Floating invalid operation traps are always enabled. If this trap occurs, the result register is written with an UNPREDICTABLE value.
0	Software completion (SWC) Is set when all of the other arithmetic exception bits were set by floating-operate instructions with the /S qualifier set. See Common Architecture, Chapter 4, Arithmetic Trap Completion, for rules about setting the /S qualifier in code that may cause an arithmetic trap, and Section 5.1.1 for rules about using the SWC bit in a trap handler.

5.4.1.2 Exception Register Write Mask

The exception register write mask parameter records all registers that were targets of instructions that set the bits in the exception summary register. There is a one-to-one correspondence between bits in the register write mask quadword and the register numbers. The quadword, starting at bit 0 and proceeding right to left, records which of the registers r0 through r31, then f0 through f31, received an exceptional result.

Note:

For a sequence such as:

```
ADDF    F1,F2,F3
MULF    F4,F5,F3
```

if the add overflows and the multiply does not, the OVF bit is set in the exception summary, and the F3 bit is set in the register mask, even though the overflowed sum in F3 can be overwritten with an in-range product by the time the trap is taken. (This code violates the destination reuse rule for exception completion. See Common Architecture, Chapter 4, *Arithmetic Trap Shadows*, for the destination reuse rules.)

The PC value saved in the exception stack frame is the virtual address of the next instruction. This is defined as the virtual address of the first instruction not executed after the trap condition was recognized.

5.4.2 System Entry Instruction Fault (entIF)

The instruction fault or synchronous trap entry is called for bpt, bugchk, gentrap, and opDec synchronous traps, and for a FEN fault (floating-point instruction when the floating-point unit is disabled, FEN EQ 0). On entry, a0 contains a 0 for a bpt, a 1 for bugchk, a 2 for gentrap, a 3 for FEN fault, and a 4 for opDec. No additional data is passed in a1...a2. The saved PC at (SP+00) is the address of the instruction that caused the fault for FEN faults. The saved PC at (SP+00) is the address of the instruction after the instruction that caused the bpt, bugchk, gentrap, and opDec synchronous traps.

5.4.3 System Entry Hardware Interrupts (entInt)

The interrupt entry is called to service a hardware interrupt or a machine check. Table 5–4 shows what is passed in a0...a2 and the PS<IPL> setting for various interrupts.

Table 5–4: System Entry Hardware Interrupts

Entry Type	Value in a0	Value in a1	Value in a2	PS<IPL>
Interprocessor interrupt	0	UNPREDICTABLE	UNPREDICTABLE	5
Clock	1	UNPREDICTABLE	UNPREDICTABLE	5
Correctable error	2	Interrupt vector	Pointer to Logout Area	7
Machine check	2	Interrupt vector	Pointer to Logout Area	7
I/O device interrupt	3	Interrupt vector	UNPREDICTABLE	Level of device
Performance counter	4	Interrupt vector	UNPREDICTABLE	6

On entry to the hardware interrupt routine, the IPL has been set to the level of the interrupt. For hardware interrupts, register a1 contains a platform-specific interrupt vector. That platform-specific interrupt vector is typically the same value as the SCB offset value that would be returned if the platform was running OpenVMS Alpha PALcode.

For a correctable error or machine check interrupt, a1 contains a platform-specific interrupt vector and a2 contains the kseg address of the platform-specific logout area. The interrupt vector value and logout area format are typically the same as those used by the platform when running OpenVMS Alpha PALcode.

The machine check error summary (MCES) register, shown in Figure 5–4 and described in Table 5–5, records the correctable error and machine check interrupts in progress.

Figure 5–4: Machine Check Error Status (MCES) Register

63	32 31		5 4 3 2 1 0
IMP	Reserved		D D P S M S P C C I C C E E P

Table 5–5: Machine Check Error Status (MCES) Register Bit Definitions

Bit	Symbol	Description
63–32		IMP.
31–5		Reserved.
4	DSC	Disable system correctable error in progress. Set to disable system correctable error reporting.
3	DPC	Disable processor correctable error in progress. Set to disable processor correctable error reporting.
2	PCE	Processor correctable error in progress. Set when a processor correctable error is detected. Should be cleared by the processor correctable error handler when the logout frame may be reused.
1	SCE	System correctable error in progress. Set when a system correctable error is detected. Should be cleared by the system correctable error handler when the logout frame may be reused.
0	MIP	Machine check in progress. Set when a machine check occurs. Must be cleared by the machine check handler when a subsequent machine check can be handled. Used to detect double machine checks.

The MIP flag in the MCES register is set prior to invoking the machine check handler. If the MIP flag is set when a machine check is being initiated, a double machine check halt is initiated instead. The machine check handler needs to clear the MIP flag when it can handle a new machine check.

Similarly, the SCE or PCE flag in the MCES register is set prior to invoking the appropriate correctable error handler. That error handler should clear the appropriate correctable error in progress when the logout area can be reused by hardware or PALcode. PALcode does not overwrite the logout area.

Correctable processor or system error reporting may be suppressed by setting the respective DPC or DSC flag in the MCES register. When the DPC or DSC flag is set, the corresponding error is corrected, but no correctable error interrupt is generated.

5.4.4 System Entry MM Fault (entMM)

The memory-management fault entry is called when a memory management exception occurs. On entry, a0 contains the faulting virtual address and a1 contains the MMCSR (see Section 3.9). On entry, a2 is set to a minus one (−1) for an instruction fetch fault, to a plus one (+1) for a fault caused by a store instruction, or to a 0 for a fault caused by a load instruction.

5.4.5 System Entry Call System (entSys)

The system call entry is called when a callsys instruction is executed in user mode. On entry, only registers (t8...t11) have been modified. The PC+4 of the callsys instruction, the user global pointer, and the current PS are saved on the kernel stack. Additional space for a0...a2 is allocated. After completion of the system service routine, the kernel code executes a CALL_PAL retsys instruction.

5.4.6 System Entry Unaligned Access (entUna)

The unaligned access entry is called when a load or store access is not aligned. On entry, a0 contains the faulting virtual address, a1 contains the zero extended six-bit opcode (bits <31:26>) of the faulting instruction, and a2 contains the zero extended data source or destination register number (bits<25:21>) of the faulting instruction.

5.5 PALcode Support

5.5.1 Stack Writeability and Alignment

PALcode only accesses the kernel stack. Any PALcode accesses to the kernel stack that would produce a memory-management fault will result in a kernel-stack-not-valid halt. The stack pointer must always point to a quadword-aligned address. If the kernel stack is not quadword aligned on a PALcode access, a kernel-stack-not-valid halt is initiated.

DIGITAL UNIX Software Index

Windows NT Software (II–C)

This section describes how a particular implementation of the Windows NT Alpha operating system relates to the Alpha architecture. *It is important to note the following:*

- The interfaces described in this section will change as necessary to support the Microsoft Windows NT operating system.

- Effectively, many of the interfaces described in this section are private agreements between the PALcode and the kernel. Other software should not assume that those interfaces are available.

- In particular, the interfaces in this section must not be used by software developers who are writing device drivers; instead use the portable Windows NT device driver interfaces.

- The only interfaces in this section that may be used by nonsystem software are the bpt, rdteb, and gentrap PALcode instructions.

The following chapters are included in this section:

- Chapter 1, Introduction to Windows NT Alpha Software (II–C)

- Chapter 2, Processor, Process, Threads, and Registers (II–C)

- Chapter 3, Memory Management (II–C)

- Chapter 4, Exceptions, Interrupts, and Machine Checks (II–C)

- Chapter 5, PALcode Instruction Descriptions (II–C)

- Chapter 6, Initialization and Firmware Transitions (II–C)

Contents

5 PALcode Instruction Descriptions (II–C)

6 Initialization and Firmware Transitions (II–C)

Figures

Tables

Chapter 1

Introduction to Windows NT Alpha Software (II–C)

The primary goal of the Windows NT Alpha PALcode implementation is total compatibility with the base operating system design and existing implementations of Windows NT for all processor architectures. *Maintaining compatibility with Windows NT and software portability between versions of Windows NT requires the stipulations mentioned in the introduction to this section. It is important that all software developers read those stipulations.*

The PALcode mechanism, coupled with the Windows NT Alpha design, provides binary compatibility for native system components across different processor implementations. The PALcode also provides a clean abstracted processor model that matches Windows NT requirements, requires minimal porting effort for new platforms, and provides the best possible performance while offering those features.

Windows NT Alpha is a 32-bit operating system. Therefore, the PALcode is a 32-bit implementation, with, for example, a 32-bit virtual address space. The internal processor registers are 32 bits, in canonical longword format. The page table entry (PTE) format is also 32 bits. The PALcode manages any required transformation between the 32-bit processor-independent formats and the 64-bit internal processor.

A Windows NT Alpha PALcode image is processor specific and platform independent. A single version of the PALcode (for a particular processor implementation) runs on all systems. The difference between processors is entirely hidden by the PALcode for each implementation. Thus, the PALcode interface allows the Windows NT Alpha operating system images to be binary-compatible across different processor implementations.

The PALcode image is read from the disk during the boot process, like all other components of the running operating system. The boot environment PALcode need only support the common swppal instruction to allow the operating system to load and initialize the PALcode.

Some functions and parameters must be implemented on a per-platform basis. Platform-dependent functions are implemented in the HAL (hardware abstraction layer), which is a system-specific library, loaded and dynamically linked at boot time.

The basic Windows NT Alpha design, therefore, consists of a platform-independent PALcode definition and binary-compatible kernel with system-dependent functions in the HAL.

The PALcode was designed to work smoothly and quickly with the Windows NT Alpha kernel. For example, the PALcode builds Windows NT Alpha trap frames and passes Windows NT Alpha status codes. Wherever possible, parameters and return values are passed in registers between the kernel and the PALcode.

The PALcode was also designed to keep dependencies on the kernel to a minimum. For example, only the processor control region and the kernel trap frame definition are shared between the PALcode and the Windows NT Alpha kernel.

1.1 Overview of System Components

The kernel is a binary-compatible image that can run on any Alpha processor, platform, or system. The kernel is binary compatible because of cooperation between it and other system components that provide the processor- and system-specific functions. Those cooperating components are the firmware, the OS Loader, the HAL (hardware abstraction layer), and the PALcode.

The firmware and OS Loader are the first components in the boot sequence and are responsible for establishing the environment in which the kernel, HAL, and PALcode execute. The kernel reads the configuration information provided by the firmware through the OS Loader and uses the standard interfaces provided by the HAL and the PALcode.

Firmware

The firmware contributes the following components to the boot sequence:

1. Establishes the privileged environment in which the OS Loader executes and the kernel begins executing (that is, provides memory management support and the swppal instruction).

2. Provides platform- and configuration-dependent services to the OS loader (such as I/O services) by using ARC call-back routines.

3. Creates the configuration database: devices, memory size, and so forth.

4. Reads the OS Loader from the disk and executes it.

OS Loader

The OS Loader is a linking loader that reads the component operating system images from the disk, performs necessary relocation, and binds the dynamically linked images together. The OS Loader loads the appropriate HAL and PALcode, based on the configuration information provided by the firmware.

The OS Loader loads the appropriate boot drivers as read from the operating system configuration files. The OS Loader also builds the loader parameter block structure by using information provided by the firmware. The loader parameter block includes configuration information (processor, system, device, and memory configuration) and per-processor data structures.

Once the operating system components are loaded, the OS Loader jumps to the beginning of the kernel to begin execution of the operating system. The OS Loader loads the operating system PALcode on a 64K-byte-aligned address. The kernel activates the operating system PALcode by executing the swppal instruction.

Hardware Abstraction Layer (HAL)

The HAL provides the system-specific layer between the kernel and the system hardware. The HAL provides interfaces for the following types of functions:

- Interrupt handling, including dispatch and acknowledge
- DMA control
- Timer support
- Low-level I/O support
- Cache coherency

If a processor implementation requires PALcode intervention to support any of those functions, then the PALcode must support those processor-specific functions in a system-independent manner.

PALcode

The PALcode is specific to a particular processor implementation and must hide the internal workings of the processor from the kernel. The PALcode for a particular processor may include per-processor functions, but they must be called only by the HAL.

1.2 Calling Standard Register Usage

Table 1–1: General-Purpose Integer Registers

Register Number	Symbolic Name	Volatility	Description
r0	v0	Volatile	Return value register
r1 – r8	t0 – t7	Volatile	Temporary registers
r9 – r14	s0 – s5	Nonvolatile	Saved registers
r15	s6/fp	Nonvolatile	Saved register/frame pointer
r16 – r21	a0 – a5	Volatile	Argument registers
r22 – r25	t8 – t11	Volatile	Temporary registers
r26	ra	Volatile	Return address register
r27	t12	Volatile	Temporary register
r28	at	Volatile	Assembler temporary register
r29	gp	Nonvolatile	Global pointer
r30	sp	Nonvolatile	Stack pointer
r31	zero	Constant	RAZ / writes ignored

Table 1–2: General-Purpose Floating-Point Registers

Register Number	Volatility	Description
f0	Volatile	Return value register (real part)
f1	Volatile	Return value register (imaginary part)
f2 – f9	Nonvolatile	Saved registers
f10 – f15	Volatile	Temporary registers
f16 – f21	Volatile	Argument registers
f22 – f30	Volatile	Temporary registers
f31	Constant	RAZ / writes ignored

1.3 Code Flow Conventions

The code flows are shown as an ordered sequence of instructions. The instructions in the sequence may be reordered as long as the results of the sequence of instructions are not altered. In particular, if an instruction j is listed subsequent to an instruction i and i writes any data that is used by j, then i must be executed before j.

Chapter 2

Processor, Process, Threads, and Registers (II–C)

This chapter describes structures and registers that support the processor, process, and thread environment.

2.1 Processor Status

The processor status register (PSR) defines the processor status. The PSR is shown in Figure 2–1 and described in Tables 2–1, 2–2, and 2–3.

Figure 2–1: Processor Status Register

```
31                           5 4 3 2 1 0
 ┌─────────────────────────┬──────┬─┬─┐
 │                         │      │I│M│
 │        RAZ/IGN          │ IRQL │ │O│
 │                         │      │E│D│
 │                         │      │ │E│
 └─────────────────────────┴──────┴─┴─┘
```

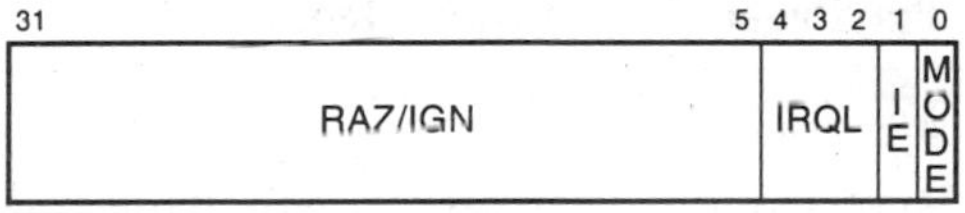

Table 2–1: Processor Status Register Fields

Field	Type	Description
IRQL	RW	Interrupt request level, in the range 0–7, as described in Table 2–2. Any interrupt disabled at a lower priority level is also disabled at a higher priority level.
IE	RW	Interrupt enable: 0 = interrupts disabled 1 = interrupts enabled A global interrupt enable to turn interrupts on and off without changing the IRQL.
MODE	RW	Processor mode: 0 = kernel mode 1 = user mode Describes the current processor privilege mode: user (unprivileged) or kernel (privileged). The processor privilege mode defines the instructions that can be executed and the memory protection that is used, as described in Table 2–3.

Table 2–2: Processor Status Register IRQL Field Summary

IRQL	Name	Description
0	PASSIVE_LEVEL	All interrupts enabled.
1	APC_LEVEL	APC software interrupts disabled.
2	DISPATCH_LEVEL	Dispatch software interrupts disabled.
3	DEVICE_LEVEL	Low-priority device hardware interrupts disabled.
4	DEVICE_HIGH_LEVEL	High-priority device hardware interrupts disabled.
5	CLOCK_LEVEL	Clock hardware interrupts disabled.
6	IPI_LEVEL	Interprocessor hardware interrupts disabled.
7	HIGH_LEVEL	All maskable interrupts disabled.

Table 2–3: Processor Privilege Mode Map

Operation	Privileged	Unprivileged
Superpage access	Yes	No
Page protection	Access to all pages	Access to only those pages with the Owner bit = 1
Privileged PALcode instructions	Yes	No

2.2 Internal Processor Register Summary

The internal processor registers in Table 2–4 are defined across all implementations. Implementation of these registers within the processor is implementation dependent.

Table 2–4: Internal Processor Register Summary

Name	Initial Value	Description
ASN	0	Address space number of owning process of current thread
GENERAL_ENTRY	0	General exception class kernel handler address
IKSP	0	Initial kernel stack pointer
INTERRUPT_ENTRY	0	Interrupt exception class kernel handler address
KGP	0	Kernel global pointer
MCES	†	Machine check error summary

Table 2–4: Internal Processor Register Summary (Continued)

Name	Initial Value	Description
MEM_MGMT_ENTRY	0	Memory management exception class kernel handler address
PAL_BASE	†	PALcode image base address
PANIC_ENTRY	0	Panic exception class kernel handler address
PCR	†	Processor control region base address
PDR	0	Page directory base address
PSR	†	Processor status register
RESTART_ADDRESS	†	Restart execution address
SIRR	0	Software interrupt request register
SYSCALL_ENTRY	0	System service exception class kernel handler address
TEB	0	Thread environment block base address
THREAD	0	Thread unique value (kernel thread address)

† The register has an architected initial value. See the register description in Table 2–5.

2.3 Internal Processor Registers

Table 2–5 lists and describes the internal processor registers.

Table 2–5: Internal Processor Registers

Name	Description
ASN	Address space number of owning process of current thread
	Bits <15:0> of the ASN register contain the address space number for the current process. Bits <31:16> are RAZ.
	The ASN is a process tag that is used by the processor to qualify each virtual translation. When translations are qualified, it is not necessary for the processor to flush all virtual translations for previous processes when performing a context swap or process swap. The swpctx and swpprocess instructions provide the ASN.
GENERAL_ENTRY	General exception class kernel handler address
	The GENERAL_ENTRY register contains the entry address (in 32-bit superpage format) for the kernel exception handler for the General class of exceptions. The wrentry instruction writes GENERAL_ENTRY.
IKSP	Initial kernel stack pointer
	The IKSP register contains the initial kernel stack address. IKSP points to the top of the kernel stack for the currently executing thread. The rdksp instruction reads IKSP and the swpksp instruction writes IKSP. IKSP is also written by swpctx and during system initialization by initpal.
INTERRUPT_ENTRY	Interrupt exception class kernel handler address
	The INTERRUPT_ENTRY register contains the entry address (in 32-bit superpage format) of the kernel exception handler for the Interrupt class of exceptions. The wrentry instruction writes INTERRUPT_ENTRY.
KGP	Kernel global pointer
	The KGP register contains the kernel global pointer, the gp value. The PALcode restores the kernel global pointer to the general-purpose register gp whenever dispatching to a kernel exception handler. The initpal instruction writes the KGP.

Table 2–5: Internal Processor Registers (Continued)

Name	Description
MCES	Machine check error summary
	The MCES register is used to report and control the current state of machine check handling. The MCES register contains multiple fields that are described in Section 4.3. The initial values for the MCES register fields DSC, DPC, and DMK are implementation specific, and all other fields set to 0. The recommended initial values are DMK = 0, DPC = 1, and DSC = 1.
MEM_MGMT_ENTRY	Memory management exception class
	The MEM_MGMT_ENTRY register contains the entry address (in 32-bit superpage format) of the kernel exception handler for the Memory Management class of exceptions. The wrentry instruction writes MEM_MGMT_ENTRY.
PAL_BASE	PALcode image base address
	The PAL_BASE register contains the physical address of the base of the currently active PALcode image. Its initial value is the address of the PALcode entry point. PAL_BASE controls which PALcode image is currently active and is written during PALcode initialization. The PAL_BASE register is illustrated and described in Section 6.2.
PANIC_ENTRY	Panic exception class kernel handler address
	The PANIC_ENTRY register contains the entry address (in 32-bit superpage format) of the kernel exception handler for the Panic class of exceptions. The wrentry instruction writes PANIC_ENTRY.
PCR	Processor control region base address
	The PCR register contains the base address (in 32-bit superpage format) of the processor control region page. The processor control region is a page of per-processor data. The PCR is passed as an initialization parameter and the rdpcr instruction reads it.

Table 2–5: Internal Processor Registers (Continued)

Name	Description
PDR	Page directory base address
	The PDR register contains the base physical address of the page directory page. The page directory page contains all of the first-level page table entries (the page directory entries or PDEs). As such, the page directory page defines an address space for a process. The swpctx and swpprocess instructions write the PDR when the address space is swapped. The initpal instruction also writes the PDR.
PSR	Processor status register
	The PSR controls the privilege state and interrupt priority of the processor. The PSR register contains multiple fields that are described in Section 2.1. The initial values for the fields in the PSR are IRQL=7, IE=1, and MODE=0 (kernel).
RESTART_ADDRESS	Restart execution address
	The RESTART_ADDRESS register contains the address where the processor resumes execution when the PALcode exits. For example, upon entry to each of the PALcode instructions, the RESTART_ADDRESS register contains the *virtual address + 4* of that instruction. The initial value of the RESTART_ADDRESS register is the kernel initialization continuation address, passed as a parameter to the initialization routine.
SIRR	Software interrupt request register
	The SIRR register indicates requested software interrupts. SIRR contains multiple fields that are defined in Section 4.2.7.
SYSCALL_ENTRY	System service exception class kernel handler address
	The SYSCALL_ENTRY register contains the entry address (in 32-bit superpage format) of the kernel exception handler for the System Service class of exceptions. The wrentry instruction writes SYSCALL_ENTRY.
TEB	Thread environment block base address
	The TEB register contains the address of the user thread environment block. Each swpctx instruction writes the TEB; the rdteb instruction reads it.

Table 2–5: Internal Processor Registers (Continued)

Name	Description
THREAD	Thread unique value (kernel thread address)
	The THREAD register contains the address of the currently executing kernel thread structure. Each swpctx instruction writes the THREAD register; the rdthread instruction reads it.

2.4 Processor Data Areas

The operating system per-processor data structure is the processor control region. The processor control region is a one-page (superpage) data structure that stores information that may be specific to a particular architecture. This information is data that is shared between the PALcode, the HAL, and/or the architecture-specific portions of the kernel. See Section 3.1 for information on the superpage.

2.4.1 Processor Control Region

The processor control region contains a number of data structures that are of importance to the PALcode, including:

- A 3064-byte region that is reserved for the PALcode and is the only per-processor data region available to the PALcode.

- The interrupt level table (ILT), which maps the interrupt enable masks for each possible interrupt request level. The PALcode may continually read these masks or may read them once and cache them inside the processor.

- The interrupt dispatch table (IDT), which contains the address of an interrupt handler for each possible interrupt vector.

- The interrupt mask table (IMT), which maps each possible pattern of interrupt requests to the highest priority interrupt vector and the corresponding synchronization level.

- The panic stack pointer.

- The restart block pointer.

- The firmware restart address.

The PALcode is responsible for initializing the PALcode base address field and several PALcode revision fields within the processor control region.

The rdpcr instruction returns the base address of the processor control region.

2.4.2 PALcode Version Control

The PALcode is responsible for writing version information in the processor control region. The PalMajorVersion, PalMinorVersion, and PalSequenceVersion are provided for maintenance and debugging. The PALcode writes these fields, but the values are implementation specific.

The kernel may use the PalMajorSpecification and PalMinorSpecification fields for check-pointing with the PALcode.

The PALcode writes the specification fields with version numbers that correspond to the version of the specification to which the PALcode image complies. Minor revisions within the same major revision are backwards compatible. The kernel may read the PalMajorSpecification and determine if it is compatible with the version of the PALcode. If the kernel is not compatible (if the PalMajorSpecification is greater than the kernel's expected PALcode major specification), the kernel runs down in a controlled manner.

The version agreement between the PALcode and the kernel is a private agreement between these two system components. No other system component, including the HAL and device drivers, may depend on any values from those fields.

2.4.3 PALcode Alignment Fixup Count

PALcode must maintain a count in the processor control region PalAlignmentFixupCount field of the total number of alignment fixups that the PALcode accomplishes. PalAlignment-FixupCount is an unsigned quadword field that is incremented by one when the PALcode fixes up an alignment fault. The field silently overflows to zero.

The kernel may use the PalAlignmentFixupCount field for determining the total number of alignment fixups on a system by adding the value in that field for each processor to the number of alignment fixups done by the kernel.

2.5 Caches and Cache Coherency

Implementations may include caches that are not kept coherent with main memory. The imb instruction provides an architected common way to make the instruction execution stream coherent with main memory. The imb instruction guarantees that subsequently executed instructions are fetched coherently with respect to main memory on only the current processor.

User-mode code that directly modifies the instruction stream, either through writes or by DMA from an I/O device, must call the appropriate Windows NT API to ensure I-cache coherency. User-mode code that uses standard APIs to modify the instruction stream works as expected and is handled by the APIs themselves.

2.6 Stacks

There are four stacks:

- Kernel stack

  Each thread is allocated its own pages for a kernel stack. The kernel stack is the two pages of virtual address space below the IKSP for a thread, where the IKSP points to the byte beyond the top of the two pages. The initial kernel stack pointer (IKSP) points to the top of the currently active kernel stack for the current thread. Two PALcode instructions provide access to the IKSP: rdksp to read the IKSP and swpksp to atomically read the current IKSP and write a new one.

Must remain valid for the currently executing thread. Software must guarantee that the kernel stack pointer remains 16-byte aligned.

- User Stack

  A per-thread stack on which all user-mode components are executed.

- Deferred procedure call (DPC) stack

  A processor-wide stack upon which all deferred procedure calls are executed. Must remain valid for the lifetime of the system.

- Panic stack

  Allows the operating system to remain coherent through a system crash. Must remain valid for the lifetime of the system.

The kernel, DPC, and panic stacks execute in kernel mode; the user stack executes in user mode.

2.7 Processes and Threads

Windows NT Alpha is designed as a multithread operating system with multiple threads executing within the same process. Each thread has its own processor context, user-mode stack, and kernel stack. Memory and the address space are shared across all threads in the same process.

The PALcode "knows" nothing about the structure of threads or processes. The PALcode implements the means to swap from one thread context to another and to allow a thread to attach to the address space of another process.

The state to accomplish these operations is passed entirely in registers. The PALcode maintains the THREAD and TEB internal processor registers. They allow threads to query about the state of the currently executing thread.

The THREAD register, a unique value identifying the current thread, is written when the thread context is swapped. The privileged instruction rdthread reads the THREAD register.

The TEB register, a user-accessible pointer to the thread environment block for the new thread, is written when thread context is swapped. The unprivileged rdteb instruction reads the TEB register. Again, the PALcode knows nothing about the structure of the thread environment block; the PALcode simply maintains the TEB register value when context is switched.

2.7.1 Swapping Thread Context to Another Thread

The swpctx instruction swaps the context from one thread to another thread. The following parameters are passed to swpctx:

Initial kernel stack pointer
Swpctx must switch to the new kernel stack for the new thread. The initial kernel stack pointer is written to the internal processor register IKSP.

THREAD internal processor register (unique thread value)

TEB internal processor register (thread environment block pointer)

These registers are maintained by the kernel and only written during a context switch. Implicitly, the values in these registers for a particular thread cannot change while that thread is executing.

PFN of the directory table base page for the new process

ASN for the new process

ASN_wrap_indicator

The PFN and ASN allow switching to a new process address space. The PFN of the directory table base page is an overloaded parameter; it is used to indicate if the process needs to be swapped.

- The PFN is set to a negative value in the kernel if the previous thread and the new thread are in the same process (address space). There is no need to swap the address space if the two threads are in the same process. The values for the ASN parameters are then UNPREDICTABLE.

- If the two threads are in different processes, the PFN is greater than or equal to zero and is used to write the PDR internal processor register. When the PFN is valid (greater than zero), the ASN must also be valid and is used to write the ASN internal processor register.

Swapping to a new process address space involves establishing a new directory pointer to the page table base page for the new process and possibly performing translation buffer operations. A set ASN_wrap_indicator signals that the PALcode must perform an invalidation operation for each cached translation in the translation buffers and virtual caches that does not have the address space match (ASM) bit set.

2.7.2 Swapping Thread Context to Another Process

The swpprocess (swap process) instruction allows a thread to attach to another process (in another address space). Swpprocess requires the PFN of the new directory table base page and the new ASN as input. Swpprocess performs the same address space swapping operation as does swpctx when the PFN of the page directory is valid.

Chapter 3

Memory Management (II–C)

3.1 Virtual Address Space

Windows NT Alpha is a 32-bit implementation with a 32-bit virtual address space, as represented in Table 3–1.

Table 3–1: Virtual Address Map

Address Range$_{16}$ (32 bits)	Permission	Description
00000000–7FFFFFFF	User and Kernel	General user address space
80000000–BFFFFFFF	Kernel	Nonmapped kernel space (32-bit superpage)
C0000000–C1FFFFFF	Kernel	Mapped, page table space
C2000000–FFFFFFFF	Kernel	Mapped, general kernel space

The address map takes advantage of the 32-bit superpage feature of the Alpha architecture. If the implementation of the 32-bit superpage is not done in hardware, it must be implemented in software (PALcode). The entire 1-GB address space mapped by the 32-bit superpage must be valid at all times for both instruction fetch and data access.

Implementation Note (Hardware):

It is strongly recommended that implementations include a hardware mapping of the 32-bit superpage for both instruction and data stream.

3.2 I/O Space Address Extension

The Windows NT Alpha kernel implementation takes advantage of the architecture's 64-bit address space to provide a nonmapped extended address for I/O space. The extended address space uses the 43-bit superpage that is available in the Alpha architecture. The superpage allows kernel mode access to an address space with a predetermined translation. Therefore, those accesses never require page table mapping or cause a translation buffer miss.

Implementation Note:

> The extended address space is particularly important to Alpha implementations that do not include the BWX extension, because the bus mapping scheme for those implementations uses a shifted physical address, where the lower address bits are used to determine the byte enables. Therefore, the effective page size is smaller. See Appendix D for information about the BWX extension.

The extended superpage provides nonmapped access to a 41-bit physical address space. The nonmapped superpage I/O accesses provide Alpha systems with a performance advantage because there is no need to write as many page table entries and to fill as many translation buffer misses as would be necessary without it. The extended address space is desirable because the likely physical address space is 34 bits or more and the 32-bit superpage can only allow accesses to 30 bits of physical address space. The extended address space is the only exception to the 32-bit virtual address map shown in Table 3–1. The extended address space is intended for I/O access only and can only be used in kernel mode. The address mapping for the extended address space is shown in Table 3–2.

Table 3–2: I/O Address Extension Address Map

Address Range$_{16}$ (64 bits)	Permission	Description
FFFFFC0000000000– FFFFFDFFFFFFFFFF	Kernel	Nonmapped kernel mode I/O extension

3.3 Canonical Virtual Address Format

All virtual addresses, with the exception of the large superpage addresses, must be in canonical longword form. The PALcode must check the faulting virtual addresses in the first level miss flows and raise an exception if the addresses are not canonical longwords. The check is required because the processor may generate 64-bit addresses that are not canonical longwords, but the common memory management code only knows about 32-bit addresses and so cannot necessarily identify or signal the exception to the offending code. The PALcode cannot simply resolve the miss by using only the lower 32 bits. When the faulting instruction is re-executed, it attempts again to access the noncanonical address. If a virtual address fails the canonical form test, the PALcode raises a general exception (see Section 4.1.7.)

3.4 Page Table Entries

Page table entries (PTEs) provide the translation from virtual addresses to their physical addresses. The PTE includes the physical address in the form of a page frame number (PFN), protection information, and performance hints. The virtual address is related to a page table entry based solely upon the position of the PTE within a set of page tables.

Two methods may be used to traverse the page tables to retrieve the corresponding PTE for a given virtual address. The first is to view the page tables as a single-level virtually contiguous table. The second is to view the page tables as a two-level physical table.

3.4.1 Single-Level Virtual Traversal of the Page Tables

For a single-level virtual traversal, a virtual address must be viewed as shown in Figure 3–1, where $2**N$ is the implementation page size:

Figure 3–1: Virtual Address (Virtual View)

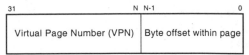

To access the corresponding PTE for a VA (virtual address) using the single-level virtual method, use the following algorithm.

```
! In the algorithm:
!     VIRTUAL_PTE_BASE = C0000000₁₆
!     PAGE_SHIFT = N
! Clear upper bits in case va is sign-extended:
va ← BYTE_ZAP( va, F0 )
! Get virtual page number:
vpn ← RIGHT_SHIFT( va, PAGE_SHIFT )
! 4 bytes per pte, offset + base:
pte_va ← VIRTUAL_PTE_BASE + ( vpn * 4)
! Do a virtual load of pte:
pte ← (pte_va)
```

3.4.2 Two-Level Physical Traversal of the Page Tables

The two-level physical method can be used to find the corresponding PTE for a virtual address when the virtual access method cannot be used (for example, if the PTE address is not valid). The key to physically traversing the page tables is the PDR internal processor register. The PDR is maintained on a per-process basis whenever process context is swapped. The PDR is the physical address of the page directory page that forms the first level of the page tables. The first level of the page tables easily fits within a single page. Each entry in the page directory page is called a PDE (page directory entry). One PDE maps one page of PTEs.

A virtual address must be viewed as shown in Figure 3–2 for a two-level, physical traversal of the page tables. In Figure 3–2, 2**N is the implementation page size, and 2**P is (PTEs per page = page size / 4).

Figure 3–2: Virtual Address (Physical View)

31	N+P N+P-1	N N-1	0
Page Directory Index (PDI)	Page Table Index (PTI)	Byte offset within page	

The following algorithm uses the two-level physical traversal method to access the corresponding PTE for a VA (virtual address).

```
!  In the algorithm:
!      PDE_SHIFT  = N + P
!      PAGE_SHIFT = N

    !  Clear upper bits in case va is sign-extended:
va ← BYTE_ZAP( va, F0 )
    !  Get pde number:
pde_index ←RIGHT_SHIFT( va, PDE_SHIFT )
    !  4 bytes per pde, index * 4  byte offset:
pde_offset ← pde_index * 4
    !  Offset + base:
pde_pa ← PDR + pde_offset
    !  Do a physical load of the page directory entry:
pde ← (pde_pa)
    !  Get PFN of pte page from pde:
pte_pfn ← pde<PFN>
    !  Get physical address of pte page:
pte_page ← LEFT_SHIFT( pte_pfn, PAGE_SHIFT)
    !  Extract page table index from virtual address:
pte_index ← va<pti>
    !  Calculate offset, 4 bytes per pte:
pte_offset ← pte_index * 4
    !  Address  base + offset:
pte_pa ← pte_page + pte_offset
    !  Do a physical load to read the pte:
pte ← (pte_pa)
```

Page directory entries are themselves page table entries and so they have the same format. There are some implications for DTB implementation because the PDEs establish a recursive mapping for addresses within the PTE address space. The implications and a description of the recursive mapping are described in Section 3.6.

3.4.3 Page Table Entry Summary

The format for a PTE is shown in Figure 3–3 and described in Table 3–3.

Figure 3–3: Page Table Entry

31		9 8 7 6 5 4 3 2 1 0
PFN		SFW	GH	G	R	D	O	V

Table 3–3: Page Table Entry Fields

Field	Description
PFN	Page frame number
SFW	Reserved for software (operating system)

Table 3–3: Page Table Entry Fields (Continued)

Field	Description
GH	Granularity hints Optional hint that provides for mapping translations larger than the standard implementation page size. These large pages must be both virtually and physically aligned. Defines the translation in terms of a multiple of the page size, where the multiplier equals 8**N, where N is the granularity hint value in the range 0–3.
G	Global translation hint (address space match) Optional hint that the indicated translation is global for all processes.
R	Reserved
D	Dirty: 0 = page is not dirty 1 = page is dirty Implemented as the inverse of fault on write (FOW). Serves double duty by causing faults for the first write to a page. Serves as a write-protect bit and as a marker that allows the operating system to track dirty pages.
O	Owner: 0 = kernel access only 1 = user access permitted Indicates whether user mode is allowed across this page, either for instruction fetch or data access. Kernel mode code has implied access to all pages that have a valid translation.
V	Valid: 0 = translation not valid 1 = valid translation

3.5 Translation Buffer Management

As shown in Table 3–4, the PALcode provides the dtbis, tbia, tbim, tbimasn, tbis, and tbisasn instructions to manage the cached virtual translations maintained in the translation buffers and virtual caches.

Table 3–4: Translation Buffer Management Instructions

Instruction	Operation
dtbis	Invalidates a single data stream translation for a specified address. It is designed for those cases when the operating system can determine that the translation is not used in the instruction stream. Implementations may advantageously use dtbis to avoid needing to invalidate instruction stream translations in both an instruction TB and a virtual I-cache.

Table 3–4: Translation Buffer Management Instructions (Continued)

Instruction	Operation
tbia	Invalidates all page table translations for both instruction and data stream access. The translations invalidated are limited to "page table translations" because it is possible that an implementation has used fixed TB entries to implement one or more of the required superpages. These fixed translations are considered "hard-wired" by the operating system and must be valid at all times.
tbim	Invalidates multiple virtual translations, passed as a parameter, for the current ASN. Tbim invalidates translations for both instruction and data stream access.
tbimasn	Invalidates multiple virtual translations for a specified address space number (ASN), passed as a parameter. The ASN may or may not be the currently executing thread. Tbimasn invalidates translations for both instruction and data stream access.
tbis	Invalidates a single translation for a specific virtual address, passed as a parameter. Tbis invalidates the translation for both instruction and data stream access.
tbisasn	Invalidates a translation for a single virtual address for a specified address space number (ASN). The ASN may or may not be for the currently executing thread. Tbisasn invalidates the translation for both instruction and data stream access.

On processors that implement physical, noncoherent instruction caches, instructions that invalidate I-stream translations must also invalidate instruction cache blocks from the physical pages that correspond to the invalidated virtual translations.

3.6 Implications of Recursive TB Mapping

Recursive virtual mapping has an implication for data translation buffer implementations: it is possible for two identical translations to be written in the DTB during the same miss handling sequence. If the DTB cannot correctly operate with two identical translations, the PALcode must include additional checks to prevent the condition from occurring.

The page tables can be viewed either as a virtual contiguous single-level table or as a two-level table that must be traversed physically. When viewed as a two-level table, the first level is a single page called the page directory page. Each page directory page entry, called a PDE, provides the first-level translation so that the TB-fill code can find the page table page that contains the PTE with the translation for the faulted virtual address. All page table pages are mapped by a PDE in the page directory page.

The page tables are recursive. The page directory page is a standard page table page and it is virtually mapped in the single-level virtual page table. Therefore, there exists one PDE that maps the page directory page. The PDE that maps the page directory page in a two-level lookup is also the PTE that maps the page directory page for the single-level virtual mapping.

This special PDE is called the root PTE or RPTE.

Assume that the processor implementation has two data stream TB miss flows — one for the misses taken in native mode and one for the misses taken in the PALcode environment. For the case when a native-mode virtual access is made to the page directory page, PALcode takes the following flows:

Native Miss Flow	PALcode Environment Miss Flow
1. {get va for PTE that maps the faulted va: VA}	
2. {get the PTE using its va} ldl rx, 0(ry) where ry ←va of PTE	
	3. {ldl rx, 0(ry) from PALcode environment faulted}
	4. {resolve this fault by making the va of the missed PTE valid}
	5. {translation for RPTE is written into the DTB}
	6. {re-execute the load that failed since the va of the PTE is now valid}
7. load completes, rx ← RPTE}	
8. {write the translation for the faulting va, VA, into the DTB}	
9. { RPTE is now in the DTB twice}	
10. {Re-execute the origina lnative-mode instruction that faulted when accessing VA}	

Since there is only one PTE, RPTE, that exhibits this behavior, the PALcode can check the faulting PTE address in the second-level fill routine to special case for RPTE. It is preferable not to slow down even the second-level fill flow. However, this is a processor implementation decision.

Chapter 4

Exceptions, Interrupts, and Machine Checks (II–C)

At certain times during the operation of a system, events within the system require the execution of software outside the explicit flow of control. When such an exceptional event occurs, an Alpha processor forces a change in control flow from that indicated by the current instruction stream. The notification process for such events is an exception, an interrupt, or a machine check.

4.1 Exceptions

4.1.1 Exception Dispatch

When the processor encounters an exception, it traps to PALcode that provides preliminary exception dispatch for the operating system. Some exceptions, such as TB miss, may be handled entirely by the PALcode without the intervention of the operating system.

The PALcode provides a simple and efficient method of dispatching to the operating system for those exceptions that require operating system action. In general, the following operations characterize exception dispatch:

1. Switch to kernel mode (if in user mode).

2. Allocate a trap frame on the kernel stack.

3. Save the necessary processor state in the trap frame.

4. Prepare arguments to the kernel exception handler using the standard argument registers where possible.

5. Set the processor state for executing the kernel (establish the stack pointer so it points to the kernel stack, establish the global pointer to point to the kernel global area).

6. Restart execution at the address of the kernel exception handler registered for the class of exception that was encountered.

4.1.2 Exception Classes

The PALcode classifies each exception into one of the following categories:

- Memory management exceptions

  Memory management exceptions, described in Section 4.1.5 , are raised for:

  - Translation not valid faults: accesses to addresses that do not have a valid translation for the currently executing context

- Access violations: accesses to addresses for which the currently executing context does not have permission for the access

- System service call exceptions

  Although not really exceptions, system service calls are handled as exceptions to allow unprivileged code to request and receive privileged services. System services may be requested from both unprivileged and privileged modes (user and kernel mode respectively). System service calls are described in Section 4.1.6.

- General exceptions

  The general exception class, described in Section 4.1.7, is the catchall category for all of the other exceptions that may be raised by unprivileged code:

  - Arithmetic exceptions

  - Unaligned memory access

  - Illegal instruction execution

  - Invalid (non-canonical virtual) address exceptions

  - Software exceptions

  - Breakpoints

  - Subsetted instruction execution

- Panic exceptions

  The panic exception class, described in Section 4.1.8, is reserved for conditions from which execution cannot reliably be continued. The following general cases of panic exceptions are anticipated:

  - Invalid kernel stack (including overflow and underflow)

  - Unexpected exceptions from PALcode

4.1.3 Returning from Exceptions

The rfe and retsys instructions are provided for returning from exceptions.

The rfe (return from exception or interrupt) instruction allows the operating system to return from an exception. Rfe may also be used to transition from kernel mode to user-mode startup code.

The rfe instruction reverses the effect of an exception by restoring the original processor state from the trap frame on the kernel stack. In addition, rfe accepts a parameter that allows it to set software interrupt requests for the execution context that is about to be reestablished

Two exception classes do not use rfe to return to the previously executing context: system service call and panic exceptions. The retsys instruction is used for returning from system service call exceptions because a system service call has different semantics with regard to the saved processor state than the other exceptions.

Panic exceptions do not return because they precipitate a controlled crash of the operating system.

4.1.4 Trap Frames

Trap frames are allocated on the kernel stack for all classes of exceptions in PALcode. The PALcode also partially writes the trap frame; the fields written are based upon the exception being handled. The kernel stack must be guaranteed to remain aligned on a 16-byte boundary, as specified in the Windows NT Alpha calling standard. The trap frame itself is guaranteed in size to be a multiple of 32 bytes. The PALcode may over-align the kernel stack pointer when allocating the trap frame in order to improve memory throughput, with consideration for the extra memory being consumed. The trap frame is structured so that writes aggregate. The register values stored in the trap frame are 64-bit values. This is required as the register set is 64 bits and may contain 64-bit values (as opposed to canonical longwords).

Trap frame definitions are shown in Table 4–1.

Table 4–1: Trap Frame Definitions

Symbolic Name	Size	Description
TrIntSp	Quadword	Stack pointer register at point of exception
TrPsr	Longword	Processor status register at point of exception
TrFir	Quadword	Exception program counter
TrIntA0	Quadword	Register a0 at point of exception
TrIntA1	Quadword	Register a1 at point of exception
TrIntA2	Quadword	Register a2 at point of exception
TrIntA3	Quadword	Register a3 at point of exception
TrIntFp	Quadword	Frame pointer register at point of exception
TrIntGp	Quadword	Global pointer register at point of exception
TrIntRa	Quadword	Return address register at point of exception

4.1.5 Memory Management Exceptions

PALcode recognizes two classes of memory management exceptions: translation not valid faults and access violations. Translation not valid faults are detected when a page table entry for a virtual address has the valid bit cleared. The invalid page table entry can be either a first- or second-level table entry. Access violations are detected by the hardware when the processor attempts to access a virtual address and that type of access is not permitted according to the protection mask in the page table entry that maps the translation for the virtual address.

The PALcode dispatches to the kernel in the same manner for each of these two classes of exceptions, according to the following description:

```
previousPSR  ← PSR
if ( PSR<Mode> EQ User ) then
        PSR<Mode>  ← kernel
        tp ← (IKSP - TrapFrameLength)! Establish trap pointer
else
        tp ← (sp - TrapFrameLength)  ! Establish trap pointer
endif
TrIntSp(tp) ← sp
TrIntFp(tp) ← fp
TrIntRa(tp) ← ra
TrIntGp(tp) ← gp
TrIntA0(tp) ← a0
TrIntA1(tp) ← a1
TrIntA2(tp) ← a2
TrIntA3(tp) ← a3
TrFir(tp) ← ExceptionPC
TrPsr(tp) ← previousPSR
sp ← tp
RESTART_ADDRESS ← MEM_MGMT_ENTRY
fp ← sp
gp ← KGP
a0 ← 1 if store; 0 if load
a1 ← faulting virtual address
a2 ← previousPSR<Mode>
a3 ← previousPSR
```

All other general-purpose registers must be preserved across the memory management exception dispatch.

If the kernel can resolve the fault, it uses the rfe instruction to restart the faulting thread, thus reissuing the instruction that faulted. Otherwise, the kernel raises the appropriate exception.

4.1.6 System Service Calls

System service calls are initiated from both user and kernel modes via the callsys instruction. The privileged retsys instruction returns from a system service back to the caller. The callsys and retsys instructions are described in Sections 5.2.3 and 5.1.21, respectively.

4.1.7 General Exceptions

General exceptions are those exceptions, other than memory management exceptions and system service call exceptions, that can be raised by hardware or software. All general exceptions are handled in approximately the same manner in the PALcode and in exactly the same manner in the lowest level kernel exception dispatch.

The following exceptions are grouped together as general exceptions:

- Arithmetic exceptions
- Unaligned access exceptions
- Illegal instruction exceptions

- Invalid (non-canonical virtual) address exceptions
- Software exceptions
- Breakpoints
- Subsetted IEEE instruction exceptions

A general exception builds a trap frame on the kernel stack and populates the exception record within the trap frame and then dispatches to the kernel general exception entry point. The common dispatch for general exceptions is shown in Section 4.1.7.8.

The differences between each type of exception are the population of the exception record and the meaning of the faulting instruction field within the trap frame. The values for each specific exception are detailed in the sections that follow.

4.1.7.1 Arithmetic Exceptions

An arithmetic trap occurs at the completion of the operation that caused the exception. Since several instructions may be in various stages of execution at any point in time, it is possible for multiple arithmetic traps to occur simultaneously. The intervening instructions (after the trigger instruction) are collectively called the *trap shadow*. See Common Architecture, Chapter 4, *Arithmetic Trap Completion*, for information.

The ExceptionPC is written to the TrFir offset of the trap frame. The Exception PC written into the trap frame is the virtual address of the first instruction after the trapping instruction that has not yet executed.

Arithmetic traps write the following information into the exception record of the trap frame, where *er* is the exception record pointer:

```
ErExceptionCode(er)          ← STATUS_ALPHA_ARITHMETIC
ErExceptionInformation<0>(er) ← FLOATING_REGISTER_MASK
ErExceptionInformation<1>(er) ← INTEGER_REGISTER_MASK
ErExceptionInformation<2>(er) ← EXCEPTION_SUMMARY
ErNumberParameters(er)← 3
ErExceptionFlags(er)   ← 0
ErExceptionRecord(er)  ← 0
```

The floating register masks indicate which floating-point registers were destinations of instructions that caused an exception. A one in the corresponding position for a register indicates that the register was the destination of an instruction that faulted. A zero indicates that the register was not the destination of an instruction that faulted. The definition of the correspondence between the floating registers and the bits in the mask is shown in Figure 4–1.

Figure 4–1: Floating-Point Register Mask (FLOAT_REGISTER_MASK)

```
 31 30 29                              2  1  0
┌──┬──┬────────────────────────────┬──┬──┐
│F │F │                            │F │F │
│3 │3 │      F29 through F2         │1 │0 │
│1 │0 │                            │  │  │
└──┴──┴────────────────────────────┴──┴──┘
```

The integer register masks indicate which integer registers were destinations of instructions that caused an exception. A one in the corresponding position for a register indicates that the register was the destination of an instruction that faulted. A zero indicates that the register was not the destination of an instruction that faulted. The definition of the correspondence between the integer registers and the bits in the mask is shown in Figure 4–2.

Figure 4–2: Integer Register Mask (INTEGER_REGISTER_MASK)

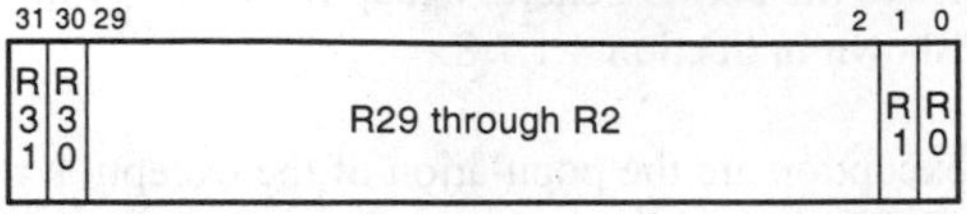

The format of the exception summary register is shown in Figure 4–3 and the fields are defined in Table 4–2.

Figure 4–3: Exception Summary Register (EXCEPTION_SUMMARY)

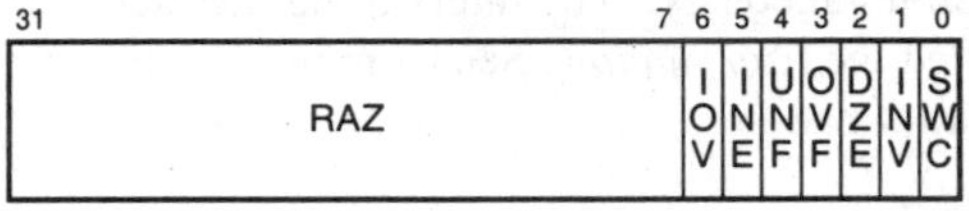

Table 4–2: Exception Summary Register Fields

Field	Name	Description
RAZ		Read as zero.
IOV	Integer overflow	Result of integer operation overflowed the destination's precision.
INE	Inexact result	Result of floating operation caused loss of precision.
UNF	Underflow	Result of floating operation underflowed the destination exponent.
OVF	Overflow	Result of floating operation overflowed the destination exponent.
DZE	Division by zero	Floating-point divide attempt with a divisor of zero.
INV	Invalid operation	One or more of the operands of a floating-point operation was an illegal value.
SWC	Software completion	The exception completion qualifier /S was selected for all of the faulting instructions.

4.1.7.2 Unaligned Access Exceptions

Unaligned access exceptions are reported to and handled by the kernel and are precise. Therefore, the address written to the faulting instruction offset of the trap frame is the virtual address of the load or store instruction that accessed the unaligned address.

The PALcode writes the following information into the exception record of the trap frame for an unaligned access exception, where *er* is the exception record pointer.

```
ErExceptionCode(er)          ← STATUS_DATATYPE_MISALIGNMENT
ErExceptionInformation<0>(er)  ← Faulting opcode
ErExceptionInformation<1>(er)  ← Destination register
ErExceptionInformation<2>(er)  ← Unaligned virtual address
ErNumberParameters(er)       ← 3
ErExceptionFlags(er)         ← 0
ErExceptionRecord(er)        ← 0
```

4.1.7.3 Illegal Instruction Exceptions

PALcode raises the following types of illegal operations as illegal instruction exceptions:

- Attempt to execute an instruction with an opcode reserved to DIGITAL.

- Attempt to execute an instruction with an unimplemented PALcode function code.

- Attempt to execute a privileged PALcode instruction from user (unprivileged) mode.

- Attempt to execute an instruction with an illegal operand.

- Attempt to execute an unimplemented/subsetted instruction.

Note:

Instructions with illegal operands cause illegal instruction exceptions to be raised only if the processor raises an exception for these operations.

Illegal instruction exceptions are precise; the faulting address written into the trap frame is the virtual address of the instruction that caused the exception.

The PALcode writes the following information into the exception record of the trap frame for an illegal instruction exception, where *er* is the exception record pointer.

```
ErExceptionCode(er)     ← STATUS_ILLEGAL_INSTRUCTION
ErNumberParameters(er)  ← 0
ErExceptionFlags(er)    ← 0
```

4.1.7.4 Invalid (Non-Canonical Virtual) Address Exceptions

The PALcode raises a general exception if the PALcode detects an invalid faulting virtual address, that is, a faulting virtual address that is not a canonical longword. The implementation must test for the non-canonical format for both data stream and instruction stream translation buffer fills.

For data stream faults, the faulting address written to the trap frame is the virtual address of the instruction that caused the reference to the invalid address.

Instruction stream invalid addresses present a more difficult problem because the exception address itself is invalid and cannot be properly interpreted by a 32-bit operating system. In the case of instruction stream virtual addresses, the ra (return address) register minus 4 (ra–4) is written to the faulting address field of the trap frame. The ra register is used because it probably yields a sane address within the correct program that faulted. Also, the (ra–4) is the most probable faulting address, as the most likely instruction to have caused the fault is: jsr ra, (rx).

The PALcode writes the following information into the exception record of the trap frame for a non-canonical virtual address fault, where *er* is the exception record pointer.

```
ErExceptionCode(er)            ← STATUS_INVALID_ADDRESS
ErExceptionInformation<0>(er)  ← 1 if store; 0 otherwise
ErExceptionInformation<1>(er)  ← invalid va<63..32>
ErExceptionInformation<2>(er)  ← invalid va<31..0>
ErNumberParameters(er)         ← 3
ErExceptionFlags(er)           ← 0
ErExceptionRecord(er)          ← 0
```

4.1.7.5 Software Exceptions

Software may raise exceptions by using the unprivileged gentrap (generate trap) instruction. The gentrap instruction is used to raise exceptions recognized (possibly) in user-mode software for conditions such as divide by zero. (The Alpha architecture does not provide an integer divide instruction; division is accomplished by specialized divide routines.

The gentrap instruction takes a single parameter that is preserved but not interpreted by the PALcode. The gentrap parameter is written into the exception record where it is interpreted by the kernel exception handler. Gentrap uses the STATUS_ALPHA_GENTRAP) status as an exception code. The kernel exception dispatcher interprets the gentrap parameter to determine the appropriate Windows NT Alpha status to raise to the currently executing thread.

The faulting address for a gentrap exception is the virtual address of the executed gentrap instruction.

The PALcode writes the following information into the exception record for a gentrap instruction, where *er* is the exception record pointer:

```
ErExceptionCode(er)            ← STATUS_ALPHA_GENTRAP
ErExceptionInformation<0>(er)  ← gentrap parameter
                                  (a0<31..0> upon execution of gentrap)
ErExceptionInformation<1>(er)  ← gentrap parameter
                                  (a0<63..32> upon execution of gentrap)
ErNumberParameters(er)         ← 2
ErExceptionFlags(er)           ← 0
ErExceptionRecord(er)          ← 0
```

4.1.7.6 Breakpoints and Debugger Support

There are several breakpoint instructions and each raises a general exception. Several of these breakpoints are implemented to support the kernel debugger and are essentially special subroutine calls. The exact semantics of these calls are not important to the PALcode; all breakpoints are handled in the same manner and are distinguished only by the breakpoint type that is written into the exception record.

All breakpoints are implemented as unprivileged PALcode instructions, which allows the kernel to decide whether the breakpoint can be taken in the current mode.

Table 4–3 lists the breakpoint mnemonics and their corresponding breakpoint types:

Table 4–3: Breakpoint Types

Mnemonic	Type	Description
bpt	USER_BREAKPOINT	User breakpoint
kbpt	KERNEL_BREAKPOINT	Kernel breakpoint
callkd	Passed in v0	Call kernel debugger

The faulting instruction address for all breakpoints is the virtual address of the breakpoint instruction.

PALcode completes the exception record for breakpoints as follows, where *er* is the exception record pointer:

```
ErExceptionCode(er) ← STATUS_BREAKPOINT
ErExceptionInformation<0>(er) ← breakpoint type
ErNumberParameters(er) ← 1
ErExceptionFlags(er)    ← 0
ErExceptionRecord(er)   ← 0
```

4.1.7.7 Subsetted IEEE Instruction Exceptions

Floating-point instructions are always enabled. Therefore, FEN (floating enable) faults are not supported.

Hardware Implementation Note:

Windows NT Alpha requires implementation of IEEE floating-point in each processor implementation. The PALcode raises an illegal instruction exception for any subsetted IEEE floating-point instruction — that is, for any IEEE floating-point instruction not implemented in hardware.

VAX floating-point format is not supported.

4.1.7.8 General Exceptions: Common Operations

The common operations for all general exceptions are as follows.

```
previousPSR  ← PSR
if ( PSR<Mode> EQ User ) then
        PSR<Mode> ← kernel
        tp ← (IKSP - TrapFrameLength)! Establish trap pointer
else
        tp ← (sp - TrapFrameLength)  ! Establish trap pointer
```

```
endif
TrIntSp(tp) ← sp
TrIntFp(tp) ← fp
TrIntGp(tp) ← gp
TrIntRa(tp) ← ra
TrIntA0(tp) ← a0
TrIntA1(tp) ← a1
TrIntA2(tp) ← a2
TrIntA3(tp) ← a3
TrPsr(tp) ← previousPSR
TrFir(tp) ← ExceptionPC
sp ← tp
RESTART_ADDRESS ← GENERAL_ENTRY
fp ← sp
gp ← KGP
a0 ← tp + TrExceptionRecord          ! pointer to exception record
a3 ← previousPSR
```

All other general-purpose registers must be preserved across the general exception dispatch.

4.1.8 Panic Exceptions

Severe problems produce panic exceptions. Severe problems are not recoverable; the operating system cannot continue executing normally. Panic exception handling shuts down the machine in a controlled manner that assists in debugging the problem. With the exception of hardware errors, panic exceptions are not expected to occur in the production operating system.

The PALcode raises a panic exception to the kernel and describes the condition that causes the panic with a bugcheck code. When the kernel receives a panic exception, it enters the kernel debugger if it is enabled.

The classes of panic exceptions are:

- Kernel stack corruption
- Unexpected exceptions in PALcode

4.1.8.1 Kernel Stack Corruption

The PALcode can recognize the following types of kernel stack corruption: invalid kernel stack, kernel stack overflow, and kernel stack underflow. The kernel stack for an executing thread must always be valid. The PALcode raises a panic exception if the processor faults when accessing the kernel stack and the page tables indicate that the kernel stack address is not valid. The PALcode may also check for kernel stack underflow and overflow and raise a panic exception if either condition is detected.

The kernel stack is the two pages of virtual address space below the IKSP for a thread, where the IKSP points to the byte beyond the top of the two pages. When raising a kernel stack corruption exception, the PALcode sets the bugcheck code to PANIC_STACK_SWITCH.

4.1.8.2 Unexpected Exceptions

The PALcode may raise a panic exception when it detects an unexpected condition caused by PALcode. Such unexpected conditions are implementation dependent. It is anticipated that those conditions indicate a bug in the PALcode or that the processor is no longer executing correctly. The PALcode raises the bugcheck code TRAP_CAUSE_UNKNOWN.

4.1.8.3 Panic Exception Trap Frame and Dispatch

The PALcode builds a trap frame for the kernel before it dispatches. The PALcode also fills in the exception record that exists within the trap frame.
The PALcode attempts to maintain all possible register state in order to assist in debugging.

The PALcode performs the following operations when dispatching a panic exception to the kernel:

```
previousPSR ← PSR
if ( PSR<Mode> EQ User ) then
        PSR<Mode> ← Kernel
endif
panicStack ← PcPanicStack(PCR)      ! Get the panic stack
tp ← (panicStack - TrapFrameLength)  ! Allocate trap frame
                                     !   on panic stack

TrIntSp(tp)   ← sp
TrIntFp(tp)   ← fp
TrIntGp(tp)   ← gp
TrIntRa(tp)   ← ra
TrIntA0(tp)   ← a0
TrIntA1(tp)   ← a1
TrIntA2(tp)   ← a2
TrIntA3(tp)   ← a3
TrPsr(tp)   ← previousPSR
TrFir(tp)   ← ExceptionPC
sp  ← tp
fp  ← sp
gp  ← KGP
a0  ← NT bugcheck code
a1  ← Exception address
a2, a3, a4  ← Bugcheck parameters
RestartAddress  ← PANIC_ENTRY
```

All other general-purpose registers must be preserved across the panic exception dispatch.

4.2 Interrupts

The PALcode supports two software interrupt levels and an implementation-specific limit of hardware interrupt sources. The Windows NT Alpha PALcode supports eight levels of interrupt priority known as interrupt request levels (IRQL). The supported IRQLs are numbered 0–7.

The platform independence of interrupt dispatch is accomplished via three tables: Interrupt

Level Table, Interrupt Mask Table, and Interrupt Dispatch Table.

4.2.1 Interrupt Level Table (ILT)

The Interrupt Level Table consists of eight entries, indexed 0–7. The index values and symbols for the entries are described in Table 2–1. Each table entry corresponds to an IRQL by its index within the table. The value of each entry is an enable value that indicates which interrupt sources are to be enabled within the processor for the corresponding IRQL. One full longword is reserved for each table entry. The interpretation of the bits within the enable mask is processor specific.

Implementation Note (Software):

The Interrupt Level Table is probably the most important optional set of data that can be cached within the processor. Implementations should consider implementing a PALcode instruction that causes the ILT to be reread and recached within the processor. Some processors may have an effectively hardwired ILT. In such a case, the HAL has no influence over which interrupts are enabled for each IRQL.

4.2.2 Interrupt Mask Table (IMT)

The Interrupt Mask Table relates a mask value of requested interrupts to both an interrupt vector and a synchronization IRQL. The table resolves implicit interrupt priorities because only one interrupt vector can be assigned for each request mask. The IMT is divided into two sub-tables as described in Table 4–4.

Table 4–4: Interrupt Mask Table (IMT)

Index Range	Interrupt Source Description
0–3	Software (2 sources)
4–131	Hardware

Each entry in the table is a longword that consists of two word values: the interrupt vector number and the synchronization level. The use of the software portion of the table is strictly defined and consistent across all processor implementations.

Implementation Note:

In an implementation, the relation between pending interrupts and their interrupt vectors and synchronization levels may be hardwired. In that case, the IMT is not used and the HAL is not able to influence the setting of priority or assignment of interrupts.

The software entries are used only if no hardware interrupts are pending. The entries must be initialized so that deferred procedure call (DPC) software interrupts are higher priority than asynchronous procedure call (APC) software interrupts. The expected initialization of the software portion of the IMT is defined in Table 4–5.

Table 4–5: Software Entries of the IMT

Index	Synchronization Level	Vector
0	PASSIVE_LEVEL = 0	Passive release vector
1	APC_LEVEL = 1	APC dispatch vector
2	DISPATCH_LEVEL = 2	DPC dispatch vector
3	DISPATCH_LEVEL = 2	DPC dispatch vector

The hardware portion of the IMT is designed for flexible use. Each implementation must define a relation f that defines a mapping of requested and enabled hardware interrupt sources to entries in the IMT. The relation f is implementation specific, but f must be a function in the mathematical sense (for each input there is a single unambiguous result). All interrupts other than software interrupts are considered hardware interrupts. Hardware interrupts can include external interrupt signals, performance counter interrupts, and correctable read interrupts.

4.2.3 Interrupt Dispatch Table (IDT)

The Interrupt Dispatch Table (IDT) has an entry for each possible interrupt vector. The possible interrupt vectors are in the range 0–255. Each entry is a longword pointer, which is the virtual address of the interrupt dispatch routine for the vector that corresponds to the index of the entry within the table. The PALcode does not read or write the IDT; it is maintained and used entirely by the kernel and HAL.

4.2.4 Interrupt Dispatch

Interrupt dispatch within the PALcode goes through the following steps:

```
        ! Mask of requested (irr) and enabled (ier) interrupt sources:
irm ← irr AND ier
        ! Retrieve value from interrupt mask table:
CASE
    Hardware Interrupt Pending :
        index = f(irm)
        sirql   ← (IMT<{index*4}>)<Synchronization IRQL>
        vector  ← (IMT<{index*4}>)<InterruptVector>
    Software Interrupt Pending:
        sirql   ← (IMT<{irm*4}>)<Synchronization IRQL>
        vector  ← (IMT<{irm*4}>)<InterruptVector>
    Otherwise:
        Passive release, restart execution
ENDCASE
Set processor to sirql IRQL
if ( processor interrupt ) then
{ acknowledge the interrupt }
endif
```

Once synchronization level has been set and the interrupt service routine has been determined, the PALcode builds a trap frame and dispatches to the kernel interrupt exception handler passing in the interrupt vector.

In the case of software interrupts:

```
previousPsr  ← PSR
if ( PSR<Mode> EQ User ) then
        PSR<Mode>  ← Kernel
        tp  ← (IKSP - TrapFrameLength)   ! Establish trap pointer
else
        tp  ← (sp - TrapFrameLength)     ! Establish trap pointer
endif
TrIntSp(tp) ← sp
TrIntFp(tp) ← fp
TrIntGp(tp) ← gp
TrIntA0(tp) ← a0
TrIntA1(tp) ← a1
TrIntA2(tp) ← a2
TrIntA3(tp) ← a3
TrFir(tp) ← ExceptionPC
TrPsr(tp) ← previousPSR
TrIntRa(tp) ← ra
sp ← tp
fp ← sp
gp ← KGP
a0 ← interrupt vector
a1 ← PCR
a2 ← synchronization IRQL
a3 ← previousPSR
RestartAddress ← INTERRUPT_ENTRY
```

In the case of hardware interrupts:

```
PreviousPSR ← PSR
if ( PSR<Mode> EQ User ) then
        PSR<Mode>  ← Kernel
        tp  ← (IKSP - TrapFrameLength)   ! Establish trap pointer
else
        tp  ← (sp - TrapFrameLength)     ! Establish trap pointer
TrIntSp(tp) ← sp
TrIntFp(tp) ← fp
TrIntGp(tp) ← gp
TrIntA0(tp) ← a0
TrIntA1(tp) ← a1
TrIntA2(tp) ← a2
TrIntA3(tp) ← a3
TrFir(tp) ← ExceptionPC
TrPsr(tp) ← previousPSR
TrIntRa(tp) ← ra
sp ← tp
fp ← sp
```

```
gp ← KGP
a0 ← interrupt vector
a1 ← PCR
a2 ← synchronization IRQL
a3 ← previousPSR
RestartAddress ← INTERRUPT_ENTRY
```

All other general-purpose register values must be preserved across interrupt dispatch.

The kernel uses the rfe instruction to restart the interrupted code sequence.

4.2.5 Interrupt Acknowledge

Interrupts are acknowledged according to their origin. Internal processor interrupts, such as software interrupts and performance counters, are acknowledged by the PALcode. System-level interrupts are acknowledged in the native interrupt dispatch routines.

4.2.6 Synchronization Functions

The swpirql, di, and ei instructions allow the kernel to affect the processor's current interrupt enable state:

- Swpirql swaps the current interrupt request level (IRQL) of the processor. Swpirql takes the new IRQL as a parameter and returns the previous IRQL.

- Di disables all interrupts without changing the current IRQL.

- Ei enables interrupts at the currently set IRQL.

Those instructions and the existence of the interrupt enable bit in the PSR are used as a global interrupt enable for all interrupts.

4.2.7 Software Interrupt Requests

The PALcode includes the software interrupt request register (SIRR), an architected internal processor register, for controlling software interrupt requests. The PALcode also includes two instructions, ssir and csir, to control the state of the SIRR register.

The format of the SIRR is shown in Figure 4–4 and the fields are defined in Table 4–6.

Figure 4–4: Software Interrupt Request Register

Table 4–6: Software Interrupt Request Register Fields

Field	Type	Description
DPC	RW	DPC software interrupt requested
APC	RW	APC software interrupt requested

The ssir and csir instructions affect the state of software interrupt requests

The ssir .instruction sets software interrupt requests by taking as a parameter the interrupt request levels to be set. Setting the appropriate bit in SIRR indicates that the corresponding software interrupt is requested. The csir instruction clears software interrupt requests by taking as a parameter the interrupt request level to be cleared. Clearing the appropriate bit in SIRR indicates that the corresponding software interrupt request has been cleared.

4.3 Machine Checks

Machine checks are initiated when the hardware detects a hardware error condition. However, machine checks are not the only way that detected hardware errors are reported. Hardware error conditions can be reported from three sources:

- At the pin level. Hardware may choose to signal errors via hardware interrupts. PAL-code delivers such hardware error interrupts to the kernel as standard interrupts, where they may be hooked by the HAL for system-specific processing. Such interrupts are not processed by the PALcode as machine checks and are not described in this section.

- From an implementation-dependent internal error interrupt. It is an implementation decision whether to deliver such an interrupt as a standard interrupt or as a machine check. The processing of an interrupt that is delivered as a machine check is described in this section.

- At the machine check hardware vector. Hardware errors that are signaled by the processor through a specific machine check hardware vector are considered machine checks and are described in this section.

The machine check condition may be correctable or uncorrectable. If uncorrectable, the hardware may choose to retry the operation that returned the error.

The PALcode recognizes the following types of machine checks:

- Correctable errors
- Uncorrectable errors
- Catastrophic errors

4.3.1 Correctable Errors

Processor correctable errors are data errors that are detected by the processor and can be reliably corrected. System correctable errors are detected and corrected by the system hardware; incorrect data is not read into the processor.

Correctable errors are maskable by the MCES internal processor register (Figure 4–5). It is recommended that correctable errors be disabled during PALcode initialization and subsequently be explicitly enabled by the HAL. Correctable errors are delivered from the PALcode to allow the HAL to log the errors. The PALcode builds a logout frame with per-processor information that assists the HAL in logging the error.

4.3.2 Uncorrectable Errors

Uncorrectable errors from the processor are detected by the processor and exhibit data errors that cannot be reliably corrected. Actual processor uncorrectable errors are defined by the processor implementation. Uncorrectable errors from the system are detected but not corrected by the system hardware.

Although uncorrectable errors are likely also to be unrecoverable, a mechanism exists in the exception record to allow one or more retries when appropriate. The HAL controls the retry count. For example, a parity error in the I-cache, although uncorrectable, may disappear after an operation retry.

The machine check exception is raised to the HAL to allow per-platform error handling. Uncorrectable errors are delivered immediately upon detection. The PALcode creates a logout frame with per-processor information to assist the HAL in handling the error condition.

4.3.3 Machine Check Error Handling

The general model for machine check handling has the following flow:

1. The PALcode corrects the error, if possible.
2. The PALcode sets the machine to a known state from which restart is possible.
3. The PALcode builds a logout frame describing the detected error.
4. The PALcode sets processor IRQL appropriately (see below).
5. The PALcode dispatches a general exception to the kernel.
6. In the case of a catastrophic error, PALcode returns control to the firmware, as described in Section 4.3.4.

The machine check error summary (MCES) register, Figure 4–5, indicates and controls the current state of the machine check handler for the processor. Table 4–7 describes the MCES register.

Figure 4–5: Machine Check Error Summary

31		5	4	3	2	1	0
Reserved		DSC	DPC	PCE	SCC	SCE	MCK

Table 4–7: Machine Check Error Summary Fields

Field	Type	Description
DMK	RW	Disable all machine checks
DSC	RW	Disable system correctable error reporting
DPC	RW	Disable processor correctable error reporting
PCE	RW	Processor correctable error reported
SCE	RW	System correctable error reported
MCK	RW	Machine check (uncorrectable) reported (see Section 4.3.4)

All machine checks (correctable and uncorrectable) are maskable via the DMK bit in the MCES register. This bit is provided only for debugging systems.

The initial value in MCES is implementation specific but, wherever possible, PALcode attempts to preserve the state of machine check enables from the previous PALcode environment during initialization.

PALcode writes the exception record with the following values for a machine check, where *er* is the exception record pointer.

```
ErExceptionCode(er)          ← DATA_BUS_ERROR
ErExceptionInformation<0>(er) ← machine check type
ErExceptionInformation<1>(er) ← pointer to logout frame
ErNumberParameters(er)       ← 2
ErExceptionFlags(er)         ← 0
ErExceptionRecord(er)        ← 0
```

The two-bit mask that shows the machine check type is shown in Table 4–8.

Table 4–8: Machine Check Types

Machine Check Type	Mask Value (Bits 0:1)
Uncorrectable with no retries	00
Correctable	01
Uncorrectable with retries	10
Reserved	11

The virtual address of the logout frame is a 32-bit superpage address, and the logout frame has a per-processor format.

The draina instruction, when coupled with appropriate implementation-specific native code, can allow software to force completion of all previously executed instructions, such that the previous instructions cannot cause machine checks to be signaled while any instructions subsequent to the draina are executed.

4.3.4 Catastrophic Errors

Although particular catastrophic conditions are specific to the processor implementation, such conditions indicate that the machine is left in a state where execution cannot be reliably restarted. They also indicate that the hardware cannot be trusted to execute properly or the state of data within the system cannot be determined.

An example of a catastrophic condition is a machine check taken while machine check handling is in progress, as indicated by a set MCK bit in the MCES register. Taking a machine check while in the PALcode environment is also considered catastrophic. In those cases, control is returned to the firmware as follows:

1. Further machine check acknowledgement is turned off and a logout frame is generated.

2. The restart block is verified:

   – If the restart block is good, the current state in the restart block is saved, the previous state is restored, and control is returned to the firmware at the restart address.

   – If the restart block is bad, the alternate path is used to re-execute the previous PAL-code image at its entry address. See Section 6.2.1.

Chapter 5

PALcode Instruction Descriptions (II–C)

The PALcode instructions generally follow the Windows NT Alpha calling standard. Arguments are passed in the argument (a0–a5) registers and return values are returned in the value (v0) register. The PALcode instructions also incorporate the following conventions into their own calling standard:

- Unless specific temporary registers are required, only the argument registers a0–a5 are considered volatile.

- Generally, all parameters are passed in registers.

The argument registers are used as volatile registers because often they contain parameters to the PALcode instructions. In strict adherence to the calling standard, the temporary registers t0–t12 could also be considered volatile in the PALcode instructions, but they are not. The temporary registers are not considered necessarily volatile because PALcode instructions generally do not need more free registers. Further, it is convenient in assembly language, from which the PALcode instructions are most frequently called, to be able to assume that temporary registers are preserved across the PALcode instruction.

All parameters to the PALcode instructions are passed in registers. If the number of parameters exceeds the available number of argument registers, additional temporary registers are used as arguments. This precludes the need for callers to build an appropriate stack frame for PALcode instructions with more than six parameters.

The RESTART_ADDRESS register indicates the next execution address when the PALcode exits. Upon entry to each of the PALcode instructions, the RESTART_ADDRESS register is considered to contain the address of the instruction immediately following the PALcode instructions.

A range of privileged PALcode instructions is reserved for processor-implementation-specific PALcode instructions that allow specialized communication between the HAL and the PALcode.

Note:

> The *Operation* part of the PALcode instruction descriptions is shown as an ordered sequence of instructions. The instructions in the sequence may be reordered as long as the results of the sequence of instructions are not altered. In particular, if an instruction j is listed subsequent to an instruction i and i writes any data that is used by j, then i must be executed before j.

5.1 Privileged PALcode Instructions

Table 5–1 summarizes the privileged PALcode instructions.

Table 5–1: Privileged PALcode Instruction Summary

Mnemonic	Description
csir	Clear software interrupt request
dalnfix	Disable alignment fixups
di	Disable interrupts
draina	Drain aborts
dtbis	Data translation buffer invalidate single
ealnfix	Enable alignment fixups
ei	Enable interrupts
halt	Halt the processor
initpal	Initialize the PALcode
initpcr	Initialize PCR data
rdcounters	Read PALcode event counters
rdirql	Read current IRQL
rdksp	Read initial kernel stack
rdmces	Read machine check error summary
rdpcr	Read processor control region address
rdpsr	Read processor status register
rdstate	Read internal processor state
rdthread	Read the current thread value
reboot	Transfer to console or previous PALcode environment
restart	Restart the processor
retsys	Return from system service call
rfe	Return from exception
ssir	Set software interrupt request
swpctx	Swap privileged thread context
swpirql	Swap IRQL
swpksp	Swap initial kernel stack
swppal	Swap PALcode
swpprocess	Swap privileged process context

Table 5–1: Privileged PALcode Instruction Summary (Continued)

Mnemonic	Description
tbia	Translation buffer invalidate all
tbim	Translation buffer invalidate multiple
tbimasn	Translation buffer invalidate multiple for ASN
tbis	Translation buffer invalidate single
tbisasn	Translation buffer invalidate for single ASN
wrentry	Write system entry
wrmccs	Write machine check error summary
wiperfmon	Write performance monitoring values

5.1.1 Clear Software Interrupt Request

Format:

csir   ! PALcode format

Operation:

```
{ a0 = Software interrupt requests to clear }

if ( PSR<Mode> EQ User ) then
        { Initiate illegal instruction exception }
endif
if ( a0<1> EQ 1 ) then
        SIRR<DPC>  ← 0
endif
if ( a0<0> EQ 1 ) then
        SIRR<APC>  ← 0
endif
```

GPR State Change:

a0–a5 are UNPREDICTABLE

IPR State Change:

SIRR ← 0 according to a0

Exceptions:

Illegal Instruction
Machine Checks

Description:

The csir instruction clears the specified bit in the SIRR internal processor register, depending on the contents of a0. See Section 4.2.7.

5.1.2 Disable Alignment Fixups

Format:

```
dalnfix                                                    ! PALcode format
```

Operation:

```
if ( PSR<Mode> EQ User ) then
        { Initiate illegal instruction exception }
endif
{ Implementation-specific state is set to generate alignment fault }
{    exceptions and to prevent alignment fault fixups by the PALcode }
```

GPR State Change:

None

IPR State Change:

None

Exceptions:

Illegal Instruction
Machine Checks

Description:

The dalnfix instruction disables alignment fault fixups in PALcode and generates alignment fault exceptions whenever an alignment fault occurs. After dalnfix is executed on a processor, all alignment faults on that processor are not fixed-up by PALcode and alignment fault exceptions are dispatched to the kernel until the ealnfix instruction is executed on that processor.

5.1.3 Disable All Interrupts

Format:

di   ! PALcode format

Operation:

```
if ( PSR<Mode> EQ User ) then
        { Initiate illegal instruction exception }
endif
PSR<IE>  ← 0
```

GPR State Change:

None

IPR State Change:

PSR<IE> ← 0

Exceptions:

Illegal Instruction
Machine Checks

Description:

The di instruction disables all interrupts by clearing the interrupt enable bit (IE) in the PSR internal processor register. The IRQL field is unaffected. Interrupts may be re-enabled via the ei instruction.

5.1.4 Drain All Aborts Including Machine Checks

Format:

draina   ! PALcode format

Operation:

```
if ( PSR<Mode> EQ User ) then
        { Initiate illegal instruction exception }
endif
{ Implementation-specific drain }
```

GPR State Change:

None

IPR State Change:

None

Exceptions:

Illegal Instruction
Machine Checks

Description:

The draina instruction facilitates the draining of all aborts, including machine checks, from the current processor. When coupled with the appropriate implementation-specific native code, draina can help guarantee that no abort is signaled for an instruction issued before the draina while any instruction issued subsequent to the draina is executing.

5.1.5 Data Translation Buffer Invalidate Single

Format:

dtbis   ! PALcode format

Operation:

```
{ a0 = Virtual address of translation to invalidate }

if ( PSR<MODE> EQ User ) then
        { Initiate illegal instruction exception }
endif
{ Invalidate all translations in the data stream for the }
{   virtual address in a0 }
```

GPR State Change:

a0–a5 are UNPREDICTABLE

IPR State Change:

None

Exceptions:

Illegal Instruction
Machine Checks

Description:

The dtbis instruction invalidates a single data stream translation. The translation for the virtual address in a0 must be invalidated in all data translation buffers and in all virtual data caches.

5.1.6 Enable Alignment Fixups

Format:

ealnfix   ! PALcode format

Operation:

```
if ( PSR<Mode> EQ User ) then
        { Initiate illegal instruction exception }
endif
{ Implementation-specific state is set to fix up alignment fault }
{    by the PALcode }
```

GPR State Change:

None

IPR State Change:

None

Exceptions:

Illegal Instruction
Machine Checks

Description:

The ealnfix instruction enables alignment fault fixups in PALcode and prevents alignment
fault exceptions. After ealnfix is executed on a processor, all alignment faults on that processor are fixed-up by PALcode and no alignment fault exceptions are dispatched to the kernel
until the dalnfix instruction is executed on that processor.

The default state is disabled alignment fixups in PALcode.

5.1.7 Enable Interrupts

Format:

ei   ! PALcode format

Operation:

```
if ( PSR<MODE> EQ User ) then
        { Initiate illegal instruction exception }
endif
PSR<IE>  ← 1
```

GPR State Change:

None

IPR State Change:

PSR<IE> ← 1

Exceptions:

Illegal Instruction
Machine Checks

Description:

The ei instruction sets the interrupt enable (IE) bit in the PSR internal processor register, thus enabling those interrupts that are at the appropriate level for the current IRQL field in the PSR.

5.1.8 Halt the Operating System by Trapping to Illegal Instruction

Format:

halt   ! PALcode format

Operation:

```
{ Initiate illegal instruction exception }
```

GPR State Change:

See Section 4.1.7.3 for illegal instruction exception handling.

IPR State Change:

See Section 4.1.7.3 for illegal instruction exception handling.

Exceptions:

Illegal Instruction

Description:

The halt instruction forces an illegal instruction exception. See the reboot instruction, Section 5.1.19, for transferring control to the console or previous PALcode environment.

5.1.9 Initialize PALcode Data Structures with Operating System Values

Format:

initpal   ! PALcode format

Operation:
```
{ a0 = Page directory entry (PDE) page, superpage 32 address }
{ a1 = Initial thread value }
{ a2 = Initial TEB value }
{ gp = Kernel global pointer }
{ sp = Initial kernel stack pointer }

if ( PSR<MODE> EQ User ) then
        { Initiate illegal instruction exception }
endif
PDR        ← (a0 BIC 80000000₁₆ )
THREAD     ← a1
TEB        ← a2
IKSP       ← sp
KGP        ← gp
PcPalBaseAddress(PCR)          ← PAL_BASE
PcPalMajorVersion(PCR)         ← PalMajorVersion
PcPalMinorVersion(PCR)         ← PalMinorVersion
PcPalSequenceVersion(PCR)      ← PalSequenceVersion
PcPalMajorSpecification(PCR)   ← PalMajorSpecification
PcPalMinorSpecification(PCR)   ← PalMinorSpecification
v0  ← PAL_BASE
```

GPR State Change:
```
v0 ← PAL_BASE
a0–a5 are UNPREDICTABLE
```

IPR State Change:
```
PDR ← a0
THREAD ← a1
TEB ← a2
IKSP ← sp
KGP ← gp
```

Exceptions:

Illegal Instruction
Machine Checks

Description:

The initpal instruction is called early in the kernel initialization sequence to establish IPR values for the initial thread PDR, THREAD, TEB, and IKSP. The IPR value KGP persists for the life of the system. In addition, initpal writes the PALcode version information into the PCR.

On return from the initpal instruction, the return value register, v0, contains the PAL_BASE register, the base address in 32-bit superpage (kseg0) format.

5.1.10 Initialize Processor Control Region Data

Format:

      initpcr   ! PALcode format

Operation:

```
if ( PSR<MODE> EQ User ) then
        { Initiate illegal instruction exception }
endif
{ Cache portions of Interrupt Level Table and Processor Control Region }
{    data in implementation-dependent manner }
```

GPR State Change:

a0–a4 are UNPREDICTABLE

IPR State Change:

None

Exceptions:

Illegal Instruction
Machine Checks

Description:

The initpcr instruction caches process-specific information, including parts of the Interrupt Level Table (ILT), for use by the PALcode. See Section 6.1.4 for information on the ILT.

5.1.11 Read the Software Event Counters

Format:

      rdcounters   ! PALcode format

Operation:

```
{ a0 = Pointer to 32-bit superpage address of counter record buffer. }
{      Address must be quadword aligned }
{ a1 = Length of buffer in bytes }

if ( PSR<MODE> EQ User ) then
        { Initiate illegal instruction exception }
endif
{ Dump event counter values to the counter record }
v0  ←  status
```

GPR State Change:

    v0 ← status
    a0–a5 are UNPREDICTABLE

IPR State Change:

    None

Exceptions:

    Illegal Instruction
    Machine Checks

Description:

For debug PALcode (see Section 5.3), rdcounters causes that PALcode to write the state of its internal software event counters into an implementation-specific counter record pointed to by the address passed in the a0 register. For production PALcode, rdcounters returns a status value of zero, indicating that it is not implemented in the current PALcode image.

On return from rdcounters, v0 contains the status as follows:

If v0 = 0	Interface is not implemented.
If v0 ≤ a1	v0 is length of data returned.
If v0 > a1	No data is returned and v0 is length of processor implementation counter record.

5.1.12 Read the Current IRQL from the PSR

Format:

    rdirql   ! PALcode format

Operation:

```
if ( PSR<MODE> EQ User ) then
        { Initiate illegal instruction exception }
endif
v0  ← PSR<IRQL>
```

GPR State Change:

    v0 ← <IRQL>

IPR State Change:

    None

Exceptions:

    Illegal Instruction
    Machine Checks

Description:

The rdirql instruction returns in v0 the contents of the interrupt request level (IRQL) field of the PSR internal processor register.

5.1.13 Read Initial Kernel Stack Pointer for the Current Thread

Format:

rdksp   ! PALcode format

Operation:

```
if ( PSR<MODE> EQ User ) then
        { Initiate illegal instruction exception }
endif
v0  ← IKSP
```

GPR State Change:

v0 ← <IKSP>

IPR State Change:

None

Exceptions:

Illegal Instruction
Machine Checks

Description:

The rdksp instruction returns in v0 the contents of the IKSP (initial kernel stack pointer) internal processor register for the currently executing thread.

5.1.14 Read the Machine Check Error Summary Register

Format:

    rdmces   ! PALcode format

Operation:

```
if ( PSR<MODE> EQ User ) then
        { Initiate illegal instruction exception }
endif
v0  ← MCES
```

GPR State Change:

    v0 ← MCES

IPR State Change:

Exceptions:

Illegal Instruction
Machine Checks

Description:

The rdmces instruction returns in v0 the contents of the machine check error summary (MCES) internal processor register.

5.1.15 Read the Processor Control Region Base Address

Format:

      rdpcr   ! PALcode format

Operation:

```
if ( PSR<MODE> EQ User ) then
        { Initiate illegal instruction exception }
endif
v0  ← PCR
```

GPR State Change:

    v0 ← PCR

IPR State Change:

    None

Exceptions:

    Illegal Instruction

    Machine Checks

Description:

The rdpcr instruction returns in v0 the contents of the PCR internal processor register (the base address value of the processor control region).

5.1.16 Read the Current Processor Status Register (PSR)

Format:

      rdpsr   ! PALcode format

Operation:

```
if ( PSR<MODE> EQ User ) then
        { Initiate illegal instruction exception }
endif
v0  ← PSR
```

GPR State Change:

v0 ← PSR

IPR State Change:

None

Exceptions:

Illegal Instruction
Machine Checks

Description:

The rdpsr instruction returns in v0 the contents of the current PSR (Processor Status Register) internal processor register.

5.1.17 Read the Current Internal Processor State

Format:

```
rdstate                                             ! PALcode format
```

Operation:

```
{ a0 = Pointer to 32-bit superpage address of state record buffer. }
{        Address must be quadword aligned }
{ a1 = Length of buffer in bytes }


if ( PSR<MODE> EQ User ) then
        { Initiate Illegal instruction exception }
endif
{ Dump internal processor state record to processor state buffer }
v0  ←  status
```

GPR State Change:

> v0 ← status
>
> a0–a5 are UNPREDICTABLE

IPR State Change:

> None

Exceptions:

> Illegal Instruction
>
> Machine Checks

Description:

The rdstate instruction writes the internal processor state to the internal processor state buffer pointed to by the address passed in the a0 register. The form and content of the internal processor state buffer are implementation specific.

On return from the rdstate instruction, the return value register, v0, contains the status as follows:

> If v0 = 0   Interface is not implemented.
>
> If v0 ≤ a1   v0 is length of data returned.
>
> If v0 > a1   No data is returned and v0 is length of processor implementation counter record.

5.1.18 Read the Thread Value for the Current Thread

Format:

    rdthread   ! PALcode format

Operation:

```
if ( PSR<MODE> EQ User ) then
        { Initiate illegal instruction exception }
endif
v0  ←  THREAD
```

GPR State Change:

v0 ← THREAD

IPR State Change:

None

Exceptions:

Illegal Instruction

Machine Checks

Description:

The rdthread instruction returns in v0 the contents of the THREAD internal processor register (for the currently executing thread).

5.1.19 Reboot — Transfer to Console Firmware

Format:

> reboot   ! PALcode format

Operation:

```
if ( PSR<MODE> EQ User ) then
        { Initiate illegal instruction exception }
endif
RestartBlockPointer  ←  PcRestartBlock(PCR )
{ If cannot verify restart block, restart previous PALcode }
{ Save general register state in saved state area }
{ Save internal processor register state in saved state area, }
{   includes PAL_BASE }
{ Save implementation-specific data in saved state area }
{ Set the saved state length in restart block }
{ Compute and store Checksum for restart block }
{ Restore previous privileged state }
PAL_BASE  ←  previous_PAL_BASE.
RESTART_ADDRESS  ←  PcFirmwareRestartAddress(PCR)
```

GPR State Change:

All registers are UNPREDICTABLE

IPR State Change:

PAL_BASE ← previous_PAL_BASE

RESTART_ADDRESS ← PcFirmwareRestartAddress(PCR)

All other registers are UNPREDICTABLE

Exceptions:

Illegal Instruction

Machine Checks

Description:

The reboot instruction stops the operating system from executing and returns execution to the boot environment. Reboot is responsible for completing the ARC Restart Block before returning to the boot environment. The PALcode must accomplish two tasks to restore the boot environment: re-establish the boot environment PALcode and restart execution in the boot environment at the Firmware Restart Address.

5.1.20 Restart the Operating System from the Restart Block

Format:

    restart   ! PALcode format

Operation:

```
{ a0 = Pointer to ARC restart block with Alpha  saved state area }

if ( PSR<MODE> EQ User ) then
        { Initiate illegal instruction exception }
endif
{ Verify restart block }
{   if invalid then return to caller }
RestartBlockPointer  ← PcRestartBlock(PCR)
{ Restore general register state from saved state area }
{ Restore internal processor register state from saved state area, }
{ Restore implementation-specific data from saved state area }
RESTART_ADDRESS  ← RbRestartAddress(RestartBlockPointer)
```

GPR State Change:

All registers are UNPREDICTABLE

IPR State Change:

RESTART_ADDRESS ← RbRestartAddress(RestartBlockPointer)

All other registers are UNPREDICTABLE

Exceptions:

Illegal Instruction
Machine Checks

Description:

The restart instruction restores saved processor state and resumes execution of the operating system.

5.1.21 Return from System Service Call Exception

Format:

```
retsys                                                    ! PALcode format
```

Operation:

```
{ a0 = Previous PSR }
{ a1 = New software interrupt requests }
{ fp = Pointer to trap frame }
{ v0 = Return status from system service }

if ( PSR<MODE> EQ User ) then
        { Initiate illegal instruction exception }
endif
if ( a1<1> EQ 1 ) then
        SIRR<DPC>  ← 1
endif
if ( a1<0> EQ 1 ) then
        SIRR<APC>  ← 1
endif
TrapFrame  ← fp
ra   ← TrIntRa(TrapFrame)
gp   ← TrIntGp(TrapFrame)
fp   ← TrIntFp(TrapFrame)
sp   ← TrIntSp(TrapFrame)
RESTART_ADDRESS  ← TrFir(TrapFrame)
PSR  ← a0
{ Clear lock_flag register }
{ Clear intr_flag register }
```

GPR State Change:

ra ← TrIntRa(TrapFrame)

gp ← TrIntGp(TrapFrame)

fp ← TrIntFp(TrapFrame)

sp ← TrIntSp(TrapFrame)

at, t0–t12, a –a5 are UNPREDICTABLE

IPR State Change:

PSR ← a0

RESTART_ADDRESS ← TrFir(TrapFrame)

SIRR ← a1<1...0>

Exceptions:

    Illegal Instruction

    Machine Checks

    Invalid Kernel Stack

Description:

The retsys instruction returns from a system service call exception by unwinding the trap frame, clearing the lock_flag and intr_flag (interrupt flag) registers, and returning to the code stream that was executing when the original exception was initiated. Retsys must return to the native code stream; it is illegal for retsys to return to the PALcode environment and that must be guaranteed not to happen. In addition, retsys accepts a parameter to set software interrupt requests that became pending while the exception was handled.

Retsys is similar to the rfe instruction, with the following exceptions:

1. Retsys need not restore the argument registers a0–a3 from the trap frame.

2. Retsys need not preserve volatile register state.

3. Retsys returns to the address in the ra register at the point of the callsys rather than the faulting instruction address (the ra was written to the faulting instruction address by callsys).

5.1.22 Return from Exception or Interrupt

Format:

```
rfe                                                    ! PALcode format
```

Operation:

```
{ a0 = Previous PSR }
{ a1 = New software interrupt requests }
{ fp = Pointer to trap frame }

if ( PSR<MODE> EQ User ) then
        { Initiate illegal instruction exception }
endif
if ( a1<1> EQ 1 ) then
        SIRR<DPC>  ← 1
endif
if ( a1<0> EQ 1 ) then
        SIRR<APC>  ← 1
endif

PSR  ← a0
TrapFrame  ← fp
a0  ← TrIntA0(TrapFrame)
a1  ← TrIntA1(TrapFrame)
a2  ← TrIntA2(TrapFrame)
a3  ← TrIntA3(TrapFrame)
ra  ← TrIntRa(TrapFrame)
gp  ← TrIntGp(TrapFrame)
fp  ← TrIntFp(TrapFrame)
sp  ← TrIntSp(TrapFrame)
RESTART_ADDRESS  ← TrFir(TrapFrame)

{ Clear lock_flag register }
```

GPR State Change:

```
a0  ← TrIntA0(TrapFrame)
a1  ← TrIntA1(TrapFrame)
a2  ← TrIntA2(TrapFrame)
a3  ← TrIntA3(TrapFrame)
ra  ← TrIntRa(TrapFrame)
gp  ← TrIntGp(TrapFrame)
fp  ← TrIntFp(TrapFrame)
sp  ← TrIntSp(TrapFrame)
```

IPR State Change:

   PSR ← a0
   RESTART_ADDRESS ← TrFir(TrapFrame)
   SIRR ← a1<1...0>

Exceptions:

   Illegal Instruction
   Machine Checks
   Invalid Kernel Stack

Description:

The rfe instruction returns from exceptions or interrupts by unwinding the trap frame, clearing the lock_flag register, and returning to the code stream that was executing when the original exception or interrupt was initiated. Rfe must return to the native code stream; it is illegal for rfe to return to the PALcode environment and that must be guaranteed not to happen. In addition, rfe accepts a parameter to set software interrupt requests that became pending while the event was handled.

5.1.23 Set Software Interrupt Request

Format:

     ssir   ! PALcode format

Operation:

```
{ a0 = Software interrupt requests to set }

if ( PSR<MODE> EQ User ) then
        {Initiate illegal instruction exception }
endif
if ( a0<1> EQ 1 ) then
        SIRR<DPC>  ← 1
endif
if ( a0<0> EQ 1 ) then
        SIRR<APC>  ← 1
endif
```

GPR State Change:

a –a5 are UNPREDICTABLE

IPR State Change:

SIRR ← a0<1...0>

Exceptions:

Illegal Instruction
Machine Checks

Description:

The ssir instruction sets software interrupt requests by setting the appropriate bits in the SIRR internal processor register. See Section 4.2.7.

5.1.24 Swap Thread Context

Format:

swpctx   ! PALcode format

Operation:

```
{ a0 = New initial kernel stack va }
{ a1 = New thread address }
{ a2 = New thread environment block pointer }
{ a3 = New address space page frame number (PFN) }
{      or a negative number }
{ a4 = ASN }
{ a5 = ASN_wrap_indicator }

if ( PSR<MODE> EQ User ) then
        { Initiate illegal instruction exception }
endif
IKSP    ← a0
THREAD  ← a1
TEB     ← a2
ASN_wrap_indicator  ← a5
if ( a3 GE 0 ) then         ! swap address space
    temp  ← SHIFT_LEFT( a3, PAGE_SHIFT )
    PDR   ← temp
    ASN   ← a4
    if ( ASN_wrap_indicator NE 0 ) then
        { invalidate all translations and virtual cache blocks }
        {   for which ASM EQ 0 }
    endif
endif

{   Where: }
{       2**PAGE_SHIFT = implementation page size }
```

GPR State Change:

a0 a5 are UNPREDICTABLE

IPR State Change:

```
IKSP ← a0
THREAD ← a1
TEB ← a2
PDR ← a3 (possibly)
ASN ← a4 (possibly)
```

Exceptions:

Illegal Instruction
Machine Checks

Description:

The swpctx instruction swaps the privileged portions of thread context. Thread context is swapped by establishing the new IKSP, THREAD, and TEB internal processor register values.

Swpctx may also swap the address space (or process) for the new thread. If the new thread is in the same process (address space) as the previous thread, the kernel passes a negative value for the page frame number (PFN) in the page directory page, indicating that the address space need not be switched. If the PFN is zero or a positive number, it is used to swap the address space, just as if swpprocess had been executed.

5.1.25 Swap the Current IRQL (Interrupt Request Level)

Format:

swpirql   ! PALcode format

Operation:

```
{ a0 = New IRQL }

if ( PSR<MODE> EQ User ) then
        { Initiate illegal instruction exception }
endif
v0  ← PSR<IRQL>
PSR<IRQL>  ← a0
```

GPR State Change:

v0 ← PSR<IRQL>
a0–a5 are UNPREDICTABLE

IPR State Change:

PSR<IRQL> ← a0

Exceptions:

Illegal Instruction
Machine Checks

Description:

The swpirql instruction swaps the current IRQL field in the PSR internal processor register for the specified new IRQL, setting the processor so that only interrupts permitted by the new IRQL are enabled. Swpirql updates the IRQL field and returns in v0 the previous IRQL.

5.1.26 Swap the Initial Kernel Stack Pointer (IKSP) for the Current Thread

Format:

```
swpksp                                                      ! PALcode format
```

Operation:

```
{ a0 = New IKSP }

if ( PSR<MODE> EQ User ) then
        { Initiate illegal instruction exception }
endif
v0  ← IKSP
IKSP  ← a0
```

GPR State Change:

```
v0 ← IKSP
a0–a5 are  UNPREDICTABLE
```

IPR State Change:

```
IKSP ← a0
```

Exceptions:

Illegal Instruction
Machine Checks

Description:

The swpksp instruction returns in v0 the value of the previous IKSP internal processor register and writes a new IKSP for the currently executing thread.

5.1.27 Swap the Currently Executing PALcode

Format:

swppal   ! PALcode format

Operation:

```
{ a0 = Physical base address of new PALcode }
{ a1-a5 = Arguments to the new PALcode environment }

if ( PSR<MODE> EQ User ) then
        { Initiate illegal instruction exception }
endif
{ load processor-dependent  parameters }
{ jump to address in a0 as a physical address in }
{   the PALcode environment }
```

GPR State Change:

at and t0–t12 are UNPREDICTABLE or contain processor-dependent parameters

IPR State Change:

None

Exceptions:

Illegal Instruction
Machine Checks

Description:

The swppal instruction swaps the currently executing PALcode by transferring to the base address of the new PALcode image (provided in a0) in the PALcode environment.

5.1.28 Swap Process Context (Swap Address Space)

Format:

```
swpprocess                                              ! PALcode format
```

Operation:

```
    { a0 = Page frame number (PFN) of new PDR }
    { a1 = Address space number (ASN) of new process }
    { a2 = Address space number wrap indicator (ASN_wrap_indicator): }
    {          zero = no wrap }
    {       nonzero = wrap }

    if ( PSR<MODE> EQ User ) then
            { Initiate illegal instruction exception }
    endif
    temp    ← SHIFT_LEFT( a0, PAGE_SHIFT )
    PDR     ← temp
    ASN     ← a1
        if ( ASN_wrap_indicator NE 0 ) then
            { Invalidate all translations and virtual cache blocks }
            {    for which ASM EQ 0 }
        endif

    {   Where: }
    {          2**PAGE_SHIFT = implementation page size }
```

GPR State Change:

a0–a5 are UNPREDICTABLE

IPR State Change:

PDR ← a0

ASN ← a1

Exceptions:

Illegal Instruction

Machine Checks

Description:

The swpprocess instruction swaps the privileged process context by changing the address
space for the currently executing thread. The address space change is accomplished by establishing a new PDR and ASN. If the ASN_wrap_indicator passed in a2 is nonzero, swpprocess
causes invalidation of all translation buffer entries and virtual cache blocks that have a clear
address space match (ASM) bit.

5.1.29 Translation Buffer Invalidate All

Format:

    tbia   ! PALcode format

Operation:

```
if ( PSR<MODE> EQ User ) then
        { Initiate illegal instruction exception }
endif
{ Invalidate all translations and virtual cache blocks }
{   within the processor }
```

GPR State Change:

a –a5 are UNPREDICTABLE

IPR State Change:

None

Exceptions:

Illegal Instruction
Machine Checks

Description:

The tbia instruction invalidates all translations and virtual cache blocks within the processor.

5.1.30 Translation Buffer Invalidate Multiple

Format:

```
tbim                                                    ! PALcode format
```

Operation:

```
{ a0 = Pointer to array of virtual addresses to invalidate }
{ a1 = Number of virtual addresses to invalidate }

if ( PSR<MODE> EQ User ) then
        { Initiate illegal instruction exception }
endif
{ Invalidate translations for virtual addresses pointed to in a0 for }
{   the number of entries in a1. Invalidate in all translation   }
{   buffers and all virtual caches }
```

GPR State Change:

a0–a5 are UNPREDICTABLE

IPR State Change:

None

Exceptions:

Illegal Instruction
Machine Checks

Description:

The tbim instruction invalidates multiple virtual translations for the current ASN. The translations for the virtual address must be invalidated in all processor translation buffers and virtual caches.

5.1.31 Translation Buffer Invalidate Multiple for ASN

Format:

tbimasn   ! PALcode format

Operation:

```
{ a0 = Pointer to array of virtual addresss to invalidate }
{ a1 = Number of virtual addesses to invalidate }
{ a2 = Address space number (ASN) }

if ( PSR<MODE> EQ User ) then
        { Initiate illegal instruction exception }
endif
{ Invalidate translations for the virtual addresses in the array }
{   pointed to in a0, for the number of entries in a1, that match the }
{   ASN in a2. Invalidate in all translation buffers and virtual caches }
```

GPR State Change:

a0–a5 are UNPREDICTABLE

IPR State Change:

None

Exceptions:

Illegal Instruction
Machine Checks

Description:

The tbimasn instruction invalidates multiple virtual translations for a specified ASN. The translations for the virtual addresses must be invalidated in all processor translation buffers and virtual caches.

5.1.32 Translation Buffer Invalidate Single

Format:

tbis   ! PALcode format

Operation:

```
{ a0 = Virtual address of translation to invalidate }

if ( PSR<MODE> EQ User ) then
        { Initiate illegal instruction exception }
endif
{ Invalidate all translations for the virtual address in a0, }
{    invalidate in all translation buffers and all virtual caches }
```

GPR State Change:

a0–a5 are UNPREDICTABLE

IPR State Change:

None

Exceptions:

Illegal Instruction
Machine Checks

Description:

The tbis instruction invalidates a single virtual translation. The translation for the passed virtual address must be invalidated in all processor translation buffers and virtual caches.

5.1.33 Translation Buffer Invalidate Single for ASN

Format:

tbisasn   ! PALcode format

Operation:

```
{ a0 = Virtual address of translation to invalidate }
{ a1 = Address space number (ASN) }

if ( PSR<MODE> EQ User ) then
        { Initiate illegal instruction exception }
endif
{ Invalidate the translation for the virtual address in a0 }
{   that matches the ASN in a1. The translation must be invalidated }
{    in all translation buffers and virtual caches }
```

GPR State Change:

a0–a5 are UNPREDICTABLE

IPR State Change:

None

Exceptions:

Illegal Instruction
Machine Checks

Description:

The tbisasn instruction invalidates a single virtual translation for a specified address space number. The translation for the passed virtual address must be invalidated in all processor translation buffers and virtual caches.

5.1.34 Write Kernel Exception Entry Routine

Format:

```
wrentry                                                    ! PALcode format
```

Operation:

```
{ a0 = Address of exception entry routine, 32-bit }
{        superpage address }
{ a1 = Exception class value }

if ( PSR<MODE> EQ User ) then
        { Initiate illegal instruction exception }
endif
case a1 begin
       0:
                PANIC_ENTRY  ← a0
                break;
       1:
                MEM_MGMT_ENTRY  ← a0
                break;
       2:
                INTERRUPT_ENTRY  ← a0
                break;
       3:
                SYSCALL_ENTRY  ← a0
                break;
       4:
                GENERAL_ENTRY  ← a0
                break;
       otherwise:
                { Initiate panic exception }
endcase;
```

GPR State Change:

a0–a5 are UNPREDICTABLE

IPR State Change:

*_ENTRY ← a0

Exceptions:

Illegal Instruction
Machine Checks
Panic Exception

Description:

The wrentry instruction provides the registry of exception handling routines for the exception classes. The address in a0 is registered for the exception class corresponding to the exception class value in a1. The kernel must use wrentry to register an exception handler for each of the exception classes. The relationship between the exception classes and class values is shown in Table 5–2.

Table 5–2: Exception Class Values

Exception Class	Value
Panic exceptions	0
Memory management exceptions	1
Interrupt exceptions	2
System service call exceptions	3
General exceptions	4

5.1.35 Write the Machine Check Error Summary Register

Format:

wrmces   ! PALcode format

Operation:

```
{a0 = New values for the machine check error }
{         summary (MCES) register. }

if ( PSR<MODE> EQ User ) then
        { Initiate illegal instruction exception }
endif
v0  ← MCES
MCES<DMK>  ← a0<5>
MCES<DSC>  ← a0<4>
MCES<DPC>  ← a0<3>
if ( a0<2> EQ 1 ) then
      MCES<PCE>  ← 0
endif
if ( a0<1> EQ 1 ) then
      MCES<SCE>  ← 0
endif
if( a0<0> EQ 1 ) then
      MCES<MCK>  ← 0
endif
```

GPR State Change:

v0 ← previous MCES

IPR State Change:

MCES ← a0

Exceptions:

Illegal Instruction
Machine Checks

Description:

The wrmces instruction writes new values for the MCES internal processor register and returns in v0 the previous values of that register.

5.1.36 Write Performance Counter Interrupt Control Information

Format:

    wrperfmon   ! PALcode format

Operation:

```
if ( PSR<MODE> EQ User ) then
        { Initiate illegal instruction exception }
endif

{ a0 - a5 contain implementation-specific input values }
```

GPR State Change:

    v0 ← implementation-dependent value

    a0–a5 are UNPREDICTABLE

IPR State Change:

    None

Exceptions:

    Illegal Instruction

    Machine Checks

Description:

The wrperfmon instruction controls any performance monitoring mechanisms in the processor and PALcode. The wrperfmon instruction arguments and actions are chip dependent, and when defined for an implementation, are described in Appendix E.

5.2 Unprivileged PALcode Instructions

Table 5–3: Unprivileged PALcode Instruction Summary

Mnemonic	Description
bpt	Breakpoint trap
callkd	Call kernel debugger
callsys	Call system service
gentrap	Generate trap
imb	Instruction memory barrier
kbpt	Kernel breakpoint trap
rdteb	Read thread environment block pointer

5.2.1 Breakpoint Trap (Standard User-Mode Breakpoint)

Format:

      bpt   ! PALcode format

Operation:

See Sections 4.1.7.8 and 4.1.7.6

GPR State Change:

See Sections 4.1.7.8 and 4.1.7.6

IPR State Change:

See Sections 4.1.7.8 and 4.1.7.6

Exceptions:

Machine Checks

Kernel Stack Invalid

Description:

The bpt instruction raises a breakpoint general exception to the kernel, setting a USER_BREAKPOINT breakpoint type.

5.2.2 Call Kernel Debugger

Format:

```
callkd                                              ! PALcode format
```

Operation:

```
{v0 = Type of breakpoint }
See Sections 4.1.7.8 and 4.1.7.6
```

GPR State Change:

```
See Sections 4.1.7.8 and 4.1.7.6
```

IPR State Change:

```
See Sections 4.1.7.8 and 4.1.7.6
```

Exceptions:

Machine Checks

Kernel Stack Invalid

Description:

The callkd instruction raises a breakpoint general exception to the kernel, setting the break-point type with the value supplied in v0. The callkd instruction implements special calls to the kernel debugger.

5.2.3 System Service Call

Format:

```
callsys                                                    ! PALcode format
```

Operation:

```
{ v0 = System service code }
{ a0-a5 = System call arguments }
previousPSR  ← PSR
if( PSR<MODE> EQ UserMode ) then
        PSR<MODE>  ← KernelMode
        tp  ← (IKSP - TrapFrameLength)    ! Establish trap pointer
else
        tp  ← (sp - TrapFrameLength)      ! Establish trap pointer
endif
TrIntSp(tp)  ← sp
TrIntFp(tp)  ← fp
TrIntRa(tp)  ← ra
TrIntGp(tp)  ← gp
TrFir(tp)    ← ra
TrPsr(tp)    ← previousPSR
gp  ← KGP
sp  ← tp
fp  ← tp
t0  ← previousPSR<MODE>
t1  ← THREAD
RESTART_ADDRESS  ← SYSCALL_ENTRY
```

GPR State Change:

```
fp ← tp
gp ← KGP
sp ← tp
t0 ← PSR
t1 ← THREAD
at and t0–t12 are  UNPREDICTABLE
```

IPR State Change:

```
PSR<MODE> ← KernelMode
RESTART_ADDRESS ← SYSCALL_ENTRY
```

Exceptions:

Machine Checks
Kernel Stack Invalid

Description:

The callsys instruction raises a system service call exception to the kernel. The system service call has the software semantics of a standard procedure call. That is, arguments are passed in argument registers and on the stack, volatile registers are considered free, and nonvolatile registers must be preserved across the call. In addition to the standard calling sequence, callsys is passed the number of the desired system service in the return value register v0. Callsys does not interpret this value, but rather passes it directly to the operating system.

Callsys switches to kernel mode if necessary, builds a trap frame on the kernel stack, and then enters the kernel at the kernel system service exception handler. See Section 4.1.6.

The argument registers must be preserved through the instruction. Standard control information, such as the previous PSR, is stored in the trap frame. Callsys then restarts execution at the kernel system service call exception entry, passing the previous mode as a parameter in the t0 register, and the current thread as a parameter in the t1 register.

5.2.4 Generate a Trap

Format:

gentrap   ! PALcode format

Operation:

```
{ a0 = Trap number that identifies exception }

See Sections 4.1.7.8 and 4.1.7.5
```

GPR State Change:

```
See Sections 4.1.7.8 and 4.1.7.5
```

IPR State Change:

```
See Sections 4.1.7.8 and 4.1.7.5
```

Exceptions:

Machine Checks
Kernel Stack Invalid

Description:

The gentrap instruction generates a software general exception to the current thread. The exception code is generated from a trap number that is specified as an input parameter. Gentrap is used to raise software-detected exceptions such as bound check errors or overflow conditions.

5.2.5 Instruction Memory Barrier

Format:

imb   ! PALcode format

Operation:

```
{ From within kernel mode, make processor }
{    instruction stream coherent with main memory }
```

GPR State Change:

None

IPR State Change:

None

Exceptions:

Machine Checks

Description:

The imb instruction may only be called from kernel mode and guarantees that all subsequent instruction stream fetches are coherent with respect to main memory on the current processor. Imb must be issued before executing code in memory that has been modified (either by stores from the processor or DMA from an I/O processor). See Common Architecture, Chapter 6.

User-mode software must not use the imb instruction, but rather use the appropriate Windows NT interface to make the I-cache coherent.

5.2.6 Kernel Breakpoint Trap

Format:

kbpt   ! PALcode format

Operation:

See Sections 4.1.7.8 and 4.1.7.6

GPR State Change:

See Sections 4.1.7.8 and 4.1.7.6

IPR State Change:

See Sections 4.1.7.8 and 4.1.7.6

Exceptions:

Machine Checks
Kernel Stack Invalid

Description:

The kbpt instruction raises a breakpoint general exception to the kernel, setting a
KERNEL_BREAKPOINT breakpoint type.

5.2.7 Read Thread Environment Block Pointer

Format:

rdteb   ! PALcode format

Operation:

v0 ← TEB

GPR State Change:

v0 ← TEB

IPR State Change:

None

Exceptions:

Machine Checks

Description:

The rdteb instruction returns in v0 the contents of the TEB internal processor register for the currently executing thread (the base address of the thread environment block). See Section 2.7.

5.3 Debug PALcode and Free PALcode

The debug PALcode is a functional superset of the production PALcode, which is specified in this document. The debug PALcode includes extra counters for performance evaluation and additional sanity checks. An unacceptable performance loss would occur if these features were implemented in production PALcode. Therefore, the debug PALcode is used in the laboratory only.

The debug PALcode contains the following additional features:

- Kernel stack underflow/overflow checking

- Special I/O address checking

- Event counters

5.3.1 Kernel Stack Checking

The debug PALcode checks for kernel stack underflow and overflow whenever it allocates a trap frame and the previous mode was kernel mode. Two pages of kernel stack are allocated for each thread.

- Underflow occurs when the thread's kernel mode stack pointer (SP) is greater than the initial kernel stack pointer (IKSP).

- Overflow is detected whenever the SP would be less than (IKSP - 2 * PAGE_SIZE).

Kernel stack underflow and overflow are indicated with a panic exception, described in Section 4.1.8.

Implementation Note:

Alpha implementations that do not include the BWX extension (described in Appendix D) cannot provide direct access to I/O space addresses (as would Intel-based systems). Instead, those Alpha implementations provide access to I/O space by allowing the standard device drivers to use address handles, provided by the HAL, that may be treated as standard I/O virtual addresses for all operations except the I/O accesses. The I/O accesses must be performed by specialized routines in the HAL that are able to convert the address handles to the actual virtual addresses used for the I/O space accesses.

By convention, the HAL uses the range of numbers $A0000000_{16}$ through $BFFFFFFF_{16}$ to represent these address handles whenever possible. This range of numbers falls into the upper half of the 32-bit superpage address range. The debug PALcode disables the 32-bit superpage in hardware and provides support for the lower half of the 32-bit superpage in PALcode (the range of addresses 80000000_{16} through $9FFFFFFF_{16}$). Addresses in the range $A0000000_{16}$ through $BFFFFFFF_{16}$ are treated as standard addresses and, since they are not mapped, cause memory management faults (translation not valid). This support in the PALcode allows easy and precise trapping of device driver code that attempts to access I/O addresses directly, without using the intended access routines provided by the HAL.

Note:

Physical system memory is limited to 512M bytes when running with the debug PALcode.

5.3.2 Event Counters

The debug PALcode provides software counters to count significant events within the PAL-code. The PALcode also provides the privileged rdcounters instruction to allow kernel-mode code to read the counters. The counted events are implementation specific but must include the following: a separate counter for each of the different PALcode instructions, TB miss counts, and interrupt counts. The format of the data returned by rdcounters is also implementation specific. However, all counters must be 64-bit counters.

Chapter 6

Initialization and Firmware Transitions (II–C)

This chapter describes the four phases of PALcode environment initialization and the PAL-code functions that provide the transition between the operating system and the firmware.

6.1 Initialization

From the perspective of the PALcode environment there are four phases of initialization:

1. Internal system-specific processor state is established before the PALcode runs.

2. PALcode initializes the internal processor state.

3. The kernel uses PALcode initialization callback instructions to prepare the PALcode to handle exceptions.

4. Interrupt tables are initialized so that standard interrupt support can be used.

6.1.1 Pre-PALcode Initialization

Firmware must set the processor and system to a known good state before the PALcode entry point is called. The firmware must initialize any internal processor registers that contain system-specific parameters such as timing or memory size information. This is necessary because the PALcode is entirely independent of the system. The firmware must ensure that all caches are coherent with main memory before calling the PALcode and that the memory system has been fully initialized.

Hardware Implementation Note:

> If system configuration information is written to write-only IPRs, those configuration IPRs cannot have any control bits that need to be written by the platform-independent operating system PALcode. If such bits were written in that manner, the firmware would have to pass the configuration information in internal processor state on a per-implementation basis. Hardware designers should consider allowing configuration registers to be read as well as written to allow the platform-independent layer to have visibility to the full internal processor state.

6.1.2 PALcode Initialization

The PALcode is entered at the first instruction at the base of the PALcode image. PALcode is called with the page frame number (PFN) of the PCR as a parameter in a1. All other argument registers must be preserved across PALcode initalization and are considered parameters to the operating system and are not interpreted by the PALcode. That is, the PALcode is free to destroy volatile general-purpose integer and floating-point registers, but must preserve the non-volatile register state across the call. Register volatility is listed in Section 1.2. The PALcode must accomplish the following initialization:

1. Deassert all interrupt requests and disable all interrupt enables (this includes software, hardware and asynchronous trap interrupts).

2. Set the processor status register (PSR) such that interrupts are enabled, interrupt request level is set to high level (7), and the mode is kernel.

3. Invalidate all virtual translation buffers.

4. Establish all required superpage mapping: 32-bit I-stream and D-stream, and 43-bit D-stream mapping.

5. Set the previous_PAL_BASE register to the previous value of the PAL_BASE register.

6. Set the PAL_BASE register to the base address of the PALcode image.

7. Set the interrupt level table so that no interrupts are enabled for all interrupt levels.

8. Initialize all architected internal processor registers to their specified initialization values.

9. Begin any required implementation-specific initialization, such as unlocking error registers.

When the PALcode has completed its initialization, it resumes execution at the address passed in the ra (return address) register.

6.1.3 Kernel Callback Initialization of PALcode

The kernel uses the initpal and wrentry instructions to call back into the PALcode with the initialization values that allow exceptions to be handled properly between the PALcode and the kernel.

The kernel uses initpal to establish system-permanent context and per-thread context for the initialization thread. The system-permanent context passed to initpal is the kernel global pointer (KGP), which is passed via the gp register.

The initialization thread data passed in initpal are the page directory page, the initial kernel stack pointer, and the initialization thread address. The page directory page and thread address are passed as standard parameters; the kernel stack pointer is passed in the sp register. The initpal instruction also initializes the PALcode information section of the processor control region.

The kernel uses wrentry to register the kernel exception entry points with the PALcode. The wrentry instruction is called once for each kernel exception entry point. Each call includes the exception entry point address and the number of the exception class it handles.

6.1.4 Interrupt Table Initialization

The interrupt table values in the processor control region are system specific and so are not initialized until HAL initialization. Until these tables are initialized, the PALcode uses interrupt tables that are initialized such that all interrupts are disabled. An implementation may choose to cach some portion of the interrupt tables within the processor. After the operating system has established the interrupt tables, an implementation may use the initpcr instruction to cache some part of those tables.

6.2 Firmware Interfaces

The firmware PALcode environment is decoupled from the operating system PALcode. The reboot/restart and swppal instructions permit the transition between the operating system and the firmware PALcode context.

6.2.1 Reboot Instruction – Transition to Firmware PALcode Context

The reboot instruction performs a controlled transition to the firmware PALcode context. Reboot essentially follows the semantics for a return to the ARC (Advanced RISC Computing) firmware environment, with the addition of Alpha support for switching to the firmware PALcode. The reboot function accomplishes the following tasks:

1. Retrieves the restart block pointer from the processor control region.

   The restart block is expected to be initialized by the firmware. The pointer to the restart block is passed by the firmware through the OS Loader to the kernel in the loader parameter block. The kernel writes the restart block pointer into the processor control region during startup. The restart block pointer must be a 32-bit superpage address.

   The firmware environment is responsible for allocating memory for the entire restart block, including the saved state area that is specific to the Alpha architecture. The firmware is also responsible for initializing the restart block, as specified by ARC.

2. Verifies the restart block and if invalid, initiates alternate restart.

   The PALcode verifies the restart block by ensuring that the restart block signature is valid and that the restart block and saved state area lengths are of sufficient size to contain the state the PALcode saves. If the PALcode determines that the restart block is not valid, an alternate restart is initiated.

   The alternate restart allows the PALcode to restore the previous PALcode base to the PAL_BASE register and to transfer control to the previous PALcode base in the PALcode environment.

   Figure 6–1 shows the structure of the PAL_BASE register.

Figure 6–1: PAL_BASE Internal Processor Register

31	PA_BITS..K		K-1..0
	ADDR		RAZ

The hardware vectors into the appropriate PALcode handlers as offsets from the base in the PAL_BASE register. The offsets for each handler and the type of handler are implementation specific, except for the reset vector. The reset vector is the PALcode initialization vector and must begin at offset 0 within the PALcode image.

Explicitly, PAL_BASE contains the value $<PA\_BITS..K>$, where PA_BITS is the physical address bits for the implementation, and $2**K$ is the minimum PALcode byte alignment for the implementation.

Note that the OS Loader uses 64K-byte boundaries, so the maximum value for K is 16. The minimum value for K is N, where $2**N$ = implementation page size.

3. Saves the general register state in the restart block.

   The saved general register state includes all 32 integer registers and all 32 floating-point registers. In addition, the floating-point control register is also saved.

4. Saves the architected internal processor register state in the restart block.

   The internal processor register state is stored in its architected format so that it may be interpreted in the firmware environment. In addition, remaining space is allocated so that the total size of the restart block is 2040 bytes. The additional space can be used for per-implementation data.

5. Saves the RESTART_ADDRESS in the restart block.

   The RESTART_ADDRESS is stored in the saved state area to allow return from reboot via the restart instruction. The HAL is responsible for populating the Version, Revision, and RestartAddress fields of the restart block header.

6. Retrieves the firmware restart address from the processor control region.

   The firmware restart address is the address to which the PALcode transfers control upon completion of the reboot. The firmware restart address is passed from the firmware through the OS Loader to the kernel and stored in the processor control region as is the restart block pointer. The firmware restart address is read from the processor control region and written to the RESTART_ADDRESS register with implementation-specific (but well-defined) interpretation.

7. Restores the PALcode base from the previous PALcode base.

   The PALcode captures the previous PALcode environment when it is first initialized. The PALcode base address is read from the PAL_BASE register and written to the previous_PAL_BASE register. When the processor executes the reboot function, it restores the previous PALcode environment by writing the value in the previous_PAL_BASE register to the PAL_BASE register.

Hardware Implementation Note:

Several restrictions are imposed on the hardware design to support this model for switching PALcode environments:

A. The currently active PALcode must be settable by writing the base address of the PALcode image to an internal processor register.

B. No implementation can require, for the base of the PALcode, an alignment of greater than 64K bytes or less than the implementation page size.

C. The internal processor register used to set the base of the PALcode must be readable for each bit that is writeable.

8. Completes the restart block by updating the boot status and the checksum.

9. Restarts execution at the firmware restart address passing a pointer to the restart block in the a0 register.

The restart instruction is provided to reverse the work done by a reboot instruction and allows the processor to restart execution. The restart function performs the inverse of the tasks that were performed in the reboot.

6.2.2 Reboot and Restart Tasks and Sequence

The tasks and sequence required for performing a reboot and restart are described below:

1. Firmware allocates restart block, initializing signature, length, ID fields, and the pointer to next restart block. Restart block pointer and firmware restart address are passed to the kernel.

2. HAL populates the Version and Revision fields during HAL initialization.

3. Some external event triggers a halt, a reboot, or a power-fail.

4. The appropriate HAL routine populates the RestartAddress field of the restart block with the address of the HAL restart routine.

5. The HAL executes the reboot instruction.

6. The PALcode saves processor state, including the RESTART_ADDRESS register (the address in the HAL of the instruction after the reboot instruction).

7. The PALcode transfers to the firmware environment.

8. The firmware initializes a restart by calling the HAL restart routine (via the address in the restart block header).

9. The HAL uses the swppal instruction to restore the operating system PALcode environment.

10. The HAL uses the restart instruction to restore complete processor state.

11. The PALcode restores state and then returns execution to the instruction after the reboot instruction in the HAL.

12. The HAL completes the restart.

6.2.3 Swppal Instruction – Transition to Any PALcode Environment

The swppal instruction is a flexible interface that allows kernel code to transition to any PAL-code environment, as contrasted with reboot, which limits the caller to transition to the previous PALcode environment.

Windows NT Alpha Software Index

P

Console Interface Architecture (III)

This part describes an architected console interface and contains the following chapters:

- Chapter 1, Console Subsystem Overview (III)
- Chapter 2, Console Interface to Operating System Software (III)
- Chapter 3, System Bootstrapping (III)

Contents

3   System Bootstrapping (III)

Figures

Tables

Chapter 1

Console Subsystem Overview (III)

On an Alpha system, underlying control of the system platform hardware is provided by a console. The console:

- Initializes, tests, and prepares the system platform hardware for Alpha system software.

- Bootstraps (loads into memory and starts the execution of) system software.

- Controls and monitors the state and state transitions of each processor in a multiprocessor system in the absence of operating system control.

- Provides services to system software that simplify system software control of and access to platform hardware.

- Provides a means for a "console operator" to monitor and control the system.

The console interacts with system platform hardware to accomplish the first three tasks. The mechanisms of these interactions are specific to the platform hardware; however, the net effects are common to all systems. Chapter 3 describes these functions.

The console interacts with system software once control of the system platform hardware has been transferred to that software. Chapter 2 discusses the basic functions of a console and its interaction with Alpha system software.

The console interacts with the console operator through a virtual display device or console terminal. The console operator may be a person or a management application. The console terminal forms the interface between the console and a console presentation layer. The functions of that presentation layer and the display formats are described in Section 1.3.

An Alpha multiprocessor system has one primary processor and one or more secondary processors. The primary processor:

- Can legally refer to the console I/O devices

- Can legally send characters to the console terminal

- Can legally receive characters from the console terminal

- Has direct access to a BB_WATCH on the system

- Is named in response to an inquiry as to which processor is primary

All other processors in the system are secondary processors.

1.1 Console Implementations

The implementation of an Alpha console varies from system to system. Regardless of implementation, the console on each system provides the functionality described in this chapter and in Chapters 2 and 3. The console may be implemented as:

- "Embedded," or co-resident in the hardware platform complex that contains the processors

- "Detached," or resident on a separate hardware platform

- Any hybrid of the above

The distinction is somewhat arbitrary. A detached console may have cooperating special code that executes on one of the processors; an embedded console may have a cooperating management application that executes on a remote machine.

Regardless of the actual implementation, each console must provide:

- A virtual display device, the default "console terminal."

  This device allows the console operator to issue commands and receive displays. With no hardware errors and with the proper console-lock setting, the default console terminal device provides reliable communication with the rest of the console.

- Reliable access to console functionality by system software and the console operator.

  All console functionality must appear to reside within the console at all times. All console functions must be accessible in a timely manner, without prior notification, and reliably.

- Secure communications with system software and the console operator.

  All console communication paths must be able to be made secure by either physical measures or encryption methods.

- A mechanism by which the console can gain control of a processor that is executing system software.

  This mechanism must preserve the execution state of system software; it must be possible for the console to gain control of the processor and subsequently continue system software execution successfully.

- A mechanism that locks the console.

  A console lock prohibits the user from accessing a selected subset (or all) of console functions. The console lock may be a console password, a key switch, jumper, or any other implementation-specific mechanism. The lock is either "locked" or "unlocked."

1.2 Console Implementation Registry

This chapter, and Chapters 2 and 3, specify required console functions. Some of these functions have attributes that may vary with console implementation; consoles may also provide more than the required functions. Console functions or attributes that may vary with implementation include:

- Supported console terminal blocks (CTBs)

- Supported environment variables

- Environment variable value formats, such as BOOT_DEV or BOOT_OSFLAGS

- Configuration data block format

- Supported callback routines

- Supported bootstrap media

- Implementation-specific HALT codes or messages

The goal of the Alpha console architecture is to promote a consistent interface across all Alpha systems. Some console functionality is inherently implementation specific and cannot be required of all Alpha systems; some may be applicable to more than one Alpha system. To prevent the proliferation of interfaces and achieve commonality of function whenever possible, the Alpha console architecture requires that:

- Any console function that is visible to system software and is not specified by these chapters must be registered with the Alpha architecture group.

- Any console function that is visible to an on-site or remote console operator (including Field Service engineers) and is not specified by these chapters must be registered with the Alpha architecture group.

- Whenever possible, implementations must use previously registered functions rather than inventing new variations.

Console functions intended for use solely by development engineering or expert-level repair and diagnosis are excluded from these requirements.

1.3 Console Presentation Layer

The following functions are assumed to be provided in the console presentation layer:

- BOOT (bootstrap the system)

- CONTINUE (continue execution)

- STARTCPU (start a given secondary)

- INITIALIZE (initialize system)

- INITIALIZECPU (initialize a given processor)

- HALTCPU (force a given processor into console I/O mode)

- HALTCRASH (cause a given processor to initiate a crash)

1.4 Messages

The console generates a binary message code to the console presentation layer to signal messages, such as audit trail or error messages. The console presentation layer interprets the binary code into something that is meaningful to the console operator.

1.5 Security

The means by which the console achieves a secure communications path with system software and with the console operator is implementation specific. Embedded consoles have the built-in capability of secure communications with system software. Detached consoles can achieve this security by residing in the same room as the Alpha system and communicating with it over a private connection. Detached consoles can also achieve security by using an encrypted protocol over a shared connection. This latter method allows a workstation over a network to function as the console.

1.6 Internationalization

Wherever possible, console implementations should support the goals of internationalization:

- Each message has a binary message code. The console presentation layer interprets the code into a meaningful message display of the appropriate language and characters.

- Consoles should avoid explicitly interpreting character set encoding (such as ISO Latin–1). Character strings are to be viewed as simple byte strings. Thus, the GETC console callback routine supports from one-to-four-byte character encodings, depending on the currently selected language and character set; the PUTS routine outputs only a byte stream.

- ASCII strings are used in certain fields of the HWRPB and certain interprocessor communications due to DEC Standard 12 and to present a common interface to system software.

- The currently selected character set encoding and language to be used for the console terminal are defined by the CHAR_SET and LANGUAGE environment variables.

- The end of a character string passed between the console and the operating system as an argument to a console callback routine is determined by passing its length.

- Console callback routines should be written to be independent from character set encoding and language. At a minimum, every implementation must support ISO Latin–1 character set encodings, which requires the following properties:

  1. The GETC console callback routine returns a one byte character (see Section 2.3.4).

  2. The PROCESS_KEYCODE console callback routine returns a one-byte character (see Section 2.3.4).

  3. English console presentation layers are strongly encouraged to use the actual values as defined in Table 2–6, rather than creating aliases.

  Other supported character set encodings are determined by platform product requirements.

- The console presentation layer is independent of the required console functionality interface.

1.7 Documentation Note

The chapters in Section III apply to both OpenVMS Alpha and DIGITAL UNIX operating systems. The few functional descriptions that are unique to one operating system are described as such. However, because of contextual equivalence in this section and in the interests of brevity, any text concerning the OpenVMS Alpha hardware privileged context block (HWPCB) applies equally to the DIGITAL UNIX privileged context block (PCB). Equivalent information for Windows NT Alpha is located in Windows NT Alpha Software (II–C), Chapter 6.

Chapter 2

Console Interface to Operating System Software (III)

This chapter describes the interactions between the console subsystem and system software. These services depend on state that is shared between the console and system software. Shared state is contained in the Hardware Restart Parameter Block (HWRPB) and a number of environment variables. The HWRPB is a data structure that is directly accessed by both the console and system software; the environment variables are indirectly accessed by system software. Specifically:

- Section 2.1 describes the HWRPB.

- Section 2.2 describes the environment variables.

- Section 2.3 describes the service, or callback, routines provided by the console to system software.

- Section 2.4 describes the communication between the console and system software.

2.1 Hardware Restart Parameter Block (HWRPB)

The Hardware Restart Parameter Block (HWRPB) is a page-aligned data structure that is shared between the console and system software. The IIWRPB is a critical resource during bootstraps, powerfail recoveries, and other restart situations. An overview of the HWRPB is shown in Figure 2–1. The individual HWRPB fields are shown in Figure 2–2 and described in Table 2–1.

The console creates the HWRPB and the required per-CPU, CTB, CRB, MEMDSC, and DSRDB offset blocks as a physically contiguous structure during console initialization. Fields within the HWRPB and the required offset blocks are updated by the console and system software during and after system bootstrapping. The console must be able to locate the HWRPB and the required offset blocks at all times. Neither the console nor system software may move the HWRPB or the required offset blocks to different physical memory locations; subsequent operation of the system is UNDEFINED if such an attempt is made.

Figure 2–1: HWRPB Overview

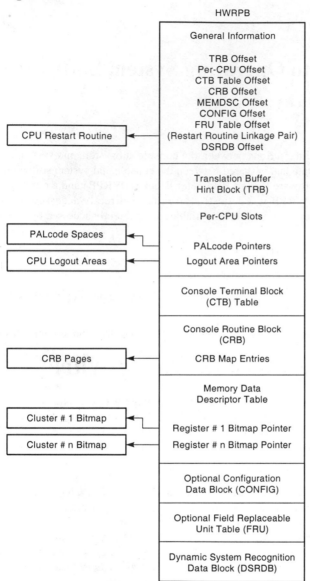

The HWRPB and the required offset blocks must comprise a virtually contiguous structure at all times. Before transferring control to system software, the console maps the HWRPB and the required offset blocks into contiguous addresses beginning at virtual address 0000 0000 1000 0000$_{16}$ in the initial bootstrap address space. If system software subsequently changes this virtual mapping, any new mapping must preserve the relative offsets of all fields and blocks; all physically contiguous pages must remain virtually contiguous. Some of the data structures located by HWRPB fields need not be contiguous with the HWRPB. The structures that may be discontiguous are the PALcode spaces, the logout areas, the CRB pages, and the memory bitmaps located by the MEMDSC table.

All offset blocks must be at least quadword aligned. The starting address of an offset block is determined by adding the contents of the HWRPB offset field to the starting address of the HWRPB. For example, the starting address of the MEMDSC block is given by:

```
MEMDSC Address = HWRPB address + MEMDSC OFFSET
              = HWRPB address + (HWRPB[200])
```

The total size of the HWRPB and the required offset blocks is on the order of 8K bytes to 16K bytes. The size is contained in the HWRPB_SIZE field at HWRPB[24]. The required offset blocks may be offset from the HWRPB in any order; the HWRPB offset fields must not be used to infer the size of the HWRPB or any offset block.

Figure 2–2: Hardware Restart Parameter Block Structure

63	32 31	0	
Physical Address of the HWRPB			:HWRPB
"HWRPB"			:+08
HWRPB Revision			:+16
HWRPB Size			:+24
Primary CPU ID			:+32
Page Size (Bytes)			:+40
Number of Extension VA Bits		Number of PA Bits	:+48
Maximum Valid ASN			:+56
System Serial Number (SSN)			:+64
System Type			:+80
System Variation			:+88
System Revision			:+96
Interval Clock Interrupt Frequency			:+104
Cycle Counter Frequency			:+112
Virtual Page Table Base			:+120
Reserved for Architecture Use			:+128
Offset to Translation Buffer Hint Block			:+136
Number of Processor Slots			:+144
Per-CPU Slot Size			:+152
Offset to Per-CPU Slots			:+160
Number of CTBs			:+168
CTB Size			:+176
Offset to Console Terminal Block Table			:+184
Offset to Console Callback Routine Block			:+192
Offset to Memory Data Descriptor Table			:+200
Offset to Configuration Data Block (If Present)			:+208
Offset to FRU Table (If Present)			:+216
Virtual Address of Terminal Save State Routine			:+224
Procedure Value of Terminal Save State Routine			:+232
Virtual Address of Terminal Restore State Routine			:+240
Procedure Value of Terminal Restore State Routine			:+248

Figure 2-2 : Hardware Restart Parameter Block Structure (Continued)

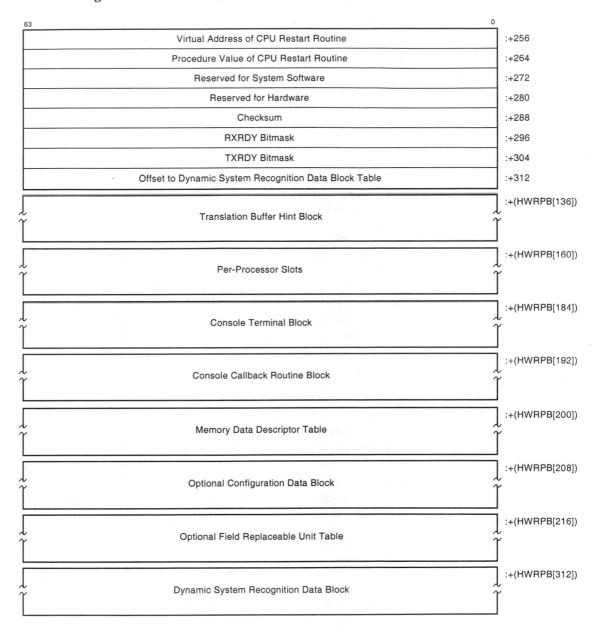

Table 2–1: HWRPB Fields

Offset	Description
HWRPB	**HWRPB PA[1]** Starting physical address of the HWRPB field. This field is used by the console to validate the HWRPB.
+08	**HWRPB VALIDATION[1]** Quadword containing "HWRPB<0><0><0>" (0000 0042 5052 5748_{16}). This field is used by the console to validate the HWRPB.
+16	**HWRPB REVISION[1]** Format of the HWRPB. See Section 2.1.1. The HWRPB revision level for this version of the architecture specification is 7.
+24	**HWRPB SIZE[1]** Size in bytes of the HWRPB and required physically contiguous TBB, per-CPU, CTB, CRB, MEMDSC, CONFIG, FRU, and DSRDB offset blocks. Unsigned field.
+32	**PRIMARY CPU ID[1,3]** WHAMI of the primary processor. System software modifies this field only at primary switch; see Section 3.5.6. Unsigned field.
+40	**PAGE SIZE[1]** Number of bytes within a page for this Alpha processor implementation. Unsigned field.
+48	**PA SIZE[1]** Size of the physical address space in bits for this Alpha processor implementation. PA SIZE must be 48 bits or less. Unsigned 32-bit field.
+52	**EXTENDED VA SIZE[2]** Size of the extended portion of the virtual address space in bits for this Alpha processor implementation. Unsigned 32-bit field. If this implementation is operating with three levels of page table, this field contains a zero, indicating that no "extension" bits exist. If this implementation is operating with a fourth level of page table, this field contains the number of additional virtual address bits that exist beyond the number that would exist if operating with only three levels of page table.
+56	**MAX VALID ASN[1]** Maximum ASN value allowed by this Alpha processor implementation. Unsigned field.

Table 2–1: HWRPB Fields (Continued)

Offset	Description
+64	SYSTEM SERIAL NUMBER[1] Full DEC STD 12 serial number for this Alpha system. This octaword field contains a 10-character ASCII serial number determined at the time of manufacture; see DEC STD 12 for format information. See Section 2.1.1.1.
+80	SYSTEM TYPE[1] Family or system hardware platform. See Section 2.1.1. Unsigned field.
+88	SYSTEM VARIATION[1,3] Subtype variation of the system. This may include the member of the system family and whether the system has optional features such as multiprocessor support or special power supply conditioning. See Sections 2.1.1 and 2.1.1.2 for optional features.
+96	SYSTEM REVISION CODE[1] DEC STD 12 revision field for this Alpha system. Four ASCII characters. See Section 2.1.1.1.
+104	INTERVAL CLOCK INTERRUPT FREQUENCY[1] Number of interval clock interrupts per second (scaled by 4096) in this Alpha system. Interrupts occur only if enabled. Unsigned field.
+112	CYCLE COUNTER FREQUENCY[1] Number of SCC and PCC updates per second in this Alpha system. See the RPCC instruction and, for OpenVMS, the CALL_PAL RSCC instruction. Unsigned field.
+120	VIRTUAL PAGE TABLE BASE[2,3] Virtual address of the base of the entire page table structure. The console sets this field at system bootstraps and restores the virtual page table base register (pointer) with this value at all processor restarts. System software is responsible for updating this field whenever the virtual page table base register (pointer) is modified. See Sections 3.4.1.3, 3.4.3.5, and 3.5.1.
+128	Reserved for architecture use; SBZ.
+136	TB HINT OFFSET[1] Unsigned offset to the starting address of the Translation Buffer Hint Block (TBB). See Section 2.1.2.
+144	NUMBER OF PER-CPU SLOTS[1] Number of per-CPU slots present. Must be a number between 1 and 64, inclusive. See Section 2.1.3 for the per-CPU slot format. Unsigned field.

Table 2–1: HWRPB Fields (Continued)

Offset	Description
+152	PER-CPU SLOT SIZE[1] Size in bytes of each per-CPU slot rounded up to the next integer multiple of 128. See Section 2.1.3. Unsigned field.
+160	CPU SLOT OFFSET[1] Unsigned offset to the first per-CPU slot in the HWRPB. See Section 2.1.3.
+168	NUMBER OF CTB[1] Number of Console Terminal Blocks (CTBs) contained in the CTB table. See Section 2.3.8.2. Unsigned field.
+176	CTB SIZE[1] Size in bytes of the largest Console Terminal Block (CTB) contained in the CTB table. See Section 2.3.8.2. Unsigned field.
+184	CTB OFFSET[1] Unsigned offset to the starting address of the Console Terminal Block (CTB) table. See Section 2.3.8.2.
+192	CRB OFFSET[1] Unsigned offset to the starting address of the Console Callback Routine Block (CRB). See Section 2.3.8.1.
+200	MEMDSC OFFSET[1] Unsigned offset to the starting address of the Memory Data Descriptor Table (MEMDSC). See Section 3.4.1.2.
+208	CONFIG OFFSET[1] Unsigned offset to the starting address of the Configuration Data Table (CONFIG). If zero, no CONFIG table exists. See Section 2.1.4.
+216	FRU TABLE OFFSET[1] Unsigned offset to the starting address of the Field Replaceable Unit Table (FRU). If zero, no FRU table exists. See Section 2.1.5.
+224	SAVE_TERM RTN VA[2,3] Starting virtual address of a routine that saves console terminal state. This routine is optionally provided by system software. See Section 3.5.7. Set to zero by the console at system bootstraps.
+232	SAVE_TERM VALUE[2,3] Procedure value of the SAVE_TERM routine optionally provided by system software. The console copies this value into R27 before invoking the routine. See Section 3.5.7. Set to zero by the console at system bootstraps.

Table 2–1: HWRPB Fields (Continued)

Offset	Description
+240	RESTORE_TERM RTN VA[2,3] Starting virtual address of a routine that restores console terminal state. This routine is optionally provided by system software. See Section 3.5.7. Set to zero by the console at system bootstraps
+248	RESTORE_TERM VALUE[2,3] Procedure value of the RESTORE_TERM routine optionally provided by system software. The console copies this value into R27 before invoking the routine. See Section 3.5.7. Set to zero by the console at system bootstraps.
+256	RESTART RTN VA[2,3] Starting virtual address of a CPU restart routine provided by system software. The console restarts system software by transferring control to this routine. See Section 3.5. Set to zero by the console at system bootstraps.
+264	RESTART VALUE[2,3] Procedure value of the CPU restart routine provided by system software. During the restart process, the console copies this value into R27 before transferring control to the CPU restart routine. See Section 3.5. Set to zero by the console at system bootstraps.
+272	RESERVED FOR SYSTEM SOFTWARE[2,3] Reserved for use by system software. Set to zero by the console at system bootstraps.
+280	RESERVED FOR HARDWARE[1] Reserved for use by hardware.
+288	HWRPB CHECKSUM[2,3] Checksum of all the quadwords of the HWRPB from offset [00] to [280], inclusive. Computed as a 64-bit sum, ignoring overflows. Used to validate the HWRPB during warm bootstraps, restarts, and secondary starts. Set by console initialization; recomputed and updated whenever a HWRPB field with offset [00] to [280], inclusive, is modified by the console or system software.
+296	RXRDY BITMASK[2,3] Secondary receive bitmask for interprocessor console communications. When transmitting a command to a secondary, the primary processor sets the RXRDY bit, which corresponds to the CPU ID of the secondary. The number of active bits in this field is determined by the number of per-CPU slots in HWRPB[144]. See Section 2.4. All bits are initialized as clear.

Table 2–1: HWRPB Fields (Continued)

Offset	Description
+304	TXRDY BITMASK[2,3] Secondary transmit bitmask for interprocessor console communications. When transmitting a message to the primary, the secondary processor sets the TXRDY bit, which corresponds to its CPU ID and requests an interprocessor interrupt to the primary. The number of active bits in this field is determined by the number of per-CPU slots in HWRPB[144]. See Section 2.4. All bits are initialized as clear.
+312	DSRDB OFFSET[1] Unsigned offset to the starting address of the Dynamic System Recognition Data Block.
+(HWRPB[136])	TB HINT BLOCK[2,3] Quadword-aligned block that describes the characteristics of the translation buffer (TB) granularity hints. See Section 2.1.2.
+(HWRPB[160])	Per-CPU SLOTS[2,3] 128 byte-aligned slots that describe each processor in the system. See Section 2.1.3.
+(HWRPB[184])	CTB TABLE[1] Quadword-aligned Console Terminal Block Table. Set at console initialization; modified by console terminal callbacks. See Section 2.3.8.2.
+(HWRPB[192])	CONSOLE CALLBACK ROUTINE BLOCK[2,3] Quadword-aligned block that describes the location and mapping of the console callback routines. Set at system bootstrap; modified by console FIXUP callback. See Section 2.3.8.1.
+(HWRPB[200])	MEMDSC[1,3] Quadword-aligned Memory Data Descriptor Table. Set at console initialization; preserved across warm bootstraps. See Section 3.4.1.2.
+(HWRPB[208])	CONFIG BLOCK[1] Optional implementation-dependent configuration block. See Section 2.1.4.

Table 2–1: HWRPB Fields (Continued)

Offset	Description
+(HWRPB[216])	FRU TABLE[1] Optional implementation-dependent field replaceable unit table. See Section 2.1.5.
+(HWRPB[312])	DSRDB[1] Quadword-aligned Dynamic System Recognition Data Block (DSRDB).

---

[1] Initialized by the console at cold system bootstrap only. Preserved unchanged by the console at all warm system bootstraps.

[2] Initialized by the console at all system bootstraps (cold or warm).

[3] May be modified by system software.

2.1.1 Serial Number, Revision, Type, and Variation Fields

The HWRPB contains several serial number, revision, type, and variation fields that describe the Alpha system platform hardware and PALcode. System software uses these fields to identify hardware-dependent support code that must be loaded or enabled. These fields are examined early in operating system bootstrap; if one of the fields contains a value that is unrecognized or incompatible with the operating system, the bootstrap attempt fails. Diagnostic software uses these fields to guide field installation and upgrade procedures and for material and parts control.

In multiprocessor systems, the processor type and PALcode revisions need not be identical for all processors. Console and system software can use these fields to determine if multiprocessor operation is viable. This evaluation may be performed by the running primary, the starting secondary, or a combination of both. For an example, see Section 3.4.3.3.

2.1.1.1 Serial Number and Revision Fields

The revision fields include:

- HWRPB revision — HWRPB[16]

  This field identifies the format of the HWRPB. Since the HWRPB is shared between the console and system software, both must agree on the field offsets, formats, and interpretations.

- System serial number and revision — HWRPB[64] and HWRPB[96]

  These fields identify the system platform hardware serial number and revision according to DEC STD 12.

  The system serial number and revision fields must be distinct from the processor serial number and revision fields in the per-CPU table, pointed to by HWRPB[152]. In particular, on multiprocessing systems, the system fields must not be simply replicated from the fields of the primary processor. The system fields must be constant regardless of which processor serves as primary and must have persistence across processor failures and/or replacement.

- Processor type and processor variation (capabilities) — SLOT[176] and SLOT[184]

  These per-CPU slot fields identify each Alpha processor and its capabilities. The type field (SLOT[176]) contains a major and minor subfield. The major subfield identifies the processor family and the minor subfield identifies the particular membership in that family.

  The variation (capabilities) field (SLOT[184]) identifies any system-specific attributes (such as local memory or cache size).

  Processor type and variation field assignments are listed in Appendix D.

- Processor Revision — SLOT[192]

  This per-CPU slot field identifies the processor hardware revision according to DEC STD 12.

- PALcode Revision — SLOT[168]

  This field identifies the PALcode revision required and/or in use by the processor. System software uses the PALcode variation and PALcode compatibility subfields. The variation subfield indicates whether the PALcode image includes extensions or functional variations necessary to a given operating system or application.

  Programming Note:
  > For example, a PALcode variation may contain a different TB fill routine. System software (and optionally the console) uses the compatibility subfield to ensure that all processors in a multiprocessor system are using compatible PALcode images.

  PALcode revisions are specific to the system platform and processor major type. The file name of distributed PALcode images must contain sufficient information to distinguish the intended system platform and processor.

- PALcode Revisions Available — SLOT[464]

  This field identifies the PALcode variant revisions that have been previously loaded on this processor. System software uses these fields to determine if a given PALcode variant and revision are present before PALcode switching. The format follows the PALcode revision field in SLOT[168].

  PALcode variation assignments are listed in Appendix D.

2.1.1.2 System Type and Variation Fields

The system type and system variation fields are HWRPB[80] and HWRPB[88].

These fields identify the Alpha system platform. System software infers attributes such as physical address offsets and I/O device locations from the system type. The system type field contains the family and member identification numbers, along with the major and minor subfield identifiers. It is described in Appendix D. The system variation field is described in Table 2–2.

The following system variations are defined:

Table 2–2: System Variation Field (HWRPB[88])

Bits	Description
63 – 16	Reserved — MBZ
15 – 10	System Type Specific (STS). Registered system identifiers for system member identification.
9	GRAPHICS — If set, indicates that the platform contains an embedded graphics processor. Initialized by the console at all cold bootstraps.
8	POWERFAIL RESTART — If set, indicates that the console should restart all available processors on a powerfail recovery. If clear, only the primary processor will be restarted. Cleared by the console at system bootstraps; may be set by system software.
7 – 5	POWERFAIL — Indicates the type of powerfail (if any) implemented by this platform. See Section 3.5.3 for more information. Defined values include:

<7:5>	Interpretation
000	Reserved
001	United
010	Separate
011	Full battery backup of system platform hardware

Initialized by the console at all cold bootstraps.

Bits	Description
4 – 1	CONSOLE — Indicates the type of console. Defined values include:

<4:1>	Interpretation
0000	Reserved
0001	Detached service processor
0010	Embedded console
Other	Reserved for future use

Initialized by the console at all cold bootstraps.

Bits	Description
0	MPCAP — If set, indicates this system platform is capable of being configured as a multiprocessor; all support for multiprocessing is present, even if only one processor is present. If clear, this system supports a uniprocessor only. Initialized by the console at all cold bootstraps.

2.1.2 Translation Buffer Hint Block

The Translation Buffer Hint Block (TBB) contains information on the characteristics of the instruction stream translation buffer (ITB) and data stream translation buffer (DTB) granularity hints (GH). All processors in a multiprocessor Alpha system must implement the same granularity hints. The granularity hint fields are listed in Table 2–3.

The TBB consists of 8 quadwords, 4 for each of the translation buffers (ITB and DTB). The 4 quadwords contain 16 word fields; each word contains the number of entries in the translation buffer that implement a combination of granularity hints (including none).

Table 2–3: Granularity Hint Fields

Offset$_{16}$	Granularity Hint
0	None
2	1 page
4	8 pages
6	1 and 8 pages
8	64 pages
A	1 and 64 pages
C	8 and 64 pages
E	1, 8, and 64 pages
10	512 pages
12	1 and 512 pages
14	8, and 512 pages
16	1, 8, and 512 pages
18	64 and 512 pages
1A	1, 64, and 512 pages
1C	8, 64, and 512 pages
1E	1, 8, 64, and 512 pages

2.1.3 Per-CPU Slots in the HWRPB

Information on the state of a processor is contained in a "per-CPU slot" data structure for that processor. The per-CPU slots form a contiguous array indexed by CPU ID. The starting address of the first per-CPU slot is given by the offset HWRPB[160] relative to the starting address of the HWRPB. The number of per-CPU slots is given in HWRPB[144]. Each per-CPU slot must be 128-byte-aligned to ensure natural alignment of the hardware privileged context block (HWPCB) at SLOT[0]. The slot size, rounded up to the nearest multiple of 128 bytes, is given in HWRPB[152].

CPU IDs are determined by the implementation.. The only requirement is that they be in the range of zero to the maximum number of processors the particular platform supports minus one.

Software Note:

OpenVMS supports CPU IDs in the range 0–31 only.

Each per-CPU slot contains information necessary to bootstrap, start, restart or halt the processor. The format is shown Figure 2–3 and Table 2–4. The hardware privileged context block (HWPCB) specifies the context in which the loaded system software will execute.

The console must initialize the per-CPU slot for the primary processor before system bootstrap. The per-CPU slot fields for secondary processors are set by a combination of the console and system software. The console updates the halt information at error halts and before processor restarts.

Slots corresponding to nonexistent processors are zeroed. There may be more per-CPU slots than are necessary in any given Alpha system. A system implementation may reserve HWRPB space for processors that are not present at system bootstrap.

An Alpha system may support internally different, yet software compatible, PALcode for different processors in a multiprocessor implementation. Each per-CPU slot contains a PALcode memory descriptor that locates the PALcode used by that processor. See Section 3.3.1 for information on PALcode loading and initialization on the primary processor and Section 3.4.3.3 for information on PALcode loading and initialization on secondary processors.

The starting address of a per-CPU slot is calculated by:

```
Slot Address = {CPU ID * slot size}   + offset      + HWRPB base
             = {CPU ID * HWRPB[152]}  + HWRPB[160]  + #HWRPB
```

The address may be physical or virtual.

Figure 2–3: Per-CPU Slot in HWRPB

63		0	
Bootstrap/Restart HWPCB			:SLOT
Per-CPU State Flag Bits			:+128
PALcode Memory Length			:+136
PALcode Scratch Length			:+144
Physical Address of PALcode Memory Space			:+152
Physical Address of PALcode Scratch Space			:+160
PALcode Revision Required by Processor			:+168
Processor Type			:+176
Processor Variation			:+184
Processor Revision			:+192
Processor Serial Number			:+200
Physical Address of Logout Area			:+216
Logout Area Length			:+224
Halt PCBB			:+232
Halt PC			:+240
Halt PS			:+248
Halt Argument List (R25)			:+256
Halt Return Address (R26)			:+264
Halt Procedure Value (R27)			:+272
Reason for Halt			:+280
Reserved for Software			:+288
Interprocessor Console Buffer Area			:+296
PALcode Revisions Available Block			:+464
Processor Software Compatibility Field			:+592
Reserved for Architecture Use			:+600

Table 2–4: Per-CPU Slot Fields

Offset	Description
SLOT	HWPCB[1,2] Hardware privileged context block (HWPCB) for this processor. See Table 3–8 for the contents as set by the console.
+128	STATE FLAGS[1,2] Current state of this processor. See Table 2–5 for the interpretation of each bit.
+136	PALCODE MEMORY SPACE LENGTH[3,4,5] Number of bytes required by this processor for PALcode memory. Unsigned field.
+144	PALCODE SCRATCH SPACE LENGTH[3,4,5] Number of bytes required by this processor for PALcode scratch space. Unsigned field.
+152	PA OF PALCODE MEMORY SPACE[2,3,5] Starting physical address of PALcode memory space for this processor. PALcode memory space must be page aligned. See Section 3.3.1 or Section 3.4.3.3.
+160	PA OF PALCODE SCRATCH SPACE[2,3,5] Starting physical address of PALcode scratch space for this processor. PALcode scratch space must be page aligned. See Section 3.3.1 or Section 3.4.3.3.
+168	PALCODE REVISION[2,3,4,6] PALcode revision level for this processor:

Bits	Interpretation
63 – 48	Maximum number of processors that can share this PALcode image
47 – 32	PALcode compatibility (0–65535): 0 Unknown 1–65535 Compatibility revision
31 – 24	SBZ
23 – 16	PALcode variation (0–255)
15 – 8	PALcode major revision (0–255)
7 – 0	PALcode minor revision (0–255)

This field identifies the PALcode revision required by the console and/or processor initialization. The major and minor PALcode revisions are set at console initialization; the remaining fields are set during PALcode loading and initialization. This field must be updated after PALcode switching to reflect the new PALcode environment. See Sections 2.1.1 and Section 3.4.3.3. Also see Appendix D

Table 2–4: Per-CPU Slot Fields (Continued)

Offset	Description

+176   PROCESSOR TYPE[3,4]
Type of this processor:

Bits	Interpretation
63 – 32	Minor type
31 – 0	Major type

The processor types are defined in Appendix D.

+184   PROCESSOR VARIATION[3,4]
The following processor variations are defined:

Bit	Description
63–3	RESERVED — MBZ
2	PRIMARY ELIGIBLE (PE) — If set, indicates that this processor is eligible to become a primary processor. The processor has direct access to the console, a BB_WATCH, and all I/O devices. See Chapter 3.
1	IEEE-FP — If set, indicates this processor supports IEEE floating-point operations and data types. If clear, this processor has no such support.
0	VAX-FP — If set, indicates this processor supports VAX floating-point operations and data types. If clear, this processor has no such support.

+192   PROCESSOR REVISION[3,4]
Full DEC STD 12 revision field for this processor. This quadword field contains four ASCII characters. See Section 2.1.1.

+200   PROCESSOR SERIAL NUMBER[3,4]
Full DEC STD serial number for this processor module. This octaword field contains a 10-character ASCII serial number determined at the time of manufacture; see DEC STD 12 for format information.

+216   PA OF LOGOUT AREA[3,4]
Starting physical address of PALcode logout area for this processor. Logout areas must be at least quadword aligned.

+224   LOGOUT AREA LENGTH[3,4]
Number of bytes in the PALcode logout area for this processor.

Table 2–4: Per-CPU Slot Fields (Continued)

Offset	Description
+232	HALT PCBB[1,7] Value of the PCBB register when a processor halt condition is encountered by this processor. Initialized to the address of the hardware privileged context block (HWPCB) at offset [0] from this per-CPU slot at system bootstraps or secondary processor starts.
+240	HALT PC[1,7] Value of the PC when a processor halt condition is encountered by this processor. Zerocd at system bootstraps or secondary processor starts.
+248	HALT PS[1,7] Value of the PS when a processor halt condition is encountered by this processor. Zeroed at system bootstraps or secondary processor starts.
+256	HALT ARGUMENT LIST[1,7] Value of R25 (argument list) when a processor halt condition is encountered by this processor. Zeroed at system bootstraps or secondary processor starts.
+264	HALT RETURN ADDRESS[1,7] Value of R26 (return address) when a processor halt condition is encountered by this processor. Zeroed at system bootstraps or secondary processor starts.
+272	HALT PROCEDURE VALUE[1,7] Value of R27 (procedure value) when a processor halt condition is encountered by this processor. Zeroed at system bootstraps or secondary processor starts.
+280	REASON FOR HALT[1,7] Indicates why this processor was halted. Values include:

$Code_{16}$	Reason
0	Bootstrap, processor start, or powerfail restart
1	Console operator requested a system crash
2	Processor halted due to kernel-stack not-valid halt
3	Invalid SCBB
4	Invalid PTBR
5	Processor executed CALL_PAL HALT instruction in kernel mode
6	Double error abort encountered
7	Machine check while in PALcode environment
8 – FFF	Reserved
Other	Implementation-specific

Code is set to "0" at console initialization.

Offset	Description
+288	RESERVED FOR SOFTWARE[2] Reserved for use by system software. Zeroed at system bootstraps or secondary processor starts.

Table 2–4: Per-CPU Slot Fields (Continued)

Offset	Description
+296	RXTX BUFFER AREA Used for interprocessor console communication. See Section 2.4.
+464	PALCODE AVAILABLE[3,4] Block of 16 quadwords that list previously loaded PALcode variations that are available to the console or operating system for PALcode switching.

The first offset (SLOT[464]) is reserved for an overall firmware revision field for this processor, the format of which is determined by the HWRPB revision level found at HWRPB[16]. If HWRPB[16] contains 6 or less, the format for SLOT[464] is platform specific. If HWRPB[16] is greater than 6, the format for SLOT[464] is as follows:

Bits	Interpretation
63–48	Maximum number of processors that can share this console
47–32	Console build sequence number (0–16383)
31–24	SBZ
23–16	Variant (0 for console version)
15–8	Console major revision (0–255)
7–0	Console minor revision (0–255)

The format of each subsequent quadword follows the PALcode revision field (SLOT[168]). Each quadword is indexed by PALcode variant. If the quadword is non-zero, the PALcode variant has been loaded and the operating system may switch to that PALcode variant by passing the variant number to CALL_PAL SWPPAL.

Offset	Description
+592	PROCESSOR SOFTWARE COMPATIBILITY FIELD[8] Type of pre-existing processor that is software compatible with existing processor. Format follows SLOT[176].

Bits	Interpretation
63–32	Minor type
31–0	Major type

Table 2–4: Per-CPU Slot Fields (Continued)

Offset	Description
+600	RESERVED Reserved for DIGITAL; SBZ.

1. Initialized by the console for the primary at all system bootstraps (cold or warm) and for a secondary before processor start.
2. May by modified by system software for a secondary before processor start.
3. Initialized by the console for a secondary at cold system bootstrap only. Preserved unchanged by the console at all other times.
4. Initialized by the console for the primary at cold system bootstrap only. Preserved unchanged by the console at all other times
5. Support PALcode loading as described in Section 3.3.
6. May be modified by system software for the primary.
7. Set by the console at all processor halts.
8. Initialized by the console at cold bootstrap and never written by system software or console.

Table 2–5: Per-CPU State Flags

Bit	Description
63:24	RESERVED; MBZ.
23:16	HALT REQUESTED[1,2,3] Indicates the console action requested by system software executing on this processor. Values include:

$Code_{16}$	Reason
0	Default (no specific action)
1	SAVE_TERM/RESTORE_TERM exit
2	Cold bootstrap requested
3	Warm bootstrap requested
4	Remain halted (no restart)
Other	Reserved

Set to "0" at system bootstraps and secondary processor starts. May be set to non-zero by system software before processor halt and subsequent processor entry into console I/O mode. See Sections 3.5.7 and 3.4.5.

Bit	Description
15:9	RESERVED; MBZ.
8	PALCODE LOADED (PL)[3,4,5] Indicates that this processor's PALcode image has been loaded into the address given in the processor's slot PALcode memory space address field. See Sections 3.3.1 and 3.4.3.3.

Table 2–5: Per-CPU State Flags (Continued)

Bit	Description
7	PALCODE MEMORY VALID (PMV)[3,4,5] Indicates that this processor's PALcode memory and scratch space addresses are valid. Set after the necessary memory is allocated and the addresses are written into the processor's slot. See Sections 3.3.1 and 3.4.3.3.
6	PALCODE VALID (PV)[4,5] Indicates that this processor's PALcode is valid. Set after PALcode has been successfully loaded and initialized. See Sections 3.3.1 and 3.4.3.3.
5	CONTEXT VALID (CV)[1,3] Indicates that the HWPCB in this slot is valid. Set after the console or system software initializes the HWPCB in this slot. See Sections 3.3.1 and 3.4.3.
4	OPERATOR HALTED (OH)[1,6] Indicates that this processor is in console I/O mode as the result of explicit operator action. See Section 3.5.8.
3	PROCESSOR PRESENT (PP)[4,5] Indicates that this processor is physically present in the configuration.
2	PROCESSOR AVAILABLE (PA)[4,5] Indicates that this processor is available for use by system software. The PA bit may differ from the PP bit based on self-test or other diagnostics, or as the result of a console command that explicitly sets this processor unavailable.
1	RESTART CAPABLE (RC)[1,2,3,6] Indicates that system software executing on this processor is capable of being restarted if a detected error halt, powerfail recovery, or other error condition occurs. Cleared by the console and set by system software. See Sections 3.4.1.3, 3.4.3.6, and 3.5.1.
0	BOOTSTRAP IN PROGRESS (BIP)[1,2,3] For the primary, this bit indicates that this processor is undergoing a system bootstrap. For a secondary, this bit indicates that a CPU start operation is in progress. Set by the console and cleared by system software. See Sections 3.4.1.3, 3.4.3.6, and 3.5.1.

[1] Initialized by the console for the primary at all system bootstraps (cold or warm) and for a secondary before processor start.

[2] May be modified by system software for the primary.

[3] May be modified by system software for a secondary before processor start.

[4] Initialized by the console for primary at cold system bootstrap only. Preserved unchanged by the console at all other times.

[5] Initialized by the console for a secondary at cold system bootstrap only. Preserved unchanged by the console at all other times.

[6] Set by the console at all processor halts.

2.1.4 Configuration Data Block

Systems may have a Configuration Data Block (CONFIG). The format of the block and whether it exists in a system is implementation specific. If present, the block must be mapped in the bootstrap address space. The CONFIG offset at HWRPB[208] contains the block offset address; if no CONFIG block exists, the offset is zero. The first quadword of a CONFIG block must contain the size in bytes of the block. The second quadword must contain a checksum for the block. The checksum is computed as a 64-bit sum, ignoring overflows, of all quadwords in the configuration data block except the checksum quadword.

2.1.5 Field Replaceable Unit Table

Systems may have a field replaceable unit (FRU) table. The format of the table and whether it exists in a system is implementation specific. If present, the table must be mapped in the bootstrap address space. The FRU table offset at HWRPB[216] contains the table offset address; if no FRU table exists, the offset is zero.

2.2 Environment Variables

The environment variables provide an easily extensible mechanism for managing complex console state. Such state may be variable length, may change with system software, may change as a result of console state changes, and may be established by the console presentation layer. Environment variables may be read, written, or saved.

An environment variable consists of an identifier (ID) and a byte stream value maintained by the console. There are three classes of environment variables:

1. Common to all implementations: ID = 0 to $3F_{16}$.

   These have meaning to both the console and system software. All consoles must implement all of these environment variables.

2. Specific to a given console implementation: ID = 40 to $7F_{16}$.

   These have meaning to a given console implementation and system software implementation. Support for these environment variables is optional.

3. Specific to system software: ID = 80 to FF_{16}.

   These have meaning to a given system software application or implementation; the console passes these environment variables between the console presentation layer and the target application without interpretation. Support for these environment variables is optional.

If a console supports optional environment variables, they must be described in the relevant console implementation specification and registered with the Alpha architecture group.

The value, format, and size of each environment variable depends on the environment variable and the console implementation. The size of an environment variable value is specified in bytes. The byte stream value of most environment variables consists of an ASCII string.

The booting environment variables, BOOT_DEV, BOOTDEF_DEV, and BOOTED_DEV, contain values that can consist of multiple fields and lists. For those variables, the values are parsed as follows:

- Each field is delimited by one and only one space " " (20_{16}).

- Each list element is delimited by one and only one comma "," ($2C_{16}$).

- Any numeric quantities are expressed in decimal.

- All characters are case-blind and may be expressed in uppercase or lowercase.

Other examples of environment variables that have list values are BOOTED_OSFLAGS and DUMP_DEV.

Programming Note:

For example, BOOT_DEV might consist of "0 4 MSCP,0 1 MOP" and BOOT_OSFLAGS might consist of "7,2,28".

System software uses the console environment variable routines to access the environment variables. Each environment variable is identified by an identification number (ID). If the console resolves the ID, the associated byte stream value is returned. The console environment variable routines present system software with a consistent interface to environment variables regardless of the presentation layer and internal console representation. The console operator interacts with the console presentation layer to access environment variables. See Section 1.3 for details.

In a multiprocessor system, the console must ensure that the dynamic state created by the environment variables is common to all processors. It must not be possible for a value observed on a secondary to differ from that observed on the primary or another secondary. This is necessary to support bootstrapping, restarting a processor, and switching the primary.

Some environment variables contain critical state that must be maintained across console initializations and system power transitions. Other environment variables contain dynamic state that must be initialized at console initialization and retained across warm bootstraps. Still others contain dynamic state that is initialized at each system bootstrap.

Environment variable values that must be maintained across console initializations must be retained in some sort of nonvolatile storage. Default values for these environment variables must be set before system shipment. Thus, there are three possible values: the dynamic value, the default value retained in nonvolatile storage, and the initial default value set in nonvolatile storage before system shipment. The console need not preserve the initial default value. If console implementation preserves the initial default value, that value is accessible only to the console presentation layer; system software accesses only the dynamic and default (last written) values. The dynamic and default values may differ at any time after console initialization as the result of changes by system software or the console operator.

The internal mechanisms for representing and implementing environment variables are determined by the console and are unknown to both system software and the console presentation layer. The method of handling the required nonvolatile storage also depends on the implementation.

Table 2–6 lists the environment variables maintained by the console. Each environment ID is also assigned a symbolic name that is used to reference the environment variable elsewhere in this specification. Tables 2–7 and 2–8, respectively, list supported languages and character sets.

Table 2–6: Required Environment Variables

Environment Variable ID$_{16}$	Symbol	Description
00		Reserved
01	AUTO_ACTION[1,2]	Console action following an error halt or powerup. Defined values and the action invoked are: • "BOOT" (544F 4F42$_{16}$) bootstrap • "HALT" (544C 4148$_{16}$) halt • "RESTART" (54 5241 5453 4552$_{16}$) restart Any other value causes a halt; The default value when the system is shipped is "HALT". See Section 3.1.1.
02	BOOT_DEV[2]	Device list used by the last (or currently in progress) bootstrap attempt. The console modifies BOOT_DEV at console initialization and when a bootstrap attempt is initiated by a BOOT command. The value of BOOT_DEV is set from the device list specified with the BOOT command or, if no device list is specified, BOOTDEF_DEV. The console uses BOOT_DEV without change on all bootstrap attempts that are not initiated by a BOOT command. See Section 3.4.1.5. The format is independent of the console presentation layer.
03	BOOTDEF_DEV[1,2]	Device list from which bootstrapping is to be attempted when no path is specified by a BOOT command. See Section 3.4.1.5. The format follows BOOT_DEV. The default value when the system is shipped indicates a valid implementation-specific device or NULL (00$_{16}$).
04	BOOTED_DEV[3]	Device used by the last (or currently in progress) bootstrap attempt. Value is one of the devices in the BOOT_DEV list. See Section 3.4.1.5. The format is independent of the console presentation layer.

Table 2–6: Required Environment Variables (Continued)

Environment Variable ID$_{16}$	Symbol	Description
05	BOOT_FILE[1,2]	File name to be used when a bootstrap requires a file name and when the bootstrap is not the result of a BOOT command or when no file name is specified on a BOOT command. The console passes the value between the console presentation layer and system software without interpretation; the value is preserved across warm bootstraps. The default value when the system is shipped is NULL (00$_{16}$).
06	BOOTED_FILE[3]	File name used by the last (or currently in progress) bootstrap attempt. The value is derived from BOOT_FILE or the current BOOT command. The console passes the value between the console presentation layer and system software without interpretation.
07	BOOT_OSFLAGS[1,2]	Additional parameters to be passed to system software when the bootstrap is not the result of a BOOT command or when no parameters are specified on a BOOT command. The console preserves the value across warm bootstraps and passes the value between the console presentation layer and system software without interpretation. The default value when the system is shipped is NULL (00$_{16}$).
08	BOOTED_OSFLAGS[3]	Additional parameters passed to system software during the last (or currently in progress) bootstrap attempt. The value is derived from BOOT_OSFLAGS or the current BOOT command. The console passes the value between the console presentation layer and system software without interpretation.
09	BOOT_RESET[1,2]	Indicates whether a full system reset is performed in response to an error halt or BOOT command. Defined values and the action invoked are: • "OFF" (46 464F$_{16}$) warm bootstrap, no full system reset is performed. • "ON" (4E4F$_{16}$) cold bootstrap, a full system reset is performed. See Sections 3.4.1 and 3.4.2. The default value when the system is shipped is implementation specific.

Table 2–6: Required Environment Variables (Continued)

Environment Variable ID$_{16}$	Symbol	Description
0A	DUMP_DEV[1,2]	Device used to write operating system crash dumps. The format follows BOOTED_DEV and is independent of the console presentation layer. The value is preserved across warm bootstraps. The default value when the system is shipped indicates an implementation-specific device or NULL (00$_{16}$).
0B	ENABLE_AUDIT[1,2]	Indicates whether audit trail messages are to be generated during bootstrap. Defined values and the action invoked are: • "OFF" (46 464F$_{16}$). Audit trail messages suppressed. • "ON" (4E4F$_{16}$). Audit trail messages generated. The default value when the system is shipped is "ON."
0C	LICENSE[1,3]	Software license in effect. The value is derived in an implementation-specific manner during console initialization.
0D	CHAR_SET[1,2]	Current console terminal character set encoding. Defined values are given in Table 2–8. The default value when the system is shipped is determined by the manufacturing site.
0E	LANGUAGE[1,2]	Current console terminal language. Defined values are given in Table 2–7. The default value when the system is shipped is determined by the manufacturing site.
0F	TTY_DEV[1,2,3]	Current console terminal unit. Indicates which entry of the CTB table corresponds to the actual console terminal. The value is preserved across warm bootstraps. The default value is "0" (30$_{16}$)
10– 3F		Reserved for DIGITAL.
40 – 7F		Reserved for console implementation use.
80 – FF		Reserved for system software use.

[1] Nonvolatile. The last value saved by system software or set by console commands is preserved across system initializations, cold bootstraps, and long power outages.

[2] Warm nonvolatile. The last value set by system software is preserved across warm bootstraps and restarts.

[3] Read-only. The variable cannot be modified by system software or console commands.

Table 2–7: Supported Languages

LANGUAGE$_{16}$	Language	Character Set	GETC Bytes
0	None (cryptic)	ISO Latin–1	1
30	Dansk	ISO Latin–1	1
32	Deutsch	ISO Latin–1	1
34	Deutsch (Schweiz)	ISO Latin–1	1
36	English (American)	ISO Latin–1	1
38	English (British/Irish)	ISO Latin–1	1
3A	Espanol	ISO Latin–1	1
3C	Francais	ISO Latin–1	1
3E	Francais (Canadian)	ISO Latin–1	1
40	Francais (Suisse Romande)	ISO Latin–1	1
42	Italiano	ISO Latin–1	1
44	Nederlands	ISO Latin–1	1
46	Norsk	ISO Latin–1	1
48	Portugues	ISO Latin–1	1
4A	Suomi	ISO Latin–1	1
4C	Svenska	ISO Latin–1	1
4E	Vlaams	ISO Latin–1	1
Other	Reserved		

Table 2–8: Supported Character Sets

CHAR_SET$_{16}$	Character Set
0	ISO Latin–1
Other	Reserved.

2.3 Console Callback Routines

System software can access certain system hardware components through a set of callback routines provided by the Alpha console. These routines give system software an architecturally consistent and relatively simple interface to those components.

All of the console callback routines may be used by system software when the operating system has only restricted functionality, such as during bootstrap or crash. When invoked in this context, the console may assume full control of system platform hardware. Some of the console callback routines may be used by system software when the operating system is fully functional. Such usage imposes constraints on the console implementation.

All routines must be called by system software executing in kernel mode. All routines require that the HWRPB and the per-CPU, CTB, and CRD offset blocks are virtually mapped and kernel read/write accessible. If these conditions are not met, the results are UNDEFINED. If conditions from within user mode are not met, the results are UNPREDICTABLE. Some of the routines execute correctly only at or above certain IPLs.

The routines must never modify any processor registers except those explicitly indicated by the routine descriptions.

2.3.1 System Software Use of Console Callback Routines

The console callback routines present an environment to the operating system in which the following behavior must be implemented. These routines must:

- Not alter the current IPL
- Not alter the current execution mode
- Not disable or mask interrupts
- Not alter any registers except as explicitly defined by the routine interface
- Not alter the existing memory management policy
- Not usurp any existing interrupt mechanisms
- Be interruptible
- Ensure timely completion

Once the operating system is bootstrapped, the console must not reclaim resources transferred to that operating system. This includes both the issuing and servicing of I/O device interrupts, interprocessor interrupts, and exceptions.

It is the responsibility of the console implementation to ensure that these console callback routines may be invoked at multiple IPLs, may be interrupted, and may be invoked by multiple system software threads. The operation of these routines must appear to be atomic to the calling system software even if that software thread is interrupted.

In a multiprocessor system, some console routines may be invoked only on the primary processor. A secondary processor may invoke only a subset of these routines and then only under a limited set of conditions. These conditions are explicitly stated in the routine descriptions; if violated, the results are UNDEFINED.

2.3.2 System Software Invocation of Console Callback Routines

With the exception of the FIXUP routine, all of the routines are accessed uniformly through a common DISPATCH procedure. The target routine is identified by a function code. All console callback routines are invoked using the Alpha standard calling conventions.

Any memory management exceptions generated by incorrect mapping or inaccessibility of console callback routine parameters produce UNDEFINED results. This occurs naturally for those console callback routines that are intended for use while the operating system is fully functional; these routines execute in the unmodified context of the operating system.

For those routines intended for use only while the operating system has restricted functionality, the DISPATCH routine must ensure that any conflicts in mapping or accessibility are resolved before permitting the console to gain control of the system platform hardware.

2.3.3 Console Callback Routine Summary

The console callback routines fall into four functional groups:

1. Console terminal interaction
2. Generic I/O device access
3. Environment variable manipulation
4. Miscellaneous

The hexadecimal function code, name, and function for each routine are summarized in Table 2–9.

Table 2–9: Console Callback Routines

$Code_{16}$	Name	Function Invoked
	Console Terminal Routines	
01	GETC	Get character from console terminal
02	PUTS	Put byte stream to console terminal
03	RESET_TERM	Reset console terminal to default
04	SET_TERM_INT	Set console terminal interrupts
05	SET_TERM_CTL	Set console terminal controls
06	PROCESS_KEYCODE	Process and translate keycode
07-F		Reserved

Table 2–9: Console Callback Routines (Continued)

Code$_{16}$	Name	Function Invoked
Console Generic I/O Device Routines		
10	OPEN	Open I/O device for access
11	CLOSE	Close I/O device for access
12	IOCTL	Perform I/O device-specific operations
13	READ	Read I/O device
14	WRITE	Write I/O device
15 – 1F		Reserved
Console Environment Variable Routines		
20	SET_ENV	Set (write) an environment variable
21	RESET_ENV	Reset (default) an environment variable
22	GET_ENV	Get (read) an environment variable
23	SAVE_ENV	Save current environment variables
Console Miscellaneous Routines		
30	PSWITCH	Switch primary processor
(None)	FIXUP	Remap console callback routines
(None)	DISPATCH	Access console callback routine
32	BIOS_EMUL	Run BIOS emulation callback routine
Other		Reserved

All Alpha consoles must implement:

- All console terminal routines except PROCESS_KEYCODE.
- All console generic I/O device routines.
- All environment variable routines except SAVE_ENV.
- The FIXUP and DISPATCH miscellaneous routines.

The PSWITCH routine is required for all Alpha multiprocessor systems that support dynamic primary switching. See Section 3.5.6.

2.3.4 Console Terminal Routines

Alpha consoles provide system software with a consistent interface to the console terminal, regardless of the physical realization of that terminal. This interface consists of the console terminal block (CTB) table and a number of console terminal routines. Each CTB contains the characteristics of a terminal device that can be accessed through the console terminal routines; see Section 2.3.8.2.

There is *only one* console terminal. The CTB table may contain multiple CTBs and the console terminal routines may be used to access multiple terminal devices. Each terminal device is identified by a "unit number" that is the index of its CTB within the CTB table. The TTY_DEV environment variable indicates the unit, hence the CTB, of the console terminal. The console terminal unit is determined at system bootstrap and cannot be altered by system software. Console terminal device interrupts are delivered at the console terminal device IPL to the primary processor; interrupts can be redirected to a secondary only when switching the primary processor.

The console terminal routines permit system software to access the console terminal in a device-independent way. These routines may be invoked while the operating system is fully functional as well as during operating system bootstrap or crash. All console terminal routines are subject to the constraints given in Section 2.3.1. These routines must:

- Not alter the current IPL or current mode.

  These routines must be invoked in kernel mode at or above the console terminal device IPL.

- Not alter the existing memory management policy.

  All internal pointers must have been remapped by FIXUP.

- Not block interrupts.

  The operating system must be capable of continuing to receive hardware interrupts at higher IPLs.

- Be interruptible and re-entrant.

  These routines may be invoked at multiple IPLs and their execution may be interrupted. However, console terminal callback operations are not necessarily atomic. In the event of re-entrant invocations, it is UNPREDICTABLE whether or not the interrupted operation will fail and characters may be transmitted or received out of order.

The time required for console terminal routines to complete is UNPREDICTABLE; however, a console implementation will attempt to minimize the time whenever possible.

Software Note:

Implementations must limit the execution time to significantly less than the interval clock interrupt period. A return after partial operation completion is preferable to long latency.

When invoking these routines, system software must:

- Be executing in kernel mode at or above the console terminal device IPL.

  If these routines are invoked in other modes, their execution causes UNPREDICTABLE operation. If invoked at lower IPLs, their execution causes UNDEFINED operation.

- Be executing on the primary processor in a multiprocessor configuration.

  If these routines are invoked on secondary processors in kernel mode, their execution causes UNDEFINED operation.

- Be prepared to service any resulting console terminal interrupts, if enabled.

System software must provide valid interrupt service routines for the console terminal transmit and receive interrupts. The operating system interrupt service routines must be established before enabling interrupts; otherwise the operation of the system is UNDEFINED.

Programming Note:

Any console terminal interrupt service routines established by the console before transferring control to operating system software are not transferred to the operating system nor are they remapped by FIXUP. Any console terminal interrupts will be delivered only after the operating system lowers IPL from the console terminal device IPL.

Implementation Note:

The implementation of console terminal I/O interrupts is specific to the system hardware platform. An example of implementation-specific characteristics is console terminal SCB vectors.

2.3.4.1 GETC - Get Character from Console Terminal

Format:

char   = DISPATCH (GETC,unit)

Inputs:

GETC	= R16;	GETC function code – 01_{16}
unit	= R17;	Terminal device unit number
retadr	= R26;	Return address

Outputs:

char	= R0;	Returned character and status:	
		R0<63:61>	'000' Success, character received
			'001' Success, character received, more to be read
			'100' Failure, character not yet ready for reception
			'110' Failure, character received with error
			'111' Failure, character received with error, more to be read
		R0<60:48>	Device-specific error status
		R0<47:40>	SBZ
		R0<39:32>	Terminal device unit number returning character
		R0<31:0>	Character read from console terminal

GETC attempts to read one character from a console terminal device and, if successful, returns that character in R0<31:0>. The character is not echoed on the terminal device. The size of the returned character is from one to four bytes and is a function of the current character set encoding and language (see Table 2–7). The routine performs any necessary keycode mapping.

For implementations that support multiple directly addressable terminal devices, R17 contains the unit number from which to read the character. If the implementation does not support multiple terminal devices or if the devices are not directly addressable, R17 should be zero. The unit number from which the character was read is returned in R0<39:32>. If the implementation does not support multiple terminal devices, R0<39:32> is returned as zero.

GETC returns character reception status in R0<63:61>. If received characters are buffered by the console terminal, R0<61> is set to '1' whenever additional characters are available. If GETC returns a character without error, R0<63:62> is set to '00'. If no character is yet ready, R0<63:62> is set to '10'. If an error is encountered obtaining a character, R0<63:62> is set to '11'. Examples of errors during character reception include data overrun or loss of carrier.

When an error is returned by GETC, the contents of R0<31:0> and R0<60:48> depend on the capabilities of the underlying hardware. Implementations in which the hardware returns the character in error must provide that character in R0<31:0>. Additional device-specific error status may be contained in R0<60:48>.

When appropriate, GETC performs special keyboard operations such as turning keyboard LEDs on or off. Such action is based on the incoming stream of keycodes delivered by the console terminal.

The return address indicated by R26 should be mapped and executable by the kernel.

2.3.4.2 PROCESS_KEYCODE - Process and Translates Keycode

Format:

char = DISPATCH(PROCESS_KEYCODE,unit,keycode,again)

Inputs:

PROCESS_KEYCODE	= R16;	PROCESS_KEYCODE function code – 06_{16}
unit	= R17;	Terminal device unit number
keycode	= R18;	Keycode to be processed
again	= R19;	'1' if calling again for same keycode '0' otherwise
retadr	= R26;	Return address

Outputs:

char	= R0;	Translated character and status:	
	R0<63:61>	'000'	Success, character returned
		'101'	Failure, more time needed to process keycode
		'110'	Failure, device not supported by routine or routine not supported
		'111'	Failure, no character; more keycodes needed or illegal sequence encountered
	R0<60>	'0'	Success in correcting severe error
		'1'	Failure in correcting severe error
	R0<59:32>	SBZ	
	R0<31:0>	Translated character	

PROCESS_KEYCODE attempts to translate the keycode contained in R18 and, if successful, returns the character in R0<31:0>. The translation is based on the current character set encoding, language, and console terminal device state contained in the appropriate CTB. The translated character may be from one to four bytes. For implementations that support multiple terminal devices, R17 contains the unit number of the keyboard;otherwise, R17 should be zero.

Implementation Note:

For ISO Latin–1 character set encoding, PROCESS_KEYCODE returns a one-byte character.

PROCESS_KEYCODE returns keycode translation status in R0<63:61>. The processing falls into one of several cases:

1. The keycode, along with previous keycodes if any, translates into a character from the currently selected character set. In this case, R0<63:61> set to '000'.

2. The keycode, along with previously entered keycodes if any, does not translate into a character from the currently selected character set. This is because either:

   - Not yet enough keycodes have been entered to produce a character in the currently selected character set.

   - The keycodes entered to this point indicate a severe keyboard error status.

   - The keycodes entered to this point form an illegal or unsupported keycode sequence.

   In this case, R0<63:61> set to '111'.

3. The console terminal device for which keycode translation is being performed is not supported by the PROCESS_KEYCODE implementation or the console implementation does not support PROCESS_KEYCODE. In this case, R0<63:61> set to '110'.

4. The keycode cannot be processed in a reasonable amount of time; multiple invocations of PROCESS_KEYCODE are necessary. In this case, the routine returns with R0<63:61> set to '101'. The subsequent call(s) should be made with the same keycode in R18 and R19 set to '1'.

Implementation Note:
> It may not be possible for an implementation to perform all the actions associated with special keycodes (such as turning on LEDs) in a timely manner. The PROCESS_KEYCODE routine must return after partial completion of an operation if necessary. It is the responsibility of the console to ensure that subsequent calls make forward progress. The delay between successive operating system calls is UNPREDICTABLE, although the operating system should attempt to complete the operation in a timely fashion. See Section 2.3.4.

In all but the first case, the contents of R0<31:0> are UNPREDICTABLE.

When certain severe keyboard errors are encountered, PROCESS_KEYCODE attempts to correct them by performing special keyboard operations. Those severe errors that may be corrected are device specific and contained in the terminal device CTB. If an error is encountered and the attempt to correct the error is unsuccessful, R0<60> is set to '1'; otherwise R0<60> is set to '0'.

The keyboard state recorded in the CTB is updated appropriately as the input stream of keycodes is processed. If appropriate, PROCESS_KEYBOARD may buffer some of the keycodes in the CTB keycode buffer. The supported keyboard state changes are device specific and are listed in the device CTB.

The return address indicated by R26 should be mapped and executable by the kernel.

2.3.4.3 PUTS — Put Stream to Console Terminal

Format:

wcount = DISPATCH (PUTS,unit,address,length)

Inputs:

PUTS	= R16;	PUTS function code – 02_{16}
unit	= R17;	Terminal device unit number
address	= R18;	Virtual address of byte stream to be written
length	= R19;	Count of bytes to be written
retadr	= R26;	Return address

Outputs:

wcount	= R0;	Count of bytes written and status:		
		R0<63:61>	'000'	Success, all bytes written
			'001'	Success, some bytes written
			'100'	Failure, no bytes written Terminal error encountered
			'111'	Failure, some bytes written Terminal error encountered
		R0<60:48>	Device-specific error status	
		R0<47:32>	SBZ	
		R0<31:0>	Count of bytes written (unsigned)	

PUTS attempts to write a number of bytes to a console terminal device. R18 contains the base virtual address of the memory-resident byte stream; R19 contains its 32-bit size in bytes. The byte stream is written in order with no interpretation or special handling. The count of the bytes transmitted is returned in R0<31:0>.

Programming Note:

For multiple-byte character set encodings, the returned byte count may indicate a partial character transmission.

For implementations that support multiple terminal devices, R17 contains the unit number to which the byte stream is to be written; otherwise, R17 should be zero.

PUTS returns byte stream transmission status in R0<63:61>. If only a portion of the byte stream was written, R0<61> is set to '1'. If no error is encountered, R0<63:62> is set to '00'. If no bytes were written because the terminal was not ready, R0<63:62> is set to '10'. If an error is encountered writing a byte, R0<63:62> is set to '00'. Examples of errors during byte transmission include data overrun or loss of carrier.

When an error is returned by PUTS, additional device-specific error status may be contained in R0<60:48>.

Multiple invocations of PUTS may be necessary because the console terminal may accept only a very few bytes in a reasonable period of time.

The output byte stream located by R18 should be mapped and read accessible by the kernel; the return address indicated by R26 should be mapped and executable by the kernel.

2.3.4.4 RESET_TERM — Reset Console Terminal to default parameters

Format:

status   = DISPATCH (RESET_TERM,unit)

Inputs:

RESET_TERM	= R16;	RESET_TERM function code – 03_{16}
unit	= R17;	Terminal device unit number
retadr	= R26;	Return address

Outputs:

status   = R0;   Status:

                   R0<63>   '0'   Success, terminal reset

                             '1'   Failure, terminal not fully reset

               R0<62:0>   SBZ

RESET_TERM resets a console terminal device and its CTB to their initial, default state. All errors in the CTB are cleared. For implementations that support multiple terminal devices, R17 contains the unit number to be reset; otherwise, R17 should be zero.

The CTB describes the capabilities of the terminal device and its initial, default state. Depending on the terminal device type and particular console implementation, other terminal devices may be affected by the routine.

Programming Note:

For example, if multiple terminal units share a common interrupt, that interrupt may be disabled or enabled for all.

If the console terminal is successfully reset, RESET_TERM returns with R0<63> set to '0'. If errors are encountered, the routine attempts to return the console terminal to a usable state and then returns with R0<63> set to '1'.

The return address indicated by R26 should be mapped and executable by the kernel.

2.3.4.5 SET_TERM_CTL — Set Console Terminal Controls

Format

status   = DISPATCH (SET_TERM_CTL, unit, ctb)

Inputs

SET_TERM_CTL   = R16;   SET_TERM_CTL function code – 05_{16}

unit   = R17;   Terminal device unit number

ctb   = R18;   Virtual address of CTB

retadr   = R26;   Return address

Outputs:

status   = R0;   Status:

	R0<63>	'0'	Success, requested change completed
		'1'	Failure, change not completed
	R0<62:32>	SBZ	
	R0<31:0>	Offset to offending CTB field (unsigned)	

SET_TERM_CTL, if successful, changes the characteristics of a console terminal device and updates its CTB. The changes are specified by fields contained in a CTB located by R18. The characteristics that can be changed, hence the active CTB fields, depend on the console terminal device type.

For implementations that support multiple terminal devices, R17 contains the unit number to be reset; otherwise, R17 should be zero.

If the console terminal characteristics are successfully changed, SET_TERM_CTL returns with R0<63> set to '0'. If errors are encountered or if the terminal device does not support the requested settings, the routine attempts to return the device to the previous usable state and then returns with R0<63> set to '1' and R0<31:0> set to the offset of an offending or unsupported field in the CTB located by R18. Regardless of success or failure, the device CTB table entry always contains the current device characteristics upon routine return. SET_TERM_CTL returns the CTB located by R18 without modification.

The CTB located by R18 should be mapped and read accessible by the kernel; the return address indicated by R26 should be mapped and executable by the kernel.

2.3.4.6 SET_TERM_INT - Set Console Terminal Interrupts

Format:

status $\qquad$ = DISPATCH (SET_TERM_INT,unit,mask)

Inputs:

SET_TERM_INT	= R16;	SET_TERM_INT function code – 04_{16}
unit	= R17;	Terminal device unit number
mask	= R18;	Bit encoded mask:

R18<63:10>	SBZ	
R18<9:8>	'01'	No change to receive interrupts
	'00'	Disable receive interrupts
	'1X'	Enable receive interrupts
R18<7:2>	SBZ	
R18<1:0>	'01'	No change to transmit interrupts
	'00'	Disable transmit interrupts
	'1X'	Enable transmit interrupts

retadr	= R26;	Return address

Outputs:

status	= R0;	Status:

R0<63>	'0'	Success
	'1'	Failure, operation not supported
R0<62:2>	SBZ	
R0<0>	'1'	Transmit interrupts enabled
	'0'	Transmit interrupts disabled
R0<1>	'1'	Receive interrupts enabled
	'0'	Receive interrupts disabled

SET_TERM_INT reads, enables, and disables transmit and receive interrupts from a console terminal device and updates its CTB. For implementations that support multiple terminal devices, R17 contains the unit number to be reset; otherwise, R17 should be zero.

If the interrupt settings are successfully changed, the routine returns with R0<63> set to '0'. If the terminal device does not support the requested setting, the routine returns with R0<63> set to '1'.

Programming Note:

For example, a device that has a unified transmit/receive interrupt would not support a request to enable transmit interrupts while leaving receive interrupts disabled.

Regardless of success or failure, the routine always returns with the previous settings in R0<1:0>. The current state of the interrupt settings can be read without change by invoking SET_TERM_INT with R18<1:0> and R18<9:8> set to '01'.

The return address indicated by R26 should be mapped and executable by the kernel.

2.3.5 Console Generic I/O Device Routines

The Alpha console provides primitive generic I/O device routines for system software use during the bootstrap or crash process. These routines serve in place of the more sophisticated system software I/O drivers until such time as these drivers can be established. These routines may also be used to access console-private devices that are not directly accessible by the processor.

During the bootstrap process, these routines can be used to acquire a secondary bootstrap program from a system bootstrap device or write messages to a terminal other than the logical console terminal. When the operating system is about to crash, these routines can be used to write dump files.

These routines are *not* intended for use while the operating system is fully functional. These routines may:

- Alter the current IPL.

  The console may raise the current IPL. It may lower the current IPL only insofar as the state presented to the operating system remains consistent, as though the IPL had not been lowered. The console must ensure that interrupts that would not have been delivered at the caller's IPL are pended and delivered to the operating system at the conclusion of the callback.

- Block interrupts.

  These routines may cause any and all interrupts to be blocked or delivered to and serviced by the console for the duration of the routine execution.

- Block exceptions.

  These routines may cause any and all exceptions to be blocked or delivered to and serviced by the console for the duration of the routine execution.

- Alter the existing memory management policy.

  The console may substitute a console-private (or bootstrap address) mapping for the duration of the routine execution.

  Programming Note:
  The console must resolve any virtually addressed arguments before altering the existing memory management policy.

- Take any length of time for completion.

  The operating system cannot guarantee timeliness when invoking these routines. Any operating system timer may have expired before their return. The time necessary for completion is UNPREDICTABLE; however, a console implementation will attempt to minimize the time whenever possible.

Before returning to the invoking system software, these routines must restore any altered processor state. These routines must return to the calling system software at the IPL and in the memory management policy of that software.

System software invokes these routines synchronously. When invoking these routines, system software must:

- Be executing in kernel mode.

  If these routines are invoked in other modes, their execution causes UNPREDICTABLE operation.

- Be executing on the primary processor in a multiprocessor configuration.

  If these routines are invoked on other processors, their execution causes UNDEFINED operation.

2.3.5.1 CLOSE — Close Generic I/O Device for Access

Format:

status   = DISPATCH (CLOSE,channel)

Inputs:

CLOSE	= R16;	CLOSE function code – 11_{16}
channel	= R17;	Channel to close
retadr	= R26;	Return address

Outputs:

status	= R0;	Status:

R0<63>	'0'	Success
	'1'	Failure
R0<62:60>	SBZ	
R0<59:32>	Device-specific error status	
R0<31:0>	SBZ	

CLOSE deassigns the channel number from a previously opened block storage I/O device. The channel number is free to be reassigned. The I/O device must be reopened before any subsequent accesses.

CLOSE returns status in R0<63>. If the channel was open and the close is successful, R0<63> is set to '0'; otherwise R0<63> is set to '1' and additional device-specific status is recorded in R0<59:32>.

For magnetic tape devices, CLOSE does not affect the current tape position, nor is any rewind of the tape performed.

The return address indicated by R26 should be mapped and executable by the kernel.

2.3.5.2 IOCTL — Perform Device-Specific Operations

Format:

count   = DISPATCH (IOCTL,channel,R18,R19,R20,R21)

Inputs:

IOCTL	= R16;	IOCTL function code – 12_{16}
channel	= R17;	Channel number of device to be accessed
retadr	= R26;	Return address

For Magnetic Tape Devices Only:

operate	= R18;	Tape positioning operation:

                           '01'   For skip to next/previous interrecord gap
                           '02'   For skip over tape mark
                           '03'   For rewind
                           '04'   For write tape mark

count	= R19;	Number of skips to perform (signed)
	= R20 – R21	Reserved for future use as inputs

Outputs:

For Magnetic Tape Devices Only:

count	= R0;	Number of skips performed and status:

                          R0<63:62>   '00'   Success
                                        '10'   Failure, position not found
                                        '11'   Hardware failure
                          R0<61:60>   SBZ
                          R0<59:32>   Device-specific error status
                          R0<31:0>   Number of skips actually performed (signed)

IOCTL performs special device-specific operations on I/O devices. The operation performed and the interpretation of any additional arguments passed in R18–R21 are functions of the device type as designated by the channel number passed in R17.

For magnetic tape devices, the following operations are defined:

- '01' — IOCTL relocates the current tape position by skipping over a number of inter-record gaps. The direction of the skip and the number of gaps skipped is given by the signed 32-bit count in R19. Skipping with a count of '0' does not change the current tape position. The number of gaps actually skipped is returned in R0<31:0>.

- '02' — IOCTL relocates the current tape position by skipping over a number of tape marks. The direction of the skip and the number of marks skipped is given by the signed 32-bit count in R19. Skipping with a count of '0' does not change the current tape position. The number of tape marks actually skipped is returned in R0<31:0>.

- '03' — IOCTL rewinds the tape to the position just after the Beginning-of-Tape (BOT) marker. R0<31:0> is returned as SBZ.

- '04' — IOCTL writes a tape mark starting at the current position. R0<31:0> is returned as SBZ.

IOCTL returns magnetic tape operation status in R0<63:62>. If the operation was successful, R0<63:62> is set to '00'. If the tape positioning was not successful, the tape is left at the position where the error occurred and R0<63:62> is set to '10'. Tape positioning may fail due to encountering a BOT marker (R18 '01' or '02'), encountering a tape mark (R18 '01'), or running off the end of the tape. If a hardware device error is encountered, the final position of the tape is UNPREDICTABLE and R0<63:62> is set to '11'. In the event of an error, additional device-specific status is recorded in R0<59:32>.

The return address indicated by R26 should be mapped and executable by the kernel.

2.3.5.3 OPEN — Open Generic I/O Device for Access

Format:

channel   = DISPATCH (OPEN,devstr,length)

Inputs:

OPEN	= R16;	OPEN function code – 10_{16}
devstr	= R17;	Starting virtual address of byte string that contains the device specification
length	= R18;	Length of byte buffer
retadr	= R26;	Return address

Outputs:

channel	= R0;	Assigned channel number and status:

R0<63:62>   '00'   Success

                  '10'   Failure, device does not exist

                  '11'   Failure, error, device cannot be accessed or prepared

R0<61:60>   SBZ

R0<59:32>   Device-specific error status

R0<31:0>   Assigned channel number of device

OPEN prepares a generic I/O device for use by the READ and WRITE routines. R17 contains the base virtual address of a byte string that specifies the complete device specification of the I/O device. The length of the string is given in R18. The format and contents of the device specification string follow that of the BOOTED_DEV environment variable.

The routine assigns a unique channel number to the device. The channel number is returned in R0 and must be used to reference the device in subsequent calls to the READ, WRITE, and CLOSE routines.

OPEN returns status in R0<63:62>. If the I/O device exists and can be prepared for subsequent accesses, R0<63:62> is set to '00'. If the device does not exist, R0<63:62> is set to '10'. If the device exists, but errors are encountered in preparing the device, R0<63:62> is set to '11' and additional device-specific status is recorded in R0<59:32>. In the latter two failure cases, the channel number returned in R0<31:0> is UNPREDICTABLE.

All console implementations must support at least two concurrently opened generic I/O devices. Additional generic I/O devices may be supported.

For magnetic tape devices, OPEN does not affect the current tape position, nor is any rewind of the tape performed.

Multiple channels cannot be assigned to the same device; the second and any subsequent calls to OPEN fail with R0<63:62> set to '11' and R0<31:0> as UNPREDICTABLE. The status of the first opened channel is unaffected.

The input string located by R17 should be mapped and read accessible by the kernel; the return address indicated by R26 should be mapped and executable by the kernel.

2.3.5.4 READ — Read Generic I/O Device

Format:

    rcount   = DISPATCH (READ,channel,count,address,block)

Inputs:

READ	= R16;	READ function code – 13_{16}
channel	= R17;	Channel number of device to be accessed
count	= R18;	Number of bytes to be read (should be multiple of the device's record length) (unsigned)
address	= R19;	Virtual address of buffer to read data into
block	= R20;	Logical block number of data to read (used only by disk devices)
retadr	= R26;	Return address

Outputs:

rcount	= R0;	Number of bytes read and status:

                    R0<63>   '0'   Success
                                        '1'   Failure
                    R0<62>   '1'   EOT or Logical End of Device condition encountered
                                        '0'   Otherwise
                    R0<61>   '1'   Illegal record length specified
                                        '0'   Otherwise
                    R0<60>   '1'   Run off end of tape
                                        '0'   Otherwise
                    R0<59:32>   Device-specific error status
                    R0<31:0>   Number of bytes actually read (unsigned)

READ causes data to be read from the generic I/O device designated by the channel number in R17 and written to a memory buffer pointed to by R19. The 32-bit transfer byte count, hence length of the buffer, is contained in R18. The buffer must be quadword aligned, virtually mapped, and resident in physical memory.

READ returns transfer status in R0<63:60> and the number of bytes actually read, if any, in R0<31:0>. If the routine is successful, R0<63> is set to '0'. If an error is encountered in accessing the device, R0<63> is set to '1'. Additional device-specific status may be returned in R0<59:32>.

The transfer byte count should be a multiple of the record length of the device. If the specified byte count is not a multiple of the record length, R0<61> is set to '1'. If the count exceeds the record length, the count is rounded down to the nearest multiple of the record length and READ attempts to read that number of bytes. If the record length exceeds the count, it is

UNPREDICTABLE whether READ attempts to access the device. If no read attempt is made, R0<63> is set to '1'.

For magnetic tape devices, READ does not interpret the tape format or differentiate between ANSI formatted and unformatted tapes. The routine reads the requested transfer byte count starting at the current tape position. READ terminates when one of the following occurs:

- The specified number of bytes have been read. In this case, R0<63:60> is set to '0000'.

- An interrecord gap is encountered. In this case, the tape is positioned to the next position after the gap and R0<63:60> is set to '0000'.

- A tape mark is encountered. In this case, the tape is positioned to the next position after the tape mark and R0<63:60> is set to '0100'. (After calling READ and finding a tape mark, the caller can determine if the logical End-of-Volume or an empty file section has been found by calling READ again. The condition exists if the second READ returns with zero bytes read and a tape mark found.)

- The routine runs off the end of tape. In this case, R0<63:60> is set to '1001'.

READ ignores End-of-Tape (EOT) markers.

For disk devices, READ does not understand the file structure of the device. The routine reads the requested transfer byte count starting at the logical block number specified by R20. The transfer continues until either the specified number of bytes has been read or the last logical block on the device has been read. If the logical end of the device is encountered, then R0<63:62> is set to '01'.

For network devices, READ interprets and removes any device-specific or protocol-specific packet headers. If a packet has been received, the remainder of the packet is copied into the specified buffer. If a packet has not been received, the routine returns with R0<31:0> set to '0'. Only those network packets that are specifically addressed to this system and are of the specified protocol type are returned; broadcast packets are not returned. The actual packet size is dependent on the device and protocol; the characteristics of the network device and protocol are specified at the time of the channel OPEN.

The buffer pointed to by R19 should be mapped and write accessible by the kernel; the return address indicated by R26 should be mapped and executable by the kernel.

2.3.5.5 WRITE — Write Generic I/O Device

Format:

wcount   = DISPATCH (WRITE,channel,count,address,block)

Inputs:

WRITE	= R16;	WRITE function code – 14_{16}
channel	= R17;	Channel number of device to be accessed
count	= R18;	Number of bytes to be written (should be multiple of the device's record length) (unsigned)
address	= R19;	Virtual address of buffer to read data from
block	= R20;	Logical block number of data to be written (used only by disk devices)
retadr	= R26;	Return address

Outputs:

wcount   = R0;   Number of bytes written and status:

R0<63>	'0'	Success
	'1'	Failure
R0<62>	'1'	EOT or Logical End of Device condition encountered
	'0'	Otherwise
R0<61>	'1'	Illegal record length specified
	'0'	Otherwise
R0<60>	'1'	If run off end of tape
	'0'	Otherwise
R0<59:32>	Device-specific error status	
R0<31:0>	Number of bytes actually written (unsigned)	

WRITE causes data to be written to the generic I/O device designated by the channel number in R17 and read from a memory buffer pointed to by R19. The 32-bit transfer byte count, hence length of the buffer, is contained in R18. The buffer must be quadword aligned, virtually mapped, and resident in physical memory.

WRITE returns transfer status in R0<63:60> and the number of bytes actually written, if any, in R0<31:0>. If the routine is successful, R0<63> is set to '0'. If an error is encountered in accessing the device, R0<63> is set to '1'. Additional device-specific status may be returned in R0<59:32>.

The transfer byte count should be a multiple of the record length of the device. If the specified byte count is not a multiple of the record length, R0<61> is set to '1'. If the count exceeds the record length, the count is rounded down to the nearest multiple of the record length and WRITE attempts to write that number of bytes. If the record length exceeds the count, it is

UNPREDICTABLE whether WRITE attempts to access the device. If no write attempt is made, R0<63> is set to '1'.

For magnetic tape devices, WRITE does not interpret the tape format or differentiate between ANSI formatted and unformatted tapes. The routine writes the requested transfer byte count starting at the current tape position. WRITE terminates when any of the following occur:

- The specified number of bytes has been written without detecting an End-of-Tape (EOT) marker. In this case, R0<63:60> is set to '0000'.

- The specified number of bytes has been written and an End-of-Tape (EOT) marker was detected. In this case, R0<63:60> is set to '0100'.

- The routine runs off the end of tape. In this case, R0<63:60> is set to '1001'.

For disk devices, WRITE does not understand the file structure of the device. The routine writes the requested transfer byte count starting at the logical block number specified by R20. The transfer continues until either the specified number of bytes has been written or the last logical block on the device has been written. If the logical end of the device is encountered, then R0<63:62> is set to '01'.

For network devices, WRITE appends any device-specific or protocol-specific headers. The routine transmits the specified requested transfer bytes with the proper network protocol over the appropriate network. The actual packet size is dependent on the device and protocol; the characteristics of the network device and protocol are specified at the time of the channel OPEN.

The buffer pointed to by R19 should be mapped and write accessible by the kernel; the return address indicated by R26 should be mapped and executable by the kernel.

2.3.6 Console Environment Variable Routines

System software accesses the environment variables indirectly through console callback routines. These routines may be invoked while the operating system is fully functional as well as during operating system bootstrap or crash. The GET_ENV, SET_ENV, and RESET_ENV routines are subject to the constraints given in Section 2.3.1. These routines must:

- Not alter the current IPL or current mode.

  These routines must be invoked in kernel mode.

- Not alter the existing memory management policy.

  All internal pointers must be remapped by FIXUP.

- Not block interrupts.

  The operating system must be capable of continuing to receive hardware and software interrupts.

The constraints on SAVE_ENV differ; see Section 2.3.6.3.

The time necessary for these routines to complete is UNPREDICTABLE; however, a console implementation will attempt to minimize the time whenever possible.

Software Note:

Implementations must limit the execution time of these routines to significantly less than the interval clock interrupt period.

The console implementation must ensure that any access to an environment variable is atomic. The console implementation must resolve multiple competing accesses by system software as well as competing accesses by system software and the console presentation layer.

When invoking these routines, system software must be executing in kernel mode. If these routines are invoked in other modes, their execution causes UNPREDICTABLE operation.

These routines may be invoked on both the primary and secondary processors in a multiprocessor configuration. It is recommended that system software serialize competing accesses to a given environment variable; a stale value may be returned if GET_ENV is invoked simultaneously with SET_ENV or RESET_ENV.

2.3.6.1 GET_ENV — Get an Environment Variable

Format:

status   = DISPATCH (GET_ENV,ID,value,length)

Inputs:

GET_ENV	= R16;	GET_ENV function code – 22_{16}
ID	= R17;	ID of environment variable
value	= R18;	Starting virtual address of buffer to contain returned value
length	= R19;	Number of bytes in buffer (unsigned)
retadr	= R26;	Return address

Outputs:

status	= R0;	Status:		
		R0<63:61>	'000'	Success
			'001'	Success, byte stream truncated
			'110'	Failure, variable not recognized
		R0<60:32>	SBZ	
		R0<31:0>	Count of bytes returned (unsigned)	

GET_ENV causes the value of the environment variable specified by the ID in R17 to be returned in the byte stream specified by the virtual address in R18. The size in bytes of the input buffer is contained in R19.

GET_ENV returns status in R0<63:61>. If the environment variable is recognized, R0<63:62> is set to '00', its current value is copied into the byte stream, and R0<31:0> is set to the number of bytes copied. If the value must be truncated, R0<61> is set to '1'. If the variable is not recognized, R0<63:61> is set to '110' and R0<31:0> is set to '0'.

The byte stream indicated by R18 should be mapped and write accessible by the kernel; the return address indicated by R26 should be mapped and executable by the kernel.

2.3.6.2 RESET_ENV — Reset an Environment Variable

Format:

status $= \text{DISPATCH} (\text{RESET\_ENV},\text{ID},\text{value},\text{length})$

Inputs:

RESET_ENV	= R16;	RESET_ENV function code – 21_{16}
ID	= R17;	ID of environment variable
value	= R18;	Starting virtual address of byte stream to contain returned value
length	= R19;	Number of bytes in buffer (unsigned)
retadr	= R26;	Return address

Outputs:

status	= R0;	Status:	
		R0<63:61>	'000' Success
			'001' Success, byte stream truncated
			'100' Failure, variable read-only
			'101' Failure, variable read-only, byte stream truncated
			'110' Failure, variable not recognized
		R0<60:32>	SBZ
		R0<31:0>	Count of bytes returned (unsigned)

RESET_ENV causes the environment variable specified by the ID in R17 to be reset to the system default value and that default value to be returned in the byte stream specified by the virtual address in R18. The size in bytes of the input buffer is contained in R19.

RESET_ENV returns status in R0<63:61>. If the environment variable is successfully reset to the default value, R0<63:62> is set to '00'. If the variable is recognized but read-only, the value is unchanged and R0<63:62> is set to '10'. In both cases, the default value is copied into the byte stream and R0<31:0> is set to the number of bytes copied; if the value must be truncated, R0<61> is set to '1'. If the variable is not recognized, R0<63:61> is set to '110' and R0<31:0> is set to '0'.

The byte stream indicated by R18 should be mapped and write accessible by the kernel; the return address indicated by R26 should be mapped and executable by the kernel.

2.3.6.3 SAVE_ENV - Save Current Environment Variables

Format:

status	= DISPATCH (SAVE_ENV)

Inputs:

SAVE_ENV	= R16;	SAVE_ENV function code – 23_{16}
retadr	= R26;	Return address

Outputs:

status	= R0;	Status:

R0<63:61>	'000' Success, all values saved
	'001' Success, some bytes saved, additional values to be saved
	'110' Failure, routine unsupported
	'111' Failure, error encountered saving values
R0<60:0>	SBZ

SAVE_ENV attempts to update the nonvolatile storage of those environment variables that must be retained across console initializations and system power transitions.

Programming Note:

For example, SAVE_ENV may cause an EEPROM to be updated. That update may write all "NV" environment variable values to the EEPROM, or may only write those variables that have been modified since the last update or console initialization.

This routine is not subject to the constraints given in Section 2.3.6. The console may usurp operating system control of the system platform hardware, but must restore any such control or altered state before return. The console must not service any interrupts or exceptions that are otherwise intended for the operating system.

The nonvolatile storage update may take significant time and multiple invocations of SAVE_ENV may be necessary. The time necessary for this routine to complete is UNPREDICTABLE. A console implementation will attempt to minimize the time whenever possible and must return in a timely fashion. The routine must return after partial operation completion if necessary. It is the responsibility of the console to ensure that subsequent calls make forward progress. The operating system may delay for extended periods between subsequent calls; the console must not rely on timely invocations of SAVE_ENV.

Implementation Note:

Implementations must limit the execution time of these routines to significantly less than the interval clock interrupt period. A return after partial operation completion is preferable to long latency.

SAVE_ENV returns status on the update in R0<63:61>. When the update has successfully completed and all relevant variables have been saved, the routine returns with R0<63:61> set to '000'. If SAVE_ENV returns after only a partial update to ensure timely response, R0<63:61> set to '001'. If an unrecoverable error is encountered, the routine returns with R0<63:61> set to '111'. The contents of the nonvolatile storage are UNDEFINED.

Implementation of SAVE_ENV is optional. If the console does not support SAVE_ENV, the routine returns with R0<63:61> set to '110'.

On a multiprocessor system with an embedded console, the routine must be invoked on each processor in the configuration. Section 3.8.1

It is recommended that system software ensure that calls to SET_ENV or RESET_ENV are not issued while an update operation is in progress on any processor. It is UNPREDICTABLE whether the updated environment value is saved.

The return address indicated by R26 should be mapped and executable by the kernel. This routine does not affect the current value of any environment variable maintained by the console.

2.3.6.4 SET_ENV — Set an Environment Variable

Format:

status	= DISPATCH (SET_ENV,ID,value,length)

Inputs:

SET_ENV	= R16;	SET_ENV function code - 20_{16}
ID	= R17;	ID of environment variable
value	= R18;	Starting virtual address of byte stream containing value
length	= R19;	Number of bytes in buffer (unsigned)
retadr	= R26;	Return address

Outputs:

status	= R0;	Status:		
		R0<63:61>	'000'	Success
			'100'	Failure, variable read-only
			'110'	Failure, variable not recognized
			'111'	Failure, byte stream exceeds value length
		R0<60:31>	SBZ	
		R0<31:0>	Maximum value length (unsigned)	

SET_ENV causes the environment variable specified by the ID in R17 to have the value specified by the byte stream value pointed to by the virtual address in R18. The size in bytes of the input buffer is contained in R19.

SET_ENV returns status in R0<63:61>. If the environment variable is successfully set to the new value, R0<63:61> is set to '000'. If the variable is not recognized, R0<63:61> is set to '110'. If the variable is read-only, the value is unchanged and R0<63:61> is set to '100'. If the input buffer exceeds the maximum value length, the value is unchanged and R0<63:61> is set to '111'. In all cases, the maximum value length is returned in R0<31:0>.

The byte stream indicated by R18 should be mapped and read accessible by the kernel; the return address indicated by R26 should be mapped and executable by the kernel.

2.3.7 Miscellaneous Routines

2.3.7.1 FIXUP — Fixup Virtual Addresses in Console Routines

Format:

status   = FIXUP (NEW_BASE_VA, HWRPB_VA)

Inputs:

NEW_BASE_VA	= R16;	New starting virtual address of the console callback routines
HWRPB_VA	= R17;	New starting virtual address of the HWRPB
retadr	= R26;	Return address

Outputs:

status	= R0;	Status:		
		R0<63>	'0'	Success
			'1'	Failure
		R0<62:0>	SBZ	

FIXUP adjusts virtual address references in all other console callback routines using the new starting virtual address in R16, the new starting virtual address of the HWRPB in R17, and the current contents of the CRB. See Section 2.3.8.1.2 for a full description of FIXUP usage and functionality.

If FIXUP is successful, it returns with R0<63> set to '0'. If FIXUP is not successful, console internal state has been compromised. The console attempts a cold bootstrap if the state transition in Figure 3–1 indicates a bootstrap and the BOOT_RESET environment variable is set to "ON" ($4E4F_{16}$). Otherwise, the system remains in console I/O mode.

This routine must be called in kernel mode and in the context of the existing memory mapping; otherwise its execution causes UNPREDICTABLE or UNDEFINED operation.

Software Note:

FIXUP must be called while the original address space mapping is in effect.

The return address indicated by R26 should be mapped and executable by the kernel.

2.3.7.2 PSWITCH — Switch Primary Processors

Format:

status = DISPATCH (PSWITCH,action)

Inputs:

PSWITCH	= R16;	PSWITCH function code – 30_{16}
action	= R17;	Action requests:

R17<63:2> SBZ

R17<1:0>	'01'	Transition from primary
	'10'	Transition to primary
	'11'	Switch primary

cpu_id	= R18;	New primary CPU ID
retadr	= R26;	Return address

Outputs:

status	= R0;	Status:

R0<63>	'0'	Success
	'1'	Failure, operation not supported
R0<62:0>		Implementation-specific error status

PSWITCH attempts to perform any implementation-specific functions necessary to support primary switching. R17 indicates the requested primary transition action. R18 contains the CPU ID (WHAMI IPR) of the new primary.

PSWITCH is invoked by the old primary, the secondary that is to become the new primary, or both. See Section 3.5.6 for a full description of PSWITCH usage, functionality, and error returns.

If PSWITCH is successful, it returns with R0<63> set to '0'. If PSWITCH is unsuccessful for any reason, it returns with R0<63> set to '1' and implementation-specific status in R0<62:0>.

PSWITCH is invoked at the highest IPL level or it produces UNDEFINED results. The return address indicated by R26 should be mapped and executable by the kernel.

2.3.7.3 BIOS_EMUL — Run BIOS Emulation Callback

Format:

status   = DISPATCH (BIOS_EMUL, int86, input_flags, x86_regs, additional_data)

Inputs

func_code	= R16;	BIOS_EMUL function code – 32_{16}
int86	= R17;	BIOS interrupt number (also called the BIOS service number)
input_flags	= R18;	The following input flags:

         R18<63:5>   SBZ

         R18<4>   '1'   Use data in R20

                            '0'   Ignore R20

         R18<3:1>   Type of BIOS emulator to service the call:

'000'	16-bit emulator type
'001'	32-bit emulator type
'010'	64-bit emulator type
'011'	Reserved
'100'	Reserved
'101'	Reserved
'110'	Reserved
'111'	Reserved

         R18<0>   Type of call:

'1'	Emulator type inquiry
'0'	Service

x86_regs	= R19;	Virtual address of x86 register data block that represents the x86 register set for BIOS calls.

                                          Use the appropriate register structure for the type of BIOS emulator:

                                          16-bit emulator — Use register structure 1 (Figure 2–4)

                                          32-bit emulator — Use register structure 2 (Figure 2–4)

                                          64-bit emulator — Not defined for this version of the architecture

Additional_data	= R20;	Virtual address of additional argument data. Specific to BIOS call
Retaddr	= R26;	Return address

Outputs:

status   = R0   Status:

If R18<0> = 0, R0 has the following meaning:

R0<63>	'0'	Callback supported
	'1'	Callback not supported
R0<62>	'0'	Emulator type supported
	'1'	Emulator type not supported
R0<61>	'0'	Service number supported
	'1'	Service number not supported

R0<60:56>   SBZ

R0<55:0>   Implementation-specific

If R18<0> = 1, R0 has the following meaning:

R0<63>	'0'	Callback supported
	'1'	Callback not supported

R0<62:59>   SBZ

R0<58:56>   Return console's emulator type:

'000'	No emulator in this console
'001'	16-bit emulator in this console
'010'	32-bit emulator in this console
'011'	64-bit emulator in this console

R0<55:0>   SBZ

The resulting x86 register state from the BIOS call is placed in the data block located at x86_regs (R19). Success or failure of the BIOS call is specific to the attempted call and the expected result in x86_regs.

The BIOS_EMUL callback provides access to the BIOS emulator, allowing emulation of the x86 INT assembler instruction.

The int86 value specifies the BIOS interrupt number to be emulated. A data block representing the x86 register set is used as input and is updated on return because operation of BIOS calls requires setting the x86 register set before the BIOS call and receiving data in them as the result of a BIOS call.

Programming Notes:

If a platform or pre-existing version of the firmware does not support BIOS_EMUL, R0<63> returns '1' .

The caller can determine the type of BIOS emulator in the console by setting R18<0> to '1'. BIOS_EMUL returns the type in R0<58:56>.

Because multiple BIOS emulators can be built into the console, use R18<3:1> to specify the type of BIOS emulator and register structure. If the console does not support a specified type, R0<63> and R0<62> return '1'.

BIOS_EMUL supports only INT10 service calls, and for any other service number, R0<63> returns '1'.

The caller should maintain the integrity of the register structure as input/output across multiple calls. The routine uses the register structure values as passed and returns the end values in the same structure.

The return address indicated by R26 should be mapped and kernel-executable.

Figure 2–4: BIOS Emulator Register Structures

Register Structure 1

31	24 23	16 15	8 7	0	
SBZ	SBZ	AH	AL		VA
SBZ	SBZ	BH	BL		+4
SBZ	SBZ	CH	CL		+8
SBZ	SBZ	DH	DL		+12
SBZ	SBZ	SP			+16
SBZ	SBZ	BP			+20
SBZ	SBZ	SI			+24
SBZ	SBZ	DI			+28
SBZ	SBZ	CS			+32
SBZ	SBZ	DS			+36
SBZ	SBZ	SS			+40
SBZ	SBZ	ES			+44
SBZ	SBZ	FLAGS			+48
SBZ	SBZ	IP			+52

Register Structure 2

31	24 23	16 15	8 7	0	
		EAX			VA
		EBX			+4
		ECX			+8
		EDX			+12
		ESP			+16
		EBP			+20
		ESI			+24
		EDI			+28
SBZ	SBZ	CS			+32
SBZ	SBZ	DS			+36
SBZ	SBZ	SS			+40
SBZ	SBZ	ES			+44
		EFLAGS			+48
		EIP			+52

Background Notes on BIOS Emulation:

- BIOS

  BIOS, or Basic Input Output System, is firmware that initializes the hardware and sets it to a known state or to a state that is chosen by the hardware vendor or the system user. The BIOS code performs a power-up self-test (POST), configures buses and devices, and provides an interface to boot the operating system. BIOS code can also provide a set of functions that allows other system software to program devices to a given mode or state. Those functions are device-dependent, but follow an industry standard that is supported by most hardware vendors. Most BIOS code is written in the x86 assembly language.

- BIOS Emulation

  To support standard BIOS firmware (x86-based) on Alpha-based platforms, the Alpha console has a built-in emulator that emulates the x86 instruction set. The emulator supports VGA BIOS functions and is limited to the less complex, INT10, VGA BIOS calls. The emulator supports a large number of third-party graphics cards on Alpha-based platforms.

  The emulator can be 16 bit or 32 bit. A 16-bit emulator limits its support to the 16-bit register and instruction sets. A 32-bit emulator supports the 32-bit register and instruction sets, as well as the 16-bit instruction set.

- BIOS_EMUL Callback Routine

  The BIOS_EMUL callback routine provides a generic interface to the BIOS emulator. It provides a mechanism to request the console's BIOS emulator type and returns appropriate status and error codes that indicate supported and unsupported arguments. Operating systems require this interface to support third-party graphics cards for different Alpha platforms.

  Commodity PC graphics cards (SVGA) rely heavily on the BIOS to set the graphics mode. Vendors generally do not document how to set a graphics mode by register programming (like 1280x1024), but instead refer to the BIOS INT10 call, which is used to set up the card. Without the interface provided by BIOS_EMUL, the operating system has no access to BIOS emulation, and the graphics cards must be programmed by specialized code in the driver. Further, BIOS_EMUL allows the operating system to maintain support for graphics cards when vendors release new versions, because the interface lets the operating system continue to correctly interact with any changed mode parameters.

2.3.8 Console Callback Routine Data Structures

The console and system software share two data structures that are necessary for the console callback routines: the Console Routine Block (CRB) and the Console Terminal Block (CTB) table. Both are located by offset fields in the HWRPB as shown in Figure 2–5.

The CRB locates all addresses necessary for console callback routine function. The base physical address of the CRB is obtained by adding the CRB OFFSET field at HWRPB[192] to the base physical address of the HWRPB. The CRB format is shown in Figure 2–6 and described in Table 2–10.

The CTB table contains information necessary to describe the console terminal devices. The base physical address of the CTB table is obtained by adding the CTB TABLE OFFSET field at HWRPB[184] to the base physical address of the HWRPB. The CTB format is shown in Figure 2–7 and described in Table 2–11.

Figure 2–5: Console Data Structure Linkage

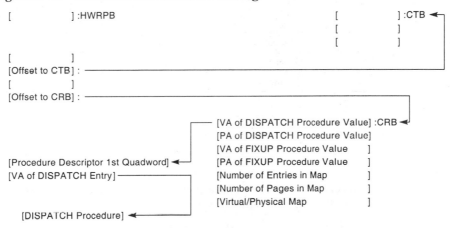

2.3.8.1 Console Routine Block

Before transferring control to system software, the console ensures that the console callback routines, console-private data structures, and associated local I/O space locations are mapped into region 0 of initial bootstrap address space. All necessary pages are located by the console routine block (CRB).

Figure 2–6: Console Routine Block

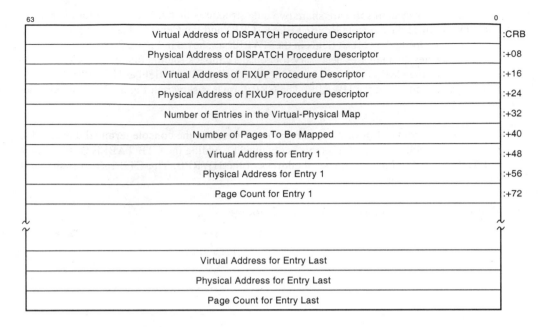

63	0	
Virtual Address of DISPATCH Procedure Descriptor		:CRB
Physical Address of DISPATCH Procedure Descriptor		:+08
Virtual Address of FIXUP Procedure Descriptor		:+16
Physical Address of FIXUP Procedure Descriptor		:+24
Number of Entries in the Virtual-Physical Map		:+32
Number of Pages To Be Mapped		:+40
Virtual Address for Entry 1		:+48
Physical Address for Entry 1		:+56
Page Count for Entry 1		:+72
Virtual Address for Entry Last		
Physical Address for Entry Last		
Page Count for Entry Last		

Table 2–10: CRB Fields

Offset	Description
CRB	DISPATCH VA — The virtual address of the OpenVMS procedure descriptor for the DISPATCH procedure
+08	DISPATCH PA — The physical address of the OpenVMS procedure descriptor for the DISPATCH procedure.
+16	FIXUP VA — The virtual address of the OpenVMS procedure descriptor for the FIXUP procedure.
+24	FIXUP PA — The physical address of the OpenVMS procedure descriptor for the FIXUP procedure.
+32	ENTRIES — The number of entries in the virtual-physical map. Unsigned integer.
+40	PAGES — The total number of physical pages to be mapped. Unsigned integer.

Table 2–10: CRB Fields (Continued)

Offset	Description
+48	ENTRY — Each entry identifies a collection of physically contiguous pages to be mapped. Each map entry consists of three quadwords:

Offset	Name	Description
+00	ENTRY_VA	Base virtual address for entry
+08	ENTRY_PA	Base physical address for entry
+16	ENTRY_PAGES	Number of contiguous physical pages to be mapped. Unsigned integer.

The CRB must be quadword aligned. The DISPATCH and FIXUP addresses must be quadword aligned; all unused bits should be zero. The ENTRY addresses must be page aligned and all unused bits should be zero.

The DISPATCH and FIXUP procedure descriptors located by DISPATCH_PA, DISPATCH_VA, FIXUP_PA and FIXUP_VA must be contained within the pages located by the first virtual-physical map entry.

2.3.8.1.1 Console Routine Block Initialization

Before transferring control to system software, the console initializes all fields of the CRB. The console fills in all physical and virtual address fields, the number of entries in the virtual-physical map (ENTRIES), the total number of pages to be mapped (PAGES), and the virtual addresses contained in the OpenVMS procedure descriptors for the DISPATCH and FIXUP procedures.[1] PAGES is the sum of the contents of all ENTRY_PAGES fields.

All addresses are initially mapped within region 0 of the initial bootstrap address space. These addresses include the contents of the CRB and all addresses contained within the DISPATCH and FIXUP procedure descriptors. The mapping must permit kernel access with appropriate read/write/execute access. The KRE, KWE, and FOx PTE fields are never subsequently altered by system software. The initial mapping need not be virtually contiguous.

2.3.8.1.2 Console Routine Remapping

When the console transfers control to the system software, the console callback routines may be invoked by the system software without additional setup. All necessary virtual mappings into initial bootstrap address space must be performed by the console before transferring control.

The system software may virtually remap the console callback routines. Remapping permits the system software to relocate the routines to virtual addresses other than those assigned in initial bootstrap address space. Relocation requires that the console adjust (or fix up) various internal virtual address references.

---

1 The OpenVMS calling standard specifies that the second quadword of a procedure descriptor contains the entry address (virtual) of the procedure itself.

The system software invokes the FIXUP routine to enable the console to perform the necessary internal relocations. The FIXUP routine virtually relocates all console routines and adjusts any console-private virtual address pointers such as those used to locate a local I/O device or HWRPB data structure. If system software virtually remaps the HWRPB, FIXUP must be invoked before calling any other console callback routine; it is recommended that system software remap both the HWRPB and the console routines together. Calling the console callback routines after the HWRPB has been remapped from its original bootstrap address location results in UNDEFINED operation of the system.

To remap the console callback routines, the system software and the console cooperate as follows:

1. System software must be executing on the primary processor in a multiprocessor system.

2. System software determines the new base virtual address of the HWRPB; this remapping is optional. System software does not perform any remapping of the HWRPB at this step.

   System software need not remap the memory data descriptor table located by HWRPB[200]. See Section 2.1 for a description of the HWRPB and its size.

3. System software determines the new base virtual address of the console callback routines. The CRB entries will be mapped into a set of virtually contiguous pages. The CRB PAGES field (CRB[40]) is used to determine the number of pages that must be mapped. System software does not perform any remapping of the console callback routines at this step.

4. System software passes control to the console by calling FIXUP (NEW_BASE_VA, NEW_HWRPB_VA), initiating the remapping. NEW_BASE_VA is the new base virtual address as established in step 3. HWRPB_VA is the new starting virtual address of the HWRPB as established in step 2. The remapping process is only initiated at this step; do not attempt to access the HWRPB or CRB using the new VAs.

5. The console first locates the HWRPB, then locates the CRB using the CRB OFFSET field. The console then locates all internal pointers and adjusts them. All linkage sections and other console-internal pointers must be modified. These data structures can be located during FIXUP because the initial bootstrap address space mapping is in effect; any console-internal pointers are valid until modified.

   System software need not remap the optional CONFIG block or FRU table located by HWRPB OFFSET fields. If these blocks will subsequently be used by the console, they must be located by console-internal pointers and those pointers must be modified during FIXUP.

   DISPATCH and FIXUP are not uniquely remapped by the system software. The FIXUP must update the DISPATCH and FIXUP procedure descriptors located by CRB[8] and CRB[24]. The physical pages containing the procedure descriptors and the routines themselves must be included in the virtual-physical map.

   The relative virtual address offsets of the pages located by the entry map are not guaranteed to be retained across the FIXUP. The initial bootstrap address mapping of the physical pages located by the entry map is not required to be virtually contiguous. The system software remapping is required to be virtually contiguous. Any offsets that cross physical pages may have to be modified by FIXUP.

6. The console returns from FIXUP. If the FIXUP was not successful, console internal state has been compromised. The console attempts a cold bootstrap if the state transition in Figure 3–1 indicates a bootstrap and the BOOT_RESET environment variable is set to "ON" ($4E4F_{16}$). Otherwise, the system remains in console I/O mode.

7. System software updates each virtual-physical map entry of the CRB:

   A. The PTE and TB entries that correspond to the range of old virtual address are invalidated using the old ENTRY_VA and ENTRY_PAGES values.

   B. The new starting virtual address is written into the ENTRY_VA. This virtual address is computed by adding the NEW_BASE_VA to the sum of the PAGE_COUNTs of each preceding entry.

   C. New PTEs are constructed for each physical page. The new PTE FOx and protection fields are copied from the original bootstrap address PTE.

   Programming Note:
   It is the responsibility of the console to judiciously set both the protection and FOx bits in the bootstrap address PTE. In particular, if the console sets the FOE bit, there is no architectural guarantee that the console exception handler will gain control as a result, nor is there any obvious appropriate response for the operating system handler.

8. System software updates the DISPATCH and FIXUP VA's. The first virtual-physical map entry locates the physical page that contains the DISPATCH and FIXUP procedure descriptors.

9. System software updates all PTEs and invalidates all appropriate TB entries associated with the remapped HWRPB and any remapped OFFSET blocks.

At the completion of this process, the console callback routines are remapped and may again be used by system software. Since FIXUP itself is relocated, system software may remap the routines more than once.

2.3.8.2 Console Terminal Block Table

The Console Terminal Block (CTB) table indicates the current identity and characteristics of each console terminal device. The CTB table is the only data structure shared by the console and system software that describes the terminal devices accessible by console callback routines.

The CTB table contains an array of CTBs. Each CTB is a quadword-aligned structure with format as shown in Figure 2–7 and described in Table 2–11. The index of the CTB in the CTB table is the unit number of the terminal device. The CTB format consists of two parts: a header and a device-specific segment. The format of the header is common to all CTBs; the format of the device-specific segment is dependent on the unique device type.

There is *only one* console terminal. The console terminal unit is selected by the console presentation layer before bootstrapping the operating system. See Section 1.3. Once the operating system is bootstrapped, the console terminal unit should not be changed by the console presentation layer. Any attempt to do so results in UNDEFINED operation of the console. Specifically, if the console presentation layer halts the operating system, alters the console terminal unit, then restarts or continues operating system execution, the operation of the console is UNDEFINED. The console terminal unit is identified by the TTY_DEV environment variable.

During console initialization, the console:

1. Locates all console terminal devices.

2. Selects the console terminal.

3. Builds a CTB for each.

4. Initializes the CTB OFFSET field of the HWRPB.

5. Initializes each console terminal device.

6. Records the default state of each console terminal device in its CTB.

7. Records the unit number of the console terminal in the TTY_DEV environment variable.

Whenever the console changes the state of a console terminal device, the console must update its CTB to reflect the change. The console may record extended status on character transfers (GETC/PUTS) in the CTB.

System software uses the CTB to determine console terminal device characteristics. System software never directly modifies the contents of a CTB; such modifications can result in UNDEFINED operation of the console terminal device either as the result of a subsequent call to a console terminal routine or as the result of a console internal need to access a console terminal device (for example, as the result of a halt). System software calls the SET_TERM_CTL console terminal routine to change console terminal device characteristics.

Figure 2–7: Console Terminal Block

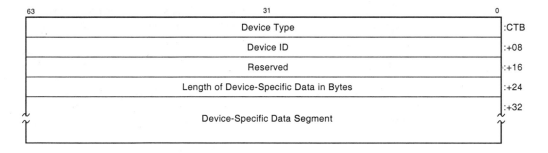

Table 2–11: CTB Fields

Offset	Description
CTB	DEVICE TYPE — Console terminal device type and format of the device-specific segment. Defined device types are:

Type	Description
0	No console present
1	Detached service processor
2	Serial line UART
3	Graphics display with LK keyboard connected to serial line UART
4	Multipurpose
Other	Reserved

Offset	Description
+08	DEVICE ID — The physical device and channel that sends and receives the console terminal stream. This field is necessary for configurations that include multiple-channel devices or multiple single-channel devices. The field has two subfields:

Bits	Description
<63:32>	Device index
<31:0>	Channel index

For implementations that support only a single directly connected console terminal device, this field is set to zero. The device ID is not necessarily related to the console terminal device unit number.

Offset	Description
+16	RESERVED — This field is reserved for future expansion and may not be used by the console or system software.
+24	DSD LENGTH — This field specifies the number of bytes in the device-specific data field, DSD.
+32	DSD — This field contains device-specific data associated with the unique console terminal type. Device-specific data may include such parameters as baud rate, flow control enable, and the current state of the CAPS LOCK key. The DSD field should contain only those items that must be shared between the console and system software.

2.4 Interprocessor Console Communications

This section considers only those communications between a running processor and a console processor. Communications paths between running processors are external to the console. Communications paths between console processors are internal to the console.

Commands are transmitted from a running primary to a console secondary; messages (and requests) are transmitted from a console secondary to a running primary. Commands and messages are passed via receive (RX) and transmit (TX) buffers contained in each per-CPU slot of the HWRPB. The use of these buffers is controlled by the Receive Buffer Ready (RXRDY) and Transmit Buffer Ready (TXRDY) flags.

The transmit and receive buffers are named from the point of view of the console secondary. The console secondary receives commands in the RX buffer and transmits messages in the TX buffer.

2.4.1 Interprocessor Console Communications Flags

The Receive Buffer Ready (RXRDY) and Transmit Buffer Ready (TXRDY) flags are used to control the interprocessor console communications. The RXRDY and TXRDY flags are gathered into bitmasks in the HWRPB at HWRPB[296] and HWRPB[304], respectively. The TXRDY bitmask allows a running primary to quickly determine which, if any, of the console secondaries are trying to send messages.

The running primary sets the appropriate RXRDY flag to indicate to the receiving console secondary that a command is contained in the secondary's RX buffer. The secondary is assumed to be polling its RXRDY flag. The RXRDY flag is cleared by the secondary after the command has been read from the RX buffer and before executing the command.

A console secondary sets its TXRDY flag to indicate to the running primary that a message is contained in the secondary's TX buffer. The console generates an interprocessor interrupt to the primary to notify it that a message is ready. System software clears the TXRDY flag after the message has been read from the TX buffer and before processing the message.

Implementation Note:

The TXRDY bitmask minimizes interprocessor interrupt service overhead by reducing the number of required memory lookups.

2.4.2 Interprocessor Console Communications Buffer Area

Each per-CPU slot of the HWRPB includes an RXTX Buffer Area that provides the communications path between processors. The buffer area is controlled by the RXRDY and TXRDY flags. The format is shown in Figure 2–8 and described in Table 2–12.

Figure 2–8: Inter-Console Communications Buffer

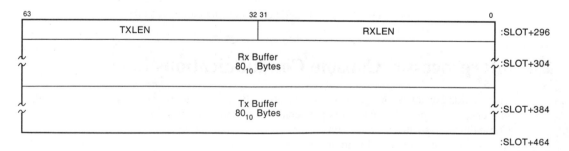

Table 2–12: Inter-Console Communications Buffer Fields

Offset	Description
SLOT+296	RXLEN — If the bit corresponding to this processor is set in the RXRDY bit-mask at HWRPB[296], the RXLEN field contains the length in bytes of the command in the RX buffer.
+300	TXLEN — If the bit corresponding to this processor is set in the TXRDY bit-mask at HWRPB[304], the TXLEN field contains the length in bytes of the message in the TX buffer
+304	RX BUFFER — Buffer used by this console secondary to receive a command from the running primary. Only command data is passed through this buffer; a console secondary does not receive messages from the running primary. Commands must end with "<CR><LF>" ($0A0D_{16}$).
+384	TX BUFFER — Buffer used by this console secondary to transmit a message to the running primary. Only message data is passed through this buffer; a console secondary does not send commands to the running primary. Messages must end with with the console secondary's prompt, "<CR><LF>Pnn>>>" ($3E3E$ $3Enn$ $nn50$ $0A0D_{16}$)

2.4.3 Sending a Command to a Secondary

The running primary manipulates the secondary's RXRDY flag and RX buffer in the following manner to send a command to a console secondary.

Programming Note:

The RXRDY flag is a software lock variable; the primary and the secondary must use LDQ_L/STQ_C instructions to set and clear bit n. See Common Architecture (I), Chapter 5.

In the following sequence, the console secondary is assumed to have CPU ID = n.

1. The primary examines bit n of the RXRDY bitmask. If the bit is clear, proceed to step 3.

2. The primary polls bit n of the RXRDY bitmask until clear or until some timeout is reached. If a timeout occurs, system software reports an error and takes appropriate action.

3. The primary moves the text of the desired console command into the RX buffer in the secondary's HWRPB slot (the nth per-CPU slot).

4. The primary sets the length of the command into the RXLEN field in the secondary's HWRPB slot (the nth per-CPU slot).

5. The primary sets bit n of the RXRDY bitmask to indicate there is a command waiting.

6. The secondary is assumed to be polling bit n of the RXRDY bitmask.

7. When the secondary notices that bit n of the RXRDY bitmask is set, it removes the command from its RX buffer.

8. The secondary clears bit n of the RXRDY bitmask, indicating that its RX buffer is again available.

9. The secondary attempts to process the command.

2.4.3.1 Sending a Message to the Primary

The console secondary manipulates its TXRDY flag and TX buffer in the following manner to return a message to the running primary.

Programming Note:

The TXRDY flag is a software lock variable; the primary and the secondary must use LDQ_L/STQ_C instructions to set and clear bit n. See Common Architecture (I), Chapter 5.

Again, the console secondary is assumed to have CPU ID = n.

1. The secondary examines bit n of the TXRDY bitmask. If the bit is clear, proceed to step 3.

2. The secondary polls this bit until it clears or until a long timeout occurs. (See step 7.)

3. The secondary moves the text of its response message into the TX buffer in the secondary's HWRPB slot (the nth per-CPU slot).

4. The secondary sets the length of the message into the TXLEN field in the secondary's HWRPB slot (the nth per-CPU slot).

5. The secondary sets bit n of the TXRDY bitmask to indicate there is a message waiting.

6. The secondary issues an interprocessor interrupt to the primary. This is always done; the primary need not poll for bits in the TXRDY bitmask.

7. The secondary polls the TXRDY bitmask until bit n clears or until a long timeout expires. This prevents the secondary from performing any action that might cause the message to be lost before the primary can process it.

   Programming Note:
   The secondary may be restarted once it has transmitted the error halt message to the primary. However, it must wait for the primary to have a reasonable chance to respond to the interprocessor interrupt and process the message before the restart proceeds, because that message is important visible evidence of the error halt condition. On the other hand, the secondary should not wait too long for the primary to respond because the primary may be affected by the same condition that caused the secondary to error halt. Hence, the need for a timeout that is of reasonable length.

8. As a result of the interprocessor interrupt, the primary eventually checks for console messages by examining the TXRDY bitmask. The primary notices that bit n of the TXRDY bitmask is set.

9. The primary removes the message from the TX buffer.

10. The primary clears bit n of the TXRDY bitmask, indicating that the TX buffer is again available.

The primary attempts to process the message.

Chapter 3

System Bootstrapping (III)

This chapter describes the net effects of the action of the console to control the system platform hardware. The major system state transitions and the role of the console in controlling those transitions are described in Section 3.1.1. When power is applied to an Alpha system, the console initializes the system as explained in Section 3.2. The console actions necessary to bootstrap system software include processor initialization (Section 3.4.1.5), memory sizing and testing (Section 3.4.1.1), building an initial virtual address space (Section 3.4.1.2), and loading the bootstrap (Section 3.6). The console actions to restart system software are described in Section 3.5.

3.1 Processor States and Modes

3.1.1 States and State Transitions

An Alpha processor can be in one of five major states:

1. Powered off — no system power supplied to the processor

2. Halted — operating system software execution suspended

3. Bootstrapping — attempting to load and start the operating system software

4. Restarting — attempting to restart the operating system software

5. Running — operating system software functioning

As shown in Figure 3–1, the transitions between the major states are determined by the current state and by a number of variables and events, including:

- Whether power is available to the system

- The console AUTO_ACTION environment variable, which specifies a "Halt action" (see CALL_PAL HALT)

- The console lock setting

- The Bootstrap–in–Progress (BIP) flags

- The Restart–Capable (RC) flags

- The CALL_PAL HALT instruction

- Console commands

Figure 3–1: Major State Transitions

Action Causing Transition to Final State	Initial State				
	Off	Halted	Booting	Restart	Running
Powerfail	Off	Off	Off	Off	Off
A and Power Restored	Halted				
B and Power Restored	Booting				
C and Power Restored	Restart				
BOOT and Console Is Locked		Booting			
START or CONTINUE (and) Console Is Unlocked		Running			
Bootstrap Fails or D			Halted		
Bootstrap Succeeds			Running		
D				Halted	
Restart Fails				Booting	
Restart Succeeds				Running	
A and Processor Halts or D					Halted
B and Processor Halts					Booting
C and Processor Halts					Restart

(The five rightmost columns constitute the Final State.)

Key to Figure 3–1

A   Console is unlocked and AUTO_ACTION is "HALT".

B   Console is unlocked and AUTO_ACTION is "BOOT".

C   Console is unlocked and AUTO_ACTION is "RESTART" or console is locked.

D   Console is unlocked, the processor is forced into console I/O mode.

To effect major state transitions, the console obeys these rules:

- If the console is unlocked when power is restored or when the processor halts, enter the state selected by the console AUTO_ACTION environment variable.

- If the console is locked when power is restored or when the processor halts, attempt a processor restart.

- When processor restart fails, attempt a bootstrap of that processor. One cause of a failed restart is the processor's RC flag being clear when the console attempts the restart.

- When system bootstrap fails, halt. One cause of a failed bootstrap is the processor's BIP flag being set before the console attempting the bootstrap. Only the processor that failed bootstrap will halt.

- When system bootstrap or processor restart succeeds, the processor starts running.

- When the primary processor is halted and the console is unlocked, the console BOOT command causes a system bootstrap.

- When a secondary processor is halted and the console is unlocked, the console START –CPU command causes the console to attempt to start that processor running.

- When a processor is halted and the console is unlocked, the console CONTINUE command causes the processor to continue running as though no halt was incurred.

- If the console is unlocked and a specified processor is running or booting or restarting, that processor is halted by a console HALT –CPU command.

  Implementation Note:

  > In an embedded console implementation, the primary processor must be forced into the console I/O mode before issuing the HALT –CPU command.

3.1.2 Major Modes

In addition to the major states, the console and processor are described as being in one of three modes:

1. Program I/O mode

   The processor is running. The processor interprets instructions, services interrupts and exceptions, and initiates I/O operations under the control of the operating system.

2. Console I/O mode

   The processor is halted or bootstrapping or restarting. The console provides control over the system; the operating system has either relinquished control or has yet to gain control. The operating system does not service interrupts or exceptions or initiate I/O operations. The actions of the console are determined by internal console state and commands from the console operator.

3. Console Initialization mode

   The console has yet to acquire control of the processor. The console itself may also require initialization, such as when power is first applied to the system.

A given processor may be in one of four modes:

- Primary processor in program I/O mode or "running primary"

- Primary processor in console I/O mode or "console primary"

- Secondary processor in program I/O mode or "running secondary"

- Secondary processor in console I/O mode or "console secondary"

As noted in Section 1.1, implementations must include a mechanism to force a processor executing in program I/O mode into console I/O mode.

3.2 System Initialization

An Alpha system must be initialized when power is restored. System initialization also occurs as the result of a system bootstrap when the BOOT_RESET environment variable is set to "ON", or as the result of the console INITIALIZE command. Initialization involves all implementation-specific, system-wide actions necessary to allow the system to boot system software on the primary processor. Table 3–1 summarizes the effects of initialization as seen by system software.

Initialization may include initialization of the console itself. During console initialization, the console must build the HWRPB and all associated data structures necessary to permit the console to accept console commands and boot system software.

System initialization may also include any necessary system bus, processor, or I/O device initialization. The initialization of a processor performed as part of system initialization is not necessarily that performed just before transfer of control to the operating system bootstrap. See Section 3.4.1.5 for a description of processor initialization as seen by system software.

Table 3–1: Effects of Power-Up Initialization

Processor State	Initialized State
BIP and RC flags	Cleared
Reason for halt code	'0' (bootstrap)
Integer and floating-point registers	UNPREDICTABLE
System memory	Unaffected if preserved by battery backup; otherwise, UNPREDICTABLE
Environment variables	Unaffected if nonvolatile; otherwise, set to default
BB_WATCH	Unaffected
I/O device registers	UNPREDICTABLE

3.3 PALcode Loading and Switching

3.3.1 PALcode Loading

The console loads PALcode into good memory within a memory cluster that is not available to system software. If PALcode scratch space is required, the console allocates good memory within a memory cluster that is not available to system software. PALcode memory and scratch space are at least page aligned. The console records the starting physical address and length of PALcode memory and scratch space and then sets the PALcode Memory Valid (PMV) flag in the per-CPU slot of the primary processor. The PMV flag indicates that the PALcode descriptors are valid.

After PALcode loading and initialization, the console sets the PALcode Loaded (PL) and PALcode Valid (PV) flags in the primary's per-CPU slot. The PL flag indicates that PALcode has been loaded; the PV flag indicates that any necessary PALcode initialization has been performed.

PALcode loading and initialization are implementation specific. The PALcode source may be a special console device, ROM, a system device, a communications line, or any other implementation-specific source. The state of the console and system must be such that the source is accessible. The console determines the PALcode variant in an implementation-specific fashion; console implementations that are dependent on a given variant load that variant. Console and platform implementations may select any PALcode variant and may load multiple PALcode variants.

Note:

> DIGITAL UNIX supports PALcode switching but does not support PALcode loading. Any platform that supports DIGITAL UNIX must either use the DIGITAL UNIX variant as the default or must load (but need not switch to) the DIGITAL UNIX variant before system bootstrap.

The means by which any PALcode internal state is initialized is implementation specific.

3.3.2 PALcode Switching

PALcode switching is accomplished when one ("current") PALcode transfers control to another ("new") PALcode. PALcode switching can be initiated by the console or the operating system software.

Note:

> OpenVMS Alpha does not support PALcode switching. Any platform that supports OpenVMS Alpha must either use the OpenVMS Alpha variant as the default or must switch to the OpenVMS Alpha variant before system bootstrap.

PALcode switching is performed by PALcode without intervention from the console or operating system software. The current PALcode must be able to locate the new PALcode image. The new PALcode may perform minimal sanity checks.

To support PALcode switching, all PALcode images must implement a PALcode switching entry point at the image base (offset 0). During PALcode switching, the new PALcode image receives control from the current PALcode image at this offset.

For the purposes of switching, a PALcode image is identified by one of the following:

- PALcode variant

   PALcode variants are in the range $0 <$ variant < 256 and permit switching between cooperating, previously loaded PALcode images. PALcode variants are interpreted by the current PALcode without assistance from the console or operating system.

- The physical address of the switching entry point.

   Entry point addresses are used whenever the operating system or console must load a PALcode image. Entry point addresses must meet the alignment requirements of the processor implementation and may occupy the lowest memory page.

System software initiates PALcode switching during system bootstrap whenever the variant required is not identical to that supplied by the console. Once a new variant has been established by system software, the console must restore that variant across all subsequent transitions from console I/O mode to program I/O mode. The console must ensure that the system software PALcode variant appears unchanged when:

1. A processor is restarted.

2. A secondary processor is started.

3. The operator forces a processor into console I/O mode, then continues program execution (HALT followed by CONTINUE).

4. System software invokes a callback routine that requires transition to console I/O mode.

System software is never required to restore a PALcode variant. The console may switch PALcode at entries to console I/O mode, but must restore the variant established by system software at subsequent re-entry to program I/O mode.

3.3.2.1 PALcode Switching Procedure

PALcode switching proceeds as follows:

1. The current PALcode is entered by the CALL_PAL SWPPAL instruction. The PALcode image identifier (variant or switching entry point address) is contained in R16. Registers R17 through R21 contain parameters that are passed without change to the new PALcode image. The interpretation of R17 through R21 is specific to the new PALcode image.

2. If the current PALcode is not supplied by DIGITAL and does not support PALcode switching, the current PALcode sets R0 = 1 and returns from the CALL_PAL SWPPA instructionL.

3. The current PALcode determines if R16 contains a PALcode variant or switching entry point address. If the latter, execution continues at step 7.

4. The current PALcode validates the PALcode variant. If unsuccessful, the operation fails, the current PALcode sets R0 = 1 and returns from the CALL_PAL SWPPAL instruction.

5. The current PALcode determines if the PALcode associated with the PALcode token has been loaded. If not, the operation fails, the current PALcode sets R0 = 2 and returns from the CALL_PAL SWPPAL instruction.

6. The current PALcode determines the base physical address associated with the PALcode token.

7. The current PALcode branches to the new PALcode image at the switching entry point (physical) address determined in step 3 or 6.

8. The new PALcode performs any necessary implementation-specific PALcode initialization.

9. The new PALcode invalidates all TB entries and establishes the new memory management algorithm. (For example, DIGITAL UNIX PALcode loads the VPTB with a value supplied to the CALL_PAL SWPPAL instruction.)

10. The new PALcode performs any implementation-specific actions using the entry parameters contained in R17 through R21. The resulting changes in processor state are summarized for each PALcode variant in Section 3.3.2.3.

11. The new PALcode clears R0 and passes control to the code thread determined by the entry parameters. Control is always passed in kernel mode with interrupts disabled or blocked.

If a hardware failure occurs when accessing any of the addresses specified by the calling arguments or other dependent locations, a hardware reset and system initialization are performed.

Implemention Note:

A common implementation is that the switching entry point is identical to the hardware reset entry. PALcode must distinguish the two cases. In the case of hardware reset, PALcode must perform any necessary hardware initialization and pass control to the console. In the case of switching, PALcode must pass control to the code thread determined by the entry parameters.

Notes:

- System software must update the PALcode revision field (SLOT[168]) after PALcode switching. The console uses that field to determine if PALcode must be switched (to the system software-specific image) before passing control on system restarts.

  Similarly, system software may need to update the PALcode revision field in the per-CPU slot (SLOT[168]) of each secondary processor before starting the secondary. There is only one system restart routine. The console uses the PALcode revision field to determine if PALcode must be switched (to the system software-specific image) before passing control on secondary processor starts.

- PALcode switching is initiated by invoking the CALL_PAL SWPPAL instruction. before invoking SWPPAL, the caller should ensure that the system is quiescent. It is recommended that SWPPAL be invoked with interrupts either disabled or blocked. After a successful PALcode switch, the operating system may need to update the VPTB field in the HWRPB or restart HWPCB in each per-CPU slot.

- PALcode switching does not implicitly load PALcode. During system bootstrap, the operating system must ensure that the desired PALcode variant is loaded. If loading is required, the operating system must allocate sufficient physically contiguous physical memory for the new PALcode image and any additional PALcode scratch space, then load the PALcode image in an implementation-specific manner.

- After a PALcode switch, the operating system may need to invoke the FIXUP console callback routine. FIXUP must be invoked after any operation that affects virtual address translation and before subsequent invocations of other callback routines. See Section 2.3.7.1.

3.3.2.2 Specific PALcode Switching Implementation Information

OpenVMS Alpha does not currently support PALcode switching. DIGITAL UNIX supports PALcode switching as shown in Table 3–2.

Table 3–2: DIGITAL UNIX PALcode Switching

Register	CALL_PAL swppal Parameter Usage
R17 (a1)	New PC
R18 (a2)	New PCBB
R19 (a3)	New VPTB

3.3.2.3 Processor State at Exit for DIGITAL UNIX from PALcode Switching Instruction

Table 3–3: Processor State for DIGITAL UNIX at Exit from swppal

Processor State		At Exit from swppal:
ASN	Address space number	ASN in PCB passed to swppal
FEN	Floating enable	FEN in PCB passed to swppal
IPL	Interrupt priority level	7
MCES	Machine check error summary	Zero
PCBB	Privileged context block	Address of PCB passed to swppal
PC	Program counter	PC passed to swppal
PS	Processor status	IPL=7, CM=K
PTBR	Page table base register	PTBR in PCB passed to swppal
Unique	Processor unique value	Unique in PCB passed to swppal
WHAMI	Who-Am-I	Unchanged
Sysvalue	System value	Unchanged
KSP	Kernel stack pointer	KSP in PCB passed to swppal
Other IPRs		UNPREDICTABLE
R0		Zero
Integer and floating-point registers		UNPREDICTABLE, except SP and R0

3.4 System Bootstrapping

This section describes the operations performed by the Alpha console to locate, load, and transfer control to a primary bootstrap. The responsibilities of the console and the initial state seen by system software are presented for multiprocessor and uniprocessor environments. The actions of the console for cold bootstrap (full hardware initialization) and warm bootstrap (partial hardware initialization) are described.

A system bootstrap can occur as the result of a powerfail recovery, a processor halt, or an INITIALIZE or BOOT console command. See Section 3.1.1 for a complete description of these state transitions.

3.4.1 Cold Bootstrapping in a Uniprocessor Environment

This section describes a cold bootstrap in a uniprocessor environment. A system bootstrap is a cold bootstrap when any of the following occur:

- Power is first applied to the system.
- The bootstrap is requested by system software.
- A console INITIALIZE command is issued and the AUTO_ACTION environment variable is set to "BOOT".
- The BOOT_RESET environment variable is set to "ON".

The console must perform the following steps in the cold bootstrap sequence.

1. Perform a system initialization
2. Size memory
3. Test sufficient memory for bootstrapping
4. Determine whether to configure a standard three-level page table or an extended four-level page table structure
5. Load PALcode
6. Build a valid Hardware Restart Parameter Block (HWRPB)
7. Build a valid Memory Data Descriptor table in the HWRPB
8. Initialize bootstrap page tables and map initial regions
9. Locate and load the system software primary bootstrap image
10. Initialize processor state on all processors
11. Transfer control to the system software primary bootstrap image

The steps leading up to the transfer of control to system software may be performed in any order. The final state seen by system software is defined, but the implementation-specific sequence of these steps is not. Before beginning a bootstrap, the console must clear any internally pended restarts to any processor.

3.4.1.1 Page Table Structure Configuration

An Alpha implementation must support a mode of operation whereby the virtual address format contains three levels of page table fields, plus a byte-within-page field.

An Alpha implementation additionally may support an extended mode of operation whereby the virtual address format contains four levels of page table fields, plus a byte-within-page field.

The console must support a mechanism that lets the user specify the desired mode of operation. The console then configures the system accordingly, as it prepares the bootstrap environment for software. This mechanism must be persistent, such that once specified, the user's choice remains in force for all subsequent bootstraps or until the user chooses a different mode of operation.

3.4.1.2 Memory Sizing and Testing

Memory sizing is the responsibility of the console. The console must also test sufficient memory to permit control to be passed to the primary bootstrap image. The results of console memory sizing and testing are passed to system software in the Memory Data Descriptor (MEMDSC) table located by HWRPB[200].

The MEMDSC table contains one or more memory cluster descriptors. Each memory cluster descriptor describes a physically contiguous extent of physical memory that contains no holes. Cluster descriptors are ordered by increasing physical address; the range of PFNs described by cluster N is of lower address than the range of PFNs described by cluster N+1.

The MEMDSC table must be quadword aligned and both physically and virtually contiguous. The MEMDSC table format is shown in Figure 3–2; the memory cluster descriptor format is shown in Figure 3–3. The size of the MEMDSC table can be determined by the number of clusters contained in MEMDSC[16]. The size of the table and the offset to the last quadword of the table are given by:

```
MEMDSC_SIZE = ((7 * MEMDSC[10_16]) + 3) * 8
MEMDSC_END  = MEMDSC_SIZE -8
```

The memory within a cluster is either available to system software or reserved for console use. Usage within a cluster cannot be mixed; if the cluster contains a page reserved for console use, system software cannot allocate any page within the cluster. The memory cluster descriptor contains a cluster usage field that indicates the cluster availability to system software. The primary bootstrap image must reside in clusters available to system software.

The memory within each cluster may be fully tested, partially tested, or untested by the console. If the memory is untested, no cluster memory bitmap is built. The console must test enough memory to allow the primary bootstrap image to be loaded and control to be passed to that image. This memory includes:

- PALcode memory and scratch areas
- CPU logout areas
- Memory bitmaps

- HWRPB and all offset blocks
- Console CRB map entries
- Bootstrap address space page tables
- Primary bootstrap image
- One page for the initial bootstrap stack

Any additional memory testing by the console is implementation specific. It is the responsibility of system software to test any memory not tested by the console.

A cluster bitmap is built if the cluster is available to system software and the console tests any memory within the cluster. Each page in the cluster is represented by a bit in the bitmask. A '1' in the bitmap means that the corresponding page is "good"; the page was tested without error. A '0' in the bitmap means that the corresponding page is "bad"; the page is either untested or was tested but encountered correctable (Corrected Read Data) errors or hard (Read Data Substitute) errors.

Cluster bitmaps must be at least quadword aligned and must be an integral number of quadwords; any unused bits in the highest addressed quadword must be zero.

Implementation Notes:

Every implementation cannot be required to test all of memory before booting the operating system. Partial memory testing is recommended whenever testing is time-consuming and would significantly delay the bootstrapping process; the choice is implementation specific. The high-water mark mechanism allows implementations to completely size memory without testing all of it and indicate to the operating system where testing ended.

Clusters reserved for the use of the console and PALcode do not have associated bitmaps. If such a cluster would contain a large number (three or more) of contiguous pages that encounter soft read errors or are otherwise unsuitable for console and PALcode, the console should consider breaking the bad pages into a separate cluster. This cluster should be made available for use by system software, which can possibly reclaim the pages for use.

The console does not alter the Memory Data Descriptor table or any bitmaps across warm bootstraps. This permits system software to propagate information on system software memory testing and intermittent errors across operating system bootstraps. For example, system software could set the "bad" bit of a page that incurred repeated CRD errors.

Figure 3–2: Memory Cluster Descriptor Table

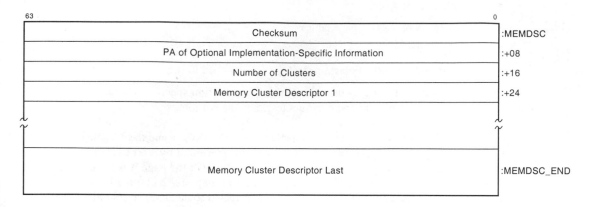

63	0	
Checksum		:MEMDSC
PA of Optional Implementation-Specific Information		:+08
Number of Clusters		:+16
Memory Cluster Descriptor 1		:+24
Memory Cluster Descriptor Last		:MEMDSC_END

Table 3–4: Memory Cluster Descriptor Table Fields

Offset	Description
MEMDSC	CHECKSUM — Checksum of all the quadwords from offset MEMDSC+8 through MEMDSC_END. Computed as a 64-bit sum, ignoring overflows. The checksum does not include any of the cluster bitmaps or any optional implementation-specific data.
+08	IMP_DATA_PA — Physical address of additional implementation-specific information (if any). If no additional implementation-specific information exists, the field must contain a zero.
+16	CLUSTERS — Number of clusters in the Memory Cluster Descriptor table. Unsigned integer.
+24	CLUSTER — Each Memory Cluster Descriptor describes an extent of physical memory. See Figure 3–3.

Figure 3–3: Memory Cluster Descriptor

63	0	
Starting PFN of Cluster		:MEMC
Count of Pages in Cluster		:+08
Count of Tested Pages in Cluster Bitmap		:+16
VA of Cluster Bitmap or Zero		:+24
PA of Cluster Bitmap or Zero		:+32
Checksum of Cluster Bitmap		:+40
Usage of Cluster		:+48
		:+56

Table 3–5: Memory Cluster Descriptor Fields

Offset	Description
MEMC	PFN — Starting PFN of the memory cluster.
+08	PAGES — Number of pages in the memory cluster. Unsigned integer.
+16	TESTED_PAGES — Number of tested memory pages in the cluster. If only a limited extent of the cluster memory was tested, a bitmap is built, and this field indicates the number of pages that were tested.
+24	BITMAP_VA — Starting virtual address of the cluster memory testing bitmap in the bootstrap address space. If the memory is untested, no bitmap is built and this field is set to zero.
+32	BITMAP_PA — Starting physical address of the cluster memory testing bitmap. If the memory is untested, no bitmap is built and this field is set to zero.
+40	BITMAP_CHECKSUM — Checksum of the cluster memory testing bitmap. Computed as a 64-bit sum, ignoring overflows, over the PAGES active bits only.
+48	USAGE — Indicates whether the cluster is available for use by system software. <ul><li>If USAGE<0> is '0', system software may allocate and use the cluster.</li><li>If USAGE<0> is '0' and USAGE<1> is '1', the cluster is available for use by the system software, but is in nonvolatile memory.</li><li>If USAGE<0> is '1', the cluster is reserved for console use and must not be allocated by system software.</li><li>USAGE<63:2> should be zero.</li></ul>

3.4.1.3 Bootstrap Address Space

All system software, including the primary bootstrap image, runs in a virtual memory environment. The console creates the initial page tables that define the initial bootstrap address space for the primary bootstrap. System software may replace this bootstrap address space at any time after the console passes control to the primary bootstrap image.

The bootstrap address space consists of four regions. All regions must be located in good memory within clusters that are available to system software. The regions are:

Region 0

This region maps all console or PALcode data structures that must be shared with system software. These structures include the HWRPB in its entirety, all blocks located by HWRPB offsets, the console callback routines, and all memory bitmaps. Region 0 begins at address 256MB, virtual address $0000\ 0000\ 1000\ 0000_{16}$. The starting address of the HWRPB is the base of Region 0.

Region 1

The primary bootstrap image is loaded into this region. The region must be at least large enough to load system software plus three pages. The three additional pages are used as an initial bootstrap stack and stack guard pages. The stack guard pages are virtually adjacent to the bootstrap stack page and marked no-access. All other pages in the region are mapped and valid. Region 1 begins at address 512MB, virtual address $0000\ 0000\ 2000\ 0000_{16}$.

Software Note:
> This region must be set to the size of the primary bootstrap image plus 3 pages for OpenVMS Alpha and at least 256K bytes for DIGITAL UNIX.

Region 2

This region, or "page table space," contains the bootstrap address space page tables. Region 2 begins at address 1GB, virtual address $0000\ 0000\ 4000\ 0000_{16}$. The range depends on the page size:

Page Size	Page Table Space Address Range
8KB	1GB to 1GB+8MB
16KB	1GB to 1GB+16MB
32KB	1GB to 1GB+32MB
64KB	1GB to 1GB+64MB

This region includes the Level 2 and Level 3 page tables used to map all three regions comprising bootstrap address space. The Level 2 page table maps itself as a Level 3 page table. The address of the Level 2 page table page and the PTE within the page that is used for self-mapping also depend on the page size.

Page Size	Virtual Address of Level 2 Page Table	L2PTE Number Used for Self-Mapping
8KB	1GB+1MB	128
16KB	1GB+512KB	32
32KB	1GB+256KB	8
64KB	1GB+128KB	2

Implemention Note:
> Region 2 allows the primary bootstrap code to start with 32-bit pointers that execute in a 32-bit context. Thus, Region 2 allows primary bootstrap software to be written with 32-bit-oriented language compilers.

The initial page tables that map the virtual address regions are shown in Figure 3–4 and illustrated in Figure 3–5.

Region 3

This region maps the entire page table structure, including all levels of page table, that would be required to map the entire virtual address space supported by this implementation. The most significant page table is self-mapped by the second PTE in the page. If booted with a three-level page table configuration, this is the Level 1 page table. If booted with a four-level page table configuration, this is the Level 0 page table.

Region 3 exists to support virtual page table lookup for Translation Buffer misses. Region 3 exists at a virtual address that is inaccessible to code that is compiled to support only a 32-bit virtual address space. As such, Region 3 is not the primary page table space that is presented to bootstrap software.

Programming Note:

Due to the self-mapping, Region 3 maps all page table pages. The Level 2 and Level 3 page table pages are in both Region 2 and Region 3.

Page Size	Virtual Address of Page Table Space (VPTB) (Three-Level PT)	(Four-Level PT)
8KB	8GB	8TB
16KB	64GB	128TB
32KB	512GB	2048TB
64KB	4TB	32768TB

Figure 3–4:   Initial Virtual Memory Regions

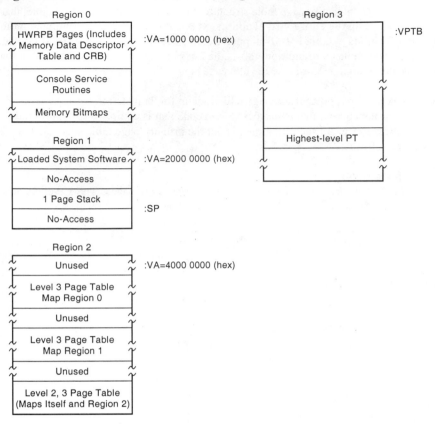

All valid pages allow read/write access from kernel mode and deny all access from other modes. All fault bits (FOR, FOW, FOE) are clear, as well as Address Space Match (ASM) and Granularity Hint (GH). ·

The self-mapping of the Level 2 page table excludes any higher-level page table from Region 2. If operating in the mode of three levels of page table, this is just the Level 1 page table. In this case, the Level 1 page table has two active PTEs. The first L1PTE points to the PFN of the Level 2 page table page, which maps page table space (Region 2). The second L1PTE contains the PFN of the Level 1 page table itself, thus defining Region 3. Only these two entries within the Level 1 page table are valid; all other Level 1 PTEs are zero.

If operating in the mode of four levels of page table, both a Level 0 and Level 1 page table exist and both are excluded from Region 2. In this case, the Level 0 page table has two active PTEs. The first L0PTE points to the PFN of the Level 1 page table page. The second L0PTE contains the PFN of the Level 0 page table itself, thus defining Region 3. The Level 1 page table has one active PTE. The first L1PTE points to the PFN of the Level 2 page table page, which maps page table space (Region 2). Only the first two entries within the Level 0 page table, and the first entry within the Level 1 page table, are valid; all other Level 0 and Level 1 PTEs are zero.

Figure 3–5: Three-Level Initial Page Tables

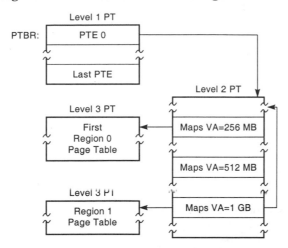

The level 2 PT maps Region 2 (page table space) at 1 GB. The level 2 PT maps itself as its own level 3 PT.

The level 1 PT is not mapped.

The self-mapping of the Level 2 page table also causes the addresses of the Level 2 and Level 3 PTEs for a given virtual address to be functions of that address. For every virtual address within the bootstrap address space, there is exactly one location within page table space for the Level 2 PTE that maps that virtual address, and exactly one location for the Level 3 PTE that maps that virtual address.

Thus, the Level 2 and Level 3 PTE virtual addresses for a given virtual address (VA) within bootstrap address space can be calculated given the page size. The following bit range definitions provide convenient notation for referring to the constituent parts of a virtual address. For example, VA<L2> is equivalent to VA<32:23> for an 8K byte page size.

VA:	L1	L2	L3	Byte in Page

Page Size	L0[1]	L1	L2	L3
8KB	52:43	42:33	32:23	22:13
16KB	57:47	46:36	35:25	24:14
32KB	62:51	50:39	38:27	26:15
64KB	63:55	54:42	41:29	28:16

[1] L0 pertains only to the mode where four levels of page table have been configured.

The base of page table space is a constant value:

1. `PT_Base = 1GB`

   The virtual address of the Level 3 PTE (L3PTE_VA) of any virtual address (VA) is given by:

2. `L3PTE_VA(VA) = PT_Base + (page_size*VA<L2>) + (8*VA<L3>)`

   Thus, the virtual address of the Level 3 PTE that maps the lowest address of page table space is given by:

   ```
   L3PTE_VA(PT_Base) = PT_Base + (page_size * PT_Base<L2>)
   ```

   Since the Level 2 page table is self-mapped, the above is also the base virtual address of the Level 2 page table. Thus:

3. `L2PT_Base = PT_Base + (page_size * PT_Base<L2>)`

   Finally, the virtual address of the Level 2 PTE (L2PTE_VA) of any virtual address (VA) is given by:

   ```
   L2PTE_VA(VA) = L2PT_Base + (8 * VA<L2>)
   ```

4. `L2PTE_VA(VA) = PT_Base + (page_size * PT_Base<L2>) + (8 * VA<L2>)`

3.4.1.4 Bootstrap Flags

The Bootstrap-in-Progress (BIP) and Restart-Capable (RC) processor state flags in the primary processor's per-CPU slot are used to detect failed bootstraps. If the primary re-enters console I/O mode while the BIP flag is set and the RC flag is clear, the bootstrap attempt fails, and the subsequent console action is determined by Figure 3–1.

The console sets the BIP flag and clears the RC flag before transferring control to system software. System software sets the RC flag to indicate that sufficient context has been established to handle a restart attempt. System software clears the BIP flag to indicate that the bootstrap operation has been completed. The RC flag should be set before clearing the BIP flag. Table 3–6 gives the console interpretation of BIP and RC flags.

Table 3–6: Console Interpretation of BIP and RC flags

BIP	RC	Interpretation at Entry to Console I/O Mode
set	clear	Failed bootstrap
set	set	Halt condition encountered during bootstrap, restart processor
clear	clear	Failed restart
clear	set	Halt condition encountered, restart processor

3.4.1.5 Loading of System Software

The console is responsible for loading system software at the base of Region 1 beginning at virtual address 512MB. This software is expected to be a primary bootstrap program that is responsible for loading other system software, but may be diagnostic or other special-purpose software. Section 3.6 contains descriptions of the format of each supported bootstrap medium.

The console uses the BOOT_DEV environment variable to determine the bootstrap device and the path to that device. Environment variables contain lists of bootstrap devices and paths; each list element specifies the complete path to a given bootstrap device. If multiple elements are specified, the console attempts to load a bootstrap image from each in turn.

The console uses the BOOTDEF_DEV, BOOT_DEV, and BOOTED_DEV environment variables as follows:

- At console initialization, the console sets the BOOTDEF_DEV and BOOT_DEV environment variables to be equivalent. The format of these environment variables depends on the console implementation and is independent of the console presentation layer; the value may be interpreted and modified by system software.

- When a bootstrap results from a BOOT command that specifies a bootstrap device list, the console uses the list specified with the command. The console modifies BOOT_DEV to contain the specified device list.

  Note:
  > This may require conversion from the presentation layer format to the registered format.

- When a bootstrap is the result of a BOOT command that does not specify a bootstrap device list, the console uses the bootstrap device list contained in the BOOTDEF_DEV environment variable. The console copies the value of BOOTDEF_DEV to BOOT_DEV.

- When a bootstrap is not the result of a BOOT command, the console uses the bootstrap device list contained in the BOOT_DEV environment variable. The console does not modify the contents of BOOT_DEV.

- The console attempts to load a bootstrap image from each element of the bootstrap device list. If the list is exhausted before successfully transferring control to system software, the bootstrap attempt fails and the subsequent console action is determined by Figure 3–1.

- The console indicates the actual bootstrap path and device used in the BOOTED_DEV environment variable. The console sets BOOTED_DEV after loading the primary bootstrap image and before transferring control to system software. The BOOTED_DEV format follows that of a BOOT_DEV list element.

- If the bootstrap device list is empty, BOOTDEF_DEV or BOOT_DEV are NULL (00_{16}), and the action is implementation specific. The console may remain in console I/O mode or attempt to locate a bootstrap device in an implementation-specific manner.

The BOOT_FILE and BOOT_OSFLAGS environment variables are used as default values for the bootstrap file name and option flags. The console indicates the actual bootstrap image file name (if any) and option flags for the current bootstrap attempt in BOOTED_FILE and BOOTED_OSFLAGS and environment variables. The BOOT_FILE default bootstrap image file name is used whenever the bootstrap requires a file name and either none was specified on the BOOT command or the bootstrap was initiated by the console as the result of a major state transition. The console never interprets the bootstrap option flags, but simply passes them between the console presentation layer and system software.

3.4.1.6 Processor Initialization

Before control is transferred to system software, certain IPRs and other processor state must be initialized as shown in Table 3–7 and Section 3.3.2.3 for each PALcode variant. Processor initialization is performed by the console before booting a processor, before restarting a processor, or as the result of the INITIALIZE –CPU console command.

The Context Valid (CV) flag in the processor's per-CPU slot must be valid for processor initialization to be successful. If the CV flag is clear, the HWPCB contained in the per-CPU slot is not valid, and the console must not transfer control to system software. If this or any error occurs in initializing the processor, the console retains control of the system and generates the binary error message ERROR_PROC_INIT.

Table 3–7: Processor Initialization

Processor State		Initialized State
ASN	Address Space Number	Zero
ASTEN[1]	AST Enable	ASTEN in processor's HWPCB
ASTSR[1]	AST Summary	ASTSR in processor's HWPCB
FEN	Floating Enable	FEN in processor's HWPCB
IPL	Interrupt Priority Level	Highest
MCES	Machine Check Error Summary	8 (bit 3=1)
PCBB	Privileged Context Block	Address of processor's HWPCB
PS	Processor Status	IPL=highest, VMM=0, CM=K, SW=0
PTBR	Page Table Base Register	PFN value in processor's HWPCB
SISR[1]	Software Interrupt Summary	Zero
WHAMI	Who-Am-I	CPU identifier
SCC[1]	System Cycle Counter	Zero
SP	Kernel Stack Pointer	KSP in processor's HWPCB
Other IPRs		UNPREDICTABLE
Cache, instruction buffer, or write buffer		Empty or valid
Translation buffer		Invalidated
Main memory		Unaffected
Integer and floating-point registers		Unaffected, except SP
Reason for Halt code		Unaffected
BIP and RC flags		Unaffected
Environment variables		Unaffected

[1] OpenVMS Alpha only.

3.4.1.7 Transfer of Control to System Software

Before transferring control to system software, the console must define valid hardware privileged context for that software. The console builds that context in the hardware privileged context block (HWPCB) in the primary processor's per-CPU slot. The initialized context is summarized in Table 3–8 and Section 3.3.2.3 for each PALcode variant.

The initial KSP points to the lowest addressed quadword in the higher addressed stack guard page (top-of-stack) of Region 1 of the bootstrap address space. The PTBR points to the Level 1 page table page. All other scalar and floating-point register contents are UNPREDICTABLE.

After building the HWPCB for the primary processor, the console sets the Context Valid (CV) flag in the primary's per-CPU slot. All other bootstrap information is passed from the console to system software by environment variables. See Section 2.2 for more details.

Table 3–8: Initial HWPCB contents

HWPCB Field	Initialized State
KSP	Top-of-stack (contents of SP)
ESP[1]	UNPREDICTABLE
SSP[1]	UNPREDICTABLE
USP	UNPREDICTABLE
PTBR	PFN of Level 1 page table
ASN	Zero
ASTSR[1]	Zero
ASTEN[1]	Zero (all disabled)
FEN	Zero (disabled)
PCC	Zero
Unique value	Zero
PALcode scratch	Implementation specific

[1] OpenVMS Alpha systems only.

Control is transferred to system software in kernel mode at the highest IPL with virtual memory management enabled. Control is transferred to the first longword of the system software image loaded into Region 1, virtual address $0000\ 0000\ 2000\ 0000_{16}$. Before transferring control, the console ensures that the SP contains the KSP value in the HWPCB. System software should assume that the stack is initially empty.

The transfer of control transitions the primary processor from the halted state into the running state and from console I/O mode into program I/O mode. The rest of the uniprocessor bootstrap process is the responsibility of system software.

3.4.2 Warm Bootstrapping in a Uniprocessor Environment

The actions of the console on a warm bootstrap are a subset of those for a cold bootstrap. A system bootstrap will be a warm bootstrap whenever the BOOT_RESET environment variable is set to "OFF", and console internal state permits.

The console performs the following steps in the warm bootstrap sequence:

1. Locate and validate the Hardware Restart Parameter Block (HWRPB)

2. Locate and load the system software primary bootstrap image

3. Initialize processor state on all processors

4. Initialize bootstrap page tables and map initial regions

5. Transfer control to the system software primary bootstrap image

At warm bootstrap, the console does not load PALcode, does not modify the Memory Data Descriptor table, and does not reinitialize any environment variables. If the console cannot locate and validate the previously initialized HWRPB, the console must initiate a cold bootstrap. Before beginning a bootstrap, the console must clear any internally pended restarts to any processor.

Programming Note:

Warm bootstrap permits system software to preserve limited context across bootstraps.

3.4.2.1 HWRPB Location and Validation

After console initialization, the console must preserve the location of the HWRPB in an implementation-specific manner. On warm bootstraps and restarts, the console locates the HWRPB and verifies it by ensuring that:

1. The first quadword of the table contains the physical address of the table.

2. The second quadword of the table contains "HWRPB" ($0000\ 0042\ 5052\ 5748_{16}$).

3. The quadword at offset HWRPB[288] contains the 64-bit sum, ignoring overflows of the quadwords from offset HWRPB[00] to HWRPB[280], inclusive, relative to the beginning of the potential HWRPB.

4. The quadword at offset [0] of the MEMDSC block contains the 64-bit sum, ignoring overflows, of the quadwords from MEMDSC+8 through MEMDSC_END of that block. The MEMDSC block is located by the MEMDSC offset at HWRPB[200]. See Figure 3–2.

5. As described in Section 2.1.4, if a CONFIG table exists, it is located by the CONFIG offset at HWRPB[208]. The quadword at offset [8] of the optional CONFIG table contains the 64-bit sum, ignoring overflows, of the quadwords from CONFIG+16 through CONFIG_END of that table.

If one or more of the above conditions is not true, the HWRPB is not valid. The warm bootstrap (or restart) fails. The subsequent console action is determined by Figure 3–1. If a bootstrap is indicated, a cold bootstrap will be performed.

The console must not search memory for a HWRPB; searching memory constitutes a security hole.

3.4.3 Multiprocessor Bootstrapping

Multiprocessor bootstrapping differs from uniprocessor bootstrapping primarily in areas relating to synchronization between processors. In a shared memory system, processors cannot independently load and start system software; bootstrapping is controlled by the primary processor.

3.4.3.1 Selection of Primary Processor

The primary processor is selected by the console during system initialization before any access to main memory by any processor. Selection of the primary processor may be done in any fashion that guarantees choosing exactly one primary processor.

Once a primary processor has been selected, the secondary processors take no further action until appropriately notified by the primary processor. In particular, secondary processors must not access main memory.

3.4.3.2 Actions of Console

After selection, the console proceeds to bootstrap the primary processor, after the normal uniprocessor bootstrap as described in Section 3.4.1.

The console must correctly initialize all HWRPB fields used for synchronization or communication between the processors. The console must initialize the PRIMARY CPU ID field at HWRPB[32], zero the TXRDY and RXRDY bitmasks at HWRPB[296] and HWRPB[304], and recompute the HWRPB checksum at HWRPB[288].

The console must also initialize each per-CPU slot for the secondary processors. The console must:

- Clear the BIP, RC, OH, and CV flags
- Clear the Halt Request code field
- Set the PP flag if the processor is present
- Set the PA flag if the processor is present and available for use by system software
- Set the PMV and PL flags if the console has loaded PALcode on this processor
- Set the PV flag if the console has initialized PALcode on this processor
- Set the PE processor variation flag if the processor is eligible to become a primary

After initializing each processor's per-CPU slot, the console must notify each console secondary processor of the existence and location of the valid HWRPB.

3.4.3.3 PALcode Loading on Secondary Processors

Most console implementations load PALcode on all secondary processors before bootstrapping the primary processor. Console implementations may delay the loading or initialization of PALcode on a secondary processor. If delayed, PALcode loading and initialization require the cooperation of system software executing on the running primary and the console executing on behalf of the secondary.

The console secondary must have performed any necessary initialization as described in Section 3.4.3.5. All interprocessor console communications follow the mechanisms described in Section 2.4.

The following procedure applies only to initial PALcode loading on a console secondary. The PALcode variant to be loaded must be identical to that of the running primary processor before any PALcode switching by system software. This procedure cannot be used to load operating system-specific PALcode variants:

1. The console secondary initializes the PALcode memory and scratch space length fields in its per-CPU slot.

2. The console secondary sets the PALcode major revision, minor revision, and compatibility subfields in the PALcode revision field in its per-CPU slot.

3. The console secondary notifies the primary that PALcode loading is requested by transmitting a message to the running primary as described in Section 2.4.

4. The console secondary polls the PALcode Memory Valid (PMV) flag in its per-CPU slot.

5. The running primary detects the console secondary request.

6. The running primary verifies that the Processor Available (PA) flag is set in the secondary's per-CPU slot. If the flag is not set, the operation fails.

7. The running primary compares the major and minor revision subfields of the PALcode revision field in its per-CPU slot to that in the secondary's per-CPU slot. If the revision levels do not match, the running primary proceeds to step 12.

8. The running primary compares the number of processors currently sharing its PALcode image to the maximum contained in the subfield of the PALcode revision field of its per-CPU slot. If the current number is the maximum, no additional console secondary can share the PALcode image. The running primary proceeds to step 12.

   Programming Note:
   The running primary can determine the number of processors currently sharing a given PALcode image by counting the number of per-CPU slots with the same valid PALcode memory space descriptors. A PALcode memory space descriptor is valid if the PALcode Loaded (PL) flag is set in the per-CPU slot.

9. The running primary copies the PALcode memory and scratch space descriptors from its per-CPU slot into the secondary's per-CPU slot.

10. The running primary copies the PALcode variation, compatibility, and maximum number of processors subfields of the PALcode revision field from its per-CPU slot into the secondary's per-CPU slot.

11. The running primary sets the PALcode Loaded (PL) flag in the secondary's per-CPU slot, then proceeds to step 13.

12. The running primary allocates physical memory for PALcode memory and scratch areas and records the addresses in the secondary's per-CPU slot.

13. The running primary sets the PALcode Memory Valid (PMV) flag in the secondary's per-CPU slot.

14. The console secondary observes that the PMV flag is set in its per-CPU slot.

15. If the PL flag in its per-CPU slot is not set, the console secondary loads PALcode into the allocated PALcode memory and scratch space. In this case, the console secondary sets the PALcode Loaded (PL) flag in its per-CPU slot.

16. The console secondary ensures that any required implementation-specific PALcode initialization is performed.

17. The console secondary sets the PALcode Valid (PV) flag in the secondary's per-CPU slot.

The PALcode memory and scratch space must be page aligned. If not allocated by the console before system bootstrap, the allocation management of PALcode memory for secondary processors is the responsibility of system software.

It is the responsibility of console and system software to ensure that the initially loaded PALcode variation and revision levels of all processors are compatible. This may be performed by the primary before starting the secondary, by the starting secondary, or any combination thereof. PALcode images of the same PALcode variation but different revision levels are compatible if the PALcode revision compatibility subfields match.

3.4.3.4 Actions of the Running Primary

System software executing on the primary processor must initialize the HWPCB for each secondary processor. The HWPCB contains the necessary privileged context for the execution of system software and successful restarts. The HWPCB must be initialized before requesting that the console secondary perform any START command. After initializing the HWPCB, system software sets the Context Valid (CV) flag.

Once the PALcode is valid on a console secondary, the secondary waits for a START (or other) command from the running primary. System software issues the necessary console commands that instruct the secondary to begin executing software. The exchange of commands and messages between the running primary and a secondary is described in Section 2.4.

System software may start secondary processors at any time. In particular, secondary processors may be started before or after switching PALcode on the running primary. If system software switches to an operating system-specific PALcode before starting a secondary processor, system software must update the PALcode revision field in the per-CPU slot (SLOT[168]) of each secondary before starting the secondary. See Section 3.3.1.

Programming Note:

All commands sent to a console secondary are implicitly targeted to the secondary.

3.4.3.5 Actions of a Console Secondary

After failing to become the primary, a console secondary uses an implementation-specific mechanism to determine when a valid HWRPB has been constructed in main memory. The console secondary then locates the HWRPB in an implementation-specific manner.

Once the HWRPB is located, the secondary locates its per-CPU slot using its CPU ID as an index. The secondary verifies that its slot exists by comparing its CPU ID to the number of per-CPU slots at HWRPB[144]. If its CPU ID exceeds the number of per-CPU slots, the secondary must not leave console mode or continue to access main memory. If PALcode loading is necessary, the console secondary follows the procedure given in Section 3.4.3.3.

Once PALcode is valid, the console secondary waits for a START (or other) command from the running primary by polling the appropriate flag in the RXRDY bitmask. The exchange of commands and messages between the running primary and a secondary is described in Section 2.4.

In response to a START command, the console secondary:

1. Verifies that the Context Valid (CV) flag is set in its per-CPU slot.

2. Sets the Bootstrap-in-Progress (BIP) flag in its per-CPU slot.

3. Clears the Restart-Capable (RC) flag in its per-CPU slot.

4. Initializes the processor.

5. If necessary, switches to the system software specific PALcode variant identified in the PALcode revision field in the per-CPU slot.

6. Loads the privileged context specified by the HWPCB in its per-CPU slot.

7. Loads the procedure value at HWRPB[264] into R27.

8. Clears R26 and R25.

9. Loads the virtual page table base (VPTB) register with the value stored in HWRPB[120].

10. Transfers control to the CPU Restart routine, whose virtual address is stored in HWRPB[256].

The CV flag indicates that the HWPCB in the slot contains valid hardware privileged state for system software. If the CV flag is not set, the processor remains in console I/O mode.

The console uses the PALcode revision field in the per-CPU slot to determine if system software has switched PALcode to a system software-specific variant. The console must restore that variant before passing control to the CPU restart routine.

3.4.3.6 Bootstrap Flags

The Bootstrap-in-Progress (BIP) and Restart-Capable (RC) processor state flags in the console secondary processor's per-CPU slot are used to control error recovery during secondary starts. If the secondary re-enters console I/O mode while the BIP flag is set and the RC flag is clear, the start attempt fails. Failed starts are equivalent to failed bootstraps, and the subsequent console action is determined by Figure 3–1. See Section 3.4.1.3 and Table 3–6.

3.4.4 Addition of a Processor to a Running System

A processor may be added to a running system at any time if a slot has been provided for it in the HWRPB. The new console secondary processor follows the secondary start procedure given in Sections 3.4.3.3 and 3.4.3.5, with one minor difference. If no PALcode loading is necessary, the console secondary sends a ?STARTREQ? message to the running primary. This message notifies the primary that a new processor has been added to the configuration. After sending the ?STARTREQ? message, the console secondary waits for a START (or other) command from the running primary. See Section 2.4 for a description of interprocessor console communication.

3.4.5 System Software Requested Bootstraps

System software can request that the console perform a system bootstrap. This request can be made on any processor in a multiprocessor system and overrides the setting of the AUTO_ACTION and BOOT_RESET environment variables.

To request a bootstrap, system software sets one of the codes requested by the bootstrap in the Halt Request field of its per-CPU slot, then executes a CALL_PAL HALT instruction. If a cold bootstrap is requested, the "Cold Bootstrap Requested" code ('2') is set; the "Warm Bootstrap Requested" ('3') code is set to request a warm bootstrap.

Instead of initiating the normal error halt processing described in Section 3.5.4, the console initiates the appropriate system bootstrap as described in Sections 3.4.1 and 3.4.2. The bootstrap attempt is unconditional; the AUTO_ACTION or the BOOT_RESET environment variables do not affect the bootstrap attempt.

3.5 System Restarts

The console is responsible for restarting a processor halted by powerfail or by error halt. The console follows the same sequence for a primary or secondary processor.

3.5.1 Actions of Console

The console begins the restart sequence by locating and then validating the HWRPB, using the procedure given in Section 3.4.2.1. If the HWRPB is not valid, the restart attempt fails. See Section 3.1.1 for console actions at major state transitions.

If the HWRPB is valid, the console uses the processor CPU ID as an index to calculate the address of that processor's HWRPB slot. The console:

1. Verifies that the processor's PALcode Valid (PV) flag is set. If the PV flag is clear, PALcode is not valid, and the restart attempt fails.

2. Verifies that the processor's Context Valid (CV) flag is set. If the CV flag is clear, the HWPCB does not contain valid software context for the restart, and the restart attempt fails.

3. If the Reason for Halt is anything other that "powerfail restart", the console examines the processor's Restart-Capable (RC) flag. If RC is set, the console proceeds with the restart at step 5. If RC is clear, system software is not capable of attempting the restart, and the restart attempt fails.

   Ignoring the RC flag for powerfail restart avoids unnecessary bootstraps that are caused by repeated power failures that in turn, are caused by a bouncing power supply that prevents software from having sufficient time to set the RC flag.

4. Examines the Bootstrap-in-Progress (BIP) flag. If BIP is clear, and the AUTO_ACTION environment variable is "BOOT", a system bootstrap is attempted. Otherwise, the processor remains in console I/O mode. See Figure 3–1.

5. Examines the PALcode revision field in its per-CPU slot. If the revision field does not match the PALcode revision in use by the console, the console must switch PALcode before passing control to the CPU Restart routine.

6. Loads the privileged context specified by the HWPCB in its per-CPU slot.

7. Loads the procedure value at HWRPB[264] into R27.

8. Clears R26 (return address) and R25 (argument information).

9. Loads the virtual page table base (VPTB) register with the value stored in HWRPB[120].

10. Transfers control to the CPU Restart routine, whose virtual address is stored in HWRPB[256].

On all restart attempt failures the console initiates the action indicated by Figure 3–1. The PV and CV flags should never be clear for the primary processor; if either flag is clear, then the restart fails. Also, no PALcode or system software is loaded during a restart.

It is the responsibility of system software to complete the restart operation and to set the RC flag at the point where a subsequent restart can be handled correctly.

3.5.2 Powerfail and Recovery — Uniprocessor

On Alpha systems, the system power supply conditions external power and transforms it for use by the processor, memory, and I/O subsystems. Backup options are available on some systems to supply power after external power fails. The backup option may supply power to all of the system platform hardware or only a subset. The effect of an external power failure depends on the backup option:

- If no backup option exists, the processor cannot be restarted after power is restored. The processor must be bootstrapped or left halted in console I/O mode.

- If the backup option maintains power to all of the system platform hardware, execution of system software is unaffected by the power failure. It must be possible for system software to determine that a transition to backup power has occurred.

- If the backup option maintains only the contents of memory and keeps system time with the BB_WATCH, the power supply must request a powerfail interrupt. After requesting the interrupt, the power supply must continue to supply power to the processor for an implementation-specific period to allow system software to save state.

  Powerfail recovery is possible only if adequate system state is preserved during an interruption of power to the processor. System software must save all volatile state and perform any operating system-specific actions necessary to ensure later successful recovery.

When power is restored, the console determines that the HWRPB is still valid, then examines the console lock and AUTO_ACTION environment variable. If the console is locked, and AUTO_ACTION environment variable is "RESTART", the console attempts an operating system restart. See Section 3.1.1.

The processor may lose state when power is lost. For example, if a processor is halted when power fails, the action on power-up is still determined by the console switches and environment variables. The system does not necessarily stay halted.

Software Note:

As explained in OpenVMS Alpha Software (II-A), Chapter 6, and DIGITAL UNIX Software (II-B), Chapter 5, a powerfail interrupt is delivered at an appropriate IPL to the interrupt service routine located at SCB offset 640_{16} for that operating system.

3.5.3 Powerfail and Recovery — Multiprocessor

There are two basic approaches to powerfail recovery on multiprocessor systems:

- United — all available processors effectively experience the powerfail event identically.
- Split — each available processor effectively experiences independent powerfail events.

A processor is "available" if the Processor Available (PA) flag is set in the processor's per-CPU slot. The powerfail system variation flag at HWRPB[88] indicates the type of powerfail and restart action.

A multiprocessor Alpha system that supports powerfail recovery must implement the united powerfail mode. The split mode may be implemented optionally as an alternative, selected at system bootstrap.

Software Note:

OpenVMS Alpha supports only the united powerfail and recovery mode at this time. Powerfail recovery is possible only when the primary is restarted; all secondaries should remain in console I/O mode.

3.5.3.1 United Powerfail and Recovery

In united powerfail and recovery mode, all available processors experience powerfail interrupts, halts, and restorations uniformly. If one available processor experiences a powerfail event, all other available processors experience that event. Therefore, if one processor powerfails and recovers, all processors must do so. Even if a separately powered processor does not actually lose power, that processor will still receive the powerfail interrupt and must be restarted as if power had been lost.

When power is restored and a restart is to be attempted, the console must determine whether to restart all available processors or only the primary processor. The console determines the appropriate action by the Powerfail Restart (PR) flag in the system variation field of the HWRPB[88]. If the PR flag is set, the console attempts to restart all available processors; if PR is clear, the console attempts to restart only the primary processor. In both cases, it is the responsibility of system software to coordinate and synchronize further powerfail recovery.

3.5.3.2 Split Powerfail and Recovery

In split powerfail and recovery mode, only the available processors that actually experience a loss of power will experience a powerfail interrupt and subsequent recovery. Available processors that are separately powered and do not lose power do not experience a powerfail interrupt.

When power is restored and a restart is to be attempted, the console must determine whether to restart any available processor or only the primary processor. As in the united mode, the console determines the appropriate action by the Powerfail Restart (PR) flag in the system variation field of the HWRPB[88]. If the PR flag is set, the console attempts to restart any available processor. If PR is clear, the console attempts to restart only the primary processor; on a secondary, the console sends the ?STARTREQ? message and waits for a START (or other command) from the running primary as discussed in Section 3.4.3.5. Again, system software has the responsibility for further coordination and synchronization of powerfail recovery.

3.5.4 Error Halt and Recovery

A number of serious error conditions can prevent a processor from executing the current thread of software. Such error conditions are detected by PALcode and halt the processor.

When a halt is encountered, the console must ensure that the processor hardware state is visible to the console operator and to system software after a subsequent restart attempt. This state includes the current values in PS, PC, SP, PCBB, HWPCB, all integer registers, all floating-point registers, and the name of the halt condition. The console must:

1. Ensure that the contents of the integer and floating-point registers appear unaffected.

2. Write the current hardware context to the HWPCB located by the current PCBB.

3. Write the current PS, PC, and PCBB register contents into the processor's per-CPU slot.

4. Write the current R25, R26, and R27 register contents into the processor's per-CPU slot.

5. Set the appropriate code into the Reason for Halt field of the processor's per-CPU slot.

The values of R25, R26, and R27 must be explicitly saved in the per-CPU slot to permit the console to invoke the CPU restart routine.

Section 3.1.1 and Table 2–4 list the defined halt conditions that transition an Alpha processor from the running state to a halted state and that may lead to an attempt to restart the processor. Each condition is passed to the operating system in the Reason for Halt quadword of the processor's HWRPB slot.

When an error halt occurs, the console examines the console lock setting. If the console is locked, the console attempts a restart. If unlocked, the console action is determined by the setting of the AUTO_ACTION environment variable (see Figure 3–1). See Section 3.5.1 for a description of the restart attempt process.

The processor must be initialized after an error halt. If the processor starts running after an error halt without an intervening processor initialization, the operation of the processor is UNDEFINED. The effects of processor initialization are summarized in Table 3–7.

An error halt directly affects only the processor that incurred it, although multiple processors may simultaneously and coincidentally incur their own error halt conditions. If restarts are enabled, each halted processor must be independently restarted by the console. The restarts of individual processors may occur in a different order than the error halts occurred, but if the console restarts any halted processor, it must restart all halted processors in a timely fashion unless a bootstrap is requested in the meantime. A bootstrap nullifies any pending restarts in the multiprocessor.

3.5.5 Operator Requested Crash

When the operating system does not respond to normal program requests, the console operator may request that the console request an operating system crash. A console requested crash differs from a console halt of a processor in that system software can write a crash dump.

The console operator interacts with the console presentation layer and requests the crash with a HALT –CRASH command. The console converts this command to an error halt restart of system software. After gaining control of the processor, the console preserves the hardware state (see Section 3.5.4). The console passes the crash request to system software by using the "Console Operator requests system crash" code in the Reason for Halt field in the primary's per-CPU slot. It is the responsibility of the system software restart routine to initiate the crash in an implementation-specific fashion.

3.5.6 Primary Switching

System software may find it necessary to replace the primary processor with one of the running secondary processors without bootstrapping the system. This "switch" of the running primary may be caused by an error encountered by the primary or by a program request. Switching a running primary must be initiated by system software; the console cannot force a switch to occur.

Support for primary switching is optional to system software, console implementations, and system platforms. The system platform hardware must permit the selected secondary to assume the functions of a primary. The selected secondary must have direct access to the console, a BB_WATCH, and all I/O devices. Direct access to the console ensures that the secondary can access console I/O devices and the console terminal. Direct access to a BB_WATCH ensures that the secondary can act as the system timekeeper. Direct access to all I/O devices ensures that the secondary can initiate I/O requests to and receive I/O interrupts from all I/O devices, and that the secondary can reinitialize all devices as part of powerfail recovery

If the processor is eligible to become a primary, the console will set the Primary Eligible (PE) processor variation flag in the processor's per-CPU slot during processor initialization. See Table 2–4.

Primary switching requires cooperation between system software and the console. System software is responsible for the selection of the new primary and any necessary redirection of I/O interrupts. The console is responsible for any necessary configuration of the console terminal or other console device interface.

3.5.6.1 Sequence on an Embedded Console

The sequence of events differs depending on the type of console implementation. On a system with an embedded console, the operation proceeds as follows:

1. System software performs any actions specific to system software synchronization.

2. System software executing on the old primary ensures that the console terminal is in a quiescent state. In particular, character reception from the terminal must be suspended.

3. System software selects the new primary. The selected secondary must be eligible as indicated by the PE processor variation flag in its per-CPU slot.

4. System software executing on the old primary invokes the PSWITCH console callback specifying the "transition from primary" action.

5. The console attempts to perform any necessary hardware state changes to transform the old primary into a secondary.

   Hardware/Software Coordination Note:
   An example of such a hardware state change is disabling a console UART physically located on the processor board.

6. If the state change is completed, PSWITCH returns success status. System software may proceed with the primary switch at step 8.

7. If the state change is not effected, PSWITCH returns failure status. System software must take other appropriate action.

8. System software executing on the old primary notifies system software on the selected secondary of the successful PSWITCH completion.

9. System software executing on the selected secondary invokes the PSWITCH console callback specifying the "transition to primary" action.

10. The console verifies that the selected secondary is eligible to become a primary and attempts to perform any necessary hardware state changes to transform the old secondary into the new primary.

11. If the state change is completed, PSWITCH returns success status. System software may proceed with the primary switch at step 13.

12. If the state change is not effected, PSWITCH returns failure status. System software must select a different potential primary or take other appropriate action.

13. System software executing on the selected secondary reactivates the console terminal. In particular, character reception from the terminal is re-enabled.

14. System software performs any additional system reconfiguration, updates the PRIMARY CPU ID field at HWRPB[32], recomputes the HWRPB checksum at HWRPB[288], and performs any actions specific to system software synchronization.

3.5.6.2 Sequence on a Detached Console

On a system with a detached console, the operation is similar, but only one call to PSWITCH is required. Additional calls to PSWITCH with the "switch primary" action may result in UNDEFINED operation. The operation proceeds as follows:

1. System software performs any actions specific to system software synchronization.

2. System software executing on the old primary ensures that that the console terminal is in a quiescent state. In particular, character reception from the terminal must be suspended.

3. System software selects the new primary. The selected secondary must be eligible as indicated by the PE processor variation flag in its per-CPU slot.

4. System software executing on any processor invokes the PSWITCH console callback specifying the "switch primary" action and the CPU ID of the new primary.

5. The console verifies that the selected secondary is eligible to become a primary and attempts to perform any necessary hardware state changes to transform the old primary into a secondary and to transform the selected secondary into the primary.

6. If the state change is completed, PSWITCH returns success status. System software may proceed with the primary switch at step 9.

7. If the state change is not effected and the resulting hardware state permits a return to system software, PSWITCH returns failure status. System software must select a different potential primary or take other appropriate action.

8. If the state change is not effected and the resulting hardware state does not permit a return to system software, the console takes the action associated with a failed restart.

9. System software executing on the selected secondary reactivates the console terminal. In particular, character reception from the terminal is re-enabled.

10. System software performs any additional system reconfiguration, updates the PRIMARY CPU ID field at HWRPB[32], recomputes the HWRPB checksum at HWRPB[288], and performs any actions specific to system software synchronization.

3.5.7 Transitioning Console Terminal State During HALT/RESTART

Abrupt transitions from program I/O mode to console I/O mode may occur. Such transitions may be caused by execution of a CALL_PAL HALT instruction, a catastrophic error, or a console operator forcing the processor into console I/O mode. Upon transition to console I/O mode, the console must be able to regain control of the console terminal, even though system software may have changed the device characteristics.

The console may seize control of the console terminal without regard to system software when the transition is such that no return to program I/O mode is possible. Such transitions are normally associated with a catastrophic error.

If system software execution may be continued, the console must be able to restore the existing state of the console terminal. The console must regain and subsequently relinquish control of the console terminal with the cooperation of system software.

Hardware/Software Coordination Note:

This is particularly desirable on workstations when the console operator forces the processor into console I/O mode.

System software may provide SAVE_TERM and RESTORE_TERM routines that can be called by the console to save and restore the state of the console terminal. To provide these optional routines, system software loads the SAVE_TERM and RESTORE_TERM starting virtual address and procedure descriptor fields in the HWRPB and recomputes the HWRPB checksum at HWRPB[288]. At system bootstraps, the console sets these fields to zero.

The console calls SAVE_TERM and RESTORE_TERM in kernel mode at the highest IPL in the memory management policy established by system software. The console loads the routine procedure value into R27, clears R25 and R26, and then transfers control to system software at the starting virtual address. The procedure value and starting virtual address for SAVE_TERM are contained in HWRPB[224] and [232]; those for RESTORE_TERM are contained in HWRPB[240] and [248]. These routines are invoked only on the primary processor and only upon an unexpected entry into console I/O mode. The console must preserve sufficient hardware state to permit the processor to be restarted before invoking these routines. See Section 3.5.4.

Exit from these routines must be accomplished by using the CALL_PAL HALT instruction to return the processor to console I/O mode; these routines do not use the RET subroutine return instruction. Before exiting, these routines must set the "SAVE_TERM/RESTORE_TERM exit" code ('1') in the Halt Request field of the primary's per-CPU slot and indicate success ('0') or failure ('1') status in R0<63>. The console will not attempt to continue system software if a failure status is returned.

SAVE_TERM and RESTORE_TERM may be called when system software has encountered an unexpected CALL_PAL HALT or other halt condition; system state may be corrupt. These routines must be written with few or no dependencies on possibly corrupt system state.

Hardware/Software Coordination Note:

A console terminal on a serial line may or may not have state that needs to be saved. A console terminal on a workstation may require the system software to "roll down" the current screen to expose the "console window" and "roll up" the "console window" to expose the current screen.

3.5.7.1 SAVE_TERM — Save Console Terminal State

Format:

status   = SAVE_TERM

Inputs:

R27   = Procedure value (HWRPB[232])

Outputs:

status   = R0;   status:

	R0<63>	'0'	Success, terminal state saved
		'1'	Failure, terminal state not saved
	R0<62:0>	SBZ	

SAVE_TERM is called by the console after an unexpected entry to console mode. The routine performs any implementation-specific and device-specific actions necessary to save the state of the console terminal as established by system software. When the routine exits and console I/O mode is restored, the console is free to modify the existing console terminal state in any manner.

3.5.7.2 RESTORE_TERM — Restore Console Terminal State

Format:

status   = RESTORE_TERM

Inputs:

R27   = Procedure value (HWRPB[248])

Outputs:

status   = R0;   Status:

R0<63>	'0'	Success, terminal state restored
	'1'	Failure, terminal state not restored
R0<62:0>	SBZ	

RESTORE_TERM is called by the console just before continuing system software. The routine performs any implementation-specific and device-specific actions necessary to restore the state of the console terminal as established by system software.

3.5.8 Operator Forced Entry to Console I/O Mode

The console operator can force a processor into console I/O mode with a HALT -CPU command. When a processor enters console I/O mode in this way, the console sets the Operator Halted (OH) flag in its per-CPU slot. The console does not update the Reason for Halt or any other processor halt state in its per-CPU slot. The console sets the OH flag only as the result of an explicit operator action. The OH flag is not set on transitions to console I/O mode that result from error halt conditions, powerfails, CALL_PAL HALT instructions in kernel mode, console operator requests of a system crash, or software-directed processor shutdowns.

The console clears the OH flag before returning to program I/O mode as the result of a CONTINUE or BOOT command. The console may clear OH flag if an error halt or operator-induced condition is encountered that precludes a subsequent CONTINUE command. Such a condition is treated as an error halt (see Section 3.5.4).

3.6 Bootstrap Loading and Image Media Format

An Alpha console may load a primary bootstrap image from one or more of the device classes listed in Table 3–9. Subsequent sections describe how the console locates, sizes, and loads the bootstrap image for each device class.

Table 3–9: Bootstrap Devices and Image Media

Device Class	Data Link	Protocol
Local Disk	N/A	Bootblock
Local Tape	N/A	ANSI Bootblock

Table 3–9: Bootstrap Devices and Image Media (Continued)

Device Class	Data Link	Protocol
Network	NI, FDDI	MOP Bootp
ROM	N/A	ROM Bootblock

As explained in Section 3.4.1.4, the console attempts to load a bootstrap image from each element of a bootstrap device list until a successful image load is achieved. If the bootstrap image cannot be located or if the load fails for any reason, the console retains control of the system, generates the binary error message AUDIT_BSTRAP_ABORT, and then attempts to load a bootstrap image from the next bootstrap device list element. After a bootstrap image is successfully located and loaded, the console transfers control to system software as described in Section 3.4.

As the loading of the bootstrap image proceeds, the console optionally generates an audit trail of progress messages. The ENABLE_AUDIT environment variable controls audit trail generation. The audit trail begins with the AUDIT_BOOT_STARTS message. The audit trail continues with messages that are specific to the bootstrap device. Each consists of a binary message code that is interpreted by the console presentation layer.

3.6.1 Disk Bootstrapping

An Alpha primary bootstrap may be loaded from a directly accessed disk device. The console loads the "boot block" contained in the first logical block (LBN 0) of the disk. The boot block contains the starting logical block number (LBN) of the primary bootstrap program and the count of contiguous LBNs that make up that image.

The first 512 bytes of the boot block are structured as shown in Figure 3–6. The console loads the primary bootstrap without knowledge of the operating system file system. The boot block is (previously) initialized by the operating system. The actual size of a logical block is device-specific and may exceed 512 bytes.

Figure 3–6: Alpha Disk Boot Block

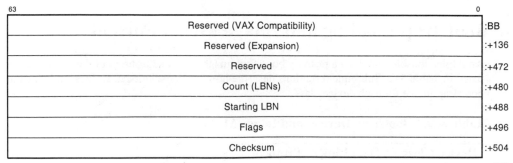

63	0	
Reserved (VAX Compatibility)		:BB
Reserved (Expansion)		:+136
Reserved		:+472
Count (LBNs)		:+480
Starting LBN		:+488
Flags		:+496
Checksum		:+504
		:+512

A local disk bootstrap proceeds as follows:

1. The console reads the boot block from LBN 0 of the specified disk device.

2. The console validates the boot block CHECKSUM; if the checksum is not validated, the bootstrap image load attempt aborts. The console computes the checksum of the first 63 quadwords in the block as a 64-bit sum, ignoring overflow. The computation includes both reserved regions. The computed checksum is compared to the CHECK-SUM.

3. The console generates the AUDIT_CHECKSUM_GOOD message if the audit trail is enabled.

4. The console ensures that the FLAG quadword is zero; otherwise the bootstrap image load attempt aborts.

5. The console ensures that the COUNT is non-zero; otherwise the bootstrap image load attempt aborts. The count field indicates the number of contiguous logical blocks that contain the primary bootstrap.

6. The console generates the AUDIT_LOAD_BEGINS message if the audit trail is enabled.

7. The console reads the primary bootstrap image specified by COUNT and STARTING LBN into system memory; in any error occurs, the bootstrap image load attempt aborts.

    The transfer begins at the logical block given by the STARTING LBN; a contiguous COUNT number of logical blocks is read. The image is read into a virtually contiguous system memory buffer; the starting virtual address is 0000 0000 2000 0000$_{16}$. (See Section 3.4.1.2.)

    Errors include device hardware errors, the specified STARTING LBN not being present on the disk, or unexpectedly encountering the last logical block on the disk during the read.

8. The console generates the AUDIT_LOAD_DONE message when the load has completed; the message is generated only if the audit trail is enabled.

9. The console prepares to transfer control to the bootstrap program as described in Section 3.4.1.6.

Implementation Notes:

Unlike the VAX boot block support, *no* native Alpha code is contained in the boot block; the boot block contains *only* the LBN descriptor for the Alpha primary bootstrap image. An Alpha boot block can contain pointers to primary bootstrap images for both VAX and Alpha simultaneously.

Because the boot block includes an LBN and block count, the console need have no knowledge of the operating system file system or on-disk structure.

The first 136 bytes of the boot block are currently used by the VAX disk boot block mechanism. The next 80 bytes are not currently used either by VAX or Alpha boot blocks. For future expansions, VAX boot blocks should expand towards higher addresses and Alpha boot blocks expand towards lower addresses; each region remains contiguous. These 216 bytes are ignored by the Alpha console except for the purposes of computing the boot block checksum.

The boot block FLAGS word is reserved for future expansion. Flag<0> is reserved to indicate a discontiguous bootstrap image; Flag <63:1> are reserved for future definition. There are no current plans by any DIGITAL operating system to have a discontiguous primary bootstrap image.

3.6.2 Tape Bootstrapping

An Alpha primary bootstrap may be loaded from a directly accessed tape device. Before loading the primary bootstrap, the console must determine the tape format and locate the primary bootstrap on the tape. The console:

1. Rewinds the tape on the specified tape device to the beginning of the tape (BOT).

2. Reads the first record.

3. Determines the record length.

   – If the record length is 80 bytes, the tape may be an ANSI-formatted tape. The console proceeds as described in Section 3.6.2.1.

   – If the record length is 512 bytes, the tape is "boot blocked." The console proceeds as described in Section 3.6.2.2.

   – If the length is other than 80 or 512 bytes, the bootstrap image load attempt aborts.

3.6.2.1 Bootstrapping from ANSI-Formatted Tape

Before loading the primary bootstrap image from an ANSI-formatted tape, the console must ensure that the format is valid. To verify that a given record contains a particular ANSI label, the console checks for the ASCII label name string at the beginning of the record. For example, a record containing a VOL1 label begins with the ASCII string "VOL1." All other record bytes are ignored when verifying the label.

A primary bootstrap image file name may be specified explicitly on a BOOT command or implicitly by the BOOT_FILE environment variable. If no file name is specified, the first file located will be used.

A local ANSI-formatted tape bootstrap proceeds as follows:

1. The console verifies that the first record contains a VOL1 label; if the verification fails, the bootstrap image load attempt aborts.

2. The console generates the AUDIT_TAPE_ANSI message if the audit trail is enabled.

3. If no file name was specified, the console advances the tape position to the End-of-Tape (EOT) side of the the first tape mark. The console proceeds to step 5.

4. If a file name was specified, the console attempts to locate that file on the tape. If the file cannot be located, the attempt to load the bootstrap image aborts. The console compares the specified file name with the file name present in each HDR1 label on the tape. At the first match, the console proceeds to step 5.

   The console searches for the specified file, starting with the second tape record. The console reads 80-byte records from the tape until it encounters an HDR1 label, then proceeds as follows:

A. The console generates the AUDIT_FILE_FOUND<filename> message, where <filename> is the value of the HDR1 label. The message is generated only if the audit trail is enabled.

B. The console compares the specified file name with the 17-character File Identifier Field found in the HDR1 label.

C. If a match occurs, the console advances the tape position to after the next tape mark and proceeds to step 5. (Any HDR2 or HDR3 labels are ignored.)

D. If no match occurs, the console advances the tape position over the next three tape marks and reads the next record. If another tape mark is found, the logical end of volume has been encountered and the attempt to load the bootstrap image aborts. Otherwise, the record should be the HDR1 label for the next file on the tape and the console proceeds at step A.

The console aborts the attempt to load the bootstrap image whenever an unexpected tape mark is encountered, the tape runs off the end, or a hardware error occurs.

5. The console generates the AUDIT_LOAD_BEGINS message if the audit trail is enabled.

6. The console reads the primary bootstrap image from tape into system memory; if any error occurs or if the tape runs off the end, the attempt to load the bootstrap image aborts.

The transfer from tape begins at the current tape position and continues until a tape mark is encountered. The image is read into a virtually contiguous system memory buffer; the starting virtual address is 0000 0000 2000 0000$_{16}$. (See Section 3.4.1.2.)

7. The console checks that the bootstrap file was properly closed by:

A. Reading the record after the tape mark and verifying that the record is an EOF1 label. If not, the attempt to load the bootstrap image aborts.

B. Searching for a subsequent tape mark. If a tape mark is not found, the bootstrap file was improperly closed and the attempt to load the bootstrap image aborts. (Any EOF2 and EOF3 labels are ignored.)

8. The console generates the AUDIT_LOAD_DONE message if the audit trail is enabled.

9. The console prepares to transfer control to the bootstrap as described in Section 3.4.1.6. The console does not rewind or otherwise change the position of the tape after reading the bootstrap image.

3.6.2.2 Bootstrapping from Boot-Blocked Tape

Bootstrapping from a boot-blocked tape is similar to the local disk bootstrapping described in Section 3.6.1. The first tape record must be 512 bytes and must follow the format given for disk boot blocks as shown in Figure 3–6. The STARTING LBN and FLAGS fields are MBZ for tape boot boot blocks.

All tape records that comprise the primary bootstrap must be 512 bytes in size. If the console encounters records of any other size, the attempt to load the bootstrap image aborts.

A local tape boot block bootstrap proceeds as follows:

1. The console generates the AUDIT_TAPE_BBLOCK message if the audit trail is enabled.

2. The console validates the boot block CHECKSUM; if the checksum is not validated, the attempt to load the bootstrap image aborts. The console computes the checksum of the first 63 quadwords in the block as a 64-bit sum, ignoring overflow. The computation includes both reserved regions and the MBZ fields. The computed checksum is compared to the CHECKSUM at [BB+504].

3. The console generates the AUDIT_CHECKSUM_GOOD message if the audit trail is enabled.

4. The console ensures that the COUNT is non-zero; otherwise the attempt to load the bootstrap image aborts. The count field indicates the number of subsequent 512-byte records that contain the primary bootstrap.

5. The console generates the AUDIT_LOAD_BEGINS message if the audit trail is enabled.

6. The console reads the count field subsequent records from the tape into system memory. The attempt to load the bootstrap image aborts if the console encounters any error, encounters any record size other than 512 bytes, or the tape runs off the end.

   The image is read into a virtually contiguous system memory buffer; the starting virtual address is $0000\ 0000\ 2000\ 0000_{16}$. (See Section 3.4.1.2.)

7. The console generates the AUDIT_LOAD_DONE message if the audit trail is enabled.

8. The console prepares to transfer control to the bootstrap as described in Section 3.4.1.6. The console does not rewind or otherwise change the position of the tape after reading the bootstrap image.

3.6.3 ROM Bootstrapping

An Alpha console may support bootstrapping from read-only memory (ROM). Bootstrap ROM is assumed to appear in multiple discontiguous regions of the physical address space. A given ROM region may contain multiple bootstrap images. A given bootstrap image must not span ROM regions.

Each ROM bootstrap image is page aligned and begins with a boot block as shown in Figure 3–7. The ROM boot block is similar to the local disk and tape boot block shown in Figure 3–6.

Figure 3–7: Alpha ROM Boot Block

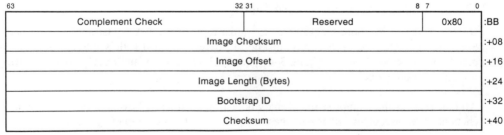

A ROM bootstrap proceeds as follows:

1. The console locates the specified ordinal ROM bootstrap image; if the bootstrap image cannot be located, the attempt to load the bootstrap image aborts.

    The console locates the ROM bootstrap image by searching ROM regions beginning with the ROM region with the lowest physical address and proceeding upward to the ROM region with the highest physical address.

    The search proceeds as follows:

    A. The console verifies that the page contains a ROM bootstrap image:

        –   The low-order byte of the first quadword must be 80_{16}.

        –   The high-order longword of the first quadword must be the one's complement of the low-order longword.

        –   The sixth quadword must contain the checksum of the first five quadwords. The checksum is computed as a 64-bit sum, ignoring overflow.

    B. The console generates the AUDIT_BOOT_TYPE<string> message for each valid boot block, if the audit trail is enabled. The <string> is the ISO Latin–1 string contained in the BOOTSTRAP ID quadword.

    C. If the specified ordinal image number has been reached, the console proceeds to step 2.

    D. Otherwise, the console uses the IMAGE LENGTH at [BB+24] to determine the offset to the next ROM region page to be searched. The console repeats the process at step A.

2. The console computes the starting physical address of the bootstrap image by adding the physical address OFFSET at [BB+16] to the starting physical address of the boot block [BB].

3. The console verifies the accessibility of each page of the bootstrap image. If any page is inaccessible, the attempt to load the bootstrap image is aborted.

4. The console generates the AUDIT_BSTRAP_ACCESSIBLE message if the audit trail is enabled.

5. If requested, the console validates the IMAGE CHECKSUM at [BB+08]; if the checksum is not validated, the attempt to load the bootstrap image aborts. The console computes the checksum of all quadwords in the bootstrap image as a 64-bit sum, ignoring overflow. The existence and implementation of the mechanism for requesting this validation is implementation specific.

6. The console generates the AUDIT_BSTRAP_GOOD message if the audit trail is enabled.

7. If requested, the console copies the bootstrap image from ROM into system memory (RAM). The image is copied into a virtually contiguous buffer starting at virtual address 0000 0000 2000 0000$_{16}$. (See Section 3.4.1.2.) The console generates the AUDIT_LOAD_BEGINS message before beginning the copy and the AUDIT_LOAD_DONE after the copy completes successfully if the audit trail is enabled.

8. The console prepares to transfer control to the bootstrap as described in Section 3.4.1.6.

3.6.4 Network Bootstrapping

An Alpha system may support bootstrapping over one or more network communication devices and data link protocols. The console actions depend on the network device, data link protocol, and remote server capabilities.

An Alpha system can use the DIGITAL Network Architecture Maintenance Operations Protocol (MOP), or the BOOTP–UDP/IP network protocol, to bootstrap an Alpha system. See the MOP or BOOTP–UDP/IP specification for a detailed description.

A network bootstrap proceeds as follows:

1. The console determines if a bootstrap file name is to be used. The file name is taken from the BOOT command or the BOOT_FILE environment variable. If no file name is specified on the BOOT command and BOOT_FILE is null, no file name will be used.

2. The console generates the AUDIT_BOOT_REQ<filename> message if the audit trail is enabled.

3. The console issues the appropriate (MOP or BOOTP–UDP/IP) bootstrap request message(s).

4. The console receives an appropriate response (MOP or BOOTP–UDP/IP) from a remote bootstrap server. If no such response is received, the attempt to load the bootstrap image abortss.

5. The console generates the AUDIT_BSERVER_FOUND message if the audit trail is enabled.

6. The bootstrap load proceeds, using the appropriate network protocol.

7. When the console receives the first portion of the bootstrap image, the console generates the AUDIT_LOAD_BEGINS message if the audit trail is enabled.

8. The console loads the initial portion of the bootstrap image into a virtually contiguous system memory buffer; the starting virtual address is $0000\ 0000\ 2000\ 0000_{16}$. (See Section 3.4.1.2.)

9. When the bootstrap image has been loaded, the console generates the AUDIT_LOAD_DONE message if the audit trail is enabled.

10. The console prepares to transfer control to the bootstrap program as described in Section 3.4.1.6.

If any error occurs, the attempt to load the bootstrap image aborts.

3.7 BB_WATCH

The following list offers important points about BB_WATCH:

1. BB_WATCH is the correct name for this entity. Although incorrect terminology, TOY, TODR, and watch chip, when used in the context of an Alpha system, are equivalent in meaning to the BB_WATCH.

2. System software must directly manipulate the BB_WATCH through an implementation-dependent interface.

3. System software makes the decision where to acquire known time; if a BB_WATCH is present, it may be used as the provider of known time.

4. Systems are not required to have a BB_WATCH.

   Software Note:
   However, all systems that support OpenVMS Alpha or DIGITAL UNIX on Alpha must have a BB_WATCH.

5. If a BB_WATCH is present in a system, it meets the following requirements:

   –   It has an accuracy of at least 50 ppm regardless of whether power is applied to the system.

   –   It has a resolution of at least 1 second (that is, it is read and written in units of a second or better).

   –   Changing the entirety of the time maintained by the BB_WATCH takes under 1 second.

   –   It has battery backup to survive a loss of power.

6. A BB_WATCH is always accessible to the primary processor. That is, a processor must be able to access a BB_WATCH directly (it must not need to go through another processor to access it) in order to be a candidate for primary processor.

7. The number of BB_WATCH entities in a system is either one for the entire system or one for each processor in the system; which of the two options a system chooses is implementation dependent. If the latter option is chosen (one BB_WATCH per processor), writing one BB_WATCH does not update another.

8. Although writing the BB_WATCH takes less than one second, it may not be a fast operation. Software should avoid frequently writing the BB_WATCH lest it negatively impact performance.

9. The processor and its PALcode never changes the value of BB_WATCH except under the direction of system software. (The console, boot programs, and remote console clients are not system software.) The console, its PALcode, and any console application (including a diagnostic supervisor) never changes BB_WATCH except under the direction of the console operator — even when the CPU is halted, the processor is being initialized, or the BB_WATCH has an invalid time.

Programming Note:

The Primary-Eligible (PE) bit in the per-CPU slot of the HWRPB for each processor indicates, among other things, whether the CPU has access to a BB_WATCH. See Chapter 2.

The description of primary switching details the actions taken in a multiprocessor system, including the requirement for the primary processor to have access to the BB_WATCH.

3.8 Implementation Considerations

3.8.1 Embedded Console

In an embedded console implementation, the console executes on the same processor as the operating system. In such an implementation, the state transitions as experienced by the processor are more conceptual. For example, the processor acting as the console will be executing instructions when in the halted state. The processor may also field console I/O mode exceptions and interrupts.

An embedded console may be implemented as an extension of PALcode or as a distinct software entity. The console may execute from dedicated RAM or ROM on the processor or, after console initialization, may execute from main memory.

An embedded console implementation must include a mechanism by which the primary processor can be forced into console I/O mode from program I/O mode. This enables the console operator to gain control of the system regardless of the state of the system software. See Section 1.1 for recommended and required mechanisms.

3.8.1.1 Multiprocessor Considerations

In a multiprocessor system, selection of the primary processor occurs before any access to main memory by any of the processors. At system cold start, each of the processors will be executing in console I/O mode. The necessary memory for console execution must be independent of main memory; the console must be executing from dedicated console RAM or ROM and/or a suitably configured processor cache.

The selection of the console primary requires one or more hardware registers with state that is shared by all processors. One possible example is a mutex contained in a single-bit register accessed only with LDQ_L/STQ_C instructions. The primary successfully gains ownership of the mutex. Implementations should include mechanisms for operator override of the selection process and for recovery if the selection process fails.

Once a console primary has been selected, the console secondaries take no further action until appropriately notified by the primary. In particular, console secondaries must not access main memory. The console primary is responsible for building the HWRPB and any console-internal data structures (such as environment variables) for the secondaries. When these structures have been initialized, the console primary must be able to signal one or more of the secondaries by additional hardware register(s).

The console primary allocates a HWRPB in main memory, initializes it, and stores its physical address in an implementation-specific, nonvolatile manner. The console primary then indicates the presence of the HWRPB and its location to all secondaries by an implementation-specific mechanism.

On system restarts, the console primary identifies itself by comparing its WHAMI register contents with the Primary CPU ID value stored in the HWRPB.

When executing in console I/O mode, all processors must observe the same values of all console environment variables. The values of the AUTO_ACTION and BOOT_RESET environment variables are particularly important. After failing to become the console primary processor, a console secondary waits to be notified that a valid HWRPB exists. Upon such notification by the primary, the console secondaries use the address provided by the primary to locate the HWRPB. The primary may be in either program I/O mode or console I/O mode.

On cold bootstrap, a console secondary must not access main memory until notified by the primary that a valid HWRPB exists. Thus, there must exist a mechanism that is not based on main memory whereby the primary may signal each of the secondaries. On warm bootstrap or restart, a secondary processor must locate its per-CPU slot in the HWRPB and poll its RXRDY bit.

Console processors must locate the HWRPB without searching memory; such a search constitutes a security hole. One possible implementation is to use an environment variable or other shared console data structure. The address of the HWRPB must be nonvolatile across power failures in systems that support powerfail recovery.

Console implementations that support SAVE_ENV must be able to execute the routine simultaneously on each processor. System software use of SAVE_ENV requires care. System software must invoke SAVE_ENV on all available processors, but cannot ensure that the nonvolatile storage is updated on processors that are not available at the time of update. If mismatch occurs, the console uses the nonvolatile values preserved by the primary processor.

3.8.2 Detached Console

In a detached console implementation, the console executes on a separate and distinct hardware platform. A detached console may have cooperating special code that executes on one of the processors in the system configuration.

Detached console implementations should provide a keep-alive function. System software should be able to detect failures of the path between the system platform and the console. The mechanism may be a single dedicated signal or periodic message exchange. System software should be able to continue to execute if a keep-alive failure occurs, and restoration of the connection (or console state) should not cause a system crash or other major state transition. The console should buffer any messages if a keep-alive failure occurs until reconnection occurs.

Detached consoles may maintain a local console log. The logging device and format are implementation specific.

Console Interface Index

C

D

Appendixes

The following appendixes are included in the *Alpha Architecture Reference Manual*:

- Appendix A, Software Considerations
- Appendix B, IEEE Floating Point Conformance
- Appendix C, Instruction Summary
- Appendix D, Registered System and Processor Identifiers
- Appendix E, Waivers and Implementation-Dependent Functionality

Contents

A Software Considerations

B IEEE Floating-Point Conformance

C Instruction Summary

D Registered System and Processor Identifiers

E Waivers and Implementation-Dependent Functionality

Figures

Tables

Software Considerations

A.1 Hardware-Software Compact

The Alpha architecture, like all RISC architectures, depends on careful attention to data alignment and instruction scheduling to achieve high performance.

Since there will be various implementations of the Alpha architecture, it is not obvious how compilers can generate high-performance code for all implementations. This chapter gives some scheduling guidelines that, if followed by all compilers and respected by all implementations, will result in good performance. As such, this section represents a good-faith compact between hardware designers and software writers. It represents a set of common goals, not a set of architectural requirements. Thus, an Appendix, not a Chapter.

Many of the performance optimizations discussed below provide an advantage only for frequently executed code. For rarely executed code, they may produce a bigger program that is not any faster. Some of the branching optimizations also depend on good prediction of which path from a conditional branch is more frequently executed. These optimizations are best determined by using an execution profile, either an estimate generated by compiler heuristics, or a real profile of a previous run, such as that gathered by PC-sampling in PCA.

Each computer architecture has a "natural word size." For the PDP-11, it is 16 bits; for VAX, 32 bits; and for Alpha , 64 bits. Other architectures also have a natural word size that varies between 16 and 64 bits. Except for very low-end implementations, ALU data paths, cache access paths, chip pin buses, and main memory data paths are all usually the natural word size. As an architecture becomes commercially successful, high-end implementations inevitably move to double-width data paths that can transfer an *aligned* (at an even natural word address) pair of natural words in one cycle. For Alpha , this means 128-bit wide data paths will eventually be implemented. It is difficult to get much speed advantage from paired transfers unless the code being executed has instructions and data appropriately aligned on aligned octaword boundaries. Since this is difficult to retrofit to old code, the following sections sometimes encourage "over-aligning" to octaword boundaries in anticipation of high-speed Alpha implementations.

In some cases, there are performance advantages to aligning instructions or data to cache-block boundaries, or putting data whose use is correlated into the same cache block, or trying to avoid cache conflicts by not having data whose use is correlated placed at addresses that are equal modulo the cache size. Since the Alpha architecture will have many implementations, an exact cache design cannot be outlined here.

In each case below, the performance implication is given by an order-of-magnitude number: 1, 3, 10, 30, or 100. A factor of 10 means that the performance difference being discussed will likely range from 3 to 30 across all Alpha implementations.

A.2 Instruction-Stream Considerations

The following sections describe considerations for the instruction stream.

A.2.1 Instruction Alignment

Code PSECTs should be octaword aligned. Targets of frequently taken branches should be at least quadword aligned, and octaword aligned for very frequent loops. Compilers could use execution profiles to identify frequently taken branches.

Quadword I-fetch implementors should give first priority to executing aligned quadwords quickly. Octaword-fetch implementors should give first priority to executing aligned octawords quickly, and second priority to executing aligned quadwords quickly. Dual-issue implementations should give first priority to issuing both halves of an aligned quadword in one cycle, and second priority to buffering and issuing other combinations.

A.2.2 Branch Prediction and Minimizing Branch-Taken — Factor of 3

In many Alpha implementations, an unexpected change in I-stream address will result in about 10 lost instruction times. "Unexpected" may mean any branch-taken or may mean a mispredicted branch. In many implementations, even a correctly predicted branch to a quadword target address will be slower than straight-line code.

Compilers should follow these rules to minimize unexpected branches:

1. Branch prediction is implementation specific. Based on execution profiles, compilers should physically rearrange code so that it has matching behavior.

2. Make basic blocks as big as possible. A good goal is 20 instructions on average between branch-taken. This requires unrolling loops so that they contain at least 20 instructions, and putting subroutines of less than 20 instructions directly in line. It also requires using execution profiles to rearrange code so that the frequent case of a conditional branch falls through. For very high-performance loops, it will be profitable to move instructions across conditional branches to fill otherwise wasted instruction issue slots, even if the instructions moved will not always do useful work. Note that using the Conditional Move instructions can sometimes avoid breaking up basic blocks.

3. In an if-then-else construct whose execution profile is skewed even slightly away from 50%-50% (51-49 is enough), put the infrequent case completely out of line, so that the frequent case encounters *zero* branch-takens, and the infrequent case encounters *two* branch-takens. If the infrequent case is rare (5%), put it far enough away that it never comes into the I-cache. If the infrequent case is extremely rare (error message code), put it on a page of rarely executed code and expect that page *never* to be paged in.

4. There are two functionally identical branch-format opcodes, BSR and BR, as shown in Figure A–1.

Figure A–1: Branch-Format BSR and BR Opcodes

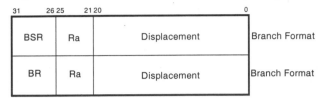

Compilers should use the first one for subroutine calls, and the second for GOTOs. Some implementations may push a stack of predicted return addresses for BSR and not push the stack for BR. Failure to compile the correct opcode will result in mispredicted return addresses, and hence make subroutine returns slow.

5. The memory-format JSR instruction, shown in Figure A–2, has 16 unused bits. These should be used by the compilers to communicate a hint about expected branch-target behavior (see Common Architecture, Chapter 4).

Figure A–2: Memory-Format JSR Instruction

If the JSR is used for a computed GOTO or a CASE statement, compile bits <15:14> as 00, and bits <13:0> such that (updated PC+Instr<13:0>*4) <15:0> equals (likely_target_addr) <15:0>. In other words, pick the low 14 bits so that a normal PC+displacement*4 calculation will match the low 16 bits of the most likely target longword address. (Implementations will likely prefetch from the matching cache block.)

If the JSR is used for a computed subroutine call, compile bits <15:14> as 01, and bits <13:0> as above. Some implementations will prefetch the call target using the prediction and also push updated PC on a return-prediction stack.

If the JSR is used as a subroutine return, compile bits <15:14> as 10. Some implementations will pop an address off a return-prediction stack.

If the JSR is used as a coroutine linkage, compile bits <15:14> as 11. Some implementations will pop an address off a return-prediction stack and also push updated PC on the return-prediction stack.

Implementors should give first priority to executing straight-line code with no branch-takens as quickly as possible, second priority to predicting conditional branches based on the sign of the displacement field (backward taken, forward not-taken), and third priority to predicting subroutine return addresses by running a small prediction stack. (VAX traces show a stack of two to four entries correctly predicts most branches.)

A.2.3 Improving I-Stream Density — Factor of 3

Compilers should try to use profiles to make sure almost 100% of the bytes brought into an I-cache are actually executed. This requires aligning branch targets and putting rarely executed code out of line.

A.2.4 Instruction Scheduling — Factor of 3

The performance of Alpha programs is sensitive to how carefully the code is scheduled to minimize instruction-issue delays.

"Result latency" is defined as the number of CPU cycles that must elapse between an instruction that writes a result register and one that uses that register, if execution-time stalls are to be avoided. Thus, with a latency of zero, the instruction writes a result register and the instruction that uses that register can be multiple-issued in the *same* cycle. With a latency of 2, if the writing instruction is issued at cycle N, the reading instruction can issue no earlier than cycle N+2. Latency is implementation specific.

Most Alpha instructions have a non-zero result latency. Compilers should schedule code so that a result is not used too soon, at least in frequently executed code (inner loops, as identified by execution profiles). In general, this will require unrolling loops and inlining short procedures.

Compilers should try to schedule code to match the above latency rules and also to match the multiple-issue rules. If doing both is impractical for a particular sequence of code, the latency rules are more important (since they apply even in single-issue implementations).

Implementors should give first priority to minimizing the latency of back-to-back integer operations, of address calculations immediately followed by load/store, of load immediately followed by branch, and of compare immediately followed by branch. Give second priority to minimizing latencies in general.

A.3 Data-Stream Considerations

The following sections describe considerations for the data stream.

A.3.1 Data Alignment — Factor of 10

Data PSECTs should be at least octaword aligned, so that aggregates (arrays, some records, subroutine stack frames) can be allocated on aligned octaword boundaries to take advantage of any implementations with aligned octaword data paths, and to decrease the number of cache fills in almost all implementations.

Aggregates (arrays, records, common blocks, and so forth) should be allocated on at least aligned octaword boundaries whenever language rules allow. In some implementations, a series of writes that completely fill a cache block may be a factor of 10 faster than a series of writes that partially fill a cache block, when that cache block would give a read miss. This is true of write-back caches that read a partially filled cache block from memory, but optimize away the read for completely filled blocks.

For such implementations, long strings of sequential writes will be faster if they start on a cache-block boundary (a multiple of 128 bytes will do well for most, if not all, Alpha implementations). This applies to array results that sweep through large portions of memory, and to register-save areas for context switching, graphics frame buffer accesses, and other places where exactly 8, 16, 32, or more quadwords are stored sequentially. Allocating the targets at multiples of 8, 16, 32, or more quadwords, respectively, and doing the writes in order of increasing address will maximize the write speed.

Items within aggregates that are forced to be unaligned (records, common blocks) should generate compile-time warning messages and inline byte extract/insert code. Users must be educated that the warning message means that they are taking a factor of 30 performance hit.

Compiled code for parameters should assume that the parameters are aligned. Unaligned actuals will cause run-time alignment traps and very slow fixups. The fixup routine, if invoked, should generate warning messages to the user, preferably giving the first few statement numbers that are doing unaligned parameter access, and at the end of a run the total number of alignment traps (and perhaps an estimate of the performance improvement if the data were aligned). Users must be educated that the trap routine warning message means they are taking a factor of 30 performance hit.

Frequently used scalars should reside in registers. Each scalar datum allocated in memory should normally be allocated an aligned quadword to itself, even if the datum is only a byte wide. This allows aligned quadword loads and stores and avoids partial-quadword writes (which may be half as fast as full-quadword writes, due to such factors as read-modify-write a quadword to do quadword ECC calculation).

Implementors should give first priority to fast reads of aligned octawords and second priority to fast writes of full cache blocks.

A.3.2 Shared Data in Multiple Processors — Factor of 3

Software locks are aligned quadwords and should be allocated to large cache blocks that either contain no other data or read-mostly data whose usage is correlated with the lock.

Whenever there is high contention for a lock, one processor will have the lock and be using the guarded data, while other processors will be in a read-only spin loop on the lock bit. Under these circumstances, *any* write to the cache block containing the lock will likely cause excess bus traffic and cache fills, thus affecting performance on all processors that are involved and the buses between them. In some decomposed FORTRAN programs, refills of the cache blocks containing one or two frequently used locks can account for a third of all the bus bandwidth the program consumes.

Whenever there is almost no contention for a lock, one processor will have the lock and be using the guarded data. Under these circumstances, it might be desirable to keep the guarded data in the *same* cache block as the lock.

For the high-sharing case, compilers should assume that *almost all* accesses to shared data result in cache misses all the way back to main memory, for each distinct cache block used. Such accesses will likely be a factor of 30 slower than cache hits. It is helpful to pack correlated shared data into a small number of cache blocks. It is helpful also to segregate blocks written by one processor from blocks read by others.

Therefore, accesses to shared data, including locks, should be minimized. For example, a four-processor decomposition of some manipulation of a 1000-row array should avoid accessing lock variables every row, but instead might access a lock variable every 250 rows.

Array manipulation should be partitioned across processors so that cache blocks do not thrash between processors. Having each of four processors work on every fourth array element severely impairs performance on any implementation with a cache block of four elements or larger. The processors all contend for copies of the *same* cache blocks and use only one quarter of the data in each block. Writes in one processor severely impair cache performance on all processors.

A better decomposition is to give each processor the largest possible contiguous chunk of data to work on (N/4 consecutive rows for four processors and row-major array storage; N/4 columns for column-major storage). With the possible exception of three cache blocks at the partition boundaries, this decomposition will result in each processor caching data that is touched by *no* other processor.

Operating-system scheduling algorithms should attempt to minimize process migration from one processor to another. Any time migration occurs, there are likely to be a large number of cache misses on the new processor.

Similarly, operating-system scheduling algorithms should attempt to enforce some affinity between a given device's interrupts and the processor on which the interrupt-handler runs. I/O control data structures and locks for different devices should be disjoint. Observing these guidelines allows higher cache hit rates on the corresponding I/O control data structures.

Implementors should give first priority to an efficient (low-bandwidth) way of transferring isolated lock values and other isolated, shared write data between processors.

Implementors should assume that the amount of shared data will continue to increase, so over time the need for efficient sharing implementations will also increase.

A.3.3 Avoiding Cache/TB Conflicts — Factor of 1

Occasionally, programs that run with a direct-mapped cache or TB will thrash, taking excessive cache or TB misses. With some work, thrashing can be minimized at compile time.

Note:

No Alpha processor through and including the 21264 has implemented a direct-mapped TB.

In a frequently executed loop, compilers could allocate the data items accessed from memory so that, on each loop iteration, all of the memory addresses accessed are either in *exactly the same* aligned 64-byte block or differ in bits VA<10:6>. For loops that go through arrays in a common direction with a common stride, this requires allocating the arrays, checking that the first-iteration addresses differ, and if not, inserting up to 64 bytes of padding *between* the arrays. This rule will avoid thrashing in small direct-mapped data caches with block sizes up to 64 bytes and total sizes of 2K bytes or more.

Example:

```
   REAL*4 A(1000),B(1000)
   DO 60 i=1,1000
60 A( i ) = f(B( i ))
```

Figures A–3, A–4, and A–5 show bad, better, and best allocation in cache, respectively.

BAD allocation (A and B thrash in 8 KB direct-mapped cache):

Figure A–3: Bad Allocation in Cache

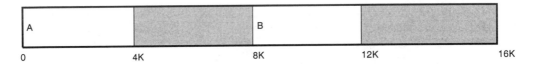

BETTER allocation (A and B offset by 64 mod 2 KB, so 16 elements of A and 16 of B can be in cache simultaneously):

Figure A–4: Better Allocation in Cache

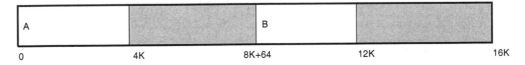

BEST allocation (A and B offset by 64 mod 2 KB, so 16 elements of A and 16 of B can be in cache simultaneously, *and* both arrays fit entirely in 8 KB or bigger cache):

Figure A–5: Best Allocation in Cache

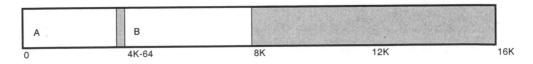

In a frequently executed loop, compilers could allocate the data items accessed from memory so that, on each loop iteration, all of the memory addresses accessed are either in *exactly the same 8 KB* page, or differ in bits VA<17:13>. For loops that go through arrays in a common direction with a common stride, this requires allocating the arrays, checking that the first-iteration addresses differ, and if they do not, inserting up to 8K bytes of padding *between* the arrays. This rule will avoid thrashing in direct-mapped TBs and in some large direct-mapped data caches with total sizes of 32 pages (256 KB) or more.

Usually, this padding will mean *zero* extra bytes in the executable image, just a skip in virtual address space to the next-higher page boundary.

For large caches, the rule above should be applied to the I-stream, in addition to all the D-stream references. Some implementations will have combined I-stream/D-stream large caches.

Both of the rules above can be satisfied simultaneously, thus often eliminating thrashing in all anticipated direct-mapped cache/TB implementations.

A.3.4 Sequential Read/Write — Factor of 1

All other things being equal, sequences of consecutive reads or writes should use ascending (rather than descending) memory addresses. Where possible, the memory address for a block of 2**Kbytes should be on a 2**K boundary, since this minimizes the number of different cache blocks used and minimizes the number of partially written cache blocks.

To avoid overrunning memory bandwidth, sequences of more than eight quadword load or store instructions should be broken up with intervening instructions (if there is any useful work to be done).

For consecutive reads, implementors should give first priority to prefetching ascending cache blocks and second priority to absorbing up to eight consecutive quadword load instructions (aligned on a 64-byte boundary) without stalling.

For consecutive writes, implementors should give first priority to avoiding read overhead for fully written aligned cache blocks and second priority to absorbing up to eight consecutive quadword store instructions (aligned on a 64-byte boundary) without stalling.

A.3.5 Prefetching — Factor of 3

Prefetching can be directed toward a cache block (a cache line) in the primary cache.

Alpha hardware, beginning with the 21164 (EV5) and subsequent, supports cache block prefetching. Cache block prefetching is performed by the following load operations to the R31 or F31 register:

Table A–1: Cache Block Prefetching

Type	Instructions	Operation
Normal Prefetch	LDL R31, xxx (Rn)	If the load operation hits in the Dcache, the instruction is dismissed; otherwise, the addressed cache block is allocated into the Dcache.
Prefetch with Modify Intent	LDS F31, xxx (Rn)	If the load operation hits a dirty, modified, Dcache block, the instruction is dismissed. Otherwise, the addressed cache block is allocated into the Dcache for write access — its dirty and modified bits are set.
Prefetch, Evict Next	LDQ R31, xxx (Rn)	Prefetch a cache block and mark that block in an associated cache to be evicted on the next cache fill to an associated address. (This operation is useful to prefetch data that is not to be repeatedly referenced.)

A.4   Code Sequences

The following section describes code sequences.

A.4.1 Aligned Byte/Word (Within Register) Memory Accesses

The instruction sequences given in Common Architecture, Chapter 4, for byte-within-register accesses are worst-case code. More importantly, they do not reflect the instructions available with the BWX extension, described in the Common Architecture, Chapter 4, Byte Manipulation Instructions, and in Appendix D. If the BWX extension instructions are available, it is wise to consider them rather than the sequences that follow.

The following sequences are appropriate if the BWX extension instructions are not available.

In the common case of accessing a byte or aligned word field at a known offset from a pointer that is expected to be at least longword aligned, the common-case code is much shorter. "Expected" means that the code should run fast for a longword-aligned pointer and trap for unaligned. The trap handler may at its option fix up the unaligned reference.

For access at a known offset D from a longword-aligned pointer Rx, let D.lw be D rounded down to a multiple of 4 ((D div 4)*4), and let D.mod be D mod 4.

In the common case, the intended sequence for loading and zero-extending an aligned word is:

```
LDL    R1,D.lw(Rx)          ! Traps if unaligned
EXTWL  R1,#D.mod,R1         ! Picks up word at byte 0 or byte 2
```

In the common case, the intended sequence for loading and sign-extending an aligned word is:

```
LDL     R1,D.lw(Rx)             ! Traps if unaligned
SLL     R1,#48-8*D.mod,R1       ! Aligns word at high end of R1
SRA     R1,#48,R1               ! SEXT to low end of R1
```

Note:

The shifts often can be combined with shifts that might surround subsequent arithmetic operations (for example, to produce word overflow from the high end of a register).

In the common case, the intended sequence for loading and zero-extending a byte is:

```
LDL     R1,D.lw(Rx)             !
EXTBL   R1,#D.mod,R1            !
```

In the common case, the intended sequence for loading and sign-extending a byte is:

```
LDL     R1,D.lw(Rx)             !
SLL     R1,#56-8*D.mod,R1       !
SRA     R1,#56,R1               !
```

In the common case, the intended sequence for storing an aligned word R5 is:

```
LDL     R1,D.lw(Rx)             !
INSWL   R5,#D.mod,R3            !
MSKWL   R1,#D.mod,R1            !
BIS     R3,R1,R1                !
STL     R1,D.lw(Rx)             !
```

In the common case, the intended sequence for storing a byte R5 is:

```
LDL     R1,D.lw(Rx)             !
INSBL   R5,#D.mod,R3            !
MSKBL   R1,#D.mod,R1            !
BIS     R3,R1,R1                !
STL     R1,D.lw(Rx)             !
```

A.4.2 Division

In all implementations, floating-point division is likely to have a substantially longer result latency than floating-point multiply. In addition, in many implementations multiplies will be pipelined and divides will not.

Thus, any division by a constant power of two should be compiled as a multiply by the exact reciprocal, if it is representable without overflow or underflow. If language rules or surrounding context allow, multiplication by the reciprocal can closely approximate other divisions by constants.

Integer division does not exist as a hardware opcode. Division by a constant can always be done via UMULH of another appropriate constant, followed by a right shift. A subroutine can do general quadword division by true variables. The subroutine could test for small divisors (less than about 1000 in absolute value) and for those, do a table lookup on the exact constant and shift count for an UMULH/shift sequence. For the remaining cases, a table lookup on about a 1000-entry table and a multiply can give a linear approximation to 1/divisor that is accurate to 16 bits.

Using this approximation, a multiply and a back-multiply and a subtract can generate one 16-bit quotient digit plus a 48-bit new partial dividend. Three more such steps can generate the full quotient. Having prior knowledge of the possible sizes of the divisor and dividend, normalizing away leading bytes of zeros, and performing an early-out test can reduce the average number of multiplies to about five (compared to a best case of one and a worst case of nine).

A.4.3 Byte Swap

When it is necessary to swap all the bytes of a datum, perhaps because the datum originated on a machine of the opposite byte numbering convention, the simplest sequence is to use the VAX floating-point load instruction to swap words, followed by an integer sequence to swap four pairs of bytes. Assume as shown below that an aligned quadword datum is in memory at location X and is to be left in R1 after byte-swapping; temp is an aligned quadword temporary, and "." (period) in the comments stands for a byte of zeros. Similar sequences can be used for data in registers, sometimes doing the byte swaps first and word swap second:

```
                                ; X  = ABCD EFGH
    LDG    F0,X                 ; F0 = GHEF CDAB
    STT    F0,temp
    LDQ    R1,temp              ; R1 = GHEF CDAB
    SLL    R1,#8,R2             ; R2 = HEFC DAB.
    SRL    R1,#8,R1             ; R1 = .GHE FCDA
    ZAP    R2,#55(hex),R2       ; R2 = H.F. D.B.
    ZAP    R1,#AA(hex),R1       ; R1 = .G.E .C.A
    OR     R1,R2,R1             ; R1 = HGFE DCBA
```

For bulk swapping of arrays, this sequence can be usefully unrolled about four times and scheduled, using four different aligned quadword memory temps.

A.4.4 Stylized Code Forms

Using the same stylized code form for a common operation improves the readability of compiler output and increases the likelyhood that an implementation will speed up the stylized form.

A.4.4.1 NOP

The universal NOP form is:

```
    UNOP            ==       LDQ_U   R31,0(Rx)
```

In most implementations, UNOP should encounter no operand issue delays, no destination issue delay, and no functional unit issue delays. (In some implementations, it may encounter an operand issue delay for Rx.) Implementations are free to optimize UNOP into no action and zero execution cycles.

If the actual instruction is encoded as LDQ_U Rn,0(Rx), where *n* is other than 31, and such an instruction generates a memory-management exception, it is UNPREDICTABLE whether UNOP would generate the same exception. On most implementations, UNOP does not generate memory management exceptions.

The standard NOP forms are:

```
NOP            ==      BIS     R31,R31,R31
FNOP           ==      CPYS    F31,F31,F31
```

These generate no exceptions. In most implementations, they should encounter no operand issue delays and no destination issue delay. Implementations are free to optimize these into no action and zero execution cycles.

A.4.4.2 Clear a Register

The standard clear register forms are:

```
CLR            ==      BIS     R31,R31,Rx
FCLR           ==      CPYS    F31,F31,Fx
```

These generate no exceptions. In most implementations, they should encounter no operand issue delays and no functional unit issue delay.

A.4.4.3 Load Literal

The standard load integer literal (ZEXT 8-bit) form is:

```
MOV #lit8,Ry    ==    BIS R31, lit8, Ry
```

The Alpha literal construct in Operate instructions creates a canonical longword constant for values 0..255.

A longword constant stored in an Alpha 64-bit register is in canonical form when bits <63:32>=bit <31>.

A canonical 32-bit literal can usually be generated with one or two instructions, but sometimes three instructions are needed. Use the following procedure to determine the offset fields of the instructions:

```
val  =  <sign-extended, 32-bit value>

low  = val <15:0>
tmp1 = val - SEXT(low)          ! Account for LDA instruction

high = tmp1 <31:16>
tmp2 = tmp1 - SHIFT_LEFT( SEXT(high,16) )
```

```
if tmp2 NE 0 then
    ! original val was in range 7FFF8000₁₆..7FFFFFFF₁₆
        extra = 4000₁₆
        tmp1 = tmp1 - 40000000₁₆
        high = tmp1 <31:16>
else
        extra = 0
endif
```

The general sequence is:

```
LDA  Rdst, low(R31)
LDAH Rdst, extra(Rdst)          ! Omit if extra=0
LDAH Rdst, high(Rdst)           ! Omit if high=0
```

A.4.4.4 Register-to-Register Move

The standard register move forms are:

```
MOV  RX,RY      ==      BIS  RX,RX,RY
FMOV FX,FY      ==      CPYS FX,FX,FY
```

These move forms generate no exceptions. In most implementations, these should encounter no functional unit issue delay.

A.4.4.5 Negate

The standard register negate forms are:

```
NEGz Rx,Ry      ==      SUBz   R31,Rx,Ry    ! z = L or Q
NEGz Fx,Fy      ==      SUBz   F31,Fx,Fy    ! z = F G S or T
FNEGz Fx,Fy     ==      CPYSN  Fx,Fx,Fy     ! z = F G S or T
```

The integer subtract generates no Integer Overflow trap if Rx contains the largest negative number (SUBz/V would trap). The floating subtract generates a floating-point exception for a non-finite value in Fx. The CPYSN form generates no exceptions.

A.4.4.6 NOT

The standard integer register NOT form is:

```
NOT Rx,Ry       ==      ORNOT  R31,Rx,Ry
```

This generates no exceptions. In most implementations, this should encounter no functional unit issue delay.

A.4.4.7 Booleans

The standard alternative to BIS is:

```
OR  Rx,Ry,Rz     ==      BIS     Rx,Ry,Rz
```

The standard alternative to BIC is:

```
ANDNOT  Rx,Ry,Rz ==      BIC     Rx,Ry,Rz
```
The standard alternative to EQV is:

```
XORNOT  Rx,Ry,Rz ==      EQV     Rx,Ry,Rz
```

A.4.5 Exception and Trap Barriers

The EXCB instruction allows software to guarantee that in a pipelined implementation, all previous instructions have completed any behavior related to exceptions or rounding modes before any instructions after the EXCB are issued. In particular, all changes to the Floating-point Control Register (FPCR) are guaranteed to have been made, whether or not there is an associated exception. Also, all potential floating-point exceptions and integer overflow exceptions are guaranteed to have been taken.

The TRAPB instruction guarantees that it and any following instructions do not issue until all possible preceding traps have been signaled. This does not mean that all preceding instructions have necessarily run to completion (for example, a Load instruction may have passed all the fault checks but not yet delivered data from a cache miss).

EXCB is thus a superset of TRAPB.

A.4.6 Pseudo-Operations (Stylized Code Forms)

This section summarizes the pseudo-operations for the Alpha architecture that may be used by various software components in an Alpha system. Most of these forms are discussed in preceding sections.

In the context of this section, pseudo-operations all represent a single underlying machine instruction. Each pseudo-operation represents a particular instruction with either replicated fields (such as FMOV), or hard-coded zero fields. Since the pattern is distinct, these pseudo-operations can be decoded by instruction decode mechanisms.

In Table A–2, the pseudo-operation codes can be viewed as macros with parameters. The formal form is listed in the left column, and the expansion in the code stream is listed in the right column.

Some instruction mnemonics have synonyms. These differ from pseudo-operations in that each synonym represents the same underlying instruction with no special encoding of operand fields. As a result, synonyms cannot be distinquished from each other. They are not listed in the table. Examples of synonyms are: BIC/ANDNOT, BIS/OR, and EQV/XORNOT.

Table A–2: Decodable Pseudo-Operations (Stylized Code Forms)

Pseudo-Operation in Listing		Meaning	Actual Instruction Encoding	
BR	target	Branch to target (21-bit signed displacement)	BR	R31, target
CLR	Rx	Clear integer register	BIS	R31, R31, Rx
FABS	Fx, Fy	No-exception generic floating absolute value	CPYS	F31, Fx, Fy
FCLR	Fx	Clear a floating-point register	CPYS	F31, F31, Fx
FMOV	Fx, Fy	Floating-point move	CPYS	Fy, Fy, Fy
FNEG	Fx, Fy	No-exception generic floating negation	CPYSN	Fx, Fx, Fy
FNOP		Floating-point no-op	CPYS	F31, F31, F31
MOV	Lit, Rx	Move 16-bit sign-extended literal to Rx	LDA	Rx,lit(R31)
MOV	{Rx/Lit8}, Ry	Move Rx/8-bit zero-extended literal to Ry	BIS	R31,{Rx/Lit8},Ry
MF_FPCR	Fx	Move from FPCR	MF_FPCR	Fx, Fx, Fx
MT_FPCR	Fx	Move to FPCR	MT_FPCR	Fx, Fx, Fx
NEGF	Fx, Fy	Negate F_floating	SUBF	F31, Fx, Fy
NEGF/S	Fx, Fy	Negate F_floating, semi-precise	SUBF/S	F31, Fx, Fy
NEGG	Fx, Fy	Negate G_floating	SUBG	F31, Fx, Fy
NEGG/S	Fx, Fy	Negate G_floating, semi-precise	SUBG/S	F31, Fx, Fy
NEGL	{Rx/Lit8}, Ry	Negate longword	SUBL	R31,{Rx/Lit},Ry
NEGL/V	{Rx/Lit8}, Ry	Negate longword with overflow detection	SUBL/V	R31, {Rx/Lit}, Ry
NEGQ	{Rx/Lit8}, Ry	Negate quadword	SUBQ	R31,{Rx/Lit},Ry
NEGQ/V	{Rx/Lit8}, Ry	Negate quadword with overflow detection	SUBQ/V	R31,{Rx/Lit},Ry
NEGS	Fx, Fy	Negate S_floating	SUBS	F31, Fx, Fy
NEGS/SU	Fx, Fy	Negate S_floating, software with underflow detection	SUBS/SU	F31, Fx, Fy
NEGS/SUI	Fx, Fy	Negate S_floating, software with underflow and inexact result detection	SUBS/SUI	F31, Fx, Fy
NEGT	Fx, Fy	Negate T_floating	SUBT	F31, Fx, Fy
NEGT/SU	Fx, Fy	Negate T_floating, software with underflow detection	SUBT/SU	F31, Fx, Fy

Table A–2: Decodable Pseudo-Operations (Stylized Code Forms) (Continued)

Pseudo-Operation in Listing		Meaning	Actual Instruction Encoding	
NEGT/SUI		Negate T_floating, software with underflow and inexact result detection	SUBT/SUI	F31,Fx, Fy
NOP		Integer no-op	BIS	R31, R31, R31
NOT	{Rx/Lit8}, Ry	Logical NOT of Rx/8-bit zero-extended literal storing results in Ry	ORNOT	R31, {Rx/Lit}, Ry
SEXTL	{Rx/Lit8}, Ry	Longword sign-extension of Rx storing results in Ry	ADDL	R31, {Rx/Lit}, Ry
UNOP		Universal NOP for both integer and floating-point code	LDQ_U	R31,0(Rx)

A.5 Timing Considerations: Atomic Sequences

A sufficiently long instruction sequence between LDx_L and STx_C will never complete, because periodic timer interrupts will always occur before the sequence completes. The following rules describe sequences that will eventually complete in all Alpha implementations:

- At most 40 operate or conditional-branch (not taken) instructions executed in the sequence between LDx_L and STx_C.

- At most two I-stream TB-miss faults. Sequential instruction execution guarantees this.

- No other exceptions triggered during the last execution of the sequence.

Implementation Note:

On all expected implementations, this allows for about 50 μsec of execution time, even with 100 percent cache misses. This should satisfy any requirement for a 1-msec timer interrupt rate.

IEEE Floating-Point Conformance

A subset of IEEE Standard for Binary Floating-Point Arithmetic (754-1985) is provided in the Alpha floating-point instructions. This appendix describes how to construct a complete IEEE implementation.

The order of presentation parallels the order of the IEEE specification.

B.1 Alpha Choices for IEEE Options

Alpha supports IEEE single, double, and optionally (in software) extended double formats. There is no hardware support for the optional extended double format.

Alpha hardware supports normal and chopped IEEE rounding modes. IEEE plus infinity and minus infinity rounding modes can be implemented in hardware or software.

Alpha hardware does not support optional IEEE software trap enable/disable modes. See the following discussion about software support.

Alpha hardware supports add, subtract, multiply, divide, convert between floating formats, convert between floating and integer formats, compare, and square root. Software routines support remainder, round to integer in floating-point format, and convert binary to/from decimal.

In the Alpha architecture, copying without change of format is not considered an operation. (LDx, CPYSx, and STx do not check for non-finite numbers; an operation would.) Compilers may generate ADDx F31,Fx,Fy to get the opposite effect.

Optional operations for differing formats are not provided.

The Alpha choice is that the accuracy provided by conversions between decimal strings and binary floating-point numbers will meet or exceed IEEE standard requirements. It is implementation dependent whether the software binary/decimal conversions beyond 9 or 17 digits treat any excess digits as zeros.

Overflow and underflow, NaNs, and infinities encountered during software binary to decimal conversion return strings that specify the conditions.

Alpha hardware supports comparisons of same-format numbers. Software supports comparisons of different-format numbers.

In the Alpha architecture, results are true-false in response to a predicate.

Alpha hardware supports the required six predicates and the optional unordered predicate. The other 19 optional predicates can be constructed from sequences of two comparisons and two branches.

Alpha hardware supports infinity arithmetic with the compare instructions (CMPTyy). When a /S qualifier is included, Alpha hardware may optionally support infinity arithmetic when infinity operands are encountered and, together with overflow disable (OVFD) and division by zero disable (DZED), when infinity is to be generated from finite operands. Otherwise, Alpha hardware supports infinity arithmetic by trapping. That is the case when an infinity operand is encountered and when an infinity is to be created from finite operands by overflow or division by zero. An OS completion handler (interposed between the hardware and the IEEE user) provides correct infinity arithmetic.

When a /S qualifier is included, Alpha hardware may optionally support NaNs and invalid operations, controlled by the INVD option. Otherwise, Alpha hardware supports NaNs and invalid operations by trapping when a NaN operand is encountered and when a NaN is to be created. An OS completion handler (interposed between the hardware and the IEEE user) provides correct Signaling and Quiet NaN behavior.

In the Alpha architecture, Quiet NaNs do not afford retrospective diagnostic information.

In the Alpha architecture, copying a Signaling NaN without a change of format does not signal an invalid exception (LDx, CPYSx, and STx do not check for non-finite numbers). Compilers may generate ADDx F31,Fx,Fy to get the opposite effect.

Alpha hardware fully supports negative zero operands and follows the IEEE rules for creating negative zero results except for underflow. When a /S qualifier is included, Alpha hardware may optionally support underflow and denormalized numbers, controlled by the UNFD option. Otherwise, Alpha hardware supports underflow and denormalized numbers by trapping when a denormalized operand is encountered, when a denormalized result is created, and when an underflow occurs. An OS completion handler (interposed between the hardware and the IEEE user) provides correct denormalized and underflow arithmetic.

Except for the optional trap disable bits in the FPCR, Alpha hardware does not supply IEEE exception trap behavior; the hardware traps are a superset of the IEEE-required conditions. An OS completion handler (interposed between the hardware and the IEEE user) provides correct IEEE exception behavior.

In the Alpha architecture, tininess is detected by hardware after rounding, and loss of accuracy is detected by software as an inexact result.

In the Alpha architecture, user signal handlers are supported by compilers and an OS completion handler (interposed between the hardware and the IEEE user), as described in the next section.

B.2 Alpha Support for OS Completion Handlers

Alpha floating-point trap behavior is statically controlled by the /S, /U, and /I mode qualifiers on floating-point instructions. Changing these options usually requires recompiling. Instructions with any valid qualifier combination that includes the /S qualifier can be dynamically controlled by the optional trap disable bits and denormal control bits in the FPCR.

Each Alpha implementation may choose how to distribute support for the completion modes (/S, /SU, /SV, /SUI, and /SVI), between hardware and software. An implementation may minimize hardware complexity by trapping to implementation software for support of exceptions and non-finites. An implementation may choose increased floating-point performance at the cost of increased hardware complexity by providing hardware support for exceptions and non-finites.

However completion mode support is distributed, application software on any system that meets the Alpha architecture specification will see consistent floating-point semantics because Alpha implementation software provides support for any floating-point feature that is not directly supported by the hardware.

Each Alpha operating system must include an OS completion handler that does software completion of instructions that have any valid qualifier combination that includes the /S qualifier, and that finishes the computation of any floating-point operation that is not completed by the hardware. The OS completion handler is responsible for providing the result specified by the architecture. The handler either continues execution of the application program or signals an exception to the application.

If the exception summary parameter of an arithmetic trap indicates that an instruction requiring software completion caused the trap, the operating system must finish the operation. An OS completion handler uses the register write mask parameter to ignore instructions in the trap shadow and to locate the trigger instruction of the arithmetic trap. The handler then uses the trigger instruction input register values to compute the result in the output register and to record any appropriate signal status. The handler then continues execution with the instruction following the trigger instruction, unless the application has requested execution of an optional signal handler.

It is recommended that the OS completion handler report an enabled IEEE exception to the user application as a fault, rather than as a trap. When reported as a fault, the reported PC points to the trigger instruction, rather than after the trigger instruction. Regardless of whether an enabled fault occurs, it is recommended that the completion trap handler set the result register and status flags to the IEEE standard nontrapping results, as defined in the IEEE Standard section in Common Architecture, Chapter 4. That behavior makes it possible for the user application to continue from a fault by stepping over the trigger instruction.

The Floating-Point Control Register (FPCR) contains several trap disable bits and denormal control bits. Implementation of these bits in the FPCR is optional. A system that includes these bits may choose to complete computations involving non-finite values without the assistance of software completion. Operating systems use these FPCR bits to enable hardware completion of instructions with any valid qualifier combination that includes /S in those cases where the operating system does not require a trap to do exception signaling.

To get the optional full IEEE user trap handler behavior, an OS completion handler must be provided that implements the exception status flags, dynamic user trap handler disabling, handler saving and restoring, default behavior for disabled user trap handlers, and linkages that allow a user handler to return a substitute result. OS completion handlers can use the FP_Control quadword, along with the floating-point control register (FPCR), to provide various levels of IEEE-compliant behavior.

OS completion handlers provide two options for special handling of denormal numbers in instructions that are compiled with any valid qualifier combination that includes the /S qualifier. These options are controlled by bits defined by implementation software in the IEEE Floating-Point Control (FP_C) Quadword.

- The first option maps all denormal results to a true zero value. That option is useful for improving the performance of IEEE compliant code that does not need gradual underflow and for mixing IEEE instructions that both include and do not include the /S qualifier.

- A second option treats all denormal input operands as if they were signed zeros. That option is useful for improving the performance of IEEE compliant code that encounters spurious denormal values in uninitialized data.

The optional UNDZ and DNZ (denormal control) bits in the FPCR can assist hardware to improve the performance of these denormal handling options.

B.2.1 IEEE Floating-Point Control (FP_C) Quadword

Operating system implementations provide the following support for an IEEE floating-point control quadword (FP_C), illustrated in Figure B–1 and described in Table B–1.

Figure B–1: IEEE Floating-Point Control (FP_C) Quadword

```
63                              23 22 21 20 19 18 17 16        7  6  5  4  3  2  1  0
+----------------------------+---------------------+----------+---------------------+-+
|                            |D  I  U  O  D  I     |          |D  I  U  O  D  I     | |
|        Reserved            |N  N  N  V  Z  N      | Reserved |N  N  N  V  Z  N      | |
|                            |O  E  F  F  E  V      |          |O  E  F  F  E  V      | |
|                            |S  S  S  S  S         |          |E  E  E  E  E         | |
+----------------------------+---------------------+----------+---------------------+-+
```

- The operating system software completion mechanism maintains the FP_C. Therefore, the FP_C affects (and is affected by) only those instructions with any valid qualifier combination that includes the /S qualifier.

- The FP_C quadword is context switched when the operating system switches the thread context. (The FP_C can be placed in a currently switched data structure.)

- Although the operating system can keep the FP_C in a user mode memory location, user code may not directly access the FP_C.

- Integer overflow (IOV) exceptions are controlled by the INVE enable mask bit (FP_C<1>), as allowed by the IEEE standard. Implementation software is responsible for setting the INVS status bit (FP_C<17>) when a CVTTQ or CVTQL instruction traps into the software completion mechanism for integer overflow .

- At process creation, all trap enable flags in the FP_C are clear. The settings of other FP_C bits, defined in Table B–1 as reserved for implementation software, are defined by operating system software.

At other events such as forks or thread creation, and at asynchronous routine calls such as traps and signals, the operating system controls all assigned FP_C bits and those defined as reserved for implementation software.

Table B–1: Floating-Point Control (FP_C) Quadword Bit Summary

Bit	Description
63–48	Reserved for implementation software.
47–23	Reserved for future architecture definition.
22	Denormal operand status (DNOS) A floating arithmetic or conversion operation used a denormal operand value. This status field is left unchanged if the system is treating denormal operand values as if they were signed zero values. If an operation with a denormal operand causes other exceptions, all appropriate status bits are set.
21	Inexact result status (INES) A floating arithmetic or conversion operation gave a result that differed from the mathematically exact result.
20	Underflow status (UNFS) A floating arithmetic or conversion operation underflowed the destination exponent.
19	Overflow status (OVFS) A floating arithmetic or conversion operation overflowed the destination exponent.
18	Division by zero status (DZES) An attempt was made to perform a floating divide operation with a divisor of zero.
17	Invalid operation status (INVS) An attempt was made to perform a floating arithmetic, conversion, or comparison operation, and one or more of the operand values were illegal.
16–12	Reserved for implementation software.
11–7	Reserved for future architecture definition.
6	Denormal operand exception enable (DNOE) Initiate an INV exception if a floating arithmetic or conversion operation involves a denormal operand value. This exception does not signal if the system is treating denormal operand values as if they were signed zero values. If an operation can initiate more than one enabled exception, the denormal operand exception has priority.

Bit	Description
5	Inexact result enable (INEE) Initiate an INE exception if the result of a floating arithmetic or conversion operation differs from the mathematically exact result.
4	Underflow enable (UNFE) Initiate a UNF exception if a floating arithmetic or conversion operation underflows the destination exponent.
3	Overflow enable (OVFE) Initiate an OVF exception if a floating arithmetic or conversion operation overflows the destination exponent.
2	Division by zero enable (DZEE) Initiate a DZE exception if an attempt is made to perform a floating divide operation with a divisor of zero.
1	Invalid operation enable (INVE) Initiate an INV exception if an attempt is made to perform a floating arithmetic, conversion, or comparison operation, and one or more of the operand values is illegal.
0	Reserved for implementation software.

B.3 Mapping to IEEE Standard

There are five IEEE exceptions, each of which can be "IEEE software trap-enabled" or disabled (the default condition). Implementing the IEEE software trap-enabled mode is optional in the IEEE standard.

The assumption, therefore, is that the only access to IEEE-specified software trap-enabled results will be generated in assembly language code. The following design allows this, but *only* if such assembly language code has TRAPB instructions after each floating-point instruction, and generates the IEEE-specified scaled result in a trap handler by emulating the instruction that was trapped by hardware overflow/underflow detection, using the original operands.

There is a set of detailed IEEE-specified result values, both for operations that are specified to raise IEEE traps and those that do not. This behavior is created on Alpha by four layers of hardware, PALcode, the operating-system completion handler, and the user signal handler, as shown in Figure B–2.

Figure B–2: IEEE Trap Handling Behavior

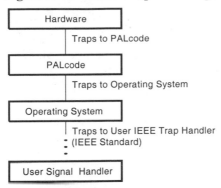

The IEEE-specified trap behavior occurs *only* with respect to the user signal handler (the last layer in Figure B–2); any trap-and-fixup behavior in the first three layers is outside the scope of the IEEE standard.

The IEEE number system is divided into finite and non-finite numbers:
The finites are normal numbers:

- –MAX..–MIN, 0, 0, +MIN..+MAX

- The non-finites are:

- Denormals, +/– Infinity, Signaling NaN, Quiet NaN

Alpha hardware must treat minus zero operands and results as special cases, as required by the IEEE standard.

If the DNZ (denormal operands to zero) bit in the FPCR is set or if the OS completion handler is treating denormal operands as zero, then IEEE trap handling is done as if each denormal operand had the corresponding signed zero value.

Table B–2 specifies, for the IEEE /S qualifier modes, which layer does each piece of trap handling. The table describes where the hardware and PALcode can trap to the OS completion handler. However, for IEEE operations with any valid qualifier combination that includes the /S qualifier, the system may choose not to trap to the OS completion handler, provided that any applicable exception is disabled by the trap disable bits in the FPCR and the hardware and PALcode can produce the expected IEEE result as modified by the denormal control bits in the FPCR. See Common Architecture, Chapter 4, for more detail on the hardware instruction descriptions.

Table B–2: IEEE Floating-Point Trap Handling

Alpha Instructions	Hardware[1]	PAL-Code	OS Completion Handler	User Signal Handler
FBEQ FBNE FBLT FBLE FBGT FBGE	Bits Only – No Exceptions			
LDS LDT	Bits Only—No Exceptions			
STS STT	Bits Only—No Exceptions			
CPYS CPYSN	Bits Only—No Exceptions			
FCMOVx	Bits Only—No Exceptions			
ADDx SUBx INPUT Exceptions:				
Denormal operand	Trap	Trap	Supply sum	[Denormal Op[2]]
+/-Inf operand	Trap	Trap	Supply sum	–
QNaN operand	Trap	Trap	Supply QNaN	–
SNaN operand	Trap	Trap	Supply QNaN	[Invalid Op]
+Inf + –Inf	Trap	Trap	Supply QNaN	[Invalid Op]
ADDx SUBx OUTPUT Exceptions:				
Exponent overflow	Trap	Trap	Supply +/–Inf +/–MAX	[Overflow[3]] Scale by bias adjust
Exponent underflow and disabled	Supply +0	–	–	–[4]
Exponent underflow and enabled	Supply +0 and trap	Trap	Supply +/–MIN denorm +/–0	[Underflow[3]] Scale by bias adjust
Inexact and disabled	–	–	–	–
Inexact and enabled	Supply sum and trap	Trap	–	[Inexact]
MULx INPUT Exceptions:				
Denormal operand	Trap	Trap	Supply prod.	[Denormal Op[2]]
+/-Inf operand	Trap	Trap	Supply prod.	–
QNaN operand	Trap	Trap	Supply QNaN	–
SNaN operand	Trap	Trap	Supply QNaN	[Invalid Op]
0 * Inf	Trap	Trap	Supply QNaN	[Invalid Op]

Table B–2: IEEE Floating-Point Trap Handling (Continued)

Alpha Instructions	Hardware[1]	PAL-Code	OS Completion Handler	User Signal Handler
MULx OUTPUT Exceptions:				
Exponent overflow	Trap	Trap	Supply +/–Inf +/–MAX	[Overflow[3]] Scale by bias adjust
Exponent underflow and disabled	Supply +0	–	–	–
Exponent underflow and enabled	Supply +0 and Trap	Trap	Supply +/–MIN denorm +/–0	[Underflow[3]] Scale by bias adjust
Inexact and disabled	–	–	–	–
Inexact and enabled	Supply prod. and trap	Trap	–	[Inexact]
DIVx INPUT Exceptions:				
Denormal operand	Trap	Trap	Supply quot.	[Denormal Op[2]]
+/ Inf operand	Trap	Trap	Supply quot.	–
QNaN operand	Trap	Trap	Supply QNaN	–
SNaN operand	Trap	Trap	Supply QNaN	[Invalid Op]
0/0 or Inf/Inf	Trap	Trap	Supply QNaN	[Invalid Op]
A/0	Trap	Trap	Supply +/– Inf	[Div. Zero]
DIVx OUTPUT Exceptions:				
Exponent overflow	Trap	Trap	Supply +/–Inf +/– MAX	[Overflow[3]] Scale by bias adjust
Exponent underflow and disabled	Supply +0	–	–	–
Exponent underflow and enabled	Supply +0 and trap	Trap	Supply +/– MIN denorm +/–0	[Underflow[3]] Scale by bias adjust
Inexact and disabled	–	–	–	–
Inexact and enabled	Supply quot. and trap	Trap	–	[Inexact]
CMPTEQ CMPTUN INPUT Exceptions:				
Denormal operand	Trap	Trap	Supply (=)	[Denormal Op[2]]
QNaN operand	Trap	Trap	Supply False for EQ, True for UN	–
SNaN operand	Trap	Trap	Supply False/ True	[Invalid Op]

Table B–2: IEEE Floating-Point Trap Handling (Continued)

Alpha Instructions	Hardware[1]	PAL-Code	OS Completion Handler	User Signal Handler
CMPTLT CMPTLE INPUT Exceptions:				
Denormal operand	Trap	Trap	Supply ≤ or <	[Denormal Op[2]]
QNaN operand	Trap	Trap	Supply False	[Invalid Op]
SNaN operand	Trap	Trap	Supply False	[Invalid Op]
CVTfi INPUT Exceptions:				
Denormal operand	Trap	Trap	Supply Cvt	[Denormal Op[2]]
+/–Inf operand	Trap	Trap	Supply 0	[Invalid Op]
QNaN operand	Trap	Trap	Supply 0	–
SNaN operand	Trap	Trap	Supply 0	[Invalid Op]
CVTfi OUTPUT Exceptions:				
Inexact and disabled	–	–	–	–
Inexact and enabled	Supply Cvt and trap	Trap	–	[Inexact]
Integer overflow	Supply Trunc. result and trap if enabled	Trap	–	[Invalid Op[5]]
CVTif OUTPUT Exceptions:				
Inexact and disabled	–	–	–	–
Inexact and enabled	Supply Cvt and trap	Trap	–	[Inexact]
CVTff INPUT Exceptions:				
Denormal operand	Trap	Trap	Supply Cvt	[Denormal Op[2]]
+/–Inf operand	Trap	Trap	Supply Cvt	–
QNaN operand	Trap	Trap	Supply QNaN	–
SNaN operand	Trap	Trap	Supply QNaN	[Invalid Op]
CVTff OUTPUT Exceptions:				
Exponent overflow	Trap	Trap	Supply +/–Inf +/–MAX	[Overflow[3]] Scale by bias adjust
Exponent underflow and disabled	Supply +0	–	–	–
Exponent underflow and enabled	Supply +0 and trap	Trap	Supply +/– MIN denorm +/–0	[Underflow[3]] Scale by bias adjust
Inexact and disabled	–	–	–	–
Inexact and enabled	Supply Cvt and trap	Trap	–	[Inexact]

Table B–2: IEEE Floating-Point Trap Handling (Continued)

Alpha Instructions	Hardware[1]	PAL-Code	OS Completion Handler	User Signal Handler
SQRTx INPUT Exceptions				
Negative nonzero operand	Trap	Trap	Supply QNan	[Invalid Op]
+/–0	Supply +/–0	–	–	–
+ Denormal operand	Trap	Trap	Supply SQRT	[Denormal Op[2]]
– Denormal operand	Trap	Trap	Supply QNaN	[Denormal Op/ Invalid Op]
+ Infinity operand	Trap	Trap	Supply +Inf	–
– Infinity operand	Trap	Trap	Supply QNaN	[Invalid Op]
QNaN operand	Trap	Trap	Supply QNaN	–
SNaN operand	Trap	Trap	Supply QNaN	[Invalid Op]
SQRTx OUTPUT Exceptions				
Exponent overflow	Not possible			
Exponent underflow	Not possible			
Inexact and disabled	–	–	–	–
Inexact and enabled	Supply SQRT	Trap	–	[Inexact]

[1] This column describes the minimum necessary hardware support.

[2] [Denormal Op] signals have priority over all other signals.

[3] [Overflow] and [Underflow] signals have priority over [Inexact] signals.

[4] An implementation could choose instead to trap to PALcode and have the PALcode supply a zero result on all underflows.

[5] An implementation could choose instead to trap to PALcode on extreme values and have the PALcode supply a truncated result on all overflows.

Other IEEE operations (software subroutines or sequences of instructions) are listed here for completeness:

> Remainder
> Round float to integer-valued float
> Convert binary to/from decimal
> Compare, other combinations than the four above

Table B–3 shows the IEEE standard charts. In the charts, the second column is the result when the user signal handler is disabled; the third column is the result when that handler is enabled. The OS completion handler supplies the IEEE default that is specified in the second column. The contents of the Alpha registers contain sufficient information for an enabled user handler to compute the value in the third column.

Table B–3: IEEE Standard Charts

Exception	User Signal Handler Disabled (IEEE Default)	User Signal Handler Enabled (Optional)
Invalid Operation		
(1) Input signaling NaN	Quiet NaN	
(2) Mag. subtract Inf.	Quiet NaN	
(3) 0 * Inf.	Quiet NaN	
(4) 0/0 or Inf/Inf	Quiet NaN	
(5) x REM 0 or Inf REM y	Quiet NaN	
(6) SQRT(negative non-zero)	Quiet NaN	
(7) Cvt to int(ovfl)	Low-order bits	
(8) Cvt to int(Inf, NaN)	0	
(9) Compare unordered	Quiet NaN	
Division by Zero		
x/0, x finite <>0	+/–Inf	
Overflow		
Round nearest	+/–Inf.	Res/2**192 or 1536
Round to zero	+/–MAX	Res/2**192 or 1536
Round to –Inf	+MAX/–Inf	Res/2**192 or 1536
Round to +Inf	+Inf/–MAX	Res/2**192 or 1536
Underflow		
Underflow	0/denorm	Res*2**192 or 1536
Inexact		
Inexact	Rounded	Res

Instruction Summary

This appendix summarizes all instructions and opcodes in the Alpha architecture. All values are in hexadecimal radix.

C.1 Common Architecture Instruction Summary

This section summarizes all common Alpha instructions. Table C–1 describes the contents of the Format and Opcode columns in Table C–2.

Table C–1: Instruction Format and Opcode Notation

Instruction Format	Format Symbol	Opcode Notation	Meaning
Branch	Bra	oo	*oo* is the 6-bit opcode field
Floating- point	F-P	oo.fff	*oo* is the 6-bit opcode field *fff* is the 11-bit function code field
Memory	Mem	oo	*oo* is the 6-bit opcode field
Memory/ func code	Mfc	oo.ffff	*oo* is the 6-bit opcode field *ffff* is the 16-bit function code in the displacement field
Memory/ branch	Mbr	oo.h	*oo* is the 6-bit opcode field h is the high-order two bits of the displacement field
Operate	Opr	oo.ff	*oo* is the 6-bit opcode field *ff* is the 7-bit function code field
PALcode	Pcd	oo	*oo* is the 6-bit opcode field; the particular PALcode instruction is specified in the 26-bit function code field.

Table C–2 shows qualifiers for operate format instructions. Qualifiers for IEEE and VAX floating-point instructions are shown in Sections C.2 and C.3, respectively.

Table C–2: Common Architecture Instructions

Mnemonic	Format	Opcode	Description
ADDF	F-P	15.080	Add F_floating
ADDG	F-P	15.0A0	Add G_floating
ADDL	Opr	10.00	Add longword
ADDL/V		10.40	
ADDQ	Opr	10.20	Add quadword
ADDQ/V		10.60	
ADDS	F-P	16.080	Add S_floating
ADDT	F-P	16.0A0	Add T_floating
AMASK	Opr	11.61	Architecture mask
AND	Opr	11.00	Logical product
BEQ	Bra	39	Branch if = zero
BGE	Bra	3E	Branch if ≥ zero
BGT	Bra	3F	Branch if > zero
BIC	Opr	11.0	Bit clear
BIS	Opr	11.20	Logical sum
BLBC	Bra	38	Branch if low bit clear
BLBS	Bra	3C	Branch if low bit set
BLE	Bra	3B	Branch if ≤ zero
BLT	Bra	3A	Branch if < zero
BNE	Bra	3D	Branch if ≠ zero
BR	Bra	30	Unconditional branch
BSR	Mbr	34	Branch to subroutine
CALL_PAL	Pcd	00	Trap to PALcode
CMOVEQ	Opr	11.24	CMOVE if = zero
CMOVGE	Opr	11.46	CMOVE if ≥ zero
CMOVGT	Opr	11.66	CMOVE if > zero
CMOVLBC	Opr	11.16	CMOVE if low bit clear
CMOVLBS	Opr	11.14	CMOVE if low bit set
CMOVLE	Opr	11.64	CMOVE if ≤ zero
CMOVLT	Opr	11.44	CMOVE if < zero
CMOVNE	Opr	11.26	CMOVE if ≠ zero
CMPBGE	Opr	10.0F	Compare byte
CMPEQ	Opr	10.2D	Compare signed quadword equal
CMPGEQ	F-P	15.0A5	Compare G_floating equal
CMPGLE	F-P	15.0A7	Compare G_floating less than or equal
CMPGLT	F-P	15.0A6	Compare G_floating less than
CMPLE	Opr	10.6D	Compare signed quadword less than or equal
CMPLT	Opr	10.4D	Compare signed quadword less than
CMPTEQ	F-P	16.0A5	Compare T_floating equal
CMPTLE	F-P	16.0A7	Compare T_floating less than or equal
CMPTLT	F-P	16.0A6	Compare T_floating less than
CMPTUN	F-P	16.0A4	Compare T_floating unordered
CMPULE	Opr	10.3D	Compare unsigned quadword less than or equal
CMPULT	Opr	10.1D	Compare unsigned quadword less than
CPYS	F-P	17.020	Copy sign
CPYSE	F-P	17.022	Copy sign and exponent
CPYSN	F-P	17.021	Copy sign negate
CTLZ	Opr	1C.32	Count leading zero
CTPOP	Opr	1C.30	Count population
CTTZ	Opr	1C.33	Count trailing zero
CVTDG	F-P	15.09E	Convert D_floating to G_floating
CVTGD	F-P	15.0AD	Convert G_floating to D_floating
CVTGF	F-P	15.0AC	Convert G_floating to F_floating

Table C-2: Common Architecture Instructions (Continued)

Mnemonic	Format	Opcode	Description
CVTGQ	F-P	15.0AF	Convert G_floating to quadword
CVTLQ	F-P	17.010	Convert longword to quadword
CVTQF	F-P	15.0BC	Convert quadword to F_floating
CVTQG	F-P	15.0BE	Convert quadword to G_floating
CVTQL	F-P	17.030	Convert quadword to longword
CVTQS	F-P	16.0BC	Convert quadword to S_floating
CVTQT	F-P	16.0BE	Convert quadword to T_floating
CVTST	F-P	16.2AC	Convert S_floating to T_floating
CVTTQ	F-P	16.0AF	Convert T_floating to quadword
CVTTS	F-P	16.0AC	Convert T_floating to S_floating
DIVF	F-P	15.083	Divide F_floating
DIVG	F-P	15.0A3	Divide G_floating
DIVS	F-P	16.083	Divide S_floating
DIVT	F-P	16.0A3	Divide T_floating
ECB	Mfc	18.E800	Evict cache block
EQV	Opr	11.48	Logical equivalence
EXCB	Mfc	18.0400	Exception barrier
EXTBL	Opr	12.06	Extract byte low
EXTLH	Opr	12.6A	Extract longword high
EXTLL	Opr	12.26	Extract longword low
EXTQH	Opr	12.7A	Extract quadword high
EXTQL	Opr	12.36	Extract quadword low
EXTWH	Opr	12.5A	Extract word high
EXTWL	Opr	12.16	Extract word low
FBEQ	Bra	31	Floating branch if = zero
FBGE	Bra	36	Floating branch if ≥ zero
FBGT	Bra	37	Floating branch if > zero
FBLE	Bra	33	Floating branch if ≤ zero
FBLT	Bra	32	Floating branch if < zero
FBNE	Bra	35	Floating branch if ≠ zero
FCMOVEQ	F-P	17.02A	FCMOVE if = zero
FCMOVGE	F-P	17.02D	FCMOVE if ≥ zero
FCMOVGT	F-P	17.02F	FCMOVE if > zero
FCMOVLE	F-P	17.02E	FCMOVE if ≤ zero
FCMOVLT	F-P	17.02C	FCMOVE if < zero
FCMOVNE	F-P	17.02B	FCMOVE if ≠ zero
FETCH	Mfc	18.8000	Prefetch data
FETCH_M	Mfc	18.A000	Prefetch data, modify intent
FTOIS	F-P	1C.78	Floating to integer move, S_floating
FTOIT	F-P	1C.70	Floating to integer move, T_floating
IMPLVER	Opr	11.6C	Implementation version
INSBL	Opr	12.0B	Insert byte low
INSLH	Opr	12.67	Insert longword high
INSLL	Opr	12.2B	Insert longword low
INSQH	Opr	12.77	Insert quadword high
INSQL	Opr	12.3B	Insert quadword low
INSWH	Opr	12.57	Insert word high
INSWL	Opr	12.1B	Insert word low
ITOFF	F-P	14.014	Integer to floating move, F_floating
ITOFS	F-P	14.004	Integer to floating move, S_floating
ITOFT	F-P	14.024	Integer to floating move, T_floating
JMP	Mbr	1A.0	Jump
JSR	Mbr	1A.1	Jump to subroutine
JSR_COROUTINE	Mbr	1A.3	Jump to subroutine return

Table C–2: Common Architecture Instructions (Continued)

Mnemonic	Format	Opcode	Description
LDA	Mem	08	Load address
LDAH	Mem	09	Load address high
LDBU	Mem	0A	Load zero-extended byte
LDWU	Mem	0C	Load zero-extended word
LDF	Mem	20	Load F_floating
LDG	Mem	21	Load G_floating
LDL	Mem	28	Load sign-extended longword
LDL_L	Mem	2A	Load sign-extended longword locked
LDQ	Mem	29	Load quadword
LDQ_L	Mem	2B	Load quadword locked
LDQ_U	Mem	0B	Load unaligned quadword
LDS	Mem	22	Load S_floating
LDT	Mem	23	Load T_floating
MAXSB8	Opr	1C.3E	Vector signed byte maximum
MAXSW4	Opr	1C.3F	Vector signed word maximum
MAXUB8	Opr	1C.3C	Vector unsigned byte maximum
MAXUW4	Opr	1C.3D	Vector unsigned word maximum
MB	Mfc	18.4000	Memory barrier
MF_FPCR	F-P	17.025	Move from FPCR
MINSB8	Opr	1C.38	Vector signed byte minimum
MINSW4	Opr	1C.39	Vector signed word minimum
MINUB8	Opr	1C.3A	Vector unsigned byte minimum
MINUW4	Opr	1C.3B	Vector unsigned word minimum
MSKBL	Opr	12.02	Mask byte low
MSKLH	Opr	12.62	Mask longword high
MSKLL	Opr	12.22	Mask longword low
MSKQH	Opr	12.72	Mask quadword high
MSKQL	Opr	12.32	Mask quadword low
MSKWH	Opr	12.52	Mask word high
MSKWL	Opr	12.12	Mask word low
MT_FPCR	F-P	17.024	Move to FPCR
MULF	F-P	15.082	Multiply F_floating
MULG	F-P	15.0A2	Multiply G_floating
MULL	Opr	13.00	Multiply longword
MULL/V		13.40	
MULQ	Opr	13.20	Multiply quadword
MULQ/V		13.60	
MULS	F-P	16.082	Multiply S_floating
MULT	F-P	16.0A2	Multiply T_floating
ORNOT	Opr	11.28	Logical sum with complement
PERR	Opr	1C.31	Pixel error
PKLB	Opr	1C.37	Pack longwords to bytes
PKWB	Opr	1C.36	Pack words to bytes
RC	Mfc	18.E000	Read and clear
RET	Mbr	1A.2	Return from subroutine
RPCC	Mfc	18.C000	Read process cycle counter
RS	Mfc	18.F000	Read and set
S4ADDL	Opr	10.02	Scaled add longword by 4
S4ADDQ	Opr	10.22	Scaled add quadword by 4
S4SUBL	Opr	10.0B	Scaled subtract longword by 4
S4SUBQ	Opr	10.2B	Scaled subtract quadword by 4
S8ADDL	Opr	10.12	Scaled add longword by 8
S8ADDQ	Opr	10.32	Scaled add quadword by 8
S8SUBL	Opr	10.1B	Scaled subtract longword by 8

Table C–2: Common Architecture Instructions (Continued)

Mnemonic	Format	Opcode	Description
S8SUBQ	Opr	10.3B	Scaled subtract quadword by 8
SEXTB	Opr	1C.00	Sign extend byte
SEXTW	Opr	1C.01	Sign extend word
SLL	Opr	12.39	Shift left logical
SQRTF	F-P	14.08A	Square root F_floating
SQRTG	F-P	14.0AA	Square root G_floating
SQRTS	F-P	14.08B	Square root S_floating
SQRTT	F-P	14.0AB	Square root T_floating
SRA	Opr	12.3C	Shift right arithmetic
SRL	Opr	12.34	Shift right logical
STB	Mem	0E	Store byte
STF	Mem	24	Store F_floating
STG	Mem	25	Store G_floating
STS	Mem	26	Store S_floating
STL	Mem	2C	Store longword
STL_C	Mem	2E	Store longword conditional
STQ	Mem	2D	Store quadword
STQ_C	Mem	2F	Store quadword conditional
STQ_U	Mem	0F	Store unaligned quadword
STT	Mem	27	Store T_floating
STW	Mem	0D	Store word
SUBF	F-P	15.081	Subtract F_floating
SUBG	F-P	15.0A1	Subtract G_floating
SUBL	Opr	10.09	Subtract longword
SUBL/V		10.49	
SUBQ	Opr	10.29	Subtract quadword
SUBQ/V		10.69	
SUBS	F-P	16.081	Subtract S_floating
SUBT	F-P	16.0A1	Subtract T_floating
TRAPB	Mfc	18.0000	Trap barrier
UMULH	Opr	13.30	Unsigned multiply quadword high
UNPKBL	Opr	1C.35	Unpack bytes to longwords
UNPKBW	Opr	1C.34	Unpack bytes to words
WH64	Mfc	18.F800	Write hint — 64 bytes
WMB	Mfc	18.4400	Write memory barrier
XOR	Opr	11.40	Logical difference
ZAP	Opr	12.30	Zero bytes
ZAPNOT	Opr	12.31	Zero bytes not

C.2 IEEE Floating-Point Instructions

Table C–3 lists the hexadecimal value of the 11-bit function code field for the IEEE floating-point instructions, with and without qualifiers. The opcode for the following instructions is 16_{16}, except for SQRTS and SQRTT, which are opcode 14_{16}.

Table C–3: IEEE Floating-Point Instruction Function Codes

	None	/C	/M	/D	/U	/UC	/UM	/UD
ADDS	080	000	040	0C0	180	100	140	1C0
ADDT	0A0	020	060	0E0	1A0	120	160	1E0
CMPTEQ	0A5							
CMPTLT	0A6							
CMPTLE	0A7							
CMPTUN	0A4							
CVTQS	0BC	03C	07C	0FC				
CVTQT	0BE	03E	07E	0FE				
CVTST	See below							
CVTTQ	See below							
CVTTS	0AC	02C	06C	0EC	1AC	12C	16C	1EC
DIVS	083	003	043	0C3	183	103	143	1C3
DIVT	0A3	023	063	0E3	1A3	123	163	1E3
MULS	082	002	042	0C2	182	102	142	1C2
MULT	0A2	022	062	0E2	1A2	122	162	1E2
SQRTS	08B	00B	04B	0CB	18B	10B	14B	1CB
SQRTT	0AB	02B	06B	0EB	1AB	12B	16B	1EB
SUBS	081	001	041	0C1	181	101	141	1C1
SUBT	0A1	021	061	0E1	1A1	121	161	1E1

	/SU	/SUC	/SUM	/SUD	/SUI	/SUIC	/SUIM	/SUID
ADDS	580	500	540	5C0	780	700	740	7C0
ADDT	5A0	520	560	5E0	7A0	720	760	7E0
CMPTEQ	5A5							
CMPTLT	5A6							
CMPTLE	5A7							
CMPTUN	5A4							
CVTQS					7BC	73C	77C	7FC
CVTQT					7BE	73E	77E	7FE
CVTTS	5AC	52C	56C	5EC	7AC	72C	76C	7EC
DIVS	583	503	543	5C3	783	703	743	7C3
DIVT	5A3	523	563	5E3	7A3	723	763	7E3
MULS	582	502	542	5C2	782	702	742	7C2
MULT	5A2	522	562	5E2	7A2	722	762	7E2
SQRTS	58B	50B	54B	5CB	78B	70B	74B	7CB
SQRTT	5AB	52B	56B	5EB	7AB	72B	76B	7EB
SUBS	581	501	541	5C1	781	701	741	7C1
SUBT	5A1	521	561	5E1	7A1	721	761	7E1

	None	/S
CVTST	2AC	6AC

Table C–3: IEEE Floating-Point Instruction Function Codes (Continued)

	None	/C	/V	/VC	/SV	/SVC	/SVI	/SVIC
CVTTQ	0AF	02F	1AF	12F	5AF	52F	7AF	72F
	/D	/VD	/SVD	/SVID	/M	/VM	/SVM	/SVIM
CVTTQ	0EF	1EF	5EF	7EF	06F	16F	56F	76F

Programming Note:

To use CMPTxx with software completion trap handling, specify the /SU IEEE trap mode, even though an underflow trap is not possible. To use CVTQS or CVTQT with software completion trap handling, specify the /SUI IEEE trap mode, even though an underflow trap is not possible.

C.3 VAX Floating-Point Instructions

Table C–4 lists the hexadecimal value of the 11-bit function code field for the VAX floating-point instructions. The opcode for the following instructions is 15_{16}, except for SQRTF and SQRTG, which are opcode 14_{16}.

Table C–4: VAX Floating-Point Instruction Function Codes

	None	/C	/U	/UC	/S	/SC	/SU	/SUC
ADDF	080	000	180	100	480	400	580	500
CVTDG	09E	01E	19E	11E	49E	41E	59E	51E
ADDG	0A0	020	1A0	120	4A0	420	5A0	520
CMPGEQ	0A5				4A5			
CMPGLT	0A6				4A6			
CMPGLE	0A7				4A7			
CVTGF	0AC	02C	1AC	12C	4AC	42C	5AC	52C
CVTGD	0AD	02D	1AD	12D	4AD	42D	5AD	52D
CVTGQ	See below							
CVTQF	0BC	03C						
CVTQG	0BE	03E						
DIVF	083	003	183	103	483	403	583	503
DIVG	0A3	023	1A3	123	4A3	423	5A3	523
MULF	082	002	182	102	482	402	582	502
MULG	0A2	022	1A2	122	4A2	422	5A2	522
SQRTF	08A	00A	18A	10A	48A	40A	58A	50A
SQRTG	0AA	02A	1AA	12A	4AA	42A	5AA	52A
SUBF	081	001	181	101	481	401	581	501
SUBG	0A1	021	1A1	121	4A1	421	5A1	521

	None	/C	/V	/VC	/S	/SC	/SV	/SVC
CVTGQ	0AF	02F	1AF	12F	4AF	42F	5AF	52F

C.4 Independent Floating-Point Instructions

Table C–5 lists the hexadecimal value of the 11-bit function code field for the floating-point instructions that are not directly tied to IEEE or VAX floating point. The opcode for the following instructions is 17_{16}.

Table C–5: Independent Floating-Point Instruction Function Codes

	None	/V	/SV
CPYS	020		
CPYSE	022		
CPYSN	021		
CVTLQ	010		
CVTQL	030	130	530
FCMOVEQ	02A		
FCMOVGE	02D		
FCMOVGT	02F		
FCMOVLE	02E		
FCMOVLT	02C		
MF_FPCR	025		
MT_FPCR	024		

C.5 Opcode Summary

Table C–6 lists all Alpha opcodes from 00 (CALL_PAL) through 3F (BGT). In the table, the column headings that appear over the instructions have a granularity of 8_{16}. The rows beneath the leftmost column supply the individual hex number to resolve that granularity.

If an instruction column has a 0 (zero) in the right (low) hex digit, replace that 0 with the number to the left of the backslash in the leftmost column on the instruction's row. If an instruction column has an 8 in the right (low) hexadecimal digit, replace that 8 with the number to the right of the backslash in the leftmost column.

For example, the third row (2/A) under the 10 column contains the symbol INTS*, representing all the integer shift instructions. The opcode for those instructions would then be 12_{16} because the 0 in 10 is replaced by the 2 in the leftmost column. Likewise, the third row under the 18 column contains the symbol JSR*, representing all jump instructions. The opcode for those instructions is 1A because the 8 in the heading is replaced by the number to the right of the backslash in the leftmost column.

The instruction format is listed under the instruction symbol. The symbols in Table C–6 are explained in Table C–7.

Table C–6: Opcode Summary

	00	**08**	**10**	**18**	**20**	**28**	**30**	**38**
0/8	PAL* (pal)	LDA (mem)	INTA* (op)	MISC* (mem)	LDF (mem)	LDL (mem)	BR (br)	BLBC (br)
1/9	Res	LDAH (mem)	INTL* (op)	\PAL\	LDG (mem)	LDQ (mem)	FBEQ (br)	BEQ (br)
2/A	Res	LDBU (mem)	INTS* (op)	JSR* (mem)	LDS (mem)	LDL_L (mem)	FBLT (br)	BLT (br)
3/B	Res	LDQ_U (mem)	INTM* (op)	\PAL\	LDT (mem)	LDQ_L (mem)	FBLE (br)	BLE (br)
4/C	Res	LDWU (mem)	ITFP*	FPTI*	STF (mem)	STL (mem)	BSR (br)	BLBS (br)
5/D	Res	STW (mem)	FLTV* (op)	\PAL\	STG (mem)	STQ (mem)	FBNE (br)	BNE (br)
6/E	Res	STB (mem)	FLTI* (op)	\PAL\	STS (mem)	STL_C (mem)	FBGE (br)	BGE (br)
7/F	Res	STQ_U (mem)	FLTL* (op)	\PAL\	STT (mem)	STQ_C (mem)	FBGT (br)	BGT (br)

Table C–7: Key to Opcode Summary

Symbol	**Meaning**
FLTI*	IEEE floating-point instruction opcodes
FLTL*	Floating-point Operate instruction opcodes
FLTV*	VAX floating-point instruction opcodes
FPTI*	Floating-point to integer register move opcodes
INTA*	Integer arithmetic instruction opcodes
INTL*	Integer logical instruction opcodes
INTM*	Integer multiply instruction opcodes
INTS*	Integer shift instruction opcodes
ITFP*	Integer to floating-point register move opcodes
JSR*	Jump instruction opcodes
MISC*	Miscellaneous instruction opcodes
PAL*	PALcode instruction (CALL_PAL) opcodes
\PAL\	Reserved for PALcode
Res	Reserved for DIGITAL

C.6 Common Architecture Opcodes in Numerical Order

Table C–8: Common Architecture Opcodes in Numerical Order

Opcode		Opcode		Opcode	
00	CALL_PAL	11.26	CMOVNE	14.014	ITOFF
01	OPC01	11.28	ORNOT	14.024	ITOFT
02	OPC02	11.40	XOR	14.02A	SQRTG/C
03	OPC03	11.44	CMOVLT	14.02B	SQRTT/C
04	OPC04	11.46	CMOVGE	14.04B	SQRTS/M
05	OPC05	11.48	EQV	14.06B	SQRTT/M
06	OPC06	11.61	AMASK	14.08A	SQRTF
07	OPC07	11.64	CMOVLE	14.08B	SQRTS
08	LDA	11.66	CMOVGT	14.0AA	SQRTG
09	LDAH	11.6C	IMPLVER	14.0AB	SQRTT
0A	LDBU	12.02	MSKBL	14.0CB	SQRTS/D
0B	LDQ_U	12.06	EXTBL	14.0EB	SQRTT/D
0C	LDWU	12.0B	INSBL	14.10A	SQRTF/UC
0D	STW	12.12	MSKWL	14.10B	SQRTS/UC
0E	STB	12.16	EXTWL	14.12A	SQRTG/UC
0F	STQ_U	12.1B	INSWL	14.12B	SQRTT/UC
10.00	ADDL	12.22	MSKLL	14.14B	SQRTS/UM
10.02	S4ADDL	12.26	EXTLL	14.16B	SQRTT/UM
10.09	SUBL	12.2B	INSLL	14.18A	SQRTF/U
10.0B	S4SUBL	12.30	ZAP	14.18B	SQRTS/U
10.0F	CMPBGE	12.31	ZAPNOT	14.1AA	SQRTG/U
10.12	S8ADDL	12.32	MSKQL	14.1AB	SQRTT/U
10.1B	S8SUBL	12.34	SRL	14.1CB	SQRTS/UD
10.1D	CMPULT	12.36	EXTQL	14.1EB	SQRTT/UD
10.20	ADDQ	12.39	SLL	14.40A	SQRTF/SC
10.22	S4ADDQ	12.3B	INSQL	14.42A	SQRTG/SC
10.29	SUBQ	12.3C	SRA	14.48A	SQRTF/S
10.2B	S4SUBQ	12.52	MSKWH	14.4AA	SQRTG/S
10.2D	CMPEQ	12.57	INSWH	14.50A	SQRTF/SUC
10.32	S8ADDQ	12.5A	EXTWH	14.50B	SQRTS/SUC
10.3B	S8SUBQ	12.62	MSKLH	14.52A	SQRTG/SUC
10.3D	CMPULE	12.67	INSLH	14.52B	SQRTT/SUC
10.40	ADDL/V	12.6A	EXTLH	14.54B	SQRTS/SUM
10.49	SUBL/V	12.72	MSKQH	14.56B	SQRTT/SUM
10.4D	CMPLT	12.77	INSQH	14.58A	SQRTF/SU
10.60	ADDQ/V	12.7A	EXTQH	14.58B	SQRTS/SU
10.69	SUBQ/V	13.00	MULL	14.5AA	SQRTG/SU
10.6D	CMPLE	13.20	MULQ	14.5AB	SQRTT/SU
11.00	AND	13.30	UMULH	14.5CB	SQRTS/SUD
11.08	BIC	13.40	MULL/V	14.5EB	SQRTT/SUD
11.14	CMOVLBS	13.60	MULQ/V	14.70B	SQRTS/SUIC
11.16	CMOVLBC	14.004	ITOFS	14.72B	SQRTT/SUIC
11.20	BIS	14.00A	SQRTF/C	14.74B	SQRTS/SUIM
11.24	CMOVEQ	14.00B	SQRTS/C	14.76B	SQRTT/SUIM

Table C–8: Common Architecture Opcodes in Numerical Order (Continued)

Opcode		Opcode		Opcode	
14.78B	SQRTS/SUI	15.12F	CVTGQ/VC	15.521	SUBG/SUC
14.7AB	SQRTT/SUI	15.180	ADDF/U	15.522	MULG/SUC
14.7CB	SQRTS/SUID	15.181	SUBF/U	15.523	DIVG/SUC
14.7EB	SQRTT/SUID	15.182	MULF/U	15.52C	CVTGF/SUC
15.000	ADDF/C	15.183	DIVF/U	15.52D	CVTGD/SUC
15.001	SUBF/C	15.19E	CVTDG/U	15.52F	CVTGQ/SVC
15.002	MULF/C	15.1A0	ADDG/U	15.580	ADDF/SU
15.003	DIVF/C	15.1A1	SUBG/U	15.581	SUBF/SU
15.01E	CVTDG/C	15.1A2	MULG/U	15.582	MULF/SU
15.020	ADDG/C	15.1A3	DIVG/U	15.583	DIVF/SU
15.021	SUBG/C	15.1AC	CVTGF/U	15.59E	CVTDG/SU
15.022	MULG/C	15.1AD	CVTGD/U	15.5A0	ADDG/SU
15.023	DIVG/C	15.1AF	CVTGQ/V	15.5A1	SUBG/SU
15.02C	CVTGF/C	15.400	ADDF/SC	15.5A2	MULG/SU
15.02D	CVTGD/C	15.401	SUBF/SC	15.5A3	DIVG/SU
15.02F	CVTGQ/C	15.402	MULF/SC	15.5AC	CVTGF/SU
15.03C	CVTQF/C	15.403	DIVF/SC	15.5AD	CVTGD/SU
15.03E	CVTQG/C	15.41E	CVTDG/SC	15.5AF	CVTGQ/SV
15.080	ADDF	15.420	ADDG/SC	16.000	ADDS/C
15.081	SUBF	15.421	SUBG/SC	16.001	SUBS/C
15.082	MULF	15.422	MULG/SC	16.002	MULS/C
15.083	DIVF	15.423	DIVG/SC	16.003	DIVS/C
15.09E	CVTDG	15.42C	CVTGF/SC	16.020	ADDT/C
15.0A0	ADDG	15.42D	CVTGD/SC	16.021	SUBT/C
15.0A1	SUBG	15.42F	CVTGQ/SC	16.022	MULT/C
15.0A2	MULG	15.480	ADDF/S	16.023	DIVT/C
15.0A3	DIVG	15.481	SUBF/S	16.02C	CVTTS/C
15.0A5	CMPGEQ	15.482	MULF/S	16.02F	CVTTQ/C
15.0A6	CMPGLT	15.483	DIVF/S	16.03C	CVTQS/C
15.0A7	CMPGLE	15.49E	CVTDG/S	16.03E	CVTQT/C
15.0AC	CVTGF	15.4A0	ADDG/S	16.040	ADDS/M
15.0AD	CVTGD	15.4A1	SUBG/S	16.041	SUBS/M
15.0AF	CVTGQ	15.4A2	MULG/S	16.042	MULS/M
15.0BC	CVTQF	15.4A3	DIVG/S	16.043	DIVS/M
15.0BE	CVTQG	15.4A5	CMPGEQ/S	16.060	ADDT/M
15.100	ADDF/UC	15.4A6	CMPGLT/S	16.061	SUBT/M
15.101	SUBF/UC	15.4A7	CMPGLE/S	16.062	MULT/M
15.102	MULF/UC	15.4AC	CVTGF/S	16.063	DIVT/M
15.103	DIVF/UC	15.4AD	CVTGD/S	16.06C	CVTTS/M
15.11E	CVTDG/UC	15.4AF	CVTGQ/S	16.06F	CVTTQ/M
15.120	ADDG/UC	15.500	ADDF/SUC	16.07C	CVTQS/M
15.121	SUBG/UC	15.501	SUBF/SUC	16.07E	CVTQT/M
15.122	MULG/UC	15.502	MULF/SUC	16.080	ADDS
15.123	DIVG/UC	15.503	DIVF/SUC	16.081	SUBS
15.12C	CVTGF/UC	15.51E	CVTDG/SUC	16.082	MULS
15.12D	CVTGD/UC	15.520	ADDG/SUC	16.083	DIVS

Table C–8: Common Architecture Opcodes in Numerical Order (Continued)

Opcode		Opcode		Opcode	
16.0A0	ADDT	16.182	MULS/U	16.5A3	DIVT/SU
16.0A1	SUBT	16.183	DIVS/U	16.5A4	CMPTUN/SU
16.0A2	MULT	16.1A0	ADDT/U	16.5A5	CMPTEQ/SU
16.0A3	DIVT	16.1A1	SUBT/U	16.5A6	CMPTLT/SU
16.0A4	CMPTUN	16.1A2	MULT/U	16.5A7	CMPTLE/SU
16.0A5	CMPTEQ	16.1A3	DIVT/U	16.5AC	CVTTS/SU
16.0A6	CMPTLT	16.1AC	CVTTS/U	16.5AF	CVTTQ/SV
16.0A7	CMPTLE	16.1AF	CVTTQ/V	16.5C0	ADDS/SUD
16.0AC	CVTTS	16.1C0	ADDS/UD	16.5C1	SUBS/SUD
16.0AF	CVTTQ	16.1C1	SUBS/UD	16.5C2	MULS/SUD
16.0BC	CVTQS	16.1C2	MULS/UD	16.5C3	DIVS/SUD
16.0BE	CVTQT	16.1C3	DIVS/UD	16.5E0	ADDT/SUD
16.0C0	ADDS/D	16.1E0	ADDT/UD	16.5E1	SUBT/SUD
16.0C1	SUBS/D	16.1E1	SUBT/UD	16.5E2	MULT/SUD
16.0C2	MULS/D	16.1E2	MULT/UD	16.5E3	DIVT/SUD
16.0C3	DIVS/D	16.1E3	DIVT/UD	16.5EC	CVTTS/SUD
16.0E0	ADDT/D	16.1EC	CVTTS/UD	16.5EF	CVTTQ/SVD
16.0E1	SUBT/D	16.1EF	CVTTQ/VD	16.6AC	CVTST/S
16.0E2	MULT/D	16.2AC	CVTST	16.700	ADDS/SUIC
16.0E3	DIVT/D	16.500	ADDS/SUC	16.701	SUBS/SUIC
16.0EC	CVTTS/D	16.501	SUBS/SUC	16.702	MULS/SUIC
16.0EF	CVTTQ/D	16.502	MULS/SUC	16.703	DIVS/SUIC
16.0FC	CVTQS/D	16.503	DIVS/SUC	16.720	ADDT/SUIC
16.0FE	CVTQT/D	16.520	ADDT/SUC	16.721	SUBT/SUIC
16.100	ADDS/UC	16.521	SUBT/SUC	16.722	MULT/SUIC
16.101	SUBS/UC	16.522	MULT/SUC	16.723	DIVT/SUIC
16.102	MULS/UC	16.523	DIVT/SUC	16.72C	CVTTS/SUIC
16.103	DIVS/UC	16.52C	CVTTS/SUC	16.72F	CVTTQ/SVIC
16.120	ADDT/UC	16.52F	CVTTQ/SVC	16.73C	CVTQS/SUIC
16.121	SUBT/UC	16.540	ADDS/SUM	16.73E	CVTQT/SUIC
16.122	MULT/UC	16.541	SUBS/SUM	16.740	ADDS/SUIM
16.123	DIVT/UC	16.542	MULS/SUM	16.741	SUBS/SUIM
16.12C	CVTTS/UC	16.543	DIVS/SUM	16.742	MULS/SUIM
16.12F	CVTTQ/VC	16.560	ADDT/SUM	16.743	DIVS/SUIM
16.140	ADDS/UM	16.561	SUBT/SUM	16.760	ADDT/SUIM
16.141	SUBS/UM	16.562	MULT/SUM	16.761	SUBT/SUIM
16.142	MULS/UM	16.563	DIVT/SUM	16.762	MULT/SUIM
16.143	DIVS/UM	16.56C	CVTTS/SUM	16.763	DIVT/SUIM
16.160	ADDT/UM	16.56F	CVTTQ/SVM	16.76C	CVTTS/SUIM
16.161	SUBT/UM	16.580	ADDS/SU	16.76F	CVTTQ/SVIM
16.162	MULT/UM	16.581	SUBS/SU	16.77C	CVTQS/SUIM
16.163	DIVT/UM	16.582	MULS/SU	16.77E	CVTQT/SUIM
16.16C	CVTTS/UM	16.583	DIVS/SU	16.780	ADDS/SUI
16.16F	CVTTQ/VM	16.5A0	ADDT/SU	16.781	SUBS/SUI
16.180	ADDS/U	16.5A1	SUBT/SU	16.782	MULS/SUI
16.181	SUBS/U	16.5A2	MULT/SU	16.783	DIVS/SUI

Table C–8: Common Architecture Opcodes in Numerical Order (Continued)

Opcode		Opcode		Opcode	
16.7A0	ADDT/SUI	18.4000	MB	1F	PAL1F
16.7A1	SUBT/SUI	18.4400	WMB	20	LDF
16.7A2	MULT/SUI	18.8000	FETCH	21	LDG
16.7A3	DIVT/SUI	18.A000	FETCH_M	22	LDS
16.7AC	CVTTS/SUI	18.C000	RPCC	23	LDT
16.7AF	CVTTQ/SVI	18.E000	RC	24	STF
16.7BC	CVTQS/SUI	18.E800	ECB	25	STG
16.7BE	CVTQT/SUI	18.F000	RS	26	STS
16.7C0	ADDS/SUID	18.F800	WH64	27	STT
16.7C1	SUBS/SUID	19	PAL19	28	LDL
16.7C2	MULS/SUID	1A.0	JMP	29	LDQ
16.7C3	DIVS/SUID	1A.1	JSR	2A	LDL_L
16.7E0	ADDT/SUID	1A.2	RET	2B	LDQ_L
16.7E1	SUBT/SUID	1A.3	JSR_COROUTINE	2C	STL
16.7E2	MULT/SUID	1B	PAL1B	2D	STQ
16.7E3	DIVT/SUID	1C.00	SEXTB	2E	STL_C
16.7EC	CVTTS/SUID	1C.01	SEXTW	2F	STQ_C
16.7EF	CVTTQ/SVID	1C.30	CTPOP	30	BR
16.7FC	CVTQS/SUID	1C.31	PERR	31	FBEQ
16.7FE	CVTQT/SUID	1C.32	CTLZ	32	FBLT
17.010	CVTLQ	1C.33	CTTZ	33	FBLE
17.020	CPYS	1C.34	UNPKBW	34	BSR
17.021	CPYSN	1C.35	UNPKBL	35	FBNE
17.022	CPYSE	1C.36	PKWB	36	FBGE
17.024	MT_FPCR	1C.37	PKLB	37	FBGT
17.025	MF_FPCR	1C.38	MINSB8	38	BLBC
17.02A	FCMOVEQ	1C.39	MINSW4	39	BEQ
17.02B	FCMOVNE	1C.3A	MINUB8	3A	BLT
17.02C	FCMOVLT	1C.3B	MINUW4	3B	BLE
17.02D	FCMOVGE	1C.3C	MAXUB8	3C	BLBS
17.02E	FCMOVLE	1C.3D	MAXUW4	3D	BNE
17.02F	FCMOVGT	1C.3E	MAXSB8	3E	BGE
17.030	CVTQL	1C.3F	MAXSW4	3F	BGT
17.130	CVTQL/V	1C.70	FTOIT		
17.530	CVTQL/SV	1C.78	FTOIS		
18.0000	TRAPB	1D	PAL1D		
18.0400	EXCB	1E	PAL1E		

C.7 OpenVMS Alpha PALcode Instruction Summary

Table C–9: OpenVMS Alpha Unprivileged PALcode Instructions

Mnemonic	Opcode	Description
AMOVRM	00.00A1	Atomic move from register to memory
AMOVRR	00.00A0	Atomic move from register to register
BPT	00.0080	Breakpoint
BUGCHK	00.0081	Bugcheck
CHMK	00.0083	Change mode to kernel
CHME	00.0082	Change mode to executive
CHMS	00.0084	Change mode to supervisor
CHMU	00.0085	Change mode to user
CLRFEN	00.00AE	Clear floating-point enable
GENTRAP	00.00AA	Generate software trap
IMB	00.0086	I-stream memory barrier
INSQHIL	00.0087	Insert into longword queue at head interlocked
INSQHILR	00.00A2	Insert into longword queue at head interlocked resident
INSQHIQ	00.0089	Insert into quadword queue at head interlocked
INSQHIQR	00.00A4	Insert into quadword queue at head interlocked resident
INSQTIL	00.0088	Insert into longword queue at tail interlocked
INSQTILR	00.00A3	Insert into longword queue at tail interlocked resident
INSQTIQ	00.008A	Insert into quadword queue at tail interlocked
INSQTIQR	00.00A5	Insert into quadword queue at tail interlockedresident
INSQUEL	00.008B	Insert entry into longword queue
INSQUEL/D	00.008D	Insert entry into longword queue deferred
INSQUEQ	00.008C	Insert entry into quadword queue
INSQUEQ/D	00.008E	Insert entry into quadword queue deferred
PROBER	00.008F	Probe for read access
PROBEW	00.0090	Probe for write access
RD_PS	00.0091	Move processor status
READ_UNQ	00.009E	Read unique context
REI	00.0092	Return from exception or interrupt
REMQHIL	00.0093	Remove from longword queue at head interlocked
REMQHILR	00.00A6	Remove from longword queue at head interlocked resident
REMQHIQ	00.0095	Remove from quadword queue at head interlocked
REMQHIQR	00.00A8	Remove from quadword queue at head interlocked resident
REMQTIL	00.0094	Remove from longword queue at tail interlocked
REMQTILR	00.00A7	Remove from longword queue at tail interlocked resident
REMQTIQ	00.0096	Remove from quadword queue at tail interlocked
REMQTIQR	00.00A9	Remove from quadword queue at tail interlocked resident
REMQUEL	00.0097	Rcmove entry from longword queue
REMQUEL/D	00.0099	Remove entry from longword queue deferred
REMQUEQ	00.0098	Remove entry from quadword queue
REMQUEQ/D	00.009A	Remove entry from quadword queue deferred
RSCC	00.009D	Read system cycle counter
SWASTEN	00.009B	Swap AST enable for current mode
WRITE_UNQ	00.009F	Write unique context
WR_PS_SW	00.009C	Write processor status software field

Table C–10: OpenVMS Alpha Privileged PALcode Instructions

Mnemonic	Opcode	Description
CFLUSH	00.0001	Cache flush
CSERVE	00.0009	Console service
DRAINA	00.0002	Drain aborts
HALT	00.0000	Halt processor
LDQP	00.0003	Load quadword physical
MFPR_ASN	00.0006	Move from processor register ASN
MFPR_ESP	00.001E	Move from processor register ESP
MFPR_FEN	00.000B	Move from processor register FEN
MFPR_IPL	00.000E	Move from processor register IPL
MFPR_MCES	00.0010	Move from processor register MCES
MFPR_PCBB	00.0012	Move from processor register PCBB
MFPR_PRBR	00.0013	Move from processor register PRBR
MFPR_PTBR	00.0015	Move from processor register PTBR
MFPR_SCBB	00.0016	Move from processor register SCBB
MFPR_SISR	00.0019	Move from processor register SISR
MFPR_SSP	00.0020	Move from processor register SSP
MFPR_TBCHK	00.001A	Move from processor register TBCHK
MFPR_USP	00.0022	Move from processor register USP
MFPR_VPTB	00.0029	Move from processor register VPTB
MFPR_WHAMI	00.003F	Move from processor register WHAMI
MTPR_ASTEN	00.0026	Move to processor register ASTEN
MTPR_ASTSR	00.0027	Move to processor register ASTSR
MTPR_DATFX	00.002E	Move to processor register DATFX
MTPR_ESP	00.001F	Move to processor register ESP
MTPR_FEN	00.000B	Move to processor register FEN
MTPR_IPIR	00.000D	Move to processor register IPRI
MTPR_IPL	00.000E	Move to processor register IPL
MTPR_MCES	00.0011	Move to processor register MCES
MTPR_PERFMON	00.002B	Move to processor register PERFMON
MTPR_PRBR	00.0014	Move to processor register PRBR
MTPR_SCBB	00.0017	Move to processor register SCBB
MTPR_SIRR	00.0018	Move to processor register SIRR
MTPR_SSP	00.0021	Move to processor register SSP
MTPR_TBIA	00.001B	Move to processor register TBIA
MTPR_TBIAP	00.001C	Move to processor register TBIAP
MTPR_TBIS	00.001D	Move to processor register TBIS
MTPR_TBISD	00.0024	Move to processor register TBISD
MTPR_TBISI	00.0025	Move to processor register TBISI
MTPR_USP	00.0023	Move to processor register USP
MTPR_VPTB	00.002A	Move to processor register VPTB
STQP	00.0004	Store quadword physical
SWPCTX	00.0005	Swap privileged context
SWPPAL	00.000A	Swap PALcode image
WTINT	00.003E	Wait for interrupt

C.8 DIGITAL UNIX PALcode Instruction Summary

Table C–11: DIGITAL UNIX Unprivileged PALcode Instructions

Mnemonic	Opcode	Description
bpt	00.0080	Breakpoint trap
bugchk	00.0081	Bugcheck
callsys	00.0083	System call
clrfen	00.00AE	Clear floating-point enable
gentrap	00.00AA	Generate software trap
imb	00.0086	I-stream memory barrier
rdunique	00.009E	Read unique value
urti	00.0092	Return from user mode trap
wrunique	00.009F	Write unique value

Table C–12: DIGITAL UNIX Privileged PALcode Instructions

Mnemonic	Opcode	Description
cflush	00.0001	Cache flush
cserve	00.0009	Console service
draina	00.0002	Drain aborts
halt	00.0000	Halt the processor
rdmces	00.0010	Read machine check error summary register
rdps	00.0036	Read processor status
rdusp	00.003A	Read user stack pointer
rdval	00.0032	Read system value
retsys	00.003D	Return from system call
rti	00.003F	Return from trap or interrupt
swpctx	00.0030	Swap privileged context
swpipl	00.0035	Swap interrupt priority level
swppal	00.000A	Swap PALcode image
tbi	00.0033	Translation buffer invalidate
whami	00.003C	Who am I
wrent	00.0034	Write system entry address
wrfen	00.002B	Write floating-point enable
wripir	00.000D	Write interprocessor interrupt request
wrkgp	00.0037	Write kernel global pointer
wrmces	00.0011	Write machine check error summary register
wrperfmon	00.0039	Performance monitoring function
wrusp	00.0038	Write user stack pointer
wrval	00.0031	Write system value
wrvptptr	00.002D	Write virtual page table pointer
wtint	00.003E	Wait for interrupt

C.9 Windows NT Alpha Instruction Summary

Table C–13: Windows NT Alpha Unprivileged PALcode Instructions

Mnemonic	Opcode	Description
bpt	00.0080	Breakpoint trap
callkd	00.00AD	Call kernel debugger
callsys	00.0083	Call system service
gentrap	00.00AA	Generate trap
imb	00.0086	Instruction memory barrier
kbpt	00.00AC	Kernel breakpoint trap
rdteb	00.00AB	Read TEB internal processor register

Table C–14: Windows NT Alpha Privileged PALcode instructions

Mnemonic	Opcode	Description
csir	00.000D	Clear software interrupt request
dalnfix	00.0025	Disable alignment fixups
di	00.0008	Disable interrupts
draina	00.0002	Drain aborts
dtbis	00.0016	Data translation buffer invalidate single
ealnfix	00.0024	Enable alignment fixups
ei	00.0009	Enable interrupts
halt	00.0000	Trap to illegal instruction
initpal	00.0004	Initialize the PALcode
initpcr	00.0038	Initialize processor control region data
rdcounters	00.0030	Read PALcode event counters
rdirql	00.0007	Read current IRQL
rdksp	00.0018	Read initial kernel stack
rdmces	00.0012	Read machine check error summary
rdpcr	00.001C	Read PCR (processor control registers)
rdpsr	00.001A	Read processor status register
rdstate	00.0031	Read internal processor state
rdthread	00.001E	Read the current thread value
reboot	00.0002	Transfer to console firmware
restart	00.0001	Restart the processor
retsys	00.000F	Return from system service call
rfe	00.000E	Return from exception
swpirql	00.0006	Swap IRQL
swpksp	00.0019	Swap initial kernel stack
swppal	00.000A	Swap PALcode
swpprocess	00.0011	Swap privileged process context
swpctx	00.0010	Swap privileged thread context
ssir	00.000C	Set software interrupt request
tbia	00.0014	Translation buffer invalidate all
tbim	00.0020	Translation buffer invalidate multiple
tbimasn	00.0021	Translation buffer invalidate multiple ASN
tbis	00.0015	Translation buffer invalidate single
tbisasn	00.0017	Translation buffer invalidate single ASN
wrentry	00.0005	Write system entry
wrmces	00.0013	Write machine check error summary
wrperfmon	00.0032	Write performance monitoring values

C.10 PALcode Opcodes in Numerical Order

Opcodes 00.0038_{16} through $00.003F_{16}$ are reserved for processor implementation-specific PALcode instructions. All other opcodes are reserved for use by DIGITAL.

Table C–15: PALcode Opcodes in Numerical Order

Opcode$_{16}$	Opcode$_{10}$	OpenVMS Alpha	DIGITAL UNIX	Windows NT Alpha
00.0000	00.0000	HALT	halt	halt
00.0001	00.0001	CFLUSH	cflush	restart
00.0002	00.0002	DRAINA	draina	draina
00.0003	00.0003	LDQP	—	reboot
00.0004	00.0004	STQP	—	initpal
00.0005	00.0005	SWPCTX	—	wrentry
00.0006	00.0006	MFPR_ASN	—	swpirql
00.0007	00.0007	MTPR_ASTEN	—	rdirql
00.0008	00.0008	MTPR_ASTSR	—	di
00.0009	00.0009	CSERVE	cserve	ei
00.000A	00.0010	SWPPAL	swppal	swppal
00.000B	00.0011	MFPR_FEN	—	—
00.000C	00.0012	MTPR_FEN	—	ssir
00.000D	00.0013	MTPR_IPIR	wripir	csir
00.000E	00.0014	MFPR_IPL	—	rfe
00.000F	00.0015	MTPR_IPL	—	retsys
00.0010	00.0016	MFPR_MCES	rdmces	swpctx
00.0011	00.0017	MTPR_MCES	wrmces	swpprocess
00.0012	00.0018	MFPR_PCBB	—	rdmes
00.0013	00.0019	MFPR_PRBR	—	wrmces
00.0014	00.0020	MTPR_PRBR	—	tbia
00.0015	00.0021	MFPR_PTBR	—	tbis
00.0016	00.0022	MFPR_SCBB	—	dtbis
00.0017	00.0023	MTPR_SCBB	—	tbisasn
00.0018	00.0024	MTPR_SIRR	—	rdksp
00.0019	00.0025	MFPR_SISR	—	swpksp
00.001A	00.0026	MFPR_TBCHK	—	rdpsr
00.001B	00.0027	MTPR_TBIA	—	—
00.001C	00.0028	MTPR_TBIAP	—	rdpcr
00.001D	00.0029	MTPR_TBIS	—	—
00.001E	00.0030	MFPR_ESP	—	rdthread
00.001F	00.0031	MTPR_ESP	—	—
00.0020	00.0032	MFPR_SSP	—	tbim
00.0021	00.0033	MTPR_SSP	—	tbimasn
00.0022	00.0034	MFPR_USP	—	—
00.0023	00.0035	MTPR_USP	—	—
00.0024	00.0036	MTPR_TBISD	—	ealnfix
00.0025	00.0037	MTPR_TBISI	—	dalnfix
00.0026	00.0038	MFPR_ASTEN	—	—
00.0027	00.0039	MFPR_ASTSR	—	—
00.0029	00.0041	MFPR_VPTB	—	—
00.002A	00.0042	MTPR_VPTB	—	—
00.002B	00.0043	MTPR_PERFMON	wrfen	—
00.002D	00.0045	—	wrvptptr	—
00.002E	00.0046	MTPR_DATFX	—	—
00.0030	00.0048	—	swpctx	rdcounters

Table C–15: PALcode Opcodes in Numerical Order (Continued)

Opcode$_{16}$	Opcode$_{10}$	OpenVMS Alpha	DIGITAL UNIX	Windows NT Alpha
00.0031	00.0049	—	wrval	rdstate
00.0032	00.0050	—	rdval	wrperfmon
00.0033	00.0051	—	tbi	—
00.0034	00.0052	—	wrent	—
00.0035	00.0053	—	swpipl	—
00.0036	00.0054	—	rdps	—
00.0037	00.0055	—	wrkgp	initpcr
00.0038	00.0056	—	wrusp	—
00.0039	00.0057	—	wrperfmon	—
00.003A	00.0058	—	rdusp	—
00.003C	00.0060	—	whami	—
00.003D	00.0061	—	retsys	—
00.003E	00.0062	WTINT	wtint	—
00.003F	00.0063	MFPR_WHAMI	rti	—
00.0080	00.0128	BPT	bpt	bpt
00.0081	00.0129	BUGCHK	bugchk	—
00.0082	00.0130	CHME	—	—
00.0083	00.0131	CHMK	callsys	callsys
00.0084	00.0132	CHMS	—	—
00.0085	00.0133	CHMU	—	—
00.0086	00.0134	IMB	imb	imb
00.0087	00.0135	INSQHIL	—	—
00.0088	00.0136	INSQTIL	—	—
00.0089	00.0137	INSQHIQ	—	—
00.008A	00.0138	INSQTIQ	—	—
00.008B	00.0139	INSQUEL	—	—
00.008C	00.0140	INSQUEQ	—	—
00.008D	00.0141	INSQUEL/D	—	—
00.008E	00.0142	INSQUEQ/D	—	—
00.008F	00.0143	PROBER	—	—
00.0090	00.0144	PROBEW	—	—
00.0091	00.0145	RD_PS	—	—
00.0092	00.0146	REI	urti	—
00.0093	00.0147	REMQHIL	—	—
00.0094	00.0148	REMQTIL	—	—
00.0095	00.0149	REMQHIQ	—	—
00.0096	00.0150	REMQTIQ	—	—
00.0097	00.0151	REMQUEL	—	—
00.0098	00.0152	REMQUEQ	—	—
00.0099	00.0153	REMQUEL/D		—
00.009A	00.0154	REMQUEQ/D	—	—
00.009B	00.0155	SWASTEN	—	—
00.009C	00.0156	WR_PS_SW	—	—
00.009D	00.0157	RSCC	—	—
00.009E	00.0158	READ_UNQ	rdunique	—
00.009F	00.0159	WRITE_UNQ	wrunique	—
00.00A0	00.0160	AMOVRR	—	—
00.00A1	00.0161	AMOVRM	—	—
00.00A2	00.0162	INSQHILR	—	—
00.00A3	00.0163	INSQTILR	—	—
00.00A4	00.0164	INSQHIQR	—	—
00.00A5	00.0165	INSQTIQR	—	—

Table C–15: PALcode Opcodes in Numerical Order (Continued)

Opcode$_{16}$	Opcode$_{10}$	OpenVMS Alpha	DIGITAL UNIX	Windows NT Alpha
00.00A6	00.0166	REMQHILR	—	—
00.00A7	00.0167	REMQTILR	—	—
00.00A8	00.0168	REMQHIQR	—	—
00.00A9	00.0169	REMQTIQR	—	—
00.00AA	00.0170	GENTRAP	gentrap	gentrap
00.00AB	00.0171	—	—	rdteb
00.00AC	00.0172	—	—	kbpt
00.00AD	00.0173	—	—	callkd
00.00AE	00.0174	CLRFEN	clrfen	

C.11 Required PALcode Opcodes

The opcodes listed in Table C–16 are required for all Alpha implementations. The notation used is oo.ffff, where *oo* is the hexadecimal 6-bit opcode and *ffff* is the hexadecimal 26-bit function code.

Table C–16: Required PALcode Opcodes

Mnemonic	Type	Opcode
DRAINA	Privileged	00.0002
HALT	Privileged	00.0000
IMB	Unprivileged	00.0086

C.12 Opcodes Reserved to PALcode

The opcodes listed in Table C–17 are reserved for use in implementing PALcode.

Table C–17: Opcodes Reserved for PALcode

Mnemonic		Mnemonic		Mnemonic	
PAL19	19	PAL1B	1B	PAL1D	1D
PAL1E	1E	PAL1F	1F		

C.13 Opcodes Reserved to DIGITAL

The opcodes listed in Table C–18 are reserved to DIGITAL.

Table C–18: Opcodes Reserved for DIGITAL

Mnemonic		Mnemonic		Mnemonic	
OPC01	01	OPC02	02	OPC03	03
OPC04	04	OPC05	05	OPC06	06
OPC07	07				

Programming Note:

The code points 18.4800 and 18.4C00 are reserved for adding weaker memory barrier instructions. Those code points must operate as a Memory Barrier instruction (MB 18.4000) for implementations that precede their definition as weaker memory barrier instructions. Software must use the 18.4000 code point for MB.

C.14 Unused Function Code Behavior

Unused function codes for all opcodes assigned (not reserved) in the Version 5 Alpha architecture specification (May 1992) produce UNPREDICTABLE but not UNDEFINED results; they are not security holes.

Unused function codes for opcodes defined as reserved in the Version 5 Alpha architecture specification produce an illegal instruction trap. Those opcodes are 01, 02, 03, 04, 05, 06, 07, 0A, 0C, 0D, 0E, 14, 19, 1B, 1C, 1D, 1E, and 1F. Unused function codes for those opcodes reserved to PALcode produce an illegal instruction trap only if not used in the PALcode environment.

C.15 ASCII Character Set

Table C-19 shows the 7-bit ASCII character set and the corresponding hexadecimal value for each character.

Table C-19: ASCII Character Set

Char	Hex Code	Char	Hex Code	Char	Hex Code	Char	Hex Code
NUL	0	SP	20	@	40	`	60
SQH	1	!	21	A	41	a	61
STX	2	"	22	B	42	b	62
ETX	3	#	23	C	43	c	63
EOT	4	$	24	D	44	d	64
ENQ	5	%	25	E	45	e	65
ACK	6	&	26	F	46	f	66
BEL	7	'	27	G	47	g	67
BS	8	(	28	H	48	h	68
HT	9	)	29	I	49	i	69
LF	A	*	2A	J	4A	j	6A
VT	B	+	2B	K	4B	k	6B
FF	C	,	2C	L	4C	l	6C
CR	D	-	2D	M	4D	m	6D
SO	E	.	2E	N	4E	n	6E
SI	F	/	2F	O	4F	o	6F
DLE	10	0	30	P	50	p	70
DC1	11	1	31	Q	51	q	71
DC2	12	2	32	R	52	r	72
DC3	13	3	33	S	53	s	73
DC4	14	4	34	T	54	t	74
NAK	15	5	35	U	55	u	75
SYN	16	6	36	V	56	v	76
ETB	17	7	37	W	57	w	77
CAN	18	8	38	X	58	x	78
EM	19	9	39	Y	59	y	79
SUB	1A	:	3A	Z	5A	z	7A
ESC	1B	;	3B	[	5B	{	7B
FS	1C	<	3C	\	5C	|	7C
GS	1D	=	3D	]	5D	}	7D
RS	1E	>	3E	^	5E	~	7E
US	1F	?	3F	_	5F	DEL	7F

Registered System and Processor Identifiers

This appendix contains a table of the processor type assignments, PALcode implementation information, and the architecture mask (AMASK) and implementation value (IMPLVER) assignments.

D.1 Processor Type Assignments

The following processor types are defined.

Table D–1: Processor Type Assignments

Major Type		Minor Type	
1 =	EV3		
2 =	EV4 (21064)	0 =	Pass 2 or 2.1
		1 =	Pass 3 (also EV4s)
3 =	Simulation		

4 =	LCA Family:
	    LCA4s (21066)
	    LCA4s embedded (21068)
	    LCA45 (21066A, 21068A)		

		0 =	Reserved
		1 =	Pass 1 or 1.1 (21066)
		2 =	Pass 2 (21066)
		3 =	Pass 1 or 1.1 (21068)
		4 =	Pass 2 (21068)
		5 =	Pass 1 (21066A)
		6 =	Pass 1 (21068A)

Table D–1: Processor Type Assignments (Continued)

Major Type		Minor Type	
5 =	EV5 (21164)	0 =	Reserved (Pass 1)
		1 =	Pass 2, 2.2 (rev BA, CA)
		2 =	Pass 2.3 (rev DA, EA)
		3 =	Pass 3
		4 =	Pass 3.2
		5 =	Pass 4
6 =	EV45 (21064A)	0 =	Reserved
		1 =	Pass 1
		2 =	Pass 1.1
		3 =	Pass 2
7 =	EV56 (21164A)	0 =	Reserved
		1 =	Pass 1
		2 =	Pass 2
8 =	EV6 (21264)	0 =	Reserved
		1 =	Pass 1
9 =	PCA56 (21164PC)	0 =	Reserved
		1 =	Pass 1

For OpenVMS Alpha and DIGITAL UNIX, the processor types are stored in the Per-CPU Slot Table (SLOT[176]), pointed to by HWRPB[160].

D.2 PALcode Variation Assignments

The PALcode variation assignments are as follows:

Table D–2: PALcode Variation Assignments

Token	PALcode Type	Summary Table
0	Console	N/A
1	OpenVMS Alpha	Console Interface (III), Chapter 3
2	DIGITAL UNIX	Console Interface (III), Chapter 3
3–127	Reserved to DIGITAL	
128–255	Reserved to non-DIGITAL	

D.3 Architecture Mask and Implementation Values

The following bits are defined for the AMASK instruction.

Table D–3: AMASK Bit Assignments

Bit	Meaning
0	Support for the byte/word extension (BWX) The instructions that comprise the BWX extension are LDBU, LDWU, SEXTB, SEXTW, STB, and STW.
1	Support for the square-root and floating-point convert extension (FIX) The instructions that comprise the FIX extension are FTOIS, FTOIT, ITOFF, ITOFS, ITOFT, SQRTF, SQRTG, SQRTS, and SQRTT.
2	Support for the count extension (CIX) The instructions that comprise the CIX extension are CTLZ, CTPOP, and CTTZ.
8	Support for the multimedia extension (MVI) The instructions that comprise the MVI extension are MAXSB8, MAXSW4, MAXUB8, MAXUW4, MINSB8, MINSW4, MINUB8, MINUW4, PERR, PKLB, PKWB, UNPKBL, and UNPKBW.
9	Support for precise arithmetic trap reporting in hardware. The trap PC is the same as the instruction PC after the trapping instruction is executed.

The following values are defined for the IMPLVER instruction.

Table D–4: IMPLVER Value Assignments

Value	Meaning
0	21064 (EV4) 21064A (EV45) 21066A/21068A (LCA45)
1	21164 (EV5) 21164A (EV56) 21164PC (PCA56)
2	21264 (EV6)

Waivers and Implementation-Dependent Functionality

This appendix describes waivers to the Alpha architecture and functionality that is specific to particular hardware implementations.

E.1 Waivers

The following waivers have been passed for the Alpha architecture.

E.1.1 DECchip 21064, DECchip 21066, and DECchip 21068 IEEE Divide Instruction Violation

The DECchip 21064, DECchip 21066, and DECchip 21068 CPUs violate the architected handling of IEEE divide instructions DIVS and DIVT with respect to reporting Inexact Result exceptions.

Note:

The DECchip 21064A, DECchip 21066A, and DECchip 21068A CPUs are compliant and require no waiver. The DECchip 21164 is also compliant.

As specified by the architecture, floating-point exceptions generated by the CPU are recorded in two places for all IEEE floating-point instructions:

1. If an exception is detected and the corresponding trap is enabled (such as ADD/U for underflow), the CPU initiates a trap and records the exception in the exception summary register (EXC_SUM).

2. The exceptions are also recorded as flags that can be tested in the floating-point control register (FPCR). The FPCR can only be accessed with MTPR/MFPR instructions and an explicit MT_FPCR is required to clear the FPCR. The FPCR is updated irrespective of whether the trap is enabled or not.

The DECchip 21064, DECchip 21066, and DECchip 21068 implementations differ from the above specification in handling the Inexact condition for the IEEE DIVS and DIVT instructions in two ways:

1. The DIVS and DIVT instructions with the /Inexact modifier trap unconditionally and report the INE exception in the EXC_SUM register (except for NaN, infinity, and denormal inputs that result in INVs). This allows for a software calculation to determine the correct INE status.

2. The FPCR <INE> bit is *never* set by DIVS or DIVT. This is because the DECchip 21064, DECchip 21066, and DECchip 21068 do not include hardware to determine that particular exactness.

E.1.2 DECchip 21064, DECchip 21066, and DECchip 21068 Write Buffer Violation

The DECchip 21064, DECchip 21066, and DECchip 21068 CPUs can be made to violate the architecture by, under one contrived case, indefinitely delaying a buffered off-chip write.

Note:

> The DECchip 21064A, DECchip 21066A, and DECchip 21068A CPUs are compliant and require no waiver. The DECchip 21164 is also compliant.

The CPUs in violation can send a buffered write off-chip when one of the following conditions is met:

1. The write buffer contains at least two valid entries.

2. The write buffer contains one valid entry and 256 cycles have elapsed since the execution of the last write.

3. The write buffer contains an MB or STx_C instruction.

4. A load miss hits an entry in the write buffer.

The write can be delayed indefinitely under condition 2 above, when there is an indefinite stream of writes to addresses within the same aligned 32-byte write buffer block.

E.1.3 DECchip 21264 LDx_L/STx_C with WH64 Violation

The DECchip 21264 violates the architected relationship between the LDx_L and STx_C instructions when an intervening WH64 instruction is executed.

As specified by the common architecture, in Section 4.2.4:

> If any other memory access (ECB, LDx, LDQ_U, STx, STQ_U, WH64) is executed on the given processor between the LDx_L and the STx_C, the sequence above may always fail on some implementations; hence, no useful program should do this.

The DECchip 21264 varies from that description, with regard to the WH64 instruction, as follows:

> If any other memory access (ECB, LDx, LDQ_U, STx, STQ_U) is executed on the given processor between the LDx_L and the STx_C, the sequence above may always fail on some implementations; hence, no useful program should do this.

> If a WH64 memory access is executed on any given 21264 processor between the LDx_L and STx_C, and:

> - The WH64 access is to the same aligned 64-byte block that STx_C is accessing, and

> - No CALL_PAL REI, rei, or rfe instruction has been executed since the most-recent LDx_L (ensuring that the sequence cannot occur as the result of unfortunate coincidences with interrupts)

then, the load-locked/store-conditional sequence may sometimes fail when it would otherwise succeed and sometimes succeed when it otherwise would fail; hence no useful program should do this.

E.2 Implementation-Specific Functionality

The following functionality, although a documented part of the Alpha architecture, is implemented in a manner that is specific to the particular hardware implementation.

E.2.1 DECchip 21064/21066/21068 Performance Monitoring

Note:

> All functions, arguments, and descriptions in this section apply to the DECchip 21064/21064A, 21066/21066A, and 21068/21068A.

PALcode instructions control the DECchip 21064/21066/21068 on-chip performance counters. For OpenVMS Alpha, the instruction is MTPR_PERFMON; for DIGITAL UNIX and Windows NT Alpha, the instruction is wrperfmon.

The instruction arguments and results are described in the following sections. The scratch register usage is operating system specific.

Two on-chip counters count events. The bit width of the counters (8, 12, or 16 bits) can be selected and the event that they count can be switched among a number of available events. One possible event is an "external" event. For example, the processor board can supply an event that causes the counter to increment. In this manner, off-chip events can be counted.

The two counters can be switched independently. There is no hardware support for reading, writing, or resetting the counters. The only way to monitor the counters is to enable them to cause an interrupt on overflow.

The performance monitor functions, described in Section E.2.1.2, can provide the following, depending on implementation:

- Enable the performance counters to interrupt and trap into the performance monitoring vector in the operating system.

- Disable the performance counter from interrupting. This does not necessarily mean that the counters will stop counting.

- Select which events will be monitored and set the width of the two counters.

- In the case of OpenVMS Alpha and DIGITAL UNIX, implementations can choose to monitor selected processes. If that option is selected, the PME bit in the PCB controls the enabling of the counters. Since the counters cannot be read/written/reset, if more than one process is being monitored, the rounding error may become significant.

E.2.1.1 DECchip 21064/21066/21068 Performance Monitor Interrupt Mechanism

The performance monitoring interrupt mechanism varies according to the particular operating system.

For the OpenVMS Alpha Operating System

When a counter overflows and interrupt enabling conditions are correct, the counter causes an interrupt to PALcode. The PALcode builds an appropriate stack frame. The PALcode then dispatches in the form of an exception (not in the form of an interrupt) to the operating system by vectoring to the SCB performance monitor entry point through SCBB+650 (HWSCB$Q_PERF_MONITOR), at IPL 29, in kernel mode.

Two interrupts are generated if both counters overflow. For each interrupt, the status of each counter overflow is indicated by register R4:

R4 = 0 if performance counter 0 caused the interrupt
R4 = 1 if performance counter 1 caused the interrupt

When the interrupt is taken, the PC is saved on the stack frame as the old PC.

For the DIGITAL UNIX Operating System

When a counter overflows and interrupt enabling conditions are correct, the counter causes an interrupt to PALcode. The PALcode builds an appropriate stack frame and dispatches to the operating system by vectoring to the interrupt entry point entINT, at IPL 6, in kernel mode.

Two interrupts are generated if both counters overflow. For each interrupt, registers a0..a2 are as follows:

a0 = osfint$c_perf (4)
a1 = scb$v_perfmon (650)
a2 = 0 if performance counter 0 caused the interrupt
a2 = 1 if performance counter 1 caused the interrupt

When the interrupt is taken, the PC is saved on the stack frame as the old PC.

For the Windows NT Alpha Operating System

When a counter overflows and interrupt enabling conditions are correct, the counter causes an interrupt to PALcode. The PALcode builds a frame on the kernel stack and dispatches to the kernel at the interrupt entry point.

E.2.1.2 Functions and Arguments for the DECchip 21064/21066/21068

The functions execute on a single (the current running) processor only and are described in Table E–1.

- The OpenVMS Alpha MTPR_PERFMON instruction is called with a function code in R16, a function-specific argument in R17, and status is returned in R0.
- The DIGITAL UNIX wrperfmon instruction is called with a function code in a0, a function specific argument in a1, and status is returned in v0.
- The Windows NT Alpha wrperfmon instruction is called with input parameters a0 through a3, as shown in Table E–1.

Table E–1: DECchip 21064/21066/21068 Performance Monitoring Functions

Function	Register Usage		Comments
Enable performance monitoring			Enable takes effect at the next IPL change
DIGITAL UNIX			
	Input:	a0 = 1	Function code
		a1 = 0	Argument
	Output:	v0 = 1	Success
		v0 = 0	Failure (not generated)
OpenVMS Alpha			
	Input:	R16 = 1	Function code
		R17 = 0	Argument
	Output:	R0 = 1	Success
		R0 = 0	Failure (not generated)
Windows NT Alpha			
	Input:	a0 = 0	Select counter 0
		a0 = 1	Select counter 1
		a1 = 1	Enable selected counter
Disable performance monitoring			Disable takes effect at the next IPL change
DIGITAL UNIX			
	Input:	a0 = 0	Function code
		a1 = 0	Argument
	Output:	v0 = 1	Success
		v0 = 0	Failure (not generated)
OpenVMS Alpha			
	Input:	R16 = 0	Function code
		R17 = 0	Argument
	Output:	R0 = 1	Success
		R0 = 0	Failure (not generated)

Function	Register Usage		Comments
Windows NT Alpha			
	Input:	a0 = 0	Select counter 0
		a0 = 1	Select counter 1
		a1 = 0	Disable selected counter

Select desired events (mux_ctl)

DIGITAL UNIX

	Input:	a0 = 2	Function code
		a1 = mux_ctl	*mux_ctl* is the exact contents of those fields from the ICCSR register, in write format, described in Table E–2.
	Output:	v0 = 1	Success
		v0 = 0	Failure (not generated)

OpenVMS Alpha

	Input:	R16 = 2	Function code
		R17 = mux_ctl	*mux_ctl* is the exact contents of those fields from the ICCSR register, in write format, described in Table E–2.
	Output:	R0 = 1	Success
		R0 = 0	Failure (not generated)

Windows NT Alpha

	Input:	a2 = PCMUX0	For ICCSR<PCMUX0> field when a0 = 0
		a2 = PCMUX1	For ICCSR<PCMUX1> field when a0 = 1
		a3 = PC0	For ICCSR<PC0> field when a0 = 0
		a3 = PC1	For ICCSR<PC1> field when a0 = 1

Select performance monitoring options

DIGITAL UNIX

	Input:	a0 = 3	Function code
		a1 = opt	Function argument *opt* is: <0> = log all processes if set <1> = log only selected if set
	Output:	v0 = 1	Success
		v0 = 0	Failure (not generated)

Table E–1: DECchip 21064/21066/21068 Performance Monitoring   Functions (Continued)

Function	Register Usage		Comments
OpenVMS Alpha			
Input:	R16 = 3		Function code
	R17 = opt		Function argument *opt* is: <0> = log all processes if set <1> = log only selected if set
Output:	R0 = 1		Success
	R0 = 0		Failure (not generated)

Table E–2: DECchip 21064/21066/21068 MUX Control Fields in ICCSR Register

Bits	Option	Description	
34:32	PCMUX1	Event selection, counter 1:	
		Value	**Description**
		0	Total D-cache misses
		1	Total I-cache misses
		2	Cycles of dual issue
		3	Branch mispredicts (conditional, JSR, HW_REI)
		4	FP operate instructions (not BR, LOAD, STORE)
		5	Integer operates (including LDA, LDAH into R0–R30)
		6	Total store instructions
		7	External events supplied by pin

Bits	Option	Description
11:8	PCMUX0	Event selection, counter 0:

Value	Description
0	Total issues divided by 2
1	Unused
2	Nothing issued, no valid I-stream data
3	Unused
4	All load instructions
5	Unused
6	Nothing issued, resource conflict
7	Unused
8	All branches (conditional, unconditional, JSR, HW_REI)
9	Unused
10	Total cycles
11	Cycles while in PALcode environment
12	Total nonissues divided by 2
13	Unused
14	External event supplied by pin.
15	Unused

Bits	Option	Description
3	PC0	Frequency setting, counter 0:

Value	Description
0	2**16 (65536) events per interrupt
1	2**12 (4096) events per interrupt

Bits	Option	Description
0	PC1	Frequency setting, counter 1:

Value	Description
0	2**12 (4096) events per interrupt
1	2**8 (256) events per interrupt

E.2.2 DECchip 21164/21164PC Performance Monitoring

Unless otherwise stated, the term "21164" in this section means implementations of the 21164 at all frequencies.

PALcode instructions control the DECchip 21164/21164PC on-chip performance counters. For OpenVMS Alpha, the instruction is MTPR_PERFMON; for DIGITAL UNIX and Windows NT Alpha, the instruction is wrperfmon.
The instruction arguments and results are described in the following sections. The scratch register usage is operating system specific.

Three on-chip counters count events. Counters 0 and 1 are 16-bit counters; counter 2 is a 14-bit counter. Each counter can be individually programmed. Counters can be read and written and are not required to interrupt. The counters can be collectively restricted according to the processor mode.

Processes can be selectively monitored with the PME bit.

E.2.2.1 Performance Monitor Interrupt Mechanism

The performance monitoring interrupt mechanism varies according to the particular operating system.

For the Windows NT Alpha Operating System

When a counter overflows and interrupt enabling conditions are correct, the counter causes an interrupt to PALcode. The PALcode builds a frame on the kernel stack and dispatches to the kernel at the interrupt entry point.

For the OpenVMS Alpha Operating System

When a counter overflows and interrupt enabling conditions are correct, the counter causes an interrupt to PALcode. The PALcode builds an appropriate stack frame. The PALcode then dispatches in the form of an exception (not in the form of an interrupt) to the operating system by vectoring to the SCB performance monitor entry point through SCBB+650 (HWSCB$Q_PERF_MONITOR), at IPL 29, in kernel mode.

An interrupt is generated for each counter overflow. For each interrupt, the status of each counter overflow is indicated by register R4:

    R4 = 0 if performance counter 0 caused the interrupt
    R4 = 1 if performance counter 1 caused the interrupt
    R4 = 2 if performance counter 2 caused the interrupt

When the interrupt is taken, the PC is saved on the stack frame as the old PC.

For the DIGITAL UNIX Operating System

When a counter overflows and interrupt enabling conditions are correct, the counter causes an interrupt to PALcode. The PALcode builds an appropriate stack frame and dispatches to the operating system by vectoring to the interrupt entry point entINT, at IPL 6, in kernel mode.

An interrupt is generated for each counter overflow. For each interrupt, registers a0..a2 are as follows:

a0 = osfint$c_perf (4)
a1 = scb$v_perfmon (650)
a2 = 0 if performance counter 0 caused the interrupt
a2 = 1 if performance counter 1 caused the interrupt

E.2.2.2 Windows NT Alpha Functions and Argument

The functions for Windows NT Alpha execute on only a single (the current running) processor. The wrperfmon instruction is called with the following input registers:

Input Register	Contents (Bits)	Meaning
a0	63–0	The register in Table E–3, which contains the value to be written to the hardware PMCTR register.
a1	0	When a1 = 0, write a0 to the hardware PMCTR register.
		When a1 = 1, read the hardware PMCTR register. The returned PMCTR register is written to register v0.
a2	2–0	Has meaning when PCSEL1 in Table E–3 has the value 0xF. Contents are determined by processor type:

Processor	Contents	Reference
21164	CBOX1	Table E–15
21164PC	PM0_MUX	Table E–17

Input Register	Contents (Bits)	Meaning
a3	2–0	Has meaning when PCSEL2 in Table E–3 has the value 0xF. Contents are determined by processor type:

Processor	Contents	Reference
21164	CBOX2	Table E–16
21164PC	PM1_MUX	Table E–18

Table E–3: Bit Summary of PMCTR Register for Windows NT Alpha

Bits	Name	Meaning		
63–48	CTR0	Counter 0 value		
47–32	CTR1	Counter 1 value		
31	PCSEL0	Counter 0 selection:		
		Value	**Meaning**	
		0	Cycles	
		1	Issues	
30		Must be set to one[1]		
29–16	CTR2	Counter 2 value		
15–14	CTL0	Counter 0 control:		
		Value	**Meaning**	
		0	Counter disable, interrupt disable	
		1	Counter enable, interrupt disable	
		2	Counter enable, interrupt at count 65536	
		3	Counter enable, interrupt at count 256	
13–12	CTL1	Counter 1 control:		
		Value	**Meaning**	
		0	Counter disable, interrupt disable	
		1	Counter enable, interrupt disable	
		2	Counter enable, interrupt at count 65536	
		3	Counter enable, interrupt at count 256	
11–10	CTL2	Counter 2 control:		
		Value	**Meaning**	
		0	Counter disable, interrupt disable	
		1	Counter enable, interrupt disable	
		2	Counter enable, interrupt at count 16384	
		3	Counter enable, interrupt at count 256	

Table E–3: Bit Summary of PMCTR Register for Windows NT Alpha (Continued)

Bits	Name	Meaning
9–8	MODE_SELECT[1]	Select modes in which to count:
7–4	PCSEL1	Counter 1 selection. See Table E–13
3–0	PCSEL2	Counter 2 selection. See Table E–14

For MODE_SELECT:

Value	Meaning
0	Count all modes
1	Count PALmode only
2	Count all modes except PALmode
3	Count only user mode

[1] Windows NT Alpha uses bits 30 and 9–8 differently than as documented in the 21164 Hardware Reference Manual; it uses the processor executive mode to run user (nonprivileged) code. Therefore, bit 30 is always set to one and bits 9–8 are used to select the mode.

E.2.2.3 OpenVMS Alpha and DIGITAL UNIX Functions and Arguments

The functions execute on a single (the current running) processor only and are described in Table E–4.

The OpenVMS Alpha MTPR_PERFMON instruction is called with a function code in R16, a function-specific argument in R17, and status is returned in R0.

The DIGITAL UNIX wrperfmon instruction is called with a function code in a0, a function specific argument in a1, and status is returned in v0.

Table E–4: OpenVMS Alpha and DIGITAL UNIX Performance Monitoring Functions

Function	Register Usage		Comments
Enable performance monitoring; do not reset counters			
DIGITAL UNIX			
	Input:	a0 = 1	Function code value
		a1 = arg	Argument from Table E–5
	Output:	v0 = 1	Success
		v0 = 0	Failure (not generated)
OpenVMS Alpha			
	Input:	R16 = 1	Function code value
		R17 = arg	Argument from Table E–5
	Output:	R0 = 1	Success
		R0 = 0	Failure (not generated)

Table E–4: OpenVMS Alpha and DIGITAL UNIX Performance Monitoring Functions (Continued)

Function	Register Usage		Comments

Enable performance monitoring; start the counters from zero

DIGITAL UNIX

	Input:	a0 = 7	Function code value
		a1 = arg	Argument from Table E–5
	Output:	v0 = 1	Success
		v0 = 0	Failure (not generated)

OpenVMS Alpha

	Input:	R16 = 7	Function code value
		R17 = arg	Argument from Table E–5
	Output:	R0 = 1	Success
		R0 = 0	Failure (not generated)

Disable performance monitoring; do not reset counters

DIGITAL UNIX

	Input:	a0 = 0	Function code value
		a1 = arg	Argument from Table E–6
	Output:	v0 = 1	Success
		v0 = 0	Failure (not generated)

OpenVMS Alpha

	Input:	R16 = 0	Function code value
		R17 = arg	Argument from Table E–6
	Output:	R0 = 1	Success
		R0 = 0	Failure (not generated)

Select desired events (MUX_SELECT)

DIGITAL UNIX

	Input:	a0 = 2	Function code value
		a1 = arg	Argument from Table E–7 or E–8
	Output:	v0 = 1	Success
		v0 = 0	Failure (not generated)

OpenVMS Alpha

	Input:	R16 = 2	Function code value
		R17 = arg	Argument from Table E–7 or E–8
	Output:	R0 = 1	Success
		R0 = 0	Failure (not generated)

Function	Register Usage		Comments
Select Processor Mode options			
DIGITAL UNIX			
	Input:	a0 = 3	Function code value
		a1 = arg	Argument from Table E–9
	Output:	v0 = 1	Success
		v0 = 0	Failure (not generated)
OpenVMS Alpha			
	Input:	R16 = 3	Function code value
		R17 = arg	Argument from Table E–9
	Output:	R0 = 1	Success
		R0 = 0	Failure (not generated)
Select interrupt frequencies			
DIGITAL UNIX			
	Input:	a0 = 4	Function code value
		a1 = arg	Argument from Table E–10
	Output:	v0 = 1	Success
		v0 = 0	Failure (not generated)
OpenVMS Alpha			
	Input:	R16 = 4	Function code value
		R17 = arg	Argument from Table E–10
	Output:	R0 = 1	Success
		R0 = 0	Failure (not generated)
Read the counters			
DIGITAL UNIX			
	Input:	a0 = 5	Function code value
		a1 = arg	Argument from Table E–11
	Output:	v0 = val	Return value from Table E–11
OpenVMS Alpha			
	Input:	R16 = 5	Function code value
		R17 = arg	Argument from Table E–11
	Output:	R0 = val	Return value from Table E–11

Table E–4: OpenVMS Alpha and DIGITAL UNIX Performance Monitoring Functions (Continued)

Function	Register Usage		Comments
Write the counters			
DIGITAL UNIX			
	Input:	a0 = 6	Function code value
		a1 = arg	Argument from Table E–12
	Output:	v0 = 1	Success
		v0 = 0	Failure (not generated)
OpenVMS Alpha			
	Input:	R16 = 6	Function code value
		R17 = arg	Argument from Table E–12
	Output:	R0 = 1	Success
		R0 = 0	Failure (not generated)

Table E–5: 21164/21164PC Enable Counters for OpenVMS Alpha and DIGITAL UNIX

Bits	Meaning When Set
2	Operate on counter 2
1	Operate on counter 1
0	Operate on counter 0

Table E–6: 21164/21164PC Disable Counters for OpenVMS Alpha and DIGITAL UNIX

Bits	Meaning When Set
2	Operate on counter 2
1	Operate on counter 1
0	Operate on counter 0

Table E–7: 21164 Select Desired Events for OpenVMS Alpha and DIGITAL UNIX

Bits	Name	Meaning
63:32		MBZ
31	PCSEL0	Counter 0 selection:

Value	Meaning
0	Cycles
1	Issues

Bits	Name	Meaning
30:25		MBZ
24:22	CBOX2	CBOX2 event selection (only has meaning when event selection field PCSEL2 is value <15>; otherwise MBZ). CBOX2 described in Table E–16.
21:19	CBOX1	CBOX1 event selection (only has meaning when event selection field PCSEL1 is value <15>; otherwise MBZ). CBOX1 described in Table E–15.
18:8		MBZ
7:4	PCSEL1	Counter 1 event selection. PCSEL1 described in Table E–13.
3:0	PCSEL2	Counter 2 event selection. PCSEL2 described in Table E–14.

Table E–8: 21164PC Select Desired Events for OpenVMS Alpha and DIGITAL UNIX

Bits	Name	Meaning
63:32		MBZ
31	PCSEL0	Counter 0 selection:

Value	Meaning
0	Cycles
1	Issues

Bits	Name	Meaning
30:14		MBZ
13:11	PM1_MUX	PM1_MUX event selection (only has meaning when event selection field PCSEL2 is value <15>; otherwise MBZ). PM1_MUX is described in Table E–18.
10:8	PM0_MUX	PM0_MUX event selection (only has meaning when event selection field PCSEL1 is value <15>; otherwise MBZ). PM0_MUX is described in Table E–17.

Table E–8: 21164PC Select Desired Events for OpenVMS Alpha and DIGITAL UNIX (Continued)

Bits	Name	Meaning
7:4	PCSEL1	Counter 1 event selection. PCSEL1 described in Table E–13.
3:0	PCSEL2	Counter 2 event selection. PCSEL2 described in Table E–14.

Table E–9: 21164/21164PC Select Special Options for OpenVMS Alpha and DIGITAL UNIX

Bits	Meaning
63:31	MBZ
30	Stop count in user mode
29:10	MBZ
9	Stop count in PALmode
8	Stop count in kernel mode
7:1	MBZ
0	Monitor selected processes (when clear monitor all processes)

Setting any of the "NOT" bits causes the counters to not count when the processor is running in the specified mode. Under OpenVMS Alpha, "NOT_KERNEL" also stops the count in executive and supervisor mode, except as noted below:

NOT_BITS			Counters Operate Under These Modes When Bits Set:
K	**U**	**P**	
0	0	0	K E S U P
0	0	1	K E S U
0	1	0	K E S P
0	1	1	K E S
1	0	0	U P
1	0	1	U
1	1	0	P
1	1	1	E S (here "NOT_KERNEL" stops kernel counter only)

Note:

DIGITAL UNIX counts user mode by using the executive counter; that is, the count for executive mode is returned as the user mode count.

Table E–10: 21164/21164PC Select Desired Frequencies for OpenVMS Alpha and DIGITAL UNIX

Table E–10 contains the selection definitions for each of the three counters. All frequency fields are two-bit fields with the following values defined:

Bits	Meaning When Set
63:10	MBZ
9:8	Counter 0 frequency:

Value	Meaning
0	Do not interrupt
1	Unused
2	Low frequency (2**16 (65536) events per interrupt)
3	High frequency (2**8 (256) events per interrupt)

Bits	Meaning When Set
7:6	Counter 1 frequency:

Value	Meaning
0	Do not interrupt
1	Unused
2	Low frequency (2**16 (65536) events per interrupt)
3	High frequency (2**8 (256) events per interrupt)

Bits	Meaning When Set
5:4	Counter 2 frequency:

Value	Meaning
0	Do not interrupt
1	Unused
2	Low frequency (2**14 (16384) events per interrupt)
3	High frequency (2**8 (256) events per interrupt)

Bits	Meaning When Set
3:0	MBZ

Table E–11: 21164/21164PC Read Counters for OpenVMS Alpha and DIGITAL UNIX

Bits	Meaning When Returned
63:48	Counter 0 returned value
47:32	Counter 1 returned value
31:30	MBZ
29:16	Counter 2 returned value
15:1	MBZ
0	Set means success; clear means failure

Table E–12: 21164/21164PC Write Counters for OpenVMS Alpha and DIGITAL UNIX

Bits	Meaning
63:48	Counter 0 written value
47:32	Counter 1 written value
31:30	MBZ
29:16	Counter 2 written value
15:0	MBZ

Table E–13: 21164/21164PC Counter 1 (PCSEL1) Event Selection

The following values choose the counter 1 (PCSEL1) event selection:

Value	Meaning
0	Nothing issued, pipeline frozen
1	Some but not all issuable instructions issued
2	Nothing issued, pipeline dry
3	Replay traps (ldu, wb/maf, litmus test)
4	Single issue cycles
5	Dual issue cycles
6	Triple issue cycles
7	Quad issue cycles
8	Flow change (all branches, jsr-ret, hw_rei), where: If PCSEL2 has value 3, flow change is a conditional branch If PCSEL2 has value 2, flow change is a JSR-RET

Table E-13: 21164/21164PC Counter 1 (PCSEL1) Event Selection (Continued)

The following values choose the counter 1 (PCSEL1) event selection:

Value	Meaning
9	Integer operate instructions
10	Floating point operate instructions
11	Load instructions
12	Store instructions
13	Instruction cache access
14	Data cache access
15	For the 21164, use CBOX1 event selection in Table E-15. For the 21164PC, use PM0_MUX event selection in Table E-17.

Table E-14: 21164/21164PC Counter 2 (PCSEL2) Event Selection

The following values choose the counter 2 (PCSEL2) event selection:

Value	Meaning
0	Long stalls (> 15 cycles)
1	Unused value
2	PC mispredicts
3	Branch mispredicts
4	I-cache misses
5	ITB misses
6	D-cache misses
7	DTB misses
8	Loads merged in MAF
9	LDU replays
10	WB/MAF full replays
11	Event from external pin
12	Cycles
13	Memory barrier instructions
14	LDx/L instructions
15	For the 21164, use CBOX2 event selection in Table E-16. For the 21164PC, use PM1_MUX event selection in Table E-18.

Table E–15: 21164 CBOX1 Event Selection

The following values choose the CBOX1 event selection.

Value	Meaning
0	S-cache access
1	S-cache read
2	S-cache write
3	S-cache victim
4	Unused value
5	B-cache hit
6	B-cache victim
7	System request

Table E–16: 21164 CBOX2 Event Selection

The following values choose the CBOX2 event selection.

Value	Meaning
0	S-cache misses
1	S-cache read misses
2	S-cache write misses
3	S-cache shared writes
4	S-cache writes
5	B-cache misses
6	System invalidates
7	System read requests

Table E–17: 21164PC PM0_MUX Event Selection

The following values choose the PM0_MUX event selection and perform the chosen operation in Counter 0.

Value	Meaning
0	B-cache read operations
1	B-cache D read hits
2	B-cache D read fills
3	B-cache write operations
4	Undefined
5	B-cache clean write hits
6	B-cache victims
7	Read miss 2 launched

Table E–18: 21164PC PM1_MUX Event Selection

The following values choose the PM1_MUX event selection and perform the chosen operation in Counter 1.

Value	Meaning
0	B-cache D read operations
1	B-cache read hits
2	B-cache read fills
3	B-cache write hits
4	B-cache write fills
5	System read/flush B-cache hits
6	System read/flush B-cache misses
7	Read miss 3 launched

Appendix Index

Master Index†

A

Aborts, forcing, (I) 6–5

Absolute longword queue, (II-A) 2–21

Absolute quadword queue, (II-A) 2–24

Access control violation (ACV) fault, (II-A) 6–10
    has precedence, (II-A) 3–13
    memory protection, (II-A) 3–8
    service routine entry point, (II-A) 6–27

Access violation fault, (II-B) 3–12, (II-C) 4–3

ACCESS(x,y) operator, (I) 3–7

Add instructions
    add longword, (I) 4–25
    add quadword, (I) 4–27
    add scaled quadword, (I) 4–28
    See also Floating-point operate

ADDF instruction, (I) 4–110

ADDG instruction, (I) 4–110

ADDL instruction, (I) 4–25

ADDQ instruction, (I) 4–27

Address space, (II-C) 3–1

Address space match (ASM)
    bit in PTE, (II-A) 3–5, (II-B) 3–5, (II-C) 3–5
    TBIAP register uses, (II-A) 5–27
    virtual cache coherency, (I) 5–4
    with context switch, (II-C) 2–10, (II-C) 5–35

Address space number (ASN) register, (II-A) 5–5,
    (II-C) 2–4
    at processor initialization, (III) 3–20
    defined, (II-B) 1–3
    described, (II-B) 3–11
    in HWPCB, (II-A) 4–2
    in initial HWPCB, (III) 3–21
    in process context, (II-B) 4–1
    privileged context, (II-A) 2–91
    range supported, (II-A) 3–12
    TBCHK register uses, (II-A) 5–25

TBIS register uses, (II-A) 5–28
translation buffer with, (II-A) 3–11
virtual cache coherency, (I) 5–4
with context switch, (II-C) 2–10
with PALcode switching, (III) 3–8

Address translation
    algorithm to perform, (II-A) 3–9
    page frame number (PFN), (II-A) 3–8
    page table structure, (II-A) 3–8, (II-C) 3–2
    performance enhancements, (II-A) 3–10
    physical, (II-B) 3–7
    translation buffer with, (II-A) 3–11
    virtual, (II-B) 3–9
    virtual address segment fields, (II-A) 3–8

ADDS instruction, (I) 4–111

ADDT instruction, (I) 4–111

AFTER, defined for memory access, (I) 5–12

Aligned byte/word memory accesses, A–9

ALIGNED data objects, (I) 1–9

Alignment
    atomic byte, (I) 5–3
    atomic longword, (I) 5–2
    atomic quadword, (I) 5–2
    D_floating, (I) 2–6
    data alignment trap, (II-A) 6–15
    data considerations, A–4
    double-width data paths, A–1
    F_floating, (I) 2–4
    G_floating, (I) 2–5
    instruction, A–2
    longword, (I) 2–2
    longword integer, (I) 2–12
    memory accesses, A–9
    program counter (PC), (II-A) 6–6
    quadword, (I) 2–3
    quadword integer, (I) 2–12
    S_floating, (I) 2–8
    stack, (II-A) 6–31
    T_floating, (I) 2–9
    when data is unaligned, (II-A) 6–28
    X_floating, (I) 2–10

---

†. Each section of this manual includes an index of only that section, and following this Master Index is
an index of the Alpha instruction set and the PALcode instructions for each documented operating system.

overriding, (III) 3–27
state transitions and, (III) 3–1
with cold bootstrap, (III) 3–9
with error halts, (III) 3–30
with system restarts, (III) 3–28

B

BB_WATCH
    at power-up initialization, (III) 3–4
    requirements, (III) 3–42
    with powerfail interrupts, (III) 3–28
    with primary console switching, (III) 3–31
    with primary-eligible (PE) bit, (III) 3–43

BEFORE, defined for memory access, (I) 5–12

BEQ instruction, (I) 4–20

BGE instruction, (I) 4–20

BGT instruction, (I) 4–20

BIC instruction, (I) 4–42

Big-endian addressing, (I) 2–13
    byte operation examples, (I) 4–54
    byte swapping for, A–11
    extract byte with, (I) 4–51
    insert byte with, (I) 4–55
    load F_floating with, (I) 4–91
    load long/quad locked with, (I) 4–9
    load S_floating with, (I) 4–93
    mask byte with, (I) 4–57
    store byte/word with, (I) 4–15
    store F_floating with, (I) 4–95
    store long/quad conditional with, (I) 4–12
    store long/quad with, (I) 4–15
    store S_floating with, (I) 4–97

Big-endian data types, X_floating, (I) 2–10

BIS instruction, (I) 4–42

BITMAP_CHECKSUM, memory cluster field, (III) 3–13

BITMAP_PA, memory cluster field, (III) 3–13

BITMAP_VA, memory cluster field, (III) 3–13

BLBC instruction, (I) 4–20

BLBS instruction, (I) 4–20

BLE instruction, (I) 4–20

BLT instruction, (I) 4–20

BNE instruction, (I) 4–20

Boolean instructions, (I) 4–41
    logical functions, (I) 4–42

Boolean stylized code forms, A–14

Boot block on disk, (III) 3–36

Boot environment, restoring, (II-C) 5–23

Boot sequence, establishing, (II-C) 1–2

BOOT_DEV environment variable, (III) 2–25
    with loading system software, (III) 3–19

BOOT_FILE environment variable, (III) 2–26, (III) 3–38
    with loading system software, (III) 3–19

BOOT_OSFLAGS environment variable, (III) 2–26
    with loading system software, (III) 3–19

BOOT_RESET environment variable, (III) 2–26
    at system initialization, (III) 3–3
    at warm bootstrap, (III) 3–22
    overriding, (III) 3–27
    with cold bootstrap, (III) 3–9

BOOTDEF_DEV environment variable, (III) 2–25
    with loading system software, (III) 3–19

BOOTED_DEV environment variable
    with loading system software, (III) 3–19

BOOTED_FILE environment variable, (III) 2–26
    with loading system software, (III) 3–19

BOOTED_OSFLAGS environment variable, (III) 2–26
    with loading system software, (III) 3–19

BOOTP-UDP/IP network protocol, (III) 3–42

Bootstrap address space
    regions, (III) 3–13

Bootstrap-in-progress (BIP) flag
    at multiprocessor boot, (III) 3–23
    at power-up initialization, (III) 3–4
    at processor initialization, (III) 3–20
    per-CPU state contains, (III) 2–22
    state transitions and, (III) 3–1
    with failed bootstrap, (III) 3–18
    with secondary console, (III) 3–26

Bootstrapping, (III) 3–1
    adding processor while running system, (III) 3–26
    address space at cold, (III) 3–13
    boot block in ROM, (III) 3–40
    boot block on disk, (III) 3–36
    cold in uniprocessor environment, (III) 3–9
    control to system software, (III) 3–21
    failure of, (III) 3–18
    from disk, (III) 3–36
    from magtape, (III) 3–38
    from MOP-based network, (III) 3–42
    from ROM, (III) 3–40
    implementation considerations, (III) 3–44
    loading page table space at cold, (III) 3–14
    loading primary image, (III) 3–35
    loading system software, (III) 3–18
    MEMC table at cold boot, (III) 3–12
    multiprocessor, (III) 3–23
    PALcode loading at cold, (III) 3–13
    processor initialization, (III) 3–20
    request from system software, (III) 3–27
    state flags with, (III) 3–18
    system, (III) 3–3
    unconditional, (III) 3–27
    warm, (III) 3–22

BPT (PALcode) instruction, (II-A) 2–4
    required recognition of, (I) 6–4

PROCESS_KEYCODE console terminal routine, (III) 2–36

Processor
  adding to running system, (III) 3–26
  states and modes, (III) 3–1

Processor available (PA) flag
  at multiprocessor boot, (III) 3–23
  per-CPU state contains, (III) 2–22

Processor base (PRBR) register, (II-A) 5–19

Processor communication, (I) 5–14

Processor control block (PRCB)
  at initialization, (II-C) 6–2

Processor control region, (II-C) 2–7
  interrupt tables with, (II-C) 2–7

Processor control region base (PCR) register
  at initialization, (II-C) 6–2
  initializing, (II-C) 5–12
  returning contents of, (II-C) 5–19

Processor correctable errors, (II-C) 4–16
  reporting, (II-C) 4–18

Processor cycle counter (PCC) register, (I) 3–3
  for Digital UNIX, (II-B) 1–4
  for OpenVMS Alpha, (II-A) 1–2
  in initial HWPCB, (III) 3–21
  RPCC instruction with, (I) 4–143
  system cycle counter with, (II-A) 2–17
  See also Charged process cycles

Processor data areas, (II-C) 2–7

Processor hardware interrupt, service routine entry points, (II-A) 6–29

Processor initialization, (III) 3–20

Processor issue constraints, (I) 5–12

Processor issue sequence, (I) 5–12

Processor modes, (II-A) 3–1, (II-C) 2–1, (III) 3–3
  AST pending state, (II-A) 5–8
  change to executive, (II-A) 2–6
  change to kernel, (II-A) 2–7
  change to supervisor, (II-A) 2–8
  change to user, (II-A) 2–9
  controlling memory access, (II-A) 3–7
  enabling executive mode reads, (II-A) 3–5
  enabling executive mode writes, (II-A) 3–4
  enabling kernel mode reads, (II-A) 3–5
  enabling supervisor mode reads, (II-A) 3–5
  enabling supervisor mode writes, (II-A) 3–4
  enabling user mode reads, (II-A) 3–4
  enabling user mode writes, (II-A) 3–4
  page access with, (II-A) 3–2
  PALcode state transitions, (II-A) 6–37

Processor present (PP) flag
  at multiprocessor boot, (III) 3–23
  per-CPU state contains, (III) 2–22

Processor stacks, (II-A) 6–7

Processor state transitions, (II-A) 6–37

Processor state, defined, (II-A) 6–5

Processor state, internal, initialized, (II-C) 6–1

Processor status (PS) register
  at processor initialization, (III) 3–20
  bit meanings for, (II-B) 5–2
  bit summary, (II-A) 6–6
  bootstrap values in, (II-A) 6–6
  current, (II-A) 6–5
  defined, (II-A) 1–1, (II-B) 1–4
  explicit reading/writing of, (II-A) 6–5
  in process context, (II-B) 4–1
  in processor state, (II-A) 6–5
  saved on stack, (II-A) 6–5
  saved on stack frame, (II-A) 6–7
  with PALcode switching, (III) 3–8
  WR_PS_SW instruction, (II-A) 2–20

Processor status (PSR) register, (II-C) 2–1, (II-C) 2–6
  returning contents of, (II-C) 5–20

Processor type assignments, D–1

Processor uncorrectable errors, (II-C) 4–17

Processor unique value, (III) 3–8

Processor unique value (unique) register
  in initial HWPCB, (III) 3–21
  with PALcode switching, (III) 3–8

Processor, per-CPU slot field for
  halt, (III) 2–19
  revision, (III) 2–18
  serial number, (III) 2–18
  software compatibility, (III) 2–20
  type, (III) 2–18
  variation, (III) 2–18

Processors, switching primary, (III) 2–62

Program counter (PC) register, (I) 3–1
  alignment, (II-A) 6–6
  current PC defined, (II-A) 6–2
  defined, (II-B) 1–4
  explicit reading of, (II-A) 6–7
  in process context, (II-B) 4–1
  in processor state, (II-A) 6–5
  saved on stack frame, (II-A) 6–7
  with arithmetic traps, (II-A) 6–14, (II-B) 5–1
  with EXCB instruction, (I) 4–138
  with faults, (II-A) 6–9
  with interrupts, (II-A) 6–2
  with machine checks, (II-A) 6–23
  with PALcode switching, (III) 3–8
  with synchronous traps, (II-A) 6–15

Program I/O mode, (III) 3–3

Protection code, (II-A) 3–7, (II-B) 3–6

Protection modes, (II-A) 6–7

PS. See Processor status

PS<SP_ALIGN> field, (II-A) 2–14

Pseudo-ops, A–14

PSR. See Processor status register

modes for, (III) 3–3

Security holes, (I) 1–7
    with UNPREDICTABLE results, (I) 1–8

Seg0, mapping of, (II-B) 3–1

Seg1, mapping of, (II-B) 3–1

Self-relative longword queue, (II-A) 2–21

Self-relative quadword queue, (II-A) 2–25

Sequential read/write, A–8

Serialization, MB instruction with, (I) 4–142

SET_ENV variable routine, (III) 2–60

SET_TERM_CTL terminal console routine, (III)
    2 41

SET_TERM_INT console terminal routine, (III)
    2–42

SEXT(x) operator, (I) 3–9

SEXTB instruction, (I) 4–60

SEXTW instruction, (I) 4–60

Shared data (multiprocessor), A–5
    changed vs. updated datum, (I) 5–6

Shared data structures
    atomic update, (I) 5–7
    ordering considerations, (I) 5–9
    using memory barrier (MB) instruction, (I) 5–9

Shared memory
    accessing, (I) 5–11
    defined, (I) 5–10

Shift arithmetic instructions, (I) 4–46

Sign extend instructions, (I) 4–60

Single-precision floating-point, (I) 4–62

SLL instruction, (I) 4–45

Software (SW) field, in PS register, (II-A) 6–6

Software completion bit, exception summary register,
    (II-A) 6–13, (II-B) 5–6, (II-C) 4–6

Software considerations, A–1
    See also Performance optimizations

Software exceptions, (II-C) 4–8

Software interrupt request (SIRR) register, (II-C)
    2–6
    clearing, (II-C) 5–4
    described, (II-A) 5–22
    format for, (II-C) 4–15
    interrupt arbitration, (II-A) 6–35, (II-A) 6–36
    protocol for, (II-A) 6–19
    See also Software interrupts

Software interrupt summary (SISR) register
    at processor initialization, (III) 3–20
    described, (II-A) 5–23
    protocol for, (II-A) 6–19

Software interrupts, (II-A) 6–19
    asynchronous system traps (AST), (II-A) 6–20

protocol between summary and request, (II-A)
    6–19
recording pending state of, (II-A) 5–23
request (SIRR) register, (II-A) 6–19
requesting, (II-A) 5–22, (II-C) 4–15
requests after exception handling, (II-C) 5–25,
    (II-C) 5–27
service routine entry points, (II-A) 6–29
setting, (II-C) 5–29
summary (SISR) register, (II-A) 6–19
supported levels of, (II-A) 5–22

Software traps, generating, (II-A) 2–11

SP. See Stack pointer

SQRTF instruction, (I) 4–128

SQRTG instruction, (I) 4–128

SQRTS instruction, (I) 4–129

SQRTT instruction, (I) 4–129

Square root instructions
    IEEE, (I) 4–129
    VAX, (I) 4–128

SRA instruction, (I) 4–46

SRL instruction, (I) 4–45

ssir (PALcode) instruction, (II-C) 5–29
    sets software interrupts, (II-C) 4–16

Stack alignment, (II-A) 6–31

Stack alignment (SP_ALIGN), field in saved PS,
    (II-A) 6–6

Stack frames, (II-A) 6–7, (II-B) 5–3

Stack pointer (SP) register
    defined, (II-A) 1–1, (II-B) 1–4
    linkage for, (II-B) 1–1

State flags, per-CPU slot field for, (III) 2–17

STATUS_ALPHA_ARITHMETIC code, (II-C) 4–5

STATUS_ALPHA_GENTRAP code, (II-C) 4–8

STATUS_BREAKPOINT code, (II-C) 4–9

STATUS_DATATYPE_MISALIGNMENT code,
    (II-C) 4–6

STATUS_ILLEGAL_INSTRUCTION code, (II-C)
    4–7

STATUS_INVALID_ADDRESS code, (II-C) 4–7

STB instruction, (I) 4–15

STF instruction, (I) 4–95
    when data is unaligned, (II-A) 6–28

STG instruction, (I) 4–96
    when data is unaligned, (II-A) 6–28

STL instruction, (I) 4–15
    when data is unaligned, (II-A) 6–28

STL_C instruction, (I) 4–12
    when data is unaligned, (II-A) 6–28
    when guaranteed ordering with LDL_L, (I)
    4–14

reporting, (II-C) 4–18

System crash, requesting, (III) 3–31

System cycle counter (SCC) register
    at processor initialization, (III) 3–20
    reading, (II-A) 2–17

System entry addresses, (II-B) 5–4

System initialization, (III) 3–3

System restarts, (III) 3–27
    error halt and recovery, (III) 3–30
    forcing console I/O mode, (III) 3–35
    powerfail and recovery (multiprocessor), (III)
        3–29
    powerfail and recovery (split), (III) 3–29
    powerfail and recovery (uniprocessor), (III)
        3–28
    powerfail and recovery (united), (III) 3–29
    primary switching, (III) 3–31
    requesting a crash, (III) 3–31
    RESTORE_TERM routine, (III) 3–33, (III)
        3–35
    restoring terminal state, (III) 3–33
    SAVE_TERM routine, (III) 3–33, (III) 3–34
    saving terminal state, (III) 3–33

System serial number, HWRPB field for, (III) 2–7

System service call exceptions, (II-C) 4–4
    returning from, (II-C) 5–25

System service exception address
    (SYSCALL_ENTRY) register, (II-C) 2–6

System uncorrectable errors, (II-C) 4–17

System value (sysvalue) register, (II-B) 1–5
    with PALcode switching, (III) 3–8

System variation field (HWRPB)
    bit summary, (III) 2–13

System, HWRPB field for
    revision code, (III) 2–7, (III) 2–11
    serial number, (III) 2–11
    type, (III) 2–7, (III) 2–12
    variation, (III) 2–7, (III) 2–12

Sysvalue. See System value

T

T_floating data type
    alignment of, (I) 2–9
    exceptions, (I) 2–9
    format, (I) 2–9
    MAX/MIN, (I) 4–65
    NaN with S_floating convert, (I) 4–88
    when data is unaligned, (II-A) 6–28

Tape. See Magtape

TB hint offset, HWRPB field for, (III) 2–7

TB. See Translation buffer

TBB. See Translation buffer hint block

tbi (PALcode) instruction, (II-B) 2–24

with TBs, (II-B) 3–10

tbia (PALcode) instruction, (II-C) 3–6, (II-C) 5–36

tbim (PALcode) instruction, (II-C) 3–6, (II-C) 5–37

tbimasn (PALcode) instruction, (II-C) 3–6, (II-C)
    5–38

tbis (PALcode) instruction, (II-C) 3–6, (II-C) 5–39

tbisasn (PALcode) instruction, (II-C) 3–6, (II-C)
    5–40

Temporary PALcode registers, (II-C) 5–1

Terminal console
    setting controls, (III) 2–41

Terminals
    setting interrupts for, (III) 2–42

TEST(x,cond) operator, (I) 3–10

TESTED_PAGES, memory cluster field, (III) 3–13

Thread environment block base (TEB) register,
    (II-C) 2–6
    initializing, (II-C) 5–12
    returning contents of, (II-C) 5–53
    with context switch, (II-C) 2–10, (II-C) 5–31

Thread unique value (THREAD) register, (II-C) 2–7
    initializing, (II-C) 5–12
    returning contents of, (II-C) 5–22
    with context switch, (II-C) 2–10, (II-C) 5–31

Timeliness of location access, (I) 5–17

Timer support, HAL interface fpr, (II-C) 1–3

Timing considerations, atomic sequences, A–16

Translation
    physical, (II-B) 3–7
    virtual, (II-B) 3–9

Translation buffer (TB), (II-B) 3–10
    address space number with, (II-A) 3–11
    at context switch, (II-C) 2–10
    fault on execute, (II-A) 6–12
    fault on read, (II-A) 6–11
    fault on write, (II-A) 6–11
    granularity hint in PTE, (II-A) 3–5
    invalidate all, (II-C) 5–36
    invalidate multiple, (II-C) 5–37
    invalidate single, (II-C) 5–39
    invalidate single data, (II-C) 5–8
    management of, (II-C) 3–5
    recursion in, (II-C) 3–6
    with invalid PTEs, (II-A) 3–12

Translation buffer check (TBCHK) register
    described, (II-A) 5–25
    with translation buffer, (II-A) 3–12

Translation buffer hint block (TBB), (III) 2–10, (III)
    2–13

Translation buffer invalidate all (TBIA) register
    described, (II-A) 5–26
    with translation buffer, (II-A) 3–12

Translation buffer invalidate all process (TBIAP)

W

X

Y

Z

RPCC 4–143
RS 4–150

S4ADDL 4–26
S4ADDQ 4–28
S4SUBL 4–38
S4SUBQ 4–40
S8ADDL 4–26
S8ADDQ 4–28
S8SUBL 4–38
S8SUBQ 4–40
SEXTB 4–60
SEXTW 4–60
SLL 4–45
SQRTF 4–128
SQRTG 4–128
SQRTS 4–129
SQRTT 4–129

SRA 4–46
SRL 4–45
STB 4–15
STF 4–95
STG 4–96
STL 4–15
STL_C 4–12
STQ 4–15
STQ_C 4–12
STQ_U 4–17
STS 4–97
STT 4–98
STW 4–15
SUBF 4–130
SUBG 4–130
SUBL 4–37
SUBQ 4–39
SUBS 4–131

SUBT 4–131

TRAPB 4–144

UMULH 4–36
UNPKBL 4–156
UNPKBW 4–156

WB 4–147
WH64 4–145

XOR 4–42

ZAP 4–61
ZAPNOT 4–61